"THE ONLY UNAVOIDABLE SUBJECT OF REGRET"

"The Only Unavoidable Subject of Regret"

GEORGE WASHINGTON, SLAVERY, AND THE
ENSLAVED COMMUNITY AT MOUNT VERNON

Mary V. Thompson

UNIVERSITY OF VIRGINIA PRESS

Charlottesville and London

University of Virginia Press
© 2019 by the Rector and Visitors of the University of Virginia
All rights reserved
Printed in the United States of America on acid-free paper

First published 2019

3 5 7 9 8 6 4 2

Library of Congress Cataloging-in-Publication Data
Names: Thompson, Mary V., 1955–   author.
Title: "The only unavoidable subject of regret": George Washington, slavery, and
the enslaved community at Mount Vernon / Mary V. Thompson.
Description: Charlottesville : University of Virginia Press, 2019. |
Includes bibliographical references and index.
Identifiers: LCCN 2018046407 | ISBN 9780813941844 (cloth : alk. paper) |
ISBN 9780813941851 (ebook)
Subjects: LCSH: Washington, George, 1732–1799—Relations with slaves. |
Slaves—Virginia—Mount Vernon (Estate)—History—18th century. |
Mount Vernon (Va. : Estate)—History—18th century.
Classification: LCC E312.17 .T4665 2019 | DDC 973.4/1092—dc23
LC record available at https://lccn.loc.gov/2018046407

Cover art: *Potomak Front of Mount Vernon* (detail), watercolor and
ink over graphite, William Russell Birch, c. 1801–1803.
(Courtesy of Mount Vernon Ladies' Association)

For my husband, Anthony Marrs Bates,
who has been with me through good days and many struggles,
for almost as long as I've been working on this project.

For Jane Brown (1889–1996),
a dear neighbor and the daughter of a couple who had been enslaved.
Thank you, Miss Jane, for teaching me that a person could "live in slavery"
without being a slave in their heart. Your friendship, your positive spirit,
and your ringing testimony of God's love for you were inspirational.
I'm looking forward to sitting and talking with you again one day.

For the unknown and unexpected West African ancestor
who provided 0.9 percent of my DNA.
I so wish I could talk to you.

CONTENTS

ILLUSTRATIONS

Figures

Tables (in Appendix)

PREFACE

In the formation of the United States, there have been a few processes that shaped—and continue to shape—the way Americans see themselves. One of the best-known of these influences, for example, was the frontier, which contributed to the idea of American exceptionalism, that we were destined by God for great things, that we would not be limited by geography to a tiny sliver of land along the Atlantic Coast. It may also be responsible for the celebration of rugged individualism, leading, at its best, to the concept that each person has it within him- or herself to become anything that person wants, and, at its worst, to the belief that those who fail to succeed have only themselves to blame. The fact that we started out as colonies of several European countries may account for two paradoxical, but related, ideas: the inferiority complex many Americans feel in relation to the older and arguably more sophisticated cultures of our mother countries, and also the conviction that, having broken away from the most powerful of them by means of an almost assuredly doomed-from-the-start revolution, that we are better than they and have nothing to learn from those cultures.

Lastly, there is the fact that, for roughly 250 years, this country was built on the labor of unfree people, leading to a number of consequences that extend to this very day. According to some estimates, as many as 75 percent of all new arrivals in the British colonies were unfree, because they were working for a few years as indentured servants to pay back the cost of their travel to the New World, because they were convicts sentenced to labor for others in a foreign land, rather than face either a prison term at home or execution, or because they were enslaved for life.[1] While the first two forms of unfree labor gradually faded, leaving few traces in our collective memory, slavery was something altogether different.

Slavery was nothing new in the world; as an institution it had existed for thousands of years and in many cultures, so it was not something invented in America. But in the Americas—not just the present-day United States but throughout North and South America—slavery took a turn it had not in the rest of the world. Here it developed into a race-based institution, which for individuals held within its bonds was permanent and hereditary. Out of this system came views that people whose ancestors immigrated from Europe were naturally superior to people whose ancestors came from Africa; that black people were less capable, less intelligent, less cultured; and that expectations for them should be kept low. Those ideas meant that for generations after slaves were freed by means of a bloody civil war, they and their descendants were kept from voting, denied an education, segregated from those who considered themselves naturally better, more talented, more capable.

Slavery has been described as America's original sin: the activity or state of mind that took America from the Edenic promise of its beginning, brought it to a debased and far lesser condition than it might have had, and continues to plague the nation today.[2] As early as the Constitutional Convention in the summer of 1787, Virginia delegate George Mason declared that slavery brought "the judgment of heaven on a Country. As nations cannot be rewarded or punished in the next world they must be in this. By an inevitable chain of causes & effects providence punishes national sins, by national calamities."[3] One of our most respected and beloved American presidents, Abraham Lincoln, came close to saying as much when he described the Civil War as "the woe due to those by whom the offense [of slavery] came," and suggested that the conflict might well go on "if God wills that it continue, until all the wealth piled by the bond-man's two hundred and fifty years of unrequited toil shall be sunk, and until every drop of blood drawn with the lash, shall be paid by another drawn with the sword."[4] For many years, this "original sin" was unacknowledged and, even today, because of the scars it left, can be difficult to discuss. But the Christian church has taught for two millennia that healing from sin can only come through acknowledgment of what happened, or confession, if you will. Psychology has essentially told us the same thing for the last century. And for those who are victims, rather than perpetrators, of sin, both religion and psychology prescribe understanding and forgiveness as the only way to move past the trauma and grow to one's fullest potential.

Learning the truth of what happened in the past is the first step in acknowledging the resulting social dysfunction and psychic scars that still plague us and allowing them to heal. Historians have been working very hard for roughly eight decades to ensure that the story of slavery in the Americas is told. Much of that work, however, was done at the university level and has only within the past thirty years or so begun to make its way from the academy to other institutions of learning such as museums.

And it is only now that much of that story is making its way to a mass audience.

What that mass audience, in the form of the roughly 1 million visitors who come to Mount Vernon each year, often wants is an answer to the questions, "Was George Washington a good slave owner?" or "He was good to his slaves, wasn't he?" To anyone looking at this book to provide those answers, let me just say upfront that some of the worst things one thinks about in terms of slavery—whipping, keeping someone in shackles, tracking a person down with dogs, or selling people away from their family—all of those things happened either at Mount Vernon or on other plantations under Washington's management. The story of this man and the enslaved people who lived at this site is complicated, but it is worth getting to know the real human beings involved, both the one who was our first president and those who knew him through the lens of America's original sin.

This book is the result of many years of study undertaken as part of my job at Mount Vernon. My interest in the topic, however, began many years before. It was during my early years in elementary school that I first learned about slavery and the legacy of prejudice that still endured, as the nation commemorated the centennial of the war that abolished slavery in the United States, even as the civil rights movement played out each night on the evening news. My interest in history had early been fostered by my father, but it was in graduate school at the University of Virginia that I fell in love with African American history. There I started learning the academic story of slavery, partly through a seminar cotaught by Robert Cross and Steve Innes, and, most importantly, by a course called Slave Systems taught by Joseph Miller. The latter was probably the best class I have ever been privileged to take, and I will always be grateful to Mr. Miller (at "Mr. Jefferson's University" everyone, including professors, is addressed as Mr. or Ms., to maintain the ideal of democratic equality) for opening up this new world to me, as well as for the kindness and understanding he showed to all of his students. I came to work at Mount Vernon shortly before receiving my degree from the University of Virginia and immediately faced an interesting situation as no one spoke of slaves—they were "servants"—and I could see that roughly thirty-five to forty years of historiography were unacknowledged. Things would change at Mount Vernon in the ensuing years, and I am pleased that I have been here to see and be part of that transformation.

This volume began life in 1993 as a series of essays on slave life at Mount Vernon, written as background for a group of incoming interns who would be working on reconstructing George Washington's sixteen-sided barn and growing appropriate crops in the fields surrounding it, in an area formerly known as Hell Hole but now called the Pioneer Farm site. My supervisor, the estate's longtime curator Christine Meadows, gave the go-ahead to spend about four months pulling together and making sense of the research I had been doing for several years at that point. In addition to serving as the basis for the interpretation at the Pioneer Farm, the essays were also the foundation for Mount Vernon's slave life tours, its first-person interpreters who portray specific enslaved individuals, and several museum exhibits.

Since then, I have continued to research this topic while consulting the works of other historians as they became available and responding to comments and suggestions made by colleagues throughout the country. Foremost among those to whom I owe a debt of gratitude is Christine Meadows, who gave a younger colleague the opportunity to put her training to use, studying a much-neglected area of the estate's history. Second, my thanks to Mount Vernon's supervisory team, including current president and CEO Curt Viebranz; the founding director of the Fred W. Smith National Library for the Study of George Washington, Doug Bradburn; Mount Vernon's former executive director James C. Rees; and current senior vice president for historic preservation and collections, Carol Borchert Cadou, for giving me the time to bring this project to fruition. Carol's predecessor, Linda Ayres, has always been very supportive of my research efforts, and our former head librarian Joan Stahl was a delight as a colleague and a real cheerleader. One memorable evening, our vice president for education Allison Wickens did yeoman's duty as she oversaw the printing of two copies of the manuscript for the University of Virginia Press on the "good" copier on the third floor while I sent chapter after chapter to that location from my desk two floors below. When putting the final draft together, one of her staff members, Zerah Jakub Burr, "had my back" as she stood over me to make sure we got things paginated something close to all right. Samantha Snyder, our able access services librarian, provided additional assistance with the mystery of thumb drives. And, as always, Licensing Director Beverly Addington helped with her very Texas way of looking at the world. John Gibbs, the cataloguer in the library, kept me going with jokes and salt-water taffy. I also have to thank Sandy Newton, formerly the secretary to the regent of the Mount Vernon Ladies' Association, and Beverly Peterson, one of Mount Vernon's many volunteers, former school principal, and fellow animal-lover, for their many years of pushing, encouraging, and, yes, nagging me to get this done. I could not have done it without you.

Outside Mount Vernon are other colleagues who deserve thanks as well. First in importance are Scott Casper, the "dean of everything" at the University of Maryland, Baltimore County, and Jean B. Lee from the history department at the University of Wisconsin–Madison, for reading over earlier drafts and suggesting changes and ways of improving the project. Scott—who has become something of an unofficial member of the Mount Vernon staff—was especially helpful in assisting me to organize what had been standalone essays into what I hope is a more coherent whole. Both Phil Morgan from Johns Hopkins University and Peter Wood, who is retired from Duke, had been "heroes" of mine for years; their statements that "You MUST publish this" (from the former) and "You ARE publishing this, aren't you" (from the latter) made me terribly happy. Phil was also gracious enough to read the full draft once more in the spring of 2015, when he offered a number of cogent suggestions. Woody Holton, now at the University of South Carolina, was an enthusiastic supporter of this project—so much so that I periodically received messages from him through one of his grad students (when she was working on a fellowship here at Mount Vernon) to "finish the f-ing book already. I want to read it." Ira Berlin from the University of Maryland was incredibly helpful many years ago when, learning that I was upset that a couple of other historians were finishing their works on slavery at Mount Vernon ahead of mine, he reminded me that all of us bring to our work our own unique personalities and gifts, which means that, even looking at the same exact sources, we often choose to highlight different aspects of an issue. All of those insights are valuable in learning about the past. In addition, I must not forget Edna Medford of Howard University, for her interest and support over the years. Peter Henriques, now retired from his longtime teaching position at George Mason University, and Lorena Walsh, who spent years doing research for Colonial Williamsburg—years in which she helped to transform our knowledge of the colonial Chesapeake—served as academic readers for my book manuscript. It is so much better for your suggestions.

Lastly, to my dear Tony and several generations of furry ones at home, much love and thanks for your graciousness in dealing with an often obsessed, exhausted, and frazzled historian.

"THE ONLY UNAVOIDABLE SUBJECT OF REGRET"

Introduction

On January 1, 1795, a Welsh Baptist minister—and committed abolitionist—named Morgan John Rhys wrote down his thoughts shortly after paying a visit to Mount Vernon. George and Martha Washington were not home at the time, because he was then serving his second term as president of the United States, so they were living in the temporary capital, Philadelphia. Less than a month before, Washington had written his farm manager to ensure that it was clearly understood that visitors who fit the category of tourists were welcome during the family's absence: "I have no objection to any sober, & orderly persons gratifying their curiosity in visiting the buildings, Gardens &ca about Mount Vernon."[1] As one of those sober and orderly people, Reverend Rhys enjoyed his visit to the Washingtons' home, although he could never forget that it was a plantation built and maintained by the labor of people who were enslaved. He wrote of his time there, "If Mount Vernon was not the house of bondage to so many men, I would call it a little paradise. The mansion modest. The garden neat, the meandering of the Potomac—distant hills and extensive fields combine to render the prospect delightful and would present a happy retirement for one of the greatest men in the Universe."[2]

More than two hundred years later, Mount Vernon is one of the most visited historic homes in America, welcoming about 1 million visitors each year (in comparison, Graceland, the home of Elvis Presley, welcomes about 600,000 visitors annually, while 754,407 went to Hearst Castle in fiscal year 2014).[3] Washington's estate is also uniquely situated to introduce the subject of slavery to an international audience. While it is the estate's connection to George Washington that brings people in, and its proximity to the District of Columbia that makes it easy to get to, once these tourists enter the grounds, they learn that they are on an eighteenth-century plantation that was once home to hundreds of enslaved people, or a "house of bondage to . . . many." For many visitors, both American and international, this may well be the only southern plantation they ever have the opportunity to see.

Environmental Setting

Two hundred years ago, Mount Vernon was without a doubt George Washington's favorite place in the world. His home was located on a hill overlooking the Potomac River, at a spot from which, about a mile distant, he could see the colony and later state of Maryland. Bursting with spawning fish in the spring and wintering ducks and geese later in the year, the river was a major transportation route at a time when unpaved roads made travel by land uncomfortable and fatiguing. The cultivated fields, pastures, and woodlands surrounding the estate provided food and fuel and were home to many wild animals (deer, foxes, raccoons, opossums, rabbits, and squirrels) and birds (quails, pigeons, doves, owls, and eagles). Ships plying the river, bringing cargoes from all over the world, could be seen heading for the nearby seaport towns of Georgetown, sixteen miles to the north; Alexandria, about nine miles in the same direction; or perhaps by the last years of Washington's life, to the new Federal City, roughly halfway between the other two.

At the end of Washington's life in 1799, Alexandria, the closest of these cities, was home to 2,748 inhabitants, of whom 2,153 (78.3%) were white, 543 (19.8%) were enslaved, and another 52 (1.9%) were free blacks. An active community, filled with shops selling consumer goods made by local artisans, stores offering imported luxuries, warehouses where agricultural produce headed from Virginia to Europe, and almost three hundred taverns, Alexandria drew people, whether free, indentured, or enslaved, from the surrounding countryside.[4] Founded during George Washington's boyhood, there was still a rough quality to the town, even late in his life. In addition to its "superb wharves" and "vast warehouses," visitors wrote about the "vast number of houses" being built there, providing work for carpenters and masons, as the "hammer and trowel were at work everywhere." Others remarked on the unpaved streets, the clay soil of which became "so slippery it is almost impossible to walk in them" when it rained. One

Frenchman commented that there was more luxury to be seen in Alexandria than in Baltimore but qualified the statement by saying that it was "a miserable luxury," where it was not unusual to see "servants in silk stockings, and their masters in boots."[5]

Another European complained that "Alexandria is one of the most wicked places I ever beheld in my life; cock—fighting, horse racing, with every species of gambling and cheating, being apparently the principal business going forward." As evidence for this assertion, he offered, "this little place contains no less than between forty and fifty billiard tables. Here is one protestant church, where service is performed once a month; one presbyterian, methodist and roman catholic chapel." And the people were even worse, "proud and imperious as possible, and esteem but little such white people as are obliged to labour for a livelihood, all the drudgery being done by their wretched negro slaves."[6]

Perhaps one of the other factors making Alexandria so wicked was the fact that it was also a good place to purchase slaves. In September 1762, for example, the *Maryland Gazette* announced the upcoming sale in Alexandria of "a parcel of very healthy Gambia slaves," who had been "Just Imported" in a ship called the *Royal Charlotte,* under the command of Captain Bartholomew Fabre. The two Scottish businessmen advertising the sale were John Kirkpatrick, who had served as George Washington's military secretary during the French and Indian War, and his brother Thomas.[7]

Growth and Transformation of a Plantation

The land at Mount Vernon had been in Washington's family since 1674. By his lifetime, small bands of Native Americans still lived in the area, but much of the Algonquian population around Mount Vernon had been wiped out as a result of new diseases brought by European settlers, by conflicts with groups of northern Indians (primarily Susquehannocks and their Iroquois allies), and by warfare with the colonists, including seventeenth-century members of the Washington family.[8] The Mount Vernon property, then about 2,126 acres, came under George Washington's control in 1754, when he began renting the estate from the widow of his older half-brother Lawrence who had died two years before. When Lawrence's widow, Ann Fairfax Washington Lee, died in 1761, Washington inherited the entire Mount Vernon estate. In the next forty-five years, he aggressively purchased land in the neighborhood. At his death in December 1799, the estate totaled eight thousand acres and was home to more than three hundred individuals, living in small clusters on five separate farms.

At the Mansion House Farm, George Washington's home was surrounded by kitchen, pleasure, and experimental gardens, which provided vegetables, fruits, and herbs for his table, beautiful flowers, and exotic plants sent by correspondents from around the world; stables, where fine horses and mules were bred; a greenhouse filled with tropical plants; and buildings where various trades were carried out, such as blacksmithing, carpentry, coopering (barrel making), food production and preservation, spinning, weaving, and shoemaking. While some crops were grown there, most of the Mansion House Farm was given over to these crafts, as well as woods, meadows, and beautiful vistas. It was on the four outlying quarters—Dogue Run, Muddy Hole, Union (formed from two earlier farms known as Ferry Farm and French's Farm), and River (earlier called The Neck or Neck Plantation) Farms, located in a radius about 1.5 to 3 miles from the mansion—that crops were raised to support the entire plantation, both by supplying the needs of those living at home and through sales to others.

Like many Virginians of his generation, George Washington started out as a tobacco farmer, raising this New World plant as a cash crop for sale in England and Europe. (By the time the American colonies broke their political ties to the British government, 85 percent of the tobacco grown in those colonies was being resold by British firms to the European mainland.) Money earned from the sale of tobacco to British merchants was used to buy material goods ranging from cloth and furniture to foodstuffs, silver, and tools, which were sent by ship back to the colony. The fact that the system seemed to work so well meant that people put their money into growing tobacco, rather than building a more diversified economy. As historian Bruce A. Ragsdale explains, "The predominance of tobacco culture and a plantation system of agriculture impeded the creation of domestic markets, local manufactures, an indigenous commercial class, and a more skilled and flexible labor force." Although indebtedness to the British merchants at the hub of the trading system was something of a given, recessions could slash prices paid to the planters, while the fact that they were still reliant on those same merchants to supply them with manufactured and consumer goods resulted in rapidly increasing debt. By the first year of the American Revolution, per capita debt in the tobacco colonies of Virginia and Maryland was three times higher than the average for all the rest of Britain's North American colonies.[9]

Not every planter found himself in debt or was in debt for the same reasons. Through her decades of work on plantation management, historian Lorena S. Walsh uncovered a mix of additional reasons for indebtedness. William Byrd II, for example, was not especially interested in farming or in

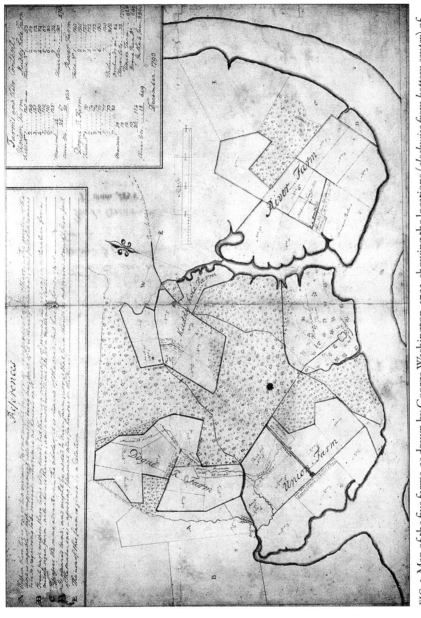

FIG. 1. Map of the five farms, as drawn by George Washington, 1793, showing the locations (*clockwise from bottom center*) of Mansion House, Union, Dogue Run, Muddy Hole, and River farms. (Courtesy of the Huntington Library)

improving his estates, while his political ambitions led him to waste a good deal of money in England trying to win a government appointment. Others ran into trouble when they used credit to finance the expansion of their lands and labor force, instead of paying cash, and then were unwilling to use profits to pay back their debts. In some families, attempts to set up children with plantations and slaves of their own or, in the case of daughters, with sizeable dowries put strains on the estates of their parents. In many cases, an unwillingness to admit what was happening and to cut expenses also played a factor.[10]

Relatively quickly, Washington, like other large planters, could see problems with tobacco as a staple crop. As with the monoculture of any crop, continuous cultivation of tobacco, which was very labor intensive to produce, depleted the soil of nutrients. Reliance on a single crop that was vulnerable to damage resulting from bad weather, disease, or insects left planters in a precarious situation. They were also vulnerable to merchants who might try to take advantage of distance and ignorance to fill their orders for consumer goods with shoddy, overpriced, and potentially out-of-fashion merchandise. For example, in a letter to the firm of Robert Cary & Company written in the summer of 1761, George Washington brought up several complaints. In fulfilling one order, his agent had sent—and charged Washington for—twenty-four whipsaws when he had only asked for two, leading Washington to note that "what I shall do with the abundant overplus I really know not as I apprehend it will be a difficult matter to dispose of such a quantity in this part of the Country." This reminded him of another complaint, this time about a piece of furniture, a liquor case, ordered in September 1760:

> Another thing occurs which must not escape unnoticed—and that is, A Case bought of Phil Bell at the price of 17 Guineas—Surely, here must be as great a mistake, or as great an Imposition as ever was offer[e]d by a Tradesman. The Case is a plain one, and such as I cou[l]d get made in this Country (where work of all kinds is very dear) of the same stuff, and equally as neat for less than four Guineas—is it possible then that 16 Gall[o]n Bottles with ground Stoppers can cost 13 Guineas? I think I might safely answer No. I wou[l]d have sent it back immediately, but being convinced that there must be some mistake in the Case I have postpon[e]d that resolution till you can made a proper enquiry into it, and advice me thereon.

Washington still was not done. He also groused that Cary and Company's "Corrispondants in Liverpool" were "a little negligent of your Orders and I am the Sufferer by it—for I have never receiv[e]d any Salt from thence not-withstanding my repeated application's for these two years past."[11] Today, with a grocery store within walking distance for many people, this might not sound like a major complaint, but salt was more than just a condiment on the table. It was absolutely necessary to preserve food, enabling people to eat, and not starve, through each season of the year.

Washington shared another aspect of the colonial tobacco trade with his peers—indebtedness to his English agents. Orders for goods for Mount Vernon averaged more than £300 per year, which, according to some estimates, means that Washington spent the modern equivalent of $2–3 million dollars in a five-year period in the early 1760s. In early 1759, Washington married a young widow, Martha Dandridge Custis, who brought a large fortune to the marriage. Like many newlyweds, the couple poured money into their home and soon found themselves in debt. By 1763, four years after the wedding, the money Washington had acquired through his marriage was gone. The following year he learned that he owed Cary & Company more than £1,800, on which he would be charged 5 percent interest.[12]

By 1765, Washington was looking for a way to change the equation, musing about substituting "some other Article in place of Tobacco" and inquiring about the sales possibilities for hemp and flax.[13] As one of the wealthier planters in the colony, Washington could afford the transition to something new, and by the late 1760s, he turned from tobacco to grains, largely wheat and corn. Through the next thirty years, he experimented with different types of manures, various cultivation techniques, and a series of crop rotation schemes in an attempt to find a sustainable agricultural system that would be the best balance of crop yield, income from the sale of those crops, and care of the land itself. His reading of the latest books on agriculture and his correspondence with leading agronomists, both in England and America, provided further encouragement for these innovations.[14] He also diversified his ways of making money, adding a mill so that he could sell flour, as well as profiting by grinding the grain of his neighbors. His fisheries provided food for his own table, fed his slaves, and provided income as preserved fish were sold to others. He increased cloth production on the plantation to reduce reliance on foreign sources of manufacture.[15]

Impact of Change

All of the changes George Washington put into place had an impact, not only on the types of work being done on the plantation but also on the people doing that work. While he may have come up with the ideas through his reading and conversations with others, his plans became reality only after they were carried out by others. For instance, late eighteenth-century agronomists encouraged the increased use of animals to pull plows and harrows. When Washington did that at Mount Vernon, it meant that his laborers had to change the way they had been working. Animals had to be trained, and people needed to learn how to handle them. Planting other crops, such as pumpkins, among hills of corn required different techniques than the fieldworkers were accustomed to using. Unlike with grains, those seeds could not be broadcast or thrown but had to be planted individually. A field thus planted would, unlike a field of wheat but much like tobacco, have to be hoed and weeded on a fairly regular basis.

Surviving letters from the late 1780s provide some insight into the problems Washington experienced in trying to introduce new equipment and methods. That year, Arthur Young, one of the foremost proponents of scientific agriculture in England, sent Washington a new type of plow. Washington later wrote Young to say that he was very happy with the plows and found that "they answer the description which you gave me of them." He noted, however, that this was "contrary to the opinion of almost every one who saw them before they were used, for it was thought their great weight would be an insuperable objection to their being drawn by two Horses."[16] In another letter, Washington mentioned being forced to seek ways to "overcome the ill-founded prejudice" of his laborers—the slaves—against the new plows.[17]

About this same time, Young sent plans for a barnyard, which included a two-story barn with a floor for threshing wheat with flails. Washington had such a barn constructed at Union Farm. Prior to its completion, wheat and other grains were separated from the stalks by threshing outside, a labor-intensive task in which workers beat the stalks with wooden flails. Another method used to accomplish the same purpose was to have draft animals tread out the grain by walking over the stalks in a circle. This latter approach required less human labor, freeing workers for use elsewhere. The problem with both these methods, however, was that by doing the work outside, the grain got dirty and was vulnerable both to theft and the elements. By moving the operation indoors, Washington hoped to prevent spoilage and theft. Unfortunately, the laborers who were supposed to do the threshing indoors were not happy with the new arrangement. Washington complained to a friend in the fall of 1793 that, despite having "one of the most convenient Barns in this, or perhaps in any other Country, where 30 hands may with great ease be employed in threshing . . . notwithstanding, when I came home . . . I found a treading yard not 30 feet from the Barn door, the

Wheat again brought out of the Barn and horses treading it out in an open exposure liable to the vicissitudes of weather."[18] While it is understandable that the enslaved workers preferred to let horses do this tedious job, what may not be so obvious is that, as Washington originally envisioned the process, working conditions inside the barn would have quickly deteriorated for anyone trying to thresh there, as dust and grain flew up into the air and made breathing difficult. There were probably valid reasons for the slaves' reluctance to accept this innovation.

Washington was forced to compromise. He was finally able to get what he wanted by constructing an elaborate treading barn on his Dogue Run Farm. In building this new structure, which had sixteen sides and was thus an initial challenge to his brick masons and carpenters, Washington envisioned that the grain would be treaded out on the second floor of the structure using draft animals, and that the kernels would fall through the carefully spaced floorboards into a secure and dry storage area on the first floor. Only one laborer—the person driving the horses—would have been exposed to the dusty working conditions, as opposed to thirty at the earlier barn.[19] In this telling example, Washington was forced to alter his planned improvements so that they were compatible with the preferences of his slaves.

FIG. 2. Nineteenth-century photograph of the original sixteen-sided barn. (Courtesy of the Mount Vernon Ladies' Association)

The story of Mount Vernon cannot, therefore, be told properly without also telling the story of the many people who worked on this site. At Mount Vernon, as on so many other plantations in Virginia, those laborers were primarily enslaved. It was through their work that the buildings, including the mansion house, were constructed; crops were planted, cared for, harvested, and taken to market; large schools of fish were taken from the river and preserved for food and sale; and land animals, used for transportation, recreation, food, clothing, and stud, were looked after, and the Washingtons subsequently enriched. Like the Washingtons, the slaves too called this land home, living out their lives, making friends, forming families, raising children, and, like the Washingtons, being buried in its soil.

George Washington was born in 1732 into a world in which slavery was simply a fact of life. The first Africans had arrived in Virginia more than one hundred years earlier, and contrary to long-held beliefs among several generations of historians, new research has shown that most were enslaved from the outset.[20] The basic outlines of the legal status of slaves in Virginia were clarified in the 1660s and 1670s, with the passage of legislation stating that whether children born in Virginia were free or enslaved depended on the condition of their mother (1662); that conversion to Christianity and subsequent baptism would not result in freedom for a slave (1667); that masters would have almost total control over how their slaves were disciplined and would not be prosecuted if a slave died while being punished (1669); and that the government would police slaves and owners would be reimbursed for any slaves who were killed while being recaptured (1672).[21] As noted by historian John C. Coombs, "even before the supposedly critical turning points of statutory recognition of slavery in the 1660s and the beginning of direct African deliveries in the mid-1670s, only a handful of blacks in Virginia were held in the capacity as servants. . . . The normative condition for 'negroes' was enslavement." And, with few exceptions, that period of enslavement lasted for the lifetime of the individual.[22]

Until the 1690s, most slaves had come to Virginia by way of commerce with other English colonies in the Caribbean, rather than directly from Africa. At this time, the Royal Africa Company had a monopoly on the transatlantic slave trade, but that advantage was challenged at the turn of the eighteenth century. Once the market was opened to others, there were dramatic changes. In the words of historian William A. Pettigrew, "the company's demise increased the number of Africans transported, which

Africans were enslaved, where they went, and who transported them." He likewise noted that "a free trade in slaves also provided the mainland American colonies with an adequate supply of slaves for the first time."[23]

Statistics on the number of slaves arriving in the Chesapeake region reinforce this picture, with the trade showing relatively slow growth up until the last quarter of the seventeenth century: 100 people from 1626 to 1650 versus 2,900 from 1651 to 1675. The trade more than tripled between 1675 and 1700, with the importation of 9,200 slaves, and then exploded in the eighteenth century: 30,000 people from 1701 to 1725; 54,000 from 1726 to 1750; and 31,000 from 1751 to 1775. Following the start of the American Revolution, the numbers dropped dramatically: in the last quarter of the eighteenth century, only 500 slaves came into Virginia from overseas.[24]

The rapid increase in the number of slaves being imported to the Chesapeake in the eighteenth century can also be seen in the greater Mount Vernon neighborhood. When George Washington began cultivating the land there in 1754, the population of the surrounding county, known as Fairfax, was about 6,500 of whom a little more than 1,800, or about 28 percent, were slaves of African origin. The proportion of slaves in the population as a whole rose throughout the century; by the end of the American Revolution, over 40 percent of the people in Fairfax County were enslaved.[25]

The story of the Washington family in America began in the mid-1650s, when two young men, John and Lawrence Washington, arrived in Virginia. Their family had been loyal to the deposed king, Charles I, during the English Civil War, and the brothers saw little future for themselves in England as long as Oliver Cromwell and Parliament were in control of the government. Thus, they set out to make their fortunes in the colonies. Both quickly established themselves, volunteering for public service and marrying well as stepping-stones to advancement. Although there is earlier evidence that the family owned slaves in the seventeenth century, the first specific mention of slaves in the family wills came with the death of John Washington's grandson Augustine, who died in 1743 leaving land and slaves to his widow and children. One of those children, the eldest son of his second marriage, was George Washington, who was due to inherit the 280-acre farm near Fredericksburg, Virginia, upon which the family was then living, and "ten negro Slaves" from his father.[26]

By this time, the family was ensconced in the wealthiest 10 percent of the Virginia population and were considered part of the "second tier" of the Virginia aristocracy, having little prominence or influence outside their home county.[27] George Washington's earliest biographer, his former military aide David Humphreys, voiced the opinion many years later that "the children of opulent families" in Virginia "were in danger of becoming indolent & helpless from the usual indulgence [of] giving a horse & a servant to attend them, as soon as they could ride; if not imperious & dissipated from the habit of commanding slaves & living in a measure without control." Humphreys believed that those Virginians who were educated in the colony rather than England, "who had fortitude enough to resist the temptations to which they were exposed in their youth, have commonly been distinguished by success in their various professions." He then indicated that there were "many Virginians, besides [Washington]" who were "the most remarkable examples of application & perseverance, which this age has produced."[28] The fact that Washington chose not to comment on these statements when he did suggest corrections to or clarification of other passages from the draft indicates that he largely agreed with Humphreys.

It would be several years before George Washington actually took possession of the slaves in his father's bequest. About 1750, the division of Augustine Washington's slaves was finally made, perhaps brought on by the fact that eighteen-year-old George had made his first land purchase with money earned from surveying. There had been some natural increase among the family's slaves in the ensuing seven years, so the young man actually acquired eleven slaves, valued at £202.10.0. (For Washington's acquisition of slaves, see table 1.)[29] The death of George Washington's older half-brother, Lawrence, in 1752 brought another group of slaves in two parts: the first included four adults and two children in 1754, while the second was made up of three adults and two children in 1762.[30]

As a young adult, George Washington purchased several additional slaves, but it was after his marriage to Martha Dandridge Custis in January 1759 that Washington's overall wealth—and his slaveholdings—increased dramatically.[31] His young bride was the widow of a wealthy planter, Daniel Parke Custis, whose multiple plantations were located over one hundred miles south of Mount Vernon, in six counties along the York River and on the Eastern Shore of Virginia. Like George Washington, Custis was a fourth-generation Virginian, but his family was much wealthier and had fewer children than the Washingtons; by the time of his father's death in 1749, Daniel was the sole surviving heir, his sister having died five years before. He was a good businessman who specialized in growing high-quality tobacco for the British market. The solid reputation of his product was the result of personally supervising such factors as seed selection, the sorting and packing of the crop, and being responsive to problems noted by his customers. The income from exported tobacco was supplemented by the production of grains (corn, wheat, oats) for sale locally and in the West Indies, as well as sales of livestock and related products (meat, butter, and wool), and income from the operation of three gristmills and a commercial fishery. Unlike many other planters, whose families were newer to Virginia, Custis inherited so many slaves that he had no need to purchase more, saving him a considerable amount of money. Many of the Custis slaves had been born in Virginia, and as a result of fairly balanced sex ratios on his older properties, the enslaved population on his estates grew rapidly through natural increase, rather than purchase. Fearing debt, Custis was careful with his money, and while he avoided borrowing for himself, he made additional income by lending to neighboring plantation owners. Historian Lorena Walsh notes that "few other Chesapeake planters had the capital, fiscal discipline, and financial expertise to benefit from a similarly distributed asset portfolio." Her examination of the plantation financial records for 1757–59 shows that those plantations were doing very well: while expenditures totaled £1,934.94 in those years, overall income came to £4,581.15.[32]

Daniel Custis died suddenly in the summer of 1757 at the age of forty-six. As careful as he was with money, he had not drawn up a will, a fact that would have serious ramifications for both his family and those they enslaved for decades to come. This unexpected death left his twenty-six-year-old widow with two very young children to raise alone, as well as the management of over seventeen thousand acres of land and almost three hundred slaves. Her dower share of the Custis estate brought her a life interest in one-third of her late husband's property, including eighty-four slaves: one man and five women who worked in the house; the child of one of those women; five male tradesmen; thirteen slaves on a Custis quarter in New Kent County, Virginia; twenty-four slaves in York County; twenty-one in King William County; and fourteen in Hanover County. Of these people, at least the six described as house servants, the child, and the tradesmen appear to have accompanied their mistress to her new home at Mount Vernon shortly after the marriage. Still others were brought up to Mount Vernon later (for example, twenty-two came north from the Custis plantations in 1770).[33]

Perhaps a couple of points about legal issues would be helpful at this point. According to eighteenth-century English laws of coverture, an unmarried woman or widow could own and "convey property, make a valid contract, sue or be sued, execute a deed, and make a will." Although not always true in practice, in theory a married woman "could do none of these things without her husband's consent or participation."[34] The important thing to remember about dower property is that neither the widow nor any subsequent husband she might marry actually owned it. Ordinarily, because married women could not own property, a remarriage would mean that the new husband automatically took possession of any property (land, slaves, or whatever) that the widow brought to the marriage. Because the widow of a man who died without a will only had a life interest in one-third of his property, she did not own it but could only manage it as long as she remained a widow. If she remarried, her new husband would not own the dower property either, but he would take over management of it. The owner was the estate of the first husband and eventually his heirs.[35]

In addition to the enslaved people from the Custis estate, during the twenty-one years prior to the start of the Revolution, George Washington purchased more than sixty slaves.[36] At least some of the African-born slaves were acquired directly from slave ships, which landed their human cargos on the Maryland side of the Potomac River. Washington, like many other Virginians in the area, took advantage of the fact that a substantially higher duty was charged on newly imported Africans in Virginia, a fee that was paid by the purchaser rather than the importer, and was applied to the sales price, which varied depending on the value of an individual slave. In contrast, there were a number of years when the duty in Maryland was as much as 15 percent less than that exacted by Virginia, made even better by the fact that it was applied per head, without regard to factors that influenced purchase price. The fact that Virginia required no duties for slaves imported from another colony for a person's own use made going across the border to acquire slaves particularly tempting. In at least one or two instances, Washington's friend Alexandria merchant John Carlyle purchased newly imported Africans for him in Maryland, leading historian Donald M. Sweig to point out the questionable nature of the transaction: "That Washington was not actually transporting the slaves himself and that Carlyle was not importing them for his own use, both legal requirements for duty-free importation, seems to have been overlooked or ignored."[37]

In addition to these people, an unknown number of enslaved people belonging to members of George and Martha Washington's extended families were also at Mount Vernon for varying lengths of time. For example, when Martha Washington headed to Valley Forge in the early months of 1778, one of the slaves accompanying her was a young man named Tom, who belonged to cousin Lund Washington but was then riding "as a postill[i]on for Mrs. Washington."[38] Almost a decade later, on January 12, 1787, George Washington recorded in his diary that his nephew and farm manager, George Augustine Washington, set off after dinner for New Kent County, Virginia, "in order to receive & bring up some Negroes which his Wife's Father Colo. Bassett had given him."[39] Following George Augustine's death, two of his carpenters, Gabriel and Reuben, were still working on projects with both hired and indentured carpenters at Mount Vernon, although his uncle intended to pay for their time.[40] Washington ordered his farm manager to "guard against" two other slaves from that family, Charles and an unnamed young man working in the stable, because he believed they were "impudent & self willed, & care not how extravagantly they feed, or even waste," citing one instance in which the younger fellow had used hay, rather than straw, as bedding for one horse.[41] Altogether, historians Philip D. Morgan and Michael L. Nicholls estimate that Washington owned and/or managed about 670 slaves during the course of his lifetime (see tables 2–4).[42]

The men, women, and children who made up this first generation of enslaved residents during George Washington's proprietorship of Mount Vernon included a mix of peoples, with varying degrees of acculturation to the dominant English culture. Some were newly arrived Africans coming either directly from that continent or after being put aboard another vessel in the West Indies. Although it is unlikely, a few others may have come after years of enslavement in the West Indies or Caribbean, whether they had been born there or in Africa.[43] Another group had been born on other plantations in Virginia, as the second or third generation of their families in America, and had only known life as slaves.

Africans in Virginia

From the arrival of the first Africans at Jamestown in 1619 through the beginning of the American Revolution, which includes the years when Washington was building up his workforce, over 95 percent of enslaved people were coming into Virginia on ships primarily originating in the British ports of Bristol (45.6%), London (32.0%), and Liverpool (18.0%), with the rest hailing from elsewhere in England, Barbados, and America (Virginia, Maryland, Rhode Island, Philadelphia, and Boston).[44] Analysis of Atlantic slave trade voyages during this same period shows that the largest number came into the Chesapeake from the Bight of Biafra, also known as the Bight of Bonny (58,000 people from what are now eastern Nigeria, Cameroon, Equatorial Guinea, and northern Gabon), followed, in descending order, by Senegambia (39,000; today Guinea-Bissau, Gambia, and Senegal), West Central Africa (26,000; modern Gabon, Republic of the Congo, Democratic Republic of the Congo, and Angola), the Gold Coast (18,000; modern Ghana), the Windward Coast (5,500; now Liberia and Côte d'Ivoire), Sierra Leone (4,500; today Guinea-Bissau, Sierra Leone, and western Liberia), and the Bight of Benin (4,000; now eastern Ghana, Togo, Benin, and western Nigeria), with another 2,900 coming from the island of Madagascar off the coast of East Africa.[45] The cargoes of newly enslaved people who were shipped to the Americas from ports in West Africa were typically made up of clusters from the same ethnic groups, rather than individuals from disparate backgrounds speaking a variety of languages. Often they had been captured hundreds of miles inland before being brought to ships waiting on the coast.[46] This makes it difficult, without additional information such as records listing their tribal connections or their original names, to precisely determine their ethnic backgrounds. According to one historian, the lack of "valid, direct evidence [of ethnicity] from the British mainland colonies" is a result of the "scant attention paid to African ethnicities in English-language documents."[47]

Regardless of precisely where they began their lives, Washington's African-born slaves stood out from others who were born in North America. One aspect of this difference was simply physical. Four men who ran away from Mount Vernon in August 1761 were described in a runaway advertisement as Africans. Two had been purchased directly from the ship carrying them from their homeland two years before, while the other two had lived for some time in Virginia (one in Williamsburg and King George County and the other in Middlesex) before they came into the possession of George Washington. Two of the four are described as having tribal cuts on their faces, filed teeth, and/or decorative scarring on their backs.[48] Another African-born slave, a carpenter named Sambo Anderson, was described as having gold earrings and a face with high cheek bones, embellished with tattooing and tribal scars.[49] Anderson was one of at least two slaves at Mount Vernon—as an elderly man, the other was known as "Father Jack"—who claimed to have come from royal families in their homelands. From the experiences of other people in the Chesapeake, we know that slaves with similar claims to royal backgrounds sometimes looked down on fellow slaves, a reaction that might have made it difficult to form new relationships and become part of a community.[50]

The fact that Anderson continued to be called by his original name, a very common one in West Africa even today, is intriguing.[51] People from this part of the world are often named for either the day of the week on which they were born or for their birth order within their family. Sambo is a name used among two largely Muslim groups: the Hausa people in what is now northwestern Nigeria and southern Niger, and the Fulani or Fulbe, who are mainly in the eastern parts of Guinea and Senegal. Signifying a second son, the name can also be found among other ethnic groups in this part of Africa.[52] Historian Ira Berlin has noted that it was typical in eighteenth-century Virginia to provide African-born slaves with English or classical names, taking care, as one planter recorded, that they "always go by ye names we gave them," as a way of "stripping the newly arrived Africans of their identity and inheritance."[53] Insisting on the use of his African name so that he did not become just another of the many men called "Sam" was also a way for Anderson to resist his enslavement.

For many decades, historians have vehemently debated the degree to which African traditions and customs survived in the Americas. Writing fourteen years after World War II, Stanley M. Elkins, for example, saw evidence for very little cultural transfer from Africa. He wrote of the work of anthropologist Melville Herskovits that, "despite much dedicated field work . . . [Herskovits] has been put to great effort to prove that in North American Negro society any African cultural vestiges have survived at all." Using psychological studies of concentration camp survivors and military prisoners of war, Elkins argued that the repeated series of shocks to which newly enslaved people were subjected—things like capture, separation from loved ones, long journeys to an African port, travel across the ocean, severe regimentation, exposure to the elements and squalid conditions, being stripped of one's name and social position, and harsh or violent treatment—resulted in such extreme trauma that, for a survivor, "nearly every prior connection had been severed. Not that he had really 'forgotten' all these things . . . but none of it any longer carried much meaning. The old values, the sanctions, the standards, already unreal, could no longer furnish him guides for conduct, for adjusting to the expectation of a complete new life." Through what is now known as Stockholm Syndrome, Elkins believed that the slave, like a hostage, came to see his master as a kind of good father figure.[54]

Almost fifty years later, historian Philip Morgan explained that African traditions certainly survived in North America but in slightly different ways depending on local conditions. He noted that during the last half of the seventeenth century, "many of the earliest blacks in both the Chesapeake and the Lowcountry assumed the customs and attitudes of their white neighbors and acquaintances." They were followed by later waves of unwilling African immigrants who "faced a double challenge," of adjusting "not only to new surroundings but to the rules and customs already worked out by the earliest [African] migrants." In the Carolina Lowcountry, however, the sheer numbers of these newcomers meant that the earlier "assimilationist slave culture . . . was swept aside by a rising tide of African slaves." The nature of slavery there, which featured a denser population of slaves on plantations, where they had a combination of more autonomy and freedom of both time and movement than elsewhere in British North America, meant that African cultural elements could thrive. This was in decided contrast to the situation in the Chesapeake, where the earlier "assimilationist slave culture" had taken "much firmer root." When large numbers of new Africans began arriving in Virginia and Maryland in the late seventeenth century, they were too widely scattered and isolated to maintain as many of the traditions from their homelands as the enslaved people in the Lowcountry.[55]

More recently, Michael A. Gomez has found numerous examples of the continuation of African culture in British North America, which is understandable given figures showing that, over the course of George Washington's lifetime, the number of African-born slaves compared to those born in America ranged from a bit less than half (about four out of ten) when he was born to about 20 percent (two out of ten) in the year he died. These cultural survivals even existed in New England, where slaves made up only 2–3 percent of the overall population in the first half of the eighteenth century, but the fact that they tended to be concentrated or clustered in particular geographic areas meant that socializing was easier than might be expected, as was maintaining elements of African culture: "In the pursuit of an African-derived way of life, eighteenth-century black New Englanders proved that plantations boasting of thousands were not always necessary. If black folk could get from one farm to the next on a regular basis and within a reasonable amount of time, they could and did re-create a distinctive culture, their propinquity to whites notwithstanding."[56]

In addition to their exotic appearance and family backgrounds, there is evidence that African-born slaves brought their own marriage customs, foods and/or methods of preparing them, folktales, and religious beliefs to Mount Vernon. We know from other Virginia plantations that they may also have brought African ways of working, as well as African forms of material goods, such as making specialized baskets for carrying things on their heads.[57] There is fragmentary evidence that at least some elements of languages spoken in Africa may have come to Mount Vernon as well. The name of a child born very late in Washington's life, which appears to be of Arabic origin, is discussed in greater detail in a later chapter. In another example, we see that one of the Mount Vernon seamstresses may have used an African word in a tense and stressful situation. The age at which a person arrived in Virginia made a big difference in how quickly they were able to acculturate to Anglo-American society and also influenced how well African cultural traits may have survived. For instance, when Daniel Parke Custis advertised for two runaway slaves in 1755, he noted that one of them, a man then about thirty years old originally from Angola, spoke very good English, which Custis attributed to the fact that "he was imported very young."[58]

In addition to newly imported slaves, still other enslaved people at Mount Vernon, like Washington's longtime valet and butler, the brothers William (Billy) and Francis (Frank) Lee, were acquired at sales held after colonists died, as their estates were broken up.[59] Having been through at least one owner prior to coming to Mount Vernon, most of these individuals would presumably have been either African-born slaves who were already at least somewhat acculturated to life in the colonies or the children—or even grandchildren—of those unwilling immigrants. At least some of them would have been, like the Lee brothers, of mixed racial background. Over the forty-five years George Washington managed Mount Vernon, these diverse groups of people—born in Africa, the Caribbean, or colonies in North America—would become coworkers, friends, enemies, neighbors, sweethearts, spouses, parents, aunts, uncles, grandparents—in short, a community.

The world they helped to create was finite in time, and its dismemberment began with the death of George Washington in 1799 and the subsequent freeing in 1801 of those individuals who had belonged to him. It ended finally when Martha Washington breathed her last in 1802 and the remaining slaves reverted to the Custis estate, eventually being divided among her four grandchildren.[60] In the following pages we begin to explore the world of the Mount Vernon slaves. Because of the limitations of the surviving sources, much of the information is presented from the point of view of George Washington and others who supervised the African American community at Mount Vernon. Only occasionally can the voice of one of the slaves be heard; their thoughts and feelings must often be inferred from their actions.

Sources

Mention of "the limitations of the surviving sources" should not obscure the fact, however, that Mount Vernon is richly blessed with incredible sources. Much of the documentation on this subject exists because of George Washington's extended absences from the plantation he so dearly loved. During both the Revolution and the presidency, and to a lesser extent during the French and Indian War, he kept track of events at home through letters from his farm managers. After the Revolution, even when he was home, Washington required weekly reports from these men, which recorded tremendous detail about the workings of the plantation. Many of these individuals were relatives: Washington's younger brother, John Augustine Washington I, who managed the estate between 1755 and 1758; third cousin Lund Washington, who ran the estate between 1765 and the first years after the Revolution; and nephews George Augustine Washington, Howell Lewis, Robert Lewis, and Lawrence Lewis, the first of whom came to help from the mid-1780s until his death early in 1793, while the next two assisted their uncle for brief periods during the second term of his presidency, and the last came on the scene following Washington's final retirement. Other farm managers—Humphrey Knight, James Bloxham, Anthony Whiting, William Pearce, and James Anderson—were hired and brought with them varying degrees of experience in, and comfort with, managing an enslaved workforce (see table 5).

In addition to managerial correspondence, Washington was a meticulous record keeper who maintained a diary for most of his life and kept records of both out-of-pocket expenses and major purchases from abroad. Filling out the picture presented by these financial papers are Martha Washington's letters and instructions to various family members and servants, inventories, wills, descriptions of the plantation, and even descriptions of individual slaves recorded by guests of the Washingtons. Finally, through their correspondence and memories of life on this plantation, Martha Washington's grandchildren helped to flesh out aspects of both the Washingtons' personalities and those of a number of individual slaves, as well as information on daily routines in the household.

Despite the large number of surviving plantation manuscripts from Mount Vernon, there were two major losses of original documents in the late eighteenth and early nineteenth centuries. The first took place after the death of Lund Washington in 1796, when his widow, Elizabeth, followed his wishes and destroyed much of his correspondence with George Washington. Just a few years after the loss of those letters, sometime between George Washington's death in 1799 and Martha's in 1802, Martha Washington consigned forty years of correspondence between herself and her husband to the flames.[61] While it was not uncommon at the time for the remaining spouse to destroy the correspondence of a deceased partner (both Thomas Jefferson and James Monroe, for example, did the same thing following the deaths of their wives), and the desire to maintain some degree of privacy is perfectly understandable, the loss to the historical record has been incalculable.[62]

Visitors to Mount Vernon were in an interesting position. Generally of the same social status as the Washingtons, they were often, especially after the Revolution, from outside the South. Slavery was for many of these people something of a novelty, and a number of them took the time to talk to the slaves and record their impressions. While the response of the slaves to questions about their happiness and feelings for their master was often positive, they were very likely hesitant to voice negative feelings to someone who might relay the information back to the Washingtons. Several years after the Revolution, a houseguest remarked that George Washington was "revered and beloved by all around him." The man went on to note, after a discussion of the house servants, that "smiling content animated and beamed on every countenance in his [Washington's] presence."[63] Another gentleman who visited Mount Vernon in 1793 reported that, in his opinion, the slaves there received better rations than on other plantation. One morning he went for a walk during which he "saw and conversed with many of them . . . who seem well contented in their Situation and most attached to their Master."[64] The nephew of John Hancock, Washington's fellow revolutionary, noted in a letter that there were "upwards of 500 slaves" at Mount Vernon, an overestimation, and that "they are all as happy as Lords."[65] As is shown in a later chapter, by no means were "all" the enslaved people at Mount Vernon "happy," a fact they conclusively demonstrated by their actions on numerous occasions.

Among several important descriptions left by visitors, two in particular stand out for the insights they provide. Both were written by upper-class Europeans for whom slavery was something outside their experience. The first, Louis-Philippe, the exiled duc d'Orleans and future king of France, came to America during the throes of the French Revolution and spent a few days at Mount Vernon in 1797, along with a servant named Beaudoin. The two Frenchmen were intrigued with the institution of slavery. They recorded information about the number and fertility of the Mount Vernon slaves, the hopes for freedom in the slave community, proselytizing among them by several religious groups, punishment, and the feelings of enslaved individuals about relatives who ran away.[66] The second invaluable account was written by Julian Ursyn Niemcewicz, a Polish nobleman whose two weeks with the Washingtons in 1798 resulted in a journal that provides invaluable details about all facets of life at Mount Vernon—and especially slavery. He had long intimate conversations with both George and Martha Washington, toured the estate with the farm manager, and observed the activities of the slaves on their day off.

These varying types of sources provide the raw material for understanding different questions about slave life. Sources such as the surviving Mount Vernon slave lists are tremendously important because through them it is possible to learn something about the broad outlines of slave life on this particular plantation. Unlike sources such as diaries and letters, this type of manuscript is invaluable for allowing historians to determine the range of experiences for a given population at a given time, or even through time, as was the case with slave lists drawn up by George Washington in 1786 and 1799. Unlike earlier lists produced prior to the Revolution for tax purposes, these lists, compiled for Washington's own benefit as he struggled first to reacquaint himself with the enslaved community after the war and thirteen years later as he made preparations for his own death, provide information on gender, age, occupation, and family relationships.[67] This kind of source also makes it possible to a certain extent to make inferences based on the data extracted about some emotional aspects of slave life here, for example, the importance to the enslaved community of having large segments of the population living on the same farm for more than a decade. What these lists cannot reveal, however, is much about individual experiences and a given individual's reaction to the events in their lives. To flesh out the slave experience at Mount Vernon, it is necessary to turn to those other, more narrative sources—diaries, letters, newspapers. Unlike most historic sites without that wealth of resources, Mount Vernon has been blessed with almost too many. It is also important, in order to put the Mount Vernon slaves and their experiences into context, to look at sources from other plantations.

Coming Chapters

The chapters which follow start with one of the most important aspects in the lives of enslaved people—the personality and character of their master or mistress—and the nature of management on the plantation. From there, the perspective changes to look at various aspects of the material, family, and work lives of the slaves. Finally, there is an examination of the many ways George Washington tried to influence the behavior of his slaves and their methods of resisting that management. My intention is that the reader will come away with an understanding of the fact that the institution of slavery was lived by very real people. Each enslaved person brought to the experience his or her own unique background, personality, abilities, family situation, moral standards, and dreams, as did the white people with whom the slave had dealings. All of these factors can, and did, have an impact on how they both experienced, and responded to, the "peculiar institution." There is a tendency to see only the large numbers involved in the story of slavery in the United States and forget the experiences of individual people. I hope that by the time readers arrive at the last page, they will feel that they know both the Washingtons and the enslaved community at Mount Vernon much better.

Themes

Throughout these chapters several recurring themes appear. Over the many years there were slaves at Mount Vernon, African-born slaves were trying to adjust to captivity, while their American-born descendants became more and more acculturated to life in the new world. From her study of an Alabama community founded after the Civil War by former slaves from Africa, historian Sylviane A. Diouf learned that these people who were captured as children, teenagers, and young adults never got over the shock of being taken and spent the remainder of their lives trying to recreate the world they were forced to leave behind.[68] Something similar might well have been happening at George Washington's Mount Vernon, for elements of African culture do appear. At the same time, both African- and American-born slaves were marrying one another, as well as people, both free and enslaved, who lived off the plantation, thus expanding their family/kinship networks into the larger Fairfax County area. In the case of the dower slaves, they would have left behind a web of family and friends in and around the Custis properties in the Tidewater. Together these disparate groups of people learned new ways of working and prospering within their own and the dominant society, which at Mount Vernon included a mix of people who either came themselves—or their ancestors had—primarily from England, Scotland, Ireland, and Germany. Workmen hired for specific jobs might bring assistants who added even more diversity, as when in the spring of 1770 laborer Thomas Byrd arrived "to work with my People" on Washington's millrace, along with a Native American (very likely Cherokee) called Sciagusta, who was described as "a prisoner from the Indians."[69] In the process, these diverse groups of people were creating a uniquely American community.

Just as it is impossible to understand George Washington's life without studying his relationship to slavery and individual slaves, there is also a need to examine Washington in order to better understand the lives of the slaves at Mount Vernon. One aspect of his life that had a very real bearing on his slaves was the fact that he spent years as a military officer, something that influenced his expectations and management style but also led him to change his ideas about slavery. Another recurring theme is the conflict between George Washington, who was trying to get as much work done as possible in the hopes of, at a bare minimum, growing enough to sustain the lives of several hundred people, and perhaps even prospering as well, and many of his slaves who were trying to resist him personally, his ways of doing things, and the institution of slavery itself.

There were also changes going on during Washington's lifetime in the way slave owners viewed their relationships with their slaves. Historian Philip Morgan has written that the concept of patriarchy is a key to understanding interactions between masters and slaves in eighteenth-century British colonies. Unlike the case with hired and indentured workers, slaves were not covered by contracts in their relationships with their masters. Like family members, they were subject to the control of the *pater familias,* the male head of the household, who considered them dependents. Morgan suggests that "being part of a household served to cushion slaves from the full force of free market commercialism. Harsh profit-and-loss purgatives had not yet voided the world of its traditional notions of duty, mutuality, and patriarchal care." He notes, however, that ideas about the master-slave relationship were changing in the years that Washington was a slave owner, from patriarchalism to paternalism. Where patriarchal masters emphasized "order, authority, unswerving obedience, and were quick to resort to violence when their authority was questioned," those who were more paternalistic may not have been any less authoritarian or violent but tended to see themselves as more solicitous or generous toward their slaves. Paternal masters in general had a more sentimental vision of their relationships with their bondsmen, expecting gratitude, and even love, from their slaves while taking a strong interest in their religious welfare. Morgan also notes that "patriarchs never underestimated their slaves' capacity to rebel; unlike paternalists, they rarely boasted of the submissiveness or docility of their slaves." Neither did they believe "the fiction of the contented and happy slave." By the nineteenth century, paternalism was perhaps closer to the norm, but elements of both views can be seen in Washington's relationships with his slaves.[70]

Throughout this story, readers may find themselves shocked by continual reminders that slaves were considered property. There are some very pointed statements making this relationship quite clear. For example, following Washington's defeat at Fort Necessity, he complained in two letters about losing "valuable Papers, cloathg, Horses, & seve[ra]l other things . . . of no inconsiderable value." Among those other things was "a valuable Servt," who was wounded in the battle; that unidentified slave died of his injuries within just a few days.[71] Many such references appear in conversations about borrowing money and settling debts. In October 1769, Washington wrote about a neighbor, John Posey, who had run up a lot of debts and needed to sell his plantation and "twenty-five choice SLAVES," as well as horses, cattle, sheep, hogs, furniture, and agricultural tools, in order to pay off his creditors. Any money from the sales would be given to Washington, who was helping to settle these debts. In discussing the situation, Washington conflated the man's slaves and livestock when he suggested that the present season was a perfect time to sell Posey's slaves to pay off those debts, because "his Negroes & stock never can be disposed of at a more favourable juncture than in the Fall when they are fat and lusty and must soon fall of[f] [lose weight] unless well fed which I am sure cannot happen in the present case for very good reasons too obvious to mention [Posey's debts]."[72] A few years later, Washington discussed loaning money to James Mercer, for which the borrower's slaves served as collateral. He noted that "Negro's are a very uncertain and precarious Security" and asked, "Is there any Land unincumber[e]d that you could give a Mortgage on? if there is I had rather have it, if the Title is clear and indisputable and of sufficient value than Negroes; but am content notwithstanding to have a fresh Mortgage on the same Negroes if they are still living and under no legal disability."[73] Fourteen years later, Washington was attempting to use a certificate from the state of Virginia reimbursing him for one of his slaves, who had been executed in 1781, as well as the interest on that certificate in order to pay his taxes because he was short of cash.[74]

There are times in these chapters, especially when discussing oral history, when the documentable facts do not support the family story that has been passed down. In several of these cases, I follow the evidence as far as I can with the resources at hand and the reader may be left in the air about a certain question. It may be that researchers elsewhere can help to pin down these traditions or explain the discrepancies better than I—and I welcome their input.

Why does it matter what happened on one Virginia plantation two centuries in the past? To begin with, George Washington, the man who owned that plantation, was an incredibly important figure in his own lifetime and remains so to this day. In the words of historian Joseph J. Ellis: "Benjamin Franklin was wiser than Washington; Alexander Hamilton was more brilliant; John Adams was better read; Thomas Jefferson was more intellectually sophisticated; James Madison was more politically astute. Yet each and all of these prominent figures acknowledged that Washington was their unquestioned superior. Within the gallery of greats so often mythologized and capitalized as Founding Fathers, Washington was recognized as *primus inter pares,* the Foundingest Father of them all."[75] As Americans continue to turn to the founding generation for insights into what they intended the United States to be, and as the country continues to experience racial turmoil, studying how the "Foundingest Father of them all" handled the issue of slavery over the course of a lifetime may suggest a way forward to his political descendants.

One of the things I hope this book does is to give readers the basic historical information they need in order to answer the question of how George Washington should be judged by history on the issue of slavery. This is more than just an academic question. In the fall of 1997, the historical community, and seemingly much of the country as a whole, were rocked by the news that the name of a school in New Orleans had been changed from George Washington to Charles Richard Drew Elementary School. This change was made in order to conform to a 1992 schoolboard policy of not naming schools for individuals who were slave owners "or others who did not respect equal opportunity for all." For weeks afterward, the papers were filled with editorials and letters either condemning or supporting the schoolboard's actions. One writer declared with glee that the New Orleans school had "struck a blow for learning, scholarship and inclusiveness" by kicking "George Washington out of the consciousness of the public-school kids of New Orleans, and good riddance. The father of our country is not a fit role model anymore because in addition to being the father of our country, he was the master of several hundred slaves."[76] More recently, almost five hundred professors and students at the University of Virginia asked that the head of that institution stop quoting Thomas Jefferson, who founded the university, because of his "slave-owning past." In response, President Teresa Sullivan noted, "Quoting Jefferson (or any historical figure) does not imply an endorsement of all the social structures and beliefs of his time, such as slavery and the exclusion of women and people of color from the University." She went on to say that the school had a "long-standing tradition of open discourse" and endorsed the right to "speak out on issues that matter to all of us, including the University's complicated Jeffersonian legacy."[77]

While I can understand the disgust many people in our society feel about slavery and their inability to fathom how anyone could "own" another person, judging a person from another time and culture by the standards of one's own time is quite naive. Not only does it take a person, in this case Washington, out of the context of the time in which he lived, but on the question of slavery, takes him out of human history as a whole (this is discussed further in later chapters).

It also denies the experiences of people who were themselves enslaved. In the story of his enslavement in Louisiana in the nineteenth century, Solomon Northup noted that there were significant differences between slave owners. In discussing William Ford, the first man to purchase him, Northup wrote,

> In many northern minds, perhaps, the idea of a man holding his brother man in servitude, and the traffic in human flesh, may seem altogether incompatible with their conceptions of a moral or religious life. . . . They are led to despise and execrate the whole class of slaveholders, indiscriminately. But I was sometime his slave, and had an opportunity of learning well his character and disposition, and it is but simple justice to him when I say, in my opinion, there never was a more kind, noble, candid, Christian man than William Ford. The influences and associations that had always surrounded him, blinded him to the inherent wrong at the bottom of the system of Slavery. He never doubted the moral right of one man holding another in subjection. Looking through the same medium with his fathers before him, he saw things in the same light. Brought up under other circumstances and other influences, his notions would undoubtedly have been different. Nevertheless, he was a model master, walking uprightly, according to the light of his understanding, and fortunate was the slave who came to his possession. Were all men such as he, Slavery would be deprived of more than half its bitterness.[78]

In contrast, Northup found Ford to be a very different kind of slave owner than a later one, Edwin Epps. The latter he described as "a man in whose heart the quality of kindness or of justice is not found. A rough, rude energy, united with an uncultivated mind and an avaricious spirit, are his prominent characteristics." Northup went on to say that Epps "could have stood unmoved and seen the tongues of his poor slaves torn out by the roots—he could have seen them burned to ashes over a slow fire, or gnawed to death by dogs, if it only brought him profit. Such a hard, cruel, unjust man is Edwin Epps."[79]

Finally, another reason for examining the issue of slavery at Mount Vernon is that, contrary to what many people believe, slavery is not a dead institution. Sadly, it is still a fact of life in our modern world. While slavery and the slave trade were outlawed by the United Nations in 1948, they continued into the late 1950s in the Arabian Peninsula, Southeast Asia, Africa, and South America. Since 1994, there have been news reports of slave trading in Mauritania and the Sudan, as well as stories coming out of Brazil, the former Soviet Union, and North Korea of women and children being sold into brothels in Southeast Asia, India, China, South America, and the

Middle East.[80] There have been, in addition, tales of involuntary servitude coming out of cities and farms in the United States.[81] According to one magazine article, 27 million people in the world today are still living in slavery, 100,000 of them in the United States alone.[82] Given the long legacy of slavery in world history, this may be a perennial fight, but perhaps learning about one of the greatest men who ever lived, the enslaved people who shared Mount Vernon with him, and his struggle to do what was right will inspire a new generation to take up the cause of liberty today.

1

"I Never See That Man Laugh to Show His Teeth"

George and Martha Washington as Slave Owners

Throughout human history and across many different cultures, the personality of a master or mistress and the way they managed their slaves were two of the most important factors in how those they enslaved experienced the institution of slavery. In his description of slave life on the West Indian island of Antigua in 1784, a visiting Italian nobleman commented that "their treatment, whether more or less cruel, depends on the disposition of those who live on the plantation."[1] In the case of an enslaved person, the management structure on a given plantation and the personality of an owner influenced not just the nature of the workday but also virtually every facet of life. It makes sense, therefore, to begin the study of slave life at Mount Vernon by looking closely at the management of the estate.

George and Martha Washington

For many modern Americans, George Washington was the quintessential leader, the charismatic head of a rebel army, and the only man who could be trusted at the head of the new government formed after the war. Through the sheer force of his personality and his embodiment of an ideal, he kept together a poorly equipped and ill-prepared army until its eventual triumph over the greatest military power of the day. Because of the nature of their relationship, the slaves who labored for him at his home saw at once the same and a very different man.

According to one member of Congress, George Washington organized his plantation very much as he did his army during the Revolution. Senator William Maclay of Pennsylvania, a staunch anti-Federalist who generally had nothing nice to say about the first president, cattily recorded in his diary a bit of gossip passed on by an acquaintance who had visited Mount Vernon:

> [Mount Vernon] . . . is under different overseers. Who may be stiled Generals—under Whom are Grades of Subordinate Appointments descending down thro Whites Mulattoes Negroes Horses Cows Sheep Hogs &ca. it was hinted that all were named. The Crops to be put into the different fields, &ca., and the hands Horses Cattle &ca. to be Used in Tillage pasturage &ca. are arranged in a Roster calculated for 10 years. the Friday of every Week is appointed for the Overseers, or we will say the Brigadier Generals to make up their returns. not a day's Work, but is noted What, by Whom, and Where done, not a Cow calves or Ewe drops her lamb, but is registered. Deaths &ca. Whether accidental or by the hands of the Butcher, all minuted. Thus the etiquette and arrangement of an army is preserved on his farm.[2]

Maclay was not the only one of Washington's contemporaries to see echoes of his military experience in the organization and management of Mount Vernon. A former neighbor, Englishman Richard Parkinson, believed that keeping order on a plantation required the same "severe discipline" as an army and credited Washington's success at managing enslaved workers not only to his industrious, methodical nature but also to his "being brought up in the army."[3]

Washington was very much a "hands-on" manager who kept close watch on all aspects of the plantation, from how well various crops were doing to whether the clothes being made for the slaves were of the correct type. Thoughts of his plantation were never far from his mind. During a two-day visit with the family of one of Martha Washington's granddaughters in the new Federal City, for instance, he suddenly decided to set out for Mount Vernon "between seven and eight o'clock in the morning in a great hurry to see the effect the last rains had had on his fields."[4] A houseguest from England in the fall of 1785 described Washington as "quite a Cincinnatus" who "often works with his men himself—strips off his coat and labors like a common man . . . condescending even to measure . . . things himself."[5]

One of the best illustrations of just how personally involved Washington could get comes from the reminiscences of an assistant to French sculptor Jean Antoine Houdon who visited Mount Vernon later that same fall.

Known as Beglair, the Frenchman was watching the harvest of a crop when one of the slaves reported that he was unable to work because his arm, which had been injured, was in a sling. According to Beglair, Washington put one hand in his pocket and raked with the other, admonishing the slave to watch him: "Since you still have one hand free, you can guide a rake. See how I do it: I have one hand in my pocket and with the other I work. If you can use your hand to eat, why can't you use it to work?"[6] While his actions in this instance may strike modern readers as insensitive to a person who was injured, Washington expected the slaves at Mount Vernon to share his own work ethic and applied the same criteria to their work as he did to his own. In other words, knowing how essential it was to the survival of the plantation to harvest the crop, and how limited the time to complete that work, he would have raked whether his arm was hurt or not.

Washington's management style may have been formed during his years with the army in the French and Indian War, but it was perfected on the plantation prior to the Revolution, and reached its highest development after that war. An early letter to a military subordinate, written when Washington was only twenty-six, hinted at the mature style to come: "You will take care therefore to keep up Discipline at the same time use lenity, to prevent discontent & Desertion. Be vigilent, & keep your Men Sober; observe Order and Regularity in the Garrison; which keep clean & wholesome; and as your numbers will be few, keep a regular and strict watch."[7] These instructions, so appropriate for the small and struggling army on the frontier, applied equally well to Washington's plantation thirty years later, where the free white population was outnumbered by enslaved Africans and African Americans by a factor of about ten to one.

In the 1770s, as commanding general of the Continental Army during the Revolution, Washington continued to keep a "regular and strict watch" on those he led. He frequently observed details that concerned him and consequently ordered changes in routine practices that might seem unworthy of notice to a modern commanding officer. By way of comparison, Washington was in roughly the same position as General Dwight Eisenhower in the Second World War, with charge over the military forces, including not only the army but the navy and marines as well, of more than one country. There were, of course, significant changes in military organization over the years, and Eisenhower was dealing with a considerably larger force. Still it is difficult to imagine the supreme allied commander taking the time to write detailed instructions on such things as the construction of huts; the placement and maintenance of latrines; sweeping the lanes and buildings in camp; the proper disposal of "Offal and Carrion," including dead horses; and how the men carried their kettles.[8] No matter was too small to escape Washington's attention, including the personal habits of his troops. At Morristown, he ordered that "no Soldier shall bath[e] in the heat of the day, nor stay long in the water at a time."[9] Finding those instructions too nebulous, however, about a year later, Washington directed that none of his troops remain "longer than ten minutes in the Water."[10]

Attention to Detail

For most of the years he was in residence at Mount Vernon, George Washington made a daily circuit of his farms. While he may not have gotten to every one of the five every day, in the course of a week he checked progress at each and later recorded his observations in a diary. In a letter to a friend following his retirement from the presidency, he described his typical daily schedule:

> I begin my diurnal course with the Sun. . . . If my hirelings are not in their places at that time I send them messages expressive of my sorrow for their indisposition—then having put these wheels in motion, I examine the state of things farther. . . . By the time I have accomplished these matters, breakfast . . . is ready. This over, I mount my horse and ride round my farms, which employs me until it is time to dress for dinner.[11]

George Washington was not the only plantation owner who felt a need to keep a sharp eye on everyday operations. Shortly after he took control of some land he inherited from his father, Martha Washington's son, John Parke Custis, complained that he had been "struggling with every Inconvenience, that a Person can meet with in coming to a Plantation in every respect out of Order." In a letter that must have gladdened the heart of the stepfather who raised him, Custis wrote that he had "found by experience already, that the Master's Eye is necessary in most Things."[12] This too had a military precedent. During the Revolution, Washington wrote to one of his generals, Alexander McDougall, to say how much he appreciated the latter's belief in the importance of keeping "Officers constantly in the Feild" with their men, that "I shall order a sufficient Number of Horsemen[']s Tents or small Marque's for the Officers," so that "they will then have no excuse for Absence, except want of health."[13]

By his own admission, George Washington kept such close personal watch on the plantation because he felt that was the only way to prevent problems from occurring or, once they had begun, to stop them at an early stage, before things went seriously wrong. As he reminded a new farm manager in the fall of 1793, nothing was inconsequential. It was necessary to look into "the smaller matters belonging to the Farms—which, though individually may be trifling, are not found so in the aggregate, for there is no addage more true than an old Scotch one, that 'many mickles make a muckle.'"[14] He complained of one hired white overseer that the man was too much of a social creature, both making and receiving frequent visits from friends. Such behavior took his attention from his business, leaving the slaves on the farm to their own devices. Little work was done, and several slaves were punished as a consequence, something which would not, in Washington's opinion, have been necessary if the overseer had done his job properly. Besides being unpleasant, Washington realized that punishment, or "correction," would never replace the time that was lost and often led to "evils which are worse than the disease."[15] In a similar vein, he cautioned another overseer that "he must stir early and late, as I expect my people will work from daybreaking until it is dusk in the evening; and, that the only way to keep them at work without severity, or wrangling, is always to be with them."[16] When he used the words "always to be with them," Washington meant that work, especially occupations that required "skill, and attention," were to be done "under . . . the immediate eye of the Overseers."[17]

Washington also scrutinized the work of his supervisory staff. Farm managers were instructed to keep a close eye on the activities of the overseers and to let them know immediately when something was being done incorrectly.[18] Overseers and other supervisors at Mount Vernon were issued paper and required to report weekly, in writing, to their employer about work done on the farms under their care, how many man-days were required for each task, and how much time was lost to illness. These reports were given to Washington at the end of the week, or to the farm manager if Washington were away from home. Although often busy with national affairs, Washington admitted that he was "anxious for the[se] weekly remarks." While chairing the Constitutional Convention, he asked one manager, his nephew George Augustine Washington, to transcribe the overseers' reports "between Saturday and Monday Night," so that they could be in the mail by Tuesday morning and get to him in Philadelphia by Friday. Some years later, as president, he suggested that the reports be taken to the post office in Alexandria on Wednesday, making it possible for them to go out on the Thursday morning post headed for Philadelphia, where they would arrive on Saturday. He noted that it "is more convenient for me to receive them on Saturdays than any other day; because between that and the departure of the [south-bound] Post on Monday, which gets into Alexandria on Wednesday, I can write with less interruption than at any other time."[19] Washington advised his subordinates that he wanted the reports not for "mere curiosity, or gratification of the moment; but that I may see into, and be informed of the State of things at any past period, by having recourse to them hereafter; as they are all preserved."[20]

Washington routinely questioned his farm managers about how the crops were coming, the status of various assignments, and whether the plantation's workforce was being kept sufficiently busy. Their answers, however, often did not contain enough detail to satisfy him, and on several occasions, Washington gave explicit instructions to his farm managers about his desired method for responding to letters. Farm manager Anthony Whiting, in particular, seems to have had an especially difficult time understanding what his employer wanted. After several weeks of dropping hints about questions to which Washington had never gotten an answer, he complained to Whiting that he had not received any of the information he had requested about the number and type of bricks on hand for a planned new barn at his Dogue Run Farm and suggested a remedy for their communication problem:

> That you may never forget directions that are given, it would be well to extract them from my letters, and place them in a pocket memorandum book, that they may be easily and frequently resorted to; without this, they may, when a letter is laid by go out of your mind, to my disappointment; and I would have nothing left undone which is required to be done, without being informed of it, and the reasons assigned; that I may judge of their weight.[21]

There must not have been much improvement. Several months later, Washington reiterated his advice about the memorandum book and gave Whiting some additional pointers, suggesting that he make notes on a "piece of waste paper, or a Slate" about the points to be answered in his letters to his employer.[22]

Whiting apparently did not understand what Washington was saying or chose to ignore the advice, because three months later his employer felt it necessary to be even more specific:

> My mind is impressed with many things, which you have been required to give answers to, which have never been received; and this will forever be the case if you depend upon the mere reading [of] a letter when you set down to answer it; without first noting on a slate or a piece of waste paper, every point as you come to it, that requires to be touched upon;

crossing it when complied with; or to stand uncrossed if you are unable to give an answer at that moment until you can do it at another time.[23]

The following year, a recently hired manager who replaced the then-deceased Whiting was given similar instructions. Washington felt that using the method he described was the best way to guarantee that "no part of a long letter can ever escape notice by not carrying the whole in your memory, when you sit down to write, or by being called off while you are writing it."[24] These stipulations are particularly interesting for the light they shed on how Washington, who freely admitted that "my memory is too treacherous to be relied on" in the absence of written documentation, very likely kept track of his own voluminous correspondence, on subjects ranging from the theory and practice of agriculture to family gossip, where to find housewares at the best price, fashions in interior decorating, and the permutations of politics.[25]

George Washington was a stickler for detail. During the presidency, he often complained about the lack of certain facts he needed from Mount Vernon: "I wanted to know the quantity [of potatoes] which grew in each lot, and in a particular manner, the quantity that grew among the Corn at that place; that I might see and compare the Crop of Corn and the Crop of Potatoes together; but it would seem as if my blundering Overseers would forever put it out of my power to ascertain facts from the accuracy of experiments."[26]

He also questioned information given in the weekly reports. In the summer of 1793, nephew Howell Lewis, then acting as temporary manager of the estate, was directed to pay closer attention to what he wrote in his reports:

> I see by the Report respecting the Ditchers that one of them is working at Union farm in the room of Cupid; but no mention is made of the latter, whether Sick, absent, or dead. . . . In the Mansion house report you make Godrey sick six days, (which is the whole week), and yet, he appears to be engaged in business some part of the week. I mention these matters not with a view to find fault, but to sh[o]w the advantages of correctness.[27]

This incredible capacity for registering detail was noted in several tales related by former slaves. Many years after his master's death, one "venerable old colored man, 77 years of age" remembered that the "slaves . . . did not quite like" Washington, primarily because "he was so exact and so strict. . . .

The most close attention must be paid to the condition of all the roads, fences, buildings, &c.; and if a rail, a clapboard, or a stone was permitted to remain out of its place, he complained; sometimes in language of severity." Perhaps to soften the effect of his recollections on his white audience, the old man added that Washington was "however . . . a most excellent man."[28] Many years after the fact, enslaved carpenter Sambo Anderson gave an example of how this attention to detail once led to additional work for himself:

> At one time, when he was building a corn house at Mount Vernon, he had the frame up and was setting the studding at the gable ends, but had not been particular to use his plumb. His master came riding along, and glancing at the building, said, "Sambo, that studding is not plumb; knock it off and use your plumb, and always do your work correctly." Sambo told me that he did not believe any man could have told the defect with his naked eye but his master, "but," said he, "his eye was a perfect plumb ball."[29]

Time

It was not unusual for households headed by masters accustomed to keeping track of time, as recorded by the hours and minutes of a clock or watch, to find themselves supervising people from both Europe and Africa whose preindustrial sense of time was marked by movements of the sun, moon, stars, and seasons.[30] Especially for slaves working in and about the mansion, clock time or the Washington family's sense of time became an important influence on their daily work. In his memoir of growing up in the Washington household, Martha Washington's grandson repeatedly stressed his step-grandfather's punctuality, undoubtedly because he and the young man had butted heads over the issue of timeliness. As George Washington Parke Custis recalled many years later, Washington was "punctual in everything and made every one punctual about him." Among the examples of people who became punctual in response were crowds who came out to see the president on his 1791 southern tour, as well as the manager of the theater in Philadelphia, and those being wined and dined in the president's house.[31] Congressional chaplain Ashbel Green recorded that during the presidency, "In private, as well as in public, [Washington's] punctuality was observable. He had a well regulated clock in his entry, by which the movements of his whole family, as well as his own were regulated." Green remembered that at the president's official Thursday afternoon dinners, Washington "allowed five minutes for the variation of time pieces, and after they were expired he would wait for no one." When late-arriving congressmen finally showed up, only to find the meal well underway, Washington's "only apology was, 'Sir, or Gentlemen, we are too punctual for you'; or in pleasantry, 'Gentlemen, I have a cook, who never asks whether the company has come, but whether the hour has come.'"[32]

At Mount Vernon, the household was kept on schedule by a bell, rung to alert everyone—family members, guests, and servants (white and black)—to the approach of a meal. Houseguest Winthrop Sargent recalled being summoned to breakfast by "the great Bell," which was probably similar to those at two contemporary Virginia plantations, Monticello and Sabine Hall. A resident at the latter noted that the bell there, which weighed over sixty pounds, was "always rung at meal Times."[33] Dinner was also announced by the sounding of a bell. George Washington wrote a friend in 1763 of his sadness that a promised visit to Mount Vernon had not occurred: "A constant Watch was kept untill the accustomed Bell gave the signal for Dinner, and said it was time to look no more."[34] The bell was first rung fifteen minutes before dinner. Many years later, Martha's grandson remembered that, in his later years, Washington generally rode his horse at a moderate pace except when running late for dinner, when "the most punctual of men would display the horsemanship of his better days, and a hard gallop bring him up to time, so that the sound of his horse's hoofs and the first dinner-bell should be heard together at a quarter to three o'clock"[35]

Of course, being on time to meals meant that a number of tasks had to be finished before the diners entered the room: the table had to be set with linens, china, silver, and glassware; food had to be prepped and cooked before placing it on serving dishes and taking it to the table at the appointed time. In his discussion of the work done by "Father Jack," an elderly African-born slave at Mount Vernon, Custis recalled that the old man supplied fish for the Washingtons' table but often fell asleep while waiting in his boat for the fish to bite. This led in turn to conflict with the cook, Hercules, who might face severe consequences if the meal was not ready in time:

> But the slumbers of Father Jack were occasionally attended by some inconvenience. The domestic duties at Mount Vernon were governed by clock time. Now, the cook required that the fish should be forthcoming at a certain period, so that they might be served smoking on the board precisely at three o'clock. He would repair to the river bank, and make the accustomed signals; but, alas, there would be no response; the old fisherman was seen quietly reposing in his canoe, rocked by the

gentle undulations of the stream, and dreaming, no doubt of events "long ago." The unfortunate *artiste* of the culinary department, grown furious by delay, would now rush down to the water's edge, and, by dint of loud shouting, would cause the canoe to turn its prow to the shore. Father Jack, indignant at its being even supposed that he was asleep upon his post, would rate those present on his landing with, "What you all meck such a debil of a noise for, hey; I wa'nt sleep, only noddin.'"[36]

The Distaff Side

While George Washington kept close watch on the overall operation of the plantation, his wife managed the domestic side of things. At least two historians have suggested that Martha Washington took a much harsher approach to slaves than did her husband. According to Henry Wiencek, she "had been schooled better than he in the rigid mental discipline of slavery," a schooling that led to a rift in the couple's relationship at the end of their lives over the issue of manumitting their slaves.[37] Unfortunately for that argument, there is little to no evidence of such disharmony between the Washingtons. More recently, Lauren F. Winner looked at the prayer journal of Elizabeth Foote Washington, who lived at Mount Vernon from November 1779, when she married cousin/farm manager Lund Washington, until sometime in 1784, when the couple moved to their own nearby plantation, Hayfield. In an entry written about the time of the move in the summer of 1784, Elizabeth expressed a desire to deal with fairness and kindness toward her slaves and never to rebuke them in front of anyone else. She never wanted to use "harsh expressions, because they are in my power,— such as fool—Blockhead—vile wretches." Winner notes that, although Elizabeth "did not single out and name those slaveowners who did deride their slaves with [such] epithets . . . it is reasonable to suppose that [she] may have been thinking about the mistress she would have seen up close during the five years of marriage she lived at Mount Vernon: Martha Custis Washington." Winner also observes that, while Martha Washington was away from Mount Vernon for most of this time, Elizabeth would still have seen her during her visits home, which totaled slightly more than a year through the end of the war, and then was with her for roughly nine months before moving to Hayfield.[38] Surviving evidence from Mount Vernon, however, suggests that Martha Washington was strict but does not support the contention that she was verbally abusive.

In her immediate family, and especially in the eyes of her grandson, Martha Washington had a reputation as an "admirable" manager, a firm but fair mistress whose "household was remarkable for the excellence of its domestics." Like her husband, on a typical day she rose at dawn, going first to the kitchen to oversee the preparation of breakfast and then stopping by the laundry and other buildings related to her tasks, such as the dairy and smokehouse. Sometime after breakfast, probably about 8 o'clock, she met with the cooks to decide the menu for the main meal of the day, dinner, which was eaten in midafternoon. In the late morning or early afternoon, she often gathered a group of young female slaves in her bedroom and taught them to sew or supervised older enslaved women as they knitted, sewed, or cut out clothing. She was back in the kitchen again before bedtime to supervise the mixing and kneading of bread.[39]

In contrast to Martha Washington's organizational ability, remembered with such fondness by her grandson, was the situation at his home, Arlington House, under the supervision of his daughter, Mary Anna Randolph Custis Lee. Mary's husband, Robert E. Lee, once apologized in advance to a friend, writing, "Tell the ladies . . . that Mrs. L is somewhat addicted to laziness and forgetfulness in her Housekeeping, But they may be certain she does her best. Or, in her Mother's words, 'The Spirit is willing but the flesh is weak.'"[40] Things were so bad that a visiting friend from New York noted that she would not like living in the South because of the "responsibility and *bother* of those servants [the slaves]." The friend went on to give the following example of the chaos that could ensue without strict supervision:

> Just fancy waiting tea (with company in the house from a long ride) until 8 oclo[ck] [about one to two hours later than normal] *because* they *could'nt find anything to milk the cow in.* Mrs Lee was fairly provoked when they told her they had gone to the dairy-maid & to this, that & the other & could'nt get a pan, & exclaimed "Why did'nt you come to me *the maid of all.*" Such shiftlessness is incredible to Northern housekeepers.[41]

Where George Washington was often remembered as stern and distant with his slaves, their relationship with his wife was warmer, and her role was, perhaps even more than his, that of a mediator. Martha Washington did favors for and tried to help the enslaved people she knew best—those who worked in and around the house—and was willing to forgive them for actions she would have considered an offense. When the Washington family went north during the presidency, Martha apparently promised the wife of Austin, one of the domestic slaves sent up there, that he would not be kept away indefinitely and that she would ensure that he was able to come home to be with his family.[42] Martha Washington developed especially close ties with the maids and seamstresses with whom she spent many hours, while either teaching them to sew or working on sewing projects together. She was extremely upset when one of those young women, her maid Oney Judge, ran away during the presidency. George Washington spent the next three years trying to get Oney to come home, with promises that, should she return of her own free will, "her late conduct will be forgiven by her Mistress."[43] When Charlotte, another seamstress, was listed as sick for several weeks in the work reports, it was Martha Washington, then in Philadelphia as first lady, who noticed and asked that the doctor be called in to take care of her if necessary.[44]

Despite her reputation as an excellent housewife, Martha Washington was happy to turn over a lot of those household duties to others. She admitted shortly after the family returned to Mount Vernon at the end of the presidency, without the services of either a steward or the family cook, Hercules, who had recently escaped, that she was dealing with "inconvenience" and "drudgery." To her younger sister she confided that her household duties "takes up the greatest part of my time . . . altogether I am sadly plaiged."[45]

Assisting her with management of such things as upkeep on the mansion, production and service of food for the table, and domestic textile production were a varied mix of younger relatives, such as niece Frances Bassett Washington and granddaughter Nelly Custis, as well as hired housekeepers and the wives of some of the hired men. For instance, in 1788, when George Washington was trying to acquire an indentured Dutch gardener, he noted that "I should prefer a single man, but have no objection to one who is married provided his wife understands spinning &c. and will indent as her husband does."[46] Occasionally, the wife of a hired worker had specific duties, such as supervising slaves at tasks like dairying and textile production.[47] George Washington, however, expressed exasperation with their talents. In a discussion of ways to prevent theft of fabric while clothing was being cut out, a frustrated Washington vented about the supervisory skills of two of those wives: "How far the Gardener[']s wife, or Allison[']s wife is to be depended upon in a business of this sort, I know not; but this I know, it is as little as either of them can do for the inconvenience I sustain by their living there, and the attendance they receive from my People."[48]

Much as her husband did, Martha Washington kept track of what was happening at Mount Vernon while she was away. Passages such as "Mrs. Washington desires you will direct Old Doll to distil a good deal of Rose and Mint Water, &c.; and we wish to know whether the Linnen for the People is all made up?" are fairly common in George Washington's letters to his farm managers. In her own letters on domestic topics, Mrs. Washington might order a thorough cleaning of the kitchen, china, and glassware prior to a visit home; insist that Frank Lee, the butler, "clean every part of the House constantly every week sellers and all"; or ask housemaid Caroline Branham to air the bedclothes and "brush and clean all the places and rooms that they were in."[49]

When she was away from home, Martha Washington seems to have read the weekly reports from Mount Vernon with as much interest and attention to detail as her husband. In a letter to one of his farm managers, George Washington noted that the seamstresses had not made as many shirts the previous week as they were expected to do. Whether Martha Washington noticed the discrepancy and pointed it out to her husband or he found something suspicious and asked for her opinion is unknown, but her husband continued, "Mrs. Washington says their usual task was to make nine with Shoulder straps, and good sewing. . . . Their work ought to be well examined, or it will be most shamefully executed, whether little or much of it be done."[50] She was more likely to have caught the shortfall than he, because preparation of clothing by and for the slaves fell under her purview, as it did for many other mistresses on southern plantations. For instance, some if not all of the twenty-six shirts for male slaves logged into the storehouse near the Mount Vernon mansion on August 18, 1787, as coming "from Mrs Washington" may actually have been made by her.[51]

Martha Washington was generally as critical of the slaves' work and as skeptical of their motives as her husband. She once complained about the supervision her former daughter-in-law's slave was giving that family's children, commenting that "it was a very careless trick in Mrs Stuart[']s maid, to let the children break the Looking glass."[52] She noted in one letter that the enslaved women doing the washing on the estate "always idle half th[e]ir time away about th[e]ir one business and wash so bad that the cloths are not fitt to use." The seamstresses came in for their share of complaints as well. One of these women, Charlotte, was thought to pretend illness, or "lay herself up for as little as any one will."[53] Disappointed that a sewing task was not done as she thought it should have been, Mrs. Washington commented that "it was but little more trouble for Charlot[te] . . . she is so indolent that she will doe nothing but what she is told she knows how work should be done." She went on to say that "I cannot find how it is possible for her and Caroline to be althogether taken up in making the people[']s cloth[e]s—if you suffer them to goe on so idele they will in a little time doe nothing but work for themselves."[54] Martha Washington expressed her doubts about the butler, Frank Lee, on occasion, cautioning her niece, "I fear there is not much dependance on him."[55]

Both George and Martha Washington's experiences with slaves, instead of opening their eyes to reasons why an enslaved person might not want to meet expectations or standards set by their owners—wanting to work at tasks to benefit themselves and their families rather than the Washingtons or a desire for independence—led the Washingtons to generalize about the basic character of all black people, rather than the effects of living in slavery. In a discussion with a friend about the duties of a hired steward at Mount Vernon, Martha noted that this person was expected to supervise the cooks and domestic servants in and around the mansion, which would require "instructions in some cases and looking after in all." The steward had to be "trust worthy—careful of what is committed to him—sober and attentive," which she considered "essential requisite[e]s in any large family, but more so among blacks—many of whom will impose when they can do it."[56] Two years earlier, in a letter to her niece, who was helping to manage domestic affairs at Mount Vernon during the presidency, Martha Washington tried to comfort the younger woman about the death of one of her enslaved children and expressed a hope that "you will not find in him much loss," reminding her that "the Blacks are so bad in th[e]ir nature that they have not the least grat[i]tude for the kindness that may be sh[o]wed them."[57] This last remark suggests that Mrs. Washington had probably been very angry—and even hurt—over the years, when slaves for whom she had interceded or done a favor later did something to resist the system, as when Charlotte's workload fell below the expected level.

Her husband expressed similar frustration when his wife's maid, Oney Judge, escaped from the executive mansion during the presidency. As he wrote to one correspondent, "the ingratitude of the girl, who was brought up and treated more like a child than a Servant . . . ought not to escape with impunity if it can be avoided."[58] Just how seriously George Washington took ingratitude can be seen in a letter written many years earlier in which he confessed to Virginia governor Robert Dinwiddie that he felt "nothing is a greater stranger to my Breast, or a Sin that my Soul abhors, than that black and detestable one Ingratitude."[59] Further examples of George Washington's generalizations about black people lacking knowledge and foresight, being thoughtless, and not mindful of their reputations are discussed in later chapters.

Martha Washington's attitude also needs to be seen in the context of the hierarchical, class-conscious society in which she had grown up, because she harbored similar feelings about hired whites. During the presidency, when farm manager William Pearce and his family were living in the mansion, Mrs. Washington informed her favorite niece that she would not be coming home to Mount Vernon in the summer of 1794 because her husband was making only a quick visit to the plantation and "it would be very inconvenient to me to be th[e]re without him." She then confided, "besides I should not like to have any thing to do with Mr Pearce[']s Family in the House."[60] Her attitude toward the Pearces, whom she had never met, softened a bit after the president got back to Philadelphia, bringing a good report about William Pearce. In her next letter to her niece, Martha Washington commented that she hoped her husband would be less "anxious about his plantation Business as he has confidence in Mr Pears—I am sorry to hear that his daughter is so ill.... I am pleased with your putting out such things as is necessary for the use of the House—and should like that Mr Pear[c]e should have any thing for his sick child that he can want that is in the House."[61]

Temper

George Washington's statement about Oney Judge's ingratitude points to another aspect of his personality that had an impact on the lives of Mount Vernon's slaves. A number of George Washington's contemporaries described a fierce temper lurking just beneath a generally calm surface. Ordinarily, he was emotionally reserved among whites of his own social class. For example, in a letter filled with advice for a nephew studying in faraway Philadelphia, he counseled the young man to "be courteous to all, but intimate with few, and let those few be well tried before you give them your confidence."[62] To a German count who came to America during the Revolution, Washington appeared "very distant" and sparing of words.[63] About a decade later, the wife of Vice President John Adams found the newly elected president to be "a singular example of modesty and diffidence. He has a dignity which forbids Familiarity mixed with an easy affibility which creates Love and Reverence."[64]

Those who knew the private Washington, however, knew a very different side to his personality. Martha Washington's grandson, who was raised at Mount Vernon by the Washingtons, was asked years later whether "children felt at home" with his step-grandfather. He replied that though George was always kind, they "felt they were in the presence of one, who was not to be trifled with."[65] Two of the best-known artists to capture Washington's likeness took note of his temper as well. Jean Antoine Houdon's famous bust of Washington was based on his subject's appearance during a disagreement with a horse trader who, Washington believed, was trying to take advantage of him.[66] About a decade later, a visitor from England discussed the American president's physical appearance with artist Gilbert Stuart, who had recently painted what was to become the most popular portrait of George Washington:

> All his features . . . were indicative of the strongest and most ungovernable passions, and had he been born in the forests it was [Stuart's] opinion that he would have been the fiercest man amongst the savage tribes. In this Mr. Stuart has given a proof of his great discernment and intimate knowledge of the human countenance; for although General Washington has been extolled for his great moderation and calmness, during the very trying situations in which he has so often been placed, yet those who have been acquainted with him the longest and most intimately say, that he is by nature a man of a fierce and irritable disposition; but that, like Socrates, his judgment and great self-command have always made him appear a man of a different cast in the eyes of the world.[67]

More than a decade after Washington's death, Thomas Jefferson, his former secretary of state who had known and worked with him for years, wrote a lengthy and detailed description of his personality in which he mentioned the temper that could so suddenly erupt: "His temper was naturally high toned; but reflection and resolution had obtained a firm and habitual ascendancy over it. If ever, however, it broke its bonds, he was most tremendous in his wrath."[68] In a series of letters about the first president written about that time, Dr. Benjamin Rush and John Adams discussed Washington's anger resulting from political attacks in the newspapers. According to Rush, Jefferson once told him that he had seen Washington throw a copy of "the *Aurora* hastily upon the floor with a 'damn' of the author, who had charged him with the crime of being a slaveholder." Adams responded, "I have heard much of Washington's impatience under the lash of scribblers, some of it from his own mouth. Mr. [Tobias] Lear related to me one morning the General's ripping and rascalling Philip Freneau for sending him his papers full of abuse."[69]

The "severity" of Washington's language toward those who worked for him, mentioned earlier by the slave who recorded Washington's concern with loose clapboards and downed fence rails, was recalled by several people who knew him privately and seems to have affected military subordinates and hired whites as well as slaves. In one wartime incident, Washington's temper got the best of him after his aide, Alexander Hamilton, arrived late for a meeting. As the young man came up the stairs, he found himself face to face with an irate Washington, who greeted him angrily with "Colonel Hamilton, you have kept me waiting at the head of the stairs these 10 minutes. I must tell you, sir, you treat me with disrespect." Hamilton's temper was aroused, and he responded, "I am not conscious of it, sir, but since you have thought it necessary to tell me so, we part." Hamilton resigned but Washington thought enough of him several years later to make him secretary of the treasury during his first administration as president.[70] Englishman Richard Parkinson noted his amazement at the "utterance of [Washington's] words" the first time he observed his famous neighbor interacting with the slaves at Mount Vernon, for he "spoke as differently as if he had been quite another man, or had been in anger."[71] The wife of a British ambassador who visited the Washingtons both officially in Philadelphia and at home in Virginia wrote in her journal that the American president, whom she had grown to admire very much, tended to control his emotions, or "passions," in public, "but in private and particularly with his servants, its violence sometimes broke out."[72] Perhaps it was for this reason that another acquaintance noted that Washington's servants "seemed to watch his eye and to anticipate his every wish; hence a look was equivalent to a command."[73]

While his family and colleagues could certainly attest to Washington's temper, it did not have the same implications for them as for servants, either free or enslaved, who were occasionally the targets of that anger. White servants risked losing their positions, housing, and food allowance. However, because skilled labor was often in short supply, especially in cities, they could usually find a new employer within a fairly short time or go into business for themselves. For a slave, the situation was more perilous. A master who was angry with a slave could punish him physically, abolish privileges such as visits to or by relatives or trips outside the plantation, or sell him away from everyone he knew, family and friends alike. In other words, the consequences for a slave were considerably worse than for a workman who was free.

Mitigation

Other aspects of slavery and slave owning at this period may have served to mitigate the effects of George Washington's temper. Like many other slave owners in late eighteenth-century Virginia, Washington saw himself as a patriarch at the head of a household made up of relatives as well as the people, both free and enslaved, who labored for him, but elements of the paternalism that characterized slavery in the nineteenth century may have been creeping in as well. Unlike in other parts of the New World, slave owners in the Chesapeake were not generally absentee landlords for whom slaves were simply the machinery by which they raised cash crops. On the contrary, masters in this area usually lived on one of the plantations they owned, where they could know both the domestic and fieldworkers very well. While their other farms or quarters might be some distance away, most were within the same colony or state, and there was the opportunity to know the people enslaved there as well, or at least better than someone living in England could know their human property in the West Indies.[74] By the end of his life, George Washington had been the proprietor of Mount Vernon for over forty years and had known as many as three generations of the same enslaved families. These were real people to him.

As did others of their social class, both of the Washingtons habitually referred to the slaves at Mount Vernon, and the hired whites as well, as part of their family. For instance, in May 1795, George Washington wrote to his farm manager after learning of the deaths of two slaves: "I am sorry to find by your last reports that there ha[ve] been two deaths in the family since I left Mount Vernon; and one of them a young fellow. I hope every necessary care and attention was afforded him."[75] Martha Washington too typically spoke of the slaves at Mount Vernon as members of her family. She informed a friend several months after her husband's death that "we have had an uncommon sickly autumn; all my family whites, and Blacks, have been very sick, many of [them] very ill—thank god they have all recovered again and I was so fortunate as not [to] loose any of them."[76] It is important, however, not to take references to "family" too literally. As Martha Washington's youngest granddaughter later recalled, "The Gen'l never called his negroes *his children,* I know for a certainty. He was a generous & noble master & they feared & loved him."[77]

There are indications that slaves and other servants may have been considered somewhat childlike and humorous. Martha Washington's grandson related that during the battle of Monmouth, George Washington turned to his officers and called their attention to a small hill where their valets, including his body servant, Billy Lee, who was looking through a telescope, had gathered to watch the battle. The general suggested that this mounted group, which probably included both free whites and slaves, was a tempting target, commenting, "See those fellows collecting on yonder height; the enemy will fire on them to a certainty." British gunners soon sent a cannon ball tearing through the trees toward the little group of servants, who quickly scattered, causing "even the grave countenance of the general-in-chief to relax into a smile."[78]

Despite his best efforts to conceal it, Washington's sense of humor did not go unnoticed by his slaves. In the 1830s, a visitor to Mount Vernon spent several minutes talking with an elderly former slave near Washington's tomb. The two men discussed the burial of one hundred slaves or "people of colour" in the area in front of the Washington family vault. Their rather disjointed conversation continued for some minutes, when the old man remarked about his former master, "I never see that man laugh to show his teeth—he done all his laughing inside."[79] While Washington may well have been self-conscious about his teeth, which were a source of pain and concern for much of his life, this description also suggests that he was consciously trying to keep up a stern front in the presence of those who labored for him. The affectionate humor with which he responded to these cases may have led him to respond with less harshness to those to whom he was especially close and/or saw as amusing, much as parents or teachers might go easier on the child who can make them laugh. It might also be seen, however, as related to a view of enslaved people that looked down on and perhaps expected less from them.

While use of the term "family" did not indicate that the Washingtons considered the slaves and hired workers their equals, historian Jane C. Nylander, writing about the situation of household servants in New England at this period, suggests that this broad use of the word conveys the idea of mutual responsibility. The servants, and one might extrapolate to include slaves, were providing services for which, like a family member, they were given certain goods or services in return, such as medical care when sick, clothing, a dwelling of some sort, food, and, in the case of servants, wages. Employers or masters were also responsible, not unlike parents, for the behavior of the people in their employ within the larger community.[80] Another scholar, Annette Gordon-Reed, has noted, however, that at least in the South at this period, "family" referred to people over whom planters "exercised power" and for whom they took "responsibility."[81] Patriarchy could be something of a two-edged sword. In the words of historian Philip Morgan, "At its most elevated, the patriarchal ethos was an uplifting creed, with the master offering to protect, guard, and care for his dependents, but, at its worst, it consisted of little more than sanctions, punishments, 'menaces and imprecations.'"[82]

Being considered "family," to whatever degree that meant to a given slave owner, might have softened the treatment accorded to slaves in the eighteenth-century Chesapeake, but it also created a problem for them. The master or mistress who looked at an adult slave as someone who needed to be taken care of essentially saw that person as a child who was incapable of looking after him- or herself. In other words, they were seen as perpetual children, not as adults with the capacity for earning a living and making decisions on their own. Aside from the unfairness of such a view on the part of a master, it also threatened the self-view of the slaves, some of whom may well have felt that they could not make it as free people.

This perhaps explains the situation at Mount Vernon about a year after George Washington's death. At that time, while making plans to free her late husband's slaves, Martha Washington confided in her old friend Abigail Adams that she was terribly worried about what would become of them: "One hundred and fifty of them are now to be liberated, men with wives & young children who have never seen an acre beyond the farm are now about to quit it, and go adrift into the world without horse Home or Friend. Mrs. Washington is distrest for them . . . and very many of them are already mis[e]rable at the thought of their Lot. . . . She feels a parent & a wife."[83] Of course, as is detailed in later chapters, slaves at Mount Vernon traveled away from the plantation for a number of reasons, including business for the Washingtons, selling produce from their gardens and things they had made, as well as to contract marriages with people on other estates. While they would not have owned horses and would be leaving their homes shortly after Adams's visit, they had work skills and a network of both whites and blacks in the neighborhood as business associates, relatives, and friends. The Mount Vernon slaves were thus hardly in the position of small children being abandoned in the woods.

The irony, of course, is that the Washingtons, like others of their class, had themselves been cared for and supported by these slaves. Both Mrs. Washington and those slaves who were worried at the thought of gaining their freedom failed to see that they were dependent on one another. All were victims of a worldview that saw blacks as less than competent adults—and the consequences did not end with emancipation.

Thoughtfulness

Another mitigating factor in George Washington's relationship with the slaves at Mount Vernon was his consideration of them. As a boy he had copied out a list of rules for proper behavior in society. One of those precepts noted that "those of high Degree" should treat craftsmen and "Persons of low Degree" "with aff[a]bility and Courtes[y], without Arrogancy."[84] He insisted on punctuality at meal times, in part to keep those slaves who served in the mansion from having to do extra, unnecessary work. As he reminded his step-grandson, who had approached him for permission to hunt before breakfast: "It is not only disagreeable, but it is also very in-convenient, for servants to be running here, & there, and they know not where, to summon you to them, when their duties, and attendance, on the company who are seated, render it improper."[85]

On one trip to Richmond after the Revolution, Washington was forced by the muddy roads and bad weather to stay for the night at Stafford Court House. The next day, in a letter to a nephew, he noted that he had not yet resumed his journey because he was "waiting a while for a cessation of rain, rather than to take Joe [Richardson, his postilion] out in it."[86] Many years after Washington's death, African-born carpenter Sambo Anderson told a neighbor that "his master was very particular and the most correct man that ever lived." As an example of what he meant by this, he said that, while living at Mount Vernon, he kept a little boat for traveling on some of the small bodies of water in the area. Occasionally, George Washington would borrow Anderson's boat, "but he was never the man to take it without ask-ing me if he could use it. Then he was so particular to place the boat just where he took it from. If it happened to be high tide when he took it, and low tide on his return, I have known him to drag the boat twenty yeard, so as to place it exactly where he took it from."[87]

A letter written during the settlement of his mother's estate shows Wash-ington's unwillingness to force a slave who wanted to stay with him to go elsewhere, even if it meant a financial loss. Early in his presidency, Wash-ington informed his sister, Betty, that an unnamed male slave who had belonged to their mother was living at Mount Vernon, and that because the man had "never stayed elsewhere" and apparently had a family there, "I should be glad to keep him." George continued,

> He must I should conceive be far short in value of the fifth of the other negroes which will be . . . divided, but I shall be content to take him as my proportion of them—and, if from a misconception either of the number or the value of these negroes it should be found that he is of greater value than falls to my lot I shall readily allow the difference, in order that the fellow may be gratified, as he never would consent to go from me.[88]

Even during his final illness, as he lay on his deathbed, Washington exhib-ited thoughtfulness toward those around him, including the slaves. When he became ill in the early morning hours of December 14, 1799, he would not allow Mrs. Washington to call one of the servants to help him because he was afraid Martha would catch cold. Some hours later, during the after-noon, realizing that Christopher Sheels, the young slave who worked as his body servant, had been in the room all day and standing for the entire time, Washington asked him to have a seat.[89]

As with other facets of Washington's personality, the consideration shown to his slaves was simply an extension of the way he treated everyone. One visitor to Mount Vernon recorded that upon his arrival at the plantation in January 1785, he was suffering from a severe cold and bad cough, which got worse when he went to bed. After a while, the door to his room opened and George Washington himself came in with a bowl of hot tea to help ease the visitor's symptoms. The poor guest was "mortified and distressed beyond expression." In his opinion, Washington's hospitable gesture, "occurring in common life with an ordinary man, would not have been noticed; but as a trait of the benevolence and private virtue of Washington, it deserves to be recorded."[90] Thirteen years later, another guest, knowing that the Washingtons habitually went to bed early, made a move to retire to his room about nine o'clock. When his host noticed that there was no servant about, Washington proceeded to get a candle for the young man and directed the guest to his room. In recording this incident, the flabbergasted guest remarked, "Think of this!"[91] In the first case, Washington may have shown courtesy not only to the guest, for whom he left his bedroom in a private wing to make the dark, cold trek to the main part of the house, but also to the slave he did not ask to get up in the middle of the night to prepare and serve the tea. In the second, probably aware that the house servants would be finishing up their work and getting ready to go to their own beds, he once again saw to the care of a visitor himself without bothering his slaves.

Servants belonging to others also benefited from Washington's thoughtfulness. Artist and engineer Benjamin Henry Latrobe immigrated to the United States in 1795 and visited Mount Vernon the following year. After breakfast on the morning he was to leave the estate, Latrobe stood on the steps outside the west door of the mansion, talking with Washington for about an hour on the subject of establishing a university in the newly constructed Federal City. At 10 o'clock, Washington seemed anxious to get to work, so the young guest signaled to one of the Mount Vernon slaves that he needed his horses. When Latrobe's own servant brought the horses up to the door, Washington approached the man to make sure that he had had breakfast before they set off.[92]

Approachability

The Mount Vernon slaves found the Washingtons approachable about their concerns, which ran the gamut from new occupations to offsite marriages, borrowing things from George, and even complaints about their rations. During the presidency, Kate at Muddy Hole Farm asked the president during one of his visits home if she could be given the position of midwife for the women on the estate, a request that Washington sanctioned as long as her qualifications were adequate.[93] He supported appeals by slaves at Mount Vernon who wished to marry individuals living off the plantation, both free and enslaved, a fact that resulted in almost one quarter of the married adults at Mount Vernon (22.9%) having spouses who did not belong to either the Custis estate or Washington. In 1799, for example, Alce, a spinner who lived at the Mansion House Farm, was married to Charles, a free black, while her daughter Anna had a husband in Georgetown.[94]

Even as a fairly young man, Washington heard his slaves' appeals for favors. One Sunday during the spring fishing season in 1760, the slaves asked to borrow a seine, which was not being used at the time, because Sunday was their regular day off from work. Although he reported that they "caught little or no Fish," the incident is significant because, as one historian described it, "some Negro, trusting in the kindness of the master, had asked a favor and it was granted."[95] Many years later, the Mount Vernon slaves even came to Washington with their grievances. When the cornmeal ration was changed in the early 1790s from "a heaping and squeezed peck . . . of unsifted meal" to a sifted, "struck peck only," presumably a level peck, Washington received numerous complaints from his slaves. He initially attributed the grumbling to the fact that sifted cornmeal left them no "husks" to feed to their chickens, but a conversation with Davy Gray, an enslaved overseer, convinced him that the people were genuinely hungry. Washington ordered his manager to look into the situation and admitted that his "feelings" had been hurt by the complaints.[96] In this case, Washington's actions testified to the trust he placed in Gray, which is discussed further in another chapter.

Much as Virginia planter Landon Carter compared information on gardening techniques with one of his elderly slaves, Washington also listened to his slaves' ideas about the work done on the estate.[97] In the spring of 1786, during what had been a difficult planting season because of the weather, Washington rode one morning to two of his outlying farms. Noticing that the newly planted peas were not doing well at Muddy Hole, he recorded that "some of my Negroes" attributed the fact that the crop had "come up very indifferently and looked badly" to its "being planted too early whilst the earth was too cool."[98] About two months later, Washington found "Chinch bugs" infesting much of the corn in the field. On one of the farms, however, the corn near a fence had been interplanted with Irish potatoes and seemed to be "much better & more uniform than in any other part of the field." Again, he discussed the situation with his slaves, noting in his diary that "whether it [the relatively good condition of that corn] has been occasioned by dunging, or otherwise, I could get no distinct acct. Some of the Negros ascribed it to this cause & it is more probable than that the Potatoes should have been the cause of it."[99]

Emotional Ties

Despite the differences of status and culture, there is evidence that affectionate ties developed between the Washingtons and some of their enslaved laborers. Colonel David Humphreys, one of George Washington's military aides, was with him for two important arrivals at Mount Vernon: the first in September 1781, after an absence of over six and a half years at war, as Washington made his way to the climactic battle at Yorktown; the second on Christmas Eve 1783 at the very end of the Revolution. It is unclear which episode Humphreys had in mind when in a poem about his former commanding officer, he described the actions of the slaves who were present at the homecoming: "Return'd from war, I saw them round him press, And all their speechless glee by artless signs express."[100] In his commentary on this scene, biographer James Thomas Flexner noted that, while it could be "interpreted, as have similar accounts concerning other celebrated slaveholders, to demonstrate that the proprietor was loved by his Negroes," still he cautioned, "Since the slaves left almost no written records, their emotions can only be fathomed through imaginations too easily colored by the preconceptions of the imaginers. Certain it is that a yearning for the proprietors' presence could be purely practical. The owners served as a court of appeal from often brutal overseers."[101] In considering this episode, it is also necessary to remember that the Mount Vernon slaves were welcoming home not just their master but his equally long-absent enslaved manservant, William Lee, who was their kinsman and friend.

A related scene, but reflecting the opposite end of the emotional spectrum, took place several years later at the beginning of George Washington's presidency. One of his young nephews, Robert Lewis, came to Mount Vernon to escort Martha Washington and her two youngest grandchildren to New York, shortly after his uncle's inauguration. In his diary account of the trip, Lewis described the new first lady's departure from Mount Vernon in the spring of 1789. For several days, the household had been in a state of confusion, occasioned by "packing,—and making all the necessary preparations for the intended peregrinations to N.Y." On the afternoon of May 16, following an early dinner and completion of "all necessary arrangements," which Lewis noted were "greatly retard[e]d," the travelers finally got underway about three in the afternoon. A considerable number of slaves, including not only house servants but fieldworkers as well, gathered to bid Mrs. Washington farewell. A granddaughter who was there that day later wrote, "I remember well what I felt when the Negroes came to take leave of their Mistress, to bid her farewell, & bless her for all her goodness to them—I see them now, many bent down with years, & infirmities, their heads silver'd by time uncover'd as they bow'd, & their voices resound in my ears, 'God bless you all' as the Carriage drove off."[102] Eliza Parke Custis had a propensity for melodrama, and by the time she wrote down her reminiscences a number of years had intervened to color her recollections, but her statements are corroborated by Robert Lewis, whose journal entry would have been written within hours of the events taking place. Lewis reported at the time that many of the Mount Vernon slaves, whom he described as "poor wretches," were "much affected" and "greatly agitated" about Martha Washington's departure. Perhaps not surprisingly, Lewis noted that his aunt was "equally so."[103]

Perhaps the best example of an affectionate relationship between master and slave at Mount Vernon was George Washington's association with William, or Billy, Lee, his valet, who was described by a contemporary as being "always at his [Washington's] side."[104] Purchased from Mary Smith Ball Lee in 1768, Billy Lee accompanied George Washington to war, serving faithfully for all eight years of the Revolution. Washington never forgot Lee's loyalty. Several years after the war, although he was not fond of the woman Lee had married in Philadelphia, Washington tried to get a passage for her to Mount Vernon, because of his feelings of affection and appreciation for Billy, who had "lived with me so long and followed my fortunes through the War with fidelity."[105] When Washington again left Mount Vernon for the presidency, Lee wanted to go along, even though two accidents in the intervening years had left him an invalid. Washington's secretary wrote that the president would prefer for Lee to remain at Mount Vernon, because he would probably due to his infirmity be of little use in the busy executive mansion and might even need someone to look after him. However, Tobias Lear wrote, "if he is still anxious to come on . . . the President would gratify

FIG. 3. Engraving of George Washington, by Valentine Green,
after John Trumbull, 1781, with Billy Lee in the background.
(Courtesy of the Mount Vernon Ladies' Association)

him Altho' he will be troublesome. He has been an old and faithful Servant this is enough for the President to gratify him in every reasonable wish."[106] Ten years later, in one of his final acts, Washington rewarded Lee for his faithfulness, making him the only one of the Mount Vernon slaves to be freed outright upon Washington's death. This provision of freedom and an annuity of thirty dollars was given "as a testimony of my sense of his attachment to me, and for his faithful services during the Revolutionary War."[107]

An unfortunate series of incidents from early in the year 1793 shows something of the closeness that developed between Martha Washington and another enslaved person, the seamstress Charlotte, in the many hours they spent together. A visitor to Mount Vernon once described the cama-raderie in the Washington bedchamber in the late morning as Mrs. Washington worked with a small group of women to clothe the inhabitants of the estate:

> On one side sits the chambermaid with her knitting, on the other a little colored pet, learning to sew, an old, decent woman with her table and shears cutting out the negroes winter clothes, while the good old lady [Mrs. Washington] directs them all, incessantly knitting herself, & pointing out to me several pair of nice coloured stockings & gloves she had just finished, & presenting me with a pair half done, begs me to finish, & wear for her sake.[108]

In his weekly report to George Washington, farm manager Anthony Whiting informed his employer that following a disagreement with Charlotte, she had become insolent with him and he had whipped her with a hickory switch he used for a riding crop. Two days later, the hired gardener's wife, who was supervising the seamstresses in Mrs. Washington's absence, reported to Whiting that she had sent some work to Charlotte but that Charlotte had refused to do it and sent the work back. Whiting admitted that he then whipped Charlotte again and that she had not done any work since, "under a pretence of her finger receiving a blow & was Swelld." Charlotte was outraged by the treatment she had received, stating that she had not been whipped for fourteen years. She was threatening to talk to Martha Washington about these incidents with Whiting, which were contrary to George Washington's general practice on the estate.[109]

Ordinarily, at least at this period, no one was allowed to punish a slave at Mount Vernon unless the case had been investigated and "the def[endan]t found guilty of some bad deed."[110] This policy would have been a means of preventing personality disputes such as this one between overseers and slaves from escalating out of control, which could lead to potentially serious physical and emotional consequences. Whiting seemingly was writing in order to get his side of the story to the Washingtons before Charlotte could. Interestingly, but perhaps not surprising given his military background, George Washington initially backed Whiting in this matter, writing that "your treatment of Charlotte was very proper, and if She, or any other of the Servants will not do their duty by fair means, or are impertinent, correction (as the only alternative) must be administered."[111] Whiting died about five months later.[112] The following month, as Washington was searching for a replacement farm manager, he made the comment that "if I could [find] a man as well qualified for my purposes as the late Mr. Whitting . . . I should esteem myself very fortunate."[113] By December 1793, still less than a year after the incident between Charlotte and Whiting, Washington's opinion about the late manager had changed completely. In a letter of advice written to Whiting's successor, he noted the importance of setting a good example and made the comment that, "unhapp[i]ly this was not set (from what I have learnt lately) by Mr. Whiting, who, it is said, drank freely, kept bad company at my house and in Alexandria, and was a very debauched person."[114] The Washingtons had just spent about six weeks at Mount Vernon in the fall, from September 14 through October 28, and it is almost impossible not to think that Charlotte was finally able to have her talk with Martha Washington and thus influence the president's opinion of his deceased supervisor.[115]

At least one of the younger members of the Washington-Custis family acknowledged similar attachments to, as well as frustrations with, the slaves with whom she came into contact as a child, and there is no reason to think that the others did not have similar experiences. Eldest granddaughter Eliza Parke Custis consoled herself as a little girl by thinking about her "Grandmama" Washington and "Mammy Molly, my old Nurse, who always overwhelm'd me with caresses, when I visited Mt Vernon, & from whom I was ever afflicted to part." During one serious childhood illness, Eliza remembered being ill with a "nervous fever" and unable to walk, when "Mammy Molly came to nurse me, my Grandmother often visited me, & I almost regretted getting well which was to take them from me." But she also remembered other "servants" laughing at her from the hallway, when her young father would stand her on the table when she was only three or four years old, to entertain his guests after dinner by singing some "very improper" songs he and a friend had taught her. Several years later, following her father's death, her mother's remarriage, and the birth of a new half-sibling, other "servants of the House encited some jealousy by making me observe my Mother[']s fondness for her infant."[116]

As in Charlotte's case, when a slave had a grievance against an overseer, he or she could turn to the Washingtons to redress a perceived wrong. During a visit home during the presidency, George Washington was approached by his slaves who had a conflict with an overseer, centered around complaints that they were not receiving their usual ration of fish. A storehouse had been broken into and the fish stolen, ostensibly, the slaves suggested, as a "pretence to cover a more nefarious mode of disposing of them." They accused overseer Hyland Crow of stealing the fish intended for themselves and selling it. Since Washington had no way at that point of determining the truth, he ordered his farm manager to "lay in a sufficiency [of fish] for my people this year; secure them well; and let only one person have access to them for delivery, and to be responsible." The key to the storehouse would be locked up at the mansion house with the other keys and the fish distributed to the overseers for the slaves at each farm on a regular basis.[117] Embezzling rations may not have been Crow's only misdeed. Several months after the incident with the stolen fish, Washington discussed the character of this same overseer in a letter to a relative, noting that he had received "too frequent complaints of ill treatment [at the hands of this individual], though I must acknowledge I never discovered any marks of abuse" on the slaves. The recipient of this letter may have decided that this particular overseer was too much of a risk, because he did not hire Crow.[118]

Reputation

Another factor influencing George Washington's relationships with the enslaved people at Mount Vernon was very much peculiar to Washington himself—specifically, his popular image. Washington had always been concerned with his reputation. As a teenager, he copied out over one hundred rules of etiquette and polite behavior, based on a sixteenth-century French Jesuit work, which were said to have influenced him throughout his life. While following many of these rules would help a person to be seen as a respectable individual of good reputation, rule 56 dealt specifically with public image: "Associate yourself with Men of good Quality if you Esteem your own Reputation; for 'tis better to be alone than in bad Company."[119] Many years later as an adult, Washington would write that "the good opinion of honest men, friends to freedom and well-wishers to mankind, wherever they may be born or happen to reside, is the only kind of reputation a wise man would ever desire."[120]

Washington's reputation grew to a national and even international level through the years of the American Revolution. As that long conflict finally wound to a successful conclusion, many people sent letters of congratulation to the American commander on his accomplishments. One of his dearest colleagues, General Nathanael Greene, the commander of the Southern Department of the Continental Army, wrote to Washington at that time to let him know that in South Carolina, "You were admired before; you are little less than adored now."[121] That adoration stretched at least as far as Europe. A few years later, during the early days of Washington's presidency, the Marquis de Lafayette sent the key to the Bastille, a political prison in France, to his former commander, who was then serving as president of the United States. The young Frenchman made the presentation in these words: "Give me leave, my dear General, to present you with a picture of the Bastille just as it looked a few days after I had ordered its demolition, with the main key of the fortress of despotism. It is a tribute which I owe as a son to my adopted father, as an aid-de-camp to my general, as a missionary of liberty to its patriarch."[122]

Washington's reputation as the patriarch of liberty was compromised, or at least threatened, by his position as a slaveholder. In the years after the Revolution, many people came to Mount Vernon simply to see this great man in his own home. In one year, 1798, the Washingtons had at least 656 guests for dinner and 677 guests who stayed overnight. Guests were present for dinner almost 66 percent of the time that year; beds were needed for them on 183 of 310 days.[123] There were so many visitors that Washington, in a letter to his mother concerning reasons why she would be unhappy living with him, made the oft-repeated comment that his home "may be compared to a well resorted tavern, as scarcely any strangers who are going from north to south, or from south to north, do not spend a day or two at it."[124] As these individuals came from across the country and Europe to visit him and write about their experiences, any negative interactions they might have seen between Washington and the estate's enslaved population could have been used to undermine his reputation. Concern for how he appeared to outside eyes might well have influenced Washington's behavior toward his slaves in the latter part of his life.

One of the surviving manuscripts from George Washington's presidential papers shows a strategy he may have come up with to soften the impact of his use of enslaved people in the executive mansion. Written in New York in the spring of 1790, Washington's estimate of "yearly expenditures" for keeping four enslaved men and two enslaved women from Mount Vernon at work in the presidential household came to a total of $438. In addition to paying for two suits of livery, two hats, two surtouts (overcoats), and one pair of boots each for individuals named Giles, Paris, and Christopher Sheels, the figures also included paying a salary of five dollars each per month to Austin, Giles, and Paris, and four dollars each per month to Sheels, Oney Judge, and Moll.[125] There is no evidence that Washington actually paid these salaries, but why would he have considered it? Because the hired, indentured, and enslaved workers in the presidential household lived and worked in very close quarters, salaries may have been considered a method of making the differences in status among the three classes of labor appear less obvious, something that might also have been beneficial in northern cities, where slavery was diminishing in importance and frowned upon. Washington would not have been the only southern slave owner to pay his enslaved workers in the North. Thomas Jefferson paid wages to Monticello slaves James and Sally Hemings when they worked for him in Paris, and to both James and their brother Robert Hemings when they worked in Jefferson's New York and Philadelphia households during Washington's administration. James Hemings was also paid a salary for cooking in the White House when Jefferson was president.[126]

Duplicity and Plans for the Future

These concerns for public image led both George and Martha Washington to practice duplicity toward their slaves. On April 5, 1791, Attorney General Edmund Randolph—another Virginian—called on Martha Washington in the Philadelphia executive mansion to let her know that three of his slaves had just told him they were going to take advantage of a law in Pennsylvania that allowed them to claim their freedom after six months' residence in that state.[127] When informed about this development, George Washington, who was then traveling in the southern states, suggested as a precaution against his and Mrs. Washington's slaves attempting a similar exodus that they be sent back to Mount Vernon. He was especially concerned because all but two of the slaves then with the family in Philadelphia were dower slaves, who belonged to the estate of Martha Washington's first husband, Daniel Parke Custis. Washington noted that "it beho[o]ves me to prevent the emancipation of them, otherwise I *shall* not only loose the use of them, but may have them to pay for"; in other words, he would have to reimburse the estate for their loss.[128]

Washington's comments on how to get around this issue are quite interesting, given his well-known—and generally deserved—reputation for honesty. He wrote that he did not think any of the family's slaves who got their freedom in this way "would be benefitted by the change in their legal status, yet the idea of freedom might be too great a temptation for them to resist. At any rate it might, if they conceived they had a right to it, make them insolent in a State of Slavery." The strategy he hit upon, which he said he wanted done "under pretext that may deceive both them and the Public," was to send them home to Mount Vernon with the story that they were either accompanying Mrs. Washington, were needed to cook for her at home, or were being given the opportunity to visit their own families and friends. This would effectively prevent any of those who were old enough to claim their freedom from meeting the residency requirement after their first six months in the state.[129] Two weeks after Randolph's initial conversation with

Martha Washington, Austin, one of the male house servants, was sent home, as she explained to her niece, for the purpose of seeing his "friends." In this instance, Mrs. Washington showed that she too was capable of deception when it came to dealings with slaves because she was using her earlier promise to Austin's wife to obscure the real reason for the trip.[130]

Washington's secretary Tobias Lear later consulted with the attorney general and fleshed out a more detailed plan to prevent any of the Mount Vernon slaves working in Philadelphia from being emancipated as a result of the Pennsylvania law in the future. That second plan differed little, however, from the strategy devised by the president and first lady. Ironically, Lear, a New Englander who opposed slavery, would later be a slave owner himself, after the death of his second wife, Martha Washington's niece Fanny Bassett Washington, if only until his stepchildren reached their majority.[131] Earlier in his employment at Mount Vernon, Lear told a friend that he was weighing the idea of buying a farm in the Mount Vernon neighborhood and cultivating "my own land—but not with Slaves—I abhor & deprecate the idea of holding one, & am convinced from the experience I have had of them that a man may hire his labourers to more advantage than he can employ Negroes as Slaves."[132] Lear was greatly troubled by both the Washingtons' plan to prevent the slaves in the presidential mansion from claiming their freedom and his part in it, and confided to George Washington that "no consideration should induce me to take these steps to prolong the slavery of a human being, had I not the fullest confidence that they will at some future period be liberated, and the strongest conviction that their situation with you is far preferable to what they would probably obtain in a state of freedom." The fact that Lear had "fullest confidence" in a future liberation of the Mount Vernon slaves indicates that the two men had previously talked at length about slavery and the strength of Washington's intention to manumit his enslaved property.[133]

Those emancipation plans were a direct result of the transformation in Washington's views about slavery, which also had an impact on his day-to-day dealings with the Mount Vernon slaves. Over the course of his life, he gradually changed from a young man who accepted slavery as a matter of course into a person who decided never again to buy or sell another slave and held hopes for the eventual abolition of the institution. This important transformation has been the subject of works by several other historians, but there is new information to consider and it is examined in detail in both the next and the final chapters.[134]

2

"A Plant of Rapid Growth"

New Ideas and a Change of Heart

Prior to the American Revolution, George Washington was involved in a number of business ventures that suggest he viewed slaves as nothing more than property. For example, he was one of the managers of a raffle at which the property of an old friend, Bernard Moore, was sold to pay back creditors, including the Custis estate. Among the things being auctioned off that December day in 1769 were fifty-five slaves, including six families and five women with one or more children. The enumeration of prizes to be won clearly showed that families were being split up in a rather cavalier manner.[1] Two years later, Washington agreed to make a long-term, interest-free loan so that Moore could "purchase Slaves for the immediate Support of his Family."[2]

There were several factors that might have led to Washington's early, unthinking acceptance of slavery as an institution. As he was growing up, most of the people with whom he and his family associated were probably either already slave owners, or if not, would have aspired to become slave owners. With the Bible largely serving as the primer for young people in Virginia in the eighteenth century, Washington and his contemporaries were exposed at an early age to additional cultures in which slavery was a fact of life.[3] Early in the Old Testament, for example, the patriarch Abraham has a child with his "bondwoman" Hagar.[4] Abraham's great-grandson Joseph, a son of Jacob, is sold by his older brothers to Midianite traders, who sell him in turn as a slave to an Egyptian official.[5] Several centuries later, Moses led the Israelites out of slavery in Egypt through a series of events chronicled in the book of

Exodus and frequently recalled elsewhere in the Bible.[6] In the New Testament, the "merchants of the earth" are depicted weeping over the destruction of Babylon, where they can no longer sell their merchandise, including "cinnamon, and odours, and ointments, and frankincense, and wine, and oil, and fine flour, and wheat, and beasts, and sheep, and horses, and chariots, and slaves, and souls of men."[7] During this period, people might be enslaved as war captives or, if in debt, could sell themselves or family members in order to pay off money owed.[8]

Throughout the Bible, while there are references to slavery, there are no direct indictments of it as an institution. Saint Paul's epistle to Philemon deals with the treatment of a runaway slave who was voluntarily returning to his owner after both men became Christians. Paul encouraged Philemon to receive Onesimus back not as a servant but rather as "a brother beloved."[9] Elsewhere, "servants" are told to "count their own masters worthy of all honour," and if their masters are fellow-believers, not to "despise them, because they are brethren; but rather do them service, because they are faithful and beloved, partakers of benefit."[10]

While slavery is never condemned or forbidden, there are statements that provide seeds for a new way of thinking, perhaps even as far as the abolition of slavery, much as Thomas Jefferson's phrase in the Declaration of Independence that "all men are created equal" has propelled an expansion of rights to many groups Jefferson probably never intended. In Genesis, the reader is told that "God created man in his [own] image, in the image of God created he him; male and female created he them."[11] Most explicit are the words of Saint Paul stating that "for ye are all the children of God by faith in Christ Jesus. . . . There is neither Jew nor Greek, there is neither bond [slave] nor free, there is neither male nor female: for ye are all one in Christ Jesus."[12]

Another source of instruction for small children were authors and stories from ancient Greece and Rome, both societies in which human beings were enslaved. Looking at just one such book aimed primarily at children and young people, the fables of Aesop feature short stories about people and animals ending with a moral point. A number of these stories deal with slavery. In one, the rivalry between a boar and a horse is settled when a man makes a deal with the horse to get revenge on his enemy. The man proposes that the horse let him saddle and bridle the horse and then let the man ride on the horse's back with a lance to kill the boar. The horse agrees to this plan and his enemy is eliminated, but at the cost of his own enslavement. In another tale, a sick man promises the gods to sacrifice a thousand bullocks if they will only heal him. As a test of the man's honesty, the gods restore his health, only to find him offering "so many Pieces of Paste made up in the Shape of Oxen" upon an altar instead of the real thing. As punishment, the man is given a dream telling him to go to the coast, where he will find a large treasure. While he is searching for this prize, the man is captured by pirates and sold into slavery. In a third tale, a rooster, following a successful battle against another rooster, flies to the top of the house to crow about his win when an eagle swoops in and carries him off, leaving the loser to take over the barnyard for himself. Aesop explains that "it fares often with the greatest of Monarchs, as with these Cocks; he that is Victorious to Day, may be a Slave tomorrow."[13] All of these stories taught eighteenth-century children that slavery was something that happened to people who let their emotions get the better of their ability to think, or were greedy, or prideful, and may well have led their young readers to believe that enslavement was justified as a form of punishment.

Inklings of Change

Washington may well have been in his thirties before he ever heard anything critical of slavery. That criticism came from his longtime friend and neighbor George Mason of Gunston Hall Plantation, who wrote in 1765:

> The Policy of encouraging the Importation of free People & discouraging that of Slaves has never been duly considered in this Colony, or we shou'd not at this Day see one Half of our best Lands in most Parts of the Country remain unset[t]led, & the other cultivated with Slaves; not to mention the ill Effect such a Practice has upon the Morals & Manners of our People: one of the first Signs of the Decay, & perhaps the primary Cause of the Destruction of the most flourishing Government that ever existed was the Introduction of great Numbers of Slaves—an Evil very pathetically described by the Roman Historians—but 'tis not the present Intention to expose our Weakness by examining this Subject too freely.[14]

Washington's first public statement on the subject nine years later was less a critique of slavery than of the slave trade. As tensions mounted with Britain, and after Virginia's royal governor dissolved the House of Burgesses, Washington served as chairman of a "general Meeting of the Freeholders and Inhabitants of the County of Fairfax" to determine what actions he and his fellow citizens were willing to undertake to support Boston, especially in regard to banning commerce with the mother country. The document they drew up and signed, known as the Fairfax County Resolves, included as the seventeenth item the belief "that during our present Difficulties and Distress, no Slaves ought to be imported into any of the British Colonies on this Continent; and We take this Opportunity of declaring our most earnest Wishes to see an entire stop for ever put to such a wicked cruel and unnatural Trade."[15]

Probably the biggest factor in the evolution of Washington's views on slavery was the Revolutionary War, in which he risked his life, his family, a sizable fortune, and a stable future fighting to obtain freedom from England, based on some relatively new and idealistic concepts about the rights of man. During the conflict, his views on slavery were radically altered, evidence that he truly believed the wartime rhetoric about freedom and liberty. Washington himself made use of this language and could hardly fail to see the irony when he expressed the view to an old friend in the summer of 1774 that the British authorities, "from whom we have a right to Seek protection," were "endeavouring by every piece of Art & despotism to fix the Shackles of Slavry upon" the Americans.[16] Two years later, in orders to his soldiers at Cambridge, he reminded them that "it is a noble Cause we are engaged in, it is the Cause of virtue and mankind," and that "freedom, or Slavery must be the result of our conduct."[17] In July of the same year, Washington challenged the army with the idea that the time had almost arrived "which must probably determine, whether Americans are to be, Freemen, or Slaves." In contrast to their lives as freemen, who would have "any property they can call their own," defeat would mean being "consigned to a State of Wretchedness from which no human efforts will probably deliver them." He closed by challenging them to "sh[o]w the whole world, that a Freeman contending for Liberty on his own ground is superior to any slavish mercenary on earth."[18]

If the Americans could not see it for themselves, the enemy did not hesitate to point out the rebels' hypocrisy on the matter of slavery. One of the best-known statements on the subject was Samuel Johnson's quip, "How is it that we hear the loudest *yelps* for liberty among the drivers of negroes?"[19] Washington's slave owning was used as another reason to hold this foremost leader of the Revolution in contempt. Responding to a wartime rumor that George Washington had been captured by the British, an English traveler in American named Nicholas Cresswell responded with sarcasm. After noting that Washington's "great caution will always prevent him being made a prisoner to our inactive General," Cresswell described the American commander as "a most surprising man, one of Nature's geniuses, a Heaven-born General, if there is any of that sort." What really irked Cresswell was "that a Negro-driver [another phrase for an overseer or foreman] should, with a ragged Banditti of undisciplined people, the scum and refuse of all nations on earth, so long keep a British General at bay, nay, even, oblige him, with as fine an army of Veteran Soldiers as ever England had on the American Continent, to retreat—it is astonishing. It is too much. By Heavens, there must be double-dealing somewhere."[20]

When Washington wrote a few years after the close of the war that "liberty, when it begins to take root, is a plant of rapid growth," he was simply noting what he had found to be true in his own life.[21] Within three years of the start of the war, Washington, who was then forty-six years old and had been a slave owner for thirty-five years, confided in a cousin back in Virginia that he longed "every day . . . more and more to get clear of" the ownership of slaves.[22] The only option he had for doing that at this point was to offer them for sale (as is shown later, Virginia slave owners were unable to free their enslaved property until 1782). As he explained a few months later, "it would be a matter of very little consequence to me, whether my property is in Negroes, or loan office Certificates," but in trying to decide about selling them off, he admitted to having "scruples" arising from "a reluctance in offering these people at public vendue, and on account of the uncertainty of timeing the sale well." He also believed that "if these poor wretches are to be held in a state of slavery, I do not see that a change of masters will render it more irksome, provided husband and wife, and Parents and children are not separated from each other, which is not my intentions to do."[23] About a decade later, Washington refused to purchase a particular slave, commenting that he already had "as many Slaves as I wish," and that he was not willing to exchange others for him "because I do not think, it would be agreeable to their inclinations to leave their Conne[ct]ions here, and it is inconsistent with my feelings to compel them."[24] These scruples would have important implications for the management of Mount Vernon.

During the war Washington traveled to parts of the country that were, in the words of historian Ira Berlin, "societies with slaves" rather than the "slave society" in Virginia where Washington had grown up. Berlin notes that in the latter, "slavery stood at the center of economic production" and every relationship, from "the most intimate connections between men and women to the most public ones between ruler and ruled, all relationships mimicked those of slavery." By contrast, in New England and the mid-Atlantic colonies, "slaves were marginal to the central productive process; slavery was just one form of labor among many."[25] It was also during the war that Washington saw black soldiers in action, fighting alongside whites in the Continental Army. In fact, within seven months of taking command of the army, Washington approved the enlistment of free black soldiers, something he and the other general officers had originally opposed.[26] They began in late 1775 by reenlisting free blacks, who had fought in the army previously and been let go, much to their disappointment, when Congress disapproved of their presence.[27] Five years later, Washington proposed a method for reorganizing two Rhode Island regiments, noting that objections could best be handled by dividing the black soldiers who made up the one unit evenly between the two and making up the difference with new recruits, so "as to abolish the name and appearance of a Black Corps," in essence integrating the army.[28]

During the Revolution, Washington was exposed to the views of several idealistic young men who ardently opposed slavery and whose opinions he valued. John Laurens of South Carolina, West Indian–born Alexander Hamilton, and the French nobleman the Marquis de Lafayette were three young officers close to Washington and not afraid to give him their opinions. They were together for days on end in tight quarters, ate together on a daily basis, and are known to have spent hours at and after dinner talking. Laurens, for example, proposed the formation of an African American corps in his home state after service in which the soldiers would receive their freedom.[29] Early in 1782, when trying to determine what the British would do next and thinking that they might send reinforcements to Charleston, Washington wrote to Laurens, "I know of nothing which can be opposed to them with such a prospect of success as the Corps you have proposed should be levied in Carolina."[30]

A little more than two years after the end of the war, Washington's former aide Alexander Hamilton had become one of the earliest supporters of the Society for Promoting the Manumission of Slaves and had signed a petition to the New York legislature calling for the abolition of the slave trade, something he referred to as "a commerce . . . repugnant to humanity, and . . . inconsistent with the liberality and justice which should distinguish a free and enlightened people."[31] Laurens, sadly, died during the war, but Hamilton and another of Washington's favorites, the Marquis de Lafayette, continued to correspond about the abolition of slavery. When Lafayette learned about the formation of the manumission society from a New York newspaper, he wrote to his former brother in arms that he felt the wording "against the slavery of negroes" was done "in such a way as to give no offense to the moderate Men in the Southern States," an acknowledgment of the sensitivity of the issue in American politics. Knowing Hamilton's views on the subject, Lafayette noted that "as I ever Have Been partial to my Brethren of that Colour, I wish if you are one in the Society, you would move, in your own Name, for my Being Admitted on the List."[32]

The Revolution also brought Washington into contact with a gifted young woman, Phillis Wheatley, who would have opened his eyes to, or at the very least led him to question, the latent abilities of the Africans and African Americans with whom he had lived since childhood. Captured and enslaved as a girl of seven or eight in Africa, Wheatley was brought to Boston where she was purchased by a tailor, John Wheatley, as a servant for his wife. Both Susanna Wheatley and her daughter, Mary, are credited with instructing the young maid, using the Bible and the literature of classical Greece and Rome as textbooks. Treated very much as a member of the family and assigned only light duties, Phillis blossomed under the Wheatleys' encouragement and began writing poetry by the time she was about thirteen. Four years later, one of her poems, written on the death of the international preacher and evangelist George Whitefield, was published. At twenty, the young woman was taken to London in the hope that the sea air would improve her health. There, one of her correspondents, Selina Hastings, the Countess of Huntingdon, who was a prominent figure in both the Anglican evangelical movement and Methodism, introduced Wheatley to English society. During this same period, a book of Wheatley's works was published in England under the title *Poems on Various Subjects, Religious and Moral.* Before she could be presented to King George III at court, however, she learned that Mrs. Wheatley was very ill back in Boston and returned to America to care for the woman who had given her the gift of an education in the last months before her death in March 1774.[33]

About a year and half later, in October 1775, Phillis Wheatley sent a letter to George Washington from Providence, Rhode Island. Assuring him that she wished "your Excellency all possible success in the great cause you are so generously engaged in," she enclosed a long, laudatory poem she had written in his honor. Perhaps a bit formal and flowery for modern tastes, the poem includes numerous classical allusions and closes with the words,

> Proceed, great chief, with virtue on thy side,
> Thy ev'ry action let the goddess guide.
> A crown, a mansion, and a throne that shine,
> With gold unfading, Washington! be thine.

Four months later, Washington sent both the letter and poem on to his friend Joseph Reed in Philadelphia, and they were later published in at least two newspapers in the colonies.[34] Washington also wrote directly to Wheatley, thanking her for her work and inviting her to visit him at his headquarters. He went on to say, "I shall be happy to see a person so favour[e]d by the Muses, and to whom nature has been so liberal and beneficent in her dispensations."[35]

Between the end of the Revolution and the start of his presidency, abolitionists began approaching Washington on the subject of slavery. Often they brought or sent pamphlets for Washington to read; by the end of his life he had a small collection of these works by such authors as Anthony Benezet, George Buchanan, Thomas Clarkson, Bryan Edwards, and Granville Sharp, written between 1776 and 1793.[36] At other times, they came seeking his support for their cause. On May 26, 1785, two Methodist bishops, Thomas Coke and Francis Asbury, arrived at Mount Vernon to ask Washington to sign an antislavery petition they were planning to present to the Virginia legislature. Coke recorded their conversation in his diary, noting that their host "received us very politely, and was very open to access." After dinner they spoke privately with him about "the grand business on which we came," showed him the petition, and asked him to sign it "if the eminence of his station did not render it inexpedient for him to sign any petition." Washington replied that he shared their feelings about slavery and "had signified his thoughts on the subject to most of the great men of the State," presumably in person, rather than in writing. He went on to explain that he did not "see it proper to sign the petition," however, but would let the Virginia assembly know how he felt about slavery if they ever took up the subject for consideration.[37] A little over five months after their meeting with Washington, the Methodists' petition was read in the Virginia legislature on November 8, 1785; it was rejected by that body two days later. The following day, James Madison informed Washington about the response to the proposed legislation:

> The pulse of the H[ouse]. of D[elegates]. was felt on thursday with regard to a general manumission by a petition presented on that subject. It was rejected without dissent but not without an avowed patronage of its principle by sundry respectable members. A motion was made to throw it under the table, which was treated with as much indignation on one side, as the petition itself was on the other. There are several petitions before the House against any Step towards freeing the slaves, and even praying for a repeal of the law which licences particular manumissions.[38]

The news of such division in the legislature must have been unsettling to Washington, for whom concensus was important. Regarding another issue taken up that same year, Washington told friends that while he was a firm supporter of freedom of religion, he had no problem with a proposed bill that would force people to pay for the support of the beliefs they professed, whether they were Christians, Jews, Muslims, or whatever. He admitted, however, that he wished the bill had never been taken up for consideration and hoped it would quietly die. He feared it was "impolitic," because, although it was popular with a majority in the state, it was viewed with "disgust" by "a respectable minority," including two friends, George Mason and James Madison, whose opinions he valued highly.[39]

A young Quaker, Robert Pleasants, challenged Washington on the issue of slavery in December 1785, citing religious reasons for the American leader to emancipate his slaves. Pleasants, a leader of the abolition movement in Virginia, had manumitted eighty of his own slaves several years earlier. He began his letter by citing concerns about Washington's reputation and went on to say that he found it strange that Washington, "who could forego all the Sweets of domestic felicity . . . and expose thy Person to the greatest fatigue & dangers in that cause [liberty], should now withhold that inestimable blessing from any who are absolutely in thy power, & after the Right of freedom, is acknowledg'd to be the natural & unalienable Right of all mankind." He suggested that perhaps Washington's hesitation in this instance was not the result of "interested motives," that is, money, but rather of "long custom, the prejudices of education towards a black skin, or that some other important concerns may have hitherto diverted thy attention from a Subject so Noble and interesting, as well to thy own Peace & reputation, as the general good of that People, and the community at large." Pleasants then offered his opinion that Washington should not delay in freeing his slaves because it was "a Sacrifi[c]e which I fully beli[e]ve the Lord is requiring of this Generation." Pleasants went on to say that he wished "that thou may not loose the op[po]rtunity of Crowning the great Actions of thy Life, with the sattisfaction of, 'doing to Others as thou would (in like Situation) be done by,' and finally to transmit to future ages a Character, equally famous for thy Christian Virtues, as thy worldly achievements." After reminding Washington of a coming day of judgment, Pleasants closed by hoping Washington would not think him presumptuous, stating that he had no selfish motives for "offering these hints to his serious consideration" other than "what may arise from the pleasure of hearing he had done those things—which belong to his present & future happiness, and the good of those over whom Providence hath placed him."[40]

A decade later, during Washington's second term as president, a Welsh Baptist minister came to Mount Vernon in his absence to visit the estate.

An ardent abolitionist, Reverend Morgan John Rhys later sent a letter to a friend in which described the beautiful setting. Despite the praise, however, Rhys severely criticized Washington for hypocrisy:

> Had the President of the United States been at home, I [would have addressed him] thus "Thou great man Washington! what meaneth the ble[a]ting of these black sheep and the lowing of these Negro oxen that till thy ground? Say not, they belong to thy wife; they are entailed to her relatives as an inheritance. Such paltry excuses are beneath thy character."
>
> The great defender of Liberty should give an example to his neighbors, worthy of himself. How much more honourable to pay wages and let them support themselves. Experience evinces even in this country, that it would be more profitable to the employer.[41]

Over and over again, Washington privately reiterated his conviction that the best way to effect the elimination of slavery was through the legislature, which he hoped would set up a program of gradual emancipation, for which he would gladly give his vote. As he assured his friend Robert Morris in 1786, he hoped that no one would read his opposition to the methods of certain abolitionists, in this case the Quakers, as opposition to abolition as a concept:

> I hope it will not be conceived from these observations, that it is my wish to hold the unhappy people who are the subject of this letter, in slavery. I can only say that there is not a man living who wishes more sincerely than I do, to see a plan adopted for the abolition of it—but there is only one proper and effectual mode by which it can be accomplished, & that is by Legislative authority: and this, as far as my suffrage will go, shall never be wanting.[42]

The Meaning of Race

The years between the end of the war and Washington's death were also a time when he and others were examining ideas about race, investigating and debating the differences among various peoples and what those might mean. Much of this can be seen in questions about the origins of Native Americans, another group about whom Washington changed his views over the course of his life. Washington was intrigued to learn from his Baltimore agent Tench Tilghman in 1785, for instance, that the Chinese crew members of a newly arrived ship "are exactly the Indians of North America, in Colour, Feature—Hair and every external Mark." Washington quickly responded that he had always had the impression from what he had read that "the Chinese though droll in shape & appearance, were yet white." Tilghman promptly responded, "The Chinese of the Northern provinces are fairer than those of the south, but none of them are of the European Complexion."[43] This would really have given Washington something to think about, because he knew, just on the basis of his purchases, that the Chinese had long had an advanced civilization and were the source of luxury goods such as silk fabrics, ivory fans, lacquered dressing glasses, and fine porcelains that were the envy of the world.[44] If they looked not like Europeans but like the Native peoples of the Americas, with whom he had considerable experience on the frontier, he would almost have been forced to wonder what nonwhite people were capable of.

A few months after his exchange with Tilghman, Washington was approached by the Marquis de Lafayette, writing on behalf of Catherine the Great of Russia, in order to obtain information about Indian languages for a universal dictionary. Although extremely busy, Washington jumped into the project, asking for help from a number of correspondents throughout the country. As he had known it would, the project took several years to complete. In a letter to Washington accompanying his contribution for the dictionary, Richard Butler, the superintendent of Indian affairs for the Northern District, also discussed theories about the ancient inhabitants of America and how the contemporary tribes had come to live where they did, surmising that the Iroquois "may be of Tarter [Mongol] Origins or descent . . . as they may have come from the Northern parts of Asia across to our Continent, and stre[t]ched, some along the Seacoast by Hudson's Bay, & others by the way of the Lakes from the high north Latitudes where the Asiatic & American Continents approach each other and their language differs exceedingly from all the Southern Indians."[45] Washington replied that Butler's observations about the remains of older civilizations and "other traces of the country's being once inhabitted by a race of people more ingenious, at least, if not more civilized than those who at present dwell there, have excited the attention and enquirries of the curious to learn from whence they came, whither they are gone and something of their history."[46]

A few years later, Reverend Jonathan Edwards, who had grown up in Stockbridge, Massachusetts, among the Mohicans, with whom his father served as a missionary, sent Washington a copy of a dictionary he had compiled on the Mohican language. In Washington's thank you letter, he wrote that he had "long regretted that so many Tribes of the American Aborigines should have become almost or entirely extinct, without leaving such vestiges, as that the genius & idiom of their Languages might be traced." He went on to say that language might give clues to the "descent or kindred of nations, whose orig[i]ns are lost in remote antiquity or illiterate darkness."[47] When he forwarded the information for the dictionary to Lafayette, Washington let slip some clues to the contemplative, visionary side of his personality, which his quietness in public tended to hide:

> Should the present or any other efforts of mine to procure information respecting the different dialects of the Aborigines in America, serve to reflect a ray of light on the obscure subject of language in general, I shall be highly gratified. For I love to indulge the contemplation of human nature in a progressive state of improvement and melioration: and if the idea would not be considered as visionary and chimerical, I could fondly hope that the present plan of the great Potentate of the North, might, in some measure, lay the foundation for that assimilation of language, which, producing assimilation of manners and interests, should one day remove many of the causes of hostility from amongst mankind.[48]

Washington had additional opportunities to think about race during his presidency, when the public's attention was drawn to a number of cases in which people in America seemed to be changing from black to white. Artist Charles Willson Peale, who had painted both Washington and members of his family since before the Revolution, published an "Account of a Black Man Turned White" in a Philadelphia newspaper in 1791. Peale had met the man, whose name was James, several months before in Somerset County, Maryland, and investigated his story of being born to a black mother and white father, and having been "a black or very dark mulatto colour 'till he was about 18 years of age, when some white spots appeared on his skin . . . and gradually increased." Peale noted that James's skin was "of a clear wholesome white, fair, and what could be called, *a better skin,* than any of a number of white people who were present, at different times when I saw him." The artist exhibited his now-lost portrait of James in both a local tavern and his own museum, and sent an account of the case to the American Philosophical Society in Philadelphia prior to the publication of his article, which was picked up by at least two other newspapers.[49] Today, James would have been diagnosed with vitiligo, a disease characterized by the loss of skin color in patches or blotches, caused when cells that produce melanin either die or stop working. The condition can affect any part of the body, including the hair, inside the mouth and nose, and even the eyes.[50]

There is no direct evidence that Washington knew of James's situation, but he had been a member of the American Philosophical Society since 1780. Although not the most active member, probably because of the press of other duties, he happily accepted membership in the organization, corresponded with other members, suggested two of his foreign correspondents for membership, and passed along a pamphlet he thought would be interesting for their library.[51] At the time of his death, he had a portrait of the society's president David Rittenhouse hanging in the dining room at Mount Vernon, suggesting the admiration Washington had for his work.[52] Peale's relationship with Washington continued throughout this period, with the production of several portraits, notably of Washington during the Constitutional Convention and again as president in 1795. Washington also supported Peale's museum in Philadelphia by paying visits; making donations directly to the collection, in the form of a pair of Chinese golden pheasants in 1787 and a Hawaiian crested helmet covered in feathers in 1792; and through the payment of subscriptions to the museum.[53] So while it is not possible to prove that Washington knew about James, he certainly was moving in circles that gave him the opportunity learn about this case.

Five years later, Washington came into personal contact with Henry Moss, whose case was similar to that of James. In July 1796, Moss, who also had vitiligo, was traveling to Philadelphia by way of Winchester, Virginia. Born about 1774 in Virginia, he was the son of a black father and a mother who was described as a "dark mulatto," and had perhaps been with the army during the Revolution as a waiter to a Colonel John Neville. While in Winchester, Moss was seen by several hundred people "who could not refrain from expressing their surpri[s]e and astonishment at the wonderful change which the Almighty Hand of Omnipotence has wrought in him." It was reported that Moss carried "certificates . . . to prove his having been born black, how long he continued in that state, when the change commenced, how it progressed, &c."[54] Moss reached Philadelphia by September 1796, where more details of his story emerged. He had been "born of a full African complexion" and was in his mid- to late thirties when his skin began to gradually change. One person wrote that he had seen Moss several times and even examined him with a magnifying glass, noting that "his African complexion has changed, in most parts of his body, to that of a fair European."[55]

Moss became very well known both through his travels and exhibitions and through publications about him in newspapers, periodicals, and the journals of groups such as the American Philosophical Society, where

Dr. Benjamin Rush discussed his and similar cases. According to historian Joanne Pope Melish, more than a dozen similar cases were brought to the public's attention between 1788 and 1810. At the same time, American seamen were being enslaved by the Barbary pirates and the public was wondering if living in a different environment was gradually changing black people to white in North America, and might not bring about a similar change to captive white Americans in North Africa. As Melish notes, people were questioning the meaning of race and asking, "Could enslavement transform whites into a servile people, as dependent and instrumental as black slaves? If so, physical characteristics might not be a reliable indicator of 'aptitude' for enslavement." All of this brought up questions that "tested environmental explanations of difference against hypothetical inner (or innate) and fixed ones, and they probed the validity of external, physical markers in locating essential human identity." Not only were all these questions being discussed around Washington, but he was serving as president as the sailors were being captured and Moss was actually "examined and viewed" by both Washington and his secretary of state Thomas Jefferson.[56]

Two years after he saw Henry Moss, George Washington wrote to Secretary of War James McHenry about rumors that had come to his attention concerning Democratic-Republican Virginians enlisting in the army to foment sedition against the government. In this letter, the retired president made the observation that "you could as soon scrub the blackamore white, as to change the principles of a profess[sed] Democrat," who would "leave nothing unattempted to overturn the Government of this Country."[57] Professor Charles D. Martin has argued that Washington's "employment of the proverb contradicts the fading blackness of Henry Moss that he witnessed just two years before, in essence denying the transformation as an impossibility, a heresy against the doctrine of fixed essences." Martin believes that Washington saw the "figure of the white Negro . . . as a symbol of an untrustworthy transformation and an unimaginable rebellion in the hierarchies of the natural order."[58]

This argument seems a bit of a stretch. Washington had grown up around black bodies and would have known that scrubbing was not enough to cause this change in skin color. Migration, whether forced or voluntary, to a different part of the world, with a totally different climate and culture, was another question entirely. Washington was aware of arguments that environmental factors could influence changes in appearance. Shortly before he wrote to McHenry, Washington sent six sheep from Mount Vernon to a correspondent in Antigua, with the comment that "it is a fact well ascertained . . . that the Woolly tribe of animals change their coating whenever they are removed to hot Climates," going from what he described as "fur to a coarse wool & then to hair." Washington thought that it would be "curious to observe the gradation and time required for this process of nature" and sent the gift so that "the fact may be established under your own eyes."[59] If this sort of change could happen in the animal kingdom, why not with men?

Washington's change of heart about slavery tracks well with a similar change in his ideas about Native Americans. By the end of his life, George Washington had gone from being a boy who found Indian people "comicle" and "ignorant" to someone who considered them "Savages" and the "cruel & blood thirsty Enemy upon our Backs," and then finally to seeing them as part of the new country.[60] He encouraged them to take up both the settled, agricultural way of life and the religion of the majority of the American population.[61] Most telling of the change in his perception of Native Americans is a long letter written toward the end of his administration as president in which he was quite clear that he understood the problems facing these people, known to him over the years as both enemies and allies, and was sympathetic to their position. He noted that they were "not without serious causes of complaint, from the encroachments which are made on their lands by our people; who are not to be restrained by any law now in being, or likely to be enacted." Reminding the recipient that the Indians had "no Press thro' which their grievances are related," he struck a cautionary note, writing, "it is well known, that when one side only of a Story is heard, and often repeated, the human mind becomes impressed with it, insensibly." He expressed the opinion that the gifts provided to the tribes annually by the government were "not given so much with a view to purchase peace, as by way of retribution for injuries, not otherwise to be redressed." Going on to enumerate those grievances, he cited "the continual pressure of land speculators and settlers on one hand; and . . . the impositions of unauthorised, and unprincipled traders (who rob them in a manner of their hunting) on the other." After suggesting some measures to improve the situation, he suggested that "we might hope to live in peace and amity with these borderers; but not whilst our citizens, in violation of law and justice, are guilty of the offences I have mentioned, and are carrying on unauthorised expeditions against them; and when, for the most attrocious murders, even of those of whom we have the least cause of complaint, a Jury on the frontiers, can hardly be got to listen to a charge, much less to convict a culprit."[62]

It is hard to believe that these experiences with other ethnic groups and such profound changes of heart about both slavery and Native Americans would not have also influenced Washington's relationships and interactions with the slaves at Mount Vernon. It is my contention that the depth and serious-ness of those changes are revealed by a corresponding alteration in Wash-ington's religious observances in the last fifteen years of his life. According to two letters written by Martha Washington's youngest granddaughter, based on conversations with her mother, Eleanor Calvert Custis Stuart, who had been a member of the Mount Vernon household for many years, George Washington regularly took communion with his wife before he took command of the Continental Army, while after the war he would exit the church just before the start of the communion service, leaving Mrs. Washington inside to take part in the religious ritual.[63]

There were, perhaps, many reasons for this change, but one thing that has influenced many other church members to stop taking communion over the years is the sense of having an ongoing sin in their life, something they believe to be wrong but which they either cannot or will not give up.[64] Washington had certainly come to believe that slavery was wrong, but it was more than that. Being a slave owner led to doing other things that were sinful, things mentioned earlier such as buying slaves in another colony to circumvent Virginia taxes or the scheme to keep slaves in the presidential household from claiming their freedom under Pennsylvania law by send-ing them home to Mount Vernon on a regular basis, a plan that required lying to them. Several years before he did that, Washington indicated that honesty was an important part of how he saw himself when he wrote, "I do not recollect that in the course of my life I ever forfeited my word, or broke a promise made to any one."[65] What must those actions have cost his own soul?

Giving up slavery was not as easy as one might think, especially when doing so might jeopardize the very country that Washington had spent so many years of his life to bring into being. According to Thomas Jeffer-son, in a conversation with Attorney General Edmund Randolph during Washington's presidency, George Washington had confided that "on the hypothesis of a separation of the Union into Northern and Southern . . . he had made up his mind to remove and be of the Northern."[66] The fact that such a separation was even being discussed must have been terribly painful for Washington, who very much believed the United States had been brought into being by the actions of God and had written that "the man must be bad indeed who can look upon the events of the American Revolution without feeling the warmest gratitude towards the great Author of the Universe whose divine interposition was so frequently manifested in our behalf—And it is my earnest prayer that we may so conduct ourselves as to merit a continuance of those blessings with which we have hitherto been favoured."[67] Washington, theologically speaking, was between a rock (his belief that slavery was wrong) and a hard place (the fact that the southern states still supported slavery and might leave the union he believed God had brought into being if the institution of slavery was threatened). A later chapter explores Washington's attempts to heal the conflict his change of heart had brought into his life.

3

"To Remain Constantly with the People"

Hired, Indentured, and Enslaved Supervisors

In the spring of 1823, Martha Washington's youngest granddaughter, Nelly Custis Lewis, shared some thoughts about what life had been like at Mount Vernon during the lifetimes of her grandparents. She began by noting the size of the plantation—eight thousand acres divided into four working farms (she omitted the Mansion House Farm). Nelly described how each farm was supervised by its own overseer, who was in turn answerable to the farm manager: "This Manager kept a weekly account of every occurrence on the different Farms. The overseers were accountable to the Manager for every thing—were completely under his direction & this Manager render'd an account of his stewardship to the Gen'l himself."[1]

For the majority of the enslaved laborers on the estate, the supervisors with whom they had the most contact were the farm managers, overseers (both free and enslaved), and hired or indentured craftsmen who directly managed and often lived near the laborers. In addition to having several hundred enslaved laborers at Mount Vernon, slightly more than three hundred hired and indentured workers either supervised or labored beside them on the plantation during the last forty years or so of the eighteenth century.[2] Of this number, at least thirty-six can be identified as immigrants: there were eleven from Ireland, nine from England, eight from Germany, five from Scotland, and three from France.[3] While most of the hired and indentured people were of European extraction, a handful of others are known to have had African or Native American backgrounds.[4] At least twenty-two of the supervisors came to Mount Vernon as indentured servants, a condition similar to slavery in that those who were indentured were unfree but with some important differences—indentured servitude was for a limited amount of time, rather than life, and it was not hereditary. Indenture was also a condition that was more or less voluntary, something that the chattel slavery practiced in Virginia certainly was not. It is believed that 80–90 percent of white people arriving in the Chesapeake came as servants, so some of the hired people at Mount Vernon may well have been indentured initially but had paid back their time and changed their status before they worked for Washington.[5]

At least six of the indentured servants at Mount Vernon were convicts.[6] This figure is hardly surprising: about 25 percent of all British immigrants to North America in the eighteenth century were convicts. Historian A. Roger Ekirch estimates that during this period, fifty thousand people were sentenced to transportation to the colonies by English courts.[7] George Washington had been acquainted with convict servants since childhood. His birthplace, Westmoreland County, Virginia, appears to have had the largest number of transported felons of any county in the colony—over 550 apparently arrived there between 1731 and 1746, roughly the period when he was growing up.[8] As a child, Washington was taught "reading, writing and accounts . . . by a convict servant whom his father bought for a schoolmaster."[9]

Not all the hired and indentured workers were men. There were at least eight women who served as midwives, two of whom were enslaved to others, while the remainder were the wives of white craftsmen and managers.[10] Another six women worked as housekeepers in the mansion, as did two men.[11]

Farm Managers

At the top of the Mount Vernon organization chart were Washington's farm managers, who occupied a position directly below himself and Martha Washington. Responsible for seeing that all the work ordered by Washington was carried out in a timely fashion and in the manner he directed, the farm managers were also expected to maintain order on the plantation. As he was seeking to fill a vacancy in this job in the summer of 1793, Washington sketched out what he expected. The most essential requirement of his managers was a compleat knowledge of the farming business in its various branches; an ability to plan and direct generally the business of four or five large farms, adjoining each other, but under sep[a]rate Overseers; and a sufficient acquaintance with business and [accounts] to enable him to buy and sell, with discretion and judgment, such things as may be wanted for the use of the Estate, and to be disposed of from it; and to keep an Account of the same.[12]

Washington noted that the necessary qualifications included many years of experience, as well as "a residence of some years in a part of the Country where the labour is done by negroes." He did not believe it was necessary for a farm manager to be a "complete Clerk, or particularly conversant in mercantile transactions" in order to handle the business aspects of the job, but was more concerned to find someone who possessed "perfect honesty, sobriety and industry," traits he considered "indispensable." Because the manager would be living on the Mansion House Farm, Washington preferred a single man to someone with a family, and wanted a person between thirty-five and forty-five years old, "as that period seems most likely to unite experience with activity."[13]

In exchange for all this responsibility, the farm managers were paid roughly two to four times the salary of the individual overseers and tradesmen. Looking at the last years of George Washington's life, for example, farm manager James Anderson received a base salary of £140 per year, while William Stewart, an overseer, made £60; overseer Joseph Cash and miller Patrick Callahan were each paid £50 annually; and John Ehlers, the gardener, got £36.[14]

Over the years, these men—and all the farm managers were men—brought experience in managing agricultural tasks and workers from previous jobs in both Great Britain and America. One of the most prominent farm managers to appear in George Washington's papers was actually his third cousin Lund Washington, who was five years younger than his employer. Prior to coming to Mount Vernon, Lund spent two years managing what was described as "a large Estate" owned by a Mr. Beverly in Albemarle County, Virginia. Washington then moved on to the management of Ravensworth in Fairfax County, which was owned by Henry Fitzhugh. He was hired to work at Mount Vernon in 1765, where he would remain for the next twenty years, most notably during the difficult years of the American Revolution.[15]

As Mount Vernon's farm manager during the war, Lund had to deal with problems that none of the others faced. Shortly before the conflict began, George Washington embarked on a plan to enlarge the mansion house at

Mount Vernon, which Lund, with input from Martha Washington, was responsible for completing. New wings were added at the north and south ends of the mansion containing, respectively, a large two-story room for entertaining and a study and master bedroom. In addition, there were plans to replace the existing outbuildings closest to the mansion with larger ones and to develop service lanes, redo the approach to the mansion, and enlarge the gardens.[16] Not all of these projects were finished by the end of the war. Lund also faced a potential smallpox epidemic, wartime shortages of salt and alcohol, threats of destruction by British ships, and a change in attitude by those enslaved at Mount Vernon.

During the first half of George Washington's presidency, the Mount Vernon estate was managed by two people: Washington's nephew George Augustine Washington and a hired Englishman, Anthony Whiting. Washington expressed great trust in the two men, who shared a malady, consumption (tuberculosis), which would result in their deaths within months of one another in 1793.[17] George Augustine did not have the level of experience that Washington generally required of his farm managers, but he had the benefit of several years of direct supervision by his uncle in the years between the end of the Revolution and the beginning of the presidency, which gave the young man a solid understanding of what was expected. George Augustine was the oldest son of George Washington's youngest full brother, Charles Washington, and Charles's wife, Mildred Thornton Washington. The young man did have military experience, having served as an officer during the American Revolution, most notably as an aide-de-camp to the Marquis de Lafayette in 1781.[18] He began showing symptoms of the disease that would eventually claim his life in the spring of 1782, when he went to Mount Vernon to recuperate.[19] Concern for his nephew led George Washington to suggest that the young man either join Nathanael Greene's army in the south or try to get to the West Indies, but George noted that there was no need that late in the war for George Augustine to rejoin his unit: "There is no duty for you to return to at present, consequently there can be no cause for your anxiety to rejoin the Army, but if there was, ill health is a sufficient plea for absence; and an attempt to recover it, a consideration to which every other should yield."[20] George Augustine spent the last summer of the war in Rhode Island and a large part of the following year in the West Indies, in the hope that the sea air would heal his lungs.[21] By the fall of 1785, George Augustine was sufficiently recovered to marry Frances (Fanny) Bassett, Martha Washington's favorite niece.[22]

Anthony Whiting, the man hired to assist George Augustine, was an English immigrant who brought considerable experience in farm management with him to Mount Vernon. Whiting initially applied to oversee Washington's Ferry and French's Farms (the latter purchased in October 1786 from Washington's neighbor Mrs. French; the two farms were later known collectively as Union Farm) in the spring of 1790, telling George Augustine that he had much "knowledge as a manager and produced as proof of it a certificate from General Dickinson and Mr Cadwalader." George Augustine found Whiting "conversant in the business he profess he said that he had been entrusted with the entire management of General Cadwalader[']s estate and for sometime had no assistant."[23] General John Cadwalader had died in 1786, so Washington contacted another member of that family to follow up on the prospective employee's management of that estate in Kent County, Maryland.[24] Congressman Lambert Cadwalader of New Jersey informed the president that Whiting had "a competent knowledge in the business of agriculture" and understood "the economy of a farm." Cadwalader believed him "to be industrious" and had "no distrust" of his "honesty," but there was a caveat. Washington informed Whiting that Cadwalader had also indicated that "he thought you were too much given to your pleasures—however of the impropriety of this he hoped and believed you were convinced, and of course would reform."[25]

George Augustine Washington signed articles of agreement with Whiting on May 20, 1790.[26] Three months later, George Augustine was ready to move Whiting to the position of overseer at the Mansion House Farm, telling his uncle that, after having "attentively examined" Whiting's conduct, he had found "nothing that would lead me to distrust his integrity, sobriety or industry and as to his capacity being superior for the general superintendence of business on an extensive scale I have not a doubt."[27]

Within weeks of George Augustine's death on February 5, 1793, Washington learned about the precarious state of Anthony Whiting's health. In a letter to the newly widowed Fanny Bassett Washington, he noted that a letter from Dr. James Craik, written on March 6, had revealed that Whiting was "confined to his bed by a more violent return of his old disorder (Spitting blood) than ever." Having received no letters from Whiting about his condition, Washington assumed that his farm manager was too sick to write, which confirmed Dr. Craik's report that the case was "critical and dangerous."[28]

Whiting's condition continued to deteriorate, leading Washington to leave Philadelphia for a quick trip home to Mount Vernon in June 1793. In a letter to James Madison, Thomas Jefferson reported that "the President . . . sets off this day to Mount Vernon, and will be absent about a fortnight. The death of his manager, hourly expected, of a consumption, is the call."[29]

Unfortunately, it was too soon for word to have reached Philadelphia that Whiting had died two days before.[30]

In the immediate aftermath of Whiting's death, George Washington turned temporarily to another nephew, Howell Lewis, who was then working for him as a secretary in the presidential mansion. Lewis was the youngest of eleven children born to Washington's sister Betty and her husband, Fielding Lewis. The young man had initially been hired in the spring of 1792, because his uncle had the impression that "he was spending his time rather idly" and also needed an income after having been "very slenderly provided for by his father," who died in 1782 when Howell was about eleven. Lewis would return to his secretarial job for his uncle by early in 1794.[31]

Whiting's permanent successor, William Pearce, would turn out to be the farm manager who probably best fit Washington's expectations for the job. Despite the pitfalls of not having an experienced manager onsite for a time while he conducted the search for a new one, Washington "thought it better to bear this temporary evil than to engage one immediately who might not have all the requisite qualifications" needed at Mount Vernon. Washington made inquiries in several parts of the country but thought that someone with experience on Maryland's Eastern Shore would work best, "for there seems to be more large Estates cultivated altogether in the farming System there than in other parts of the Country; and that—reclaiming Swamps; raising Grass, Ditching, Hedging & particular attention to Stock of all kinds—are the great pursuits of my Estate." Pearce would leave Washington's employ in the second half of 1796 because of health reasons. In a letter to his successor, Washington's reluctance to see Pearce go is evident: "I ought to have added, that the only cause of Mr. Pearces leaving my business is, an increasing Rheumatic affection which he says will not allow him to discharge his duty as he conceives he ought; for which reason, and thinking it the part of an honest man to retire."[32]

Pearce's replacement as farm manager, James Anderson, was a Scotsman who worked for George Washington primarily during his retirement years after the presidency (Anderson arrived in January 1797). Like Lund Washington and William Pearce before him, Anderson had accrued considerable experience in farm management before coming to Mount Vernon. He described his early life and experience in a letter to Washington dated September 11, 1796:

My Father was a Farmer in Scotland on the River Forth nearly 40 miles above Edinh And at the Age of 21 thinking the business more fully understood upon the English border I agreed with a Gentleman,

Famous in Farming, feeding Horned Cattle & Sheep, in Summer on Grass, and in Winter on Potatoes, Turnip & Hay, Had a good Dairy, properly managed. [W]ith Him I was an apprentice 2 Years at the expiry of which I took the management of a large Estate posses[sed] by His uncle an old Gentn which I conducted for 3 Years. And I bel[ie]ve with approbation. For 19 Years after I farmed on my own account, 18 of which I was also largely in the Grain line, And had several manufacturing Mills. But by the failure of a Sett of Distillers in 1788 I nearly lost all, And many more were ruined.[33]

Anderson came to the United States in 1791 with a large family composed of his wife, Helen Gordon, and their seven children (three sons and four daughters), who were born between 1776 and 1787.[34] Anderson admitted to Washington in a letter that he had even paid a visit to Mount Vernon shortly after his arrival in the country. He began renting a farm "of poor Land" in Fairfax County in the spring of the same year. Two years later, he started managing an 1,100-acre estate belonging to a Mr. Prescott in Prince William County, which was worked by fourteen or fifteen slaves. He remained there for two years before moving on to the Fredericksburg area, where he managed a larger farm (1,700 acres) and distillery for the Selden family and supervised about twenty-five slaves.[35]

Overseers

As he did when hiring farm managers, George Washington expected that he himself, or the farm managers acting on his behalf during his absences, would check into the backgrounds of potential overseers. When William Pearce hired John Groves to oversee Union Farm in 1794, he assured Washington that the man came "well recommended—from Several others as well as the Mr Masons [probably George Mason of Gunston Hall and his son Thomson Mason of Hollin Hall]."[36] Washington was not sure that he trusted the Masons in this matter, because he was determined to be a farmer, someone who cared for the land and its continued fertility, while he considered them merely planters, people who cared only for their cash crops and profits:

I wish the Overseer you have lately engaged may turn out well. The Masons may judge tolerably of his industry but they are very incompetent (in my opinion) to decide on his skill in any of the branches of farming, particularly those of Meadowing, grazing, and the care of stock; being planters themselves and little used to either. However, if he is sober, honest, industrious and docile, he may do under your immediate instructions, if you can keep him always with his people (and this I hope you will do) and make him be attentive to your orders and whatsoever is trusted to his care especially work horses and Cattle.[37]

Washington expressed considerable skepticism about another overseer, John Allison, who was hired by Pearce about the same time. In this case, although Washington did not personally know the man, he seems to have had a long acquaintance with his family, who lived near Mount Vernon: "I hope, and wish, Allison may turn out well. I know nothing of the one you have engaged, but it is a family of very little respectability, and closely connected with a set of people about my Mill, the Pools particularly, than whom I believe, a more worthless set are [nowhere] to be found." Washington also believed that it was John Allison who "spent, or rather misspent much of his time" with another of Washington's overseers, Hyland Crow.[38]

Martha Washington's granddaughter Nelly Custis Lewis absorbed much of her opinion about John Allison from her step-grandfather. Writing to a longtime friend in 1823, Lewis summed up her thoughts about Allison and his family, whom she would then have known for almost thirty years:

Allison was a common overseer, is a very common labouring man, who can just read & write sufficiently to be understood. He made some money by overseeing, raising Horses & fishing, has bought a few acres of land & has perhaps a few negro children & one or two grown negroes. He lives on the road between Mt V & Alex[andri]a—is a very common poor man—whose family are knowing in horse flesh & very apt to *romance* or *quiz,* or *tell fibs*—when occasion serves.[39]

Lewis's repeated use of the word "common" in describing Allison, together with her depiction of him as a "labouring man" and a "poor man" who was barely literate and owned only a small plot of land and just a few slaves, suggests that overseers were generally considered well below the Washingtons' social class.

Not all of the overseers, however, were considered lower class. Brothers Hezekiah and John Fairfax supervised Mount Vernon's Ferry Farm and the Mansion House Farm, respectively, in the 1780s. They were distant relatives of the aristocratic Fairfax family at neighboring Belvoir Plantation.[40] After leaving Washington's employ in 1790, John Fairfax moved to Virginia's Monongalia County. There he became a justice of the peace in 1794 and then represented the county in the Virginia House of Delegates from 1808 to 1810 and 1814 to 1815. John Fairfax came back to Mount Vernon about a month before George Washington's death, where he had dinner and spent the night in the mansion.[41]

Certain overseers were greatly trusted and were with Washington for many years. John Alton started out as Washington's body servant during the Braddock campaign and then came to work for him at Mount Vernon in the late 1750s.[42] Alton oversaw several of the Mount Vernon farms over the years; he was the overseer at River Farm when he died on December 3, 1785, from an "imposthume [abscess] in his thigh after lingering for more than 4 Months with it, and being reduced to a mere skeleton."[43] Out of gratitude for John Alton's decades of loyalty and service, Washington occasionally made cash payments to his widow and bequeathed one hundred dollars to the Altons' daughter, Ann, in his will.[44]

Several overseers were themselves enslaved—all were dower slaves. Israel Morris initially came to Mount Vernon as a carpenter from the Custis plantations in New Kent County in 1759 and quickly gained Washington's trust. By 1766, he was put in charge of Dogue Run Farm, a position he held for the next twenty-eight years.[45] Davy Gray had been the overseer "for many years" at Muddy Hole Farm before being moved to River Farm in 1785 as a temporary replacement for the recently deceased John Alton. He was back at Muddy Hole as overseer between 1792 and 1799.[46]

The man known as "Overseer Will" had charge of several farms in succession in the late 1780s. He replaced Gray at Muddy Hole in December 1785, but by the spring of 1790, farm manager George Augustine Washington recorded that he intended to move Gray from Muddy Hole to Dogue Run and swap in Will as the overseer at the former. Gray objected, begging that this change not be made and mentioning "that he did not think You [George Washington] would compell him so." His reason for asking to stay in place was that he had been seriously ill for some time with jaundice, was "very weakly and thought himself unable to take the management at D: run that he was now fixed and hoped to give you satisfaction." George Augustine commented that Gray "really appears to conduct himself well and what he says of his health I think is so, for he looks badly." He went on to say that he would not move either man until he heard from his uncle: "by continuing Will untill I heard from You no great injury could arise—tho' not much can be said of his skill he is active and perfectly disposed to execute orders—but do not think his management equal to conducting a planta[tio]n of its consequence."[47]

There are very brief hints of conflict between the hired and enslaved overseers. Shortly after his arrival at Mount Vernon in the summer of 1793, temporary farm manager Howell Lewis informed George Washington that he had completed an inspection of the five farms. After mentioning that the corn at both Union and Dogue Run Farms (under the supervision of hired overseers Highland Crow and Henry McCoy, respectively) looked clean, he noted that the corn at Muddy Hole Farm, which was overseen by the dower slave Davy Gray, "is not so clean as the other two." Gray's explanation, which Howell thought was "very good," was that "they [Crow and McCoy] have had his plows for some time, and deprived him of them, at a time, when the Corn wanted them most."[48]

Artisans

As was true of the farm managers and overseers, when hiring white craftsmen Washington was looking for someone with experience. Some of the hired supervisors came to Mount Vernon after working for other prominent employers. German gardener Johann Christian Ehlers had previously worked for at least two royal personages—George III of England at his palaces at Herrenhausen and Montbrillant in Hanover and the king of Prussia, who is not more specifically identified but would have been either Frederick II (also known as Frederick the Great) or Frederick William II—prior to coming to America in 1789.[49] As was true of other upper-level servants, Ehlers and his wife, Catherine, were entitled to eat at what was known as the "second table," or as Washington described it, "the victuals that went from my table (in the Cellar)," which would have been prepared by Lucy, one of two enslaved cooks in the kitchen beside the mansion.[50] Several years later, Washington was complaining about the pace of Ehlers's work, commenting that

> the matters entrusted to him appear to me to progress amazingly slow.
> I had no conception that there were grubs enough in the Vineyard enclosure to have employed them as many days as are reported; and sure I am that leveling the Bank ought to have taken a very little time. If it is found that the hands with the Gardener are not usefully (I mean industriously) employed, I shall with draw them; as I did not give them to him for *parade,* to be *idle,* or to keep him in *idleness.*[51]

For his part, according to his family, Ehlers found Washington to be "an autocrat."[52]

By the close of 1793, Washington had figured out what the problem was. Although he found that Ehlers "behaves well when sober, understands his business, and I believe is not naturally idle," things changed when the gardener was drinking. Washington believed the gardener had "too great a propensity to drink and behaves improperly when in liquor." Farm manager William Pearce was asked to "admonish [Ehlers] against it as much as you can."[53] Washington even wrote from Philadelphia to encourage the gardener to get control of his drinking. After first outlining the dangers of alcoholism he closed with the words, "Don't let this be your case. Sh[o]w yourself more of a man, and a Christian, than to yield to so intolerable a vice.... I am Your friend."[54]

Eleanor Forbes, a childless widow of about fifty years old who was born in England, was hired as housekeeper following Washington's retirement from the presidency. She had previously served in the official residence of Virginia governor Robert Brooke, who informed Washington's nephew Bushrod Washington that she was "honest, industrious, & well acquainted with nice as well as common Cooking and other subjects of domestic employment necessary in her profession." Brooke also related that he had found Forbes to be "active & spirited in the execution of her business—sober & honest—well acqua[i]nted with Cookery & ... capable of ordering & setting out a table." He had found both her appearance and demeanor to be "decent & respectable."[55] Brooke's recommendation indicates that the housekeeper's duties included supervision of both the cooks and scullions in the kitchen, as well as the butler and waiters at the table.

In hiring Forbes, George Washington was especially concerned that she not only had a thorough knowledge of the tasks required of a housekeeper but could also manage the slaves under her supervision and follow through on the orders given to her: "Besides care, & [a] knowledge of the duties of the Station—one who will *see* to the execution, as well as direct the measures of the Servants is indispensable in my family—One too who has spirit to enforce her orders—in doing which she will have every proper support."[56]

Although he initially felt that Forbes's requested salary of $150 per year was "unusually high," Washington was willing to pay it because of Martha Washington's "distresses for want of a good house keeper." In addition to her pay, Forbes would be given "a warm, decent & comfortable room to herself, to lodge in," as well as the same food the Washingtons ate, although she would take her meals at the second table in order to prevent the lines between the housekeeper and her employers from becoming blurred.[57] After an initial delay in getting her from Richmond, Forbes began working at Mount Vernon in December 1797 and moved into a room above the kitchen (formerly the quarters of enslaved butler Frank Lee; his wife, Lucy, the cook; and their children), comfortably, as promised, furnished with four chairs, a tea table, a mattress and bedstead, dressing glass, and fireplace equipment.[58] Within days of Forbes's arrival, George Washington was able to say that both "her appearance, and conduct hitherto, gives satisfaction" to Mrs. Washington.[59] The Washingtons continued to be pleased with her job performance, and she was still in their employ and helping to care for a suddenly and gravely ill George Washington when he died on December 14, 1799.[60]

Three brothers from Ireland came to Mount Vernon as indentured servants in the 1780s. Cornelius McDermott Roe was a stonemason and bricklayer who came to the plantation in 1784 with a two-year indenture. When that concluded, he then continued to work for Washington between 1786 and 1787, after signing a contract that called for a salary of thirty-two pounds, plus board, lodging, washing, an allowance of alcohol, clothing to be made and mended at Washington's expense from materials Roe would supply, and Washington's payment of Roe's taxes and parish levies. The artisan was also allowed to take off one day each quarter on his own business. Later, after leaving Washington's employ, Roe worked on the construction of buildings in the new Federal City, including the U.S. Capitol, work that may have come his way through a friendship with Irish architect James Hoban.[61] In addition to Cornelius, his brothers, Edward and Timothy, served as ditchers at Mount Vernon in the late 1780s.[62]

Contracts

In the case of the workforce at Mount Vernon, besides race, one of the major differences between those who were enslaved and those who were either hired or indentured was that the latter worked under contracts negotiated with George Washington—contracts that spelled out both his expectations and responsibilities toward them and theirs in relation to him.

Almost from the beginning of permanent English settlements in Virginia, indentured servants made up a distinct class in the population. They typically signed agreements of indenture in Europe and were brought to America at the expense of the company or individual who recruited them, where their services were transferred to a planter for a sum of money or tobacco. In these contracts, the prospective servant agreed to work for a given length of time in exchange for transportation to the colony; appropriate food, drink, clothing, and housing during the period of his indenture; and sometimes an award of cash or goods upon completion of his employment.[63]

The white servants at Mount Vernon in the eighteenth century, whether indentured or free, generally came to the estate with very similar agreements, which included mention of their expected workload and the provisions, including food, they were to receive from Washington. One of the earliest contracts, between George Washington and John Askew, a married joiner, provided for Washington to supply the latter with "good and wholesome provision's while he is at work" in exchange for working "from Sun rise to Sun set, allowing proper times only for Eating." The contract also stipulated that Askew at the end of the year would make up any work lost "by negligence Sickness or private business of his own the days and hours so lost." Askew promised to work wherever and whenever Washington required, and to "use his best endeavour's to instruct in the art of his trade any Negro or Negroes which the said George Washington shall cause to work with him." In exchange, Washington would "let the said John Askew and his wife live at a Plantation adjoining commonly known by the name of North[']s without paying Rent, that he will find the said John good & wholesome provisions while he is at work, and at the expiration of the twelve month fully compleated agreable to the true Intent hereof pay him the Curr[ent]t Sum of Twenty five pounds Lawful money of Virginia."[64]

An overseer, Burgess Mitchell, hired for six months in 1762, was to receive "washing lodging and provisions." In addition, Washington agreed to pay the man a salary of six pounds and his taxes. If this overseer did not meet the standards he agreed to—remaining constantly with the slaves, behaving "himself Soberly, and diligently in all respects endeavouring by a prudent and commendable conduct to gain the good esteem & liking of his said employer"—Mitchell agreed that he could be fired, forfeiting all his wages. That last provision proved to be unfortunate when Mitchell was discharged prior to completing his agreed-upon term of service.[65]

David Cowan, a gardener who came in 1773, agreed to work for Washington for an annual salary of twenty-five pounds and a promise to furnish him with "Washing, lodging and Diet." As the gardener, Cowan was expected to "work duely & truely, during that time, at the business; as also when need be, or when thereunto required, employ himself in Grafting, Budding, & pruning of Fruit Trees and Vines—likewise in Saving, at proper Seasons, and due order, Seeds of all kinds." He also agreed to "covenant and agree to behave himself Honestly, soberly, and peaceably, in the Family whilst he abides therein; and that he will not only stick close to the work himself, but make others which may be with him do so likewise; and moreover, that he will allow for all his own lost time." Cowan lasted ten months at Mount Vernon. When he left, he was owed a prorated salary of £19.7.10, minus £5, which Washington had advanced to him; £1.4.0 Cowan owed to George Washington's tailor for making him a suit of clothing; and £0.12.3 for "lost time."[66]

Records about the employment of William Roberts, who was the estate's miller for many years before, during, and after the Revolution, show that he was provided with clothing that was greater in both quantity and quality to that given to slaves on the plantation. In 1773, for example, Roberts received the following articles of clothing and food: a suit of jeans; a coat for someone named Thomas, probably a servant or slave; a coat; a waistcoat; over two hundred pounds of beef; and two bushels of salt. The following year he was provided with a pair of breeches, 3 pairs of Russia twill breeches, a coat and waistcoat; 113 pounds of beef, 2 bushels of salt, and 150 shad.[67] Between June 1775 and January 1776, he received a coat, 4 pairs of breeches, a waistcoat, a surtout coat, 210 shad, 2½ bushels of salt, and "a waistcoat for your Boy." Roberts appears to have made the following annual salaries: £60 (1777), £100 (1778), £100 (1779), and £800 (1780), the last showing the effects of extreme inflation resulting from the Revolution.[68]

Some of these contracts became quite specific about the foods to be supplied by Washington, and they, together with information from diaries, ledgers, and account books, are invaluable evidence for the diet of the hired and indentured white servants. They also give a good idea of how the basic needs of the hired people were thought to compare with those of the enslaved, the subject of a later chapter. For example, the basic rations of the hired whites can be seen in a diary entry from 1786. During the summer of that year, Washington hired a couple of men to ditch some swampy land at Dogue Run. In addition to receiving a set amount of money for each foot of ditching they did, each man was to receive a bottle of milk, 1 pint of spirits, 1¼ pounds of brown bread, and either 1 pound of salted meat or 1½ pounds of fresh meat per day.[69]

As was the case with the slaves, the white servants' diet relied heavily on salted meats and grains. There was, however, a noticeable difference in the quality of food given to servants of different ranks and more of a reliance on meats, such as pork and beef, and wheat flour, rather than the fish and cornmeal received by the enslaved. A carpenter (and sometime shoemaker) named Benjamin Buckler came to Mount Vernon in 1771, where he contracted to work for a period of ten months. Expected to work from "day break til dark," he was supposed to supervise Washington's enslaved carpenters, "to hurry and drive them on to the performance of so much work as they ought to render and for this purpose he the said Benjamin is hereby invested with sufficient power and authority which he is to make use of and to exercise with prudence and discretion." In addition to a salary of twenty-six pounds, Buckler would receive a house for himself and his family, plus three hundred pounds of pork and three barrels of corn. The summer after his contract was up, Buckler returned to Mount Vernon to help with bringing in the crop, for which he was paid £0.3.9.[70]

Jonathan Palmer agreed in 1768 to work with the enslaved carpenters and coopers, presumably as a supervisor, for four hundred pounds of meat and twenty bushels of Indian corn.[71] James Bloxham, who came from England in 1786 to work for Washington with the expectation that he would bring improved methods of agriculture to Mount Vernon, was to be supplied with six hundred pounds of pork or beef and eight hundred pounds of middling flour, which he considered a good wage.[72] A single overseer hired in 1790 was engaged for three hundred pounds of pork, one hundred pounds of beef, four bushels of corn, and one hundred pounds of middling flour.[73] Mr. Davenport, a miller with a wife and children, was to have six hundred pounds of pork plus some beef.[74]

In addition to salted meat, the white servants were frequently given the use of live animals, something that was not true for the enslaved at Mount Vernon. As part of his wages, Jonathan Palmer had the use of two milk cows, one half of whose increase was to go to George Washington.[75] Farming expert James Bloxham also had the use of two cows, plus a sow whose offspring could be eaten by Bloxham's family but were not to be sold.[76] A single overseer hired in 1790 was allowed the use of a cow and could raise chickens for his own use.[77] A similar arrangement was made with William Roberts, the miller. Lund Washington reported to his cousin in 1778, however, that Roberts was raising "great quantities of fowl" for sale, which was a violation of his contract. According to Lund, the miller was allowed "to raise for his own consumption only," but the man argued that after all the work his wife did taking care of the chickens, they should be permitted to sell the "overplus" in order to buy a "few Luxuries," such as sugar and coffee.[78]

Other contracts were tailored to the individual needs or proclivities of the parties involved. For instance, in 1786, George Washington hired a ditcher by the name of James Lawson. Their agreement stipulated that Lawson would "provide another hand," who would receive the same provisions and bread as the white servants "to be baked at the Home Hous[e] and sent twice or thrice a week. Meat to be boiled at [enslaved] Overseer Morris' Home by his wife [who was also enslaved]."[79] Overseer Edward Violet was married, and his agreement included references to his wife milking, churning, and doing other tasks about a dairy, which George Washington promised to build and furnish with the necessary milk pans, pails, and other equipment to carry on that enterprise. Mrs. Violet was also required to supervise one enslaved woman who would work with her. For this she would be allowed to keep one-fourth of the butter she made.[80] Among the things his employer agreed to provide to James Bloxham was "as much Bran as is sufficient to brew beer for his family."[81] Based on one of Washington's letters, the German gardener Johann Christian Ehlers and his wife were each "allowed a bottle of Beer a day, and this must be continued to them, that is, a quart each, for when I am from home it will no longer be bottled, though it may be brewed as usual as the occasion requires."[82]

A particularly interesting contract was drawn up in 1787 for Philip Bater, a gardener, elaborating on an understanding that he would not get drunk except at certain mutually agreed upon times: "In Consideration of these things being well and truly performed on the part of the sd. Philip Bater, the said George Washington doth agree to allow him . . . four Dollars at Christmas, with which he may be drunk 4 days and 4 nights; two Dollars at Easter to effect the same purpose; two Dollars also at Whitsontide, to be drunk two days; A Dram in the morning, and a drink of Grog at Dinner or at Noon."[83]

As evidenced by the agreement between Washington and Bater, getting and staying drunk was something of a given for the working class at holidays. Drinking and rough-housing may have played a part in a tragic occurrence that cost one Mount Vernon servant his life. Shortly after the first Christmas of the Revolution, George Washington learned from his farm manager that "John Broad [an indentured convict serving as a joiner] in a playing frolic last Sunday, got a small wound in the thigh which gives him much pain. It is very much swelled and inflamed. He thinks it will kill him, but I am of a different opinion."[84] Broad's situation deteriorated over the next month, and by the end of January the doctor had pronounced his case incurable. Further details about the incident came out at that time:

I told you he got a slight wound in his thigh on Christmass Eve in Alexandria—he was it seemes at play with Aaron (my fellow) [probably a slave] who had an Old rusty Sword in his hand, Broad with a Stick got to parr[y]ing with him, & by Chance he was prick[e]d in the thigh but so slight that it scarcely cou'd be called a wound, in short it was only skin deep & no wider than the point of a sword will make. [I]t was very Cold & I suppose it got into it—the wound festerd, the thigh swell[e]d & so did his Leg & Foot to a most amazing degree until his Leg Bursted in several places, from these places & his thigh there runs more matter than I ever see in all my life put together, he is free from pain but reduce'd to a Skeleton—he can eat hearty & sleeps but still he cannot live so says the Drs Rumney & Jenifer.[85]

The doctors were right; John Broad's death was reported in another letter about three weeks later.[86]

Over a decade later, the work report for the week ending March 20, 1790, recorded something interesting about Thomas Mahony, an Irish house carpenter and joiner who had begun his career at Mount Vernon as an indentured artisan for a period of two years and then continued to work for Washington after earning his freedom. This particular report noted that Mahony had been off from work for one day "keeping St. Patrick[']s day," but was then "3 days absent on his own Acct."[87] Mount Vernon's workforce was not unusual in regard to drinking, and for those artisans and indentured servants whose families were still in Europe, homesickness may have been a contributing factor. The newly arrived tutor on another Virginia plantation started a poem on December 27, 1774, which began,

> Both the last nights quite drunk was I,
> Pray God forgive me [of] the sin;
> But had I been in good company,
> Me in that case No man had seen.[88]

Like the slaves, white servants were sometimes suspected of stealing. For instance, in a 1790 letter, George Augustine Washington told his uncle that the contract of an overseer named William Garner had just been renewed for another term, with a few changes. The man's wages had been cut by six pounds and he was to receive fifty pounds of beef in lieu of the former privilege of killing four young pigs each year. George Augustine explained: "Suffering an Overseer to kill Shoats I think is affording them a pretext for great abuses—for when ever they are seen to do it they will offer an excuse that it is what they are allow'd—but if no such privilege is granted they can never make use of it as a plea."[89] Four years later, George Washington was concerned about the conduct of the overseer at Dogue Run and cautioned his farm manager:

When [Henry] McKoy is getting out the Oats at Dogue run, have a strict eye to him. He told me he expected 150 Bushls. from the stack, and if all the Oats which grew in what was called the new ground, went into it, there ought to be 200 at least: but what by waste, mismanagement, or something worse, I have, of late, got very little from any of my Overseers; what becomes of it is more difficult to determine.[90]

Those oats may have met the same fate as some butter that was the subject of a letter later in the year. As part of his contract, William Stuart was allowed a certain percentage of the butter made on the farm he oversaw. Washington ordered farm manager William Pearce to have Stuart take only the butter needed for use by his immediate family and bring the rest to the Mansion House Farm. After it was sold, Stuart would receive his portion of the sale price. The president wished by these means to "supercede the necessity of [Stuart's] wife's, or any other person's running to Alexandria to dispose of this article, or to enquire into the price of it." He suspected Mrs. Stuart of having "fraudulently" "furnished Butter for McKnight's Tavern," and that instead of the 25 percent allowed them, the couple had made off with at least three-quarters of the butter. It was hoped that the change in procedure would "guard me against such impositions; and . . . secure his own [Stuart's] character against suspicion and calumny."[91]

Daily Management: Expectations

Washington expected each of his hired employees to "remain constantly with the People over whom he is to look, and never stir from them during their hours of work, but at Mealtimes—He is not to go off the Plantation (except on Sundays) without asking leave," a fairly typical presumption shared by other plantation owners of the period.[92] Thirty years later, Washington reiterated in a letter to a relative that "with me, it is an established maxim, that an Overseer shall never be absent from his people but at night, and at his meals."[93] Neglect of these duties was one of his chief complaints against an overseer named Henry Jones, who was dismissed in 1792. Washington railed that the man would "meet with no more than his des[s]erts if he was made to pay for the damage my Wheat fields have sustained: for he had sufficient warning from myself, before I left home, to guard him against this evil." Washington also blamed "such inattention, and want of exertion, together with the opportunities that are given to my Negros" for thefts on the estate, going on to suggest that

> If some of the Nights in which these Overseers are frolicking, at the expence of my business, and to the destruction of my horses, were spent in watching the Barns, visiting the Negro quarters at unexpected hours, waylaying the Roads, or contriving some device by which the receivers of Stolen goods might be entrapped, and the facts proved upon them; it would be no more than the performance of a duty which I have a right to expect for the wages they draw from me; and it wd. redound much more to their own credit and reputation as good and faithful Overseers than runng. about.[94]

Not seeing the improvement he wanted, the following summer in a letter to three of his hired overseers, Washington reminded them that "your time is paid for by me, & if I am deprived of it, it is worse even than robbing my purse, because it is also a breach of trust; which every honest man ought to hold most sacred."[95] The perspective of Lund Washington as farm manager, which entailed supervising the overseers at the same time he was an employee himself, is particularly interesting because he was probably echoing his employer's opinion when he wrote, "it is a maxim with me, that he who rec[ei]ves the wages of another, hath no time which he, in right can call his own."[96]

Washington typically had a poor opinion of many of his hired workers, and references to "the inattention and carelessness of the Overseers," "the insufferable conduct of my Overseers," and "my blundering Overseers" were common.[97] Washington cautioned a new farm manager that he would soon find there was "little dependence" on his overseers and that, because they got a fixed salary or "standing wages" and were not generally "actuated by the principles of honor or honesty, and not very regardful of their characters," there was a tendency to slack off, "as *their* profits, whatever may be *mine,* are the same whether they are at a horse race or on the farm, whether they are entertaining company (which I believe is too much the case) in their own houses or are in the fields with the Negroes."[98] He complained to another manager that "too few of that class of (common) Overseers" were "overburthened" with either principle or "a regard for reputation."[99]

Washington distrusted not only the basic character of his overseers but also their care for the humanity of his slaves. He may have had good reason to worry. In contrasting the treatment of slaves at Mount Vernon with other places he had visited, a French traveler noted that in Virginia in general, "Negroes are not considered human beings."[100] After two slaves died in the spring of 1795, Washington expressed concern that they had been given "every necessary care and attention" during the course of their illness. He went on to say that he did not believe their overseer, "or indeed . . . most of his class," would ordinarily have seen to such care, complaining that "they seem to consider a Negro much in the same light as they do the brute beasts, on the farms; and often times treat them as inhumanly."[101] Several years earlier, Washington had complained about "the generality" of overseers, who neglected the slaves when they were too sick to work, "instead of comforting and nursing them when they lye on a sick bed."[102] A diary entry from thirty years before shows Washington performing the kind of actions he expected of his overseers in regard to sick slaves. On January 28, 1760, he noted that an African-born slave named Cupid, who had been purchased from a slave ship five months before, was sick with pleurisy at Dogue Run, and that he "had him brot. home [to the Mansion House Farm] in a Cart for better care of him." Two days later, Washington wrote that the patient was not doing well, and that "at Night when I went to Bed I thought him within a few hours of breathing his last." In this case the prognosis was wrong, because Cupid did survive; he was later listed in a runaway advertisement in the summer of 1761.[103]

On occasion, Washington included these concerns in the employment contracts drawn up with new supervisors. Edward Violette, who was hired to oversee one of the outlying farms, promised to "take all necessary and proper care of the Negroes committed to his management using them with proper humanity and discretion." Several years later, the contract with carpenter Benjamin Buckler gave him "sufficient power and authority" to oversee the enslaved carpenters but cautioned that this authority was to be exercised "with prudence and discretion."[104] The concerns Washington expressed about his overseers and managers were understood and shared by other plantation owners in the American South. They can also be found throughout the world in similar cultures, where overseers or stewards were caught between a landowner and an unfree labor force.[105]

Keeping One's Distance

As in so many aspects of their lives, George Washington wanted those in authority on the plantation to emulate his management style. While they were expected to be with the slaves constantly during work hours and nearby the rest of the time, Washington stressed over and over the necessity for hired whites to maintain their emotional distance from the people they were overseeing, much as he did himself. In 1794, for example, he advised his farm manager to caution a newly hired artisan "against familiarities with the Negros."[106] One of his major complaints about Thomas Green, a carpenter supervisor, was that the craftsman could not exert enough authority over the slaves because "he is too much upon a level with the Negroes to exert it." This may have been the problem with another hired white as well whom Washington found almost useless at supervising slaves: "I am persuaded he has no more authority over the Negroes . . . than an old woman would have; and is as unable to get a proper day[']s Work done by them as she would unless led to it by their own inclination wch. I know is not the case."[107]

It is very likely that Washington's concern with overfamiliarity between the hired whites and slaves on the plantation were reinforced by his military background, where officers traditionally kept their distance from the men they supervised. Too close a relationship could jeopardize the authority a leader needed in order to function properly. An officer could open himself up to charges of either favoritism toward or prejudice against particular individuals under his command. Soldiers who knew all their superior's faults might not follow him into a dangerous situation, could have such a low opinion of him that he was an object of ridicule, or might even try to blackmail him. An officer who was too intimately involved with his men could find himself unable to give orders necessary for completing a mission because he was thinking too much about the cost to his troops.

Evidence from Mount Vernon suggests that Washington was thinking of situations like these when he counseled those in authority on the plantation to keep their distance. For example, in the early 1790s the hired head carpenter, Thomas Green, had a severe drinking problem that got worse over time. Washington felt that Green's situation made it impossible for him to chastise the men he supervised because they had too much information with which to blackmail him: "He dare not find fault with those who are entrusted to his care lest they shd. retort and disclose his rascally conduct." As a consequence, "work that the same number of hands would perform in a week, takes mine a month."[108] Washington even cautioned a new farm manager about the dangers of getting too close to the overseers he supervised: "To treat them civilly is no more than what all men are entitled to, but, my advice to you is, to keep them at a proper distance; for they will grow upon familiarity, in proportion as you will sink in authority, if you do not."[109]

One of the ways Washington encouraged this emotional distance was to physically separate the living spaces of the slaves and hired whites of all types. When James Donaldson, who succeeded Thomas Green as supervisor of the Mount Vernon carpenters, arrived on the estate from Scotland before the family of his predecessor had vacated the house intended for him, he was moved into a section of the greenhouse complex, where the primary slave quarter at the Mansion House Farm was located. Washington was very unhappy with this situation because he preferred that the new man be "kept as sep[a]rate, and as distinct as possible from the Negros, who want no encouragement to mix with, and become too familiar (for no good purposes) with these kind of people."[110]

Racial or class prejudice was also involved in Washington's feelings about blacks and whites living in close proximity. Among his concerns with the Donaldson family's initial housing situation was that they "will get disgusted by living among the Negros if he [Donaldson] is still in the Green house."[111] About a year earlier, in correspondence with English agronomist Arthur Young, Washington had discussed the possibility of renting his four outlying farms. Individuals contracting for the farms would be able to hire as laborers, on an annual basis, the slaves living on those units, if they preferred this approach to importing "that class of people." Washington worried, however, about the wisdom of having a mixed workforce of free Europeans and enslaved African Americans: "It deserves consideration how far the mixing of whites and blacks together is advisable; especially where the former, are entirely unacquainted with the latter."[112]

In this instance, however, he may have been most concerned with the white laborers picking up the work habits of his slaves. Writing to his farm manager shortly after Donaldson's arrival, Washington wrote a long section on just this problem:

> I would have him cautioned against an error which I have felt no small inconvenience from; and that is, that rather than persevere in doing things right themselves, and being at the trouble of making others do the like, they will fall into the slovenly mode of executing work which is practiced by those, among whom they are. I have experienced this not only from European tradesmen, but from farmers also, who have come from England . . . yet, finding it a little troublesome to instruct the Negros, and to compel them to the practice of his modes, he slided into theirs; and at length . . . instead of using proper flails for threshing the grain, I have found my people at this work with hoop poles, and other things similar thereto.[113]

In an intriguing letter written to newly hired farm manager William Pearce in 1793, Washington provided considerable evidence that he was well aware of the strengths and weaknesses of his overseers. Of the three hired white overseers on his outlying farms that year, he probably had the nicest things to say about William Stuart at River Farm, who was described as "a sober man, and according to his own account a very honest one." Washington noted that Stuart was talkative, "has a high opinion of his own skill and management, and seems to live in peace and harmony with the Negroes who are confided to his care. He speaks extremely well of them, and I have never heard any complaint of him." Henry McKoy at Dogue Run Farm was "a sickly, slothful and stupid fellow," while Washington worried that Hyland Crow at Union Farm was paying too much attention to his own business to properly attend to Washington's, leaving the slaves on that farm "too much to themselves which produces idleness, or slight work on one side and flogging on the other; the last of which besides the dissatisfaction which it creates, has, in one or two instances been productive of serious consequences." In other words, someone probably became incapacitated or almost died because of a whipping. While at one point during the late

1780s all four of the outlying farms were overseen by enslaved men, by the time of this letter the only slave who was serving as an overseer was Davy Gray at Muddy Hole Farm. Washington saved some of his best remarks for this middle-aged man, who had worked as an overseer for many years: "Davy . . . carries on his business as well as the white Overseers, and with more quietness than any of them. With proper directions he will do very well and probably give you less trouble than any of them except in attending to his care of the stock of which I fear he is negligent as there are deaths too frequent among them."[114]

Physical Security

Maintaining the security of the keys on the estate was one of the most important tasks of those in management positions. In the summer of 1793, shortly after taking temporary command of Mount Vernon, nephew Howell Lewis received a letter from George Washington that focused on the need for security. It began with the information that presidential secretary Tobias Lear had recently been to Mount Vernon, where he personally placed a cask containing seven bushels of clover seed into the storehouse near the mansion house. When no one could find it, Washington ordered that James Butler, the overseer at the Mansion House Farm, "must be answerable for it; as I positively directed that the Key of that House should be deposited in the Key box, & never to be in his possession but when he was in the Act of delivering things out." Washington refused to suspect Butler of anything nefarious but felt that "if any of the Roguish people about that [House] (of which there are numbers . . .) have come at the key, unknown to him, it will be found that every thing else which could be sold, is gone as well as the Seed." He ordered that "a discovery, & stop must be put to these practices by the most vigilant watch; or soon, I shall not be able to retain a single article in the dwelling house." In order to prevent further "villainies," he asked that Fanny Bassett Washington, the widow of his nephew George Augustine, "let no body go to the key Box but herself, you, or Milly [Fanny's sister-in-law Mildred Gregory Washington]." If these measures were not taken, "it is impossible to answer for the damage I shall sustain if opportunities are given to others to get at Keyes, & keep them until their purposes are answered, & then return them unsuspected to their places. The Lock of the Key chest should also be examined—& never be out of her own room at Night." In addition to the keys to the storehouse, keys for the seed loft over the greenhouse were also to be kept in the key box.[115]

In addition to their responsibility for keys and locks, overseers on each of the farms were personally responsible for ensuring that equipment was kept in good shape. In the summer of 1793, George Washington mentioned in his weekly correspondence with the farm manager that "it may not be amiss to inform the several Overseers that when the Wood work of their Plows is made new & good, they must keep them in order themselves." Washington considered it "shameful to see by the Report that the Carpenters—one or other of them—are eternally going to one or the other of the Farms to do some trifle, which every other Overseer in the world does or ought to do himself."[116]

Family

The situation in regard to marriage was a bit different for hired and indentured servants and artisans than for slaves. Unlike the slaves, most of whom were married, "free laborerers" were often alone, without a wife or children. One of the most important differences was that their marriages were legally recognized, whether they were performed in America or in Europe prior to emigrating. The wives of hired workers were often expected to provide labor for Washington, and their children, unlike those of the slaves, simply increased his expenses without adding to his net worth. So it was that in 1784, when looking to hire a new miller, Washington wrote, "I do not object to the Man[']s having a family (a wife I could wish him to have) but if it was a small one, it would be preferable."[117] Four years later, when Washington sought an indentured Dutch gardener, he noted that "I should prefer a single man, but have no objection to one who is married provided his wife understands spinning &c. and will indent as her husband does and provided they have not a number of Children."[118] Occasionally, the wife of a hired worker had specific duties, often supervising slaves at tasks such as dairying and textile production.[119] In other cases, she might earn extra money by doing some sewing, selling domestic fowls, or acting as a midwife for the enslaved women. For example, in December 1765, George Washington paid Thomas Bishop's wife eight shillings for making two pairs of breeches for Breechy, a twenty-six-year-old dower slave who served as a waiter in the mansion, and for an unknown number of chickens. Two months later, Susannah Bishop was paid ten shillings for "bringing Betty to bed."[120]

As there were between enslaved families at Mount Vernon, so too were there marriages between the families of the hired workers. For example, at the end of the Revolution, farm manager Lund Washington hired Richard Burnet (later known as Richard Burnet Walker) to assist Martha Washington as housekeeper or steward. While Lund approved of his work, Burnet was lonely and found himself drawn to the home of longtime employee John Alton. The lure at the Alton home seems to have been a daughter named Ann, to whom Burnet was married in 1785.[121] In another case, Sarah (or Sally), the daughter of another longtime servant, Thomas Bishop, married hired carpenter/joiner Thomas Green, who had begun working at Mount Vernon in 1782.[122] The Washingtons may even have paid for the bride's wedding dress. About a year after Green was hired, Colonel Fitzgerald was paid £2.2.0 for "a Dark ground chintz for Bishop[']s Daughter."[123] At the end of his life, George Washington remembered both these women, who had grown up before his eyes, in his will. He made a bequest of one hundred dollars to each of them, "in consideration of the attachment" of their fathers to him "each of whom having lived nearly forty years in my family."[124]

There is evidence that some of these marriages were unhappy. William Roberts, Washington's longtime miller, wrote his employer in late November 1784 to ask if he could keep his job. He had been drinking heavily, which led not only to problems with the quality of his work but also with his wife. Roberts admitted that they had had "a Most unhapy falling out. . . . I hapned To Git to Drinking one night as She thought Two much" and there was "one Cross Questune [after] a nother."[125] Roberts left Mount Vernon, working elsewhere for well over a decade, during which there were several changes in his marital situation. In 1799, when he was again looking to hire a miller, Washington corresponded with William Booker in Richmond about the possibility of rehiring Roberts. Booker noted that Roberts was still "very fond of strong drink, and when Inoxicated, is very troublesome." Booker reported that in the years he had been away from Mount Vernon, Roberts had "Lost his wife, and married a second time, he has also Lost her." There had clearly been physical abuse: "While m[a]rried, [Roberts] was very often put in prison on account of being so Quarrelsome, and his wife was often thought to be in danger of her Life, while he was in those frolicks."[126] Despite his prior experience with Roberts, Washington did rehire the miller in the summer of 1799, but Roberts's ill health led to his being let go in mid-November.[127]

Another difficult relationship was the one between carpenter Thomas Green and his wife, Sally—also due to drinking. In 1793, Washington warned a younger family member who was then managing Mount Vernon, "You must have a particular eye to this fellow [Green], for a more worthless one does not, I believe live. Nothing but compassion for his helpless family would induce me to retain him a moment in my service."[128] Green left Washington's employ in the summer of 1794, leading Washington to write that "Green's quitting my business of his own accord . . . is . . . a lucky circumstance, as my repugnance to turning him away was on account of his helpless family. These you may suffer to remain where they are, until he can provide a place for them; or until you may have occasion for the house for his successor; provided this is not unreasonably delayed."[129] Green soon abandoned his wife and children, but Washington continued to keep an eye on their circumstances, contributing both money and advice.[130]

In addition to marriages, there is evidence for extramarital liaisons between managerial staff at Mount Vernon and both the white and African American women on the estate who came under their supervision (relations between white managers and black, enslaved women is discussed in detail in a later chapter). For example, the relationship between farm manager Lund Washington and a hired housekeeper was recorded by a later generation of the Washington family. Lund's nephew, also named Lund, was the son of Robert Washington, the older brother of George Washington's longtime manager. In 1849, when he was then eighty-two years old, the younger Lund sat down to write a history of his family in which he noted that his uncle "had a Son by a young Woman who was House Keeper at Mt. Vernon," then living near Connellsville, Pennsylvania. According to this account, the son, John Washington, came back to Virginia in 1791 to visit his father, who was then completely blind and refused to see him because he had been told that the young man had "been killed by the Indians in an expedition against them under Colo. or General Crawford." Believing that story, Lund "turned his Child away abruptly as an Imposter." The family chronicler noted that Lund's son was "a respectable Man, has been twice married, has a large family of children and Grandchildren and on different occasions has been recognized as a Washington from his remarkable likeness to the family." John Washington is said to have taken part in General Josiah Harmar's campaign against the Indians in the Northwest Territory in 1790 and to have received a pension from the state of Pennsylvania for his military service.[131]

Although the younger Lund Washington did not mention the name of the housekeeper who was the mother of John Washington, plantation records suggest that she was probably one of four women. Housekeeper Sarah Harle was at Mount Vernon for two years, starting in 1765. On May 2, 1767, a Doctor Thompson was brought to care for her, although the reason for the visit was not recorded. The doctor's fee of £2.3.6 was much higher than was typically charged for midwifery, but this could have been the result of an especially difficult labor and delivery, or the call may have had nothing to do with pregnancy. In any case, Sarah Harle left Mount Vernon in late May, just a few weeks after that doctor's call.[132] Her replacement was Rachel McKeaver, who worked as the housekeeper at Mount Vernon for ten months between November 1767 and September 1768.[133] Another possibility was McKeaver's replacement, Mary Wilson, who served as the Washingtons' housekeeper from December 1768 until June 1769.[134] Perhaps the most likely individual was Catherine Boyd, an indentured "Servant woman" who was purchased by Washington in May 1767 from the estate of Captain George Johnston. At some point after her arrival—the date is not given—Susannah Bishop was paid ten shillings each for delivering the babies of two slaves, Kate and Sue, and Catherine Boyd.[135]

Conclusion

It is clear that the hired and indentured managers, overseers, and artisans at Mount Vernon were placed in a difficult situation. Although most of them arrived with good references, as well as experience in management on other plantations, George Washington had high expectations that could be very hard to meet. They were also placed in a difficult situation between the master and his family, and the enslaved people they supervised, a position that proved untenable for some and may have led to problems with drinking for others. More of the stories of these hired and indentured workers unfold in future chapters, as the daily lives of the enslaved people they supervised are examined in greater detail.

4

"So Exact and So Strict"

Labor and the Mount Vernon Slaves

Expectations

George Washington summed up what he expected in the way of work from his slaves in a letter written on the first day of 1789. In it he informed a new overseer that his "people" were to be "at their work as soon as it is light, work till it is dark, and be diligent while they are at it." After stating his deeply ingrained belief that "lost labour is never to be regained," Washington stipulated that "every labourer (male or female) [do] as much in the 24 hours as their strength without endangering the health, or constitution will allow of."[1] In these few words, Washington described the work ethic that shaped his days almost until the moment of his death. The problem for this man, who rose at dawn in order to work at his desk before breakfast, made daily inspection tours of his farms, and ended the day with still more paperwork, was that others, both hired and enslaved, were not George Washington and did not share his values. Washington made repeated attempts to enforce compliance with his value system but was never able to suppress his slaves' efforts to fight the plantation system and thus assert their own independence and individuality, and the values of the African American community.

The Mount Vernon slaves were expected to be on the job when the sun came up, so a typical workday would have found them getting out of bed while it was still dark and returning to their quarters in the evening after dark as well. Many years after Washington's death, one of his former slaves recalled that the "sun never caught him [Washington] in bed, and he was unwilling it should find any of his people Sleeping."[2] Knowing that the slaves had two hours off for meals during the day, they probably left for their worksite almost immediately upon arising, and while they may have grabbed a corncake or two to eat quickly on the way, they would have eaten their regular breakfast some time later, as part of a mid-morning break. The dinner break seems to have been taken in the early afternoon.[3]

If they were doing as they were supposed to, the plantation's overseers were in the fields either when the slaves arrived or shortly afterward. Their employer repeatedly admonished his overseers to "remain constantly at home (unless called off by unavoidable business or to attend Divine Worship) and to be constantly with your people when there."[4] However, the overseers were unable to live up to Washington's exacting standards. He complained bitterly in 1793 about the overseer at River Farm, who was accused of not being on duty in the morning "until the Sun had warmed the Earth." Washington believed that if the overseer was late getting to work, the slaves would follow his example.[5] Later that year, in a letter to farm manager William Pearce, Washington again emphasized "the necessity of keeping these Overseers strictly to their duty, that is, to keep them from running about, and to oblige them to remain constantly with their people; and moreover, to see at what time they turn out of a morning, for I have strong suspicions that this, with some of them is at a late hour, the consequence of which to the Negroes is not difficult to foretell."[6] Washington's complaints about his overseers were not at all unusual. Another plantation owner, Landon Carter of Sabine Hall, had groused over twenty years before that the "eyes nor diligence" of an overseer were "not equal to one fourth of the Master's."[7]

When in residence at Mount Vernon, Washington very clearly did as he would have his managers and overseers do for him. Shortly after his retirement from the presidency in 1797, he described his typical day: "I begin my diurnal course with the Sun. ... If my hirelings are not in their places at that time I send them messages expressive of my sorrow for their indisposition."[8] His instructions to farm manager James Anderson in 1798 included the injunction to inspect the slave quarters and provide for those individuals who were sick "when they are really so, and to drive out those who are not."[9]

The Workday

The length of a workday "from Sun to Sun" would have changed substantially with the seasons.[10] At the spring equinox, the time between sunrise at 6:11 a.m. and sunset at 6:21 p.m.—and consequently the workday—was twelve hours and ten minutes. At the summer solstice, when the sun rose at 4:43 a.m. and set at 7:36 p.m., the time between those events had lengthened to fourteen hours and fifty-three minutes. Since a number of the grain crops were harvested at this time of year, these very long, hot days were also filled with hard work. By the fall equinox, the time between the rising and setting of the sun had fallen to twelve hours and twelve minutes. With the arrival of dawn at 7:24 a.m. and dusk at 4:50 p.m. at the winter solstice, the day was only nine hours and twenty-six minutes long. With two hours off for meals, the actual workday varied between roughly 7½ and 13 hours; over the course of a year, working a six-day week, each working adult slave put in 3,190 hours and 55 minutes of labor.[11] This would have made the workday roughly comparable to that of white laborers at the same period. For example, after several years of strife between journeymen and master furniture makers in Philadelphia, the journeymen triumphed by winning the right to a six-day week with an eleven-hour workday in 1796 (3,432 hours per year; it is not known how much time the journeymen received for meals throughout the day).[12]

Apart from its length, a "typical" workday varied considerably from person to person, because there was not simply one type of work performed by the Mount Vernon slaves. A series of lists made by George Washington in the summer of 1799 reveals that, of the 316 slaves owned either by himself or the estate of Martha Washington's first husband, or rented from a neighbor, 132 individuals, or almost 42 percent, were either too old or too young to work, a figure that may not have been unusual for a large estate in this part of the country. For example, at nearby Woodlawn Plantation, 47.67 percent of the enslaved population were found to be under the age of ten in 1830.[13] Of the remaining 184 people on the 1799 Mount Vernon slave lists, 54, or about 29 percent, were considered skilled laborers; only 14 of them were women. This figure compares favorably with the roughly 28.57 percent of skilled slaves on John Tayloe's plantations in northern Virginia in the early nineteenth century.[14] Washington's skilled laborers worked at trades, such as bricklaying (two men) and carpentry (six men), or were craftsmen like blacksmiths (two men) and coopers (three men). Still other skilled slaves were involved in food production and processing, working as cooks (one man, one woman) and dairy maids (one woman), gardeners (two men), millers (two men), and distillers (five men). A sizable group at the Mansion House Farm, made up of spinners and knitters (two men, seven women), seamstresses (one woman), and a shoemaker (one man), were responsible for producing clothing worn by other slaves on the estate, while another good-sized contingent from the same farm worked as house servants (three men, four women). Still other men dug ditches (five men), drove wagons and carts (three men), and worked as postilions (three men) for the carriage.[15] (See tables 3, 4, and 5.)

The practice of renting slaves was another way they could experience new or different types of work, a changes of scene, or management. At the end of George Washington's life, forty-one of the slaves at Mount Vernon, or slightly less than 13 percent, were rented. Of this number, forty belonged to a neighbor, Penelope Manley French; most of this group lived at Union Farm, with one single man living on Muddy Hole Farm and another at the distillery.[16] Slaves possessing a special skill or trained craftsmen were sometimes rented for short periods of time, when their talents were especially needed. Between May 1762 and October of the following year, a bricklayer named Guy was hired by Washington at the rate of thirty pounds per year. During that period, Washington provided Guy with food and quarters and billed his master, William Daingerfield, for his clothing.[17] George Washington hired Davy, an enslaved carpenter, from Lund Washington between 1767 and 1770 for eighteen pounds per year.[18] A few years later, the owner of an unnamed "negroe Fellow" who assisted with hauling the seine during the fishing season of 1773 was paid ten shillings for the man's time. In the fall of 1784, George Washington rented a "Negroe Taylor" from a Mr. Cockburn for five weeks at a cost of ten shillings per week. The timing of this man's hiring suggests that he was helping to finish the winter clothing allowance for the Mount Vernon slaves.[19]

Special skills with horses and mules led Washington to rent his stableman Peter Hardiman from Eleanor Calvert Custis Stuart, the widow of Washington's stepson. This case was a bit different from the others, however, in the length of time Hardiman was on the estate. Because Washington both needed the stableman's services and wanted to keep his family together, Hardiman was at Mount Vernon for at least thirteen years.[20] At least once during that period, Washington loaned him to a friend, William Fitzhugh, to care for the latter's racehorse, Tarquin, as he took part in races in the Virginia towns of Fredericksburg, Alexandria, and Falmouth in the fall of 1785. When he sent Hardiman back to Mount Vernon, Fitzhugh wrote that he was "happy that I have it in my Power to send him Home unhurt," suggesting perhaps that Hardiman was not just caring for the animal but was also his jockey.[21]

Enslaved people from Mount Vernon were also rented on occasion to other individuals. In November 1782, an unnamed male slave was briefly hired out to the skipper of a boat in order to help load corn, purchased from

Mount Vernon, aboard the vessel.[22] Washington seems to have believed, however, that slaves might not be properly treated by a renter. He suggested to one correspondent that he was persuaded that "every humane owner of that species of property [slaves] would rather have it in his own keeping, than suffer it to be in the possession of others."[23]

Skilled and Domestic Work

Some idea of the variety and amount of work done by the artisans, at least for the period after the Revolution, can be found in the weekly reports of the Mount Vernon farm managers, as well as in Washington's correspondence. Although the mansion itself was begun prior to his ownership of the plantation, his hired and enslaved carpenters and joiners not only made additions to the house but also constructed the outbuildings, including the stable, the greenhouse and its associated slave quarter on the Mansion House Farm, and the large barns on the outlying farms.[24] In addition, they repaired buildings; sawed wood; made planks for floors; dressed shingles; made gate posts and cogs for the "wheat machines"; and made or repaired wagon wheels, axles, tongues, boats, chicken coops, cheese presses, carts, ox and horse rollers, wheel barrows, ox yokes, harrows, troughs, rakes, wheat cradles, scythes, tool handles, plows, ladders, scaffolds, sawhorses, wine presses, blinds, packing cases, and coffins.[25] Occasionally, the carpenters even made or repaired furniture, such as work benches, a "Cupboard to hold China," and other pieces from the mansion.[26]

The coopers, who were based at the mill complex, made and mended barrels for holding solids (flour, fish, soap) and liquids (whiskey, water, and milk) and other types of vessels, such as pails or buckets and tubs. They also were dragged away to other necessary tasks, like stopping leaks in the mill dam and laying floors.[27] It may be difficult for many readers to view ditching as skilled labor, but the job required not just the ability to dig dirt but to measure ditches to the size specified by Washington. One good example of this is the ditch constructed during the week ending on February 24, 1787, which was 4 feet wide at the top, 1 foot wide at the bottom, and 1.5 feet deep. Two hired white supervisors and three slaves were able to dig 62.5 rods (1,031.25 feet or 343.75 yards) to those specifications in that one week, despite bad weather and the absence of one man on another project for three days. A few weeks later, with better weather and no one working elsewhere, two hired and six enslaved men completed 172 rods (2,838 feet or 946 yards) of a ditch of the same dimensions.[28]

From several sources it appears that the spinners produced enough yarn to make hundreds of yards of fabric each year.[29] Depending on their skill levels, each spinner made between one and six pounds of tow yarn or four pounds of stocking yarn in a week. Several spinners were put to work producing shoemaker's and sewing thread (two to four pounds each), while the knitters' output was one to two pairs of stockings each per week. The seamstresses could make from six to nine shirts per week but also produced other domestic textiles like aprons.[30] During just one week in 1786, the shoemaker worked on the heel of a shoe for one person, repaired a pair of boots for another, lengthened a circingle (a piece of horse equipage), and made seven pairs of "Shoes for Negroes."[31]

The slaves working in the mansion started their days very early and worked long into the evening. The basic duties of a chambermaid were spelled out in a manual for servants, written by prominent British cookbook author Hannah Glasse and published in Dublin in 1762:

> FIRST, take great care to know all your mistress's method and time of doing her business; and be very punctual and acute in your attendance; every thing you know will be wanting for her dress or undress, take care to have in readiness: and be sure to have all her linen well air'd, and every thing set very clean and nice; and when dress'd or undress'd, fold up every thing very neat, and keep all your things in their proper places, that whatever is called for, you may know where to find it in a minute; and when she is undress'd, take a dry cloth, and rub her cloths very clean, then fold them smooth, and lay them in their places; but if any spots appear on them take them out immediately.[32]

The next few pages of the manual focus on care of the expensive silk and woolen clothing worn by the mistress, with an emphasis on spot removal (because they could not simply be put into a wash tub with boiling water), keeping the gold and silver lace embellishing the shoes and clothes from tarnishing, and tips for washing the linen garments worn closest to the body, as well as things like delicate lace, silk stockings, and handkerchiefs. A lady's maid was also required to be ready to help with cosmetic issues, such as how to help with chapped hands, or make compounds to keep the skin smooth and fine, relieve sore feet and corns, and make the hair thick and free of grey.[33] At the end of a long day caring for the needs of Martha Washington, her maids Oney Judge and Moll probably looked forward to helping her out of her clothes and into her bed, even though they likely had to get those clothes into good shape by doing some brushing and stain removal before putting them away.[34]

Housemaids did heavier work. Among their first tasks in the morning was to light the fireplaces and clean the hearths, which meant sweeping up ashes and keeping the brass fireplace equipment sparkling. Once the fireplace had been cleaned and the fire lighted, it was time to polish the brass hardware on the door, sweep the rugs before folding them back, and sweeping the floor with damp sand. Then it was on to brushing the curtains to get the dust out; sweeping the windows and shutters; using a bellows to blow the dust off the picture frames; and dusting the walls, ornamental woodwork, and furniture. In addition to rooms, the hallways and stairwells came in for similar treatment. All of this had to be done by the time the mistress arose. Once the family was up, the housemaid was advised to get going on the bedchambers, where both the room itself and the bedding were thoroughly aired, the floors and textiles swept, and the furniture dusted. Among the many suggestions was a hint to "always leave a little clean water in your chamber chairpans, it prevents any offensive smell," a reminder of one of the housemaids' more odious tasks. After all that, the maid could remake the bed and put everything in order before moving on to the next room. The author assured readers that "this may seem a great deal of work, but is nothing, done every day, and saves you immense trouble in rubbing and scrubbing once a week as most servants do." Among the specialized knowledge expected of a housemaid were keeping furniture looking good; getting stains out of wood (both floors and furniture); cleaning paintings, frames, and oil cloths on the floor; getting stains out of expensive upholstery fabrics; cleaning brick hearths and fireplace equipment; and getting rid of bugs of various sorts.[35]

Among the most visible of the domestic staff were the men and boys working in the mansion, whose status typically was enslaved at Mount Vernon and at headquarters during the Revolution, and both enslaved and hired in the presidential mansion. They were responsible for greeting visitors, carrying trunks and bags to and from rooms, running errands, and serving at the table and sideboard during dinner. In filling these positions, both appearance and personality were factors that weighed in the balance. As far as personality was concerned, Washington several times stipulated the sort of person he preferred. In 1794, when seeking another waiting man for the executive mansion in Philadelphia, Washington noted that he was looking for a "genteel looking and well made man (not a giant or dwarf) . . . if sober, honest, good tempered, and acquainted with the duties of a house Servant, & footman."[36]

The Washingtons' table was served by varying numbers of waiters who might or might not be wearing the family's red-and-white livery, depending on the formality of the occasion and the number of diners. In a 1786 list of Mount Vernon slaves, George Washington noted the occupations of two men, Frank Lee and Austin, as "Waiters in the House."[37] Massachusetts representative Theophilus Bradbury, who was a guest at the executive mansion for one of the weekly Thursday afternoon dinners for members of Congress, recalled, "We were waited on by four or five men servants dressed in livery."[38] A breakfast during the same period was, however, attended by "one servant only . . . , who had no livery."[39] When Joshua Brooks came to Mount Vernon for dinner in 1799, three servants waited on the table.[40] Presumably those three were Christopher Sheels, Marcus, and Frank Lee, the butler, each of whom was described as a house servant on a second slave list made four months after Brooks's visit.[41]

The same work standards were undoubtedly expected of the waiters, both at Mount Vernon and in the presidential household. The latter were described in glowing terms by a dinner guest many years later as very orderly and knowledgeable about their tasks: "Nothing could exceed the order with which his [Washington's] table was served. Every servant knew what he was to do, and did it in the most quiet and yet rapid manner. The dishes and plate were removed and changed, with a silence and speed that seemed like enchantment."[42]

Some idea of the duties expected of a waiter can be found in books from the period. According to a 1788 English guide to proper behavior at meals, "a table ill-served and attended, is always a reflection on the good conduct of the mistress or master," who were thus required to pay close attention to the work of the waiters. After issuing a reminder that "a good servant will be industrious, and attend to the . . . rules in waiting; but, where he is remiss, it is the duty of the master or mistress to remind him," the author listed fourteen "rules for waiting at table." These ranged from knowing the correct way to set a table to where to stand in the dining room depending on the number of waiters available. These men were responsible for keeping the table tidy during the meal, cleaning up bits of garnish from the tablecloth as they fell, making sure that everyone had enough bread, and handing around the cruet, anticipating the wishes of the diners. The servants also had to know the proper methods of handing dishes and glasses to the diners; how to clear the table during the meal, so that it was ready for the next course; and when to bring out the finger bowls, toward the end of the meal.[43] While no such guidelines are known for the Washington household and not all were necessarily applicable, similar tasks would have been expected of the men serving the table in order to maintain a fashionable appearance.

Heredity and Heritability

A significant number of the tradesmen and domestic workers among the Mount Vernon slaves were of mixed race. A French visitor recorded in 1797 that "the general's house servants are mulattoes, some of whom have kinky hair still but skins as light as ours." The visitor took special note of "one small boy whose hair and skin were so much like our own that if I had not been told, I should never have suspected his ancestry. He is nevertheless a slave for the rest of his life."[44] This description is remarkably similar to one recorded by another exiled French noble visiting Monticello about the same period, who noted that Thomas Jefferson's house servants had "neither in their color nor features a single trace of their origin, but they are sons of slave mothers and consequently slaves."[45] The following year, Julian Niemcewicz briefly mentioned in his diary that "mulattoes are generally chosen for personal services."[46]

Other sources corroborate these visitors' impressions. While traveling with his sister-in-law in January 1760, George Washington spent the night in Dumfries, Virginia, at the home of a Scottish merchant. There he learned that Colonel Catesby Cocke, a retired gentleman in his late fifties, had been "disgusted" at Mount Vernon after seeing "an old Negroe there resembling his own Image," presumably a slave fathered by someone in Cocke's family.[47] Almost forty years later, one of the Washingtons' house servants was a young man named Marcus, described as "a bright Mulatto," rather small and thin, with dark blue eyes and long black hair.[48] William Lee, then the shoemaker but formerly George Washington's valet, was mulatto, as was the butler, Frank Lee, who was William's brother.[49] Some years earlier, Frank had been assisted by another "Molatto" "Waiter in the House" by the name of Austin.[50] When she was quite elderly, Martha Washington's former maid, Oney Judge, was described as being "nearly white" and "very much freckled."[51] An interviewer recorded that she was "a light mulatto, so light that she might easily pass for a white woman."[52] According to George Washington, Judge had a very large family at Mount Vernon. At least some of them were probably mulatto as well.[53]

An intriguing characteristic of the skilled and domestic occupations at Mount Vernon was that they were often hereditary within families. This situation is understandable when the close emotional ties that could develop between slave owners and the enslaved domestic servants with whom they had the most contact are considered. Other, more practical reasons may also have played a part in such assignments: for example, granting a favor to an elderly slave so that a relative could have a more desirable job, or because the children in a particular domestic's family were better-known than those of a fieldworker, or even the fact that the young people in that particular family already knew many aspects of a given household position because they had been taught by their parents.[54]

At Mount Vernon, the family headed by "Old Doll" is a good example of the passing on of an occupation from one generation to the next. Doll was thirty-eight years old when she came to Mount Vernon from the Custis estate near Williamsburg, shortly after the young widow Martha Dandridge Custis married George Washington in 1759.[55] In the next generation, Doll's daughter Lucy took over as one of the cooks, after Doll became too old to work. Lucy was married to Frank Lee, the butler. His brother Billy Lee, who was George Washington's valet, was injured in a series of accidents in the 1780s, which left him lame and unable to perform his duties. At this point, the third generation of the family entered the picture. Doll's other daughter, Alce or Alice, one of the spinners, had a son named Christopher Sheels, who eventually replaced Billy, his uncle by marriage, as Washington's personal servant, while Alce's daughter Anna worked alongside her producing thread.[56] The hereditary nature of some of these positions continued even after George and Martha Washington died. The young man who served as valet to Martha Washington's grandson at Arlington for many years was Philip Lee, the son of Lucy and Frank Lee, nephew to Billy Lee, and grandson of Old Doll.[57]

Doll's family was not the only one in which occupations were passed on from generation to generation. The horses at Mount Vernon were cared for by the previously mentioned Peter Hardiman, a rented slave who was married to Caroline Branham (or Brannum), a seamstress and housemaid. At the time of George Washington's death, Hardiman was assisted in the stable by their fifteen-year-old son Wilson, who was working as a groom.[58] In 1799, Ben, a young ditcher, was following in the footsteps of his father, Boatswain, who had been a ditcher on the estate for at least a dozen years.[59] At this same period, Kitty, the wife of the head carpenter, Isaac, worked at various times as both a spinner and dairymaid, tasks that two of her daughters, Sinah and Alla (or Anna), did as well.[60]

While some children seemingly learned how to do their jobs by watching their parents, still others were taught their trades by Washington's hired workers. Enslaved carpenter Sambo Anderson was trained in his profession by William Bernard Sears, an English-born craftsman who originally came to Virginia as a young indentured convict in 1752. After initially working at Gunston Hall Plantation, Sears went on to do beautiful carving at Mount Vernon and Mount Airy Plantations, as well as carving and gilding at

Pohick Church, the Washington family's parish church.[61] Training of slaves was often specifically mentioned in the contracts of skilled hired workers. For example, in the articles of agreement between Dominicus Gubner and George Washington, signed on September 20, 1770, the blacksmith was required to "Instruct . . . any Negro Slave which the said Geo. Washington shall put under him in the Shop in the Art of a Blacksmith."[62] Joiner John Askew was expected to "use his best endeavour's to instruct in the art of his trade any Negro or Negroes which the said George Washington shall cause to work with him during the twelve month."[63] Many years later, John Costalow (or Coslay) was brought to Mount Vernon from the Eastern Shore "to make and Fix Crad[les] for you, and to Instruct your people In Cradeling wheat In the manner practiced here, by Catching It In the hand and [mutilated] It straight." He was later paid $81.81 "for superintending my Cradlers in harvest and Instructing them to catch the Grain."[64] In at least one instance, two slaves—Nat, who belonged to George Washington, and Julius, a mulatto slave who belonged to and had earlier been the body servant of John Parke Custis—were indentured to local blacksmith Peter Gollatt for periods of three years and six years, respectively, in order to learn "the Art and Trade of Blacksmiths."[65]

Seasonality

While the seasonal nature of the work done by agricultural workers is fairly obvious, there was also a seasonal flow to the tasks done by the domestic staff at Mount Vernon. Early in the year, spring cleaning occupied the housekeeper or steward, a hired white woman or man, and the enslaved housemaids. Martha Washington ordered them to air the mattresses and bed hangings, rub down the bedsteads to kill any insects and other vermin who might have taken up residence during the winter, and thoroughly clean the entire house from top to bottom to get rid of the ashes and dirt that resulted from burning wood in the fireplaces and mud brought in from wet winter roads.[66] At this same time of year, the housekeeper or one of the cooks prepared rose and mint water, used for culinary and medicinal purposes, from plants grown in the garden and gathered by an elderly enslaved woman who could not do heavier work. In addition, these same workers preserved early fruits, such as cherries, gooseberries, and strawberries, for use in winter, while the spinners and seamstresses prepared fabrics and made clothing so that they and their fellow slaves would have new garments in the fall.[67]

During the summer, the butler, sometimes a hired white man but more often a slave, was ordered to do additional cleaning, paying special attention to the cellars, where foodstuffs were stored during the winter, and the airing, cleaning, and "scalding" of bedsteads to prepare them for use in fall and winter. The cook was instructed to clean the kitchen, while the textile workers were busy cutting out and sewing winter clothes and shirts, caps, and other "necessary things" for "Babe clothes" for the slaves' children, and the dairymaids were making butter and preserving it for use in the winter.[68] During the fall, drains leading from the mansion house were cleaned by the butler, who was also asked to "winterize" the cellar by putting "long litter," probably cornstalks or pumpkin vines, against the basement windows to keep out drafts, insulate both the basement and ground floor of the mansion, and help to keep the foodstuffs stored in the cellar from freezing. Both of these were common activities in other parts of the country at this time of year as well.[69]

George Washington wanted these skilled workers and house servants to keep busy throughout the day. When there were not enough specialized tasks to keep them occupied, they would often be assigned another sort of work on the Mansion House Farm. In 1792, with the family in Philadelphia during the presidency, Washington worried that butler Frank Lee would have nothing to do and ordered him not "to spend his time wholly in idleness."[70] Over the next few years, Lee was asked to collect walnuts, worked for the gardener, did some painting, may have pounded stone in preparation for rusticating the mansion house, and possibly did a little bricklaying as well. He was also involved in the care and breeding of some of George Washington's dogs, a task not usually considered part of a butler's duties. Shortly before Christmas in 1796, Washington expressed a "wish" that "Frank has taken particular care of the Tarriers.—I directed him to observe when the female was getting into heat, and let her be immediately shut up; and no other than the male Tarrier get to her."[71] When Lee's wife, Lucy, one of two cooks for the mansion table, was not busy with her usual chores, she was supposed to occupy her time with spinning and knitting. Washington ordered, in turn, that if there were not enough raw materials to supply the spinners and seamstresses, the manager was to "let them join the out door hands."[72] At one point, Washington was concerned that Ben, the enslaved miller, would not have enough to do "when the Manufacturing season is over, or the water is scarce." Washington noted that he expected the hired miller to make barrels during slow periods at the mill; he undoubtedly had something similar in mind for Ben.[73]

When time was of the essence, such as during the fishing and harvest seasons, many of the skilled workers, and anyone else who could "be best spared" were temporarily transferred to the site of the activity.[74] During the harvest of 1786, for example, three carpenters, the miller, a blacksmith, and a cooper were put to work using grain cradles (a slightly more complex form of scythe) to cut wheat, while another cooper assisted with making hay. That same year, at least two of the spinners from the Mansion House Farm helped with the harvest at Dogue Run and Muddy Hole Farms.[75] Two enslaved carpenters, Tom Davis and William (Billy) Muclus, were busy knitting and hauling seines in the spring of 1797. Several of the ditchers were occupied with unnamed chores at the fishing landing the following year, while Davis, this time listed as a bricklayer, was again hauling and rigging the seine.[76]

Fieldwork

Almost three-quarters of the working slaves at Mount Vernon spent their lives in the fields, and well over half of these workers, 61.4 percent, were women in 1799.[77] As with the skilled laborers, Washington's hired workers were expected to share their learning with the slaves they helped to manage. When he hired an English farmer in the 1780s to upgrade agricultural practices on the plantation, Washington expected James Bloxham to "instruct, as occasion may require, and opportunities offer, the labourers therein how to Plow, Sow; Mow, Reap; Thatch; Ditch; Hedge &ca in the best manner."[78] Similar instructions were given to farm manager Anthony Whiting—in largely the same words—in 1790.[79]

For those slaves who worked as general laborers, routine tasks changed with the seasons. In the spring and summer, male slaves plowed, harrowed, and rolled the ground; used the seine to catch fish; planted, sowed, and weeded crops; cut hay, clover, cornstalks, straw, and brush; burned logs; tied and heaped hemp; cradled and bound grain during the harvest; shocked wheat and oats; threshed; gathered basket splits and tanning bark; made baskets and horse collars; cut firewood; cut and mauled fence rails and posts; cleaned swamps; filled gullies; grubbed fields; and shelled corn. While they did all that, the female field hands dug post holes and made fences, heaped and burned trash, plowed and harrowed, chopped the plowed ground, grubbed meadows and cleared new ground, loaded dung in carts, gathered and spread fish offal, planted and weeded crops, bound and stacked grain during the various harvests, threshed, cut sprouts from tree stumps in fields, hoed rough or wet ground that the plows could not get to, prepared meadows for oats and timothy, cared for the cattle, picked up apples, leveled ditches, cleaned hedgerows and fields, filled gullies in the fields, spread dung, cut up cornstalks, and shelled corn.

Fall brought cooler weather in which the men harvested corn and peas, plowed and harrowed ground, sowed winter grains, threshed peas, and made livestock pens and feeding racks for the reception of livestock over the winter. Women harvested corn; cut down and piled cornstalks; chopped and began to process flax; made livestock pens; threshed rye, clover seed, peas, wheat, and oats; cleaned oat and wheat seed; and dug carrots. Although winter is often thought to be the slow time in the agricultural calendar, Washington's slaves were kept as busy as possible. Male slaves spent the shorter winter workdays on a number of tasks, including working on the millrace; digging ditches; plowing; cutting rails, posts, timber, and firewood; hauling timber and grain; killing hogs; filling the icehouse; mauling rails; sawing lumber; making fences and livestock pens; building roads; working in the new ground; framing barns; shelling corn; cutting straw; threshing wheat and rye; stripping tobacco; making baskets and horse collars; beating out hominy; tending the stable; tanning leather; and doing odd jobs. Women were helping at the icehouse; cutting and gathering cornstalks; husking and shelling corn; beating out hominy; hoeing the new ground and thinning trees in the swamp; cleaning the stable; heaping dung; carrying fence rails; grubbing the swamp, woods, and meadow; burning brush; filling gullies; plowing; killing and salting hogs; threshing wheat, rye, and clover seed; stripping tobacco; packing fish; and making basket splits.[80]

Injury on the Job

It was not unusual for slaves to be injured while performing their work. Perhaps the best-known case is that of Washington's valet Billy Lee, who was surveying with his master and several other people in the spring of 1785 when he fell and broke "the pan of his knee," that is, his kneecap. Washington noted that it was only "with much difficulty I was able to get him to Abingdon," the home of his late stepson, John Parke Custis, having been "obliged to get a sled to carry him on, as he could neither Walk, stand, or ride."[81] Sadly, about three years later while on a trip into the post office in Alexandria, Lee fell once again "at Mr. Porters door and broke the Pan of his other Knee."[82] He would eventually be permanently disabled by these falls.

Working around animals could be particularly hazardous. Horned cattle could be dangerous, and several methods were used at Mount Vernon to mitigate the risk of injury. When a bull with a "mischievous disposition" gored and disemboweled one of the wagon horses in the farm yard, the farm manager assured Washington that he would take care of the problem by first "sawing his horns pretty close" and, if that proved ineffective, by fastening a board across his horns. It appears that the bull won the contest:

> I am mistaken in the peoples being all well, [John] Knowles [an indentured bricklayer and laborer who worked for Washington for many years] has been laid up some time & not yet recover'd—they attempted to saw the Bull[']s Horns when I was out of the way, & as every thing Bishup [Thomas Bishop] does is wrong, so that was, every man, woman & child (I am told) upon the plantation assisted but the Bull prov'd too many for them, & in the Scuffle Knowles had like to have lost his life—he will be well I suppose in a few Days.[83]

While no slaves were reportedly hurt in this incident, it clearly shows the risks they faced in working with large domestic animals.

Another incident happened four days after Christmas in 1787, when the Washingtons were hosting a number of guests, including neighbor Roger West, family doctor James Craik, and several of the latter's children. That evening, West and the Craiks headed for home, but while they were on their way, a messenger was sent to intercept Dr. Craik and bring him back because the postilion, a slave named Paris, had been kicked by a horse, resulting in a broken jaw.[84] While this sort of incident might be considered something of an occupational hazard for anyone working around horses, it may be that the visiting horses, not being accustomed to Paris, were a bit skittish around him. Another possibility is that the horses were spooked by the presence of a strange animal they had never seen before. According to Washington's financial records, he paid eighteen shillings that day to "the man who brot. a Camel from Alex[andri]a for a show."[85] It is not known if the camel and his handlers spent the night on the plantation or if they went back to town immediately after the performance. In any case, it was one of the first camels imported to the United States. Not quite a year later, Craik was again sent for to treat Dolshy, a young woman at the Mansion House Farm who had been "much wounded" by one of "the Bucks in the Paddock," one of the tame deer kept by Washington in the deer park in front of the mansion.[86]

Disability

Individuals who were disabled, whether due to injury, disease, or aging, were often employed in less physically demanding work, much as "invalid" soldiers had been given lighter duties in the Continental Army during the Revolution.[87] A number of the slaves involved in the production of clothing and other textiles were identified as disabled. In the early months of 1776, a young man named Wally, who was described as "the sailer Boy," complained of back pains. Medical opinion was that the pain was caused by "disordered" kidneys, which would eventually cripple him.[88] Five years later, when Wally left Mount Vernon with a British ship, he was described as a weaver.[89]

Among those doing sewing, spinning, and knitting at Mount Vernon were "Lame Alice," "lame Peter," and Winny, who was described by Washington as being "old & almost blind."[90] Winny appears to have done other types of work before her progressive blindness made it impossible. She is probably the same woman, recorded as "Winna" who was inherited by George Washington in the division of slaves from his late father's estate in 1750. At that time, Winna was thirty years old.[91] Surviving tithables lists from before the Revolution indicate that she worked for many years at Mount Vernon as a house servant. About 1772, she seems to have left the mansion itself and worked elsewhere at the Mansion House Farm.[92] In this case, with seemingly no further information about her condition available, there is no way to know what was causing the sixty-six-year-old to lose her sight by 1786.

During the winter of 1792–93, Doll, a forty-six-year-old woman from Ferry (later Union) Farm who had been sick for a long time, was taken off the regular work list. She was initially put to work swingling flax, a task that involved hitting flax stalks with a wooden tool called a swingling stick in order to break down the fibers in preparation for spinning, one of several steps in the process of converting flax to linen thread. Sometime later, Doll was "brought in a Cart" to the Mansion House Farm so that she could be taught to knit stockings for the other slaves, an even less strenuous occupation.[93] Following the two accidents that broke his knee pans in the 1780s, Billy Lee became the shoemaker for the estate.[94]

Certain nonspecialized tasks were assigned to disabled slaves as well. While temporarily lame in the winter of 1776, Gunner spent his time carding tow for the women to spin.[95] A decade later, Washington noted in his diary during the winter of 1786 that, due to a storm that had dropped over eight inches of snow, all the women and the "Weak hands" were given the indoor assignment of "picking the Wild Onion from the Eastern shore Oat for seed."[96] When two slaves, Ruth and Ben at River Farm, were put on the sick list time and again, Washington suspected Ruth, at least, of feigning illness, but he still informed his farm manager that he did not expect either of them to do more work "than they are able to do [with]in reason." Neither was to be totally exempted from work, however, "whilst work proportioned, and adapted to their strength and situation, can be found for them."

Washington felt that to do otherwise would be a bad example for the other slaves and would lead to a sudden increase in the number of people pleading sickness as an excuse for not working.[97]

We have no idea how Washington responded to a plan devised by one of his farm managers that would have given more demanding assignments to disabled slaves. James Anderson wrote his employer in 1798 to suggest that "the Invalids" be put to work ditching, hedging, and cleaning hedges during the busy spring, when fishing and planting were of prime importance and occupied the majority of the workforce. Anderson remembered that such tasks were customarily hired out on English farms and felt that the invalids would find the work "no hardship," while it would be "a convenience" to everyone else. He believed, however, that they would rebel at first about this new work and "a little of the Rod would be necessary to set the business agoing."[98]

Washington sometimes went to considerable lengths to seek treatment for slaves who were disabled. After Christopher Sheels, then working as a carpenter, was "lame with a pain in his Hip" for one day in March 1797, he missed another day that same week so that he could go "to the Doctor for to have his pains cured."[99] In another case, one of the slaves was described in the summer before Washington's death as "getting Blind." Then only twenty-eight years old and single, Tom was one of forty slaves who were rented from Washington's neighbor Mrs. French.[100] Tom's rapidly diminishing eyesight was caused by a tumor, which by July 1799 appeared to threaten his remaining vision. Both the Washingtons' longtime friend and family doctor James Craik and others had treated the young plowman at Mount Vernon's Union Farm, "without [his] receiving much, if any benefit." Washington was so concerned about Tom's condition that he sent him to a specialist, Dr. William Baynham, a surgeon, who had been trained in both Edinburgh and London, and was then practicing in Essex County, Virginia.[101]

In turning to Baynham, who was said to have had "a national reputation as one of the ablest surgeons in the United States," Washington was seeking to provide Tom with the best care possible at the time. Washington had originally met Baynham in December 1785, when the surgeon came to Mount Vernon with a letter of introduction from an old friend, Colonel George William Fairfax, who had lived at nearby Belvoir Plantation before returning to England not long before the American Revolution began.[102] Washington renewed his relationship with Baynham in February 1799 when the latter once again came to dinner at Mount Vernon.[103] The retired president expressed considerable confidence in the doctor six months later when he wrote concerning an illness of his nephew Lawrence Lewis that "if Doctr Baynham, under whose hands he was, was unable to effect a radical cure, I should not place much confidence in Voss's Springs, as the disorder must be deep rooted."[104]

Tom was sent to Dr. Baynham at the end of July 1799.[105] Baynham operated on both eyes on the morning of August 10 but informed Washington immediately that the prognosis was not good, although the surgery had "given [Tom] the only chance, which the case admits of, of seeing better with one eye, and of preventing total blindness in the other." Baynham believed that the outcome of the procedures he performed would be clear within two weeks.[106] Eleven days later, Baynham wrote to say that he was being called away because of a serious illness in his own family, and that he was sending Tom back to Mount Vernon a few days earlier than expected. Baynham informed Washington that the tumor in the left eye was almost undoubtedly "incurable" and that "a growing film in the right [eye] threatens to overspread the transparent Cornea and thereby deprive him of the sight of this eye, in which the vision is, at present, but imperfect." He admitted that he knew "of no remedy save that which I have applied" and recommended "that nothing more be attempted but to leave it to nature." Because he felt that the operations had been undertaken on his part "rather by a wish than an expectation of relieving the poor fellow," Baynham wrote that he hoped Washington would not "take it amiss if I claim no more than a consultati[on] fee of five dollars."[107] Tom was back at Mount Vernon less than a week later when Washington wrote to thank the doctor and consoled himself with the thought that, if Tom's blindness were incurable, "I must be satisfied that I have neglected nothing to restore his sight to him."[108]

Exceptions to the Rule

The workforce at Mount Vernon did not labor every day of the year, for they were not only given regular days off but certain holidays as well. According to the reports given to Washington each week by his overseers, the slaves typically worked a six-day week and the usual day off for everyone on the estate was Sunday. This routine was comparable to practices on other Virginia plantations. Philip Vickers Fithian, a tutor at Robert Carter's Nomini Hall, noted in his journal that slaves on that estate worked in their own small garden plots "on Sundays, as they are otherwise employed on every other Day" and left a delightful description of preparations for that special day: "A Sunday in Virginia don[']t seem to wear the same Dress as our Sundays to the Northward—Generally here by five o-Clock on Saturday every Face (especially the Negroes) looks festive and cheerful—All the lower class of People, & the Servants, & the Slaves, consider it as a Day of Pleasure & amusement, & spend it in such Diversions as they severally choose."[109]

The slaves' holidays were based on the Christian calendar, with the longest being the three or four days given for Christmas.[110] Other religious holidays providing time off were Easter and Whitsunday, or Pentecost, celebrated on the fiftieth day after Easter. Because both of these holidays occur on Sunday, when the slaves were already not expected to work, the following Monday was given as an additional day off. For instance, George Washington wrote in his diary on Monday, April 7, 1760, that his "People kept [the Easter] Holliday," and in 1798, the work reports for the week ending April 14 note that the slaves were off for "Easter Monday."[111] The "Whitsun monday Holaday" was similarly recorded in the work reports dated May 30, 1795, and June 2, 1798.[112] A "Day of Fasting, Humiliation and Prayer" proclaimed by President John Adams as war threatened with France was also observed by the slaves at Mount Vernon on Wednesday, May 9, 1798.[113]

A number of incidents, several of which took place at particularly labor-intensive seasons, suggest both a certain flexibility in the general schedule and the inviolate nature of holidays on the estate. Additional free time was occasionally authorized as a reward for completing a particularly difficult job. The grain harvest, for example, was a period when a great deal of work had to be done in a short time frame, in order to prevent the loss of the crop. In 1786, when the slaves at Ferry Farm finished harvesting wheat at about noon on a hot July Wednesday, Washington ordered that his people get "the remainder of the day for them selves."[114] This is probably the explanation for the half-day "holyday" enjoyed by the slaves at River Farm in July 1796, while people on the other farms continued to labor.[115]

The Mount Vernon slaves were also compensated when they had to work on what should have been their time off. Much like the harvest, the fishing season was a period of hard, concentrated labor each spring, because the fish ran in large numbers for only a short time. In just a very few weeks, the majority of the fish the slaves would be eating for the next year had to be caught. In May 1775, the slaves were paid £0.13.6 for working their Easter Monday holiday at the fishery.[116] Many years later, in 1794 and 1797, respectively, money was paid to "the people for hauling the Seine on Holyday Sund[a]ys & Sund[a]y nights" and "Negroes Hauling on Sundays."[117] The following spring, the "Sein Haulers, Fish carriers [*unreadable word*] cleaners of Fish & Cook &ca" were paid more than ten pounds for working on four "Sundays and the Easter Holyday," while nine shillings were spent on "Hire of Negroes to Car[r]y Shad to Alex[and]ria on a Sunday" and an additional thirteen shillings went to slaves who loaded flour on board a ship during one of those Sundays, an assignment that would ordinarily have been done during the week but which the activity at the fishery very likely prevented them from doing.[118] Even after her husband's death, Martha Washington continued paying slaves for extra work. Four days after George died, a slave named Juba was given twenty-five cents, because he had waited in Alexandria all night, time he would ordinarily have had for himself, for Washington's coffin to be finished. A week later, on Christmas day 1799, the slaves who worked at the distillery received $1.16 as reimbursement for "working on Holydays."[119]

Money was not the only way a slave could be compensated for extra work. On one occasion, two of the bricklayers were given a free day in Alexandria, "as promised them" because they had worked on a Sunday at the brick kiln.[120] One study of life in eighteenth-century Antigua relates how slaves on that island forced their masters and the legislature to recognize as rights they were due, both the Sunday and Christmas holidays, as well as attendance at the markets where enslaved people sold produce and merchandise on Sundays, all of which had previously been considered privileges granted by slave owners. On at least two occasions, Antiguan slaves actually rioted over changes to their customary free time.[121] George Washington's payments to his slaves for working on Sunday, Easter, and at other times that were considered free hours indicate that a similar, if not so dramatic, process had occurred at Mount Vernon.

For those who provided essential support services for the mansion house, such as cooks, butlers, waiters, and personal servants, Sundays and holidays would not necessarily have been days of rest. Fireplaces still needed to be stoked, meals had to be cooked and served, the master's family had to be dressed and waited on. Martha Washington's granddaughter Nelly recalled that the Washington family rearranged their usual schedule somewhat on Sundays, in order to make things easier for these slaves. While they generally ate dinner, their main meal, at about 3 o'clock in the afternoon, on Sunday they ate at 2 o'clock "to accommodate his servants with a long afternoon."[122] One English household, faced with a similar problem of maintaining its customary level of service while still allowing its staff time off, is known to have allowed the house and laundry maids to alternate their Sundays off.[123] Weekly work reports were not maintained for the domestic staff at Mount Vernon, so there is no way of knowing if the house servants rotated duties on Sundays and other holidays or just what, if any, special arrangements might have been made for them. In addition to the house servants, those slaves responsible for the care of livestock could not have neglected certain chores, such as feeding and watering their charges, on holidays.

There were also accepted reasons for a slave not to work. Those who were sick or injured were not generally required to work. During the weeks ending October 17, 1792, and January 5, 1793, Charles, who was one of the ditchers, was unable to work because he was lame. He was out once more in February because his toe was "again Swelld & he very lame." This time Washington was informed by his farm manager that the problem had happened as a result of the bone being "very Much Cut & I expect rotten," indicating that infection had set in. Doctor Craik had been asked to "come down [from Alexandria] as soon as the roads Get better," because the manager feared it was going to be necessary to amputate the toe in order to save the ditcher's life.[124] Even being injured might not get a person out of work. When carpenter Sambo Anderson was "lame" in the summer of 1797, he was put to work dressing shingles at the River Farm barn, a task he could do while sitting. This was also the farm where his wife and children lived.[125]

In addition to illness, a number of slaves missed work because of the condition of their shoes and equipment. In December 1786, for example, a female slave was "confined" for a whole week because she did not have any shoes. The following month, one of the women from Dogue Run Farm was out of work for a day "getting her shoes mended." In February 1787 alone, at least fourteen days of work were lost because of the need to repair shoes. That same month, another woman from Dogue Run spent a day at the Mansion House Farm so that her plow could be repaired.[126]

On other occasions, slaves were given time off to take care of family matters. The work report for Dogue Run Farm one June recorded that a slave named Ben had been away from his post for a day to "see his mother," but the reason for the visit was not given.[127] These family-related absences often involved life-threatening situations. When her son Billy was dying in April 1792, Kate at Muddy Hole Farm was out of work for an entire week to nurse the child. Delia from Union Farm was given a similar amount of time during the serious illness of her son several years later.[128]

Weather conditions too sometimes forced extra free time for Washington's "people." The first few weeks in March 1787 were terribly wet, and as a consequence, a number of tasks were interrupted. Half a day of work was lost at one of Washington's five farms the week of March 3, and in the following weeks, additional rain prevented several slaves from planting corn and plowing. Two years earlier, heavy rains led to the suspension of all outdoor work at one point, and on other days Washington set the slaves to different tasks than he had originally intended.[129] Some idea of how bad the situation had to get before a stop was called, however, can be found in a letter to George Washington from Lund Washington. In a discussion of the preparations being made for planting, Lund commented that "although we are seldom without rain three days together and our mill swamp is over our shoes almost every where in water, yet are we ditching of it. And I am determined to keep on although the people in the ditch are up to their knees in mud and water. When it is properly done I expect it will yield a very great crop of tobacco."[130] Torrential rains were not the only weather condition known to bring work to a halt. In 1793, Gunner, from the Mansion House Farm, missed four days one week because he was "stopt by Snow" at River Farm, probably during a visit to his wife, Judy, who lived and worked at that location. The thirty working hands at River Farm lost a total of thirty-six days of work because of snow that same week.[131]

Even when the weather was not bad enough to stop all work, assignments on a particular day might change in response to conditions outside. During the wet winter of 1786, Washington recorded that the men at the Mansion House Farm had begun to bundle up faggots to be used in filling gullies, instead of moving earth as planned. The following month, the weather caused other work on the grounds to halt for a day, and all the people, not just the women and disabled workers, were set to picking onions out of the wheat.[132]

The work done by the slaves at Mount Vernon had a tremendous influence on their lives. Aside from determining the kinds of tasks a person would spend his or her life performing, as is discussed further in later chapters, whether people practiced a craft or fieldwork might be a factor in determining where they would live, how much supervision they had, whether or not they lived with their spouse and children, the quantity and quality of the material goods they received, and whether, if they could escape, there was a good chance for success.

5

"They Appear to Live Comfortable Together"

Family Life in the Mount Vernon Slave Community

George Washington's slaves undoubtedly cherished the hours when they were not working for their master. It was then that they had the time and, to a certain extent, the freedom to pursue their own interests and exercise some measure of control over their own lives. Slaves living on the four outlying farms may have had even more freedom in their private lives than those at the Mansion House Farm, where personal servants had to be available well into the evening and opportunities for close supervision by the master and his family abounded. Surviving period sources suggest that, as on other plantations, Mount Vernon slaves used their free time for building families, for play, and to enhance their overall economic position. Even in their "free time" and in the most personal aspects of their lives, however, Washington's slaves were never free of his ultimate control.

Marriage

Marriage was a basic building block of the enslaved community at Mount Vernon in the eighteenth century, as it was throughout the Chesapeake area. Here, in stark contrast with slave systems elsewhere in the Americas, a rough parity developed over the years between the numbers of males and females in the enslaved population. In an early business transaction, Washington indicated that in exchange for a shipment of flour to the West Indies, he would prefer the proceeds to be spent on slaves, if the price was right, or on tropical produce. If the money were to be expended for slaves, he preferred a mix of two-thirds men no older than twenty and one-third women no older than sixteen. Although the deal fell through and Washington got neither slaves nor produce from the islands, the letter does give an idea of the population mix Washington preferred, even if that is not what he actually had.[1]

Early in his career as a planter, the ratio of men to women was closer to what Washington wanted than it would be later. Tithables lists, which are official documents compiled annually to show the number of workers on whom each landowner had to pay taxes, are especially valuable sources in tracking this change. They enumerate adult white males and any slave, male or female, over the age of sixteen, when they were considered adults for taxation purposes (because slaves were legally considered property, there was no concept of an age of majority as there was for free people). Tithables lists for Washington's lands in Fairfax County show the presence of 28 enslaved men and 15 enslaved women in 1760; fourteen years later the numbers had risen to 68 men and 51 women, but at no time prior to the Revolution were there more working women than men.[2] By 1786, when Washington made a list of all the slaves (adults and children) on the plantation, the numbers of males and females were equal, with 108 of each sex, out of which there were 63 adult men and 62 adult women.[3] Thirteen years later, in the last months of Washington's life, there were 148 males and 168 females in the Mount Vernon slave quarters, the time when the number of slaves reached its highest point. Of these, there were 93 adult men and 98 adult women. This last slave list also indicates that roughly two-thirds of the plantation's adult slaves were married.[4]

These marriages were acknowledged by both the enslaved community and George Washington, who copied down this information from a report compiled by his farm manager. They were not, however, recognized or protected by the legal system because slaves were considered property and not persons in the eyes of the law, and property, unlike an adult human, cannot make a contract. It was important to Washington to keep track of these marriages for several reasons. First, simply for the sake of managing people, it was helpful, if not necessary, to know who a given individual's spouse was. It was not unusual for an enslaved person to run away in order to be with a spouse on another farm or quarter belonging to the same owner or even on another plantation. Knowing that could make finding the missing person much easier. Second, Washington recognized these relationships as marriages and did respect them. Third, on a practical basis, Washington needed to keep track of which slaves belonged to himself and which to the Custis estate. Children born to female dower slaves were automatically part of Martha Washington's lifetime share of her late husband's estate, regardless of who their father might be, and were subject to the laws regarding the dispersal of that property upon her death.

The decision to marry is, of course, one of the most important and far-reaching of a person's life. George Washington himself referred to marriage as "the most interesting event of one's life, the foundation of happiness or misery."[5] For a slave, it was all of that, plus the opportunity to exercise choice in a life that afforded little, if any, personal control over such basic issues as occupation, housing, clothing, and the ability to travel. Only three of fifty-four working slaves under twenty years old were married in 1799; all three were women aged eighteen or nineteen years.[6] This fact, taken together with evidence from Washington's four outlying farms, indicating that the average age when enslaved women at Mount Vernon had their first child was between twenty and twenty-one years old, suggests that female slaves probably married, or at least had their first serious relationships with the opposite sex, in their very late teens or early twenties (see table 6). Comparison with statistics from Maryland, North Carolina, South Carolina, France, and England in the eighteenth century indicates that slave women at Mount Vernon were perhaps a year or two older than their contemporaries on other American plantations and, conversely, several years younger than women in Europe at that time, when these critical life events took place.[7]

A couple planning to marry first needed permission from George Washington, at least if they lived on the plantations of other owners. Long-distance marriages necessitated a certain amount of traveling back and forth between the two plantations. Getting the permission of a master would thus be in keeping with a law, passed by the Virginia legislature in the fall of 1785, which stated that slaves could not travel away from home without a pass or letter of authorization from a master, employer, or overseer.[8] Several months before his death in 1799, George Washington wrote a neighbor, Roger West, about the marriage of one of his house servants to a young woman belonging to West: "Sometime ago the Servant who waits upon me, Christopher (calling himself Christopher Sheels) asked my permission to marry a mulatto girl belonging to you." Since Sheels had "behaved as well as servants usually do" and Washington had "heard the Girl well spoken of," "I told him I had no objection to the union, provided your consent could be obtained."[9] We do not presently know if Washington's permission was required for all marriages, even those in which both partners lived on the same farm at Mount Vernon. There is also no evidence for the type of ceremony or ritual, if one existed, that may have publicly, if not legally, united a couple in the eyes of their community.[10]

George Washington recognized the importance of slaves' marriages and families, and his writings relate a number of instances of his respect for these relationships.[11] In 1779, while trying to decide about selling some of his slaves, Washington commented that he did not especially think a change in master would make their lives more difficult, "provided husband and wife, and Parents and children are not separated from each other, which is not my intention to do."[12] Several years later he wrote that "it is . . . against my inclination . . . to hurt the feelings of those unhappy people by a separation of man and wife, or of families."[13] Among the reasons he gave for turning down the purchase of a slave in 1788 was that he did not want to trade other slaves for this individual, "because I do not think, it would be agreeable to their inclinations to leave their Connexions here, and it is inconsistent with my feelings to compel them."[14] One of Washington's primary concerns at the end of his life was that freeing his slaves would lead to the dissolution of slave families resulting from the intermarriage of his slaves and those from the estate of Martha Washington's first husband.[15]

George Washington actively, albeit sometimes reluctantly, tried to re-unite a number of enslaved couples. Shortly after the Revolution, Billy Lee, who had served as the general's body servant throughout the war, asked Washington to bring his wife, Margaret (Peggy) Thomas Lee, a free black woman who had worked in Washington's military household, to Mount Vernon from Philadelphia. Although there is no evidence that the woman ever arrived, and Washington admitted that he "never wished to see her more," he did write a friend to try to arrange a passage for her.[16] Three years later, when Washington was talking with a skilled slave named Neptune about Washington's desire to purchase him, the bricklayer became quite up-set because the sale would mean leaving his wife, who lived on another plan-tation near his former master. Washington wrote at the time that he was "unwilling to hurt the feelings of anyone" and determined that he would try to reconcile Neptune to the idea of seeing his wife only occasionally, but if he could not, Washington would send him back to his former master and pay for the time he had spent at Mount Vernon during the negotiations.[17] In still another case, George Washington rented a slave named Peter Hardi-man from the widow of his stepson, John Parke Custis. When Hardiman's time was up at Christmas 1787, Washington got permission to keep him on to work with the horses and mules "because he seems unwilling to part with his wife and Children." Hardiman was still at Mount Vernon twelve years later, with his wife, Caroline Branham.[18]

Despite the precariousness of their circumstances, the bond between the slave couples at Mount Vernon could be very strong. Long marriages were not uncommon. For instance, Hannah and Morris from Dogue Run Farm were married for thirty years.[19] There is evidence in these marriages of not only longevity but affection as well. Austin, one of the house servants who accompanied the Washingtons to Philadelphia during the presidency, died suddenly near Harford, Maryland, on his way home to Mount Vernon "to see his wife and family" at Christmas 1794. Among his effects was a piece of luggage, variously described as a valise or portmanteau, in which George Washington surmised he "probably . . . might be carrying things . . . for his wife."[20]

Some of the best evidence for the strength of these unions between enslaved individuals comes from incidents that threatened to tear them apart. Quite early in the Revolution, in settling a debt with George Washington, Daniel Jenifer Adams of Charles County, Maryland, proposed paying him off with a male slave who was a skilled shoemaker. Since Washington was then serving as commander of the Continental Army, his cousin Lund, who was managing the estate, attempted to bring the slave to Mount Vernon. Lund reported that the man "was so attach[e]d to his Wife & children that . . . he had rather Die than leave them" and declared that "he had much rather be hang'd than come to V[i]rginia."[21] Two years later, George Washington's mother, Mary Ball Washington, asked that a Mount Vernon slave named Silla be sent to her in Fredericksburg. Lund informed his cousin that he would comply with the request, but that Silla would probably be unwilling to go because of her attachment to her husband, a cooper named Jack, with whom she appeared to "live Comfortable together." Lund was "very sorry" about separating the two, but his distress was nothing compared to the pain felt by Jack, who "Cryes and Begs, say[in]g he had rather be Hang'd than separated."[22] Inclement weather may have postponed Silla's departure for a time. In the last communication to mention this incident, Lund blamed "the badness of the weather" for not sending her sooner and mentioned once more how "much distressed" Jack and Silla were about being parted.[23] Silla was nonetheless sent back to Mary Ball Washington. However, a letter written by George Washington about a year later indicates that the couple's separation was not permanent. Writing from Middlebrook, New Jersey, George instructed Lund that "in order to gratify Jack you may bring Sylla up again." At this point, Washington was renting ten slaves belonging to Mary Ball Washington after she moved from the farm where she had been living to a house in Fredericksburg; two of those people were working at Mount Vernon. Washington asked that, in exchange for Silla, Lund should "send one of my mother[']s own fellows down—the greatest Rogue of the two."[24]

Human nature being what it is, however, not every slave marriage or the families they created were stable or a source of comfort. As was discussed earlier, Washington's managers handed over reports each week detailing the work done by the slaves under their supervision, listing how many days were spent on each particular task, and how much time was lost to sickness. In one report from February 1795, a woman at River Farm named Fanny, then about twenty-six years old, was "Laid up" for an entire six-day workweek because she had been "badly beat" by her husband, Ben, who was owned by a Mr. Fowler.[25] George Washington was so incensed by this behavior that he forbade Ben from returning to Mount Vernon and ordered him whipped if he disobeyed. Four years later, according to a slave list compiled by Washington, Fanny had remarried, once again to a slave living off the plantation. This unnamed second husband belonged to a Mr. Alexander.[26]

Other sorts of personal conflict occasionally disturbed the peace of the quarters as well. Early in 1793, George Washington ordered that Will, an older male slave who served for many years as an overseer, be given command of the plantation's boat "and such other out of sight jobs, as may occur, and require confidence." In filling this position, Washington was showing preference to Will rather than Will's nephew Tom Davis. Because the two men seem to have had an ongoing personality clash, Washington cautioned his manager to "let them interfere as little as can be avoided, with each other." Described as "high spirited," Davis had disobeyed his uncle in at least one instance, a situation Washington deplored, believing that the younger man should have shown respect to Will "on two accts., namely, being his uncle, and having been an Overseer." Several weeks later, the relationship between the two men was so hostile that Davis could not be assigned to work at the fishery as long as his uncle was there.[27]

Fanny's situation illustrates something that was probably a significant stress factor in slave marriages—distance. Of the ninety-six married slaves on Washington's five farms in 1799, only thirty-six lived in the same household as their spouse and children. Another thirty-eight had spouses living on one of Washington's other farms, a situation primarily resulting from work assignments. Slaves were generally housed on the farm where they worked because "commuting" from one farm to another would have cost dearly in both lost work and time. Twenty-two other Mount Vernon slaves had, like Fanny, married people belonging to other plantations.[28] There is no indication that marriages on the estate were arranged, so in order for these couples to meet and form the attachments that would eventually lead to marriage, there must have been a certain degree of freedom for unmarried slaves to travel from farm to farm within the plantation or to the plantations of other owners, as well as occasions for socializing. Historian Herbert Gutman has found strong evidence for the existence of African American taboos forbidding marriage between close relatives, which was not the case among plantation-owning whites of the period, for whom marriage between cousins was not unusual. These norms of the African American community may well have been a significant factor in the formation of such a large number of long-distance marriages among the Mount Vernon slave population.[29]

Another, very practical factor that should not be overlooked is the gender ratio on each of the five farms. While the overall ratio on the plantation was .88 men for each woman, differing only a bit from the surrounding county where there were .96 men per woman, the situation on the individual farms was terribly skewed.[30] According to the 1799 slave lists, there were only twenty-five adult women and forty-four grown men, primarily artisans, at the Mansion House Farm and the mill. This was the only farm where there were more men than women and, as a consequence, the population of the four outlying farms was overwhelmingly female. Both Dogue Run and Muddy Hole Farms each had seven men and seventeen women, while River Farm had fifteen men and twenty-three women. At Union Farm there were another eighteen men and twenty-four women.[31] From these figures alone, it is easy to see that many people were forced to go off the farm on which they lived in order to look for a mate.

At least some slave marriages may have been based on another non-European pattern. Polygamy, while probably not common among slaves in the Chesapeake, was not completely unknown either. At least one African-born slave on a Virginia plantation belonging to Robert Carter had two wives, and travelers to eighteenth-century Maryland reported the continued practice of traditional polygynous marriages there.[32] The possibility that some slaves may have been practicing the marriage patterns they knew in Africa is something that should not be overlooked. Either a traditional African religion, some of which allowed hundreds and even thousands of wives for those who could afford them, or Islam, which permits male adherents to take up to four wives, would have given people both a tradition of polygamy and clear conscience to practice it.[33]

While husbands and wives often lived separately because of their occupations, their residences tended to be stable, at least after the Revolution. Prior to that time, when Washington was organizing his farms, the tithables lists show more movement of adult slaves from farm to farm, as new slaves were purchased and people were moved around based on need and skill. For example, of the fifty-nine adult slaves living at the Mansion House Farm in 1799, forty-six, or 78 percent, had been living on that site for at least thirteen years. Although the nature of the work on the four outlying farms was quite different from the "Home House," a similar stability of population prevailed. At the end of George Washington's life, 83.33 percent of the twenty-four adult slaves at Dogue Run had lived there since 1786, as had 71.05 percent of the thirty-eight adults at River Farm, and nineteen of twenty-four adults at Muddy Hole. At Union Farm, not counting thirty-eight slaves who were rented from a neighbor, sixteen of the seventeen adult slaves owned by George Washington and the Custis estate had lived on the same farm since at least 1786.[34] This continuity was a major factor leading to the formation of an African American community at Mount Vernon made up of extended, multigenerational families. It also enabled the development of long-term friendships. Together, these two types of stable relationships would go a long way toward creating a support network for individuals living within the boundaries of slavery, an institution in which instability and tenuousness were systemic.

Because Sunday was the weekly day off for everyone except possibly house servants, the individuals involved in these long-distance marriages could see one another and their children on Saturday night and during the day on Sunday, as well as during other holidays, such as Christmas and Easter, throughout the year.[35] Thus, the slaves at Mount Vernon were both visited by their spouses and paid visits to them, although such arrangements could always be curtailed at the desire of a master. For example, Washington had already become quite annoyed with his neighbor John Posey over several issues when he complained in the fall of 1769 that Posey had "under very frivolous pretences forbid two or three of my People who had Wives in his Family from coming there again."[36] Many years later during the presidency, feeling that affairs at Mount Vernon were getting out of control in his absence, Washington ordered his farm manager Anthony Whiting to "absolutely forbid the Slaves of others resorting to the Mansion house; such only excepted as have wives or husbands there, or such as you may particularly license from a knowledge of their being honest and well disposed." After giving them a warning, all others were to be punished "whensoever you shall find them transgressing these orders."[37]

This inter-plantation visiting seems to have been quite typical. An Englishman who lived in America for a few years at the end of the eighteenth century and was acquainted with George Washington recorded that "it is an usual practice for the negroes to go to see their wives on the Saturday night." The visitor went on to relate that because their wives were often some distance away, "these men will take a horse of any person's, and ride him from ten to fourteen miles, and sometimes leave him, at other times bring him back. This is looked upon as so slight an offen[s]e, that I never heard of an instance of any of them being brought to justice for it."[38]

Pregnancy and Childbirth

The marriages of the Mount Vernon slaves produced a large number of children, many of whom appear to have survived and flourished. As a result, the population of the plantation increased steadily, from about fifty slaves in 1759 to more than three hundred in 1799. In that latter year, on the four outlying farms the average age in the slave population was 20.94 years. Only 8.68 percent of the people were sixty years old or more, while 58.45 percent were under the age of nineteen. Fully 34.70 percent were younger than nine,[39] confirming a description recorded by a French visitor to Mount Vernon in 1797: "These unfortunates [the slaves] reproduce freely and their number is increasing. . . . These shacks swarm with pickaninnies in rags that our own beggars would scorn to wear" (see table 7).[40] Some of the Mount Vernon slaves had large families, which, when the children were grown and married, made for multigenerational extended families and led in turn to the creation of a real community among the slaves of Washington's five farms and the surrounding neighborhood. In 1799, for instance, Isaac, the head carpenter, and his wife, Kitty, a milkmaid, had nine daughters, ranging in age from twenty-seven-year-old Sinah to Levina, who was just six. Through the marriages of four of the girls, Isaac and Kitty's family was linked to slaves at Washington's mill; Tobias Lear's Walnut Tree Farm, which had formerly been part of Washington's River Farm; and possibly to others at Ferry Farm. These marriages had also given Isaac and Kitty three grandchildren.[41]

The rate of natural increase in the estate's enslaved population could be impressive (see tables 8–11). In the three and a half years from December 1775 to May 1779, thirty-one live births and one confirmed and possibly two additional miscarriages were recorded for all of George Washington's farms. Another fifty-one children were born between May 1782 and August 1787. Where it is possible to determine intervals between births for these times, in the 1770s the average interval was 17.27 months, while in the 1780s it was 21.59 months. Contrasting with this material is data taken from the slave lists compiled by George Washington in 1786 and 1799. According to figures gleaned from Washington's 1786 census, based on the experiences of twenty-three women, the average interval between births was about 33.6 months. Information about the families of thirty-eight women taken from the 1799 slave lists suggests an average interval of 38.38 months between births, with the shortest interval being 1 year and the longest being 10. The large difference between the birth intervals derived from the financial and work records, and those from the slave lists can be attributed to the fact that a list shows a static picture of the families. Unlike the weekly reports, it does not give evidence of every birth on the plantation because a certain percentage of children would have died in their early years and their brief existence was not recorded on the list. Historians studying nineteenth-century American plantations note that perhaps twice as many slave children died before reaching their fifth birthdays as did white children at the same period (for every 1,000 children ages 0–1, 137.2 slave children died versus 61.4 white children; for every 1,000 children ages 1–4, 27.7 enslaved children died as opposed to 11.8 white children), a difference due to inadequate nutrition for women during pregnancy and for small children in the first years after weaning.[42]

One set of figures from the 1799 Mount Vernon slave list is intriguing for what it says about the relationship between overall fertility rates and the opportunities slave couples had to be together. Historians studying fertility rates among slaves in the United States and West Indies in the 1830s noticed a lower birthrate in Trinidad, where the average interval between births was about 32 months, or 7.32 months longer than the average in the American South at that period. Much of this difference is attributed to the fact that slave couples in the West Indies often lived in separate households.[43] Something similar happened at Mount Vernon in the eighteenth century. The average interval between births for the eleven Mount Vernon women whose husbands lived with them was 33.24 months; for the twenty-seven who were unmarried or whose husbands either lived on another farm belonging to George Washington or on another plantation altogether, the interval averaged 40.44 months. This difference of 7.2 months in the birth interval between the two groups is almost identical to the difference between intervals noted for the 1830s in the United States and Trinidad. These figures suggest that while slave couples were able to visit one another on a regular basis on weekends, they were not, despite Washington's complaints about "nightwalking," seeing each other every evening during the week. The fact that 62.5 percent of the married slaves at Mount Vernon did not live with their spouses definitely had a negative impact on the birthrate on the five farms making up the Mount Vernon plantation. It may also have left many married women unprotected and vulnerable to sexual exploitation by overseers and other men.

Although she was frequently attended by a white midwife when she gave birth, occasionally another enslaved woman would care for a woman who was either giving birth or recuperating afterward.[44] For instance, Lynna at Dogue Run Farm had a difficult time during and after the birth of her son in February 1793. Her mother, Matilda (or Myrtilla), came over from the Mansion House Farm and together with Moll took care of her for two days about the time the baby was born; a little over a month later, Matilda was off from her regular duties for an entire week to look after Lynna, whose baby had died shortly after birth, and was now being treated by Dr. Craik for a "bad breast."[45]

A number of the midwives mentioned in Washington's financial accounts were the wives of white men who worked for him. A Mrs. Brasenton, who assisted at births in the early 1760s, was the wife of Samuel Brasenton (or Brazington), who made leather clothing for George Washington and a number of slaves at this same period.[46] Susannah Bishop, who looked after "Mill Judah in a Miscarriage" in November 1777, was the wife of an old and trusted white servant, Thomas Bishop, who had served with Washington in the French and Indian War. Elizabeth Simpson was married to Gilbert Simpson, one of Washington's tenants.[47]

The midwife might also come from another plantation. In February 1775, a female slave belonging to Mrs. French, one of George Washington's neighbors, was paid ten shillings for delivering the child of Jane at Dogue Run Farm. The same amount of money was given to another of Mrs. French's slaves in April 1783, for delivering a baby at Ferry Farm.[48] Many years later, Washington paid a slave woman belonging to Thomson Mason for looking after Sall from River Farm, when she gave birth in the summer of 1796.[49]

The midwife could even be another enslaved woman from Mount Vernon. Washington wrote to his farm manager William Pearce in the summer of 1794 to say that he had been approached by Kate from Muddy Hole Farm with the request that she be given the position of "Granny" for the other slave women. Kate had sworn that she was as qualified as any of the others who had been doing this work. Washington asked Pearce to look into her credentials and, if all was satisfactory, entrust the business to her. He noted that "this service, formerly, was always performed by a Negro woman belonging to the estate, but latterly, until now, none seemed disposed to undertake it."[50] Kate's request was granted. In the winter of 1799, she was given twenty-five cents to buy a pair of scissors to be used "to cut the Tongues of Young Children."[51] This would have been a useful piece of equipment for a midwife dealing with cases of tongue-tie, where the thin tissue connecting the underside of the tongue to the floor of the mouth is too short and tight, which restricts movement of the tongue, preventing the infant from sucking/eating properly and, if it survives, from talking properly as a toddler. A congenital and hereditary problem in as many as 11 percent of newborns, and twice as common in male infants as females, the solution is simply to cut the tissue, using either the traditional method (the midwife's fingernail) or a small pair of scissors.[52]

In particularly difficult cases, a white male doctor was brought in to assist, as when Dr. James Craik was "sent for to a laying in Woman at the river Plantation" in 1786.[53] Even the doctor could not save some patients, however. Jinny from Dogue Run Farm died in childbirth in the summer of 1794. As soon as he realized there was a problem, the farm manager summoned Craik, who stayed with his patient for two days and a night, but her baby could not be delivered and the mother succumbed.[54] Jinny's case would not have been terribly unusual in the eighteenth century, when labor and delivery were considerably more hazardous than today. Evidence from New England at this period suggests a mortality rate for women giving birth with either a midwife or physician in attendance at between four and six deaths for every thousand births, while the maternal death rate in English villages at the same time varied from ten to twenty-nine per thousand births. Hospitals in the British Isles had a particularly bad record, with the mortality rate sometimes reaching as high as two hundred per thousand births.[55] In the following century, analysis of data on slave women on southern plantations shortly before the Civil War suggests that one mother died for every one thousand births, a mortality rate that was actually lower than for white women in the same geographic area at this period.[56]

Rum was routinely sent from the storehouse near the mansion for the use of "women in child bed."[57] Whether the rum was used as an anesthetic during labor, was thought to be a restorative afterward, or was a reward for a task well done is unclear, but a traditional practice suggests that the second possibility was the most likely.[58]

Mulatto Slaves

The presence of mixed-race slaves at Mount Vernon indicates that some of the children born in the slave quarters might have been fathered by white men on the estate. Of the slaves at Mount Vernon in 1799, approximately twenty, or about 6 percent, were described in various sources specifically as mulatto, as having "yellow" complexions, or being "light black."[59] Mount Vernon was similar in this regard to Virginia as a whole, where about the time of the Revolution roughly 5 percent of Virginia slaves were mulatto.[60]

These classifications can get muddied and are not conclusive because generally the person recording this information was only looking at physical characteristics, specifically skin and/or eye color, and not asking for a personal history, which would reveal parents of different races. About half of the mulatto slaves at Mount Vernon lived and worked at Washington's Mansion House Farm, rather than in the fields.

At least some of the hired whites who worked and lived most closely with the Mount Vernon slaves probably became physically intimate with them. Two of the slaves mentioned frequently in Washington's correspondence in the 1790s were a spinner, Betty Davis, and a bricklayer named Tom Davis, known at Mount Vernon as a skilled hunter who provided wild game for the Washingtons' table.[61] About thirty years before, there had been a hired white weaver, Thomas Davis, working on the plantation.[62] The similarity in names between these three people is probably not a coincidence. At least one historian studying slavery at Mount Vernon feels that the hired weaver was probably the father of both these slaves.[63] In another case, Christopher Sheels, the young man who served as Washington's valet at the end of his life, was twenty-four years old in 1799, indicating that he was born about 1775. Interestingly, there was a hired wagon driver at Mount Vernon between December 1770 and at least July 1774 whose name is variously given as Christopher (or Christian) Sheldes (or Shade).[64] Mulatto blacksmith George Young was very likely the son of a man with the same name, who was hired by George Washington as a clerk in January 1774.[65]

Another hired man was the father of one of Martha Washington's maids. Oney Judge's mother, Betty, came to Mount Vernon at the time of the Washingtons' marriage, accompanied by her infant son Austin. They first appear in the historical record in papers dealing with the estate of Martha Washington's first husband, Daniel Parke Custis, in which they were valued together at sixty pounds.[66] Although there is no evidence about the identity of Austin's father, the surname used later by his younger sisters points to the paternity of those little girls. In 1772, George Washington took on an English tailor who signed a four-year indenture in exchange for his passage to America. That man, Andrew Judge, whose time should have been up in 1776, worked for Washington until 1781 and continues to show up in Mount Vernon financial records until at least 1784, when Washington loaned him twelve pounds.[67] Judge was probably still around because of his relationship with Betty and their little girls, Oney, who was born in 1774, and Philadelphia, known as Delphy, who came along in 1780. Betty is identified as a seamstress, so she and Judge probably worked together, or at least in proximity to one another.[68] With no surviving records from either Betty or Andrew, it is impossible to talk about the nature of their relationship, which could have run the gamut from rape or coercion to mutual attraction, respect, or even love.

A letter written by Washington in 1793 strongly suggests a carnal relationship between an overseer and those he supervised. Responding to a letter from his farm manager, George Washington replied that he was sorry to learn that "the Itch," or body mites, had spread among the slaves at one of his farms. He then went on to say that "if it was caught in the way you describe, and justice could be done, Garner [the overseer] ought to pay for it."[69] Unfortunately, the whereabouts of the initial letter from the farm manager detailing how this condition was transmitted are unknown, but the logical inference from Washington's response is that Garner was infected first and passed the mites on to others through sexual contact.

Overriding Washington's concerns about overfamiliarity between supervisors and slaves were several factors that may have encouraged these relationships. One of the most important was probably the isolation felt by many of the hired whites. As detailed earlier, Washington expected his employees to stay on the farms they oversaw most of the time, with the exception of a few hours away on Sunday to attend church if they were so inclined. This meant that they could almost never get into town to socialize with others of their own social class. Washington also discouraged his overseers from entertaining friends in their homes. Here then were men who were physically and emotionally isolated from their peers. If they had recently immigrated to the United States, they might be separated and virtually cut off from their families as well, further increasing the sense of being emotionally adrift. John Harrower, a young indentured Scotsman on another Virginia plantation at this period, put his feelings into a pathetically sad poem, likening his situation to that of a leper banished outside a camp or a prisoner, with "No fr[i]endly soul . . . My greiff to ease, or hear my moan."[70] Few of the hired whites at Mount Vernon had the education Harrower did, meaning they were unlikely to turn to books and letter-writing as a means of assuaging their loneliness and boredom. The company of enslaved women who lived near them, and with whom these men were probably closer in both social status and culture than the Washingtons, may have been seen by some as appealing. Depending on the personalities and ethical standards of the individuals involved, the ensuing relationships could have been the result of mutual attraction and affection, very real demonstrations of power and control, or even exercises in the manipulation of an authority figure. At this distance, and with the evidence at hand, there is no way to say for sure. Perhaps as a means of forestalling problems, Washington preferred to hire overseers who were married and had small families, rather than either those with large families, who would require larger salaries and benefits, or single men, who might be especially susceptible to loneliness and sexual temptation.[71]

Isolation, combined with the fact that they were working for George Washington, a man who expected those around him to follow his exacting work ethic, made for tremendous pressures on these men. Caught between two cultures, a number of them turned to drink for solace. The combination of loneliness, work pressures, and alcohol could lead to unpleasant situations. During the Revolution, the Mount Vernon farm manager noted that William Roberts, a hired miller, drank too much, causing him to neglect his work. A further complication, however, was that "when in liquor," Roberts's personality was "apt to be ill natured."[72] Some years later, George Washington complained about a hired German gardener with "too great a propensity to drink," which led him to behave "improperly when in liquor," a radical change from his habitual conduct when sober.[73] He cautioned the man, whose wife and children lived on the estate, to exercise willpower and call on his religious faith to combat "so intolerable a vice," which produced "bad behaviour, at the moment, and . . . more serious evils . . . afterward," including the infliction of pain, presumably on the man's family.[74] The contracts with several hired whites reiterated the importance Washington placed on sobriety. One of these documents, for example, contained the following agreement: "And whereas there are a number of whiskey stills very contiguous to the said Plantations, and many idle, drunken and dissolute People continually resorting [to] the same, priding themselves in debauching sober and well-inclined Persons the said Edd. Violett doth promise as well for his own sake as his employer[']s to avoid them as he ought."[75] It is not unlikely that men with so much authority over others, whose temper and judgment had been impaired by alcohol, and whose employer was a considerable distance away might coerce sexual favors from those they supervised. When Washington was on the estate, his presence probably mitigated somewhat against such abuses. Including the French and Indian War, the Revolutionary War, and two terms as president, however, he was gone for about twenty of the forty-five years he ran Mount Vernon, leaving open the possibility for unfortunate and, in his opinion, undesirable consequences.

Could other whites besides the hired workers have fathered the mulatto children on the estate? Absolutely. Not all of the Washingtons' houseguests, for example, were well-intentioned toward the slaves they found at Mount Vernon. A letter written by a young officer—and future U.S. senator from New York—suggests that at least some of them expected enslaved women to provide sexual services. After visiting at Mount Vernon for several days with Baron von Steuben in the spring of 1784, a visit lengthened by bad weather and made more miserable by the age and marital status of the members of the household, Major William North decided to pass the time writing to a friend, Ben Walker, who had once been George Washington's aide during the Revolution. The weather that week was raw and rainy, so amid gossip and complaints about everything from the boredom and the solitude to the fact that the only young woman of his social class in the mansion—Martha Washington's niece, Fanny Bassett—was engaged to George Augustine Washington, and being sequestered in his room when he was not eating or playing cards, North suddenly interjected, "Will you believe it—I have not humped a single mullato since I am here."[76] From his tone, it appears that North fully expected to engage in sex with the housemaids and was surprised about his enforced chastity. Whether this condition was due to an edict from Washington, the understandable lack of receptivity on the part of the slave women who crossed his path, or the fact that Steuben may have ordered him to be on his best behavior in this particular household is impossible to say. Even if North did not get the chance to father children with one of the enslaved women at Mount Vernon, other visitors might have.[77]

The Costin Family

Having sex with women of different ethnic backgrounds—and sometimes having children with them—was not unknown in the extended Washington, Dandridge, and Custis families.[78] At least two authors, Henry Wiencek and Helen Bryan, have recently dealt with the oral history of the Costin family, which states that Martha Washington had a half-sister, Ann Dandridge, who was "the daughter of a half-breed, (Indian and colored), her grandfather being a Cherokee chief," and John Dandridge, the father of Martha Washington. Ann and Martha are said to have "grown up together," suggesting that the two were close in age. Ann is later said to have had a child in 1780, a little boy named William Costin, fathered by a person variously described as being from "a prominent family in Virginia," as simply "a Custis," or as her nephew, Martha Washington's son, John Parke Custis. According to their family tradition, shortly after William's birth, Ann married a slave named Costin with whom she had four daughters between 1788 and 1795. When that marriage ended, Ann (or Nancy as she was also known) married a man with the surname Holmes (his given name is unknown), who fathered her next two children. Ann and her children were manumitted by

Thomas Law, the husband of Martha Washington's eldest granddaughter, Eliza Parke Custis, in the District of Columbia in the early nineteenth century. As an adult, William Costin married Philadelphia (Delphy) Judge, who was the younger sister of Martha Washington's maid Oney Judge. Delphy and their two older children would also be freed by Thomas Law. Costin maintained close ties with the white children of John Parke Custis, especially George Washington Parke Custis, who would have been his half-brother, and the latter's daughter, Mary Custis Lee. As evidence of these close ties, Wiencek mentioned a check written to William Costin by George Washington Parke Custis, which is in the collection at Tudor Place, the home of Custis's older sister, Martha Parke Custis, and her husband, Thomas Peter.[79]

The Costin family appears in several kinds of government records in the early nineteenth century. Deed books from the District of Columbia confirm that Thomas Law, the husband of Martha Washington's eldest granddaughter, manumitted several members of William Costin's family "in consideration of" small sums of money. On May 1, 1807, in exchange for ten cents, Law manumitted Margaret Costin (nineteen years old), Louisa Costin (seventeen), Caroline Costin (fifteen), Jemima Costin (twelve), Mary Holmes (eight), and Eleanor Holmes (six), who were presumably William Costin's sisters. Two months later, in exchange for one dollar, Thomas Law emancipated William's wife and children, Delphy Costin (twenty-eight years old), Louisa Costin (two), and Ann Costin (one). William Costin also purchased another former Mount Vernon slave, Leanthe "Brannan," one of the daughters of Martha Washington's maid Caroline Branham, from George Washington Parke Custis of Arlington on October 11, 1820; Costin freed her six days later.[80]

Census records also verify that the Costin family lived in the District of Columbia for decades. On August 7, 1820, William Costin was listed as the head of a household of eight free black people in Ward 4, including four men and one woman over the age of forty-five. Ten years later there were eleven free black people in Costin's home, still in Ward 4, which was headed by a couple between the ages of thirty-six and fifty-four.[81] Delphy must have died shortly thereafter, because marriage records for the District of Columbia indicate that William married Elizabeth Matthews (or Matthew) on June 6, 1838.[82] Costin worked as a messenger for the Bank of Washington for twenty-four years. He was a well-known figure in the city, and upon his death on May 31, 1842, John Quincy Adams said of him, "The late William Costin, though he was not white, was as much respected as any man in the District, and the large concourse of citizens that attended his remains to the grave, as well white as black, was an evidence of the manner in which he was estimated by the citizens of Washington." Costin's daughter Louisa Parke Costin started a school for blacks in her father's home on A Street Southeast on Capitol Hill in 1823; she would run the school until her death in 1831.[83]

Mount Vernon has known about the family's oral history since at least the 1960s, when descendants of William Costin first contacted the organization.[84] There are a number of problems with the family tradition. For starters, if Martha and Ann were close in age, Ann would have been in her late forties or early fifties at the time of Costin's birth, something which, while not impossible, is also not likely, especially given the fact that the suspected father, John Parke Custis, was then only twenty-six years old. It is even less plausible that she then gave birth to four more children through her early sixties when she was married and had two additional children, born about 1799 and 1801, with her second husband, when their mother would have been in her late sixties or early seventies.[85] Even more important is the complete absence of references to and information about either Ann Dandridge or her son in the papers of George and Martha Washington, a major factor in why two prominent outside historians both discount the story completely.[86] A whole new wrinkle was added to the Ann Dandridge–William Costin story a few years ago, however, by the discovery that in the late 1720s, Martha Washington's uncle William Dandridge took part in an expedition to determine the boundary between Virginia and North Carolina. While staying at a Nottaway Indian village, his fellow commissioner William Byrd II noted that "curiosity made him [Dandridge] try the difference between them & other Women, to the disobligation of his [shirt] Ruffles, which betray'd what he had been doing."[87] Here was period documentation that a man in the Dandridge family was involved with Native American women.

More recently, a newly acquired collection of family correspondence at Mount Vernon shows a close relationship between Costin and three of Martha Washington's grandchildren, as well as their uncle George Calvert in the early nineteenth century. For example, Eliza Parke Custis wrote to her stepson in the fall of 1808 about a situation involving William Costin, who was then operating a hack business—akin to a taxi service.[88] Apparently someone named Snowden had taken thirty dollars from "Billy" Costin, and she wanted John Law, who handled her money after she separated from his father, to do everything he could to "gratify him," because Costin needed that "money now to buy a Carriage which he can get [cheap] & his old one is near worn out." She reminded the young man that "I never apply to you, but for money due by your father, I might omit any explanation, yet I gave a full one." She indicated that she had borrowed money from "Billy, to whom I am willing to owe an obligation, from his faithful attachment to me, but I should be distress'd if he sustain'd any loss."[89]

Five years later, in a letter dated June 12, 1816, Eliza Custis's youngest sister, Nelly Custis Lewis, asked "My Friend Billy" to take the young man who had been tutoring her children from Woodlawn, her plantation near Mount Vernon, as far as Baltimore. Apparently the unnamed tutor had been "in very bad health," and Nelly noted, "I wish to employ you because I know you will be a nurse & friend to him if he requires one," but then cautioned, "this business must be a secret to all but you & I . . . I never wanted you to serve me so much as I do now—I hope you & family are well." She closed with the words, "I will ever be your friend," and then added as a postscript, "I paid $10 to Mrs Custis [Mary Fitzhugh Custis, her brother's wife] for you yesterday."[90]

A third letter in this same collection, written in 1813, is particularly important. At the bottom of a missive to Costin from George Washington's nephew Lawrence Lewis, the latter's wife, Nelly Custis Lewis, again appended a postscript containing the first reference to William Costin's mother in any of the family papers found so far. In her note, Lewis simply says, "Billy, I expect to go immediately to Philadelphia, and you must carry us in your hack. If your mother will go with me I will pay her in Pork if she likes it."[91] If Ann Dandridge was roughly the same age as Martha Washington, she would have been about eighty years old at the time this note was written, probably too old to have accompanied Lewis on such a long trip. My own feeling about Ann Dandridge is that the life stories of at least two women, probably a mother and daughter, were conflated in the family's oral history, but this is something that may well be impossible to prove.

Mixed-Race Children of the Washington and Custis Families

Probably much better known is the story of Martha Washington's first father-in-law. In his will, John Custis detailed a bequest to "my Negro boy Christoforo John otherwise called Jack born of the body of my slave Alice." He freed both Jack and his mother, and also asked his legitimate heir, Daniel Parke Custis, to look after the boy until his twentieth birthday. John Custis wanted his executors to build "a handsome Strong and convenient dwelling" for Jack on a specific tract of land, and to furnish it with "One Dozen high Russia Leather Chairs One Dozen Low Russia Chairs a Russia

Leather Couch good and Strong three Good Feather Beds and Bedsteads and furniture and two good Black Walnut Tables." As one historian has written, Custis was leaving Jack "a dreamed-of Big House as the most important step in trying to ensure his future status."[92]

The uncle of Martha Washington's grandchildren, George Calvert of Mount Albion and Riversdale plantations in Maryland, had a longstanding relationship with a slave, a woman of mixed Native American and African ancestry named Eleanor Beckett, which began a number of years before Calvert's marriage and produced at least two and probably five children. Two years after he was married, Calvert freed Beckett and their children and continued to look after them until his death in 1838.[93]

Closer to Mount Vernon, Martha Washington's grandson, George Washington Parke Custis, was commonly believed to have fathered several children with his slaves, who were often freed or otherwise cared for by Custis.[94] An 1865 newspaper article even indicated that Mary Anna Randolph Custis Lee, who was Custis's only legitimate daughter, had forty mulatto half-siblings in the Washington, DC, area. Another article, written twenty-three years later, included an interview with Maria Syphax, an elderly mulatto woman who had been enslaved at Arlington House, where she was the maid to her half-sister, Lee. According to Syphax, George Custis told her "face to face" that he was her father and noted that "he was kind to me."[95] Looking at another such case, Alexandrian Mary Gregory Powell, who was born in 1847, recalled that her family's nurse maids, Eugenia and Sarah,

> received their freedom in accordance with the agreement between Mr. George Washington Parke Custis and my father. . . . These two girls were the grandchildren of Caroline Brannum, Mrs. George Washington's maid, and it was generally believed that [Caroline's daughter] Lucy, [who was] the mother of Eugenia and Sarah [and] was lawfully married to a respectable mulatto named Harrison[,] was the daughter of [George Washington] Parke Custis and Caroline. She bore a very strong resemblance to his daughter Mary Custis who married General Robert E. Lee. These children might easily have passed for white.[96]

West Ford

The story of West Ford, a free black man who founded the nearby community of Gum Springs in the first half of the nineteenth century, is fairly well known. Ford was born in the early to mid-1780s at Bushfield Plantation, the home of George Washington's brother John Augustine Washington I,

FIG. 4. Detail of a photograph of West Ford on the East Front
of Mount Vernon, 1858. (Courtesy of the Mount Vernon
Ladies' Association)

about ninety-five miles south of Mount Vernon in Westmoreland County,
Virginia. Ford was brought to Mount Vernon when Bushrod Washington
inherited the property after Martha Washington's death in 1802. Following
his manumission, which took place in about 1805 (the exact date is unknown), Ford was put in positions of responsibility and trust by several
later generations of Washingtons at Mount Vernon. One referred to him
as "my venerable Lieutenant," and he became well-known to the thousands
of visitors who came to the estate each year. Bushrod Washington made a
bequest to him of 160 acres of land, which Ford later sold to purchase
a different tract of 214 acres, the nucleus of the free black community at
Gum Springs. Ford became very ill in the summer of 1863 and was brought
to Mount Vernon, where he died on July 20. He is traditionally thought to
have been buried in the slave burial ground, not far from the Washington family tomb. Some of Ford's descendants believe he was the son of

George Washington and an African American house servant at Bushfield named Venus, while others believe his father was Bushrod Washington, the nephew who inherited Mount Vernon after the death of Martha Washington in 1802.[97]

George Washington may have had an early relationship with an enslaved woman when he was in his early twenties, still a bachelor, and serving with the Virginia Regiment. This would have been immediately after his defeat at Fort Necessity and during a period of about five years when his romantic hopes were rebuffed by a succession of young women or their fathers.[98] Writing from Williamsburg in the summer of 1754, one of his fellow officers, a Frenchman named William La Péronie, started off a letter to Washington with the statement: "As I imagine you By this time, plung'd in the midst of dellight heaven can a[f]ford & enchanted By Charms even stranger to the Ciprian Dame I thought it would Contribu[t]e a little to the variety of yours amusement to Send you [a] few lines to peruse." In a marginal note, Péronie indicated that the person to whom he referred was "M's Nel."[99] The phrase "Ciprian Dame" was an eighteenth-century term for a prostitute, but it does not appear that Péronie is necessarily identifying Nel as a prostitute. The fact that she is described as "M's Nel" suggests several possibilities. For example, she may have been a barmaid working for a tavern owner (and/or pimp) whose first initial was "M," the mistress of a brother officer, or perhaps someone's slave. From other letters written about this time, it appears that Washington was probably in Alexandria, indicating that "Nel" was in that city or the greater Mount Vernon neighborhood. With the minimal evidence at hand, there are many unanswered questions about this mystery woman.[100]

After he left the army, married, and took up life as a planter, George Washington for several reasons was unlikely to have been physically involved with female slaves, either at Mount Vernon or at the homes of other family members. Given his feelings on the question of overfamiliarity between those in authority and the people they oversaw, as well as the moral correctness for which he is legendary, it would have been grossly out of character for Washington to have had a liaison with one of his slaves. Among the consequences for a slave owner who undertook such a relationship was that "not only would it stir anger and discontent in the [enslaved] families affected, but it would undermine the air of mystery and distinction on which so much of the authority of large planters rested," something Washington, who tended to consider every possible ramification of his actions before he made a move, would hardly have risked.[101] Washington himself, at the age of fifty-four, told a relative that if he died before Martha Washington, "there is a moral certainty of my dying without issue," indicating that he had not engaged in sexual relations outside his marriage.[102] In reading Washington's statement, it is necessary to consider that neither he nor many other white Virginians of this period would have considered children they had outside wedlock, whether the mother was enslaved or free, as legitimate issue. Still, given the problems with the few means of birth control available at this time, the only way a person could be completely sure that he had no illegitimate children would be to abstain from extramarital sex.[103]

Still, human beings do act in ways that are out of character for them or are not in their best interests, especially when tired, intoxicated, lonely, or stressed, so arguments from character are not especially strong. They also sound too much like the arguments used by Thomas Jefferson's biographers for decades in regard to the likelihood of a relationship between Jefferson and Sally Hemings.

Aside from Washington's personality, close examination of the elements of the Ford family oral history suggest that it is in error. One of the primary difficulties in proving that, however, is determining the date of West Ford's birth. He first appears in the manuscript record in a slave list dating from about the time of John Augustine Washington's death early in 1787 (there are no references to Ford or his mother in George Washington's papers). The list shows the division of the Bushfield slaves among John Augustine's three primary heirs—his two surviving sons, Bushrod and Corbin, and his widow, Hannah Bushrod Washington. Enumerated under Hannah's portion are four members of a family: Venus, valued at sixty-five pounds; her son, West, appraised for twelve pounds; and her parents, Billy and Jenny, who were valued at seventy and sixty pounds, respectively.[104] Another list, this one done about four years earlier on March 3, 1783, shows the three older members of the family but not West, indicating that he was born after that date.[105] Thus, Ford had to have been born sometime between that date and 1787, when John Augustine's slaves were divided among his heirs.

Perhaps the most important documentary evidence for West Ford's birth and his relationship with the Washington family is found in the will of John Augustine's widow, Hannah, which was drawn up in April 1801. In that document, she states,

> My dear husband left me in his will the following slaves to dispose of as I chose at my death provided I gave them to our own children[.] the slaves are as follows—Billey WHO IS dead since[,] his wife Jenny[,] their daughter [V]enus who has brought a daughter since called Bettey, these three slaves I give my beloved grandson Richard Henry Lee

Washington[.] a lad called West, son of Venus, who was born before my husband's will was made and not therein mentioned, I offered to buy him of my dear sons Bushrod and Corbin Washington, but they generously refused to sell him but presented the boy to me as a gift[,] it is my most earnest wish and desire this lad West may be as soon as possible inoculated for the small pox, after which to be bound to a good tradesman until the age of twenty one years, after which he is to be free the rest of his life.[106]

There are a number of points to be made about this statement. First, Hannah begins by giving West Ford's grandmother Jenny (his grandfather Billy had died by that time), mother Venus, and younger sister Bettey to her grandson Richard Henry Lee Washington. This gift is in accordance with her late husband's will, in which he had noted, "Billy, Jenny & Venus I impower my Wife to devise to such of my Children by her as she pleases," thus ensuring that they would stay in the Washington family.[107] They were the only such family to be singled out in that manner, just as West Ford was the only individual for whom inoculation, education in a trade, and manumission were mandated in Hannah's will.

Second, the reference to West Ford's younger sister, Bettey, is significant. The little girl was born after John Augustine made the provision about her family in his will, probably after 1787, because she does not appear in the 1787 division of John Augustine's slaves between his wife, Hannah, and sons, Bushrod and Corbin. John Augustine had signed his will on June 22, 1784, but added a codicil on November 19, 1785, dealing with the disposition of some recently purchased land and confirming the gift of two slaves to his grandchildren. He made no mention of any of West Ford's family members in the codicil. Bettey, however, was automatically included with the rest of her family as part of Hannah's estate, because she was a child of Venus, born after that provision in the 1784 will was written.

Third, when Hannah does deal with West Ford in her will, she carefully notes that he "was born before my husband's will was made and not therein mentioned." Had Ford been born any time after that, he would have been included in the provision about his family, just as his younger sister was. Hannah had to make this point because if Ford had been born before the 1784 will but was not mentioned with the rest of his family, he would have been included with the group of slaves who were to be divided between Bushrod and Corbin. This is why Hannah offered to buy him from her sons and why they, in turn, felt obliged to relinquish Ford to her. This would mean that Ford was born between March 3, 1783, and June 22, 1784. Considering a conception date of June 1782 through September 1783, West Ford could not be George Washington's child because Washington, who was then leading the Continental Army in the last phase of the American Revolution, was not in Virginia at any time during this period.[108]

Even if the date of Ford's birth was different and it was possible for George Washington to be his father, there is no evidence in Washington's papers for the kind of care taken by other members of his extended family for their mulatto offspring. From all accounts, West Ford was a nice-looking, intelligent, well-respected man. Imagine if he had been the son of George Washington, a man who by his early fifties had never had children of his own, who probably would have been, at least a little, pleased at being a father at last, even if he could not publicly claim the child. Others in his extended family did see that their mulatto children were freed and well cared for. West Ford was given special treatment by the Washington family, but all the good things that came to him—inoculation for smallpox, being taught a trade, manumission at the age of twenty-one, and the inheritance of land—came from the Bushfield branch of the Washington family, not George Washington, indicating that his father was someone at that plantation. My own belief is that Ford was the son of George Washington's nephew William Augustine Washington, who died in 1784.[109]

Childhood in the Mount Vernon Quarters

The birth of an enslaved child was often casually recorded, if it was noted at all. The weekly report for River Farm for the week ending April 21, 1787, noted that the population had increased by "1 Child a Girl—Mother Bath Suzy," and that reporting of the birth had been "omited last week."[110] The value placed on this new little life can be seen in an entry from Dogue Run Farm in which the overseer recorded the weekly changes in the population as "Increase 9 Lambs & 1 male child of Lynnas Decrease 1 male Child of Charitys & 2 Cows & Calves sent to Mansion House."[111] After the birth of a child, the mother was generally given time off to recover, which typically varied between three and five weeks.[112] During that time, she may have been expected to do a less physically demanding task, such as spinning. A letter from the overseer of the Custis properties discussed having spinning "done at Every Quarter in Bad weather & times when the wenches Lays in," but Washington's response seemingly has not survived.[113] An infant probably accompanied its mother to her worksite, at least while it was still being nursed and before it became too active to

FIG. 5. Engraving of the East Front of Mount Vernon with a slave family in the foreground. (Courtesy of the Mount Vernon Ladies' Association)

either stay happily on a blanket near where she was working or to be carried on her back.[114]

A new mother received her new blanket for the year at the time her baby was born. In 1787, for example, George Washington wrote his nephew from the Constitutional Convention to ask him to send an inventory of "new blankets your Aunt has in her Store room," because the time was fast approaching for making the distribution. Washington commented that "this is the year that *all* my people are entitled to receive them, except the Women who have had Children and been supplied on that occasion."[115] A letter written several years later suggests that if the baby lived, the woman might receive a new blanket for herself at the time of the fall distribution, but if it died, she would just have the one given at the time of the birth.[116] Washington and his Anglo-American farm managers may have seen rewarding mothers with an extra blanket as a way of encouraging them to take better care of their infants and thus increasing the survival rate for babies, or it might have been used for carrying the baby on the mother's back.

In addition to the new blanket, baby clothes were also issued. In September 1783, nine yards of "Slazy [thin or flimsy] White Linnen" were purchased "for Negroe Baby Cloaths," and in February 1794, stable manager Peter Hardiman picked up three yards of "Coarse linnen to make the negro Infants Clothes." Although there is no indication of how many garments each infant received, it does appear that the babies were given at least one shirt and cap apiece. During the presidency, Martha Washington sent "loose linning" to Mount Vernon from Philadelphia "to make Babe clothes—for the negro women" and directed that "shirts and caps and necessary things" be cut out of this fabric for them.[117] There is no indication about how, or even if, infants and toddlers were diapered. Washington's uncle Joseph Ball gave the following directions to another nephew in 1744 about clothing the babies of his slaves: "Let the Breeding Wenches have Baby Cloths; for which you may tear up old Sheets, or any other old Linen, that you can find in my house (I shall send things proper hereafter)."[118] Mothers certainly could have used rags left over from clothing they had worn in previous years, but knowing how many times a day babies need to be changed and the limited amount of time available to the slaves for washing their clothing, it is doubtful that such a source would have provided enough fabric.

The clothing provided to children, whether or not they were old enough to work, was of lesser quality than that given to adults. In a letter to farm manager William Pearce, Washington wrote that "the better sort" of linen be given to "the grown people, and the most deserving; whilst the more indifferent sort is served to the younger ones and worthless." In a similar vein, the previous year he had offered an opinion that the "11½ d linen is as good as any for the [working] boys, girls and small people, who do little or no work."[119] While enslaved children in Virginia were typically put into clothes similar to the adults at the time they started working, one clothing historian suggests that this would have occurred when the children were somewhere between seven and nine years old. Since children at Mount Vernon were a bit older than that when they started to work, there is no indication whether they continued to wear the frocks that were standard for younger slave children at this period until they entered the workforce.[120]

Naming Patterns

It is not known whether a child's family or the Washingtons chose its name, but if Mount Vernon followed the typical pattern on other plantations, parents or other relatives probably determined what to call their babies.[121] An extensive pool of names, drawn from a wide range of sources, was used at Mount Vernon over the years (see table 12). Analysis of the 1786 and 1799 plantation slave lists shows that the 357 people on those lists were given 209 different names. About half of the names are of English origin, while another quarter were taken from the Bible. Only a tiny fraction of the names (Juba and Sambo), fewer than 1 percent, appear on the surface to have been African. Historians studying slavery in the Carolinas, however, suggest that a number of common slave names that appear to be of European derivation may actually be African names, written down the way masters understood them or transposed to their closest-sounding English equivalent.[122] If we accept these historians' interpretations of these names as correct, the number of African or African-derived slave names at Mount Vernon actually rises to about 20 percent of the total. The most popular names at Mount Vernon were primarily from the groups of names that could be of English or biblical origin but may well, in reality, reflect an African background.

Historian S. Richard Dunn suggests that it is unlikely that an enslaved mother would choose names drawn from either Greek or Roman antiquity, from British place names, or from demeaning comic names (Bunny, Danger, Goodluck), which were probably picked by an owner or overseer.[123] I would argue, however, that while these names may well have been given to newly arrived Africans as replacements for their original names, as a way of showing mastery by those who controlled their lives, for the next and later generations, those same names would become family names, given to a new child out of love for a parent or grandparent, or to keep alive a sense of family connection.

At any given time, there were likely several individuals on the estate with the same name, another clue that names were being chosen by families rather than by the Washingtons, who might have tried to prevent confusion by using a larger pool of names. In order to tell these people apart in written communications and presumably in conversation, a distinguishing phrase relating to the person's family, occupation, physical appearance, or other traits was often appended to his or her name. Thus, on the 1799 slave lists, two eighteen-year-olds at Muddy Hole Farm were differentiated as "Kate long" and "Kate short," while at Dogue Run two men were known as "Long Jack" and "Carter Jack." Boatswain's one son was known as "young Boatswain," to tell him apart from his father; a younger brother was called "Matilda's Ben" to prevent confusion with "Carter Ben" and "millar Ben."[124] Hercules the cook appears to have been married to a woman known as "Lame Alice."[125]

Although slave families probably named their offspring themselves, it does appear that the Washingtons changed those names on occasion. One African-born slave acquired by George Washington prior to the Revolution and sent to work his lands on the Pennsylvania frontier was known by a name variously described as "Huntemah" or "Funty Munty" in Africa but was called Simon by the Washingtons. Given the very small percentage of names of African origin in the documentary sources from Mount Vernon, it is likely that they were replaced by more English sounding ones as a matter of course.[126] According to Martha Washington's grandson, Hercules, one of Mount Vernon's cooks, was an extremely strong man, "possessed of such great muscular power as to entitle him to be compared with his namesake of fabulous history."[127] At the time of his birth and naming, Hercules's parents could not have known how strong their son would become as an adult, nor would they have enough background in classical mythology to know the name. Custis's description suggests that the young man's physical prowess may have resulted in the name or nickname being applied to him as he grew and his strength became obvious. In a third case, the 1786 slave list shows that the youngest child of Betty at the Ferry Farm was an infant, approximately six months old, named Bill Langston. Thirteen years later, on the 1799 census, there is no teenager listed with the same name, so one might well infer that Bill had died as a baby or toddler. The following year, however, a runaway notice in the local newspaper alerted readers to the escape of Marcus, one of the house servants from Mount Vernon, who had been included on the 1799 slave lists. Marcus was described in the runaway notice as "a young lad, about 16 years of age, a bright Mulatto." The article went on to mention that "originally his name was Billy," and the author speculated that the young man "may possibly resume the same [name]."[128] For many years, George Washington's personal servant had been a mulatto slave named William, or Billy, Lee. Perhaps the thought of having another Billy serving in the house in the place of that old and respected gentleman was too much to contemplate, and the Washington family changed the young man's name to something quite different.

It was not unusual for children, both male and female, to be named for relatives, a fact which increased the likelihood that slaves were allowed to choose the names of their children. At River Farm in 1799, for example, Ben and Peg had a twenty-two-year-old son who was named for his father, while Lydia called her daughter, then eleven years old, after herself. That same year at Union Farm, Fanny's toddler son was named for his father, Charles, a ditcher at the Mansion House Farm. Kate, an eighteen-year-old at Muddy Hole Farm, bore the same name as her mother. Meanwhile, at Dogue Run, another couple named Ben and Peg gave their infant daughter the same name as her mother. Their neighbors, Dick and Charity, had a three-year-old also named Dick. Over at the Mansion House Farm, Sinah named her daughter after her own younger sister, Nancy. In the family of old Doll, the former cook, was a daughter named Alice or Alce, who gave one of her younger sons the name of his father, Charles, who was a freeman. Another of Doll's granddaughters called her own four-year-old daughter Anna, after herself. Stableman Peter Hardiman and his wife, Caroline Branham, had a small son named Peter as well. Not listed that year among Boatswain and Myrtilla's children was a boy called Boatswain, after his father, who had died several years earlier. The couple's daughter Lynna, who lived and worked at Dogue Run, had named her own daughter Matilda, after her mother, an alternate version of Myrtilla.[129] The slaves at Mount Vernon were not unique in these naming patterns. Historians studying slaves on other plantations have typically found evidence that children were named after parents or other relatives. This practice serves to underscore the importance placed on family ties within the enslaved community itself.[130]

Diseases and Accidents

Life for a new child could be hard. Following the death of a slave child belonging to her niece, Martha Washington wrote to console the young woman: "I am truly sorry that any thing should happen in your family to give you pain[.] Black children are liable to so many accidents and complaints that one is heardly sure of keeping them[.] I hope you will not find in him much loss."[131] As in any population, a certain percentage of children would have been born with problems. This was true of Eve, one of the daughters of the cook Hercules and his wife, Lame Alice. Born in 1782, Eve lived on the Mansion House Farm and was described at the age of seventeen as a "dwarf."[132] Similarly, nine-year-old Lavinia, the youngest of Isaac and Kitty's nine daughters, was listed as an "invalid" on an 1802 document showing a proposed division of the Custis dower slaves. The fact that the little girl was valued at only five pounds suggests that her condition was considered permanent.[133]

What are often thought of today as childhood diseases sickened children—and adults—at Mount Vernon in the eighteenth century, in both the quarters and the mansion. In January 1760, for example, Martha Washington and several slaves, including a carpenter named Sam, contracted measles.[134] Twenty-four years later, measles struck once again, this time threatening Washington's grandchildren.[135] Another childhood disease mentioned in the family papers was chicken pox, which afflicted one of the Custis grandchildren in the early years of the presidency.[136] The fact that these diseases are not specifically mentioned among the children in the quarters does not mean that they did not occur there.

The prevalence of respiratory and gastrointestinal problems fluctuated with the seasons, with the former being more common in winter and the latter in summer. While difficult for adults, these conditions were devastating to younger and more vulnerable members of the community. During the very difficult winter of 1791–92, manager Anthony Whiting noted that "a Great Many Children are very bad with the Hooping Cough at every Qu[arte]r."[137] Several years later, in a weekly report from 1797, farm manager James Anderson informed George Washington of the birth of three slave children and the death of a fourth from worms. Anderson assured his employer that medical help had been called in, but he complained that "the mothers are very inattentive to their Young."[138] Keeping in mind the women's work schedules, what Anderson saw as inattention may have been nothing more than fatigue and preoccupation. A mother may not have understood the instructions left by a white physician or might have been reluctant to follow them. It is also possible that what Anderson saw as neglect may have been due to differences in either the cultural expectations of mothers or child-rearing practices. In any case, there were definitely slave mothers at Mount Vernon who took real pains to care for their children. Myrtilla was working as a spinner at the Mansion House Farm when one of her sons, then fourteen years old, became very sick. George Washington ordered his manager to check that "young Boatswain" was truly ill because he felt the boy's mother might be exaggerating. Washington recalled that "under pretence once before, of a hurt by a Cart she kept him three months . . . in the house with her until he was forced out and this may be the case again."[139] Sadly, in this case it appears that young Boatswain's health really was precarious. Several months later, after being sick for five days, he died at Dogue Run Farm on November 7, 1794.[140] Other women were given time off from work to nurse their sick children. In June 1798, for instance, Delia at Union Farm, a slave rented from Washington's neighbor Mrs. French, was off for an entire week "nursing her son Daniel when sick."[141]

As Martha Washington noted in her letter, accidents of all types plagued enslaved children and adolescents. In addition to young Boatswain's above-mentioned confrontation with a cart, one young slave was described as having a hurt shoulder, while another received a broken jaw from being kicked by a horse.[142] A doctor was generally called in to deal with serious cases, as happened one spring, when James Craik charged Washington fifteen shillings for setting a fractured arm for an enslaved child.[143]

A number of these injuries resulted in permanent damage. Physical descriptions of slaves who grew up at Mount Vernon included a number of deformities, which may well have been the result of accidents, though whether they happened to them as children or adults cannot be known for sure. For example, Dick Gray, the son of Dick and Charity at Dogue Run, had a large white scar on his chest and small scars around his eyes. Between them, Bartley Clark and his sister Matilda, whose mother, Lynna, also worked at Dogue Run, had small scars on their underlip and arms, respectively. Dennis Richardson, who spent his early years at River Farm, had a small scar on his right wrist, while his neighbor Joe had "some small scars on his forehead."[144] At least some of these scars may have resulted from burns, a constant hazard in homes heated by fireplaces.[145]

Childhood

Until they joined the plantation workforce, enslaved children led a fairly unstructured existence. In 1799, nearly three-quarters of these children lived in households headed by single parents, who were almost invariably female. With their mothers away from home for most or all of the dawn-to-dusk workday, the children seem to have been largely unsupervised, except by one another, during those hours. Only at River Farm in 1795 was someone assigned to watch over the children. Hannah spent a total of six weeks "attending to young children," divided into two weeks in February, one week in May, and three weeks in December of that year.[146] Probably one of the slightly older children, or even an elderly person, looked after the children on a regular basis. Consequently, because they were not considered part of the workforce, they did not appear on the work reports. If that person were sick, Hannah may well have been called in to substitute. In any case, leaving young children in the care of their slightly older siblings was a typical pattern in agricultural, poor, and/or preindustrial communities throughout the world. It may well have been the norm in America at this period, in both the plantation South and the northern frontier. Slave children at Monticello under the age of ten, for instance, were expected to "serve as nurses," presumably for the younger children, while small children in the cabins of the Maine woods were under the care of older brothers and sisters, as their mothers took care of a never-ending round of chores.[147]

The young children appear to have spent a great deal of time playing together. Washington forbade the children at the Mansion House Farm from coming into the yards and gardens near his house, complaining that they "too frequently are breaking limbs or twigs from or doing other injury to my shrubs some of which at a considerable expence, have been propagated." There is no record of the specific games that threatened Washington's carefully designed plantings, but climbing and swinging on trees, dueling with branches, riding stick horses, and a group game called "hiding the switch," in which one child hid a stick on his person and the child who found it ran after the others and tried to hit them, were all possibilities. Despite the president's wishes, the Mount Vernon children got into these off-limits areas anyway, and Washington wanted his manager to break them of this practice.[148] There is no way of knowing from the surviving documentation, however, what measures were used to keep the little ones away from Washington's mansion or if they were successful.[149]

Other whites besides Washington had problems with the behavior of the slave children. His farm manager William Pearce was offered use of the servants' hall, the outbuilding just to the north of the mansion, during his first winter on the job, so that he would be in a better situation for learning about the management of the plantation. He informed Washington, however, that "I had Rather Live in the house you intended for me as I have Several small Children and I should Like to keep them at a distance from the Black ones and I thought I saw a great many at your mansion house."[150] Although Pearce's statement reflects a certain amount of prejudice, it may also suggest differing cultural attitudes between the Anglo- and African American communities about children's behavior. Richard Parkinson, an Englishman who spent several years in Maryland at the end of the eighteenth century, related a conversation with the wife of a Colonel Norwood on the subject of slave children. Mrs. Norwood found the children at her plantation "troublesome" because they took things from the kitchen and were dirty. "But what was much worse than all this," her own children quite naturally played with the young slaves, "who by nature appeared to be given to vice," and they "unavoidably contracted the habits of the negroes, and had their morals corrupted."[151] Given the little the slave children had to eat, something Norwood was unlikely to recognize, it is not surprising that they made off with food from the plantation kitchen, something she would have viewed as theft and thus contributed to her belief that they were plagued by vice and liable to corrupt her own children.

Slave children too young to join the workforce appear to have done small, and sometimes not so small, tasks about the plantation. During the summer of 1786, two older slaves, a cooper named Jack and the overseer Davy Gray, worked with a group of small children in bundling hay after it had been cut. Washington noted in his diary that these children "had never been taken out before" but did not say how well the little ones responded to this experience.[152] Almost fifty years after his death, an elderly nursemaid from Arlington House remembered that, as a young girl at Mount Vernon, she "would run to open the gate" for George Washington, whom she called "the Gen."[153] These little jobs included work for overseers and chores for their own families as well. With most parents working long hours away from home, there must have been a multitude of small tasks the children could do to help. Hauling water and wood and caring for younger children are all mentioned in surviving Washington documents. In the summer of 1793, Washington cautioned his overseers, William Stuart, Highland Crow, and Henry McKoy, against using any able-bodied adult slave for their own purposes. He told the men that he did not care, however, if they used one of the slave children "for the purpose of fetching wood or water, tending a child, or such like things." As soon as the child was of an age to begin fieldwork, though, Washington expected "to reap the benefit of their labour myself."[154] Later that year, when he asked his farm manager to try to break the children of coming into the yard, Washington reminded him that they had access to wood, water, and other things closer to their own quarters, indicating that they had regular responsibilities for those chores within their families.[155] Enslaved parents may also have expected their children to do such things as weed family garden plots, feed chickens or other fowls, or take care of mending, but we have no way of knowing for sure. Children may have occasionally done cooking as well. When a new overseer was hired in 1790, he was allowed "a Boy or Girl which[ever] can be most conveniently spared to cook for him."[156] The caveat about being able to spare this child suggests that they were probably old enough to be considered one of the "working boys and girls."

When the children were between eleven and fourteen years old, they became part of a transitional group called "working boys and girls" and began assisting on the farms. The variation in starting age was probably because the children grew and matured at different rates. These early duties involved a variety of tasks. In 1787, for example, five boys at the Mansion House Farm were helping the men by "Workg. upon the road & park & Cleang. brick," while three girls not only worked with them but also baked bread and carried water to the wash house. At about the same time, the boys and girls at River Farm were working in the barn and helping an adult man with driving carts and hauling rails. Other jobs done by the working children included carrying shocks of wheat and rye during the harvest; making fences; hauling manure, corn, and wheat; helping to carry oats; driving a harrow, roller, and cart; cutting down and picking cornstalks; cleaning up after the women grubbing the fields; threshing wheat; daubing houses; and getting wood.[157] For these young people, childhood, a period of relative freedom, was over.

6

"A Mean Pallet"

The Slave Quarters at Mount Vernon

Like many other guests at Mount Vernon, both during and after George Washington's lifetime, Jedidiah Morse took the time to record details about his visit to the home of this prominent American. He seems to have been fascinated with the layout of the plantation and found that the "toute ensemble"—"the whole assemblage"—of the mansion with its surrounding outbuildings "bears a resemblance to a rural village."[1] While Morse was speaking of the visual impression of the Mansion House Farm, from the viewpoint of its population, the Mount Vernon estate was in many ways several small African American villages presided over by an Anglo-American ruling class.

When Washington died in 1799, African Americans made up roughly 90 percent of the plantation's population, with more than three hundred slaves and roughly twenty to thirty whites living on the five farms comprising Mount Vernon. The largest "village" was at the Mansion House Farm, where about ninety slaves resided (about 500 acres), followed by seventy-six at Union Farm (928 acres), fifty-seven at River Farm (1,207 acres), forty-five on Dogue Run (650 acres), and forty-one at Muddy Hole (476 acres).[2] Over the years, Washington provided diverse housing arrangements for the enslaved people on the estate, with the greatest difference existing between the homes of the house servants and artisans at the Mansion House Farm and those of the fieldworkers on the four outlying farms.

Structures

In her study of eighteenth-century Virginia architecture, historian Camille Wells began by looking at landowners in Lancaster County shortly before the American Revolution. She found that fewer than 1 percent of these men owned more than two thousand acres, while 73 percent lived on fewer than two hundred. Her analysis of the houses recorded in estate records and newspaper advertisements, which are the kinds of records "dominated by the affluent," shows that the majority had no more than two rooms. She reminded readers that not just the poor lived in such small structures, writing that "small houses were also built and inhabited by those whose economic standing was quite enviable." After examining the quarters provided for hired and enslaved workers, she concluded that while "slave dwellings . . . could be very humble . . . [they were] never vastly inferior in terms of size and finish to buildings occupied by most of the Chesapeake's common planters and landless laborers. They were all just colonial Virginians with few material resources—they were poor."[3]

From surviving documentary sources, there appear to have been three basic types of slave housing used on the Mount Vernon estate that varied considerably in their style, quality of construction, and degree of privacy. The majority of house servants and skilled workers on the Mansion House Farm were assigned quarters considerably better in style and quality than slaves on the outlying farms. From considerations of privacy, however, field-workers on the four other farms had an advantage, both because of the configuration of their quarters, the largest of which probably housed no more than two families, and because of the greater distance from their master's supervision.

As on other plantations throughout the South, the most substantial buildings used for slave housing were certainly the "Big House quarters" at George Washington's Mansion House Farm. For approximately thirty years, beginning about the 1760s, the principal slave dwelling there was a two-story frame building constructed on a brick foundation, with two chimneys, one on each end, and glazed windows, known as the "Quarters [or House] for Families."[4] Located on the service lane north of the mansion, it was first depicted in a map drawn by English visitor Samuel Vaughan in 1787 and later appeared in a 1792 painting showing the east elevation (back or river side) of the mansion. While little is known about the configuration of dwelling spaces within this building, much of our knowledge of the material life of the Mount Vernon slaves results from the excavation of a cellar on this site in the 1980s. These old quarters were eventually torn

FIG. 6. A 1792 painting of the East Front of Mount Vernon with the House for Families to the right, attributed to Edward Savage. (Courtesy of the Mount Vernon Ladies' Association)

down in the 1790s, and the building materials—scantling (timbers), boards, shingles, and nails—saved for reuse.[5]

Although they were not constructed until 1792, George Washington had begun planning a different sort of quarter almost twenty years earlier, as either an addition to, or substitute for, the House for Families. The early months of his absence from home during the Revolution were a time of considerable activity at Mount Vernon, when improvements were made to the mansion house itself, many of the surviving outbuildings were constructed, and alterations were made to the gardens. Lund Washington managed the estate in George's absence and kept him apprised of the many changes underway through a series of detailed letters. In the fall of 1775, Lund asked for some direction on building a slave quarter, seemingly very much like that which was eventually put up at the greenhouse: "I suppose there is a wall to be Built in the new Garden next the Quarter[.] I think I have heard you say you design[e]d to have a House Built the whole length for Negroes perhaps you may direct that to be first done[.] If so be particular in the Wall that there may be no difficulty in joining other walls to it so as to make out the House Divisions &tc."[6]

Construction of the new quarter at the greenhouse was well underway by the spring of 1792. At that time, farm manager George Augustine Washington thought the new quarter would adequately house "all the Negro's that You would wish or find necessary to be kept at the Mansion House." He suggested that this new structure was necessary for maintaining discipline and order, "for until they are all brought together and under proper regulations it is in vain to attempt or at least to protect improvements."[7] Late in 1792 or early the following year, people began moving into the new quarter near the upper garden. From that time until George Washington's death in 1799, roughly half the slaves at the Mansion House Farm probably lived in the brick wings flanking the greenhouse, in four large rectangular rooms, each thirty-three feet nine inches by seventeen feet nine inches, a total living space of about six hundred square feet. Each of the rooms had a fireplace on one of its shorter walls and the luxury of glazed windows.[8]

Enslaved people made their homes in the greenhouse complex until December 1835, when a tremendous fire destroyed the structure. It was rebuilt in the 1950s using what little physical and documentary evidence had survived.[9] Probably the most striking and controversial feature of these reconstructed quarters was the arrangement of bunks on two sides of the room, creating a barracks-like atmosphere, which to some critics seemed to fly in the face of Washington's concern for maintaining the family life of his slaves. The communal arrangement would also have been atypical of late eighteenth-century practice on other plantations in the Chesapeake. Dormitories were primarily a feature of American slave life in the late seventeenth and early eighteenth centuries, generally on plantations that were at an early stage of their development, when there tended to be more men than women, or when there were a sizeable number of newly imported slaves from Africa. Over the course of the eighteenth century, the use of dormitories declined as sex ratios became more balanced, enabling enslaved people to form families, who were more likely to live in cabins. By the middle of the century, dormitories had largely given way to other forms of slave housing in both the Chesapeake and the Carolina Lowcountry, although their use did not completely die out even into the nineteenth century.[10]

Given his experiences in the French and Indian and Revolutionary Wars, Washington probably viewed bunks as an eminently practical solution for housing his artisans, primarily men, who were either single or had wives and children living on Mount Vernon's outlying farms or off the plantation altogether. Ideas about privacy were also quite different in the eighteenth century from what they are now. At that time both children and adults often shared rooms and even beds. For example, Englishman Andrew Burnaby, who was traveling in America shortly after the Washingtons were married, told this story about the experience of another traveler:

FIG. 7. One of the bunk rooms in the wings of the reconstructed greenhouse. (Courtesy of the Mount Vernon Ladies' Association)

A gentleman some time ago travelling upon the frontiers of Virginia, where there are few settlements, was obliged to take up his quarters one evening at a miserable plantation; where, exclusive of a negro or two, the family consisted of a man and his wife, and one daughter about sixteen years of age. Being fatigued, he presently desired them to sh[o]w him where he was to sleep; accordingly they pointed to a bed in a corner of the room where they were sitting. The gentleman was a little embarrassed but, being excessively weary, he retired, half undressed himself, and got into bed. After some time the old gentlewoman came to bed to him, after her the old gentleman, and last of all the young lady. This, in a country excluded from all civilized society, could only proceed from simplicity and innocence.[11]

Almost forty years later, in the spring of 1797, three visiting members of the French royal family, accompanied by one servant, spent a few days at Mount Vernon and then continued their journey. Later, in Leesburg, Virginia, the party met a Colonel Ball, "for whom the general [Washington] had given us a letter [of introduction]." Upon reading the note, Ball, who may well have been one of Washington's maternal relatives, insisted that the Frenchmen spend the night at his home, which was three miles away.

Although they considered Colonel Ball's house "little more than a shack," the four Frenchmen were delighted that they were offered the luxury of "a room with *two* good beds, which pleased us mightily."[12] Although these examples were considered humorous, they were not out of the ordinary in eighteenth-century America. Unlike their ancestors, many modern Americans would probably have difficulty sleeping in the same bed with a total stranger at an inn, or might be uncomfortable using a chamberpot in a room where others were present, much less one of the multiseat necessaries, like those in the Mount Vernon gardens. Privacy was a very different thing in that earlier world.

In the 1950s and early 1960s, as the Mount Vernon board and staff privately aired concerns about the reconstruction of the greenhouse quarters, they began a reexamination of the surviving documentary evidence about these structures. This undertaking, however, only contributed to the internal controversy over the appearance of these reconstructed spaces. For example, during the week of April 7, 1792, a hired carpenter and slave spent six days each on "putting up the births in new Qu[arte]r" and "planing plank for the Qu[arte]r Births," while one of the bricklayers was "laying brick foundation for the Sills of the births [in the] new Qu[arte]r." The following week, one of the hired carpenters was occupied another five days "putting up the berths."[13] "Berth" seems to have been a naval term, used in the eighteenth century to mean either a room where a group of sailors lived or a sleeping space, similar to a box or shelf, for a person to sleep on. At least one staff member felt that Washington's familiarity with bunks in military barracks would naturally have led him to use a similar arrangement at Mount Vernon.[14] Another, criticizing the construction of such features in the quarters, believed that the room was probably divided lengthwise down the middle, up to about three-quarters of the room's length. This would form two "private" spaces for sleeping and a common area near the fireplace for cooking and eating.[15] After much study and reflection, the Mount Vernon Ladies' Association chose the first approach, implying a communal living arrangement, which would have afforded little privacy but would have been practical given the nature of the enslaved population—primarily single men—on the Mansion House Farm.

Despite George Augustine Washington's statement that the new quarters could house all the slaves on the Mansion House Farm, it does not appear that everyone lived in them. Some slaves resided over the outbuildings where they worked. The cook, Lucy, for example, lived with her husband, Frank Lee, and their children in rooms over the kitchen in the fall of 1793, well after the new quarters were completed.[16] There is additional evidence that other families on the Mansion House Farm had the benefit of individual cabins, which gave the residents more privacy. Boatswain, a ditcher; his wife, Myrtilla, a spinner; and their children seem to have lived in a cabin beyond the west gate (the carriage entrance to the estate). A slave named Cupid once had a separate house near the Potomac River at a place known as Hell Hole (near Mount Vernon's present-day wharf). He appears to have died before the greenhouse quarters were completed, however, and the house was torn down, so the questions of whether he would have been moved into the new brick structure or allowed to stay in the cabin, and whether the cabin was in such condition that another family could have been moved into it, are moot.[17] A number of the Washingtons' houseguests also recorded the presence of cabins, which were probably across the lane from the greenhouse complex. In describing the estate, Isaac Weld noted that off to the sides of the mansion were "on the one side . . . the different offices belonging to the house, and also to the farm, and on the other, the cabins for the SLAVES."[18] Several years later in 1799, a young English visitor described a gravel road leading to George Washington's home, "which divides when in sight of the house, the north or left hand going to the negro huts, the south or right hand to the farm yard."[19]

The standard form of slave housing on Washington's four outlying farms, as well as that of families like Boatswain and Myrtilla's at the Mansion House Farm, were described by one eighteenth-century visitor as "log houses."[20] These cabins were daubed with mud to keep out drafts and rain and often had exterior wooden chimneys, fashioned of sticks plastered with mud.[21] In a letter to one of his farm managers in 1791 about moving a house from one farm to another, Washington directed that a "brick chimney must be put to it after it gets to Dogue run instead of the wood one it now has."[22] Since a hired white man in a supervisory position had lived in this structure when it had a wooden chimney and it was now intended for use by another supervisor, the enslaved overseer Davy Gray, it is logical to conclude that the common slaves did not as a rule have brick chimneys. One advantage of these wooden chimneys was that they could be easily pushed away from the cabin in the event of a fire, such as the one that destroyed the quarters at Muddy Hole in the summer of 1758.[23] The very flimsiness of these chimneys, however, was a danger, as well. Several slave children were injured in January 1795, for example, when a chimney, probably of this type, collapsed, perhaps from fire, poor construction, or simple wear and tear. A fourth possibility is suggested by a diary entry from the spring of 1760 in which George

Washington recorded that ten slaves had been hurt, "some very bad," when the quarters at Mount Vernon were struck by lightning. Despite the severity of the injuries, everyone survived, an outcome Washington attributed to bloodletting.[24]

Two sizes of cabins served as slave quarters at Mount Vernon. In December 1793, Washington wrote his manager about moving some of the cabins and recommended that his carpenters assist in "removing the largest kind of the Negro quarters." These were likely similar to a new quarter constructed at Muddy Hole Farm in 1776, described as "built for two familys with a Chimney in the Mid[d]le." From surviving slave cabins on other plantations, it would seem that each family in this sort of duplex arrangement lived in one room. Presumably the slaves living in these double cabins, which shared a chimney in the center, had chimneys of brick or stone, which were safer and more durable than wood. The other type of cabin being moved in 1793 must have been quite tiny because Washington thought the occupants of "the smaller ones" could move their own houses "with a little assistance of Carts." The smaller cabins very likely consisted of one room and were home to only one family.[25] Some of the cabins may also have had attached sheds, perhaps as dry storage areas for fuel supplies. In discussions about construction of new "Negroe Houses" during the Revolution, Lund Washington wanted direction from his cousin on "whether you wou[l]d have them Built with or without sheds."[26] George Washington's answer does not survive, so there is no way of knowing what he decided.

None of the slave cabins on the Mount Vernon estate have survived. An early twentieth-century photograph exists, however, showing what is said to be a slave dwelling on one of Washington's outlying farms. This log structure is a single-family cabin with a door centered on one side and a window directly to its right. A second window is visible at the end of the half-story loft. There is no way to tell from the photograph what the size of the building was, but some indication of its measurements may be gained from a 1793 description of the homes of two of Washington's enslaved black overseers. In a letter to an English friend, the American president discussed renting four of the farms that made up the Mount Vernon estate and detailed the facilities at each. The dimensions of the quarters for the black overseers at both Dogue Run and Muddy Hole Farms were described as being about sixteen by twenty feet. Divided into one room on the ground floor, with a one-room loft above, these cabins had a total living space of 640 square feet.[27] This would have made them considerably more spacious than the

FIG. 8. Early twentieth-century photograph of a slave cabin on one of the outlying farms. (Courtesy of the Mount Vernon Ladies' Association)

cabin, described in an advertisement as ten by twenty-four feet (480 square feet of living space), intended for the overseer on a Richmond County plantation in 1765.[28]

The Mount Vernon slave cabins were roughly comparable in size to slave quarters on other Virginia plantations. Along Monticello's Mulberry Row, for instance, the slave dwellings standing in 1796 varied in size from 20½ × 12 feet down to 12 × 14 feet, and featured dirt floors and wooden chimneys. At Landon Carter's plantation, Sabine Hall, an enslaved married couple lived in a cabin described as being only twelve by twelve feet. In fact, the majority of Americans of this period, not just slaves, lived in spaces that would seem incredibly small to their twenty-first century descendants. A 1785 survey of dwellings in southwestern Virginia, primarily the homes of middle-class white farmers, reveals that three-quarters of these buildings were simple wooden cabins ranging in size from sixteen by twenty to sixteen by twelve feet.[29] The typical eighteenth-century house in New England was one to one-and-a-half stories tall and measured ten by fourteen to sixteen by sixteen feet.[30] These small dwellings could well seem almost palatial to working-class residents of cities like Philadelphia, where two families might share the 432 square feet of living space available in the two stories of a 12 × 18-foot tenement.[31]

Both single and double cabins of the type used at Mount Vernon were common throughout the South. For example, a British prisoner of war held at a plantation outside of Charlottesville, Virginia, left a description of the quarters there, which were similar to those at Mount Vernon: "The houses are most of them built of wood, the roof being covered with shingles, and not always lathed and plastered within, only those of the better sort that are finished in that manner, and painted on the outside; the chimneys are often of brick, but the generality of them are wood, coated in the inside with clay; the windows of the better sort are glazed, the rest have only wooden shutters."[32]

Evidence from several documentary sources indicates that the cabins used by the Mount Vernon slaves were often poorly constructed. Lund Washington admitted in the fall of 1775 that "some of our Negroe Quarters are so very Bad, that I am oblige[d] to have them mended, so as to last this Winter."[33] Almost twenty years later, George Washington drew up a list of tasks for his carpenters, including a note that work needed to be done on the quarters at Dogue Run, where "some of the People . . . complain much of the Leakiness of their Houses."[34] The French prince Louis-Philippe recorded in the spring of 1797 that the slaves were "housed in wretched wooden shacks," while Julian Niemcewicz expressed the opinion that the "huts" could not even be called "by the name of houses. They are more miserable than the most miserable of the cottages of our peasants" back in Poland.[35] Not only were such cabins leaky and drafty, they were also dangerous. Farm manager Anthony Whiting informed Washington in the winter of 1793 that he was having the carpenters move a house, formerly used by one of the hired whites, to Muddy Hole Farm, where it would replace the one where Davy Gray, the enslaved overseer, and his family were living. The manager felt this move necessary because he was "fearfull that house of Davids Will fall if a high wind should happen and that if that Should be the case and any of the family in it may cost them there lives."[36]

Living Conditions in and around the Quarters

Regrettably, few contemporary sources give an idea of what the interior spaces of the Mount Vernon quarters were like in the eighteenth century. Perhaps the most important was left by Polish visitor Julian Niemcewicz in June 1798. While touring the estate, he stopped by the slave quarters at

Union Farm and recorded the following scene: "We entered one of the huts of the Blacks. . . . The husband and wife sleep on a mean pallet, the children on the ground; a very bad fireplace, some utensils for cooking, but in the middle of this poverty some cups and a teapot."[37] Although this description is of a cabin on one of the outlying farms, there is no reason to think that, other than the sleeping arrangements, the situation would have been very much different in the more substantial type of quarters at the Mansion House Farm. Nor were they vastly different from the furnishings of quarters in the next century. A Scotsman visiting in the Mount Vernon neighborhood in the 1820s wandered into at least two sets of slave cabins. At the first, located about ten miles from Washington's estate, he found "nothing resembling a table," while at the second, where he described the cabins as "wretched receptacles," he noted a pile of "rags on the floor" that served for a bed. As he wandered through about a dozen cabins, the visitor realized that there were differences. Some cabins were locked while others were not. Looking through "holes in the walls" of the locked cabins, presumably places where the mud chinking had fallen out, he noticed that the interiors of those were "a little cleaner, and in better order." This finding led him to the realization that "even in such slavery, there were grades of comfort, and enjoyment."[38] It also serves as a reminder that the inhabitants of those cabins were unique individuals with their own preferences and personalities.

Niemcewicz's rather bleak picture is reinforced by other sources, which indirectly describe the living conditions in the quarters as smoky and dirty. Lund Washington, for example, wrote his cousin late in 1775 to discuss a number of issues relating to management of the estate. He mentioned that there had been a problem with one of the chimneys in the mansion that was smoking and complained, "(The Sellar, new Room [Study] and dineg Room) they really smoke'd so Bad that the walls lookd as bad as any negroe Quarter."[39] More than twenty years later, George Washington expressed concern about the cleanliness of the quarters. He suggested that his farm manager keep a close watch on all aspects of the slaves' lives and specifically mentioned "inspecting the Negro quarters, as well for the purpose of detecting improper conduct in them; as to see if they are kept clean (being conducive to their health)."[40] Practices ordered by Washington during his years with the army to improve health in camp could well have been used in the quarters at Mount Vernon. These included such things as putting at least two windows in each cabin, increasing ventilation in the summer months by pulling the mud chinking from between the logs forming the walls, and burning a musket cartridge or tar in the huts each day to "purify the Air."[41]

The quarters were also dark. The glazed windows in the greenhouse complex were small and would not have let in much light. The situation would have been even worse on the outlying farms, where the windows were very likely just shuttered openings, which were kept closed in cold weather. While Niemcewicz made no mention of lighting devices (as a daytime visitor, he might easily have overlooked them), it is highly likely that the fireplace provided the only source of artificial light. Sewing and other sorts of close work would have been difficult to do indoors. As with so many other aspects of slave life at Mount Vernon, these dark quarters were not unusual. In the early 1830s, for example, at Woodlawn Plantation, the home of Nelly Custis Lewis, a slave woman named Sukey was confined to bed during the last months of her pregnancy. A seamstress, she struggled to make clothes for her mistress's grandchildren, her progress hampered by the lack of light. According to Lewis, "She is making the little shirts but until the weather is warm enough to have the door & window open in the quarter, she cannot see to hemstitch or tuck very nicely."[42]

Furnishings

As was true elsewhere in Virginia, the quarters of the Mount Vernon slaves were furnished with the few possessions they were given by the Washingtons or could acquire for themselves. Historians studying the records of eighteenth- and nineteenth-century Virginia stores have discovered a great deal of evidence about both the people engaged in such transactions and the kinds of goods provided to enslaved customers. Using money they had earned (see the next chapter for a discussion of the ways slaves acquired money) or goods they produced themselves as a means of barter, enslaved men were three times more likely to be store customers than women, and most of the customers at these local stores were either elderly or young men without children. Only a few of the slaves frequenting the shops had children younger than ten, suggesting that families with young children were either using all the foods and goods they produced themselves, leaving them with nothing to trade or barter, or that caring for young children took up any free hours that would otherwise have been used to produce marketable products. Textiles were frequently purchased and included such items as finer quality fabrics than were used for slave garments issued on the plantation, ribbons (used for decorating hair, clothing, and jewelry), small amounts of lace, handkerchiefs, stockings, gloves, bonnets, and hats. There were also purchases of materials—thread, thimbles, and carding combs—for making clothing, purses, or other sorts of things from fabric or for processing raw materials to make textiles. Besides clothing, necklaces, beads, shoes, and other items for personal adornment could be acquired from stores. Among the household goods shopkeepers supplied to slaves were a variety of objects including knives and forks, coverlets, jars, and ceramic dishes. Cheap mirrors, which had both practical, everyday functions as well as spiritual uses (in African and African American traditions, mirrors were used to capture, attract, or repel spirits, and also could give the ability to see into the future) were another favorite item in this category. Among the more unexpected items were almanacs, fiddle strings, paper, and penknives. Rum was popular among white and enslaved customers. Food items purchased in stores included sweeteners (sugar and molasses), chocolate, pepper, and alcohol. In the words of historian Ann Smart Martin, the last served as "an escape from the grueling workaday world, a means of socializing, a medicine, and a caloric supplement."[43]

Archaeological evidence from the cellar of the House for Families clearly shows that the slaves, at least at Washington's Mansion House Farm, used a variety of ceramics for food service and possibly storage. Among the vessels excavated from the cellar were fragments of mugs and cups, teapots, bowls, plates and saucers, jugs, and jars, in materials ranging from coarse earthenware and colonoware—a type of pottery possibly made by local Indians or even by the Mount Vernon slaves themselves—to slipware, tin-glazed earthenware, refined earthenware, creamware, pearlware, Rhenish stoneware, brown stoneware, and even Chinese porcelain. Slightly more than a quarter of all the ceramics found at the site were a type of white salt-glazed stoneware, used on the Washingtons' dinner table for about a decade beginning in the late 1750s.[44] Although the cups and teapot found by Niemcewicz at Union Farm in 1798 may have been purchased by the slave family themselves, their presence in the cabin might also imply that it was not just the slaves at the Mansion House Farm who benefited from donations of used, damaged, or out-of-date belongings from the master's family. Other objects found in the cellar of the House for Families, which would probably have been seen in the living areas of the quarters, were tobacco pipes; some glassware, including both wine bottles and stemware; bone-handled table knives and pewter spoons; cooking implements such as an iron pothook and fragments of an iron pot; chamberpots of both stoneware and earthenware; marbles; beads; different types of buckles and jewelry; numerous buttons; part of a bone brush; and finally gun flints and lead shot, indicating the presence of guns. While some of these objects

FIG. 9. Mended fragments of a colonoware bowl excavated at Mount Vernon. (Courtesy of the Mount Vernon Ladies' Association)

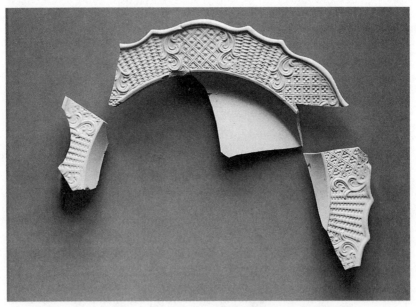

FIG. 10. Fragments of a white salt-glazed stoneware plate excavated from a slave quarter at Mount Vernon. (Courtesy of the Mount Vernon Ladies' Association)

may have been hand-me-downs from the mansion, still others could have been purchased with money earned through the sale of produce or small, homemade things like brooms. They might even have been stolen.[45]

Occasional hints as to other types of objects in the quarters can be found in George Washington's correspondence. For example, when Austin, one of the house servants, died around Christmas 1794 as he was heading to Mount Vernon from the executive mansion in Philadelphia, the tavern keeper at whose establishment he died sent Washington a list of the things Austin had had with him. Among them was a piece of luggage, variously described as a "Portmanteau" or "Valice," in which, Washington surmised, he probably was "carrying things home for his wife."[46]

Blankets

In the winter, the inhabitants of the quarters were probably quite cold. None of the living spaces in any of the three types of housing provided on the estate had more than one fireplace. To compound the problem of keeping warm, except in the case of new mothers, the slaves received at most only one blanket per year. Although these seem to have been distributed in the fall, the records are unclear as to whether everyone got one annually. In discussing the distribution of blankets in 1787, Washington complained that the prices were very high in Philadelphia, "and yet this is the year that *all* my people are entitled to receive them," implying that in other years not everyone was owed one. Similarly, several years later, Washington wrote, rather ambiguously, "All my People that want blankets (or rather all that are entitled to them) must be supplied."[47]

Apparently no attempt was made to manufacture slave blankets on the estate. Washington ordered these "dutch, or Strip'd Blanketts" from England and from American merchants in large cities up and down the Atlantic coast, and often had a difficult time finding what he wanted in the way of quality at what he considered a fair price and in sufficient quantity—in the mid-1780s, he was ordering about two hundred per year—before the temperature became chilly. For instance, he asked a northern friend for help finding blankets in the fall of 1791, and to "forward them by the first vessel which is bound to Alexandria as my Negros are teasing me for them, and the season will soon make them necessary."[48]

Storage and tracking of blankets after they arrived at Mount Vernon were among Martha Washington's responsibilities. George wrote his nephew from the Constitutional Convention in 1787 to ask that he "send me the number of New blankets your Aunt has in her Store room."[49] An undated account of the blanket distribution sometime between January 1794 and December 1796 shows that Mount Vernon purchased 150 "Large Striped Blankets" and an equal number of small striped blankets. Of those, 173 were given out in the following manner: 54 to slaves at the Mansion House Farm, 34 to Union Farm, 25 to Dogue Run Farm, 24 to Muddy Hole Farm, and another 36 at River Farm. Two more were delivered to individual slaves—Sarah and Agnes at Dogue Run—at a later time.[50]

The blankets may have been used on mattresses made of linen. In August 1784, for instance, twenty yards of linen were purchased "for Bed Ticks" for the servants, although, especially given the relatively small quantity, these were most likely intended for the hired white servants, such as the house-keeper and gardener.[51] The bedding materials used by the slaves were prob-ably similar to those on which Washington's soldiers slept during the Revo-lution. A general order from the last year of the war indicates the types of things that may have been gathered to provide a comfortable night's sleep: "The General is desirous the troops should make themselves as comfortable as possible while in the field; the encampment itself is very pleasant and healthy, straw will be issued at the rate of two bundles pr. tent, of this with the flaggs [reeds or rushes] and leaves which may be procured, convenient Matts or bedding may be formed."[52]

Sadly, Washington sometimes required the slaves to use their blankets for purposes which could, at worst, cause damage and, at best, make them terribly dirty. Several days before his death, for example, he spelled out for his farm manager the proper steps to be taken in caring for his livestock during the winter. After stressing that the stables and farm pens "ought to be kept well littered," he directed that "*Leaves,* and such spoiled Straw or weeds as will not do for food" were to be gathered for the stables, and leaves and cornstalks for the pens. In order to carry out this task, Washington ordered that "the People, with their blankets, go every evening, or as often as occasion may require, to the nearest wood and fill them with leaves for the purposes above mentioned; bottoming the beds [for the animals] with Corn Stalks, and covering them *thick* with leaves." He went on to say that doing this would, "if strictly attended to, and punctually performed, [be] of great utility in every point of view. It will save food, [m]ake the Cattle lay warm and comfortable, and produce much manure. The Hogs also in pens must be well bedded in leaves."[53] While the animals were probably very comfortable with care of this sort, one can only imagine the feelings of the enslaved people who had to use their one blanket for hauling livestock bedding.

To maintain body heat at night, slaves slept in their clothing. While traveling as a young man, Washington complained of weather and lodgings so cold that he had "never had my cloth[e]s of[f] but lay and sleep in them like a Negro." Two other strategies he used at the same time may also have been used by his slaves. Necessity forced him to stay with several lower-class white families on his journey, with whom he "lay down before the fire upon a Little Hay Straw Fodder or bairskin whichever is to be had with Man Wife and Children like a Parcel of Dogs or Catts and happy's he that gets the Birth nearest the fire."[54]

Clothing

The clothing found in the slave quarters was a combination of the rather basic items provided by the Washingtons and perhaps nicer things acquired by the slaves themselves. Among Washington's earliest letters is one dating to 1755, when he was on the frontier during the Braddock Campaign and wrote to remind his younger brother, who was managing Mount Vernon, that the slave clothing was a priority and that he should "employ Cleo's leisure hour's in mak'g them."[55] Prior to the Revolution, on at least one occasion George Washington paid a hired tailor at nearby Gum Spring for cutting out clothing for his slaves.[56] As prices went up during the war, because of a scarcity of imported cloth, the financial burden of clothing the large enslaved population at Mount Vernon was a matter of concern to Washington, who wrote a telling letter to his manager in December 1776:

> I think if there can be any possible shift made, without buying Linnen for the Negros at the enormous price you speak of, it ought to be attempted, as the price is too heavy to be borne with (if it be possible to avoid it) without making the poor Negros suffer too much—this I would not do to save any expence, as they certainly have a just claim to their Victuals and cloaths, if they make enough to purchase them.[57]

The basic clothing issued annually to enslaved people on Mount Vernon's outlying farms was comparable to that provided to slaves on other Virginia plantations at the time. Men received one wool jacket, one pair of wool breeches, two coarse linen shirts (presumably one for wearing and one for washing), one to two pairs of stockings (seemingly depending on a person's occupation), and one pair of shoes each for winter, with an additional pair of linen breeches for summer. The women each got one wool jacket, one wool skirt, two coarse linen shifts (again, one to be worn while the other was being washed), one pair of stockings, one pair of shoes for winter, and a linen skirt for the summer.[58]

One article of clothing often associated with African American women, the headscarf, does not appear to have been worn regularly in Virginia in the eighteenth century. In the fall of 1788, poet and diplomat David Humphreys was staying at Mount Vernon to draft a biography of George Washington. While there, Humphreys wrote to Thomas Jefferson about a recent visit by Eléanor François Elie, the Comte de Moustier, who was the French minister to the United States, his sister, and her son during which the local ladies were scandalized when the sister, Anne Flore Millet, the Marquise de Brehan, attended a social function wearing "a three-cornered muslin Handkerchief tied round her head, nearly in the fashion of the Negroe Women in the West Indies."[59]

Although the surviving documentation does not always show summer clothing being given out at Mount Vernon, it was definitely being ordered. As fall approached in 1759, for example, Washington asked his British agent to send "40 Yds course Jeans [a cotton fabric] or fustian [a blended linen and cotton fabric] for Summer Frocks for Negroe Servts." The order was shipped from England in March 1760. Almost thirty years later, Washington wrote to ask his agent in Philadelphia for a large quantity of British and German Osnabrig, a coarse, unbleached, plain-weave linen or hemp, "suitable for making Negroes shirts & shifts—a kind of Rolls [linen] proper for summer Petticoats & Trousers."[60]

Considering the Virginia climate, the summer clothing issued to enslaved women might have been considerably more comfortable than the multiple layers, including corsets or stays, worn by white women of the period. Within the context of the culture, however, being seen in public without a set of stays and a jacket or bodice not only emphasized the women's lack of social status but may have left them feeling physically vulnerable as well.[61] The limited number of clothes given annually to each person meant that for many months, people would be wearing fabrics that were worn, perhaps enough to see through, ripped, and tattered, a fact noted by visitors to the South, like the Italian count who wrote of rural Maryland in 1784, "Here one starts seeing the Negroes in rags and children of twelve or thirteen years almost entirely naked."[62] This too would have increased the uneasiness and sense of exposure by women and young teenagers.

Considerable fabric was needed for clothing the slaves each year. By the mid-1780s, the slaves on the estate were themselves producing enough coarse woolen cloth to supply most of the needs for that fabric. Washington informed an Alexandria neighbor in December 1785 that he was looking to buy a variety of fabrics, primarily linens, as well as some ready-made goods such as felt hats, buttons, and hose "for my Negroes," but "you will perceive no mention is made of coarse Woolens; because of these I manufacture a sufficiency to clothe my out-door Negroes."[63] As indicated by this letter, however, linen was another matter entirely. Averaging 3½ yards of Osnabrig for each adult man's shirt, 3 yards for each boy-sized shirt, 3 yards for each adult woman's shift, and 2½ to 3 yards for each girl's shift, in 1794 alone it took almost 800 yards of material just to provide these two types of basic garments for slaves on the four outlying farms.[64] The total amount of linen on hand for making slave clothing—not just shirts and shifts but also summer-weight breeches and skirts—was over 1,400 yards that year.[65] In the summer before Washington's death, his farm manager estimated that it cost two pounds to clothe each adult slave per year, while the annual expense for clothing each infant or small child was a mere two shillings.[66]

Those children who were old enough to work appear to have gotten similar clothing but not necessarily in the same quantity provided the adults. For example, two boys, Peter and Adam at River Farm, as well as other boys at Muddy Hole and Dogue Run received the same clothing allowance as the men on that farm in 1774. A girl, Else, at Muddy Hole, however, only got one shirt that same year; a boy named Paul at the Ferry Plantation was issued only a jacket, breeches, and shirt; a girl called Fanny at the same farm just got a jacket, skirt, and two shifts; and another girl, Sukey, at the mill was the recipient of a jacket and shirt.[67]

Those slaves whose work brought them into regular contact with visitors, either at Mount Vernon or in the presidential household, received clothing that was better in both quality and style—and more of it—than the fieldworkers. The men who worked in the mansion as butlers, waiters, and body servants, as well as the drivers and postilions on the family carriage would have stood out because of their clothing. They typically wore a distinctive uniform, known as livery, which was based on the three-piece suit of an eighteenth-century gentleman and would have included a coat, waistcoat or vest, and breeches. Livery was usually made of fine wool in the colors of the slave owner's coat of arms and edged with woven "livery lace."[68] George Washington's first surviving order for livery dates to the end of 1755, when he asked his British agent to send "2 Compleat Livery Suits for Servants" with enough extra cloth to make a second set for each man: "I wou'd have you choose the livery by our Arms; only, as the Field of the Arms is white[,] I think the Cloaths had better not be quite so.... The Trimmings

FIG. II. Engraving of *The Washington Family* by Edward Savage, showing a slave in livery and with his hair in a queue to the far right, 1798. (Courtesy of the Mount Vernon Ladies' Association)

and Facings of Scarlet, and a Scarlet Waistcoat. . . . If Livery Lace is not quite disus'd, I shou[l]d be glad to have these Cloaths Laced. I like that fashion best. [A]nd two Silver lac'd Hats for the above L[iver]y."[69]

This, an off-white suit trimmed with red and a red vest, would be the basic look of the Washington livery for the remainder of the century. A slave wearing this type of clothing can be seen on the far right of Edward Savage's well-known and much-copied painting *The Washington Family,* which was completed in 1796, forty-one years after George Washington's initial order.[70] At least one male house servant at Mount Vernon wore the livery of a different family—the Custises. Julius, who was the body servant of Martha Washington's son, John Parke Custis, was dressed in livery "suited to the Arms of the Custis Family," which was "blew."[71]

Looking at the clothing provided for just one person, Austin, who worked on both the carriage and in the mansion over the course of his life, the records indicate that he was given his first suit of livery in 1776, made by Washington's indentured English tailor, Andrew Judge.[72] Later that same year, Austin received another coat and pair of breeches, as well as a surtout or overcoat. Over the next six years, Austin was provided with a fustian coat and pair of shoes (1777); a suit and a pair of boots (1778); a suit and a great coat (1781); and a suit of livery, a pair of leather breeches, presumably for wear when working with the horses and carriage at the stable, and a hat (1782). Money was also spent by the Washingtons for repairs to the young man's clothing.[73] During the presidency, Austin received four pairs of stockings in 1789; 3 shirts in 1790; four pairs of stockings and two pair of hose in 1793; and eleven shirts, an unknown quantity of stockings, and a pair of shoes in 1794 (Austin died in December of the latter year).[74]

The household maids also received finer quality clothing than enslaved female laborers. An order to Washington's English agent in November 1762 requested, among many other things, that "4 Silver Bobs for Servants" be sent to Mount Vernon; the invoice sent with the completed order describes them as "4 pr Silver Ear[r]ings with Bobs" (pendants), presumably for the female house servants.[75] Three decades later, Oney Judge and Molly, maids taken to work in the presidential household, were given the following items during Washington's first term: fabric and money for making gowns, probably similar in style to those worn by the ladies in the Washington family (the fabrics included calico—a cotton fabric from India—linen, and cotton); 5 yards of lawn (a light, plain-weave fabric, "considered the finest of the white linens"), possibly for making fichus or handkerchiefs to cover the shoulders and bosoms of women in low-cut dresses but perhaps also used for aprons and caps or ruffles on a gown; stockings; cotton hose; linen fabric; shoes (one of these purchases was for cloth shoes); and "habbits" (a two-piece outfit, generally a short gown and petticoat, of matching fabric).[76] During Washington's second term the women received 14½ yards of checked fabric, probably used for utilitarian clothing (aprons, kerchiefs, and linings); stockings and shoes; a bonnet for Oney; gowns; and spectacles for Moll.[77]

Some of the slaves may have received extra clothing in the form of hand-me-downs from the Washington family. In Hannah Bushrod Washington's last will and testament, the dying woman decreed that "all my wearing apparel of every sort . . . be entirely and equally divided" among her three granddaughters. She noted, however, that "some of my most indifferent things" might be given to slaves Letty, Jenny, Suck, and Venus, "though the two last mentioned treated me with great disrespect in my last hours."[78] Although there is no direct evidence of George and Martha Washington passing old or "indifferent" clothes on to their slaves, the fact that this was done by other members of the family indicates that it was certainly a possibility and the kind of casual action that might not have been documented.

The majority of the enslaved population at Mount Vernon received their new shoes in the late fall or early winter. Among the records of goods issued from the Circle Storehouse in November 1795 were the following distributions of shoes: thirty-seven pairs to River Farm; thirty-seven pairs to Union Farm; twenty-five pairs to Dogue Run; twenty-three pairs to Muddy Hole Farm; thirty-five pairs for the artisans and other men on the Mansion House Farm; and six pairs for boys, roughly eighteen for women, and four for girls, presumably also at the Mansion House Farm.[79] Certain individuals, primarily skilled slaves or those who worked in and around the mansion, were given additional—probably better quality—shoes through-out the year. For example, on May 11, 1796, bricklayers Tom Davis and Billy Mucles and carpenters James and Sambo Anderson each received another pair of shoes.[80] Marcus, who waited on the table in the mansion, was the re-cipient of "one pair fine Shoes" from the firm of Josiah Faxon & Company on March 1, 1799.[81] In January 1800, one of the maids named Molly got "one pair Strong Shoes," which cost eighty-four cents.[82]

Given the small number of clothes issued each year, the garments worn by slaves were often dirty and torn. A French visitor to Mount Vernon in 1797 said that the quarters he saw in Virginia were swarming with little children in "rags that our own beggars would scorn to wear."[83] Another guest noted that he found the rooms at Mount Vernon small, and while everything about the mansion was clean, the servants "were dirty in dress."[84] If this was true of the servants in and about the mansion house, the condi-tion of the clothes worn on the outlying farms was probably much worse.

Yards and Gardens

The size, crowding, and darkness of the quarters would have been mitigated to a large degree by use of the yards surrounding them as additional living and work space. Studies of African American yards belonging to both enslaved and freed people show that they served a variety of functions, including socializing, doing chores (spinning, sewing, cooking, laundry, and raising and butchering animals), and serving as a play space for children and as a site for kitchen gardens. These uses reflect back to the role of yards in West Africa. According to archaeologist Barbara J. Heath, "historically in West Africa, yards were used for work, for the raising of poultry, for gardening, for socializing, and sometimes as repositories for the dead. Such patterns are seen to have continued as West Africans were brought to the Caribbean and the American South in bondage." Typically kept clean by sweeping, yards often featured ornamental plantings or were decorated in ways that made them spiritually meaningful, through the use of such things as bottle trees (either real or artificial trees ornamented with bottles and other sorts of containers and meaningful objects), intended to lure evil spirits into them, "where they cannot get out again."[85]

Evidence of the slaves' entrepreneurial activities could be seen in the grounds surrounding their homes. Near the quarters were small gardens for growing vegetables to supplement not only their diet but also their income. Various sorts of domesticated fowl would have had free run about the buildings. Outside of the "hut" at Union Farm, Julian Niemcewicz saw a "very small garden planted with vegetables . . . with 5 or 6 hens, each one leading ten to fifteen chickens." He noted that these animals were sold by the slaves in Alexandria to "procure for themselves a few amenities," which may have been anything from food luxuries such as tea or sugar to ceramics or an article of clothing.[86]

A number of other animals also inhabited the quarters. Rat and mouse remains found in the cellar of the House for Families reflect the unhealthful presence of these creatures in the quarters, while the discovery of cat bones suggests one means used by the slaves to try to deal with household vermin.[87] In addition to keeping cats to control the rodent population, the Mount Vernon slaves also raised dogs, perhaps for companionship, but also to assist them in hunting. George Washington found his slaves' ownership of dogs problematic, something discussed in detail elsewhere, and periodically ordered that those animals be exterminated.[88]

Rats appear to have been a fact of life in log structures, regardless of the social status or race of the inhabitants. A British officer imprisoned near Charlottesville recorded what life was like in a log building infested with these rodents: "The barracks swarm with rats of an enormous size, and notwithstanding each hut has a cat or two, they are very troublesome, and with every precaution, they are continually destroying the men's cloaths and bedding during the night; it is no very uncommon thing to see them running six or seven, one after the other, in the interstices of the logs with which the huts are constructed."[89]

In their search for food, rats could destroy more than textiles. During a stay with the family of a white quarrier near Stafford, Virginia, in the early nineteenth century, architect Benjamin Henry Latrobe found that rats could also ruin a person's sleep. A colony of rats living in the two-story log house discovered a basket of eggs placed under Latrobe's bed and, as he described the scene:

Storming the basket threw off the covering and got out all the eggs. . . . They covered the floor with the shells and the marks of their gluttony. Upstairs, a negro girl had laid down to sleep, with a piece of Hoecake in her hand. The rats having sufficiently regaled upon eggs made the discovery, and one of them carried off the bread. He was pursued by others who gallopped over the girl without ceremony, waked her, and set her crying. . . . The rat darted into the open drawer of a writing desk which stood on the table, and was drawn out over the edge of it. His weight overset the desk and it fell on the floor, shutting up the rat in the drawer. The noise and the cries of the girl waked every body. Mr. Robertson groped about, got hold of the desk, and in opening the drawer his finger was bit by the rat, who then made his escape. . . . There was an end of all possibility of sleeping for the remainder of the night.[90]

Health Issues

Living conditions in the quarters may have led to several types of health problems for the Mount Vernon slaves. While all of these conditions affected the white population as well, slaves' close quarters tended to encourage the spread of disease and made any sickness a community problem. Although they could not have realized why, the Washingtons considered overcrowding a "very great cause" of disease, which may have kept the quarters from becoming as crowded as they might otherwise have been.[91] Both George and Martha Washington had firsthand knowledge of how fast infectious diseases could race through a community. On January 1, 1760, Martha Washington came down with measles; within just three days, her life was despaired of and a minister was called. She was not, however, the only person at Mount Vernon to be afflicted. Several slaves had measles within two days of her getting sick, and several weeks later a slave from an outlying farm who brought some hogs to Washington contracted the disease as well. About this same time, George Washington received a letter from the overseer managing one of his quarters near Winchester that there was smallpox in the area. Within three months, smallpox was raging on his western lands, killing at least one overseer and two slaves.[92]

Immune to smallpox after contracting it as a young man, Washington traveled to these distant quarters, finding everything there in a state of "utmost confusion, disorder & backwardness." He soon had "Got Blankets and every other requisite . . . and settl[e]d things upon the best footing I cou[l]d to prev[en]t the Small Pox from Spreading—and in case of its spreading, for the care of the Negroes." He arranged to have new patients isolated from the rest of the population and a nurse to come in to look after them.[93] Some years later, perhaps as a means of preventing the spread of disease and to ensure more efficient care, Washington planned to use one of the new outbuildings in the courtyard by the mansion at Mount Vernon as a hospital for sick slaves.[94]

Smallpox again became a major issue for Washington during the Revolution. While there had been isolated outbreaks of smallpox in North America prior to the Revolution, for the most part the majority of the colonists who lived on isolated farms had never been exposed to the disease. The arrival in the country of large numbers of soldiers from Britain and Germany, where smallpox was endemic, meant that it began to spread throughout the American population. Believing that the viability of his army was threatened, Washington eventually set up a system to ensure that new recruits were inoculated with smallpox upon their enlistment, at the same time that they were being outfitted with uniforms and weapons. In this way they contracted a milder form of the disease than if they had contracted it naturally. They were consequently completely well by the time they marched off to join the main part of the army.[95]

During the early years of the war, Washington took a positive step to see that his plantation would never again be threatened by smallpox, when he ordered the inoculation of all his slaves. He was able to report to a relative that "my whole Family, I understand, are likely to get well through the disorder with no other assistance than that of Doctor Lund." Away from home with the Continental Army at the time, he assured his brother that if he had still been a member of the Virginia legislature, he would work "for a Law to compel the Masters of Families to inoculate every Child born within a certain limitted time under severe Penalties."[96] By the late 1780s, a French visitor to Mount Vernon recorded that Washington himself said that "he makes it a practice to have all his Negroes inoculated, and that he never lost one in the operation."[97] Great care still had to be taken when inoculating newly hired workmen and their families, however, because the light case of smallpox resulting from the procedure was communicable and could threaten the lives of slave children who had not yet been inoculated.[98] Unfortunately, there was little or nothing that could be done to prevent other infectious diseases, like an outbreak of influenza in the summer of 1790, when Washington's farm manager wrote that "many of the Negroes have and are confined with this troublesome Influenza."[99]

Fleas were probably present in the Mount Vernon quarters in significant numbers, attracted by rodent, feline, and canine hosts but not averse to taking up with humans. Not only were fleas a nuisance, they could transmit typhus, a disease marked by the rather generic symptoms of chills; severe headache; pain in the back, arms, and legs; fever; and sometimes coughing and vomiting.[100] While there are no specific references to typhus among George Washington's slaves, they did suffer from agues and fevers, some of which may have been caused by typhus.[101] Although Washington and his contemporaries often blamed wet summers for the agues and fevers, these warm, humid climatic conditions simply contributed to the development of the insects, which actually caused the problems.[102] In addition to typhus, agues and fevers may also have been symptoms of malaria or yellow fever, both acquired through contact with mosquitoes, which were prevalent along the river and in the marshy lands making up the Mount Vernon estate, such as Hell Hole. The slaves had contact with mosquitoes while working outdoors, and while indoors, unscreened windows meant that there would have been no relief from either mosquitoes or flies during warmer months. The latter could bring with them either typhoid fever or dysentery.[103] The "cure" for several of these debilitating conditions, characterized by the vague symptoms of chills and fever, could be almost as unpleasant as the disease. Washington suggested to one of his managers that agues and fevers be treated "after the third fit, or as soon as it intermits regularly," with "care" and an emetic to make the sufferer vomit. He had found this treatment so effective that often "the Bark" (quinine) and other medicines were unnecessary.[104]

Domestic animals likely transmitted intestinal parasites, such as roundworms, to their human owners. Both dogs and cats as well as free-roaming fowl would leave feces in the yards of the quarters, which would in turn attract more flies. One historian suggests that perhaps as many as half of the slaves in Virginia prior to the Civil War had had worms at some point in their lives.[105] There are several references to intestinal worms at Mount Vernon, one of which involved an enslaved child, Ariona, who was so ill in the spring of 1778 that her life was despaired of. Lund Washington wrote that "worms I believe is the cause of its illness." Slaves suffering from worms may have been treated with Martha Washington's remedy, which was passed down in the family for several generations. It called for putting one ounce of seeds from the wormseed plant (a perennial whose flowers and fruit are helpful in paralyzing and expelling both roundworms and threadworms and sometimes work against tapeworms and hookworms), half an ounce of rhubarb (the root of which has a laxative effect), and a tablespoon of garlic into a pint bottle filled with either wine or whiskey. After letting this mixture stand for a few days, the bottle was shaken well and the contents strained. A five-year-old child would be dosed with a small teaspoonful of the liquid, smaller children with less, and, presumably, an older child or adult would be given a larger amount. An early manuscript cookbook inherited by Martha Washington from the family of her first husband mentions that a medicinal lotion known as "oyle of worm wood," which could be made at home, was also effective against parasitic worms when applied to the stomach. In addition to wormwood, a common garden herb called tansy was known to kill worms.[106]

While the worms themselves were not fatal—something that was not realized at the time—the nutrients they took from the bodies of their young hosts weakened the children and made them more vulnerable to other diseases.[107] As with other medical conditions in the eighteenth century, there was no understanding of where the worms came from. In the case of her niece's children, Martha Washington believed overeating to be a principal cause. One wonders how she explained the presence of worms in a slave child, whose opportunities for overindulgence ranged from few and far between to nonexistent.[108]

Firewood, Water, and Necessaries

Supplies of both water and wood were readily available near the slave dwellings, at least on the Mansion House Farm. George Washington noted in the fall of 1793 that there was no reason for the slave children to come into the yards near the mansion, where their playing damaged his shrubs, because they had "wood, Water, &ct at their own doors without."[109] Manager George Augustine Washington had placed the well for the new quarter directly opposite "the center of the Green House," which would have been equally convenient for all the residents of the new quarter.[110] These practical considerations were probably similar on the four outlying farms as well. In a passage on the rearrangement of the quarters and the construction of a new house for the overseer at Union Farm, George Washington directed that a well with a pump be placed in the barn lane, "exactly half way between" the overseer's dwelling and the slave quarters situated directly across the path.[111]

Both children too young to work and adults who were physically frail, perhaps because they were elderly or recuperating from a sickness or pregnancy, supplied water for those who were working all day. When a well was repaired at the Mansion House quarter, Washington expressed concern that the mechanical components work easily, in order that "the Children, or weak people about the Quarter" would be able to draw water for themselves. In addition, certain slaves gathered wood for the rest of the community, making one less housekeeping chore to be done in the evening after long days of work. At Union Farm, one week in February, for instance, a cart spent four days "hauling wood for the people."[112]

Necessaries (outhouses) were also placed conveniently near the new Mansion House Farm quarters for the use of the inhabitants. In June 1791, Washington made up a list of carpentry work to be done on the estate, which included "building a Necessary, with two Seats for the use of the New Quarter" with materials salvaged from the demolition of the old House for Families.[113] Several years later, another necessary was constructed. In his instructions for building it, Washington again exhibited a concern for the cleanliness and consequent healthfulness of the quarters:

> Place it . . . in the drain that leads from the old brick kiln back of the Well, towards the gully leading towards the gate; that, having this advantage the offensive matter might be washed off by the Rain water that collects in the gutter. I wish you would have this done before I come home that the yard of the Quarter may be always clean and Sweet. . . . Order the other two to be well cleaned and kept in good order.[114]

Excavation of the cellar of the old House for Families revealed the presence of several types of stoneware and earthenware chamberpots, indicating that at night, at least on the Mansion House Farm, the slaves made other arrangements to prevent a trek in the dark to the necessary.[115]

Conclusion

In constructing what folklorist John Michael Vlach calls "Big House quarters," meaning the slave dwellings on the same farm as the master's house, southerners often situated them behind or to the side of the main residence, so the view as a visitor approached the mansion would not be spoiled. The overall design of the outbuildings, including the slave quarters, at Mount Vernon's Mansion House Farm certainly parallels this layout. It was not simply an aesthetic choice but also a graphic, physical way of reinforcing the fact of the master's authority and the subservient status of his workforce.[116] Even more poignantly, the layout of the buildings at Mount Vernon, where the slave quarters in the greenhouse complex to the north of the mansion are balanced by a similar building to the south—the stable—reifies the legal reality that slaves were just as much property as horses were.

Conversely, slaves tended to ignore what the plantation owner was trying to say architecturally and claimed dominion over the spaces where they lived.[117] Whether they were a means of expressing his authority or not, the quarters at Mount Vernon, as elsewhere in the South, were the place that

George Washington's slaves could call their own. Poor, dark, and dirty as the quarters were, it was there that the Mount Vernon slaves courted, raised families, visited and squabbled with neighbors, ate, drank, laughed, sang, suffered through illnesses, cried, developed their own small businesses, and died. In short, it was the one location where, with comparatively little interference from their master, they could take off the masks they habitually wore in white society and be themselves.

7

"And Procure for Themselves a Few Amenities"

Recreation and Private Enterprise in the Enslaved Community

During their time off from work, the slaves at Mount Vernon found many ways to fill their "free" hours. Each evening, on Sunday, and on their occasional holidays, the slaves were busy with activities to benefit themselves and their families rather than their master. Most important on a daily basis were "housekeeping" chores, such as tending chickens and garden plots, cooking and preserving the produce of those gardens, and caring for clothing. This latter activity was an especial concern to George Washington, when he discovered that his slaves were mending their clothes with fabric intended for other purposes. For instance, farm manager Anthony Whiting complained in 1792 that a number of bags or sacks, which would have been useful in transporting wheat to the mill, had been "Stole by the Negroes & otherwise Lost." Whiting recommended that bags purchased in the future be made of coarse sacking from Europe, "which a Negro Could not mend his Cloaths with without a discovery," and that in addition the sacks be marked on both sides.[1]

Looking after and arranging hair was an important aspect of African culture, which continued in African American society in the eighteenth century. It may have been a significant activity at Mount Vernon as well, but a lack of evidence prevents certainty on this score. A study of runaway advertisements points out that hair care was a time-consuming communal activity, undertaken primarily on Sundays, at least by slaves involved in fieldwork.[2] While surviving documents show that male slaves at Mount Vernon wore their hair both long and short, there is little information about its care and nothing about women's hairstyles. When Marcus, a young mulatto house slave, "absconded" several months after Washington's death, he was described as having "long black hair," but its style was not mentioned.[3] It may be that long hair was worn primarily by male domestics, who came in contact with visitors to the Washington home, while fieldworkers kept their hair short for practical reasons. A carpenter named Cyrus wore his hair short until he was chosen for work as a "waiting man" in the mansion. At that time, Washington directed that he be given "a strong horn comb" and "keep his head well combed, that the hair, or wool may grow long," probably so that it could be pulled back into a queue, as shown in several portraits that include slaves.[4] The well-known and much-copied portrait *The Washington Family* by Edward Savage includes a domestic slave wearing his hair in the manner requested for Cyrus. He was not the only slave to be provided with the equipment needed to look after his hair. In June 1797, Delphy, a teen-aged dower slave at the Mansion House Farm and sister of Martha Washington's maid Oney Judge, was given an unspecified amount of money so that she could buy herself a comb.[5]

Reading

For at least some of the slaves at Mount Vernon, personal time may have been taken up with learning to read or in teaching others to do so. Literacy was an invaluable skill for anyone hoping for a better position on the plantation or trying to get along in the larger society outside of Mount Vernon. While it may not have been common, it was neither unusual nor illegal for Virginia slaves at this period to be literate. In fact, those eighteenth-century pastors who actively ministered to slaves often saw it as part of their duty to teach their congregations to read, so that they could access the Bible for themselves. Beginning in 1795, the local abolition society, headquartered in Alexandria, even held Sunday classes to teach slaves of all ages reading, writing, and arithmetic. Estimates have placed the number of literate slaves at the time of the Civil War at about 5–10 percent after several decades of repressive laws forbidding people from teaching them to read and write. At this point, there is no way of knowing how many slaves were literate in the eighteenth century, when there were no such laws impeding them from learning, but one historian has estimated that perhaps as many as 15–20 percent of adult slaves could read at this period.[6]

It is unclear whether those slaves who worked as overseers on several of Washington's farms were expected to read and write, in order to draw up work reports each week and read orders from Washington. In a letter to a prospective farm manager, Washington noted that "it was always a custom when I lived at home, & it has been continued since, for each overlooker, or sub-intendent of an individual farm &c at the end of the week, to give an account in writing how his people have been employed—what they have done—what increase or decrease the Stock has sustained &c &c for which purpose each is supplied with pen, ink & paper."[7] When Will, the enslaved overseer at Muddy Hole Farm, was sick for two weeks in February 1786, the overall reports contained no information from him, simply noting, "no acc[oun]t given in."[8] It would have been the same result, however, if Will had been illiterate and unable to come to the home of the farm manager to give his report via conversation. There is clear evidence from the period after Washington's death, discussed in more detail in the final chapter, that Davy Gray, one of the longest-serving and most trusted enslaved overseers, could not write.[9] A note dropped at the time of an escape attempt in 1799, however, suggests that Christopher Sheels, the young domestic slave who succeeded William Lee as George Washington's valet, could probably read and write. Because Sheels worked closely with Washington, a certain degree of literacy may have been expected, or might have been picked up, as part of his occupation.[10]

More than just enslaved house servants and overseers could read. Caesar, a fieldworker on one of the outlying farms, ran away several times in the 1790s. On one occasion, fearing that he had attempted escape yet again, Washington commented that he thought Caesar ultimately had a good chance of success, "as he can read, if not write."[11] It is highly unlikely that Caesar would have needed to read as part of or as a consequence of his work, so he must have learned in some other way, although whether it was through another slave, his church, or some other means is impossible to say given the surviving evidence. Perhaps he had sought instruction in reading as an aid to his second career: according to Mount Vernon farm manager James Anderson, Caesar was a well-known preacher to blacks in the Mount Vernon neighborhood.[12]

It is clear that not all the Mount Vernon slaves, not even all the house servants, were literate. Many years after she ran away, enslaved lady's maid Oney Judge noted that the Washingtons had never given her any "mental . . . instruction" in all the time she was with them. She went on to relate proudly that one of her first acts upon gaining her freedom was to learn to read.[13]

Earning and Spending Money (Part 1)

A number of activities, some undertaken in the course of their occupations and others in their "off-duty" hours, helped enslaved families earn money, which could then be used to buy a range of consumer goods, including small luxuries, and thus raise their standards of living. Gifts of money, for instance, were given to three trusted slaves—Morris, who worked as an overseer; Davy Gray; and Mike—on Christmas day 1773, probably as a reward for good service during the year.[14] There is ample evidence from George Washington's financial records that he tipped slaves belonging to other owners. These were most likely domestic workers or stable hands who looked after him and his horse, while he was visiting on their plantations but might also be done for other reasons. For example, during a trip to Philadelphia in the spring of 1784, the "servants at Mr. Morris's" received £5.15.0 from Washington. A few months later, in September 1784 while traveling to his western lands, Washington gave £0.5.9 to "Servts. at Colo. Hite's," and several days later, in early October, gave 12 shillings to Joe, the serving man of Washington's longtime friend Dr. James Craik, who had accompanied him on the journey. The following month, another £0.2.9 were given to "servts. at Genl. Spotswood[']s" and £1.11.0 to "servts. at the Governor[']s."[15] Visitors to Mount Vernon probably made similar payments to the enslaved people who assisted them there.

Some slaves earned money more directly because of their positions. During his time at Mount Vernon in 1798, Julian Niemcewicz visited Washington's donkeys and mules and discussed the arrangements for boarding a mare or jenny while she was being bred. These arrangements included a fee for the person who cared for her, who in this case was the hired slave Peter Hardiman:

> We then went to see the asses. Mar[quis] de La Fayette sent to [Washington] a stallion from Malta and one from Spain with their females. They are large and handsome of their kind. The Gl. keeps up to 50 mules; these cross-bred animals are excellent for work and burdens. The asses service the mares and the jennies of the neighbors at a charge of ten dollars per season; for each female, as she is then on board, a half doll. per week is paid for her feed, which is a little dear, and besides this a ½ doll. for the boy.[16]

The ways to spend this money were as varied as the individual people themselves, but the surviving documentation suggests that better clothing, extra food, and household goods were among the possibilities. When the

Washingtons' cook Hercules went with them to Philadelphia during the presidency, he was able to make a good deal of money by selling "slops" from the kitchen. His freedom to sell remnants of the food preparation process was a holdover of a "perquisite" allowed to cooks and other domestic servants in England and France, who traditionally sold such "leftovers" as animal skins, feathers, tallow, and tea leaves to supplement their income.[17] For example, when Thomas Jefferson was looking for a French chef for the White House in 1801, he chose someone in Philadelphia who was then earning "25 dollars per month, and he has the fat and grease for his perquisite."[18] According to Martha Washington's grandson, Hercules took the proceeds of these sales and

> lavished the most of these large avails upon dress. In making his toilet his linen was of unexceptionable whiteness and quality, then black silk shorts, ditto waistcoat, ditto stockings, shoes highly polished, with large buckles covering a considerable part of the foot, blue cloth coat with velvet collar and bright metal buttons, a long watch-chain dangling from his fob, a cocked-hat, and gold-headed cane completed the grand costume of the celebrated dandy . . . of the president's kitchen.[19]

Other individuals spent their money on food, usually in the form of supplies that were better than their customary rations. Mount Vernon slaves purchased fine flour, large quantities of pork, and whiskey from Washington in the last years of his life.[20] It is also likely that they bought imported foods, such as tea, coffee, molasses, and sugar, from shops in Alexandria.

The Underground Economy

Finer clothing and other desired items could also be obtained by means of bartering goods and services. The best example of clothing acquired through this means comes from an incident involving Charlotte, a seamstress from the Mansion House Farm. It sheds light on several characteristics of slave life at Mount Vernon, including the acquisition of additional clothing, the use of African languages in the enslaved community, and the interactions between slaves and whites who were not their owners.

In the late spring of 1786, George Washington received a letter from Charles MacIver, a Highland Scot living in Alexandria whose wife had recently gotten into a dispute with Charlotte. The latter had come into town on an errand, probably for the Washingtons since she appears to have arrived in the family's "Chariot." Mrs. MacIver spotted Charlotte and another black woman strolling down the street. Insinuating that both had been drinking, the Scotswoman became irate when she thought she recognized the dress Charlotte was wearing as one that had been stolen from her several years before by an indigent young white woman. MacIver tried to closely examine the garment and started questioning Charlotte about how it came into her possession. She was not accusing Charlotte of stealing the dress, described as Indian chintz with a white ground and red stripes, only of having stolen property in her possession. It is clear that Charlotte was probably the last of several slaves to purchase the dress after it was taken, but she made the situation worse by giving several different explanations of how she came to have it. She then blew up, threatened to flog MacIver, and used a number of "abusive & contemptuous Epithets." The merchant related that, among the slurs hurled that day, Charlotte commented that she would not "*demean herself so much* as to be seen walking *with such* a Creature as my Wife, whom she called Suke," even a very short distance. Apparently this little dispute was creating something of a scene, and a Washington family friend, Sarah Carlyle Herbert, gently reminded Mrs. MacIver that it was unseemly to be shouting at another woman in the middle of the street and got her to come into the Herberts' home.[21]

A specialist in African American interpretation in museums has suggested that "Suke" was such an insult because the names Suke and Sukey were associated with slaves; Charlotte may have been trying to tell the woman that she was not behaving in accordance with her social class.[22] That explanation would be logical if the person slinging the insulting word had been Herbert, not Charlotte, and if "Sukey" had not been used as a nickname by white people during that period, including at Mount Vernon and in the Washington family.[23] Further research showed that a similar-sounding word, "juke" (as in juke box, juke dancing, and juke joint), is thought to have come into African American speech from either the word *dzug,* meaning to misbehave, which comes from the Wolof people of Senegal and Gambia, or *dzugu,* meaning wicked, from the Bambara of the upper Niger region in Mali.[24] Perhaps Charlotte was using an African word to tell Mrs. MacIver that she was behaving badly and had become the object of Charlotte's disdain.

Earning and Spending Money (Part 2)

The only detailed description of the interior of a slave dwelling at Mount Vernon sketches a scene of dire poverty, brightened by the presence of "some cups and a teapot," which could well have been purchased by the family living in the cabin.[25] Some idea of the kinds of durable goods purchased by African Americans at this period can be found in the legal papers relating to the marital breakup of a black woman named Nancy Holmes (the final name by which Martha Washington's alleged half-sister, Ann Dandridge, was known during her lifetime), whose status, whether free or slave, is unclear. The mother-in-law of former Mount Vernon slave Philadelphia (Delphy) Costin, Holmes split up with her husband in 1805. At that time, Martha Washington's eldest granddaughter, Eliza Parke Custis Law, certified that the articles belonged to Holmes, had "been obtained solely by her industry without the least assistance from her husband," and that she wished to "prevent his wasting it." The housewares she had accumulated included "one Desk, 3 tables, 8 chairs, 2 glasses, 13 pictures, 2 potts, one oven, 2 frying pans, 1 tea kettle, one & a ha[l]f dozen plates & Six teacups, 3 tea potts, 1 sugar Dish 1 cream pot 1 tea kettle 2 bedsteads 2 beds and bed cloaths 1 pr. Andirons 5 flat irons, 3 tumblers, 3 wine glasses 2 decanters 1 cloths Horse a large Wash ketle & 3 tubs."[26] Compared to descriptions of slave quarter interiors from Mount Vernon and other plantations, Holmes's home was especially well-furnished. Because she lived in Washington, DC, however, she very likely had both greater opportunity to earn extra money and access to markets or goods than enslaved people living in the country, who could get into town maybe once a week at most, and whose ability to transport furniture might be hampered by distance.

Simply being alert could bring financial rewards. For example, farm manager James Anderson placed a notice in a local paper in the fall of 1798 about a pocketbook that had been found along the road outside of Alexandria. After proving that it was his, the rightful owner could reclaim his property after paying for the advertisement and "allowing something for the Negro who found it."[27] Special jobs might also result in a tip for a slave's services. George Washington was probably not acting in an unusual manner when he left the home of his brother-in-law Burwell Bassett in the spring of 1768, and left £0.15.9 for the "Servants" who had extra duties to perform in caring for this, or any other, houseguest. When a slave belonging to James Cleveland returned a horse to Mount Vernon in the summer of 1783, he was given three shillings, which he could presumably spend as he wished. Many years later, several slaves assisted George Washington in getting his valet, Billy Lee, to the home of a friend, Dr. David Stuart, after Lee broke his knee pan while surveying with Washington in 1785. It is unclear from the surviving records whether these people were from Mount Vernon or Stuart's home, or if they just happened upon the accident, but they were given six shillings in gratitude for their aid. Washington's contemporaries, benefiting from the help of one of his slaves, would quite likely have tipped them as well.[28] Where someone of Washington's social class would have paid a slave for service with cash, a person of lower rank might barter something, as when a slave belonging to Stuart was given a dress and an apron for his wife in exchange for ferrying a young white woman, who had stolen them, across the river. It was this dress that sparked the argument between Charlotte and Mrs. MacIver.[29]

Selling things was another way of making money. Slaves living at Mount Vernon, as well as those on neighboring farms, sold foodstuffs to George Washington and in Alexandria.[30] Other slaves made small items for sale. Six pence, for example, were given to a slave named Easter in 1792 in exchange for a broom, which had presumably been made in the quarters.[31] While some of these things may have been sold door to door in the neighborhood, another destination for the goods and foodstuffs produced by the Mount Vernon slaves was the Sunday market in Alexandria, where slaves from the surrounding countryside could sell until 9:00 in the morning. This would, of course, have meant another very early morning for anyone trying to get into the city, which was approximately 9 miles away, a 1.5- to 2-hour trip on horseback. Since the slaves did not have permission to use the horses, however, this would have meant a long walk of at least three hours each way. Another possibility is that the goods were transported by water, since we know that at least two slaves, Jack the fisherman and carpenter Sambo Anderson, had small boats or canoes.[32]

The financial and social rewards of a trip to town, however, must have made the effort worthwhile. In addition to serving as a means of making money, the Sunday market was a good place to meet, exchange information, and develop relationships with slaves and free blacks, not only from the city of Alexandria but from outlying plantations as well. Descriptions of the Alexandria market in the nineteenth century speak of the "busy scene," probably similar to that in the previous century, as slaves squatted in the shade of trees "with their baskets of berries, their chickens and eggs."[33] Toward the end of George Washington's life, this privilege was tightened a bit, when farm manager James Anderson required that slaves from Mount Vernon have a special pass in order to do business at the market. Anderson was not simply being capricious but complying with a Virginia law of 1785, which forbade sales to or purchases from slaves without the permission of their owner or overseer.[34]

Fishing and hunting could also lead to financial improvement. Washington's fondness for fish was well known, even outside his household, so he was a likely customer for someone with an impressive fish to sell. He paid three shillings for two rockfish in the late summer of 1790, which had been caught by "a Negroe of Capt. Marshals."[35] Contrary to popular belief, slaves could legally own guns under certain circumstances. Prior to the Revolution, three of Landon Carter's slaves at Sabine Hall had been armed with "Guns loaded with small shot," as they sought to recapture several runaway slaves.[36] According to a Virginia statute of 1785, slaves were forbidden to keep firearms unless they were either traveling with their master or had written permission from him or their employer to have a gun. While no such documents appear to have survived from Mount Vernon, Washington clearly knew about and sanctioned the keeping of guns by at least some of his slaves.[37] He even provided shot on occasion, most likely for hunting to supply the mansion table or to rid the estate of vermin.[38]

Two references to Washington's purchases of birds from his slaves reinforce the idea that they were hunting, not only to supplement their own diet but to earn money. In the fall of 1792, two slaves, Tom Davis, a mulatto brickmason, and Sambo Anderson, the African-born carpenter, sold their master a total of eleven dozen birds.[39] Both of these men were well known as hunters. Martha Washington's grandson recalled many years later that Davis, who regularly supplied the Mount Vernon household with fresh game, had a "great Newfoundland dog" named Gunner as his hunting companion. According to George Washington Parke Custis, ducks were extremely plentiful along the Potomac in the eighteenth century, and one shot from Davis's old British musket generally brought down "as many of those delicious birds as would supply the larder for a week."[40] After Washington's death in 1799, Anderson supported himself by hunting wild game, which he sold to hotels and "the most respectable families" in Alexandria. He earned enough money from this endeavor to purchase and emancipate two slaves, both of whom were members of his family.[41] There is no reason to suppose that Anderson was not occasionally earning money from those same sources while Washington was still alive.

An interesting incident in the fall of 1787 also suggests that the Mount Vernon slaves earned a little extra money by preventing others from hunting on Washington's property. In keeping with longstanding British traditions that limited hunting on an estate to the landowner or those who had his express permission, Washington forbade hunting by outsiders and ordered his slaves to investigate immediately any gunshots heard on his land.[42] A "Party of young Gentlemen" sailed down from Alexandria to hunt ducks along the Potomac and had the misfortune to land their craft at Washington's River Farm. Three slaves belonging to the plantation, one of whom was armed with a gun, approached the young men and "insisted" that one of them shoot a squirrel, which he proceeded to do. They enticed two of the group further into the woods with the promise of more squirrels and then turned on them "in the most Violent manner" and took away their guns. As they ran off to turn the confiscated weapons over to Washington, the slaves were heard to say that they had just earned ten pounds, probably as a reward for disarming the trespassing hunters.[43]

While it may seem particularly gruesome, a perfectly acceptable means of making money was by selling teeth to dentists. Since at least the end of the Middle Ages, poor people had sold their teeth for use in both dentures and tooth transplant operations to benefit those wealthy enough to afford these procedures. Depending on their intended use, sometimes these sacrificed, marketable teeth were perfectly healthy, while still others were diseased and needed to be pulled anyway. Healthy incisors, preferably from young, healthy donors, were necessary for transplantation; teeth used in dentures could be either incisors or molars and might even be taken from corpses.[44]

Both contemporary prints and dentistry texts provide evidence for how transplantations were conducted. For the sake of efficiency, both a wealthy patient and several prospective tooth donors would be gathered in the same room. A diseased incisor would first be removed from the patient, who might need to use smelling salts in case of fainting during the process. The dentist would remove the corresponding incisor from the first donor and then try it in the socket for size. If that tooth was not a good match, the corresponding tooth would be pulled from the next donor . . . or the next, until "a reasonable fit had been achieved." For best results, the donor teeth were first rinsed in warm water. Once the best tooth had been set into the patient's gums, it was tied to those on either side to prevent it from moving. Within one to two months, if all went very well, the tooth would be firmly in place and might last up to five years.[45]

A French dentist variously referred to as Jean Pierre Le Moyer or Le Mayeur or Joseph Lemaire came to America in 1780, possibly as a naval surgeon with the French forces commanded by Jean-Baptiste-Donatien de Vimeur, Comte de Rochambeau, and treated patients in New York, Philadelphia, Baltimore, Alexandria, and Richmond over the next decade. He seems to have had an extensive practice in tooth transplants, but the results were often problematic. Looking back on his career many years later, Le Moyer noted that of 170 teeth transplanted in Philadelphia in the winter of 1785–86, a few lasted for a year or so, but most had not been successful. Transplantable teeth were hard to come by, and Le Moyer even went so far as to advertise in the New York papers in 1783 for "persons disposed to sell their front teeth, or any of them." Each tooth would net the donor two guineas (forty-two shillings). An advertisement he placed in the Richmond newspaper offered anyone but slaves a similar amount for their front teeth (technical problems made it impossible to transplant molars).[46]

The Frenchman first treated George Washington's teeth at his military headquarters in 1783. The following year, in May 1784, Washington paid several unnamed "Negroes," presumably Mount Vernon slaves, 122 shillings for 9 teeth, slightly less than one-third the going rate advertised in the papers, "on acct. of the French Dentis[t]—Doctr. Lemay."[47] Although Washington's diaries do not exist for this period, Le Moyer's correspondence with Washington and an April advertisement of his services in the Alexandria paper under the name "Lamayner" confirm his spring visit to Mount Vernon. Over the next four years, he was a rather frequent visitor on the plantation, where he appears to have been a favorite guest.[48] Whether the teeth provided by the Mount Vernon slaves were simply being sold to the dentist for any patient who needed them, or whether they were intended for Washington, is unknown at this point, although the fact that he paid for the teeth suggests that they were either for his own use or for someone in his family. Washington does seem to have overcome some initial qualms about transplantation and may have undergone the procedure after learning that one of his military aides, Colonel Richard Varick, had had four front teeth and an eye tooth replaced by Le Moyer.[49] If so, it could well be that some of the human teeth implanted to improve Washington's appearance—or even the human teeth used in at least one set of his dentures—came from his own slaves.

Pushback

Concern with his slaves' private lives came to the fore when their entrepreneurial activities threatened Washington's interests. In the fall of 1794, for example, he learned that Sally Green, the abandoned wife of one of his white carpenters and the daughter of his old servant Thomas Bishop, was thinking of moving to Alexandria to open a shop. The president feared that with her longstanding ties to the Mount Vernon slaves, the shop would be "no more than a receptacle for stolen produce" from his farms. He asked his manager William Pearce to caution Green against dealing with his slaves, for if "she deals with them at all she will be unable to distinguish between stolen, or not stolen things." He warned that if she came under any suspicion of dealing in stolen goods, "she need expect no further countenance or support from me."[50]

Washington was also troubled, and economically threatened, by the dogs kept by slaves on the plantation. In November 1792, he ordered farm manager Anthony Whiting to get to the bottom of a crime wave against the hogs and sheep: "The robberies which all your letters relate, must be stopped. . . . It is growing worse and worse every day; and if a good deal of pains is not taken to discover the thieves, and the receivers, there is no telling where the evil will end." Washington was willing to invest in bells for the sheep, as a way to make things more difficult for the thieves, but thought "this will prove but a partial remedy: the evil must be probed deeper than that."[51] The problem continued, and the following month Washington suggested another means of safeguarding his livestock:

> I not only approve of your killing those Dogs which have been the occasion of the late loss, and of thinning the Plantations of others, but give it as a positive order, that after saying what dog, or dogs shall remain, if any negro presumes under any pretence whatsoever, to preserve, or bring one into the family, that he shall be severely punished, and the dog hanged. I was obliged to adopt this practice whilst I resided at home, and from the same motives, that is, for the preservation of my Sheep and Hogs. . . . It is not for any good purpose Negros raise or keep dogs; but to aid them in their night robberies; for it is astonishing to see the command under which their dogs are.[52]

These instructions are reminiscent of English laws dating back to the Middle Ages that regulated the keeping of dogs near large feudal estates, whose owners reserved all hunting rights to themselves.[53] During the eighteenth century, the English gentry and their agents executed, by a variety of means including hanging, the illegally kept dogs used by poachers on their lands. Thomas Jefferson gave similar orders at Monticello, resulting in the destruction of dogs belonging to his slaves.[54] The fact that George Washington's slaves kept dogs, hunted with them, and were quite skilled in handling them may also be a cultural survival from Africa. In the kingdom of Massina along the Niger River, dogs were used as guards. They were likewise among the domestic animals raised by the Ijebu on the Guinea Coast.[55]

Recreation

The people enslaved at Mount Vernon also spent their nonworking hours relaxing and having fun. One favorite activity was visiting with one another. Washington asked manager William Pearce to make the slaves at the

FIG. 12. Fragments of clay pipes, marbles, and part of a jaw or mouth harp, all excavated at Mount Vernon. (Courtesy of the Mount Vernon Ladies' Association)

Mansion House Farm be very careful of fire, "for it is no uncommon thing for them to be running from one house to another in cold windy nights with sparks of fire flying, and dropping as they go along."[56] He complained to more than one manager because the slaves were too exhausted after what he called "night walking" to do the work expected of them.[57] Children may have had the opportunity to make extended visits to relatives on other farms. According to the 1786 Mount Vernon slave list, there were three fairly young unattached children at Washington's River Farm. Seven-year-old Milly and four-year-old Billy both had mothers at the Mansion House Farm, while James, who was eight, was the child of a woman at Ferry Farm. These children were too young to be part of the workforce, so their absence from home would not have been a matter of serious concern to the plantation's management, as long as their whereabouts were generally known.[58]

During these visits, the enslaved population engaged in a number of activities. A jaw or mouth harp found in the remains of the blacksmith shop could have been used by either a slave or a white servant and would have required no special training to play.[59] The cellar of an excavated slave quarter on the Mansion House Farm yielded large numbers of fragments from clay pipes, used by both sexes for smoking tobacco, though not necessarily just during leisure hours.[60] As people relaxed to the sound of music or as the aroma of tobacco filled the quarters, some individuals started telling stories. As was noted earlier, an unknown number of the plantation's slaves came originally from Africa. As an adult, Martha Washington's grandson remembered hearing stories about that far-off and exotic place from one of these people: "Father Jack was an African negro, an hundred years of age, and, although greatly enfeebled in body by such a vast weight of years, his mind possessed uncommon vigor. And he would tell of days long past, of Afric's clime, and of Afric's wars, in which he (of course the son of a king) was made captive, and of the terrible battle in which his royal sire was slain, the village consigned to the flames, and he to the slaveship."[61]

If Jack was telling such stories to the master's little grandson, he and others were almost surely relating similar tales to the children of their own families. In doing so, they passed on cultural values, building pride and giving the children a historical framework for their lives. All of these elements were instrumental in fashioning a community within the quarters, where the first generation of inhabitants had originally come from Africa and widely differing locales within Virginia itself.[62]

In addition to personal stories about life in Africa and the experience of being enslaved, there were probably other stories that on the surface seemed merely entertaining but also held deeper meaning. A young girl named Mary Gregory, who grew up in Alexandria in the 1840s and 1850s, was placed in the care of Eugenia and Sarah Harrison, the mulatto granddaughters of Martha Washington's maid Caroline Branham. As an adult, Gregory remembered that Eugenia told the story of "Brer Rabbit and the Tar Baby in almost the exact words used in Joel Chandler Harris' version."[63] Harris, the first major publisher of the Brer Rabbit stories, was from Georgia, where he had learned them from elderly local slaves as a teenager at Turnwold Plantation during the Civil War. These stories were told throughout the South and have been traced by historians and folklorists back to roots in Africa. The lessons they taught concerned the ways a relatively powerless individual, represented by Brer Rabbit, could triumph through the use of wit and intelligence over someone who was larger, more wealthy, and more powerful, for example, the fox and bear, who represented authority figures.[64] These survival skills, so necessary in the enslaved community, were very likely taught through the same stories in the quarters at Mount Vernon.

The slaves at Mount Vernon also found time for games and sports in their free hours. Among the objects recovered from the House for Families site were clay marbles.[65] Marbles are said to have been the most popular game of small black boys in the eighteenth and nineteenth centuries. It is not known whether playing this particular game of skill and, according to one scholar, gambling stopped with childhood.[66]

The Potomac River and the many creeks on the plantation provided some degree of relief from the often oppressive heat and humidity of the Virginia summer. Sadly, the only documentation for swimming or wading comes from a tragic incident in the late summer of 1778, when George Washington was notified of the death by drowning of one of his coopers. During a work break, the victim, who could not swim, had waded into the millrace in an attempt to cool off. It is clear from the attempts made to rescue him, described in more detail in the next chapter, that others in the work party could swim.[67]

Julian Niemcewicz described what may have been a team sport played by the slaves on one of their Sundays off in the summer of 1798. He recorded seeing a group of about thirty slaves, presumably adults, divided into two groups. They were playing a game he described as "prisoner's base," which involved "jumps and gambols as if they had rested all week."[68] Prisoner's base, a traditional English game dating back to the Middle Ages, is depicted in contemporary prints and was the subject of at least one song. It was played outdoors by both children and adults of all classes in the eighteenth century and appears to have been a very athletic, team version of the modern game of tag.[69]

George Washington occasionally let the slaves leave his home or plantation to attend special events. In the fall of 1784, for example, he gave six shillings so that his "Servts." could "go to the Race." Two years later, he permitted his slaves to go into Alexandria to attend the races, stipulating that responsible individuals had to remain on each of his farms, while the others were free to stagger their attendance over the several-day event. Washington was not the only plantation owner to allow such privileges; slaves belonging to his longtime friend Dr. David Stuart went to the races in October 1784.[70] Those slaves who accompanied the Washingtons to New York and Philadelphia during the presidency were given several opportunities to enjoy the entertainments available in those cities. In May 1791, Christopher Sheels and Hercules were each given a ticket to a play, and two years later Martha Washington's maids Molly and Oney Judge received a dollar "to see the tumbling feats." Just two months after that, the women were given the same amount of money to "go to the Circus." Molly and Oney must have liked what they saw there, because less than a month later, two of the men, Hercules and Austin, were given money for the same purpose.[71]

The slaves at Mount Vernon were also included, at least occasionally, in Washington family events, both happy and sad, although their roles in these cases are not always clear. In telling the story of how his grandmother, then a twenty-seven-year-old widow, came to marry George Washington, George Washington Parke Custis made sure to include the reminiscences of Cully, an elderly slave who served five generations of the family and was one of the many "domestics" "who were participants in the gay scene," perhaps because they were serving or, as Custis phrased it, "waited at the board where love made the feast and the Virginia colonel was the guest."[72]

Forty years later, one of the most memorable family events was the marriage of Custis's sister Nelly, Martha Washington's youngest granddaughter, to George Washington's nephew Lawrence Lewis. The wedding took place on the evening of February 22, 1799, George Washington's final birthday. In addition to various members of the extended family, there were a sizable number of slaves in attendance. About sixty years after the nuptials, an elderly woman who had been a dower slave and was known to the family as "Mammy," described this wedding to Agnes Lee, the bride's great-niece. While "Mammy" remembered the bride as a "celebrated beauty" dressed in "something white," she felt Nelly was outshone that day by her grandmother or "Ole Mistis." Mammy recalled that Martha Washington had worn a light flowered satin dress and spoke of her "beauty & good management." The slave also found George Washington wanting in comparison to his wife, noting that "she could not see why so much fuss was made over 'the genl, he was only a man!' a very good master she was sure, but she didn't suppose he was so much better than anyone else." Her former mistress may have risen in the elderly woman's estimation after her decision to "let all the servants come in to see" the wedding. They were more than just spectators, however. According to this woman, Martha Washington also provided them with "such good things to eat" on the day of the wedding, indicating that they partook of some special foods as well.[73] While it is doubtful that all of the slaves from the outlying farms would or even could have been invited to the festivities, it is conceivable that the approximately ninety slaves on the Mansion House Farm with whom the Washingtons were not only physically but likely emotionally close would have been included. In telling the stories about both weddings, these enslaved people were also preserving the histories and adding to the oral traditions of the Washington and Custis families.

Less than a year after Nelly's wedding, an even more significant event transpired that would ultimately have a tremendous effect on the personal lives of virtually every enslaved person at Mount Vernon. On December 14, 1799, George Washington died unexpectedly after a short illness and was buried in the family vault, following Episcopal and Masonic funeral rites, on the 18th. Frank Lee, the family's mulatto butler, and two of the other serving men from the mansion, Christopher Sheels and Marcus, were outfitted with new shoes the day after Washington's death, probably so that they would look nice while waiting on guests attending the funeral. Two other slaves, Cyrus and Wilson (the son of Peter Hardiman and Caroline Branham), took part in the funeral ceremonies. The two grooms led Washington's horse, which was carrying his saddle, holster, and pistols, in the funeral procession from the mansion to the tomb. After the entombment, the large number of nonfamily members who took part in the funeral were offered something to eat and drink. When they were gone, the "remains of the provisions" were distributed to the slaves.[74]

Religion

George Washington's writings tell us virtually nothing about the religious life of his slaves. However, an in-depth study of the enslaved community at Mount Vernon over the past several decades has led to an inescapable conclusion: in order for Washington to practice the religious toleration that was so important to him, he did not even have to leave home. The African and African American slaves who lived on the estate at the time of his death appear to have followed a variety of belief systems. Elements of Christianity, Islam, and African religions survive in Mount Vernon's documentary and archaeological records. While some slaves may have followed one of these religions exclusively, still others probably adopted and combined elements of each.

There is no evidence that George and Martha Washington provided anything in the way of religious training or services for the enslaved workers on their estate, beyond giving Sundays and a handful of Christian holidays as days off. In fact, one of the major complaints of lady's maid Oney Judge, who converted to Christianity after she ran away from the executive mansion in Philadelphia, was that the Washingtons had never given her any sort of "moral instruction."[75] A description left by a friend of Martha Washington's granddaughter Nelly detailed Martha's nighttime routine of Bible-reading, prayer, and hymn-singing in the presidential mansion in Philadelphia but is unclear about whether the enslaved maid (who might have been either Judge or Moll) was present at that point, or if she simply came in immediately afterward to help the elderly woman with changing clothes and getting into bed:

Mrs. Washington was in the habit of retiring at an early hour to her own room . . . and there, no matter what the hour, Nelly attended her. One evening my father's carriage was late in coming for me, and my dear young friend invited me to accompany her to her grandmamma's room. There, after some little chat, Mrs. Washington apologized to me for pursuing her usual preparations for the night, and Nelly entered upon her accustomed duty by reading a chapter and psalm from the old family Bible, after which all present knelt in evening prayer; Mrs. Washington's faithful maid then assisted her to disrobe and lay her head upon the pillow; Nelly then sang a verse of some soothing hymn, and leaning down, received the parting blessing for the night, with some emphatic remarks on her duties, improvements, etc. The effect of these habits and teachings appeared in the granddaughter's character through life.[76]

It would have been most unusual if Judge had been given such instruction, for eighteenth-century masters typically took little or no interest in the religious lives of their slaves, as long as they were not causing a problem. The custom of having simple household services became more common later, after the Second Great Awakening brought evangelicalism into the Episcopal church (the successor to the Anglican church) in Virginia in the last decade or so of the eighteenth century and first two decades of the nineteenth. Multiple sources, for example, show that this custom was practiced by the family of Martha Washington's grandson at Arlington Plantation, where at least the domestic slaves were usually included during family devotions, and more formal church services were even held for the slaves in a little schoolhouse on Sundays as well.[77]

One thing Washington did provide the enslaved workers at Mount Vernon was time to worship if they chose to do so on their Sundays off. The slaves at Mount Vernon did participate with organized Christian groups to some degree, although the extent of that participation is unknown. In general during the eighteenth century, while African-born slaves were largely written off as candidates for proselytizing by the Virginia legislature, primarily because of problems communicating with them, Anglican missionaries and ministers in the colony did try to work with their creole descendants, who had been born in the Americas and could understand English. Their efforts at evangelism, however, were often hampered to varying degrees by the indifference or outright hostility of masters, who, at least until about 1740, often feared that slaves who became Christian would expect to either be treated better or be freed. There were slave owners who felt it was more beneficial for slaves to spend their free time on Sundays working in their own gardens.[78] Others were concerned about the dangers of allowing more than a few enslaved people to meet at a time, an issue that was largely put to rest by implementing "more systematic surveillance."[79] It was around the fourth decade of the eighteenth century that Daniel Parke Custis and his neighbors began ensuring that slaves born on their estates near Williamsburg were initiated into the state church. Keeping in mind New Testament admonitions that slaves obey their masters and serve them cheerfully, historian Lorena Walsh has suggested that the christenings may have been an attempt to "[create] a more acculturated and servile workforce."[80]

Lending credence to Walsh's statement is a section of the prayer journal kept for many years by Elizabeth Foote Washington, the wife of longtime farm manager Lund Washington. Writing at Mount Vernon in the summer of 1784 after four years of marriage, Elizabeth wrote of her desire to have a good relationship with the enslaved women under her supervision. In cases where they had done something wrong, she wanted to

> talk to them in a kind & friendly way, pointing out their fault with calmness,—but at the same time with a steadiness that they may know I will not be impos'd upon—& I will endeavour to make them think I do not wish they should behave well for my sake, but because it will be pleasing in the eyes of the almighty—& that if they will do their business for his sake, I shall be well serv'd if they never think of me,—which is truly the case—I do most sincerely wish for their sakes—they may do their business with an earnest desire to please him—nothing would give me so great pleasure as having a truly religious family—not led away with Baptistical notions—but a religion that effectually touches the heart—no outside show.[81]

Anglican ministers in the Mount Vernon neighborhood are known to have reached out to the enslaved people in their midst. In 1749, Reverend Charles Green, the minister of Truro Parish, drew up a list of tithables in Fairfax County, Virginia. Included in that parish was the Mount Vernon estate, then under the proprietorship of George Washington's older half-brother, Lawrence. According to a note at the bottom of Green's list, "the Country born Negros are chiefly Baptized," which means that most of the slaves who had been born in America had been christened into the Anglican church.[82] Records do not seem to have survived at either Pohick Church in Truro Parish or Christ Church in Alexandria, which might document the baptism of enslaved children from Mount Vernon during George Washington's years there. At Bruton Parish Church in Williamsburg, however, at least eleven slaves "belonging to Coll. George Washington," both adults and children, are known to have been christened in the 1760s, from the plantations of the late Daniel Parke Custis, which Washington was then managing on behalf of Martha and her two minor children.[83]

A description left by a notable eighteenth-century visitor indicates that the slaves at Mount Vernon had contact of some sort with at least three other Christian denominations: Baptists, Methodists, and Quakers. Prince Louis-Philippe of France and his servant Beaudoin came to the plantation in 1797, shortly after George Washington's retirement from the presidency. There they talked with a number of the slaves and recorded that these three religious groups had raised hopes in the quarters that the slaves would be freed in the not-too-distant future. The Quakers had even approached Washington's slaves at places described as "clubs," possibly meetings of mutual aid or self-help societies, in Alexandria and Georgetown. Throughout Virginia in the last half of the eighteenth century, Baptists and Methodists actively sought new members from the enslaved community. Whether through their open acceptance of slaves into the congregation as equals or through their antislavery message, both religious communities were met with an enthusiastic response, especially from those who were younger and had been born in America. According to one study, by 1790 about one in twenty-three African Americans in Virginia had joined a church, and of this number, 80 percent were Baptists and Methodists. The presence of these two groups among the Mount Vernon slaves is, therefore, something to be expected.[84]

Lund Washington's wife, Elizabeth Foote Washington, left additional clues about Baptist inroads among her slaves. Elizabeth was one of the most evangelical members of the Washington family in the eighteenth century and did try to have household devotions with her slaves for many years. In an entry in her prayer journal, written in July 1792, several years after she and Lund moved a few miles away from Mount Vernon to their own plantation, Elizabeth expressed frustration that her slaves had "got so Baptistical in their notions, as to think they commit a crime to join with me in Prayer morning & evening." She had tried to talk to them individually about this issue,

> endeavouring to convince them—that they did not commit a crime by joining with me in Prayer—but all I can say, will not convince them—so that I am oblig'd to give out having Prayers—in my family,—which has given me great concern—but I trust as my gracious God knows the desire I had to serve him daily in my family—that I shall not be

answerable for not having family Prayers—I persever'd in it as long as I could—until it was a mere farce to attempt it any longer.

There were other issues and tensions as well. Elizabeth described the slaves as disappearing when it was time for the devotional services and looking "quite angry" if they were made to attend. The slaves had initially thought that Elizabeth's including them in family devotions meant she would "never find fault of them, nor ever reprimand them for anything at all." They eventually became disillusioned "and thought my religion was all preten[s]e," a situation that made sense to her because, "where a person professes to be a believer in Jesus, there is no . . . charity extended to them, but rather all their words & actions will be sifted, their mistakes exaggerated, & if any part of their conduct will bear a double construction it will generally be viewed in [*illegible word*] most unfavourable light."[85]

There were strong ties between the Baptists, Methodists, and Quakers and the abolition movement in Alexandria, a center for abolitionist activity in the late eighteenth century. Antislavery Quakers took an active role in the city government, and the Alexandria Society for the Relief and Protection of Persons Illegally Held in Bondage boasted more than sixty members. The society was led by Archibald M'Clean, a teacher whose classroom served as the site for its quarterly meetings. M'Clean's wife, Mary Jones, was the daughter of a prominent Baptist minister in Philadelphia and a member of the Alexandria Baptist congregation. Confirmation of Louis-Philippe's statement about the effect these groups were having on local slaves, including those from Mount Vernon, comes from Dr. Elisha Cullen Dick, one of the Washington family's physicians, who as superintendent of quarantine in 1795 attacked the abolition society for "infusing into the slaves a spirit of insurrection and rebellion."[86]

At this period in Virginia history, slaves from Mount Vernon were welcome to attend services at one of the nearby churches of these three denominations. Just a few years later, several slaves from Arlington Plantation, which belonged to George Washington Parke Custis, were among the charter members of the Alexandria Baptist Church when it was founded in 1803. About that same time, at least three slaves living at Mount Vernon and owned by Bushrod Washington, who had inherited the estate after the death of Martha Washington in 1802, were members of the same Baptist church in Alexandria.[87] This institution was founded by individuals coming from the earlier Backlick Baptist Church, located along Little River Turnpike near present-day Springfield in Fairfax County. It is possible that some of the Arlington slaves belonged to, or at least worshipped with, this earlier church, prior to Martha Washington's death and Custis's inheritance of them, when they still lived at Mount Vernon.[88]

In addition to worshipping with one or more local congregations, there is evidence that the Mount Vernon African American community developed spiritual leaders of its own, both free and enslaved, something that would not have been unusual at this period.[89] According to a runaway advertisement from the spring of 1798, Caesar, a Custis family slave from Washington's Union Farm who was thought to be forty-five to fifty years old, was a well-known preacher among the local black community in the last years of the eighteenth century. Physically, he was described as a "black negro man . . . about 5 feet 7 or 8 inches high; has a sharp aquiline nose, and some of his foreteeth stand out." Mentally, he was "plausible and artful, and can read and write." Readers were advised that "[in] the neighborhood he is so well known as to need no further description, for he frequently reads or preaches to the blacks." The advertisement recorded that he usually wore clothing of black and white homespun, a combination that might indicate his ministerial role.[90] The oral history of Charles Syphax's descendants—he was enslaved at both Mount Vernon and later at Arlington—indicates that his father was "a free black itinerant Alexandria street preacher."[91] Both Syphax's father and Caesar may have played an important part in helping the enslaved residents of the plantation deal with the hardships of their lives and find a measure of hope and meaning in their experiences.[92]

There are also several hints that religious traditions from Africa, or at least their influence, had not completely died out at Mount Vernon by the end of the eighteenth century. This would not have been unusual; evidence of similar cultural survivals have been found elsewhere in Virginia, Maryland, Kentucky, Delaware, the Carolinas, Louisiana, and even Texas. According to historian Peter Kolchin, African-born slaves generally continued to practice their native religions after their enslavement and transportation to the Americas, with these traditions surviving longest in areas where the population had a high concentration of Africans.[93] Still, religion scholar Jon Butler cautions that these survivals tended to be "not African religious systems but discrete religious practices," common to multiple cultural or ethnic groups from that continent, and followed in the mainland American colonies by individuals rather than entire communities.[94] In other words, the structure supporting the religion—things such as places of worship, priests or other leaders, schools teaching a given theology, sacred texts, and a culture accepting and nurturing followers in a given religion—were no longer available, yet certain individuals continued to practice remembered rituals or traditions.[95]

Traditional religious beliefs common to many ethnic groups living in West Africa made their way to the Americas with newly enslaved people. These shared elements included "belief in a sovereign creator and ruler of the universe, belief in divinities and ancestors who acted as intermediaries between humans and God, and reliance on practices of magic and medicine to influence events and people."[96] Physical evidence of these African religions have been found in some of the subfloor pits located under the sites of former slave cabins throughout the South including in Virginia. Pits were used for a variety of purposes by the inhabitants of the cabins: those placed in front of the hearth area were typically used to store food, especially root vegetables such as sweet potatoes, while those under the sides or corners of the room when covered with bedding became storage or hiding places for personal possessions, almost like a safe-deposit box, and were also used as shrines for private religious ceremonies. Using below-ground space for these functions was a good way to deal with the limited floor space in a cabin. A wide variety of objects, either whole or in part, could be meaningfully used in a shrine: iron tools or cooking pots, copper objects, bottles, tobacco pipes, animal bones, scissors, seashells, beads, dolls, and dishes. Some objects would be embellished with additional carving, indicating that they had some sort of spiritual significance. In certain cases, these designs appear to derive from carvings by Igbo people in Nigeria, one of the primary groups from which slaves were captured and brought to Virginia in the colonial period.[97]

Archaeologists working in the cellar of Mount Vernon's House for Families in the 1980s found at least three objects that indicate possible survivals of African religious practices. The first are the cat bones mentioned in the previous chapter. According to historian Ann Smart Martin, black cats were "strongly linked" to other beliefs about mirrors: "With some variation, the custom required catching a black cat and boiling it. When the flesh was off the bones, each bone was put in the mouth. When the 'lucky bone' was in one's mouth, one's image [presumably in the mirror] would disappear."[98] The second object was the leg bone from an owl, bearing marks from a knife cut where the talon had been removed. This same site also yielded a raccoon baculum, or penis bone, incised along one end. The carving on this bone effectively transformed it into a ceremonial or decorative object that could have been suspended from a cord around someone's neck. Both the baculum and the owl talon might be amulets of a type described by a former Maryland slave, who recalled that the "only charms that were worn [by slaves on the plantation where he was raised] were made out of bones." The well-known sexual aggressiveness of male raccoons might, for example,

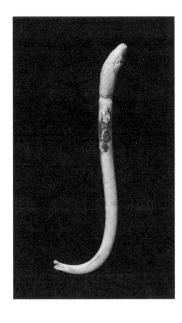

FIG. 13. Raccoon baculum (penis bone), incised near the top, probably for wearing. (Courtesy of the Mount Vernon Ladies' Association)

have led someone to see the baculum as a fertility symbol, while the owl's prowess as a nighttime hunter may have caused someone to view its talon as a valuable aid to their own hunting endeavors after dark. Archaeologists have suggested that these pieces might indicate either cultural borrowing from Native Americans or New World manifestations of an African custom.[99] Whatever the answer, these bones certainly suggest the practice of other belief systems besides, or perhaps in conjunction with, Christianity on George Washington's estate and lend credence to an undocumented neighborhood tradition that the slaves at Washington's Dogue Run Farm, at least, practiced voodoo or conjuring.[100]

Given the dominant European and Christian culture, it would have been difficult for slaves to transplant another religion to the Americas completely intact. Taking a cursory look at Islam as an example, the religion expects of its followers five basic things: the *Shahada,* a public statement of belief that "there is no true god but God, and Muhammad is the Messenger of God"; the performance of prayers at five set times of day (dawn, noon, midafternoon, sunset, and night); *Zakat,* or the giving of at least 2.5 percent of income to the poor; fasting (or abstaining from food, drink, and sex) between dawn and dusk during the month of Ramadan; and *Hajj,* pilgrimage to Mecca at least once during a believer's lifetime.[101] While making a statement of faith might or might not have been a problem depending on the situation in which it was expressed, the degree of supervision by an overseer or master could well have interfered with the requirement to pray five times each day. Determining the dates of Ramadan would very likely have been difficult given the lack of trained clergy, and trying to fast if Ramadan fell in the middle of the summer wheat harvest could have been deadly. Enslaved status would have made pilgrimage to Mecca out of the question. Aside from these requirements, with the typical workweek in Virginia being Monday through Saturday, traditional Friday prayers would have been impossible to continue in the New World without clergy to lead them and because Friday was not a day off. Given the prominence of pork in the slave diet, it might have been hard to follow Islamic dietary guidelines, though distributions of fish and occasionally mutton and beef, and the ability to hunt wild game would have made it possible.[102]

Still, other elements of Muslim religious traditions might well have survived the Middle Passage. Several female slaves at Mount Vernon appear to have had Muslim names. For example, in a list of tithables prepared by Washington in July 1774 were two female slaves, possibly a mother and daughter, known as "Fatimer" and "littler Fatimer."[103] Historically, Fatimah was the daughter of the prophet Mohammed. Her marriage to Ali, who is considered the legitimate heir of the prophet's authority by Shia Muslims, produced Mohammed's only surviving line of descendants.[104]

Twenty-five years after that tithables list, the name given to a child born shortly after George Washington's death indicates at least the continuation of some elements of Muslim culture, if not the actual practice of the religion. Late in the year 1800, a young, seemingly unmarried mulatto woman named Letty, who lived at Washington's Muddy Hole Farm, gave birth to a little girl she decided to call "Nila." This unusual name is the phonetic spelling of a Muslim woman's name, Naailah, which means "someone who acquires something" or "someone who gets what they want." In accordance with her late husband's final wishes, Martha Washington took steps at the end of 1800 to free those slaves who had belonged to him, including Letty, her three children, both her parents, and all her siblings. It may be that Nila was an old name, remembered in Letty's family or that of her baby's father, from Africa. Maybe she simply knew someone named Nila and wanted her daughter to carry the name of her friend. Perhaps, having already given birth to two little boys, Billy and Henry, Letty was delighted to finally have a daughter. Given the timing of the little girl's birth, however, it is also possible that this baby's name was bestowed in commemoration of her family's newly acquired freedom. If the latter interpretation is correct, some knowledge of Muslim tradition or a familiarity with the Arabic language could still be found in the larger African American community in Fairfax

County or Alexandria, if not at Mount Vernon itself, at the beginning of the nineteenth century.[105]

To a great extent, the religious life of the Mount Vernon plantation mirrored its social makeup. At the top were George and Martha Washington and their family, following the formal and rather reserved practices of eighteenth-century Anglicanism, which stressed the need for private devotions and service to one's church and community, through work on the vestry and charitable contributions. They, in turn, supported the religious needs of their hired and indentured employees, who hailed from England, Ireland, Scotland, Germany, and France and probably represented a wide variety of Christian denominations, by giving time off to attend church services and occasionally purchasing devotional materials for their use.[106] In contrast to the whites at the top and middle of the social scale who, whether they practiced or not, came out of a Judeo-Christian background, the African and African American slaves who made up roughly 90 percent of Mount Vernon's population may have subscribed to a more diverse system of belief, combining elements of Christianity, acquired in America, with religious traditions they brought from Africa.[107] In looking at the practice of religion at Mount Vernon, one is struck by the thought that when George Washington spoke of the need for religious toleration and freedom—writing of his belief that "every man, conducting himself as a good citizen" was "accountable to God alone for his religious opinions," and should "be protected in worshipping the Deity according to the dictates of his own conscience"—he could have been describing the situation at his own home.[108]

A Time of Rest

For those slaves who did not outlive George Washington, freedom came only through their own deaths, but there is precious little information about the rites by which their bodies were consigned to the grave. While conducting the research for the reenactment of Washington's funeral in the late 1990s, researchers at Mount Vernon found only two descriptions relating to funeral and burial customs of enslaved African Americans prior to the Civil War. One told of how, following Nat Turner's Rebellion in 1831, the community lost a number of privileges, including the opportunity "to have public funerals, unless a white person officiates. . . . Their funerals formerly gave them great satisfaction, and it was customary here to furnish the relations of the deceased with bacon, spirit, flour, sugar, and butter, with which a grand entertainment, in their way, was got up."[109] Another described how "old Aunt Henny, descendant surely of some Ethiopian queen, and freed slave of Lord Fairfax," after living to a "great age" and serving "three generations of newcomers after serving no one knows how many Fairfaxes," was laid to rest in "her last mistress' wedding gown, which she had long ago secured and d[y]ed a decent black and laid away for the purpose."[110]

The interviews done by the Works Progress Administration with elderly freed slaves during the Great Depression also provide clues to funeral and burial customs on plantations during the antebellum period. As with so many aspects of slave life, funeral and burial customs varied from plantation to plantation, depending on the wishes of the slave owner. Silas Jackson, a Virginia slave who was born in the late 1840s, later recalled that "at each funeral," his former master and mistress attended "the service conducted in the cabin where the deceased was, from there taken to the slave graveyard. A lot [was] dedicated for that purpose, situated about ¾ of a mile from the cabins near a hill."[111] In contrast, Henry James Trentham, who lived as a slave in North Carolina about the same time, remembered a different sort of funeral on the plantation where he lived: "When a slave died, there was only a few to go to the burying. They didn't have time to go, they was so busy working."[112] James V. Deane was born on a plantation in Charles County, Maryland, near the Potomac River, in 1850. He mentioned that there was a graveyard on the property where he had seen many slave funerals but noted that there was no service. Graves were marked by a simple wooden post. In contrast, Isaac Martin, who was a slave in Texas prior to the Civil War, recalled that "when anybody die, dey have a fun'rel." Everybody got off from work to attend the ceremony, at which the deceased was placed in "a ho'made coffin."[113]

At the end of their lives, the slaves at Mount Vernon were laid to rest in one of several cemeteries scattered throughout the plantation.[114] The cemetery at the Mansion House Farm is located in a quiet, wooded area near the Washington family tomb. In her description of a visit to Mount Vernon in 1833, Caroline Moore noted that "near [Washington's] Tomb, you see the burying place of his slaves containing 150 graves."[115] Five years later, another visitor recorded that an elderly slave told him that "a hundred people of colour" were buried in front of the Washington family's new tomb.[116] Both documentary and graphic evidence suggest that paling fences were present either around the entire graveyard, at least one group of graves (perhaps a family plot), or some single graves. An 1855 *Plan of Mount Vernon, the Home of Washington* by Charles Currier shows a group of twelve graves divided into two rows, running east to west, with the individual burials oriented

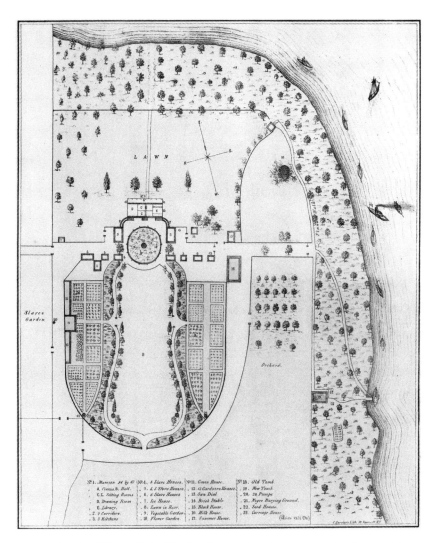

FIG. 14. An 1855 lithograph by Charles Currier showing graves at the slave burial ground at Mount Vernon (*at right, below and to the left of the docked boat in the river*), enclosed by a fence. (Courtesy of the Mount Vernon Ladies' Association)

north to south. Those graves appear to be enclosed by a fence. Nine years earlier, a visitor described seeing some "servants busy in a little grove, in front of the new tomb," where they "were enclosing with a paling a grave very neatly sodded. . . . It was the grave of a favorite servant, an aged colored woman, whose good and amiable character won respect and regard." Nearby, a workman pointed out the grave of Billy Lee, "Washington's favorite servant, who was with him in his campaigns, fulfilling his simple duties

FIG. 15. Archaeologist working in the slave burial ground at Mount Vernon. The dark rectangles are the tops of grave shafts. (Courtesy of the Mount Vernon Ladies' Association)

faithfully and affectionately. The spot is not forgotten, though the tramp of passing years has leveled the little mound." At that point, Lee had been dead for thirty-five years, plenty of time for the burial mound to subside.[117]

Grave markers present in the nineteenth century have disappeared over the years, but remote sensing of this site conducted in the 1980s revealed the presence of about fifty possible graves, oriented roughly on an east-west axis.[118] While this is the customary western model for placing bodies, there is a tradition in the local African American community that the bodies were laid this way so that they faced Africa, a way of symbolizing their desire to return home.[119] Currently, a major multiyear study of the slave burial ground is underway by Mount Vernon archaeologists in order to determine the extent and boundaries of the cemetery, as well as the exact number of people interred there. Eventually, there are plans to precisely map this area, showing the location and orientation of each burial.[120] The reference earlier to the mound covering William Lee's grave, as well as very recent discoveries at the slave burial ground, suggest that dirt was mounded over the graves in a manner similar to West African practices, which continued to be followed in African American cemeteries in the southeastern United States. This interpretation is strengthened by the discovery of upside-down crockery and a white button in association with at least two of the graves. The Mount Vernon burial ground project is expected to continue for several more years, so there should be further discoveries in the future, as well as additional publications describing and explaining these findings.[121]

Before being lowered into the grave, the bodies of both slaves and hired white servants were first placed into coffins made on the plantation.[122] For example, when a slave named Jenny or "Jinney" died in childbirth at Dogue Run in 1794, the carpenters spent half a day making a coffin for her body. The next year, fifty nails were given to Isaac, the head carpenter, to make a coffin for Lucy's son Daniel. Several years later, during the week ending April 7, 1798, the estate's carpenters reported "making a Coffin for one of the children, which came from U[nio]n Farm."[123] There is also evidence for some sort of social gathering associated with the death. When the wife of Hercules, the cook, died in 1787, Martha Washington ordered that he be given three bottles of rum "to bury his wife." It is likely that the rum was meant to be shared with other mourners at either a wake before or a meal after the funeral, though it may have been used as payment for the services of those who washed the body and otherwise prepared it for burial.[124]

Conclusion

While the Africans and African Americans who lived and worked at Mount Vernon seem to have been fairly typical of slaves on large plantations throughout Virginia, they probably had more freedom over certain aspects of their lives than the average modern visitor—raised with visions of antebellum, deep South, cotton plantations as the norm—would suspect. Individuals were given time and permission to travel locally in order to form and sustain their family relationships. In their time off from work, the

Mount Vernon slaves engaged in tasks that would earn them small sums of money to better their lives. They also enjoyed time with their friends, took part in local cultural events, and nurtured their spiritual lives. While all of this may not sound too different from the way people live today, we must never forget, as the slaves could not, that at any time their master could change his mind, rescind a certain liberty, and upend their lives.

8

"Better ... Fed Than Negroes Generally Are"

Diet of the Mount Vernon Slaves

In a letter written to English agronomist Arthur Young, George Washington described the basic diet of an eighteenth-century slave as "bread, made of the Indian Corn, Butter milk, Fish (pickled herrings) frequently, and meat now and then . . . In addition to these, ground is often allowed them for gardening, and priviledge given them to raise dung-hill fowls for their own use."[1] Washington elaborated on this basic sketch in several other letters. He informed farm manager William Pearce that he "always used to lay in a great quantity of Fish for them and when we were at home meat, fat, and other things were now and then given to them besides."[2] In his estimate of the cost of renting a neighbor's slaves for a year, Washington proposed that each of them receive a bit less than a half barrel of fish and almost twenty-two pounds of meat, issued "now and then."[3] The journal of Julian Niemcewicz gives a further breakdown of the slave rations on the estate. Slaves received "one pack [peck], one gallon of maize per week; this makes one quart a day, and half as much for the children, with 20 herrings each per month. At harvest time those who work in the fields have salt meat."[4]

It is not always easy to translate these documentary references into a quantifiable form, but it appears that each working enslaved adult at Mount Vernon would have gotten eight quarts of cornmeal and approximately thirty-six ounces of fish per week. This works out to a daily ration of a little over one quart of cornmeal and about five to eight ounces of fish. The lower number is based on the size of modern herrings, while the upper one is extrapolated from the size of those two hundred years ago. Overfishing and pollution have combined to make today's herring somewhat smaller today than previously, when each was roughly fifteen to eighteen inches long and weighed about twelve ounces.[5] Another historian, using Washington's calculations on renting slaves, suggests that the daily ration worked out to about 2 pounds of cornmeal and 8¼ ounces of fish, with the addition of about ½ pound of meat each week. According to his figures, this diet provided an average of 3,752 calories per day, comparable to the rations given to soldiers in the Continental Army during the American Revolution, as well as to Tory prisoners being held in Maryland during the same conflict.[6] Modern estimates that a medium-sized man in his twenties doing "moderately heavy agricultural labor" would need to take in between 3,200 and 4,000 calories each day suggest that, at least calorically, the rations given the slaves were adequate.[7]

The same is not necessarily true in regard to the nutritional value of the limited foods provided to the enslaved, which would have left them susceptible to compromised immune systems and disease.[8] Analysis of surviving weekly work reports from the year 1786 at Mount Vernon shows that slaves on all the farms comprising the Mount Vernon estate lost only 287 of 25,716 potential days of work, or 1.1 percent, because of illness.[9] Other sources indicate that the enslaved population on the estate was experiencing rapid natural growth, especially after the American Revolution. As was discussed in a previous chapter, at the time of Washington's death in 1799, the average age of the slaves on his four outlying farms was not quite twenty-one years, and almost 59 percent of these people were nineteen years old or younger (almost 35 percent were nine or under). Taken together, these two sets of statistics suggest a fairly healthy population. Given the deficiencies of the basic diet, the slaves themselves found ways to rectify the shortcomings in their rations.

One Mount Vernon guest, Winthrop Sargent, wrote that he considered the Mount Vernon slaves to be "better clothed and fed than negroes generally are in this Country."[10] This blanket statement is difficult to prove, however. George Washington himself believed that on small farms, where a man worked his own land with the help of two or three slaves, there was very little difference in the "manner of living" between master and slave; everyone on the place either thrived or starved together. Washington was well aware that those who owned larger places might try to cut their expenses by limiting the rations of their slaves, feeding them "on bread alone."[11] The slaves at another large eighteenth-century plantation, Robert Carter's Nomini Hall, received "a peck of Corn, & a pound of Meat a Head" each week, a ration somewhat smaller than that given to the Mount Vernon slaves. According to Philip Vickers Fithian, the tutor of Carter's children, "Mr Carter is allow'd by all, & from what I have already seen of others, I make no Doubt at all but he is, by far the most humane to his Slaves of any in these parts!" The young man was so appalled at the poor care and abuse he saw on other plantations that he could not help exclaiming at that point, "Good God! are these Christians?"[12] The slaves at Monticello had things a little better than those at Mount Vernon and were probably much better off in regard to their food rations than many others in Virginia at this time. Thomas Jefferson's adult slaves received an allotment of one peck of cornmeal, one pound of pickled beef or pork, four salted herrings, and a gill (four fluid ounces) of molasses per week.[13]

Despite the differences in the foods they were given, slaves at Mount Vernon, Nomini Hall, and Monticello all worked for extremely wealthy men. The slaves' rather tedious rations seem almost extravagant when compared to those enslaved on smaller plantations. Captured British officer Thomas Anburey made the acquaintance of several plantation owners during the war and described the typical diet of their slaves: "Their meals consist of homminy and salt, and if their master is a man of humanity, touched by the finer feelings of love and sensibility, he allows them twice a week a little fat skimmed milk, rusty bacon, or salt herring, to relish this miserable and scanty fare." According to Anburey, the master at Jones's Plantation near Charlottesville, Virginia, a neighbor of Thomas Jefferson, was an especially hard man. Instead of giving his slaves any of the rations detailed above, he made them raise all their own food: he provided them each with "an acre of ground, and all Saturday afternoon to raise grain and poultry for themselves."[14]

Starches

The basic building block of the slave diet at Mount Vernon—as it was throughout the South—was cornmeal. Large quantities of corn were needed to provide the weekly ration for the more than three hundred slaves at Mount Vernon by the end of George Washington's life. In 1790, farm manager George Augustine Washington wrote his uncle that about 620 barrels of corn would be required to feed the slaves over the next twelve months and expressed the hope that with "proper economy . . . the corn made this year will be adequate to the support of the estate."[15] By 1794, the slaves were consuming about 14 barrels of corn per week, or 728 barrels annually.[16] George Washington wanted to switch to a more English pattern of agriculture and concentrate on wheat cultivation but felt constrained because corn was the mainstay of the slaves' diet:

> I do not scruple to confess, that notwithstanding the profit which appears to result from the growth of Corn and Potatoes, or Corn and Carrots, or both, thus blended, my wish is to exclude Indian Corn altogether from my system of Cropping, but we are so habituated to the use of this grain, and it is so much better for negroes than any other, that it is not to be discarded; consequently to introduce it in the most profitable, or least injurious manner, ought to be the next consideration with the Farmer.[17]

According to artist Benjamin Henry Latrobe, who visited Mount Vernon in the summer of 1796, Washington considered corn "infinitely preferable" to wheat nutritionally, at least for his slaves, although neither man spelled out the reasoning behind that statement. Washington's experiments indicated that "though the negroes, while the novelty lasted, seemed to prefer wheat bread as being the food of their masters, they soon grew tired of it." Feeding the slaves either wheat or rye would also, in Washington's opinion, require that they have considerably more meat than they needed when given corn.[18] The Mount Vernon slaves did sometimes get wheat and other starches, but it was generally when the corn supply was running low. In 1786, for example, Washington mixed inferior grades of wheat flour with rye for his slaves.[19] The following year he instructed his nephew to use the old wheat, if it could not be sold, in order to make flour for the slaves and "if necessity obliges you[,] to resort to the Potatoes and Pease for their support."[20] Often these supplemental grains or legumes were of poor quality. During the Revolution, when farm manager Lund Washington could find markets for only the best grades of flour, the slaves and livestock at Mount Vernon were given the poorer product, which had "soured and spoiled" for want of a buyer.[21] Eating spoiled meal of any type could be risky, leading to illness and lost work. When Dundee, one of the ditchers, was sick for a day in the summer of 1798, his condition was blamed on "eating meal made of damaged corn."[22]

On occasion, especially toward the end of Washington's life, the slaves were given wheat flour, presumably unspoiled, from the mill. Davy Gray, the enslaved overseer, received 25 bushels of middling flour, valued at £0.3.9, in 1797 and another 100 bushels of the same, valued at 15 shillings, the following year. Between the fall of 1797 and the same season in 1798, the fishery made use of 3 shillings' worth of middling flour (20 bushels), while the "Mansion Negroes" and slaves at River Farm, Muddy Hole, Dogue Run, and Union Farms received 861 bushels of a lesser grade of flour called "ship stuff."[23] Another reference in a financial ledger indicates that sick slaves were indulged with a special diet, including wheat flour. In 1797, twelve bushels of middling flour was used by the "Children when Sick." Since Martha Washington's youngest grandchild was then sixteen years old and considered virtually an adult, the children referred to were undoubtedly enslaved.[24]

Although his military and political responsibilities kept George Washington away from home for long periods of time, he still monitored the rations of the slaves as closely as he could. He wrote in 1793: "I see by the Mill report for the last week, 23 bushels of meal was brought to the Mansion house, when the usual quantity for that place is 20 bushels, why was this done? If 30 bushels was brought there it would, I am persuaded be consumed, or otherwise disposed of in the week."[25] One week later, he brought up the continued discrepancy: "By the last week[']s report I see that 22 Bushels of Meal has been [brought] from the Mill. The person (old Jack) who serves it out, must acct. for the necessity of this increase; 20 bushels used to suffice, why two and 3 more now?"[26] The following year Washington noticed in a report from farm manager William Pearce that the corn crop for the year amounted to 1,639 barrels. His attention to detail required him to bring to Pearce's notice the fact that "your weekly consumption of this article is 22 barrels to the Stock, and about 14 to the Negros; amounting together to 36 barr[e]ls; which multiplied by 52, the number of weeks in a year makes 1872; and is 233 barrls. more than is made."[27]

Protein

The bounty of the eighteenth-century Potomac provided George Washington with both additional income and food for his slaves. Some idea of the riches to be found in the river were recorded by a European visitor to Mount Vernon during the Revolutionary War who saw "from General Washington's house . . . for several hours together" "hundreds, perhaps . . . thousands of sturgeon, at a great height from the water at the same instant, so that the quantity in the river must have been inconceivably great."[28] The importance of the Potomac as a food source for the Mount Vernon slaves, and the depth of their reliance on it, are evident in a 1794 letter in which Washington ordered his farm manager to "secure a sufficiency of fish for the use of my own people from the first that comes, otherwise they may be left in the lurch . . . by depending on what is called the glut."[29] Salted fish had been the standard fare of the poor and working classes in England for centuries, so in using fish as a major food source for his slaves, Washington was not only taking advantage of a local resource but following a traditional practice of the mother country.[30]

In the summer of 1798, Julian Ursyn Niemcewicz walked to the fishery during his visit and described several varieties of fish commonly eaten by the slaves. He referred to herring, one of the staples, as "the best nourishment for the Negroes." Garfish were "skinned while still alive," and their red meat, which was "little esteemed," served "only as food for negroes." The Polish visitor also saw catfish of two sorts, white and black: "The first is considered excellent, especially for broth; the second, which is black, is left for the blacks. We caught 30 of the latter kind; the hapless negroes got them all."[31] Archaeological work in the House for Families reinforced the documentary evidence that fish was a staple in the slave diet at Mount Vernon. Among the varieties of fish identified from this site were catfish, perch, redhorse, two types of gar, bony fish, sturgeon, herring, alewife, shad, sucker, pickerel, sunfish, bluegill, crappie, and bass.[32]

Shortages during the Revolutionary War caused Lund Washington considerable worry about whether there would be enough salt to preserve fish for the support of the Mount Vernon slaves. In 1776, he had on hand in several locations about 350 or 400 barrels of salt, which he refused to sell, "knowg we cou'd not get more & our people must have Fish—therefore told the [prospective buyers] I had none."[33] Two years later he wrote to inform George Washington of the tenuous situation at home: "I have but very little salt, of which we must make the most, I mean to make a Brine, and after cut[tin]g off the Head and Bellys dipping them in the Brine for but a short time, then Hang them up and cure them by smoke, or dry them in the Sun, for our people being so long accustomd to have Fish when ever they Wanted woud think it very hard to have none at all."[34] Once they were preserved, the fish were secured in a locked storage building and the keys kept at the mansion house. On a regular schedule, a quantity of fish, determined by the number of working and nonworking slaves on each of the five farms, was sent from the storehouse for distribution by the overseers.[35]

Protein was also provided in the form of pork, beef, and mutton. As on other plantations, these meats might be either of poorer quality than those eaten by whites, were foodstuffs that had not sold and were in danger of spoiling, or were less desirable cuts.[36] For instance, Lund Washington once wrote that he had cleaned and smoked a quantity of pork to make bacon, which he intended for sale: "The remainder although it will not sell the Negroes are fond of it," and he intended to distribute it to them.[37] Some of the meats given to the slaves came from older animals, whose flesh would have been tougher and stringier. A surviving farm ledger for 1797 and early 1798 records the slaughter of "an Old Bull," providing 590 pounds of meat, which was salted for use by "the people" at Muddy Hole Farm.[38] While people in the eighteenth century tended to eat parts of animals that would be unappealing to many modern Americans, such as calf's head and tongue, udder, cow heels, and tripe, the offal white people did not want found its way to the slave quarters. Washington wrote to a new farm manager in 1793 that after the hogs had been butchered and allowances given out to the overseers and white servants, what he called "the haslets and guts," meaning the heart, liver, lungs, windpipe, throat, and intestines, were to be distributed to the slaves.[39]

Extra meat rations were issued to the Mount Vernon slaves during the harvest season and were occasionally provided for the sick. Lund Washington wrote his cousin in 1776 that he "thought last year there was a Sufficiency [of meat] put up to supply our Labourers in Harvest—but we got scarcely any."[40] Almost twenty years later, George Washington sent instructions that "if the culled sheep and other useful stock cannot be sold they had better (rather than run the hazard of losing them) be salted for next harvest."[41] Many of these animals were described as old or had died in accidents; others had been killed because their "mischeffus" personalities became problematic.[42] Not all of the meat issued in the harvest was salted. One "Beef" was killed at Ferry Farm "for the use of harvest" in the summer of 1786, yielding four hundred pounds of meat. Half of this fresh meat was sent to workers at Muddy Hole, while the other half was divided between Ferry and River Farms.[43] During the summer of 1798, in addition to beef and pork, nine sheep and three lambs were provided to slaves bringing in the wheat harvest.[44] Several months earlier, a sheep from Dogue Run was sent to the Mansion House Farm, where it was "killed for the Sick."[45]

Certain slaves, primarily skilled workers and overseers, were given an allowance of meat, presumably of good quality, which was apportioned to them during or shortly after the slaughtering season. Two days before Christmas 1786, for instance, Isaac, the head carpenter who lived at the Mansion House Farm with his wife and seven daughters, was given a hog from Muddy Hole weighing eighty-four pounds "for his own use."[46] While this may have been a reward for particularly fine work done throughout the preceding year, it is more likely that the pork was considered part of Isaac's compensation for his position. In 1798, both Davy Gray at Muddy Hole Farm and Ben at Dogue Run received pork as an "allowance" from that year's kill. Gray was given three hogs, weighing 277 pounds total, while Ben got one hog weighing in at 106 pounds. Since both men worked as overseers, this meat was one of their "perks" for serving in that role. It should be noted, however, that this quantity suffers in comparison with the 500 to 1,200 pounds of meat that Washington's hired white servants generally received at the same time.[47]

Calcium

Much-needed calcium entered the diet through buttermilk, doled out occasionally by the Washingtons, as well as through vegetables the slaves grew for themselves.[48] The contract signed by a white man, Edward Violett, with George Washington required him to pay particular attention to the collection of milk and the making of butter. He was instructed to take "care tho' to let the Negroes have the benefit of the said milk after a proper use is made thereof and himself supplied."[49] There is no way of knowing how much milk the slaves actually received after the Washington household and Violett's family took what they needed. The poor quality of dairy cattle, both at Mount Vernon and throughout the South, also influenced the amount of milk the slaves received.[50] As one farm manager explained, Washington's cattle were "but indifferent and it will take some time before they can be brought to be so profitable as they ought or before much Can be made by butter the pr[e]sent stock of Cattle are too small and dwindling to Give much milk."[51]

The fact that Washington's slaves might not in the end have received very much buttermilk could actually have been something of a blessing. Medical studies have shown that a sizable percentage of adults living in sections of West Africa where the slave trade was conducted lack the enzymes necessary to digest cows' milk. Over 95 percent of the Ibo and Yoruba peoples of Nigeria are lactose intolerant, as are approximately 70–80 percent of modern African Americans (some scholars speculate that in the plantation South the figure might have been as high as almost 100 percent). Individuals with this condition can ingest only small quantities of milk products without suffering severe diarrhea.[52] According to one historian, the milk that was distributed to slaves on southern plantations probably went to only the very youngest children, whose bodies were still able to digest it.[53] There is no evidence from Mount Vernon that only children received milk, but this strong possibility should not be overlooked.

Another possible means of increasing the amount of calcium in the diet is suggested by bone evidence excavated from the cellar of the House for Families. Tooth marks found on the ends of vertebrae and long bones, like ribs, left over from meals of beef, pork, mutton, venison, and chickens may indicate that the slaves were eating the cartilage and soft ends of the bones. The practice of eating bones in just this way has been documented in both western and southern Africa, as a social custom following a meal, as well as in the West Indies, where the protocol differs slightly. A variation on this practice may also help to explain some other findings of the archaeologists studying food remains from this particular site. While the documentary evidence suggests that fish, especially herring, were the staple protein source for the slaves at Mount Vernon, analysis of the animal remains shows that fish made up only 16.78 percent of the diet, ranking third after beef (37.41 percent) and pork (24.63 percent). Conversations with several Virginians, both white and black, who either grew up in the late nineteenth and early twentieth centuries or had relatives who did have elicited the information that the bones in salted herring, when the fish is "fried hard," become soft and are not simply edible but often relished. If a majority of the slaves ate their ration of salted herring, bones and all, the remains excavated from the cellar may vastly underrepresent the percentage of fish in the diet.[54]

Hunting, Trapping, and Gardens

A considerable proportion of the foods eaten by slaves at Mount Vernon were acquired through their own efforts at night and on Sundays, the times when they were not working for the Washingtons. Excavation of the cellar of a slave quarter at the Mansion House Farm found both gunflints and lead shot, indicating that Washington's slaves had access to guns, as well as the remains of a considerable number of wild birds and mammals, which could have been either hunted or trapped. Among the identified bird species were several varieties of wild ducks, including dabbling ducks, mallards, widgeons, ruddy ducks, canvasbacks, redheads, ring-necked ducks, scaups, goldeneyes, and mergansers; coots; grouse, partridge, and pheasant; quail; and several types of pigeon. Remains of squirrels, rabbits, opossums, and raccoons also confirm the surviving documentary evidence that Mount Vernon's slaves hunted small animals.[55]

In addition to hunting and trapping, the Mount Vernon slaves also used the produce of their own garden plots and the "dung-hill fowls" they were

FIG. 16. Gun flint excavated at Mount Vernon, providing physical evidence that slaves were hunting to supplement their diets and incomes. (Courtesy of the Mount Vernon Ladies' Association)

permitted to raise to add variety and necessary nutrients to their diets, to bring in extra income to purchase small luxuries, and to retain elements of African culture in a new land. All of these factors made the gardens psychologically important to people who had little outward control over the course of their lives.[56] Julian Niemcewicz described one of these gardens outside a cabin at Union Farm in 1798: "A very small garden planted with vegetables was close by, with 5 or 6 hens, each one leading ten to fifteen chickens. It is the only comfort that is permitted them [the slaves]; for they may not keep either ducks, geese, or pigs. They sell the poultry in Alexandria and procure for themselves a few amenities."[57] The gardens did not always abut the quarters, however, and their location may have changed periodically with George Washington's plans for his estate. Late in 1792, for example, he discussed some improvements at the Mansion House Farm, "to give . . . a better appearance as the house [was] approached" from the river. It is not clear exactly what location was being considered, but it seems to have been somewhere down the hill to the south of the mansion, which is perhaps a ten-minute walk from the main slave quarter. Washington informed his farm manager that since "the home house people (the industrious part of them at least) might want ground for their truck patches, they might, for this purpose cultivate what would be cleared."[58] A Sunday market in Alexandria was the destination of many of the foodstuffs produced by the slaves at Mount Vernon.[59]

The gardens of the people enslaved at Mount Vernon were probably similar to those on other plantations in British America, and especially those in Virginia. Slaves as far away as the West Indian islands of Montserrat and Antigua used their free time on Sundays to tend the small garden plots allotted to them by their owners, where they grew foodstuffs such as yams, guinea corn, potatoes, and eddoes, or taro root, to supplement both their rations and their income.[60] A much closer example can be found in Virginia, where at Nomini Hall, tutor Philip Vickers Fithian found the slaves "digging up their small Lots of ground allow'd by their Master for Potatoes, peas &c; All such work for themselves they constantly do on Sundays, as they are otherwise employed on every other Day."[61]

Archaeological evidence shows what the slaves were growing for themselves. Between 1984 and 1985, the cellar of the House for Families at Mount Vernon yielded remains of several types of beans, peas, squash or melons, and watermelons. Twenty years later, reanalysis of the larger seeds found in the cellar showed the presence of a variety of plants, some of which were included in the weekly rations, as well as others grown in the slaves' gardens, and still more that were probably gathered from nearby forests and/or orchards: persimmons, corn, cherries, peaches, beans and/or peas, bottle gourds, wheat, black walnuts, and fragments of what could be either walnut, hickory, or pecan shells.[62]

Foodstuffs for Sale and Trade

George Washington's cash memoranda and account books are filled with references to purchases of chickens, eggs, melons, cucumbers, and honey from his slaves, as well as those belonging to neighbors, and shed further light on the nature of these gardens. For example, he paid Old Doll, the former cook, six shillings for a dozen chickens in September 1791 and purchased four melons from Nathan Gray for £0.1.8 the following year.[63] Niemcewicz seems to have been mistaken about the slaves not keeping ducks, however, for Washington purchased six from Old Doll in July 1792 and another ten from "old Sall" in September of the same year.[64] In addition to chickens, Roger supplied "Egs Mellions and Cucumber" in 1758.[65] The Mount Vernon household bought watermelons from slaves belonging to a Mrs. Coles in the summer of 1775 and from two slaves on the estate, Breechy and Tom Davis, during the summer of 1792.[66] Honey was acquired at various times from Nat, Davy Gray, Sambo Anderson, and Isaac, indicating that they might have kept bees.[67]

Slaves elsewhere in Virginia similarly profited from their "dung hill fowls" and gardens at this period. Like George Washington, Landon Carter of Sabine Hall obtained eggs and chickens from his slaves. Instead of purchasing those commodities, however, he traded for them. After his slave Nat brought him half a dozen chickens, the planter reflected, "I have been asked why I don't sell my salted Pork. . . . My Poor Slaves raise fowls, and eggs in order to exchange with their Master now and then; and, though I don't value the worth of what they bring, Yet I enjoy the humanity of refreshing such poor creatures in what they (though perhaps mistakenly) call a blessing."[68] Among the produce Thomas Jefferson's household acquired from his slaves were chickens, eggs, ducks, strawberries, apples, peaches, melons, muskmelons, watermelons, cucumbers, squash, cabbage, potatoes, beets, lettuce, "salad" (presumably greens of some sort), sprouts, greens, and "snaps" (probably green beans or some type of pea).[69]

Several intriguing notations in one of the Mount Vernon ledgers show that at least some of the slaves were using the money they earned to buy extra foodstuffs from their master. Sambo Anderson, the African-born carpenter at the Mansion House Farm, purchased a barrel of fine flour for £1.10.0 sometime between October 1, 1797, and October 1, 1798.[70] During the slaughtering season of 1798, Boatswain, a ditcher at the Mansion House Farm, paid his master $3.92 for 56 pounds of pork, while his neighbor Anderson purchased 162 pounds of pork for $11.33. About a week after these transactions and three days before Christmas, Nathaniel, a blacksmith, spent $20.71 on 35½ gallons of whiskey.[71] Whether all of the money had been earned by these three men, or if several people pooled their resources in order to make each transaction, these purchases still show a more fluid exchange between master and slave than many contemporary Americans would probably think possible.

Beverages

The surviving documentation provides less information about beverages consumed by those enslaved at Mount Vernon than about what they ate. In 1792, Washington told Englishman Arthur Young that his slaves frequently received buttermilk, the liquid remaining after butter was churned from cream.[72] Rum was doled out on a regular basis to certain skilled laborers. Each week, a manager or overseer handed out a predetermined ration of rum from the storehouse to some of the enslaved artisans. The "Joiners &

Cornelius" received a combined total of 10½ pints per week, while the shoe-maker and tailor got 3½ pints. Two pints each went to Davy Gray, Will, and Morris, enslaved overseers at the River, Muddy Hole, and Dogue Run Farms, respectively. Another two were given to head carpenter Isaac. These amounts were equal to the rations received by several hired whites, including Thomas Green, the carpenter supervisor, and the English gardener.[73]

Rum could be a reward for doing a particular task or an incentive during times of especially hard work. For instance, in 1783, prior to George Washington's return from the Revolution, Lund Washington purchased forty-eight gallons of Taffia Rum "for Harves[t]."[74] Sam and Boatswain were given rum in small increments in January 1787 for "burng the brick kiln."[75] The following month, Nat received a bottle of rum for making charcoal or "burng coal."[76] Two bottles went to slaves who were sent on an errand to Georgetown in February of that year.[77] One bottle of rum was shared by several slaves who helped free a cow stuck in the mud, and another pint delivered to those who unloaded some fish from the boat after dark.[78] Two bottles were given to Boatswain to share with his fellow ditchers in March 1787 "per the Genls Order."[79] At least six gallons were distributed to slaves working at the fishery the following month.[80] Other occasions for which rum was passed out included finishing the deer park, going into town on an errand, cutting grass, mowing and stacking hay, working on the millrace, ditching, and getting out flour.[81]

Rum was also issued to slaves who were ailing. A sick woman rented from Washington's neighbor Mrs. French was given a pint of rum in January 1787.[82] Between August 23 and September 9 of that same year, three bottles of rum were given out to women giving birth, probably as either an anesthetic or analgesic.[83]

George Washington and others in the eighteenth century saw rum not just as a reward or an incentive but as an actual necessity for the health of those doing hard labor. While this is suggested by the above cases where rum was given to sick slaves, it was more specifically spelled out in Washington's correspondence concerning his army during the Revolution. In June 1781, Washington wrote about his fears concerning the dangerous consequences of a shortage of rum: "Not a drop of Rum has yet come on, and the Physicians report that the Artificers (who labour exceedingly hard) are falling sick for want of it."[84] Two months later, the army had received very little rum, and Washington wrote another reminder: "This Article is so necessary for the Health as well as comfort of the Soldiery at this Season, that I wish it might be particularly attended to."[85] During the Yorktown campaign the following month, Washington expressed quite strongly the prevailing opinion about the health benefits of rum, when he wrote that his soldiers' "health depends upon a liberal use of Spirits in the judgment of the most Skil[l]ful Physicians, who are best acquainted with the Climate."[86]

One tantalizing notation in Washington's accounts hints that his slaves were making beer, probably for their own consumption. In the fall of 1798, Washington purchased six pounds of hops from Boatswain for $1.25.[87] Although hops can be used to make yeast, the breads used by enslaved African American are assumed to have been simple mixtures of cornmeal and water, which would not have required time to rise and were nowhere near as labor-intensive to produce as yeast breads. There would have been no incentive for the slaves to waste either space in their garden plots or their own precious free time on cultivating a crop for which they had no use. Hops, however, is a primary ingredient in the production of beer, and a type of beer made from Indian corn was known in West Africa. Its production could have been a skill that was either brought from Africa or learned on the plantation, for beer was also made by Mount Vernon's white population.[88] The slaves at Monticello are also known to have sold hops to their master's household. Two Norfolk laws of 1764 and 1773 prohibited the sale of a number of items by slaves, including beer, a fact indicating that they were brewing but also that this practice was causing problems.[89]

The slaves may actually have brewed at least two types of beer: the regular variety made with hops and persimmon beer. The latter was made by the Washington family at Mount Vernon during the Revolution, when imported beer was largely impossible to obtain. Lund Washington wrote in March 1778, "I find from experience there is a fine spirit to be made from persimmons, but neglected to gather them for that purpose, only got some for the purpose of makeg Beer."[90] The fact that persimmon seeds were the largest category of botanical materials found in the cellar of the House for Families is particularly interesting because slaves in North America are known to have used persimmons and honey locust pods for making a type of beer that came to be associated with Christmas, probably because persimmons ripen after the first frost, so they would have been in season at this time of year.[91]

Liquor, whether in the form of issued rum, wine pilfered from the mansion, whiskey purchased from the plantation's distillery, or homemade beer, was a problem for at least some of the slaves at Mount Vernon. In discussing a personality conflict between two of the men, "Overseer Will" and his nephew Tom Davis, George Washington confided to his farm manager that the older man was probably the more trustworthy of the two, although he believed both of them "will drink."[92] One of the best-known slaves at

FIG. 17. Persimmon seeds found during excavation of the slave quarters at Mount Vernon. Persimmons were used for making a type of beer. (Courtesy of the Mount Vernon Ladies' Association)

Mount Vernon had a drinking problem as well, at least in his later years. George Washington's valet Billy Lee had accompanied him throughout the eight years of the Revolutionary War and in consideration for his loyalty during that period been freed after his master's death. Unfortunately, what should have been a well-earned retirement seems to have been spoiled by an addiction to alcohol, probably the result of using liquor to dull the pain of his broken kneecaps. Lee was said to be frequently drunk and eventually suffered from delirium tremens.[93] There is no way of knowing how widespread alcoholism may have been on the plantation or the number of families affected.

Stealing Food

Slaves on plantations throughout British America, in both the eighteenth-century South and the West Indies, used theft to supplement their diet. Those at Mount Vernon were no exception.[94] Elsewhere in eighteenth-century Virginia, Landon Carter complained in 1770 that he was trying a new scheme for planting in order to protect his vegetable crops "against thieves of which I must have abundance or I could not have so many pease and beans stolen from me every year."[95]

Wine, rum, butter, milk, corn, meat in the smokehouse and on the hoof, potatoes, and fruit were all vulnerable to theft by the people enslaved at

Mount Vernon. Concerning his domestic staff, George Washington complained that "the knowledge I have of my servants is such, as to believe, that if opportunities are given them they will take off two glasses of wine for every one that is drank by . . . visitors, and tell you they were used by them."[96] Sometime earlier, in the first year of the Revolutionary War, Lund Washington reported that the rum supply had been breached: "I have sold 6 Hhds [hogsheads] of your Rum which is all you have to sell—it took one Hhd to full up those 6 and rather more. [O]ne was Broach'd when it first Come and part of it Use'd . . . three Mr. Custis had and one you remember was drawn of[f] by some rogue or other."[97] One of the enslaved women, Isaac and Kitty's daughter Sinah, was suspected of taking "a pretty ample toll of both Milk and butter" from the dairy in 1792, and Davy Gray, the enslaved overseer, was thought to have allowed some of the potatoes "to be made way with."[98] In his description of the Mount Vernon gardens, Julian Niemcewicz reported seeing a variety of fruits—berries, currants, raspberries, strawberries, gooseberries, peaches, and cherries—but found them "much inferior to ours [in Poland], which the *robins, blackbirds and Negroes* devour before they are ripe."[99]

In 1795, on a "satterday night," someone stole several pieces of bacon from the smokehouse after ripping up a board from the back of the building.[100] Upon learning of the theft, Washington wrote his farm manager with suggestions as to who the culprit might be:

> I wish you could find out the thief who robbed the Meat house at Mount Vernon, and bring him to punishment. And at the sametime secure the house against future attempts. . . . Nathan [Gray, a cook] has been suspected, if not detected, in an attempt of this sort formerly; and is as likely as any one to be guilty of it now. Postilion Joe [Richardson] has been caught in similar practices; and Sam, I am sure would not be restrain[ed] by any qualms of conscience, if he saw an opening to do the like.[101]

Unfortunately, this incident is not mentioned in any more of the surviving correspondence, and there is no way of knowing if one of these three men, or someone else entirely, was responsible for the theft.

Livestock feed was even pilfered for the benefit of the chickens Washington bought from his slaves. James Anderson, Mount Vernon's farm manager in 1798, suggested one possible explanation for why the sheep were not gaining weight as they should have been: "The Overseer, & feeder, are constantly directed by me to give such feeds, and in such plenty, as would make them [the sheep] very fatt[.] It is a great doubt with me whether these things are ever given them, there are so many fowls kept, that I believe one half of Horse, & other Cattles['] feed's goes to them."[102] Similarly, Landon Carter suspected his slaves of doing much the same thing in the summer of 1771, after his "house people" approached him with complaints that they were not receiving enough cornmeal. After some investigation, Carter concluded that there were two possible reasons for this grievance: either the miller was defrauding Carter by not providing enough for the slaves or the slaves' complaints were "a contrivance . . . to get more to feed the[i]r [own] fowls."[103]

Aside from adding variety to their diets, enslaved people stole food for a variety of reasons. First was the fact that many of the slaves experienced hunger, probably as a result of nutritional inadequacies in their basic diet. Another possibility is that the strenuousness of a given individual's work or their physical condition might mean that the rations did not meet their particular needs. For example, a fieldworker's nutritional requirements were higher than those of a woman who spent her days knitting or sewing. Women would have higher nutritional needs when pregnant or nursing than they did before becoming pregnant. Anyone who has tried to feed an adolescent boy knows that they eat more than adults of the same size. A third possibility is that the rations provided on a specific plantation were considerably less than what was considered the standard. Stealing food could also be a way of getting back at, or resisting, a way of life that seemed unfair and hopeless. It was a way for slaves to feel they had some control over their situation in life. Being able to provide additional foodstuffs through theft, and thereby adding needed variety and nutrition to the tedious rations provided by a master might also have increased an individual slave's standing, both within his or her own family and in the African American community as a whole.[104]

Cooking

Cooking situations are known to have varied from plantation to plantation in the antebellum period. Most enslaved families were permitted to cook their own food and carried their midday meals with them to the field, a system they seem to have preferred. Masters on a few plantations, however, believed that cooking reduced the amount of time available for much-needed rest, leading them to designate certain slaves to cook at least some meals for the others. As one owner explained, "To make one negro cook for all is a saving of time. If there be but ten hands and these are allowed two hours at noon, one of which is employed in cooking their dinner, for all purposes of rest that hour had as well be spent in ploughing or hoeing, and would be equal to ten hours work of one hand; whereas, the fourth of that time would be sufficient for one to cook for all." While this system might lead to an improved diet and was definitely less work, it also tended to increase the regimentation of the slaves' everyday existence, interfered with family life, and provided more opportunity for the spread of disease.[105]

Whether or not the Mount Vernon slaves cooked their own meals is unclear. There are some indications that during the harvest and when the fish were running in the spring, cooks were assigned to prepare meals for the other slaves, who were working at a frantic pace during these short seasons. Washington wrote in his diary in the summer of 1769 that he thought the number of rakers he had would be sufficient and that the rest of the people, "after the water Carriers and Cooks are taken out," could be used to stack the wheat.[106] In 1798, he paid the "Seine Haulers, Fish carriers-[*unreadable word*] cleaners of Fish, Cook &ca" £10.6.3 for having been forced, due to the nature of work at the fishery, to be on duty four Sundays and the Easter holiday, when they would normally have been off.[107]

Several people are listed as cooks in Washington's 1799 slave lists: in addition to Lucy and thirty-one-year-old Nathan Gray at the Mansion House, there were Molly, aged forty-five, at Dogue Run; Hannah, an old woman at River Farm; and sixty-two-year-old Betty at Union Farm.[108] When Betty, who was described as "Oald," was sick for almost three weeks in December 1795, another unnamed person took over her duties.[109] Lucy and Nathan did the cooking for the Washington household and the white servants who ate at "the second table." It is unclear, however, if the cooks on the outlying farms were working for fellow slaves, the overseers, or other hired whites. In 1786, for example, Washington engaged some white ditchers, agreeing to pay them a certain amount of money for each rod of ditching they produced, in addition to daily rations of milk, spirits, bread baked at the Mansion House Farm, and meat cooked by Hannah, the wife of the enslaved overseer at Dogue Run.[110] A 1790 letter from George Augustine Washington to his uncle mentions that a new overseer, who was single, had been allowed "a Boy or Girl which[ever] can be most conveniently spared to cook &ca. for him but in case butter is made and Fowls raised for the House he [the overseer] is to superintend it and the person engaged in the business is to Cook for him."[111] If the cooks at Dogue Run, River, and Union Farms in 1799 were cooking for their fellow slaves and not an overseer, there is no way to determine whether they were responsible for some or all meals on a daily basis, or only at those times, like the harvest, when the other slaves did not have the time or energy to devote to the task.

Archaeological evidence from the House for Families cellar sheds light on how foods were prepared. Boiling may well have been a standard procedure with large cuts of meat from shoulders and loins, which entered the diet during the harvest or fishing seasons, as the meat ration for a skilled artisan, or through pilfered hogs and sheep. This technique had three advantages over roasting: it reduced the saltiness of preserved meats, made the flesh of older animals more tender, and was a much less labor-intensive procedure because no one had to continually keep an eye on the pot. Parts such as feet, "wrists and ankles," "knees," backs, and heads would not have provided much in the way of meat, but the little that was there could easily have been used in one-pot meals like soups and stews, or to add a bit of flavor to pots of vegetables. In fact, using meats in this way was consistent with culinary practices in West Africa and was typical of the way these cuts were used by Anglo-Americans of the same period.[112] Aside from the "comfort factor" that comes from eating a traditional food, one-pot meals were fairly easy for a tired person to put together. A pot could be kept on the hearth most of the time, and fresh ingredients added daily. Salted fish, which made up such an important part of the slave rations at Mount Vernon, was very likely cooked as it had been in West Africa, by soaking overnight to reduce the saltiness and adding it to vegetable stews.[113] Fresh fish, chicken, and wild game could also be used in stews or eaten whole after baking or frying. Eggs might have been cooked in a number of ways—by roasting in ashes on the hearth, boiling, or frying—or could serve as ingredients in other dishes. Both eggs and smaller meats cooked quickly, and vegetables would not have been time-consuming to prepare. The intestines provided at the annual hog slaughter in late fall or early winter might have been boiled and served in a stew with vegetables or fried, while the other types of offal could well have been combined with spices and a starch, such as cornmeal, to make a type of deep-fried meatball, which was also known in the West African diet.[114]

Unlike wheat breads, the staple bread of the American slaves was made of corn. Using no yeast meant that the dough was quickly prepared, needing no time to rise and no effort to knead. These small, dense breads, often called corn- or hoe-cakes, were fashioned from the cornmeal ration and a little water. They were baked either in the ashes of the hearth or in a covered iron pot, or fried in a skillet. According to an Englishman who tried them in eighteenth-century Virginia, "I cannot say they are palateable, for as to flavor, one made of sawdust would be equally good, and not unlike it in appearance, but they are certainly a very strong and hearty food."[115] The results of a further study of beer-making among African American slaves may, however, change our assumptions about the nature of the cornbread eaten by slaves, or at least those on some of the larger plantations. It is possible to use barm (foam), a byproduct of beer-making, to leaven bread, and there was a definite link in premodern times between the production of beer and bread.[116] Among the letters of Martha Washington's granddaughter Nelly is a recipe for hoecakes in which yeast is added to the batter and left to work overnight.[117] It may well be that the slaves at Mount Vernon, as was true of the master's family, were using yeast to produce a lighter type of cornbread. In addition to bread, the cornmeal ration could also have been used for coating fried foods; thickening soups; and making African-style dumplings, gruels, and cereals.[118]

Meals

The number of meals the slaves ate per day is not known, but there is evidence that they had breakfast and dinner at least, and probably ate those meals where they worked. They likely had another meal after they returned home in the evening. One day in February 1760, Washington expressed concern that his carpenters had only cut 120 feet of wood since 10 a.m. the day before. He sat down to observe their progress and then estimated the amount of work they should be producing each day. In making his calculations, Washington noted that they generally worked "only" from "Sun to Sun" and took two hours for breakfast. Since he made no mention of dinner, the two hours for breakfast probably refers to the time allotted for both meals, since Washington did mention breakfast and dinner in regard to the slaves' schedule on other occasions.[119] This would have been comparable to the schedule at Galways Plantation on the island of Montserrat, where the slaves were at work from dawn until dusk, which usually occurred between 6:30 and 7:00 in the evening. As at Mount Vernon, the day was broken up by a two-hour respite for meals, typically divided into a break of a half hour for breakfast about 9 a.m. and one and a half hours in the middle of the day for a simple meal of boiled vegetables, which was eaten in the fields.[120]

Additional evidence for dinner comes in a letter from Lund Washington, reporting the death of one of George Washington's most valuable slaves, a cooper named James. The coopers had been assigned to help the ditchers drain a swamp, and after finishing the job one Saturday morning, they "returned from the ditch and were at their dinner." Jim finished eating before the others and went to wade in the millrace, about fifty yards from where they were sitting. After they had eaten, the others became concerned when he failed to answer their calls. Following a lengthy search, they found his body in the water. While the first part of the search was being carried out, Davy Gray, their enslaved overseer, was eating dinner at his house. From the amount of time it took Gray to get to the millrace, it would appear that his house, and presumably those of the others, were a considerable distance from the race. This suggests that the fieldworkers did not typically go home for lunch, probably because of the amount of time they would lose in traveling to and from their worksite.[121]

Not all masters, however, were so generous about mealtimes. Closer to Monticello, on a plantation outside Charlottesville, the slaves endured particularly wretched conditions:

> They are called up at day break, and seldom allowed to swallow a mouthful of homminy, or hoe cake, but are drawn out into the field immediately, where they continue at hard labour, without intermission, till noon, when they go to their dinners, and are seldom allowed an hour for that purpose. . . . After they have dined, they return to labor in the field, until dusk in the evening; here one naturally imagines the daily labor of these poor creatures was over, not so, they repair to the tobacco houses, where each has a task . . . or else they have such a quantity of Indian corn to husk. . . . Thus by their night task, it is late in the evening before these poor creatures return to their second scanty meal, and the time taken up at it encroaches upon their hours of sleep, which for refreshment of food and sleep together can never be reckoned to exceed eight.[122]

Even before enslaved Africans were brought to British North America, plants from the New World were transplanted to Africa, where they became part of the everyday diet. Corn, for example, one of the staple rations given to slaves at Mount Vernon and throughout the Chesapeake, was brought to the west coast of Africa by the Portuguese before the year 1500—well over a century before the first Africans arrived in Jamestown—in order to meet what has been described as "slave traders' growing demand for food." Historians once saw the introduction of corn to Africa as a benefit, because it matured during the traditional "hungry season" between the harvesting of the yam and sorghum crops, thus improving food availability throughout the year. As a recent book by Judith A. Carney and Richard Nicholas Rosomoff points out, however, corn was hardly "the benevolent and timely rescuer of a chronically hungry continent." Instead, while it "provided a high-yielding, quick-maturing cereal that was easily prepared and whose grains could be stored for long periods . . . it was planted to expedite and ensure delivery of slaves to New World plantation societies." These authors note that "maize can be seen as a symbol of the dehumanizing condition of chattel slaves. . . . Maize emphasized a person's demotion from human being to commodity, the loss of social status and cultural identity, of being made a kinless and orphaned servant in the Atlantic world."[123] In addition to corn, four other American foods—peanuts, sweet potatoes, squash, and pumpkins—were being grown by Igbo people in West Africa by the early to mid-seventeenth century.[124]

Many of the meats and vegetables that were standard fare for George Washington's slaves were similar to foods important in the West African diet.[125] Of those items routinely issued to or grown by the Mount Vernon slaves, quite a few were remembered in accounts written or narrated by people enslaved in Africa in the eighteenth century and brought to America. Corn, beef, mutton, and fish were typical foods of several groups along the Niger River, the Guinea Coast, the Gulf of Guinea, and in Timbuktu, while pigs were raised by other West African people.[126] Several of the domestic animals and vegetables raised by the Mount Vernon slaves themselves had been known in Africa as well. Poultry, yams, and beans were important elements of the diet in the kingdom of Benin; beans, cucumbers, and poultry were raised in the kingdom of Massina in the late eighteenth century; potatoes, yams, several varieties of poultry, and bees for honey were found on the Guinea Coast; and in Timbuktu, poultry, watermelons, and honey were plentiful.[127] An unknown but significant number of the slaves at Mount Vernon were born and raised in Africa. Finding similar foods in America must have been something of a comfort and may also have fostered the continuation of certain African culinary traditions. According to one historian, foodways "much like music and dancing, offered many slaves the opportunity to re-create in some fashion an aspect of their own culture—by experience and cultural preference a form of escape from their 'miserable condition.'"[128]

African Influence on Southern Cooking

Some years ago, when Mount Vernon was first beginning to interpret historic foodways on the tables in the mansion, we were looking to acquire good quality *faux* foods, because actual food items cannot be used in a museum setting, in order to prevent the attraction of rodents and bugs. Eventually we found a supplier offering both the experience and quality for which we were looking. There was a specific dinner we sought to replicate, described by a young man named Joshua Brookes who visited Mount Vernon on February 4, 1799: "Leg [of] boil[ed] pork, top [at head of table];

goose, bot [at foot of table]; roast beef, round cold boil[ed] beef, mutton chops, hommony, cabbage, potatoes, pickles, fried tripe, onions, etc. Table cloth wiped [crumbs brushed off], mince pies, tarts, cheese; cloth of[f], port, Madeira, two kinds [of] nuts, apples, raisins. Three servants."[129] The person making our faux foods was adamant that Washington, as a member of the upper class, would not have eaten hominy, which she termed a "slave food." This is not, however, the only description we have of Washington eating hominy or of it being served in the mansion at Mount Vernon.

In the fall of 1781, General Henry Knox left his pregnant wife, Lucy, and their seventeen-month-old son Harry, described as a "turbulent little fellow," at Mount Vernon with Martha Washington during the siege at Yorktown. In one letter to her husband, dated October 23, 1781, Lucy Knox wrote that farm manager Lund Washington would be arriving soon at Yorktown and that he "will inform you what a lovely boy your son is and he eats homine like a Virginian."[130] This letter confirms that hominy was served to people in the mansion, and moreover that it was a dish associated with—and relished by—people of all classes in Virginia. Many years later, Martha Washington's grandson told the following story about his step-grandfather:

> It was in November of the last days that the general visited Alexandria upon business, and dined with a few friends at the City hotel. Gadsby, the most accomplished of hosts, requested the general's orders for dinner, promising that there was [a] good store of canvass-back ducks in the larder. "Very good, sir," replied the chief, "give us some of them, with a chafing-dish, some hommony, and a bottle of good Madeira, and we shall not complain."[131]

Here is an instance when Washington had the option to eat something else and asked for hominy, that lowly food. The smaller lesson here is that we cannot be too dogmatic about what foods would or would not have been on the table in an elite household.

The more important lesson is that, through the work of enslaved cooks, elements of African cooking made their way onto the tables of their owners. Frying, for example, is traditionally associated with southern cooking but was a technique described as early as the fourteenth century in Mali. According to one source, "deep-frying . . . is an ancient cooking tradition in West Africa that enslaved African women likely introduced to plantation societies."[132] Looking at one quintessential southern dish, fried chicken, the only things even remotely similar from either the seventeenth-century manuscript cookbook Martha Washington inherited from her first husband's family or her copy of the English cookbook *The Art of Cookery Made*

Plain and Easy, first published in 1747 and the most popular printed cookbook in eighteenth-century America, are recipes that call for first frying either a whole chicken or one that has been cut into parts and then stewing the meat with vegetables.[133] By 1828, when the third edition of Mary Randolph's cookbook *The Virginia House-Wife* came out, it contained a recognizable recipe for what we would think of as fried chicken today—chicken that has been cut into parts, dredged in flour, seasoned with salt, fried in boiling lard, and served up on a platter with bits of fried mush (proto-hushpuppies?) and milk gravy.[134] While we cannot say for sure exactly when this change happened in Anglo-Virginia, it had occurred by the mid-eighteenth century. In the summer of 1766, for example, Virginia plantation owner Landon Carter mentioned in his diary that a relative had "eat some bite of fr[i]ed Chicken."[135]

Greens were an important part of West African cuisine, and at least one plant historian indicates that "no other cooking traditions feature them so prominently," noting that there are more than 150 indigenous species of edible greens native to that part of the African continent. They are used in stews and sauces that are served with the tubers or cereals that form the basis of the traditional diet; eaten raw, as salad; boiled for side dishes; and used for garnishing other dishes. Both mustard greens and collards are said to have made the journey from Africa to the Americas along with shiploads of slaves, where they became staples of southern cuisine.[136]

Conclusion

George Washington was determined that his slaves receive adequate provisions, both as a means of preventing theft and out of concern for them as human beings.[137] Prompted by unhappiness regarding their portions, as well as by questions from the farm manager about the quantity of food to be issued, Washington wrote from Philadelphia in the spring of 1793 that he would not make a judgment on specific amounts but emphasized the principle, "in most explicit language," that he wanted the slaves to have "plenty." He mentioned that his "feelings" had been "hurt" by those complaints, and he did not intend to be subject to the "imputation of starving my negros and thereby driving them to the necessity of thieving to supply the deficiency." He went on to note that the only reason he gave out a specific ration at all was to "prevent waste or embezzlement." He closed with the thought that "if, instead of a peck they [the slaves] could eat a bushel of Meal a week fairly, and required it, I would not withhold or begrudge it them."[138]

No immediate improvement in the situation took place, however, so the following month the president wrote again to clarify what he had done in the past and his present position on the subject. He reiterated that he did not want "my Negros" to have "an oz of meal more, nor less, than is sufficient to feed them plentifully." After going over the history of the problem, Washington closed by noting that similar complaints had come in from more than one farm, "which altogether hurt my feelings too much to suffer this matter to go on without remedy."[139]

In both letters, Washington made it clear that he wanted the slaves to have enough food to adequately meet, but not exceed, their needs. This was consistent with his views on the rations of his white servants. In 1793, Washington wrote his farm manager William Pearce with instructions to see that the hired whites "have a full sufficiency without waste, or misapplication. I am very willing to allow them enough, and of such provisions day by day, as is wholesome and good, but no more."[140] The following year, in a letter to his Philadelphia steward, Washington made a similar statement about the people—hired, indentured, and enslaved—who served in the presidential mansion: "My domestics should be plentifully fed at all times with what is wholesome and proper be[yond] which [nei]ther in quantity nor quality you are not to go."[141] The fact that the slaves felt free to approach Washington with their complaints is telling and suggests that they believed him to be fair, or at least more so than their overseers. Also revealing of Washington's personality is his twice-stated remark that he was hurt by the slaves' suggestions that he might be responsible for any reduction in their rations.

In conclusion, the diet of those enslaved at Mount Vernon was fairly typical of African American slaves on other large Virginia plantations of the eighteenth and early nineteenth centuries. While it is possible to see a good deal of oppression in the foodways of the Mount Vernon slaves—in the very tedious and nutritionally inadequate rations, and the fact that people who were exhausted from working long days were expected to grow a good deal of their food in their few "free" hours—it is also in their foodways that we see evidence of the African American community at Mount Vernon asserting its own values and fighting back. Food items were frequently stolen from the fields or storage areas on the plantation, one means of rebelling against the plantation system. With foods they raised or caught themselves forming such a large part of the slave diet, food was also one area in their lives where the people enslaved at Mount Vernon could exercise choice. More importantly, the growth, preparation, and adaptation of traditional foods allowed for the continuation of an African cultural heritage.

Transmitted to younger members of the enslaved community, these traditions were reshaped into a significant part of a uniquely African American culture. Furthermore, these same traditions had a significant influence on southern cuisine, which, as regional foods were transmitted throughout the country and the world, became American food.

9

"An Idle Set of Rascals"

Control and Resistance among the Mount Vernon Slaves

Having started this book with a close look at the people who managed Mount Vernon, followed by a detailed examination of the daily lives of those enslaved on the plantation, this chapter seeks to close the circle. The focus now shifts to the methods George Washington used to manage a labor force that had virtually no incentive to work as hard, long, or diligently as their owner expected. In response, those enslaved workers found a wide variety of ways to resist control by Washington and the lower-level managers on the estate. Just as Washington's beliefs about slavery changed during, and as a result of, the American Revolution, the slaves' response to the facts of their lives evolved as ideas about the natural rights of all men began to move through the quarters. "All men are created equal" is a powerful message that resonated among both white and black Americans at the end of the eighteenth century.

Methods of Control

In addition to having his overseers on site, Washington used a number of methods to control the labor and behavior of the Mount Vernon slaves. Threats of being demoted from a skilled position to field labor were tried occasionally, and may have proved effective, because craftsmen and house servants were often shifted to the fields during the harvest and so had a very good idea what a permanent change like that would mean. When the output of the seamstresses fell because of Martha Washington's absence during the presidency, George Washington ordered his manager to "tell them . . . from me, that what *has* been done, *shall* be done by fair or foul means. . . . Otherwise they will be sent to the several Plantations, and be placed as common laborers under the Overseers thereat."[1] The following year, Washington asked the same manager, Anthony Whiting, to talk with Billy Muclus, a bricklayer, about problems with his work. Whiting was expected to get across that if there was no improvement, Muclus would be "severely punished and placed under one of the Overseers as a common hoe Negro."[2]

Stronger coercive measures were tried as well. Physical restraints could be used to keep a slave from running away. When a man Washington considered an habitual troublemaker was sold in the West Indies in 1766, he suggested that the ship captain in whose custody the slave was placed "keep him handcuff[e]d till you get to Sea." The logical inference is that Washington himself had kept Tom in either handcuffs or leg irons to prevent his escape before he could be put on board.[3] Shackles were specifically mentioned in the case of another slave living on one of the Custis plantations near Williamsburg. According to the manager, a runaway slave known as Coachman Jamey or Jemmy was "one of the Greatest Raschals I . . . look[e]d after in all my life," and the manager proposed that if Jamey was not sold off, he should instead be sent to another of the Custis properties on the Eastern Shore and placed in "Iron Spancels," or hobbles used for cattle and horses, "if agre[e]able to you." Jamey eluded capture for "at least three months" by living off the land nearby, and was eventually tracked down and taken up with the aid of a dog.[4]

Although one houseguest recorded in his journal that Washington had prohibited the use of whips on his slaves, there is evidence that they were beaten on occasion.[5] While he was on the frontier during the French and Indian War, Washington received a letter from farm manager Humphrey Knight reporting the progress of work on the plantation in his absence. Knight wrote that he had been keeping an eye on the carpenters, watching them "all I pos[si]bly could," and hastening to add that he had "whipt em when I could see a fault."[6] More than thirty years later, then farm manager Anthony Whiting informed his employer that he "Gave . . . a very Good Whip[p]ing" with a hickory switch, which he had been using as a riding crop, to the seamstress Charlotte after she was insolent with him. When Charlotte stubbornly continued to defy him over the next few days, Whiting "Gave a little more." He closed his account of this episode with the expectation that more of the same would be necessary before Charlotte would submit, but he was "determined to lower her Spirit or skin her Back." George Washington wrote back that

FIG. 18. View of the clerk's quarters (second door on the right) at Mount Vernon. Farm manager Anthony Whiting beat an enslaved seamstress named Charlotte at this site in the winter of 1793. (Courtesy of the Mount Vernon Ladies' Association)

he considered the treatment of Charlotte to be "very proper," and that "if She, or any other of the Servants will not do their duty by fair means, or are impertinent, correction (as the only alternative) must be administered."[7] This same manager was commended the next month for the "just and proper" "correction" he gave to a slave named Ben for assaulting Sambo Anderson, one of the carpenters. While the method is not mentioned, the "correction" very likely included whipping because Washington went on to use the word "punishment" in the next sentence. Ben was not identified further, but in a letter written a few weeks later, Washington recommended "correction" as a means for dealing with "Matildas Ben," probably the same person, who was then in trouble for stealing. This young man was the fifteen-year-old son of Boatswain, a ditcher at the Mansion House Farm, and his wife, Myrtilla, one of the spinners.[8]

Washington considered these punishments and corrections just as use-ful for their deterrent value as for their effect on a particular individual. After learning, for instance, that Richmond, the son of Mount Vernon's cook Hercules, committed a "Robbery . . . on [James] Wilkes Saddle bags,"

Washington expressed his hope that the young man had been "made an example of."[9] In a similar vein, during the Revolution, Washington had ordered that soldiers sentenced to flogging receive their punishment in front of several units in order to make as great an impression, and on as many people, as possible. In one such case, when a soldier was to be punished with one hundred lashes, Washington directed that one-quarter of the sentence be given on four successive days in different parts of the line, before troops from New Hampshire, New York, New Jersey, and Massachusetts, respectively.[10] A major factor in making sure that a correction had as much effect as possible, on both the individual receiving the punishment and all who witnessed it, was that "whipping had to be used with restraint and in a coolly calculated manner."[11]

The concept of what constituted cruel punishment has, of course, changed dramatically in the centuries since Washington's death. Until the very end of the eighteenth century, whipping was a common form of punishment in both the northern and southern parts of what became the United States.[12] In the colonial Anglican church in Virginia, those who did not attend church at least once a month or who disrupted the service were subject to a fine, but if they refused to pay were given "Ten Lashes on his or her bare Back, well laid on."[13] During the American Revolution, soldiers routinely received sentences of one hundred lashes on their bare backs for a variety of infractions, ranging from desertion to "stealing and being drunk on duty," killing livestock, "using insulting language" toward and attempting to strike a superior officer, "being out of camp at an unseasonable hour and killing an ox" belonging to a local civilian, and disorderly conduct. A generation later, in 1804, just prior to the start of Meriwether Lewis and William Clark's expedition across the continent to the Pacific Ocean, three of their men were tried in military court and subjected to whipping. Two who were found guilty of being absent without leave one evening received twenty-five lashes each; a third was sentenced to fifty lashes for "being absent without leave . . . for behaving in an unbecoming manner at the ball last night . . . [and] for speaking in a language . . . after his return tending to bring into disrespect the orders of the commanding officer."[14]

Virginia law protected anyone from prosecution who killed a slave during a correction, "unless . . . it shall be proved, by the oath of at least one lawful and credible witness, that such slave was killed wilfully, maliciously, or designedly." In other words, no one would be tried unless there was proof that murder, rather than punishment, had been the intention from the beginning.[15] Socially, however, such a person might well find himself ostracized. A Frenchman who visited Thomas Jefferson's home in 1796 recorded that another plantation owner in the area had been condemned by public opinion for cruel treatment to a slave, whom he had flogged almost to the point of death. The visitor went on to say that "justice pursues this barbarous master, and all the other planters declared loudly their wish, that he may be severely punished, which seems not to admit of any doubt."[16]

Washington did institute a review system, perhaps something akin to a court martial, in order to protect his slaves from capricious and, to eighteenth-century eyes, extreme physical punishment. When his secretary Tobias Lear wrote a letter to a friend back home in New England concerning his life at Mount Vernon, he mentioned that "no whipping is allowed without a regular complaint & the def[endan]t. found guilty of some bad deed."[17] Two years later, Washington, then serving as president, asked that two slaves accused of destroying the flax at Dogue Run Farm be investigated and later punished if "found guilty." When one of the two, Jenny, later died, George Augustine Washington hastened to assure his uncle that he had conducted the inquiry himself and found her innocent. He was afraid his uncle would think she had died because of a punishment inflicted "too severely": "I mention it as you might suppose it had been done and improperly, by my intrusting it to the execution of an Overseer for, I value the opinion I hope you entertain of me to[o] highly to suppose You would think me capable of inhumanity."[18] Slave owners on other plantations tried to prevent abuses through similar means, which ranged from withholding punishment for twenty-four hours after someone was caught in an offense to instructing overseers not to "punish in a passion," limiting the number of lashes that could be given without the owner's express permission, forbidding the whipping of slaves by anyone but themselves or except in their own presence, and finally prohibiting whipping altogether.[19]

The sort of preliminary review Washington required was necessary when personality conflicts between slaves and insecure but still authority-wielding managers arose. Washington and his contemporaries were keenly aware that sadistic or temperamental individuals could find their way into supervisory positions. One young man employed by Washington's friend Dr. David Stuart proved to be a most unsatisfactory overseer, not only because of his "intolerable management" but also because of his "cruelty."[20] There were similar problems at Mount Vernon, as when during the presidency Washington expressed concerns about overseer Hyland (or Hiland) Crow. Washington advised the farm manager to ensure that Abram, one of the slaves he rented from his neighbor Mrs. French, "get his deserts" for running away. He cautioned, however, that the punishment not be entrusted to Crow, "for I have reason to believe he is swayed more by passion than by judgement in all his corrections."[21] When questioned later by a relative who contemplated hiring Crow, Washington admitted that the slaves had complained to him about "ill treatment" at the hands of this particular overseer, a man suspected of having a "hasty temper," but that he had "never discovered any marks of abuse" on them.[22]

While most of the references to physical punishment are in connection to overseers, Washington himself is known to have physically punished his slaves on occasion, something that would not be surprising given his temper—perhaps the reason he understood the problems associated with punishing out of anger and why he tried to prevent it. Several examples were recorded by artist John Gadsby Chapman, as he interviewed George Washington's nephew Lawrence Lewis during an 1833 visit to Virginia to gather information for a series of paintings relating to scenes from Washington's life for a biography by James K. Paulding. Lewis became a member of the Mount Vernon household after his uncle's retirement from the presidency and later cemented their connection by marrying Eleanor Custis in 1799. Lewis knew the slaves from Mount Vernon well, having inherited quite a few of the Custis dower slaves through his wife's share of her paternal grandfather's estate. He also served for decades as one of the executors of George Washington's estate, which made him responsible for the continued care of elderly slaves who had been freed by the terms of his uncle's will.

After telling Chapman a story about Washington's great physical strength, which he had observed himself, Lewis recalled that a few days after the incident, he asked one of the enslaved carpenters (he believed it was Isaac, who headed that group of artisans) if he had ever seen a similar display of Washington's strength. Isaac recalled that he had, just a few days before, when they were preparing logs for a construction project. Noting that some of the logs were "of great size & the heaviest timber that could be found in the woods," he remarked that "Master always, you know, marks off everything that is to be done with his own hands." Washington had previously marked one "great log" with lines showing where he wanted certain cuts made. Washington asked Isaac to turn over the log, which he attempted with help from another slave and a crow bar, but they were unable to manage it. Washington responded, "You worthless fellow what are you good for and puts his hands under it and turns it over as if it had been a half inch plank." Think for a minute how Isaac must have felt about that comment—"You worthless fellow"—especially since it was delivered in front of at least one of the men he himself supervised. Washington then drew lines on this new side and told Isaac, "when I had cut the morti[s]es half through to turn the log over again & meet them on the other side." After Isaac did the cutting on the first side, there was no one to help him to roll the log over and he could not manage it himself: "Altho' I thought my-self a portly strong man and undertook to cut the morti[s]e right through but missed by about a quarter of an inch." Isaac noted that he was "scared when I found the mischief I had done but hoped old Master would not find it out." Unfortunately, the next morning, when Washington came to the worksite, "the first thing I heard was 'Who cut this morti[s]e[?]'" Isaac "knew something was coming" but answered, "I did sir the log was heavy I could not turn it over to cut it as you directed." Noting that Washington "never said another word," Isaac reported that he "gave me such a slap on the side of my head that I whirled round like a top & before I knew where I was Master was gone." In his notes, Chapman recorded that Isaac had just died a few months earlier, in the spring of 1833.[23]

Another incident related by Lewis involved Washington's typical morn-ing routine. As did other members of the household, Lewis noted that his uncle's "habits were regular." Washington got up "before or at the dawn of day" and then, lighting a candle, went down the backstairs to his study. Lewis commented that Martha Washington said that her husband was go-ing to do "his devotions," but Lewis felt that "this no one knew for none ever intruded upon him at that early hour." Once the sun had risen suf-ficiently, Washington would blow the candle out and then ring a bell to summon a "servant," probably one of his enslaved valets, William Lee or Christopher Sheels, who "appeared with his [Washington's] boots." With-out saying a word, Washington would inspect the boots, turning "them round and round." If they were clean, he would quickly pull them on. If they were not cleaned to his specifications, however, "the servant got them about his head but without the Genl. betraying any excitement beyond the effort of the moment—in a minute afterwards he was no less calm & collected than usual."[24] In both these incidents, Washington said noth-ing and either left the scene immediately or quickly got himself under control.

Lawrence Lewis also described a much more serious incident that would have taken place in the period between Washington's return from the Revo-lution in late 1783 and his leaving to attend the Constitutional Convention in 1787:

When he [Washington] laid off and arranged the beautiful lawn in front of the house the servants were in the habit of passing and

FIG. 19. West Front of Mount Vernon, attributed to Edward Savage, 1792. (Courtesy of the Mount Vernon Ladies' Association)

unpassing without regard to the pathways and to the great injury of its beauty and regular growth of the grass—an order was issued that *no one* should walk on the grass or off the path—The General in a morning walk discovered the print of footsteps out of place, yet no one had done it. The print of the footstep was measured and examined. All the servants were called up. [A] shoe was found fitting the impression exactly and the offender was severely punished. The law was afterward respected and the offense not repeated.[25]

Although Lewis never said, the severe punishment probably involved whipping.

Not long after Washington's death, British diplomat Augustus John Foster, who served his country in the United States from 1804 to 1812, recorded that Albert Gallatin, the American secretary of the treasury, told "a story of a black Slave who said he was once saved from a caning by the General's looking at the Cane before he raised it and recollecting that it was the Cane given him by Dr. Franklin."[26] This story has the ring of truth to it, if for no other reason than the fact that, while Washington's will was widely published after his death, the story about the cane may not have been as well-known as other sections of that document. In a 1789 codicil to his will, Franklin had given a "fine crab-tree walking-stick, with a gold head curiously wrought in the form of a cap of liberty" to "my friend, and the friend

FIG. 20. Detail of the 1792 West Front showing the Washingtons, their dogs, and maybe some friends walking on the bowling green in front of the mansion. Note that there are enslaved people walking on the graveled paths around the green, a result of an order by George Washington. (Courtesy of the Mount Vernon Ladies' Association)

of mankind, *General Washington,*" who in turn bequeathed the memento to his younger brother Charles.[27] Surely seeing the liberty cap at the end of the cane and calling to mind Franklin's words, "the friend of mankind," could well have pulled Washington up short, causing him to forego harsh punishment and perhaps substitute a stern lecture.[28]

The family story told by the descendants of Sall Twine, one of the Custis dower slaves, includes a reference to another terrible punishment, branding, dating to the time of the Revolutionary War, when George Washington was with the army and Mount Vernon was being managed by his cousin Lund. Born about 1761, Sall, like many people enslaved in Virginia at the time, was aware that freedom was being promised to slaves who escaped their plantations and ran to the British. According to Sall's descendants,

> It has been told to us, General Washington held British prisoners of war on his property. We were also told that Sall befriended one in hopes of accompanying him back to Europe no matter the outcome of the war. She was most unfortunate. When the war ended, and her officer was released, she was not permitted to go with him. She protested vehemently and in order to insure that she understood she exercised no option in determining her status she was branded with a "W" on her cheek.[29]

This would have been an incredibly traumatic event in Sall's life and the story of the branding is very specific in its details, which was passed down through two hundred years of descendants. There are, however, a number of problems in trying to verify this memory.

Branding was definitely used as a punishment, both in a civilian context in seventeenth-century Virginia and in the army in the eighteenth century. For example, in March 1743, the Virginia House of Burgesses enacted legislation on the branding of servants (not slaves), stipulating that for a second offense of running away, a servant was to be branded on the cheek with the letter "R." Thirteen years later, the punishment was set at branding with an "R" but without specifying a location for the brand; the servant in question was also ordered to serve double the amount of time lost because of his or her escape. In 1758, the extra time still had to be served but the law now stipulated that the brand was to be placed on the shoulder.[30]

During Washington's presidency, desertion was a problem for the army on the frontier under the command of General Anthony Wayne, who had a reputation for being "indefatigable in disciplining his troops."[31] In a letter to Secretary of War Henry Knox, written on August 10, 1792, Wayne discussed ways to deal with the problem, including a suggestion that deserters be branded on the forehead with the word "coward." Upon learning of Wayne's plan, Washington wrote to Knox: "Concerning his idea of having a Brand, I have great doubts both as to the legality & policy of the measure; the bad impression it may make in the country, may considerably outweigh the good effects it may produce in the army."[32] In early September, Wayne sent the results of several courts martial to Knox, noting that five soldiers had been condemned to death and another "to be shaved, branded and whipt." Knox later echoed Washington when he informed Wayne that "the sentences of the Courts Martial . . . seemed absolutely necessary—Hereafter it is to be hoped there may be less call for the punishment of death. The Branding however is a punishment upon which some doubts may be entertained as to its legality. Uncommon punishments not sanctioned by Law should be admitted with caution although less severe than those authorized by the articles of War."[33]

Having examined the context, there are issues with the details in Sall's story. For example, there were several types of brands used at Mount Vernon. In order to recognize the plantation's cattle, they were typically branded on their horns, buttocks, or shoulders with the mark "GW." The location of the mark indicated where the cattle were regularly pastured: on the left buttock for Dogue Run Farm; on the right buttock for the Neck Plantation, more commonly called River Farm; on the left shoulder for Muddy Hole Farm; and on the right shoulder for the mill.[34] Washington's flour barrels were branded, according to Virginia law, with "the first letter of the mill owner's Christian name and his full surname," "G: WASHINGTON"; that brand was registered on December 21, 1772.[35] Barrels packed with preserved fish would have been "Branded with the Curer[']s name."[36] In no cases found so far has a simple "W" brand been linked to Mount Vernon.

Second, in a letter written to his wartime farm manager, George Washington chastised Lund for *not* hiring British prisoners of war:

> In one of your letters (speaking of the difficulty of getting workmen) you recommend it to me to engage some of the Enemy who were prisoners with us; many of whom you say are good workmen. Why, let me ask, when they hired themselves by the authority of Congress, and, comparatively speaking, were in your own neighbourhood, would you not do this for me? None of them were within 300 miles of me, and most of them were within from 55 to 80 miles of you.[37]

Historian Cole Jones, a specialist on the experiences and treatment of British prisoners during the Revolution, when asked about the possibility that these men might have been hired on a plantation near Mount Vernon (rather than on the plantation itself), and whether there were centralized lists of where these soldiers were kept and to whom they were hired, noted that Congress periodically allowed both British and Hessian prisoners to hire themselves out to local farmers, who would pay a security fee and room, board, and a small salary for each man hired under this program. Those closest to Mount Vernon were spread out from the towns of Winchester, Virginia, to Frederick, Maryland, and central Pennsylvania. According to Jones, "There are sadly no rosters detailing who went to work for whom. Revolutionary record keeping when it came to the prisoners was pitiful stuff, and the commissary general of prisoners was always complaining about it." In regard to the possibility of a prisoner of war working either at or near Mount Vernon, he thought it unlikely but possible. Prisoners were restricted to an eighty-mile radius from their camp. The camp closest to Mount Vernon was a little over that distance from the Washington plantation. Some of these men were working in Williamsburg, so it might have been possible that they worked on one of the Custis plantations near that city. Jones also noted that any prisoner of war working at Mount Vernon would have been an enlisted man, rather than an officer. Nor would he have been held against his will because he was working for a salary "on his own recognizance."[38]

So, what should we make of Sall Twine's family story of being branded? Marion Dobbins, who has extensive experience conducting oral history interviews in the African American community, suggests that, given the nature of oral history (and its similarities to the children's game telephone), it would not be unusual for the story to change the detail of the brand from "GW" to a simple "W."[39] Jessie MacLeod, a colleague at Mount Vernon, suggests that the story may have been a way for Sall and her descendants to embody the immense psychological pain of losing someone she cared about and, perhaps more importantly, the chance to be free.[40]

On several occasions, George Washington used the ultimate punishment—selling a slave away from his or her family and friends—or threatened to do so. When in 1766 George Washington turned over Tom to a schooner captain who was headed for the West Indies, he instructed the captain to sell Tom "in any of the Islands you may go to, for whatever he will fetch." Despite being "both a Rogue and Runaway," Tom was nonetheless "exceeding healthy, strong, and good at the Hoe" and had once worked as a gang foreman. Washington suggested that once the ship was in the open sea, or had at least gone as far as Chesapeake Bay, Tom might be uncuffed and prove "very useful to you." He hoped that Tom would "sell well, if kept clean and trim'd up a little when offer[e]d to Sale" and asked, in exchange, that the captain bring molasses, rum, limes, tamarinds, mixed sweetmeats, and the remainder of the purchase price in "good old Spirits."[41] Not long afterward, an enslaved carpenter from Mount Vernon named Sam was sold to another master in Virginia after running away four times in five years.[42] A similar fate befell Will Shag, a thirty-year-old slave on the Custis plantations near Williamsburg. Shag was a chronic runaway, described as someone who was "so lazey he will not worke and a greater Rog[u]e is not to be foun[d]." He once spent several months in Yorktown, pretending he was a freeman known as Will Jones. During one of several escape attempts, he even beat up the overseer. In July 1771, Washington's manager Joseph Valentine took out an advertisement in the newspaper declaring Shag to be an outlaw, which meant that anyone who found him could kill him. Finally, in December 1772, Washington paid for Shag's passage to Haiti, where he was to be exchanged for molasses.[43] About twenty years later, Washington threatened the previously mentioned Ben with a similar fate and, in the process, left evidence of another slave who had been sold because of his behavior. Washington ordered that Ben and his parents be told "in explicit language that if a stop is not put to his rogueries, and other villainies by fair means and shortly; that I will ship him off (as I did Waggoner Jack) for the

West Indias, where he will have no opportunity of playing such pranks as he is at present engaged in."[44] Jack had been sold off the plantation in 1791 for a quantity of wine.[45]

Carrots Rather Than Sticks

Washington believed, however, that softer methods could often have a better effect than punishment and coercion. During the Revolution, he noticed that public executions of soldiers, especially when frequent, were counterproductive. In a letter to Brigadier General Anthony Wayne written in the fall of 1779, Washington commented, "We do not see the multiplying of executions produce the effects for which they were intended; and for many reasons, it is not a desirable thing to lose men in examples of this kind, unless in cases of the most apparent necessity. I would be directed in some measure by the consequences which a pardon might occasion."[46] These military cases shed light on what Washington hoped to accomplish when punishing his slaves.

Washington's attitude about harsh punishments in regard to his slaves was not unique, however, but shared by other plantation owners, including Thomas Jefferson, who encouraged the work of his slaves through what one Monticello visitor described as "rewards and distinctions."[47] Noting at one point that vigilant attention by his overseers should prevent "irregularities and improper conduct" by the Mount Vernon slaves, Washington considered prevention to be preferable to severe treatment and "more agreeable to every feeling mind."[48] In young Ben's case, Washington counseled his manager that "admonition and advice" sometimes succeeded where "further correction" failed.[49] He occasionally tried to encourage an individual slave's pride in order to get him or her to behave as Washington desired. Before threatening the bricklayer Billy Muclus with demotion to fieldwork, Washington directed his manager to first use pride as a "stimulus to excite him to industry" and then to try "admonition."[50] In a similar vein, when Cyrus, who had been suspected of stealing horse feed, "roguery," and drinking, began to show signs of improvement, his master instructed that this change be encouraged. He then offered Cyrus the chance for a position as a "waiting man" or personal servant within the mansion as an incentive. Washington saw this as an opportunity for the young man to "exalt, and benefit himself." Several months later, he directed the manager to "again stir up the pride of Cyrus" and gave instructions for preparing Cyrus for service. Washington's tactics in this case seem to have succeeded. Cyrus was still working in the mansion in 1799, when he was given the responsibility of contacting one of the doctors treating Washington in his final illness.[51]

In addition to verbal encouragement, material incentives were also tried. When Washington sent blankets and clothing fabric to Mount Vernon from Philadelphia one fall, he told manager William Pearce that there were two qualities of each of those articles included in the shipment. He intended that "the better sort" be given to adult slaves and those who were "most deserving," while "the more indifferent sort" would be doled out to "the younger ones and worthless."[52] This was not an isolated incident. Three years earlier, he had ordered that cheaper linen be "given to the boys and girls" and "the highest price and best, to the grown and most deserving men and women."[53]

Two intriguing references from a financial ledger indicate that Washington also tried direct cash awards to his slaves. An undated notation, probably from December 1796, records that six shillings were paid to Ben at Dogue Run "for his good be[haviour] In harvest." By April of the previous year, Tom Davis at the Mansion House Farm had been given twelve shillings "by Way of [E]ncouragement at Diff[e]rent times."[54] This may also explain two payments to Davy Gray, the enslaved overseer at Muddy Hole Farm, to whom Washington gave $5.00 for an unspecified purpose in early 1798 and £1.10.0 "as a present" one year later.[55] During the harvest of 1799, two men—Ben at Dogue Run and Abraham at Union Farm—were each given one dollar "as an Encouragement for their Perseverance in Harvest."[56] Virtually all of the rewards and incentives used by Washington to encourage the kinds of behaviors he desired from his slaves were practiced by other plantation owners in eighteenth- and nineteenth-century America as well. In 1771, much like Washington, South Carolinian Henry Laurens attempted to reward what he considered proper behavior when he asked one of his overseers to let his slaves know that in the coming year, he would be sending "the best cloth . . . that ever they wore . . . for such as shall have behaved well."[57]

When all else—threats, punishment, encouragement, and reward—had been tried and failed, Washington was not too proud to accept reality. He learned early in 1795 that one of the slaves he was renting from his neighbor Mrs. French had resumed "his old tricks" and was telling people that Washington had promised him freedom after seven years of service. The president wrote his manager, detailing the reasons why he would never have made such a promise and suggesting ways of handling "French Will" in the future. Since "harsh treatment" had been ineffective in the past,

Washington thought it would be best to simply "let him piddle, and in this way . . . get what you can out of him."[58]

Resistance

Oppressed people throughout the world have typically responded to their oppression with a gamut of reactions ranging from identifying with those who oppressed them to working with their oppressors to take advantage of opportunities for better treatment or physical conditions; resisting through manipulation of flaws or weaknesses in the system to get more time off, easier work, and so on; and outright rebellion. As one twentieth-century ruler who grew up in a slave society remarked to an English friend, "Remember . . . the slave must protect himself by cunning. He is obliged to keep a foot in both camps."[59] The African American population at Mount Vernon responded in a number of ways to their status as slaves. Some individuals went along with Washington, serving him as overseers and foremen, occupations in which they themselves might be forced to take the part of the master against fellow slaves. In other cases, several generations of one family might gain the trust of the Washingtons, working at physically easier positions in the mansion. Still other slaves used the opportunities to do extra work on their days off to earn extra money to benefit themselves and their families. We now shift our focus a bit to look at the many ways the Mount Vernon slaves resisted Washington's control.

Washington's efforts to regulate the behavior of his slaves were prompted by more than just a desire to get a certain amount of work from them. Repeated references to "rogueries" and "old tricks" suggest that a significant percentage of the enslaved population at Mount Vernon were not only shirking their assigned tasks; they were doing all they could to fight the whole system as well. Methods used by the Mount Vernon slaves to rebel against both their owner and the plantation system were very like those used elsewhere in Virginia during this period and run the gamut of behaviors previously documented by historians.

PASSIVE RESISTANCE

A number of these practices were especially successful because, no matter how sure George Washington and his overseers might have been, it was virtually impossible to prove they were happening. Feigning illness as a way of getting out of work, for instance, which Washington's overseers were often incapable of diagnosing, carried far less risk than other forms of resistance. Again and again, and with increasing skepticism, Washington asked his farm managers for explanations about the illnesses of various slaves. In 1793, he wrote, "What is the matter with Old Frank, that he is always (almost) on the Sick list? I am inclined to believe that he finds the House too comfortable to quit, or he would not be so often, and so long in at a time."[60]

The following year, Washington noticed from the weekly reports that Sam had "not done a day[']s work since I left Mount Vernon" three months before. He ordered his manager to look into the case but not to contact a doctor, "for he [Sam] had Doctors enough already, of all colours and sexes, and to no effect." Washington believed the principal problem, which was supposed to be "an Asthmatical complaint," was actually "pretense" and "Laziness." If Washington was right, Sam's ploy had apparently been quite effective; his master complained that he "never could be got to work more than half his time" because of illness.[61] Several months later, upon learning that Sam was still sick, Washington spelled out his theory on diseases among the slaves and how to handle them:

> I never wish my people to work when they are really sick, or unfit for it; on the contrary, that all necessary care should be taken of them when they are so; but if you do not examine into their complaints, they will lay by when no more ails them, than ails those who stick to their business, and are not complaining, from the fatigue and drowsiness which they feel as the effect of night walking, and other practices which unfit them for the duties of the day.[62]

Over the course of his absence during the presidency, Washington became more and more concerned about the possibility that his slaves were using illness as a way to get out of work. He advised his farm manager in the summer of 1794 that a female slave, "Ruth . . . is extremely deceitful; she has been aiming for some time past to get into the house, exempt from work; but if they are not made to do what their age and strength will enable them, it will be a very bad example to others, none of whom would work if by pretexts they can avoid it."[63] In the case of another woman, Betty Davis, Washington railed that "if pretended ailments, without apparent causes, or visible effects, will screen her from work, I shall get no service at all from her; for a more lazy, deceitful and impudent huzzy, is not to be found in the United States than she is."[64] The following year, James, one of the carpenters who was described as a "very worthless fellow," was even suspected of cutting himself "on purpose" in order to "lay up." Washington complained that during the harvest, James "is sure to get a cut in the beginning of it, so as to lay him up during the continuance of it."[65] James had apparently been using this method with success for at least two decades. Washington had received a letter from home during the Revolution bearing the news that "Carpenter James by a stroke by his Broad axe has given himself such a wound a cross the ankle & heel, that I expect it will be several Months before he will be well enough to do any thing in his way again."[66] While this must have been an incredibly frustrating situation for Washington, James must have been driven by desperation or terrible anger to turn all that rage against himself and use an axe to cut his own foot. He would have been well aware that during the winter of 1775–76, John Broad, a convict carpenter-joiner, had died in great agony two months after receiving a one-inch scratch from an old sword while frolicking in Alexandria over the Christmas holidays with Aaron, a male slave of Lund Washington. In the eighteenth century, when even a tiny cut could result in tetanus or virulent systemic infection, James was risking death and perhaps trying to make a powerful statement.[67]

Concern that ailing slaves received proper medical care had been the norm for decades for the Washingtons. Prior to their marriage in 1759, Martha, then managing the estate of her late husband, had used the services of a Doctor Scott for "cur[in]g a Negroe Woman[']s Finger" and of a Dr. Kenneth McKenzie to take a look at the coachman.[68] A fairly large amount owed by the Custis estate to a Dr. James Carter suggests that he was the primary physician for the enslaved community on that family's plantations.[69] Account books dating to early in the Washingtons' marriage indicate that George Washington paid twenty-five shillings to a "Negroe Doctor" on October 3, 1759; ten shillings on both November 13, 1763 (for one of the enslaved house servants), and December 8, 1763; and fifteen shillings on August 1, 1766.[70] Since it was typical to mention the name of a white doctor called in to treat the slaves, the practitioner in these cases was probably himself African or African American and very likely enslaved. James Laurie or Lowrie was the first of a number of more formally trained doctors to look after the medical needs of both the hired and enslaved workers at Mount Vernon, but the family still occasionally used the services of a "Negro Doctr."[71]

During his presidency, Washington continually admonished his farm managers to look into illnesses carefully. If a slave were truly sick, "aid may be called in, in time," but those who were malingering were not to be "indulged in their idle habits."[72] When one of his farm managers seemed to have an especially difficult time determining bona fide illnesses from pretended ones, Washington gave him the benefit of his experience on that score:

> I never found so much difficulty as you seem to apprehend, in distinguishing between *real* and *feigned* sickness; or when a person is *much* afflicted with pain. Nobody can be very sick without having a fever, nor will a fever or any other disorder continue long upon any one without reducing them: Pain also, if it be such as to yield entirely to its force, week after week, will appear by its effects; but my people (many of them) will lay up a month, at the end of which no visible change in their countenance, nor the loss of an oz of flesh, is discoverable; and their allowance of provision is going on as if nothing ailed them. There cannot, surely, be any *real* sickness under such circumstances as I have described; nor ought such people to be improperly [i]ndulged.[73]

As with other areas where Washington's military background influenced his handling of the Mount Vernon slaves—and his handling of slaves influenced his approach to the military—there were similarities in the way he dealt with sickness during the Revolution. In 1777, Washington ordered his commanders to "visit the Sick of your Regiment often yourself and to make it [a] duty for all your Officers to do this by rotation." He noted that this would result in two benefits: "First, those that are really sick will be properly attended to, and the lazy and idle, who lay up to avoid duty, will be detected and punished."[74]

While it might seem that Washington was bordering on paranoia on this subject, his managers' weekly reports suggest that his concerns may well have had a basis in fact. A comparison of the amount of work lost because of illness when Washington was in residence at Mount Vernon with figures from periods when he was away during the presidency are illuminating. In 1786, the slaves on all the farms comprising the Mount Vernon estate lost 287 of 25,716 days of work or 1.1 percent. These figures are in marked contrast to those taken from surviving reports during Washington's presidency. Between January 1792 and November 1794, the Mount Vernon slaves were not working 10.9 percent of the time. Absenteeism due to illness increased tenfold during Washington's absence.[75] These figures might well cause a person to suspect, as Washington did, that his managers were not sufficiently diligent and that the slaves were taking advantage of this lack of care or expertise. The numbers also lend credence to Washington's complaints about other types of slave resistance on the plantation.[76]

These same figures on work lost because of illness suggest several additional points. First, comparison of the statistics from Mount Vernon in the eighteenth century with those for modern workers, who generally work fewer hours and grew up with the benefits of vaccinations, antibiotics, and other routine elements of modern medicine, indicates that the overall health of the adult slaves at Mount Vernon was probably good. For example, looking at a fairly standard benefit package used by the Mount Vernon Ladies' Association and for newly hired employees in the federal government in the late twentieth century, full-time workers were allowed to take 12 of the 260 days they worked each year as paid sick leave. While some employees may not use that much time, still others were sick more frequently and could use more leave. Twelve days a year, or 4.62 percent, therefore, was probably an average figure, which was still considerably higher than the 1.1 percent of time the Mount Vernon slaves were sick when Washington was in residence.[77]

Second, these statistics may also reveal an important point about George Washington's management of his estate. Evidence on slave illness rates for the mid-nineteenth century indicates that field hands at that period missed an average of twelve days of work per year. If they worked a six-day week, the absentee rate due to illness at that period works out to 3.85 percent. Comparison of these three sets of figures—for Mount Vernon in the 1780s, nineteenth-century plantations, and twentieth-century workers—suggests not just that the slaves were healthy but that the extremely low rate of illness when George Washington was at home was a direct result of his being on the plantation, probably because he forced or encouraged people who were not feeling well but had not become actively sick to go to work when they would rather have stayed home.[78]

Even harder to prove than feigned illness and probably used more often were procrastination and careless work. These approaches may have backfired in the long run, with claims that African Americans were lazy and clumsy workers becoming part of a stereotype that continues to this day. In the eighteenth century, however, it could lead to fairly immediate rewards, when expectations of the amount and quality of work expected by a master were lowered. For example, in a letter written in 1776, Washington's manager related some unhappy news about the potential of several slaves: "the Big Fellow you bought of Adams (jock) cannot cut with an Axe nor can he lift more than a Boy. Orford [probably Oxford] is Willing but of little service in a worck of that Kind—the one you Bought of Captn Harper is a man in years but not in Strength." Washington intended the men to work on land he owned on the frontier, but the white supervisor felt that, given the quality of the work he could expect from these fellows, he wanted to "hire two White men beside himself" and have Washington send "two other negroes besid[es] those already there."[79] In this case, as in so many others, the ploy worked. Almost twenty years later, Washington ordered farm manager Anthony Whiting to transfer a particular slave to work for the gardener because, "If Peter does *any* work at all it is in the Gardening line." Washington feared, however, that this change would be ineffective because the man would still "do nothing that he can avoid, of labour."[80] At about the same time, a planned consolidation of the quarters at Union Farm, which involved the use of rollers to move the cabins to a centralized location, was delayed for months by the "slothfulness" of Washington's enslaved carpenters.[81]

Washington eventually came to the conclusion that the majority of his slaves were genuinely clumsy and incapable of doing better work. Several times when faced with the opportunity to use new inventions to improve his agricultural operations, Washington turned them down because of reservations about his slaves' abilities. He was offered a "curiously invented plough" in the fall of 1791. Responding for his employer, secretary Tobias Lear said that Washington "would gladly become possessed of" of the plow, if he had not been convinced "from repeated experiments, that all machines used in husbandry that are of a complicated nature, would be entirely useless . . . and impossible to be introduced into common use where they are to be worked by ignorant and clumsy hands, which must be the case in every part of this country where the ground is tilled by negroes."[82] Two years later, Washington expressed doubts about the practicality of an English threshing machine "among careless Negros and ignorant Overseers." If fairly simple in construction, he thought it might prove useful but warned that "if there is any thing complex in the machinery it will be no longer in use than a mushroom is in existence."[83]

Even simple tasks were often slowed down or spoiled. While Martha Washington was away from home during the presidency, the seamstresses took advantage of her absence to make only five to six shirts apiece per week, when their usual output was nine. George Washington feared that their coworkers, lame Peter and Sarah, would do a poor job on the stockings they were knitting as well. He ordered his manager to keep an eye on them "or the Stockings will be knit too small for those for whom they are intended; such being the idleness, and deceit of those people."[84] The Mount Vernon carpenters were vilified in a letter to farm manager William Pearce in 1795. Washington characterized them as an "idle . . . set of

Rascals," virtually without equal, who would take an entire week to construct a chicken coop. In fact, he related, "buildings that are run up here [in Philadelphia] in two or three days (with not more hands) employ them [the estate carpenters] a month, or more."[85] In discussing the construction of his new barn at Dogue Run, Washington believed that the work was entirely beyond the capabilities of his "Negro Carpenters or any other bungler."[86]

Prior to the Revolution, several women on the Custis plantations may have used Martha Washington's physical distance from the place to get out of doing work they were expected to do, when they cited her as their reason for not obeying the overseer. In a letter to George Washington, the overseer complained that "at Rockahock there is a wench that is Kept for Spin[nin]g & has been all this year aspin[nin]g 47 [lb.] wool & Says that Mrs Washington ordered that she shou[l]d Spin no more th[a]n 3 [lb.] a week." Another woman, "old Nanny," refused "to Spin a thread & says her Mistress left her only to Sew."[87] With the sources at hand, it is difficult to know exactly what was going on. The women may well have been telling the truth about what Martha Washington told them. It is also possible that they were simply trying to get out of work and had been found out by the overseer. A third option is that they were deliberately playing the overseer off against Martha Washington in order to muddy the waters.

This would not be the only time an enslaved person on the estate accused an overseer of being responsible for a problem. In the summer of 1794, Peter Hardiman, who was in charge of the breeding of horses and mules, told George Washington that all mares pregnant with mule foals had given birth prematurely. Hardiman then gave an example of "a valuable Mare sent from the Mansion [H]ouse to Dogue [R]un, and rid by [Henry] McKoy into the forest doing it the night he quitted her back." Washington complained to his farm manager that "Night rides, and treading Wheat will forever deprive me of Foals," although he also considered it possible that Hardiman was using this as "an excuse for his own neglect in not attending properly to them in the covering season [when they were bred]."[88]

A related and still passive method of resistance was to take advantage of distances between specific work assignments. Washington complained bitterly on this score about Hardiman. Washington suspected him of using his special talents for working with horses and mules, their wide dispersal on Washington's different farms, and his travel time to his charges as an excuse to pursue "other objects; either of traffic or amusement, more advancive of his own pleasures than my benefit." Washington railed that it was otherwise inconceivable "that with the number of Mares I have, five and twenty of which were bought for the express purpose of breeding . . . should produce not more than Six or eight Colts a year. This I say will hardly be believed by any person who has ever been in a similar practice."[89]

The people enslaved at Mount Vernon also expressed their frustration and anger by deliberately misplacing or damaging tools and other equipment. When the president suggested, for instance, that his farm manager and nephew Howell Lewis use a particular "Machine . . . for combing off the heads of the Clover," he was told that no one could find it. Lewis had "enquired of Old Jack and all of the Overseers," and nobody had a clue to its whereabouts.[90] Sometimes nothing more dangerous was involved than just dropping a tool in the field. George Washington confessed to one manager that "nothing hurts me more than to find . . . the tools and implements laying wherever they were last used, exposed to injuries from Rain, sun, &ca."[91] He attempted to circumvent this type of resistance by having tools locked away in storage and given out as needed. Slaves were required to bring in damaged tools to the storehouse; only then, after a "satisfactory account" had been rendered of how they came to be broken, could replacements be issued. In the fall of 1792, Washington directed his manager to have "all the Tools collected from the scattered situation in which they are, and all that are not in use, put securely away." As he reminded his employee, loss or damage of the tools, "though nothing to the Overseers," was a very great expense for himself.[92] Slaves damaged or misplaced not just tools but larger pieces of equipment as well. A few months after his retirement from the presidency, Washington asked manager James Anderson to pay "more than ordinary attention" to "the Tools & Impl[e]ments of the Farms," because the carpenters were forever being "employed in making & repairing Ploughs & Carts." He blamed "abuse, more than the use of these things" for the problem and suggested greater diligence as a remedy.[93]

ACTIVE RESISTANCE

On the opposite end of the resistance spectrum were more aggressive actions. While these behaviors might be especially satisfying for a frustrated slave to carry out, they also carried greater risk of detection and punishment, simply because they were so overt. While there might be doubt about whether a person was really sick or not, being caught with stolen goods, or mouthing off to or attacking a manager were in a different league altogether. A number of these more aggressive means of resistance probably resulted from a passionate outburst of emotion, and thus the consequences were not thought through. For example, Charlotte's unfortunate feud with manager Anthony Whiting began during the annual hog slaughter. She had Davy Gray, the enslaved overseer from Muddy Hole Farm, ask Whiting on her behalf for a "spear rib as she longed for it." Whiting did not comply with her request because he "knew this to be false and thought it a piece of impudence in her which she has a great share of." Two days later, he sent ribs to every woman in the quarter, at which time Charlotte received a share. "Affronted I suppose at my not sending it on Thursday," Charlotte followed Whiting into his house, threw the "spear rib" on the floor, and told him "she wanted none of my Meat & was in short very impudent."[94] Besides insolence, Charlotte also tried to use the plantation hierarchy against the manager when she threatened to tell "Lady Washington" that Whiting had whipped her. Similar tactics were used by other slaves at Mount Vernon, who complained to George Washington about the amount of food they were being issued and insinuated that one of the overseers was stealing and then selling their rations.[95]

THEFT

One of the most frequently mentioned acts of resistance in Washington's papers is theft. There are, in fact, so many references to stealing, and of so many kinds of things, that the situation is almost humorous, with a virtual siege-mentality developing on the part of the master and his family, who seemed unable to overcome the petty and annoying larcenies going on around them. For a perpetually cash-poor farmer in a largely preindustrial society, the situation was, however, no laughing matter. When it took anywhere from three to nine months to get orders for goods filled from abroad, any manufactured item was likely to be expensive and hard to replace.[96] While it might seem that thieves would prefer to take luxury items, the loss of those things would have been noticed fairly quickly and the guilty party identified easily, bringing sure punishment on the culprit. More often, the object was something small and relatively insignificant that might not be missed right away. Also, if someone were found with a hammer or some nails on their person, it could be hard to prove that they were stealing and had not simply forgotten they had possession of them.

Those enslaved at Mount Vernon were accused of stealing a wide variety of objects over the years. Washington suspected that tools mislaid on the estate were frequently "converted into cash, rum, or other things" by his slaves, including some of the six thousand twelve-penny nails that his carpenters used in building a corn storage house at River Farm in 1793.[97] Both raw and finished materials for making clothing were also targets for theft. Washington cautioned one manager to beware of letting Caroline Branham, an enslaved seamstress and housemaid, cut out clothing fabric rather than the hired gardener's wife, because he felt she "was never celebrated for her honesty" and "would not be restrained by scruples of conscience, from taking a large toll [on the linen] if she thought it could be done with impunity."[98] All kinds of food and drink, including wine, rum, milk, butter, fruits, meat, corn, and potatoes, disappeared to be either consumed by the thieves or sold to raise money. Aware of the vulnerability of foodstuffs, Washington even expressed concern about the slow pace of construction on the Dogue Run barn, which meant that grain was still being threshed the old way, in the open yard where it was likely to be stolen.[99] Among the buildings that were broken into over the years were the greenhouse loft, the corn loft, and the smokehouse.[100]

Washington tried a number of means to prevent thefts. In 1793, for instance, he ordered his manager to mix the seeds of various grasses with sand, not only to make them easier to sow but also to keep them from being stolen and sold. He even went so far as to require sheep to be washed before they were shorn, "otherwise I shall have a larger part of the Wool stolen if washed after it is sheared."[101] Storage areas like the closets in the mansion, the stable loft, the corn loft, and the corn houses were locked and the keys kept by a trustworthy person, usually an overseer but sometimes a slave with far less authority. When "that trusty old negro Jack" died in the fall of 1795, Washington tried to find a substitute to take over management of the corn supply for the horses. At that time, he directed that one of the hired overseers be given the key to the loft, because he knew "of no black person about the house" who could be trusted. Even this measure failed on occasion, however, when those individuals charged with keeping the keys handed them over directly to the slaves who drove plows and wagons and "want grain for their work horses," rather than issuing the corn for that purpose themselves.[102] Before the seamstresses could get a new bolt of material to work with, they had to bring in both the finished product and the scraps from the previous bolt. Similar arrangements were made to protect tools and other equipment.[103] So pervasive was the problem of theft that Washington to a certain extent planned for it. In contemplating the potato crop one year, he told his manager to "be sure to reserve enough for seed, by making ample allowance for thefts, waste, and rotting."[104]

Washington and his managers often distrusted the hired and indentured whites as much as they did the slaves, and frequently suspected the free and enslaved laborers of working in concert against them.[105] One manager was informed that it "was never my custom to trust [solely] the measurement of my Corn by the Overseers," who were thought to occasionally "over report of the measurement by scantily filling the Barrel."[106] After some clover seed, which if sold "would command ready money," disappeared in 1793, Washington mused that an overseer named Butler "must have disposed of it himself." He also considered it a likely possibility, however, that Butler had kept the key, "contrary to orders," and thus "given the roguest people about the house an opportunity to come at it," a thought that led Washington to the conclusion, "there can be no doubt of their taking everything else that was saleable."[107]

Washington eventually came to believe that Alexandria was overrun with shopkeepers willing to fence stolen goods. In discussions with his farm manager about care of the sheep at Mount Vernon, Washington reflected that one proposed scheme would probably lead to the culling of his best sheep (rather than saving them for breeding), which then would end up in the shops of local butchers.[108] As he cautioned farm manager William Pearce in 1794:

> [T]o be plain, Alexandria is such a recept[a]cle for every thing that can be filched from the right owners, by either blacks or whites; and I have such an opinion of my Negros (two or three only excepted): and not much better of some of the Whites, that I am perfectly sure not a single thing that can be disposed of at any price, at that place, that will not, and is not, stolen, where it is possible; and carried thither to some of the underling shop keepers, who support themselves by this kind of traffick.[109]

These concerns continued over the next several years until in 1798, James Anderson, who was then Washington's farm manager, placed a notice to the public in the local paper. Prompted by fears that the Mount Vernon slaves were selling pilfered goods in the nearby city, any of them who wished to sell things in Alexandria in the future had to have a special certificate signed by Anderson in order to attend the Sunday market.[110]

Theft may have been so common because there were so many reasons for doing it. Where one slave might have taken something out of anger, another might simply have wanted to have possession of a pretty little object. Some of the slaves were probably, as their master suspected, stealing for business reasons, to supply shopkeepers or other middlemen in town. Still others might have stolen food because they were hungry or taken fabric to mend the few clothes they were given each year. An Englishman who spent several years in the greater Mount Vernon neighborhood suggested another reason. Slaves, and he was speaking generally, not just of George Washington's slaves, believed that

> as they work and raise all, they have a right to consume all. As I have travelled on the road, I have made it my business to converse with them, and they say, "Massa, as we work and raise all, we ought to consume all;" and to a person who does not contradict them, they will declare their mind very freely. They say, "Massa does not work; therefore he has not equal right: overseer does not work; he has no right to eat as we do."[111]

The attitude observed by this English farmer is supported by a conversation recorded at Mount Vernon the year after the Civil War ended. During his visit there, a male tourist spoke to a young black woman scrubbing clothes and found that she had been a slave of the last private owner of the estate, John Augustine Washington III, who was a great-great-nephew of George Washington. In 1866, she was working for the Mount Vernon Ladies' Association for seven dollars per month, which she thought "a good deal better n' no wages at all!" She went on to say, "You know the Bible says every one must live by the sweat of his own eyebrow. But John A. Washington, he lived by the sweat of my eyebrow."[112]

ARSON AND SABOTAGE

In addition to stealing from their master, the slaves at Mount Vernon may also have sought revenge through arson and sabotage. There were several instances when slaves may have set fire to buildings on the estate and deliberately damaged crops, but from the surviving sources we have no way of knowing what actually happened. A storage building for corn went up in flames in March 1787, leading George Washington to surmise that the cause of the blaze was "either . . . carelessness or design." While he felt that the "latter seems most likely," he noted that "whom to suspect was not known."[113] Five years later, when the carpenters' workshop burned, together with all the tools and seasoned wood inside the structure, Washington ascribed the cause to carelessness on the part of Isaac, the head carpenter. He fumed that if Isaac "had his des[s]erts, he wd. receive a severe punishment," and suggested that Isaac must have left the fire in the shop in a vigorous state or been away from it for a long time, "for such an accident to have happened before it was too late to have extinguished it."

Washington asked his manager to tell Isaac that "I sustain injury enough by their idleness; they need not add to it by their carelessness."[114] Only the week before, Washington had reminded the miller to be especially careful of fires while working at night, "because [he had found] the accident of fires is already begun." In the same letter, he complained to his manager about recent losses and seemed particularly upset that the details of a fire at his "Hound Kennels" were not given him, "as if it [a fire] was a thing of course."[115]

These incidents may have been more planned than accidental, however. Several years after Bushrod Washington took possession of Mount Vernon, a slave attempted to burn down the mansion house, possibly in retaliation "for some correction they had suffered." The northern visitor who recorded the fire wisely commented that it "is surely a miserable situation to be surrounded with a number of Slaves, however kindly they may be used, yet the very Idea of Slavery is horrible."[116]

When Jenny died in December 1790, farm manager George Augustine Washington reminded his uncle that she and another slave named Bateman were once thought "instrumental in d[e]stroying the Flax at Dogue Run." George Washington had ordered the episode investigated, and "if She was found guilty to have her punished." Nonetheless, upon digging into the matter, she was found not to be "so culpable as had been represented" and received no punishment. It is unclear from the one letter that mentions this business if the other suspect was cleared or not.[117]

MURDER: POISONING

In 1732, the year of George Washington's birth, a young planter named Ambrose Madison, then thirty-six years old, was murdered. Three slaves were arrested and tried for the crime of poisoning Madison: Pompey, who belonged to Joseph Hawkins, and two of the victim's own slaves, a man called Turk and a woman known as Dido. All three were found guilty. Pompey was hanged, while Turk and Dido were each sentenced to receive twenty-nine lashes on their bare backs and returned to their new owner, the victim's widow. According to historian Douglas Chambers, this was "the first known case of the killing of a master by slaves in Virginia" and also "the first known conviction of slaves for the use of poison against their master in Virginia. It would not, however, be the last." Ambrose Madison was the grandfather of George Washington's friend, colleague, and fellow founding father James Madison.[118]

Although there is no evidence that the Washington and Custis slaves ever took the extreme step of murdering any of the whites around them, a slave named Brunswick on one of the Custis plantations being managed by George Washington was only able to survive being poisoned by another slave through the ministrations of a "negro doctor" in the summer of 1764.[119] Whites at Mount Vernon certainly feared being poisoned. In the mid-1780s, Washington hired an old English farmer to provide agricultural advice and help him manage the estate. Perhaps because of his age, James Bloxham had a difficult time adjusting to life in Virginia. At one point, he wrote a former employer to say that he would probably be leaving America when his contract was up. He confessed that he did not like the slaves and was afraid that he was "rather in Danger of being posind [poisoned] among them."[120]

Poisoning was often suspected in cases of sudden, unexpected deaths. About this same time, former farm manager Lund Washington, now married to his cousin Elizabeth Foote, lost two "Lovely healthy daughters." Both named Lucinda, the first child lived fourteen months while the second lived for thirteen months. According to family recollections, both girls died of "Convulsion fits" after being ill for "about the same number of days." Lund was planning to free his slaves in his will, something a relative attributed to the fact that the "manumission delusion had commenced," and he was heard to say that "his Slaves should not serve anybody but himself and his Wife." Although he himself did not suspect wrongdoing in the deaths of his little girls, "an opinion was entertained that his Slaves knew of this declaration and had determined to remove the Children in order to secure its fulfilment." Lund Washington's slaves would eventually be freed by his widow.[121]

Roughly two decades before, a notorious case involving poisoning had occurred in the Mount Vernon neighborhood. At least eight slaves from the area, including people belonging to the Washingtons' longtime friend George Mason of Gunston Hall, were found guilty of conspiring to "poison their Overseers." The plot was successful, and "several Persons . . . lost their Lives in Consequence thereof." The perpetrators were executed in Alexandria, "after which their Heads were cut off, and fixed on the Chimnies of the Court-House."[122] Historian Philip J. Schwarz has suggested that the mere threat of poisoning allowed slaves to exercise a tremendous amount of power over their owners. That theory would certainly make sense in the case of Bloxham, who probably went much easier on the people he supervised out of fear for his life.[123]

Poisoning was especially feared because slaves had responsibility for cooking and serving food and thus had ample opportunity to attempt this crime. According to one eighteenth-century writer, they also had considerable knowledge of the means. On a plantation outside Charlottesville, British prisoner Thomas Anburey was told that the slaves of that household frequently poisoned one another, generally for reasons relating to love and jealousy. The type of poison used by the slaves on this plantation was never discovered, but Anburey found it remarkable that "they can administer the poison that it shall affect the life for a longer or a shorter period, agreeable to their ideas of revenge." Some of the victims "lingered out a life for six or eight months after, and others again, only a week or a fortnight."[124]

ESCAPE

Perhaps the most emphatic means used by the Mount Vernon slaves to express their anger and frustration with a system that was at heart dehumanizing was to run away. While this action was often a negative response to problems with an owner or a particular overseer, it could also be a positive action whereby someone took advantage of an opportunity to break away, go to a new location, and start life over with the identity of a free man or woman. This action was not without personal cost, however, because it meant breaking all ties with family and friends left behind. The logistics of trying to escape with small children or elderly relatives in tow prevented many women from leaving and meant that more men attempted to run away than women. The more skilled a slave was in a particular craft, the better he or she spoke English, and the more comfortably he or she dealt with the greater society outside the plantation were all factors that could lead to the success or failure of an escape attempt. According to one study, between 1760 and 1799, at least forty-seven of the slaves either owned by Washington or held as the dower property of his wife ran away; this works out to a runaway rate of about 7 percent. In the years 1797 and 1798, 2 percent of the adult slaves at Mount Vernon ran away, costing Washington only .08 percent in lost labor. In comparison, on eighteenth-century Virginia plantations as a whole, the rate of slave flight averaged from 2–4 percent in any ten-year period. The number of escapes in Virginia tended to be lower than in the Caribbean and West Indies, where studies have shown runaway rates reaching as high as 7–20 percent per decade.[125]

Among the earliest references to runaways from Mount Vernon is a newspaper advertisement from the summer of 1761 in which George Washington gave public notice that four male slaves had escaped. Whoever apprehended them would be paid a reward of forty shillings if the men were taken up before they left the county. Ever cautious where a misunderstanding could cost him money, Washington added a postscript to the effect that if the men were recaptured singly, "the Reward will be proportioned." This document is especially valuable for the descriptions it gives of the slaves, two of whom, Neptune and Cupid, had just arrived from Africa two years before and could only speak "very broken and unintelligible English." Their fellow runaways were both of African origin as well, with one actually being a "Countryman" to the first two. Jack, however, had been in Virginia several years longer and spoke "pretty good English," while the fourth and slightly older runaway, Peros, "speaks much better than either, indeed has little of his Country Dialect left." Washington believed that because there had not been "the least Suspicion, Provocation, or Difference with any Body, or the least angry Word or Abuse from their Overseers," that they would probably not linger in the neighborhood but would try to get as far away as possible. Because Peros and Jack had both lived in other parts of Virginia before coming to Mount Vernon, he thought that the men might have tried to head for those familiar neighborhoods. All four were eventually apprehended and brought back to Mount Vernon, although Neptune might have been on his own for well over a year. In May 1765, Washington reimbursed one of his overseers the sum of £3.7.3 for cash "pd Prison Fees in Maryld Neptune."[126]

From Washington's statement about the probable destinations of these four, a quarrel with or punishment by an overseer or other authority figure could impel a slave to absent himself or herself for a time but not necessarily to leave the neighborhood. In 1767, George Washington learned that a slave named Mat had run away. He had obviously not run far, however, because he had been seen once or twice, although attempts to catch him up to that point had been unsuccessful.[127] Sophia, a young teenager on Washington's Dogue Run Farm, "absconded" for six days in December 1798. There is as yet no evidence about when she returned, but she was definitely home by the time George Washington made his list of the Mount Vernon slaves the following summer.[128]

Because people often escaped in order to be with family members at a former home, the likely destination of a runaway was frequently known to those who were looking for them. When Will, an elderly man rented from Mrs. French and living at Union Farm, left in January 1795, Washington suggested that he was probably in Maryland, noting that "when he was guilty of these tricks formerly (before I had him) his walks, and harbouring place was, as I have been informed, somewhere within the circle of Broad Creek, Bladensburgh and upper Marlborough." Washington then went on, rather uncharacteristically but perhaps because of Will's age, to suggest that he did not think it "worth while (except for the sake of example, nor for that, if it stops with him) to be at *much* trouble, or at *any* expen[s]e over a trifle, to hunt him up."[129]

Escaped slaves would need to keep an eye out for patrollers. In 1766, the Virginia House of Burgesses passed a law ordering each county to set up a slave patrol composed of one officer and as many as four members of the militia. These men were required at least once a month to stop by "all negro quarters and other places suspected of entertaining unlawful assemblies of slaves, servants, or other disorderly persons." They were also expected to pick up any slave found "strolling about from one plantation to another, without a pass from his or her master, mistress or overseer." For this work, they were paid twenty pounds of tobacco for every twelve hours they were on duty. Not everyone supported this law, so it is not clear whether it was regularly enforced or not. Ten years later, Landon Carter of Sabine Hall noted that one of the burgesses had recently complained about the patrolling law, "because a poor man was made to pay for keeping a rich man[']s Slaves in order." Carter "shamed the fool so much . . . that he Slunk away; but he got elected by it."[130]

It is clear that enslaved runaways could be both assisted and harmed by other slaves. A good example is the previously mentioned case of Coachman Jamey, who ran away in 1773 from the Custis plantations near Williamsburg. After proposing that Jamey be put in "Iron Spancels" and relocated, the farm manager noted that it was useless to put them on Jamey in York because "the negro Blacksmiths in town will soon file them off w[hi]ch he will not have the same opportunity [of] on the East[er]n Shore."[131]

Runaways who hid out in the neighborhood, however, might well be informed on, apprehended, or returned by other enslaved people, probably in expectation of earning a reward. Boatswain, for example, was caught less than a week after he left Mount Vernon in the spring of 1760. He was brought back by Davy, a slave belonging to Abram Barnes. George Washington expressed his thanks to Davy for "taking up Boson" by giving him ten shillings.[132] More than a decade later, Will Shag ran away from the Custis plantations near Williamsburg. In a letter to his employer, manager Joseph Valentine reported that Shag had been taken up after he was "in formd by Sum of the young negro[s] that they saw [W]ill at Bakers Quarter."[133]

THE *SAVAGE* INCIDENT

The most atypical escape at Mount Vernon took place in the spring of 1781, when seventeen individuals took advantage of the arrival of a British warship at the plantation to make a bid for freedom. Very early in the war, the royal governor of Virginia, John Murray, fourth Earl of Dunmore, issued a "much dreaded proclamation" offering "Freedom to All Indented Servts & Slaves (the Property of Rebels) that will repair to his majesty[']s Standard—being able to bear Arms." As farm manager Lund Washington explained this hated policy, he reassured George Washington that "if there were no white Serv[an]ts in this family I shou[l]d be under no apprehension about the Slaves."[134] Lund's assessment was very wrong.

An earlier chapter explored the changes in George Washington's ideas about slavery, which were the result of his experiences during the American Revolution. That same conflict also brought similar changes to the minds of enslaved people throughout the country. Much as Washington recognized the hypocrisy of fighting for freedom and liberty while holding others in bondage, so too did the slaves at Mount Vernon—and elsewhere in America. In thinking about this time, historian Ira Berlin noted that "seizing the moment, [slaves] headed for free territory—northward to New England and southward to British lines." Still others "opportunistically chose the cause that best assured the success of *their* own cause: freedom," by enlisting either with the British Army or with American units promising freedom in exchange for their service. Berlin indicates that both men and women took advantage of the war and the movement of armies to escape slavery, commenting that the "wartime erosion of slavery encouraged direct assaults on the institution itself."[135] An excellent example of this type of flight comes from Virginia's Sabine Hall in the summer of 1776, as the Continental Congress was debating and passing the Declaration of Independence in Philadelphia. Eight enslaved men left Landon Carter's plantation on the night of June 25, taking not just themselves but two guns, bullets, gunpowder, and a canoe. Within thirteen months, at least three others from Sabine Hall took advantage of the war to liberate themselves (although this latter group were later captured). As one might imagine, considerable turmoil ensued among the plantation-owning class as a result of this change in attitude on the part of their enslaved property.[136]

In 1781, George Washington had been away from home for about six years as commander of the Continental Army and was at his military headquarters at New Windsor in New York when two letters from Virginia brought some surprising news. Lund Washington wrote first. A British frigate had landed men on the Maryland side of the Potomac, where they burned a number of "gentlemen's houses . . . in sight of Mount Vernon." Captain Thomas Graves of the *Savage* then sent a message to Mount Vernon threatening the same treatment unless he and his crew were given "a large supply of provisions." According to Lund several years after the fact, his initial response to the British demand was "that when the General engaged in the contest he had put all to stake, and was well aware of the exposed situation of his house and property, in consequence of which he had given him orders by no means to comply with any such demands, for that he would make no unworthy compromise with the enemy, and was ready to meet the fate of his neighbors."[137]

Furious at this reply, Captain Graves brought the ship closer to the shore in readiness to burn the estate but offered Lund the chance to come aboard to talk. He did so, taking "a small present of poultry" for the ship's commanding officer. During their pleasant chat, Graves "expressed his personal respect for the character of the General," commended Lund's conduct, and "assured him nothing but his having misconceived the terms of the first answer could have induced him . . . to entertain the idea of taking the smallest measure offensive to so illustrious a character as the General." He also explained that some "real or supposed provocations . . . had compelled his severity on the other side of the river." After their conversation, Lund went back to shore and "instantly d[i]spatched sheep, hogs, and an abundant supply of other articles as a present to the English frigate."[138] At some point early in these events, before Lund went on board the *Savage,* a group of slaves made their way to the ship, hoping to be emancipated on the basis of Lord Dunmore's proclamation.[139]

Although Lund Washington's letter of April 18 is missing, an enclosure listing the fourteen men and three women who escaped has survived. In addition to the foodstuffs provided by Lund, the *Savage* had also taken off "a very valuable Boat: 24 [or 22] feet Keel," and the following enslaved people: Peter, Lewis, and Frank, all of whom were described as "old"; Frederick, forty-five years old, who worked as an overseer and was "valuable"; Gunner, a brickmaker who was also about forty-five; Harry, a valuable "Horseler" of about forty; Tom and Sambo (probably Anderson), who were only twenty but "stout and Healthy"; Thomas, a seventeen-year-old house servant; Peter, age fifteen, who was described as "very likely"; Stephen, a twenty-year-old cooper; twenty-five-year-old James, who was "stout and healthy"; Watty or Wally, a weaver of twenty; Daniel, who was "very likely" at the age of nineteen; Lucy, who was twenty; Esther, a little younger at eighteen; and Deborah, who was sixteen years old.[140]

The second letter to reach Washington was from the Marquis de Lafayette, who was then trying to deflect an offensive by British land forces in Virginia. From Alexandria, the young Frenchman wrote on April 23, exhibiting less concern for the loss of Washington's enslaved property than for the example shown by Lund Washington in the face of danger:

> When the Ennemy Came to your House Many Negroes deserted to them. This piece of News did not affect me much as I little Value property—But You Cannot Conceive How Unhappy I Have Been to Hear that Mr. Lund Washington Went on Board the Ennemy's vessels and Consented to give them provisions. This Being done By the Gentleman who in Some Measure Represents you at your House will certainly Have a Bad effect, and Contrasts with Spirited Answers from Some Neighbours that Had their Houses Burnt Accordingly.
>
> You will do what you think proper about it, My dear General, But, As your friend, it Was My duty Confidentially to Mention the Circumstances.[141]

Washington was seriously disturbed by Lund's actions, writing to his cousin on April 30 that he was "very sorry to hear of your loss; I am a little sorry to hear of my own; but that which gives me most concern, is, that you should go on board the enemy[']s Vessels, and furnish them with refreshments." He went on to write,

> It would have been a less painful circumstance to me, to have heard, that in consequence of your non-compliance with their request, they had burnt my House, and laid the Plantation in ruins. You ought to have considered yourself as my representative, and should have reflected on the bad example of communicating with the enemy, and making a voluntary offer of refreshments to them with a view to prevent a conflagration. . . . I am thoroughly perswaded that you acted from your best judgment . . . but to go on board their Vessels; carry them refreshments; commune with a parcel of plundering Scoundrels, and request a favor by asking the surrender of my Negroes, was exceedingly ill-judged.[142]

Of the people who ran away to the British at this time, seven—Frederick, Frank, Gunner, Sambo Anderson, Thomas, Lucy, and Esther—were eventually returned to Mount Vernon sometime after the siege at Yorktown in the fall of 1781. Thomas had managed to get as far as Philadelphia, and Washington had to pay an unspecified amount for his "salvage." His travel expenses back to Virginia cost another twelve dollars.[143]

According to historian Alan Taylor, roughly six thousand Virginia slaves escaped to the British during the American Revolution. Of that number, about one-third gained their freedom by heading for the British lines, while another third died, probably from disease, and the final third were sent back to the plantations and masters they had left. In the latter case, those masters often sold off the returned runaways, fearing that they would be a bad influence on their fellows in the quarters. For example, six of the twenty-three slaves who escaped from Thomas Jefferson during the war were returned to him at its conclusion. Of that number, one died and the other five were sold. An exception to the rule was James Madison, who actually freed a returned slave named Billy. Commenting that the man was "too thoroughly tainted" to be around the other slaves, Madison would not consider punishing him by selling him away "merely for coveting that liberty for which we have paid the price of so much blood, and have proclaimed so often to be the right, & worthy the pursuit, of every human being."[144]

THE SUCCESSFUL RUNAWAY

In general, for most of the eighteenth century, slaves who had skills or trades they could use to support themselves and who were familiar with both white society and the English language had the best chance of making a successful escape attempt. Slaves who fit this pattern were frequently second- or third-generation African Americans working as artisans or personal servants, who were in close contact with the master and his family and had a better chance than the fieldworkers to interact with and become comfortable with the world beyond the community in the quarters. Because of the nature of their work, these slaves were likely the ones with whom the white family developed close emotional ties and to whom their owners gave special privileges. The sense of betrayal felt when such a slave escaped could be strong. At least three of the slaves who attempted to escape from the Washingtons over the years matched the above profile, and two of these individuals succeeded.

In September 1799, George Washington wrote his neighbor Roger West to inform him of a plot involving Washington's waiting man and his wife, a mulatto woman who belonged to West. The retired president had somehow come into possession of a note dropped by Christopher Sheels in the "yard" at Mount Vernon that gave some details about the planned escape on a ship from Alexandria. The note, which may have been written by Sheels's wife, confirms that at least some slaves at Mount Vernon and in the larger neighborhood could read and write. Washington asked West to do some additional investigations into the plot and to send any messages to him through a third party. He himself sent his letter to West by way of an old friend, James Craik, "to avoid the suspicion that might arise by sending a messenger with [it to your] house." By this means he hoped to keep Sheels unaware of the discovery of his escape plans, probably until all the details were known. At that point he could be confronted and apprised of the uselessness of further attempts to escape.[145]

As was typical for slaves who worked in close association with the master and his family, Sheels was probably quite comfortable with white society. He had seen something of the larger world during the years of Washington's presidency when he accompanied the family to Philadelphia.[146] He had probably been taught to read and write. Sheels had also received special treatment in the past. Two years before he made plans to run away, he had been bitten by what was presumed to have been a rabid dog. Washington sent him to Lebanon, Pennsylvania, to see Doctor William Stoy, a specialist "celebrated for curing persons bitten by mad animals." Sheels, who had been given twenty-five dollars to pay for his expenses, did not take this golden opportunity to escape. He was home within two months, at which time he returned twelve dollars to his master. A young friend and sometime member of the household, George Washington Lafayette, seems to have developed a friendship with Sheels, perhaps because the two were close in age, and wrote to say that he had crossed paths with Sheels on his way to Pennsylvania. George Washington's affection for the slave is evident in his response to the young Lafayette. He replied that Sheels had "derived so much aid from the medicine he took as to have remained perfectly well ever since." He also was so confident of Doctor Stoy's abilities that "he wou'd not again dispair of being cured of a mad dog; if the Hydrophoby was strong upon him."[147] His master's fondness for him may have been responsible for the fact that Sheels seems to have been forgiven for his escape attempt; there was, at any rate, no move to demote him. When George Washington became gravely ill three months after the plot was discovered, Sheels was with him throughout the ordeal and was at his bedside when he breathed his last.[148]

THE SUCCESSFUL RUNAWAY: HERCULES

The successful escape of Hercules, the Washington family cook, caused quite an upset within the household. Known to the family as "Uncle Harkless," the cook was described many years later as "a dark-brown man, little, if any, above the usual size, yet possessed of such great muscular power as to entitle him to be compared with his namesake of fabulous history." Hercules had been taken north in 1790 to cook for the presidential household, and while there, seems to have developed a lucrative business, the proceeds of which he then used to buy rather fancy clothes.[149] Through his years in the capital, the sales of "slops," and his purchases of clothing, Hercules would have been able to develop a network of friends and "business associates" who could help him in an escape attempt.

The Washington family exhibited their special feelings for Hercules in other ways besides the affectionate nickname with which he was known. As was mentioned in an earlier chapter, when his wife died in the summer of 1787, Martha Washington directed that three bottles of rum be given to him "to bury his wife."[150] Early in his time in the kitchen of the executive mansion, Hercules asked to have his son Richmond with him to assist as a "Scullion." This favor was granted by George Washington "not from [Richmond's] appearance or merits . . . but because he was the Son of Hercul[e]s and [the latter's] desire to have him as an assistant," and the young man was sent north in the fall of 1790.[151]

Hercules was one of several slaves in the executive mansion considered old enough to qualify under a Pennsylvania law that allowed enslaved individuals to claim their freedom after living for a minimum of six months' residence in that state. When the Washingtons decided to send these people home to Mount Vernon periodically to prevent any of them from taking advantage of the law, Hercules, having learned about the law and the ramifications of the Washingtons' actions, successfully convinced them of his loyalty. As the incident was explained to the president by his secretary:

> In my letter of the 22d of [M]ay I mentioned that Hercules was to go on to Mount Vernon a few days after that. When he was about to go, somebody, I presume, insinuated to him that the motive for sending him home so long before you was expected there, was to prevent his taking

the advantage of a six month's residence in this place. When he was possessed of this idea he appeared to be extremely unhappy—and altho' he made not the least objection to going; yet, he said he was mortified to the last degree to think that a suspicion could be entertained of his fidelity or attachment to you. [A]nd so much did the poor fellow's feelings appear to be touched that it left no doubt of his sincerity—and to sh[o]w him that there were no apprehensions of that kind entertained of him, Mrs Washington told him he should not go at that time; but might remain 'till the expiration of six months and then go home—to prepare for your arrival there. He has accordingly continued here 'till this time, and tomorrow takes his departure for Virginia.[152]

Despite those assurances from Hercules, a letter written by Washington four months before his retirement from the presidency indicates a suspicion on his part that his cook was going to run away. Following Richmond's aforementioned theft from James Wilkes in the fall of 1796, Washington expressed his hope that the young man had not been urged to do it by his father "for the purpose perhaps of a journey together." Washington asked his farm manager William Pearce to keep a discreet eye out for further evidence of escape plans.[153]

Weekly reports from Mount Vernon from the first two months of the following year show that Hercules, as well as two other house servants (Frank Lee and Cyrus), often worked several days each week with the bricklayers and gardeners. This was probably because, with the Washingtons still in Philadelphia finishing up the last few weeks of the presidency, there was simply not enough work in the mansion and kitchen to keep them busy. Being asked to do such backbreaking tasks as digging brick clay and digging out honeysuckle by the roots was logical from a managerial perspective, but would likely to have been viewed by Hercules as beneath him and as the last straw. In the weekly report dated February 25, 1797, the farm manager noted that Hercules had spent two days that week—Monday and Tuesday, February 20 and 21—digging clay for bricks and that for the remaining four days he had "absconded."[154] The fact that he very likely left Mount Vernon in the wee hours of February 22—George Washington's birthday—was a very telling statement.

As he was making his way home after the inauguration of his successor, Washington wrote with instructions for the steward in his Philadelphia household to "make all the enquiry he can after Hercules, and send him round in the Vessel if he can be discovered & apprehended."[155] One month later, a French visitor to Mount Vernon took the time to talk with the small daughter the cook left behind. Upon his suggestion that she must be very sad at the thought of never seeing her father again, the six-year-old answered that, on the contrary, she was "very glad, because he is free now."[156]

As might be expected, the response of Hercules's family was quite different from that of the Washingtons. In August 1797, a sad Martha Washington wrote her sister that "our cook Hercules went away so that I am as much at a loss for a cook as for a house keeper.—altogether I am sadly plaiged."[157] Her husband was less openly emotional, but Hercules's escape had left him with a moral dilemma: "The running off of my Cook, has been a most inconvenient thing to this family; and what renders it more disagreeable, is, that I had resolved never to become the master of another Slave by *purchase;* but this resolution I fear I must break."[158]

Rather than buying a new cook, Washington took steps to get his old one back. Learning that Hercules had run away to associates in Philadelphia, he wrote his former household steward Frederick Kitt early in 1798 with a request for his help and instructions on the best means of sending Hercules home. Washington even authorized Kitt to "hire some one who is most likely to be acquainted with his haunts, to trace them out," but warned of the need for "indirect enquiries," because "if Hercul[e]s was to get the least hint of the design he would elude all your vigilance."[159] Hercules turns up once more in the family correspondence. A little more than two years after Washington died, his widow sent a letter to Colonel Richard Varick in New York that is a bit ambiguous as to Hercules's fate: "Mrs Varick & yourself will accept my best thanks . . . for the [i]nquiries you have made respecting my old Cook Hercules, since I had the pleasure of seeing you I have been so fortunate as to engage a white cook who answers very well. I have thought it therefore better to decline taking Hercules back again."[160] Whether Varick had found Hercules or was only looking for him is unclear, in part because Varick's earlier letter is missing. What Martha Washington did not say in her note was that Hercules was part of a large group of slaves who had belonged to George Washington and whose emancipation he had provided for in his will. She had already freed those individuals almost a year previously and was thus simply giving Hercules, whether he had been located or not, his liberty as well. No additional information about his life as a freeman has come to light.[161]

THE SUCCESSFUL RUNAWAY: ONEY JUDGE

The slave whose escape caused the most emotional turmoil for the Washington family was a young mulatto woman known as Oney Judge. She had been raised at the Mansion House Farm as part of a large family and went to work as Martha Washington's maid at about ten years of age. According to George Washington, Judge was "brought up and treated more like a child than a Servant." She became an especially talented seamstress, "being perfect Mistress of her needle," and was one of the handful of household slaves brought to Philadelphia by the Washington family during the presidency. There she spent considerable time in the company of Martha Washington's youngest granddaughter, Nelly, and her friends, and accompanied the first lady on social calls.[162] Judge ran away from the Philadelphia executive mansion on the afternoon of May 21, 1796, a Saturday. Shortly after her escape, Frederick Kitt, the hired steward, placed a notice in the newspaper in which he described the twenty-year-old as "a light mulatto girl, much freckled, with very black eyes and bushy black hair," who was of medium height, "slender, and delicately formed." Kitt noted that she had "many changes of good clothes" and warned shipmasters that, trying to pass as a free woman, she might attempt to leave the city by water and would have the money for her passage. A reward was offered for her return.[163]

The escape was the subject of gossip even beyond Philadelphia. After dinner with several friends in Massachusetts, John Adams noted in his diary that, amid speculation at the table that George Washington would not serve another term as president, talk turned to "Anecdotes of Dandridge, and Mrs. W.s Negro Woman. Both disappeared—never heard of—know not where they are." Bartholomew Dandridge, Martha Washington's nephew who was serving as secretary to the president, left abruptly without explanation, about the same time as Judge. Once the young man had gotten in touch with his employer, Washington counseled that his behavior had "opened the door for variety of conjecture; some of them you may be sure not favorable." There seems to have been no connection between the two runaways, beyond the fact that they both worked in the executive mansion, and the errant Dandridge would soon return to his post.[164]

It was not true that nothing had been heard of Judge. The Washingtons had put out feelers with their acquaintances and were getting reports back. Thomas Lee, Jr., wrote to the president from New York City at the end of June to let him know that he had learned from "a free mulattoe Woman who is Cooke in a boarding house in this City kept by a Mr Marcelline" that "she is well acquain[t]ed with Oney & that she has been here" and was headed to Boston. Lee was not sure if this information was the truth or if it was intended to send him off the track of the runaway, but he notified law enforcement authorities in New York to be on the lookout for her.[165]

It is not known if Judge went to Boston first, but by early September she was in New Hampshire. Elizabeth Langdon, the only daughter of U.S. senator John Langdon, a prominent businessman and politician from that state, recognized Judge one day on the street in Portsmouth. Just as she was "about to stop and speak to her," Judge "brushed quickly by, to avoid it." According to George Washington, "Miss Langden . . . must have seen [Judge] often in the Chamber of Miss Custis," Martha Washington's youngest granddaughter. He also believed that John Langdon's wife, Elizabeth Sherburne Langdon, would have known Oney from "the occasional calls on the girl [her daughter Elizabeth] by Mrs. Washington, when she has been here [Philadelphia]," and that both Langdon women could identify her to the authorities if necessary. The president assumed that Judge had escaped with the assistance of "some one who knew what he was about, and had the means to defray the expense of it."[166] Further inquiry suggested that this accomplice was a Frenchman, "who was either really, or pretendedly deranged, and under that guise, used to frequent the family."[167]

Martha Washington seems to have been terribly upset by the loss of Judge, and her husband made several attempts on Martha's behalf over the next three years to recover the young woman. As seen earlier in chapter 1, George Washington considered Judge to be ungrateful for all the advantages she had received. His efforts to contact her were successful, and at one point she seems to have been willing to return to Mount Vernon. Negotiations broke down, however, when she made a suggestion that George Washington found completely unacceptable. Judge sent word that she would come back and "serve with fidelity during the lives of the President & his Lady if she could be freed on their decease, should she outlive them; but that she should rather suffer death than return to Slavery & [be] liable to be sold or given to any other persons."[168] Washington responded,

> To enter into such a compromise with her, as she suggested to you, is totally inadmissable, for reasons that must strike at first view: for however well disposed I might be to a gradual abolition, or even to an entire emancipation of that description of People (if the latter was in itself practicable at this moment) it would neither be politic or just to reward unfaithfulness with a premature preference; and thereby discontent before hand the minds of all her fellow-servants who by their steady attachments are far more deserving than herself of favor.[169]

Several years later, another of Martha Washington's nephews, Burwell Bassett, was even enlisted to help bring Judge back to Mount Vernon. By that time, Washington was willing to promise that if she gave him no further trouble about coming home and behaved well, she would "escape punishment for the past, & be treated according to her merits" in the future. He felt that to promise anything more would be "[an im]politic & *dangerous* precedent."[170] Judge had by then married John Staines, a mulatto sailor with whom she had a daughter named Eliza, the first of three children they would have together. She had made friends in a local church, where she learned to read, and acquired some powerful allies. When Bassett came to Portsmouth, New Hampshire, to get her, Senator John Langdon got word to her of the young man's mission and she went into hiding with friends until Bassett returned to Virginia.[171]

There may have been more than affection involved in the lengths to which the Washingtons tried to get Judge back home, having to do, as one might expect, with property rights. A Virginia law dating to October 1785 spelled out the restrictions applying to the widow of a man who died without a will, or to any subsequent husband she might take, in regard to the movement of those dower slaves in whom the widow was entitled to use for her lifetime:

XXIII. And if any widow possessed as aforesaid, shall be married to a husband who shall remove, or voluntarily permit to be removed of this commonwealth, any such slave or slaves, or any of their increase, without the consent of him or her in reversion; in such case it shall be lawful for him or her in reversion to enter into, possess, and enjoy all the estate which such husband holdeth in right of his wife's dower for and during the life of said husband.[172]

Prior to the Custis grandchildren reaching their majority and/or, in the case of the Custis granddaughters, getting married, the person who would have given permission to remove any of the dower slaves out of Virginia was probably Dr. David Stuart, the stepfather of the Custis grandchildren. It was conceivable, however, that by the spring of 1796, after two of the granddaughters had married (Martha, or Patty, as she was known, in January 1795 and Eliza in March 1796), that their new husbands might have sued because they had not been asked for permission to take the dower slaves out of the state. Had they won the suit, George and Martha Washington might have lost all of the dower property (meaning the slaves, all the land, and whatever money might have been left).

Oney Judge's is the only case in which an escaped Washington slave got to tell her story.[173] Many years later, as a very old woman, she was interviewed at least twice in the mid- to late 1840s. It was then that she revealed the identity of the ship captain who took her from Philadelphia, but she never named her connections in the city's large free black community who assisted with the escape.[174] In the interviews, Judge Staines expressed considerable bitterness toward the Washingtons. There was no problem with the way she was treated, but she simply wanted to be free; or, as expressed by one interviewer, "although well enough used as to work and living, she did not want to be a slave always."[175] According to Staines, she escaped when she did because George Washington was planning to move back to Mount Vernon upon his retirement from the presidency, and she believed that "if she went back to Virginia, she would never have a chance to escape."[176]

This explanation is quite logical, but several other factors may have played into the timing of this escape as well. Two important members of Judge's family who might have provided a reason to stay had died by this point: her older half-brother Austin, with whom she worked for years in the presidential mansions in New York and Philadelphia, expired unexpectedly in December 1794, while their mother, Betty, died after a long illness in early 1795.[177] One interviewer recorded that Martha Washington made a verbal gift of the young slave to her eldest granddaughter, Eliza Parke Custis Law, who had just been married several months before Judge escaped.[178] A second wrote that Judge "understood that after the decease of her master and mistress, she was to become the property of a grand-daughter of theirs, by the name of Custis, and that she was determined never to be her slave."[179] The information about the promised gift is noted nowhere in the Washington-Custis family correspondence. Whether the thought of working for a young woman with whom she had grown up was too much for her, or there were personality conflicts between Judge and Law or her new husband, or simply the fact that the couple lived in the new Federal City, which meant Judge would be back in the South, the fact that she was destined to go to Law was the impetus for her escape. Many years after these events, when questioned about the hardships she had faced as a free woman and whether, as a result, she regretted leaving the Washingtons, Judge Staines, who was then poor and alone, having outlived both her husband and her children, emphatically replied, "No, I am free, and have, I trust, been made a child of God by [that] means."[180] She died on February 25, 1848, in Greenland, New Hampshire.[181]

The experiences of Sheels, Hercules, and Judge illustrate an especially significant aspect of slave resistance. Here were enslaved people who were privileged in the sense that they had occupations that gave them a certain degree of prestige and the opportunity to travel. Sheels and Judge, at least, had fairly light work and were able to meet some of the most important people of their day. All three were well cared for, given special advantages, and were the objects of affectionate feelings by the Washingtons. None of this was enough. They were all willing to give up the emotional support of family and friends and a relatively comfortable life to risk physical punishment and possible demotion if caught, and considerable insecurity if they were successful, in order to have ultimate control over their own lives.

These cases also reinforce the idea that the American Revolution seared the message that freedom was a God-given right into the hearts of enslaved people throughout the country. The escape of the seventeen slaves with the British in 1781, as well as the postwar actions of Sheels, Hercules, and Judge are thus related but very different from the escapes of slaves prior to the war. Judge's acknowledgment that she "did not want to be a slave always" and her negotiations with the president of the United States about whether or not she would return to Mount Vernon reflect a very different mind-set from those earlier runaways who were simply trying to stay out of the way until a supervisor cooled down or attempting to get back to loved ones in another part of Virginia.

Conclusion

Not every slave at Mount Vernon was brave, angry, or strong enough to risk everything in a bid for freedom by running away. While feigning illness, procrastination, producing sloppy work, and damaging tools may seem petty or trifling, those actions too reveal tremendous anger and frustration. Through their behavior, the slaves at Mount Vernon were not only expressing negative emotion however. They were also trying nonverbally to define themselves as separate, both as individuals and a community, from their master or overseer and to get across the idea that their values concerning everything from the use of their time to the relative place of family and work in their lives were different.

Through the years, George Washington was involved in a continuous battle to control the behavior of his slaves. He once complained to a friend in England that his slaves had "no ambition to establish a *good* name" and were "too regardless of a *bad* one."[182] Qualities that might enhance a person's "good name" among his fellow slaves were, however, often diametrically opposed to a master's goals. A slave might care very much about his reputation within the African American community and still consider what the overseer felt about him to be irrelevant. The man who could surprise his family with sugar purchased with money from the successful theft and sale of a quantity of seeds or nails might be well regarded in the quarters and considered a rogue by his master. The enslaved community might think very highly of the woman who could get out of work by falsely claiming to be pregnant, at the same time a white supervisor thought of her as a lazy hussy. Ironically, Washington never understood that the things that motivated him to do his best—pride, concern with his reputation, material advancement—were the very things that motivated the bondsmen working for him, but that his interests and those of the enslaved community were often incompatible.

Conclusion

"More Than a Father"

Eulogy for a "Father"

On December 29, 1799, just fifteen days after George Washington's death at Mount Vernon, Reverend Richard Allen, a Methodist minister (it would be another seventeen years before he founded the African Methodist Episcopal church), took to the pulpit in Philadelphia to give a eulogy in Washington's honor. Coming as they did from a former slave, Allen's words are particularly interesting because they focus on the reputation of Washington as a lifelong slave owner. He began by noting that the nation was mourning in a "season of festivity" for the man he called "Our father and friend." He told his congregants that they especially had "particular cause to bemoan our loss," because Washington had been a "sympathising friend and tender father" who had "watched over us, and viewed our degraded and afflicted state with compassion and pity—his heart was not insensible to our sufferings. He whose wisdom the nations revered thought we had a right to liberty. Unbiased by the popular opinion of the state in which is the memorable Mount Vernon—he dared to do his duty, and wipe off the only stain with which man could ever reproach him." Allen went on to laud Washington as a man who "did not fight for that liberty which he desired to withhold from others" but instead "let the oppressed go free" and "undid every burden." Recalling Washington's role in the Revolution as "his country's deliverer," Allen asked, "by what name shall we call him who secretly and almost unknown emancipated his 'bondsmen and bondswomen'—became to them a father, and gave them an inheritance?" The minister noted that "deeds like these are not common" and that God would openly reward "such acts of beneficense." He predicted that "the name of Washington will live when the sculptured marble and the statue of bronze shall be crumbled into dust—for it is the decree of the eternal God that 'the righteous shall be had in everlasting remembrance.'"[1]

Reverend Allen's lovely eulogy emphasized a provision in George Washington's will that greatly impacted the lives of both his widow and the enslaved community at Mount Vernon. Written the summer before he died, Washington left, with the exception of a few specific bequests to others, "the use, profit and benefit of my whole Estate, real and personal," to his "dearly beloved wife Martha Washington," "for the term of her natural life." In addition, at the end of the same document, he also named "my dearly beloved wife Martha Washington" one of seven executors of his will, along with nephews William Augustine Washington, Bushrod Washington, George Steptoe Washington, Samuel Washington, and Lawrence Lewis, and step-grandson George Washington Parke Custis.[2]

One of the primary duties Washington placed on his executors was the emancipation, after Martha Washington's death, of all the slaves who had belonged to him. In accordance with state law, Washington stipulated that elderly slaves or those who were too sick to work were to be supported throughout their lives by his estate. Going beyond the law, which decreed that male slaves under the age of twenty-one and females under the age of eighteen be "supported and maintained" by the estate of the person who freed them until they reached their majority, Washington's will required that children without parents, or those whose families were too poor or indifferent to see to their education, were to be bound out to masters and mistresses who would teach them reading, writing, and a useful trade until they were ultimately freed at the age of twenty-five. Washington's language concerning the importance he placed on these duties was forceful: "And I do moreover most pointedly, and most solemnly enjoin it upon my Executors . . . to see that this clause respecting Slaves, and every part thereof be religiously fulfilled at the Epoch at which it is directed to take place; without evasion, neglect or delay, after the Crops which may then be on the ground are harvested, particularly as it respects the aged and infirm."[3]

As evidenced by Reverend Allen's sermon, the contents of George Washington's will became known very quickly, both within the United States and abroad. Quoting a Baltimore newspaper article of January 7, 1800, the *Massachusetts Mercury* reported that Washington had "directed the emancipation of his black servants, and assigned them land for their support."[4] A writer in England took a more nuanced approach to the manumission, describing it as "of a mixed nature, partly belonging to the patriot, and partly to the master of the slaves on his estate," but still finding it "humane, earnest and solemn." The author felt that the will

> explains, with infinite delicacy and manly sensibility, the true cause of his not having emancipated them in his life time; and should operate as a caution against those petty libellers, who interpret the whole of a character by a part, instead of interpreting a part by the whole. We feel ourselves at a loss which most to admire . . . the deep and weighty feeling of the general principle of universal liberty, or the wise veneration of those fixed laws in society, without which that universal liberty must forever remain impossible . . . or, lastly, the affectionate attention to the particular feelings of the slaves themselves, with the ample provision for the aged and infirm. Washington was no "architect of ruin!"[5]

Roadblocks to Manumission

The fact that Washington freed his slaves as a private citizen was largely a result of his disappointment with the government at both the state and federal levels. As much as he would like to have seen the United States as a whole take up the cause of emancipation, Washington admitted after the Revolution that he "despaired" of seeing an abolitionist spirit sweep the country. He confided to Lafayette in 1786 that "some petitions were presented to the [Virginia] Assembly at its last Session, for the abolition of slavery, but they could scarcely obtain a reading. To set them [the slaves] afloat at once would, I really believe, be productive of much inconvenience & mischief; but by degrees it certainly might, & assuredly ought to be effected & that too by Legislative authority."[6]

Washington often stated his opinion that manumission would best be accomplished as a gradual process and fleshed out his reasoning in correspondence with friends. To one friend in 1786, he expressed concern that "slaves who are happy & content to remain with their present masters, are tampered with & seduced to leave them" by abolition groups, and "masters are taken at unawar[e]s by these practices," resulting in "discontent on one side and resentment on the other."[7] Several months later, he bluntly told another, "I never mean (unless some particular circumstances should compel me to it) to possess another slave by purchase; it being among my first wishes to see some plan adopted, by the legislature by which slavery in this Country may be abolished by slow, sure, & impercept[i]ble degrees."[8] Eleven years later, upon learning that a nephew's slave had run away,

Washington voiced the opinion that "these elopements will be *much more,* before they are *less* frequent" and suggested "that the persons making them should never be retained, if they are recovered, as they are sure to contaminate and discontent others." He then confided, "I wish from my Soul that the Legislature of this State could see a policy of a gradual abolition of Slavery; it might prev[en]t much future mischief."[9] To a visiting British actor, the retired president explained that he felt education was necessary in order to prepare enslaved people for freedom:

> Till the mind of the slave has been educated to perceive what are the obligations of a state of freedom, and not confound a man's with a brute's, the gift [of liberty] would insure its abuse.... Slaves were bequeathed to us by Europeans, and time alone can change them; an event, sir, which, you may believe me, no man desires more heartily than I do. Not only do I pray for it, on the score of human dignity, but I can clearly foresee that nothing but the rooting out of slavery can perpetuate the existence of our union, by consolidating it in a common bond of principle.[10]

In addition to feeling that those who were enslaved would not be ready for freedom until they were more educated, there was another factor to consider in Washington's insistence on gradual emancipation—the effect on slave owners. From the owners' point of view, manumitting their slaves involved giving up a substantial amount of accumulated wealth. According to historian Lorena Walsh, slaves made up one-third of the capital assets of Martha Washington's first husband, but this situation was unusual in that Custis's financial wealth, excluding land, was also spread among such assets as money he had loaned out at interest, cash, and bank stocks, which made up 52 percent of his "portfolio." In contrast, enslaved people comprised over three-quarters of the capital assets of most large Virginia plantations just before the start of the Revolution.[11] For some people in the early national period, the arguments for emancipation may have convinced them that this was a matter of principle, while for others the conversation might result in internal conflict and vague moral qualms. For still others, abolishing slavery was something they would never understand. Adding to the complexity of deciding for or against manumission was the fact that owners who freed their enslaved property faced a significant financial loss.

Washington, in supporting a policy of gradual freedom, was definitely seeking to ameliorate the financial damage to slave owners, but he very likely saw this as a way of reducing opposition to the policy as well. Throughout his experiences as commander in chief of the army and later as the first president, he often reminded legislators of the fact that people cannot be expected to act outside of their financial interest for long. In a letter written at Valley Forge to a committee of the Continental Congress, Washington instructed them to remember that "a small knowledge of human nature will convince us, that, with far the greatest part of mankind, interest is the governing principle; and that, almost, every man is more or less, under its influence." He offered the opinion that "motives of public virtue may for a time, or in particular instances, actuate men to the observance of a conduct purely disinterested," but

> Few men are capable of making a continual sacrifice of all views of private interest, or advantage, to the common good. It is in vain to exclaim against the depravity of human nature on this account—the fact is so, the experience of every age and nation has proved it, and we must, in a great measure, ch[ange] the constitution of man, before we can make it otherwise. [No] institution, not built on the presumptive truth of these ma[xims,] can succeed.[12]

Similarly, a few months later, Washington noted that "men may speculate as they will—they may talk of patriotism . . . but, whoever builds upon it, as a sufficient basis, for conducting a long and bloody War, will find themselves deceived in the end." He went on to say that he did not intend to negate the idea of patriotism because "I know it exists," but "a great and lasting War can never be supported on this principle alone—It must be aided by a prospect of Interest or some reward. For a time it may, of itself, push men to action—to bear much—to encounter difficulties; but it will not endure unassisted by Interest."[13]

Many years later, when announcing his upcoming retirement from the presidency, Washington offered advice to his young countrymen. In regard to foreign relations, he recommended being impartial toward other nations in both political and commercial affairs. He also saw these relationships as impermanent, as subject to change as circumstances altered, and reminded everyone that they should "constantly [keep] in view that it is folly in one nation to look for distinterested favors from another." Much like people, countries too acted in their own interests.[14] A gradual system of manumission would take away some of the sting from the financial loss to slave owners, giving them less reason to oppose it, while also allowing younger slaves to be prepared for freedom.

The individual states had taken a variety of paths on the issue of slavery within their borders. In a fervor of emotion sparked by the Revolution, three New England states (Vermont, New Hampshire, and Massachusetts) took steps to abolish slavery outright during the war, although it is clear from the recent work of several historians that individuals continued to be held in bondage after that time. Legislatures in the upper South (Virginia, Maryland, and Delaware) made it easier for slave owners to free their slaves, something which had been impossible for a private individual to do in Virginia between 1723 and 1782. There was even a precedent for the type of gradual emancipation Washington favored. Pennsylvania had passed a law in 1780 that all slaves born there in the future would become free when they reached the age of twenty-eight. Other northern states followed suit. In the year Washington died, for example, the New York legislature agreed to free future-born enslaved men at twenty-eight and women at twenty-five years old. New Jersey, Connecticut, and Rhode Island instituted similar plans. As a result of these laws, about 75 percent of African Americans in the northern states were free by 1810.[15]

In Virginia, after 1782 when it became legal for masters there to manumit their slaves without a special action of the governor and council, many took advantage of this new law to act on their principles.[16] As we saw earlier, even large slaveholders were willing to take this step: Quaker Robert Pleasants chose to manumit his eighty slaves in the early 1780s, and in the following decade, planter Robert Carter followed suit, freeing more than five hundred enslaved people after his own religious conversion. Passed one year before the end of the Revolution, the new law resulted in rapid growth in the number of free blacks in Virginia, from about 2,000 in 1782, to 12,776 people in 1790 and 20,124 in 1800. According to historian Paul Finkelman, most of this growth came from manumissions rather than natural increase.[17]

The manumission of Washington's slaves, as laid out in his will and carried out by his widow, can also be seen as the result not just of government's failure to act but also of Washington's own inability to come up with another viable plan for liberating his slaves. From the end of the Revolution, when he finally had the time to work out a plan for emancipation, until his death sixteen years later, Washington struggled with financial problems, family issues, and the fact that he was pulled back into national and international politics, which again took him away from home, exacerbated his financial problems, and drew his attention away from the issue of those enslaved at Mount Vernon.

As he prepared to return home after the Revolution, an eight-year period during which he had received no salary, Washington was surprised to find that he was deeply in debt. From correspondence with several relatives, he learned, for example, that his cousin Lund had not followed up on hiring British prisoners of war—a cheap form of labor—to supply a lack of skilled artisans during the conflict. This meant that there were many repairs that needed to be made at Mount Vernon. Washington complained further that Lund's "aversion to going from home" meant that none of his rents had been collected from tenants, resulting in "many years arrears of rent" being due. And there was more, as he wrote to Lund:

> But if your own wages, since the charge of them in the Acct. rendered at Valley Forge, has not been received by you in the specific articles of the Crop; which does not appear by the Accots. you have lately rendered to me; I shall be more hurt, than at any thing else, to think that an Estate, which I have drawn nothing from, for eight years, and which always enabled me to make any purchase I had in view, should not have been able for the last five years, to pay the manager: And that, worse than going home to empty coffers, and expensive living, I shall be encumbered with debt.[18]

Financial problems plagued Washington throughout these years. In explaining why he could not make a loan to a friend—he simply did not have cash at his disposal—Washington described how during the war, the debts owed him were repaid with inflated (depreciated) currency, while he was now having to pay his own debts "at their intrinsic value, with interest thereon and other circumstances which are unnecessary to enumerate, I find it exceedingly difficult . . . to make my funds and expenditures accord with each other."[19]

Crop failures compounded the pain. When sending some money to his mother, Washington noted that he needed to pay £500 to various creditors—£340 of which were required for his 1786 taxes. Sadly, he wrote, "I know not where or when, I shall receive one shilling with which to pay it." He continued, "In the last two years I made no crops. In the first I was obliged to buy corn and this year have none to sell, and my wheat is so bad, I cannot either eat it myself or sell it to others, and Tobacco I make none." Although he felt he was not living extravagantly and had no "inclination . . . to live splendidly," his expenses for "the absolute support of my family and the visitors who are constantly here, are exceedingly high; higher indeed than I can support without selling part of my estate, which I am disposed to do, rather than run in debt, or continue to be so; but this I cannot do, without taking much less than the lands I have offered for sale are worth. This is really and truely my situation."[20]

By the spring of 1787, just before he left Mount Vernon to attend the Constitutional Convention, Washington admitted, "There is no source from which I derive more than a sufficiency for the daily calls of my family, except what flows from the collection of old debts, and scanty and precarious enough, God knows this is. My estate for the last 11 years has not been able to make both ends meet. I am encumbered now with the deficiency."[21]

The next fall, in response to another would-be borrower, Washington explained plainly that his "expenditures are never behind my income," and that 1787 had been a particularly difficult year, "occasioned by the severest drouth [drought] that ever was known in this neighborhood." As a result, instead of being able to sell grain, which was generally his "principal source of income," he had doubts that he could purchase enough of that commodity to "support my family," meaning here both his immediate family and the slaves, for less than five hundred pounds.[22] A couple of months later, he admitted to a relative, "I can truly say that at no period of my life have I ever felt the want of money so sensibly as now."[23] The following year brought just the opposite problem of a drought—too much water. To a friend, Irish agronomist Sir Edward Newenham, Washington wrote not long before his first inauguration, "We had last summer . . . as rainy a season, I believe as you had in Ireland. . . . Indeed the seasons with us have been uncommonly in opposite extremes for two years past. The summer before last was so dry, and last summer so wet, as to prevent me from acquiring any accurate result from many of my agricultural experiments."[24]

Perhaps the best example of the financial difficulties facing Washington at this time is the fact that he was forced to borrow money to travel to New York City for his own inauguration. About six weeks before he once again left Mount Vernon, he confided to Richard Conway of nearby Alexandria that until two years earlier, he had never before in his life "experienced the want of money," a fact he blamed on "Short Crops, and other causes not entirely within my Controul." He found it "impracticable" to collect the back rents due him "without the intervention of Suits (and these are tedious) . . . And Land, which I have offered for Sale, will not command cash at an under value." Having candidly laid out his financial situation, Washington then got to the heart of the matter:

> Under this statement I am inclined to do what I never expected to be reduced to the necessity of doing, that is, to borrow money upon interest. Five hundred pounds would enable me to discharge what I owe in Alexandria &ca.; and to leave the State (if it shall not be permitted me to remain at home in retirement) without doing this, would be exceedingly disagreeable to me. . . . Permit me to ask if it is in your power to supply me with the above, or a smaller Sum? Any security you may best like, I can give; and you may be assured, that it is no more my

inclination than it can be yours, to let it remain long unpaid. Could I get in one fourth part of the money which is due to me by Bonds, or sell any of the landed property which I am inclined to dispose of, I could do it with ease; but independently of these, my Crops and Rents if I am tolerably successful in the first, or have common justice done me in the latter would enable me to do it.[25]

The gentleman agreed to lend him the money at 6 percent interest, but Washington discovered that the sum he had asked for would only discharge the debts, not cover his expenses to New York. He therefore found it necessary to borrow another hundred pounds.[26]

The shortage of cash was an issue because manumitting the Mount Vernon slaves would take a lot of money. When Virginia passed their manumission law in May 1782, they were concerned that people might try to save themselves the expense of caring for slaves who were unable to work, for whatever reason, by freeing them. By dumping those people, former owners would transfer the costs of caring for them to the counties in which they lived, thus overwhelming the resources of those local governments. To prevent that from happening, the manumission law required that

> all slaves so set free, not being in the judgment of the court, of sound mind and body, or being above the age of forty-five years, or being males under the age of twenty-one, or females under the age of eighteen years, shall respectively be supported and maintained by the person so liberating them, or by his or her estate; and, upon neglect or refusal so to do, the court of the county where such neglect or refusal may be, is hereby empowered and required, upon application to them made, to order the sheriff to distrain and sell so much of the person's estate as shall be sufficient for that purpose.

In addition, owners were required to provide each manumitted slave with "a copy of the instrument of manumission, attested by the clerk of the county," each of which cost five shillings.[27] All of this required money Washington did not have right after the war.

Planning for a Very Different Future

Still, after his return from the Revolution, Washington investigated a variety of ways to manumit the enslaved people at Mount Vernon. He and the Marquis de Lafayette, for example, discussed taking part in an experiment to prove that a plantation could be operated using free labor. Late in the war, Lafayette suggested that the two men purchase land, which Washington's slaves would then work as tenants. Lafayette was hoping that Washington's involvement would help to make the project "a general practice." The younger man thought that if his plan were successful in the United States, it could then spread to the West Indies. In a passionate display of his sentiments, Lafayette wrote that "if it be a wild scheme, I had rather be mad in this way, than to be thought wise in the other task."[28] Washington responded warmly to Lafayette's idea, which he saw as "striking evidence of the benevolence of your Heart." He told his young friend that he would "be happy to join you in so laudable a work" but wanted to wait to discuss the details in person.[29] The two men were able to get together after the Revolution during Lafayette's 1784 visit to the United States. An early historian, who had read through Washington's wartime correspondence at Mount Vernon that summer, later wrote to his host:

> You wished to get rid of all your Negroes, & the Marquis wish[ed] that an end might be put to the slavery of all of them. I should rejoice beyond measure could your joint counsels & influence produce it, & thereby give the finishing stroke & the last polish to your political characters. Could it not be contrived that the industrious among them might be turned into copyholders on the lands of their present masters, & by having a special interest in the produce of their labors be made [mutilated] more profit than at present? A[nd] could not this in its consequences excite the lazy to exertions [tha]t might prove highly beneficial? I am not for letting them all loose upon the public; but am for gradually releasing them & their posterity from bonds, & incorporating them so in the states, that they may be a defen[s]e & not a danger upon any extraordinary occurrence.[30]

Lafayette was ready to begin the experiment the following year. In June 1785, he ordered his attorney to purchase a plantation for him in French Guiana, with the proviso that none of the slaves on the plantation be sold or exchanged. He informed Washington the next February that he had secretly acquired an estate "and am going to free my Negroes in order to Make that Experiment which you know is my Hobby Horse."[31] Washington responded warmly to the plan: "The benevolence of your heart my D[ear] Marq[ui]s is so conspicuous upon all occasions, that I never wonder at any fresh proofs of it; but your late purchase of an Estate in the Colony of Cayenne with a view of emancipating the slaves on it, is a generous and noble proof of your humanity. Would to God a like spirit would diffuse itself generally into the minds of the people of this country."[32]

Washington himself made a start at a similar experiment at Mount Vernon. In the last six years of his life, he advertised to rent the four outlying farms of his plantation, if he could find "good farmers" from England or Scotland willing to take on the project. This scheme would relieve Washington of the burden of managing the land while at the same time ensuring a stable income. In his correspondence on the matter, Washington also wrote that "many of the Negroes, male & female, might be hired by the year as labourers," if the tenants chose to use them, instead of bringing in workers from their own country.[33] Unfortunately, although he corresponded with a number of prospective tenants, none of the negotiations proved fruitful.

A series of letters written in this same period shows that Washington was similarly trying to sell 32,423 acres of his western lands along the Ohio and Great Kanawha Rivers. He admitted in a confidential note to Tobias Lear that, in addition to his freely acknowledged desire to arrange things so that "the remainder of my days may, thereby, be more tranquil & freer from cares," he also had "another motive which makes me earnestly wish for the accomplishment of these things—it is indeed more powerful than all the rest—namely to liberate a certain species of property which I possess, very repugnant to my own feelings; but which imperious necessity compels; & until I can substitute some other expedient, by which expen[s]es not in my power to avoid (however well disposed I may be to do it) can be defrayed."[34] In other words, Washington was trying to come up with enough cash to manumit the Mount Vernon slaves.

Other correspondence suggests that Washington may have been hoping to emancipate not only his own slaves but also the Custis dower slaves. To do that, he would need to sell the western lands in order to have enough cash to reimburse the Custis heirs for the value of the dower slaves, so that they too could be manumitted and none of the enslaved families (at least those in which one spouse belonged to Washington and the other to the Custis estate) broken up.[35] As a step in that direction, Washington asked farm manager William Pearce to "let me know . . . who, of the Dower Negros that are grown, have husbands and wives, and who those husbands and wives are. That is, whether these connections are, one Dower Negro with another Dower Negro; whether they are with other Negros on the Estate; or whether with the Neighbouring Negros." Once he had the list in hand, Washington asked Pearce to send "a list of all the remaining Negros on the Estate; distinguishing French's from the others; and both made out in the manner of the last, giving the ages &ca."[36]

Unfortunately, the fact that much of the communication on this topic was done in person means that the letters dealing with Washington's plans are more cryptic than they might otherwise have been. For example, about ten days after his directions to Pearce, Washington wrote to Dr. David Stuart, the stepfather of Martha Washington's grandchildren, transmitting an advertisement describing the Mount Vernon farms for rent, adding that he was "making an essay to accomplish what I communicated to you in *confidence,* when I was last in Virginia." According to historian Henry Wiencek, it looks as though Washington was first hoping to hire out the dower slaves, both to Stuart for use on Custis lands on the Eastern Shore as well as to prospective tenants renting the four outlying farms at Mount Vernon. This would temporarily split up the families until Washington could go on to the second part of the plan, the manumission of his own slaves, which he admitted to Stuart had to come later because "reasons of a political—indeed of imperious nature must make it a posterior operation."[37] Wiencek suggests that Washington was expressing concerns about the political fallout from a president freeing his slaves while in office, at a time when Washington and the Federalist Party were under attack over the Jay Treaty.[38]

Dennis Pogue, a former colleague, using an average value of forty pounds per person (based on figures from the 1780s), has suggested that Washington would have needed to come up with a little over six thousand pounds in order to compensate the Custis heirs for the loss they would sustain because of the emancipation. With a total annual profit from all of the plantation operations in 1797 amounting to only £898 pounds, Washington was forced to look to his frontier properties as the source for the money.[39]

Things looked up briefly. Writing in the late spring of 1798, Julian Niemcewicz noted during his visit to Mount Vernon that Washington had just sold 23,000 acres of land on the Kanawha River, that he had received years before as payment for his services in the French and Indian War. The sale price was $8 per acre, for a total of $184,000 at 6 percent interest. He also managed to lease some of his lands in Berkeley and Frederick Counties, Virginia, for forty pounds per hundred acres.[40] The sales agreement to which Niemcewicz referred between Washington and James Welch actually involved a long-term lease with an option to convert to an outright purchase; it was signed on December 16, 1797. Unfortunately, the prospective buyer of the Kanawha properties never paid Washington anything, and the land reverted to Washington's estate.[41]

Following his retirement from the presidency, Washington confided to a nephew his fears of financial ruin unless something changed—and quickly. In August 1799, he admitted that he had more than twice as many "working

Negros . . . than can be employed to any advantage in the farming system," but was running out of options:

> To sell the overplus I cannot, because I am principled against this kind of traffic in the human species. To hire them out, is almost as bad, because they could not be disposed of in families to any advantage, and to disperse the families I have an aversion. What is then to be done? Something must or I shall be ruined; for all the money (in addition to what I raise by Crops, and rents) that have been *received* for Lands, sold within the last four years, to the amount of Fifty thousand dollars, has scarcely been able to keep me a float.

He decided to move half the enslaved people at Mount Vernon to his lands in the western part of Virginia but had not yet decided where.[42] Only a week before his death, Washington was thinking about this problem again, noting that "I must, if Mrs Washington and myself should both survive another year, find some place to which the supernumerary hands on *this* Estate could be removed." He then asked his nephew Robert Lewis to "keep a steady eye upon all my tenements in Berkeley and Frederick; and . . . learn with precision the most favourable terms on which I could repossess such *adjoining ones,* as would work eight or ten hands to advantage."[43]

Fears for a Young Country

Two summers before he became president, Washington presided over the Constitutional Convention in Philadelphia. In that role, he heard the debate on the issue of slavery between delegates from various sections of the country and knew exactly how divisive this issue was. On July 14, 1787, in his notes on the convention, Virginian James Madison made the point that "it seemed now to be pretty well understood that the real difference of interests lay, not between the large & small but between the N. [northern] & South[er]n States. The institution of slavery & its consequences formed the line of discrimination."[44]

Over a month later, on August 21, the discussion centered on allowing a change in the draft of the Constitution to permit "a prohibition or tax on the importation of slaves." Delegate Luther Martin of Maryland requested the change for three reasons. The first had to do with the issue of representation in Congress, because "as five slaves are to be counted as 3 free men in the apportionment of Representatives," it would actually encourage the slave trade. Martin further believed that the presence of "slaves weakened one part of the Union which the other parts were bound to protect: the privilege of importing them was therefore unreasonable." The third issue went to the heart of the matter: "It was inconsistent with the principles of the revolution and dishonorable to the American character to have such a feature in the Constitution." John Rutledge of South Carolina disagreed: "The true question at present is whether the [southern] States shall or shall not be parties to the Union. If the Northern States consult their interest, they will not oppose the increase of Slaves which will increase the commodities of which they will become the carriers." Later that day, another South Carolinian, Charles Pinckney, boldly stated that "South Carolina can never receive the plan [the Constitution] if it prohibits the slave trade." He held out the possibility, however, that "if the States be all left at liberty on this subject, S. Carolina may perhaps by degrees do of herself what is wished, as Virginia & Maryland have already done."[45]

The debate continued into the following day. Virginia's George Mason noted that his state and Maryland had already abolished the importation of slaves and that North Carolina had "done the same in substance," but these actions would be "in vain if S. Carolina & Georgia be at liberty to import. The Western people are already calling out for slaves for their new lands, and will fill that Country with slaves if they can be got thro' S. Carolina & Georgia." He enumerated the "pernicious" effects of slavery, which included his belief that the institution discouraged the development of "arts & manufactures"; led people to despise hard work; prevent "the immigration of Whites, who really enrich & strengthen a Country"; and caused a deterioration in manners, leading every slave owner to be a "petty tyrant." Mason reiterated arguments he had made prior to the Revolution that slavery was sinful and threatened to bring "the judgment of heaven on a Country. As nations can not be rewarded or punished in the next world they must be in this. By an inevitable chain of causes & effects providence punishes national sins, by national calamities."[46]

General Charles Cotesworth Pinckney of South Carolina responded that if he and "all his colleagues were to sign the Constitution & use their personal influence, it would be of no avail towards obtaining the assent of their Constituents. S. Carolina & Georgia cannot do without slaves." He then came close to accusing Virginia of hypocrisy, citing her ulterior motives on the slave trade issue and commenting that, as "to Virginia she will gain by stopping the importations. Her slaves will rise in value, & she has more than she wants. It would be unequal to require S. C. & Georgia to confederate on such unequal terms." After detailing his opinion that "the importation of slaves would be for the interest of the whole Union,"

Pinckney closed by saying that it would be "reasonable" for slaves to be taxed "like other imports," but that he would "consider a rejection of the clause as an exclusion of S. Carol[in]a from the Union."[47]

Abraham Baldwin of Georgia jumped in to suggest, as had others, that this was an issue for the individual states, rather than the central government, but that if "left to herself," Georgia "may probably put a stop to the evil." This led in turn to James Wilson of Pennsylvania suggesting that "if S. C. & Georgia were themselves disposed to get rid of the importation of slaves in a short time as had been suggested, they would never refuse to Unite because the importation might be prohibited." He noted that "as the Section now stands all articles imported are to be taxed. Slaves alone are exempt. This is in fact a bounty on that article." John Dickinson of Delaware "considered it as inadmissible on every principle of honor & safety that the importation of slaves should be authorized to the States by the Constitution. The true question was whether the national happiness would be promoted or impeded by the importation, and this question ought to be left to the National Govt. not to the States particularly interested."[48]

With strong feelings on all sides, the debate continued. In the end, the delegates finally agreed not to take up this contentious issue just yet, with the Constitution stating in article 1, section 9: "The migration or importation of such persons as the several states now existing shall think proper to admit, shall not be prohibited by the Congress prior to the year one thousand eight hundred and eight, but a tax or duty may be imposed on such importation, not exceeding ten dollars for each person."[49]

If he had had any doubts before about where the country stood on the issue of slavery, Washington could have had none after the Constitutional Convention: if the issue of abolishing slavery was pushed, the country would dissolve. While he could never bring himself to publicly lead the effort to abolish slavery, probably for fear of tearing apart the country he had worked so hard to build, Washington could, and did, try to lead by setting an example and freeing the people over whom he had control.[50]

An Extraordinary "Conversation" in the Family

It is evident from both surviving correspondence and statements by friends and family members that George Washington had many conversations on the subject of freeing his slaves in the roughly twenty years before he actually took that step in his will. One letter in particular stands out. Written just over a year prior to Washington's retirement from the presidency by David Stuart, the stepfather of Martha Washington's four Custis grandchildren, it appears to continue an ongoing conversation. Stuart began by discussing Washington's plans to rent the outlying farms at Mount Vernon, which he noted would be "a very fortunate event for the country if you should: for from the immense trouble and small profits from lands and negroes, the disposition is gaining ground fast in this State among the Proprietors of such property, to get released from their slaves at least." Stuart expressed the hope that "we may at no very distant period, derive a comfortable support from the rent of our lands alone" and noted that he would "omit no opportunity of mentioning your plan to those you speak of."[51]

Stuart went on to say that he found Washington's plans in regard to the slaves "a delicate and perplexing subject." Like Washington, he agreed that both the "wellfare" of the slaves and "the safety of the country required that the plan be gradual," and then suggested a scheme of his own. Stuart felt that it would be best to "select some one of the most intelligent and responsible negroes" and rent him a farm with whatever slaves and tools were necessary, while "stipulating so much for each hand to rec[ei]ve as an encouragement for them to work, and do their duty without violence." As a "further inducement to industry and good behaviour . . . if they conducted themselves well they should be at perfect liberty at the expiration of two or three years." Someone (like Washington) with a profusion of land and slaves "might inform his other negroes that he meant to rent another farm on the same plan every year, till they were all free, or his lands all occupied, in which latter case, the ballance of the negroes would be set free on condition of paying a moderate sum to their Masters for two or three years."[52]

Stuart had other suggestions for putting this plan into motion. One of the most interesting concerned an action he felt the Virginia legislature should make, namely passing an "act enabling those destined for freedom, to bear witness against the whites in all instances at least of trespasses, and robbery committed on such a farm." He noted that "there have been instances in this Country, where some free negroes have had their houses broke open, and robbed of all they had, without being able to get any redress, tho' they knew the robbers: because, their testimony against a white man was inadmissible."[53]

Stuart then changed direction a bit, comparing the situation in Virginia to that of medieval Europe, and the "lower classes of people" on that continent to the situation of the slaves. He believed those long-ago peasants were

> not only as much debased [as the slaves], but their masters even possessed the right in many instances of taking away their lives—and another perhaps still more humiliating, of having the first night with the

daughters of all his vassalls when married—The introduction of commerce, was the happy cause [which] dispelled this execrable system—If debasement of mind therefore, is any argument against the plan, I think it may be proved that the whites were in a more debased state under the feudal system. And yet these people at present form the substantial yeomanry of those Countries where they were once so vilifyed—That the same will happen to our negroes I have no doubt—And the only thing to be regretted is, that they are not of the same colour with ourselves—But time which applies a remedy to all things, will no doubt soon find one for this.[54]

Leaving aside problems with Stuart's seeming ignorance about the sexual exploitation of enslaved women, would Washington have been comforted, as Stuart was, by his belief that things had turned out for the best despite the initial obstacles? Perhaps the comparison served as a reminder to Washington that he needed to do what he felt was right and trust to God, or time, that all would work out for the best in the future.

Freedom at Last

Emancipating the Mount Vernon slaves was a complicated business. To reiterate the problem, in the forty years of the Washingtons' marriage, the slaves on the estate had increased in number to over three hundred people. Forty of these individuals were rented from a neighbor, while a little less than half of the remainder belonged to George Washington. Except for two or three individuals, the rest were owned by the estate of Martha Washington's first husband, Daniel Parke Custis.[55] Because Custis had died without a will, both English common law and Virginia law directed that his widow receive a life interest in, or had "dower rights" to, one-third of the slaves in his estate. After her death, however, those slaves would revert to the surviving Custis heirs, who, in this case, were her four grandchildren.[56] Adding further complexity and emotional distress to this situation was the fact that during this forty-year period, the Washington and Custis slaves had intermarried, meaning that for many families, emancipation would bring great sadness, as husbands were separated from both their wives and their children, whose ownership was determined by that of their mother. About twenty couples and their children were divided for this reason, including a number of people featured in these pages: the butler Frank Lee and his wife, Lucy, the cook; head carpenter Isaac and dairy maid Kitty; their daughter Sinah and her husband, Ben the miller; Dolshy, who had been wounded by the deer, and her husband, Joe; waiter Cyrus and his wife, Lucy; and carpenter Sambo Anderson and his wife, Agnes. A few others were torn apart because they had married with slaves who were rented. George Washington admitted in his will that it was the breakup of families that kept him from emancipating his slaves earlier:

> To emancipate them during [Martha Washington's] life, would, tho' earnestly wished by me, be attended with such insuperable difficulties on account of their intermixture by Marriages with the Dower Negroes, as to excite the most painful sensations, if not disagreeable consequences from the latter, while both descriptions are in the occupancy of the same Proprietor; it not being in my power, under the tenure by which the Dower Negros are held, to manumit them.[57]

There were changes in the works within just a few months of George Washington's death. The runaway notice for Marcus, a young house slave, issued by farm manager James Anderson in April 1800, warned readers that the teenager "may attempt to pass for one of those negroes that did belong to the late general Washington, and whom Mrs. Washington intends in the fall of this year to liberate," when he was in fact one of the people "held by right of dower, by Mrs. Washington, during her life."[58] So, within four months of her late husband's death, Martha Washington was planning to free his slaves early—but why? It could be that she—ever the dutiful wife—took seriously her late husband's statement that he "earnestly wished" that his slaves would be emancipated "during her life." During the Revolution, for example, there were times when she would rather have stayed at home but faithfully set out for Washington's military headquarters when he asked her to come each year. In 1777, she wrote her newly widowed brother-in-law from Mount Vernon to assure him that "nothing in this world do I wish for more sincer[e]ly than to be with [you], but alass I am so situated at this time that I cannot le[a]ve home. . . . the General has wrote to me that he cannot come home this winter but as soon as the army under his command goes into winter quarter[s] he will send for me, if he does I must go."[59] About a year later, she learned of the severe illness of her mother and wistfully confided to a relative: "I wish I was near enough to come to see you and her. I am very uneasy at this time—I have some reason to expect that I shall take another trip to the northward. The pore General is not likely to come to see us from what I can hear—I expect to hear seertainly by the next post—if I doe I shall write to you to inform you and my friends—if I am so happy to stay at home."[60] But, like so many things in life, there may well have been a mixture of motives involved.

According to several sources, Washington's provision for freeing his slaves after his wife's death left Martha Washington in a precarious state. The first hint that her actions might have been prompted by a problem came in December 1800, some months after Marcus escaped, in a letter written by Abigail Adams, the wife of President John Adams, after a visit with Washington at Mount Vernon. Barely one year after George Washington died, Abigail Adams wrote her sister about the imminent manumission of those slaves who had belonged to George Washington. According to Adams, the slaves were being freed prior to Martha Washington's death because of fears for her safety: "[W]hat could she do. in the state in which they were left by the General, to be free at her death, she did not feel as tho her Life was safe in their Hands, many of whom would be told that it was [in their] interest to get rid of her—She therefore was advised to s[e]t them all free at the close of the year."[61]

Among those advising Martha Washington on the emancipation of her late husband's slaves were two of the other executors of his will—her grandson, George Washington Parke Custis, and George Washington's nephew Supreme Court justice Bushrod Washington—and Chief Justice John Marshall. In fact, not quite two weeks after his uncle's death, Bushrod Washington mentioned in a letter "the plan I have recommended [to Martha Washington] of getting clear of her negroes & of plantation cares & troubles."[62] Custis recorded many years later that, although the Washington slaves were to be freed "at the death of Mrs. Washington," it had been "found necessary (for *prudential* reasons) to give them their freedom in one year after the general's decease."[63] The decision to hurry the emancipation may have been prompted by an actual attempt on Martha Washington's life. According to one of Bushrod Washington's close friends and colleagues, the only time he ever failed to preside over the circuit court was a "very few years after General Washington's death," when he came into court and announced that he had to leave immediately for Mount Vernon: "It was understood that Chief Justice Marshall and Judge Washington had been urgently called to Mrs. Washington, in consequence of an attempt to set fire to Mount Vernon House, in which some of the slaves were thought to be implicated; and it was afterwards said, that Marshall and Washington advised the immediate emancipation of the slaves, as a bar to similar and worse attempts."[64] In December 1800, Martha Washington signed a deed of manumission for her deceased husband's slaves, a transaction that is recorded in the abstracts of the Fairfax County, Virginia, court records. They would become free on January 1, 1801.[65]

A list composed two months later, on March 5, 1801, shows that most of George Washington's slaves had left Mount Vernon, while others belonging to the Custis estate had been moved to other farms so that there were enough people on each to carry out the necessary work. According to this document, there were 121 enslaved adults and working age children still living at Mount Vernon: the Mansion House Farm was home to 35 (12 men, 6 boys, 14 women, and 3 girls); there were 30 at River Farm (10 men, 2 boys, 17 women, and 1 girl); 20 were living at Muddy Hole (6 men, 2 boys, 10 women, and 2 girls); and another 36 were at Union Farm (9 men, 6 boys, 18 women, and 3 girls). No one was listed as being at Dogue Run Farm, but whether that site was omitted on purpose or that was where the newly freed people who were too old or too young to work were being kept is unknown at this point.[66]

Five women were described on the 1801 list as "Free but yet Remain," indicating that they were still living at Mount Vernon, although the exact farm they were on was not mentioned. They included: thirty-two-year-old Amey from Muddy Hole Farm, who was the unmarried mother of two daughters, Rainey (eight) and Urinah (two) in 1799. Alce, forty years old and also from Muddy Hole, was listed as the mother of two boys, George (eight) and Adam (seven), and one daughter, Cecelia (two), in 1799. She was married to Sam, a cook at the Mansion House Farm, who also belonged to George Washington and was included among those who were "Passed Labour." Peg, fifty-eight years old in 1801, was living on River Farm in 1799 with her husband, "old Ben," a dower slave, who was then seventy and described as "Nearly done." Agnes was twenty-seven years old in 1801. She had been living at Dogue Run Farm and was married to a dower slave named Will at the Mansion House Farm. The last of the five, "Old Judy," was probably a fifty-seven-year-old woman in 1801 and had lived at River Farm. Her husband, a George Washington slave named Gunner, who would have been ninety-two years old that year, had lived at the Mansion House Farm, where he was listed as "Passed Labour."[67]

Financial records from the period of Martha Washington's widowhood indicate that certain aspects of life at Mount Vernon remained virtually the same. A doctor continued to treat slaves on the estate, although the physicians were now a Doctor Hamilton and Peter Hawk instead of the formerly omnipresent Dr. James Craik. Medicines were dispensed, people were bled, babies were born, teeth were drawn, and a slave was cured of "a venereal complaint." Martha Washington even spent ten dollars on "medicine & attendance on old Negro Molly," the Custis family slave who had cared for her children and grandchildren.[68] On January 12, 1801, Davy

Gray, the enslaved overseer at Muddy Hole Farm who was a dower slave, was paid $9.75 as "his proportion of ⅓d" of 32 turkeys, 20 ducks, and 42 chickens "raised by him for Mrs. Washington." The fact that Gray signed with an "X" indicates that he could not write.[69] A surviving receipt shows that at least one of the newly liberated craftsmen from Mount Vernon continued working there for a salary. Written at Woodlawn Plantation, the home of executor Lawrence Lewis, on January 12, 1803, it documents that another executor, Thomas Peter, paid George the blacksmith fifty dollars "in full for my Hire as a Smith on Mount Vernon Estate for the year 1802." George too signed with an X.[70]

Of the more than 300 slaves known to have been at Mount Vernon in 1799, fewer than half, 123 individuals, belonged to George Washington and would go free. In addition, there were another 33 slaves who had become Washington's property on the death of his brother-in-law Bartholomew Dandridge in 1785 as payment for a debt. These people were still living at the Dandridge plantation when Washington died, but he made arrangements in his will for their freedom too, after the death of Dandridge's widow. Washington asked that they be freed gradually, according to a schedule that varied depending on their ages (those over forty were to be freed immediately, those between sixteen and forty would be manumitted after another seven years of labor, and anyone under the age of sixteen would be emancipated at the age of twenty-five).[71] The 153 dower slaves at Mount Vernon would go to the Custis grandchildren after Martha Washington's death.[72] All of the rented slaves—forty individuals from Mrs. French, along with stableman Peter Hardiman from the widow of Martha Washington's son—would eventually return to their owners.[73] The one slave Martha Washington owned outright at the time of her death and could have manumitted, a mulatto man whose name is variously recorded as Elish (possibly for Elisha) or Elijah, who had been purchased by her from a Washington relative after the death of George Washington, she bequeathed to her grandson.[74]

Many questions remain about the division of the dower slaves after Martha Washington's death. Among some family papers purchased a few years ago by the Mount Vernon Ladies' Association was the draft list of a division of over 160 slaves, valued at £6,812, among the four Custis heirs, but there is no final version to know exactly how the division was accomplished.[75] The title, "List of the different Drafts of Negros," suggests that the heirs might have been submitting lists of the slaves they particularly wanted. By this time, all three of the granddaughters were married, so, in the case of all but one of them, their shares are listed as going to their husbands. The document begins with the outlier, "Lot #1 for Mrs. Law's," showing eldest granddaughter Eliza's acquisition of 43 slaves, valued in total at £1,854. Two of this group, Lavinia (the nine-year-old daughter of head carpenter Isaac and his wife, Kitty, the milkmaid) and a young man named Gefrey, are described as being invalids. In "Lot #3 Mr T Peters," the husband of second granddaughter Patty would receive 47 slaves, valued at £2,025. "Mr Lewis's d[ra]ft of Negroes" showed 36 or 37 slaves going to granddaughter Nelly's husband, Lawrence Lewis, who was also George Washington's nephew; those slaves were valued at £1,383. A note at the bottom of that list indicates that "The 4 last given . . . to satisfy him on a/c of the claim he had on G. W. P. Custis." Finally, "Mr. G W P Custis's List of Slaves" shows that 36 slaves, valued at more than £1,550, would be going to Martha Washington's youngest grandchild and only grandson. Study of the people on each list shows that the Custis heirs were making a concerted effort to keep mothers and at least their younger children together.[76]

Living in Freedom

George Washington's decision to free his slaves was not met by universal acclaim, even from supporters of abolition. Virginian William Short was an American diplomat who began his career as private secretary to Thomas Jefferson and remained close to his former employer for his entire life. An abolitionist himself, Short wrote to Jefferson less than a year after Washington's death with complaints about how the manumission was to be carried out. After introducing the topic of the future of slavery, Short stated, "I wish that Genl. Washington had considered it maturely—his example would of course have had great weight." After giving his opinion that "I do not think the manner, in which he has cut the Gordian knot,—the most advantageous either in policy or humanity," he said that "turning a number of people (grown up in chains) all at once loose on the wide world, seems to me at least impolitic—Would it not have been better for all if he had gone more gradually to work." Short felt Washington should have "provided . . . for their being in the hands of good masters—for the manumission of such as had sh[o]wn a capacity for self government—for the apprenticeship of the young . . . in fine if he had established a permanent & productive fund vested in some corporate body (for wch he might have obtained an act of the legislature)." He closed by suggesting a plan to manumit the Washington slaves in a way that might have had a larger influence on the rest of the country:

It is moreover highly probable if a fund of this sort had been established under the appellation of the Washington fund, & under legislative protection, that many people would have contributed to it, by imitation, who would of themselves never have thought of it—If Genl. Washington had left some such example, it is probable according to my way of seeing at least, that it would not have been the least important of the services for which his country has given him credit, & humanity at least would have erected him an altar.[77]

Sadly, in the opinion of other Virginians who were less wedded to the idea of freedom for all, the manumission of his slaves was one area in his life where Washington had made a serious error. Writing many years later, Pennsylvania jurist Horace Binney opined,

> At a time when there was little or no experience in the world of the effects of an unprepared emancipation of a considerable body of slaves within a community having large numbers of them, General Washington, from his predominant preference of free institutions and labor, had made this testamentary provision without duly estimating, it seems, the dangers to the intermediate life [Martha Washington], or to the slaves themselves. I understood years afterwards in the neighborhood, that no good had come from it to the slaves, and that the State of Virginia was compelled to place restraints upon emancipation within her limits, for the general good of all.[78]

A similar judgment was made by younger members of the extended Washington-Custis family in the years following the emancipation. It is unlikely that they were surprised by the actions mandated in his will because, as was his practice during both the Revolution and the presidency, Washington sought the opinions of those involved prior to making his decision. As recalled in an 1853 letter, Lawrence Lewis was summoned to Washington's study for a serious conversation, which began with the words, "Lawrence, being about to make my will, and feeling great embarrassment as to the proper disposition of my negroes, I have sent for you to ask your advice and opinion on the matter." Echoing the words of Tobias Lear in response to the plan to rotate slaves in and out of the presidential residence in Philadelphia, Lewis "expressed the opinion that they were far happier in a State of Slavery." According to him, "the General *fully concurred,* remarking, however, 'the position which I occupy before my countrymen, and a becoming deference for the opinions of a portion of them, may call for the Manumission of my Slaves, and I will take the matter into further consideration.'"[79]

Years after their emancipation, Martha Washington's grandson, George Washington Parke Custis of Arlington Plantation, wrote of the newly freed people from Mount Vernon that "although many of them, with a view to their liberation, had been instructed in mechanic trades, yet they succeeded very badly as freemen; so true is the axiom, 'that the hour which makes man a slave, takes half his worth away.'"[80] Others in the family shared his opinion. Edward George Washington Butler was the son-in-law of Custis's sister Nelly Custis Lewis. He descended from a long line of soldiers and, following his father's death, became the ward of Andrew Jackson. After leaving his own career in the army, Butler retired and settled on a sugar plantation in Louisiana called Dunboyne. Writing from there in the summer of 1853 to Louisiana historian Charles Gayarré, Butler was highly critical of Washington's decision to free his slaves:

> I speak from my own observation, and can appeal to citizens of Fairfax County, Virginia, for the truth of my assertion, when I affirm that the descendants of the latter [the Custis slaves who remained in bondage] (many of whom are in possession of the writer of this,) have been and are prosperous, contented, and happy; whilst the former—after a life of vice, dissipation and idleness—may literally be said to have disappeared from the face of the earth.

Butler went on to discuss how, after "their kind and generous master made provision for them in his will," the freed slaves would appear at Woodlawn Plantation, the home of his in-laws, "in sickness, age, and poverty," where "their wants and sufferings" would be seen to by Lawrence Lewis, the nephew and executor of George Washington, and by his "too-generous wife (the Granddaughter of Mrs. Washington)." Lewis was "often . . . called upon to release others from the jail of Alexandria for poaching [*unreadable word*] and larceny." He closed with an ironic word picture, leaving no doubt about his position on the subjects of slavery and abolition: "Strange as it may appear to the [*unreadable words*] of abolitionists and intermeddlers, it was *those in Slavery* who, on such occasions, were called upon to carry out the kind intentions and instructions of their master & mistress, and who condoled with their unhappy kinsfolk and former companions, *upon their enjoyment of the privileges and blessings of freedom.*"[81] A more distant relative, cousin and farm manager Lund Washington's nephew Lund, in a handwritten history of the family, described George Washington's emancipation of his slaves as "the . . . worst act of his public life."[82] While it is true that these well-educated, upper-class men almost certainly overlooked the social and legal barriers that prejudice against former slaves would have thrown in the way of the slaves' prospering, their own racism and southern-leaning political views were also coloring their observations.[83]

Contrary to these reports, there is evidence that some of the former Mount Vernon slaves did quite well for themselves after they were freed, buying land, supporting their families, and playing a leadership role in the free black community. In her study of slavery at Monticello, historian Lucia Stanton describes the perilous situation for free blacks in Virginia in the 1830s and 1840s and explains the importance of property ownership:

> Free blacks lived in a kind of littoral zone, alternately submerged or exposed by the tides of law and public opinion. In the struggle to adapt to this unsettled environment, property was of primary importance. Because they were denied by law other means of achieving security and social standing (free blacks in Virginia could not legally vote, hold office, attend schools, or carry weapons, among other restrictions), the acquisition, preservation, and expansion of real estate constituted a critical aspect not only of success but of survival and the maintenance of family unity.[84]

By 1811 and 1812, there were seven households of "General Washington's free negroes" living at "Free Town," in Fairfax County's Truro Parish (which included Mount Vernon). According to researchers studying this community, it was the "earliest known recorded reference to a free black settlement in Fairfax County." The former Mount Vernon residents were joined in Free Town by people who were manumitted by other slaveholders in the neighborhood, following George Washington's example. Beginning in the 1790s and building in the nineteenth century, plantation owners in Fairfax County started selling their land and moving to other places where land was cheaper and more fertile and they could start over. In doing so, many sold their lands in northern Virginia to families from northern states, often Quakers, who wanted to prove to their new neighbors that progressive farming methods and the use of hired free blacks could make farming in the area profitable again. According to historians Susan Hellman and Maddy McCoy, the Quakers "hoped to prove to southerners that successful farming did not require slave labor." As one of these Quakers later explained, "we succeeded, even beyond our expectations."[85]

Two of the grandsons of Joe Richardson, the postilion on the Washingtons' carriage, and his wife, Sall, were among the first black landowners on Mason Neck, near George Mason's Gunston Hall Plantation. Both were the sons of Joe and Sall's daughter Polly, who was only one year old when George Washington drew up the will that freed them. Polly's son Elijah Blackburn, born about 1817, purchased 20 acres in 1844 for $109; seven years later, his younger brother, Richard, born about 1821, acquired 10 acres for himself for $60. This was not a smooth process. According to historian Paula Elsey, "Elijah Blackburn had to hire a lawyer to finalize ownership of his 21 acres. The deed drawn up between him and the seller, John B. Reardon, was not filed at the courthouse before Reardon died in 1852. Blackburn's lawyer lost the receipt of sale. Reardon's widow, however, put in writing that she was 'anxious and desirous . . . Elijah Blackburn should have a good and perfect title to the said land.'"[86]

About the same time, one of the sons of carpenter Davy Jones and his wife, Edy, also became a landowner. Levi Jones bought 14 acres of land in 1844 for a total purchase price of $435. By the time the Civil War began, Levi had added another three acres. Historian Edna Greene Medford notes that

> Jones's property eventually became the southern extension of the Nauck community, a settlement which grew out of the post–Civil War sale of parcels of land to groups of freed people who had initially settled at Freedman's Village, where were housed some of the thousands of fugitives who escaped to the Union Lines during the war. In the early stages of the community's development, Jones's home served as school, church, and meeting house.[87]

At least two freed Mount Vernon slaves were both well enough known and had won enough respect to be mentioned in local obituaries on their deaths. In the summer of 1821, the *Alexandria Gazette* noted that "Francis Lee," who was the younger brother of Billy Lee and himself a butler for George Washington, had recently died at Mount Vernon. Twenty-four years later, the same paper announced the death "near Mount Vernon" of "old Samuel" (Sambo) Anderson, described as "a native African" who "had been tattooed in youth, and bore the marks to the day of his death." The deceased was said to be "aged about 100 years" and "one of the former servants of Gen. WASHINGTON, and liberated by that great man in his will."[88] In 1876, "an old citizen of Alexandria" recalled that Anderson had been given permission by Fairfax County to own a gun, which he used for hunting, much as he had for George Washington. In the early nineteenth century, the creeks and marshes near Alexandria "swarmed with game . . . and he had but little trouble to kill what he wanted." Later, the profusion of "these big gunners . . . killed and scared all the game away." Prior to that, Anderson had supplied "the most respectable families in Alexandria," as well as hotels, but he is said to have "preferred to sell to his gentlemen customers, who not only paid him his price but would make him handsome presents."[89] As a free man, he took the last name Anderson, perhaps a reflection of positive feelings toward Washington's Scottish farm manager James Anderson or James's son John. With the money Sambo Anderson earned, he is said to have purchased two slaves himself, although someone who knew him recalled that Anderson was not "as happy as he was before he became a slave holder. I know myself that he had much trouble with one of his slaves."[90] County records show that Anderson emancipated two slaves but at least one is known to have been his son, William Anderson, born about 1812, while the other, a young woman named Eliza Anderson, who was six years younger, was probably his daughter.[91] Neither the Blackburns, the Joneses, Frank Lee, nor Sambo Anderson had, in the words of Edward George Washington Butler, "disappeared from the face of the earth."[92]

The Effect of a Master's Reputation

As was evident in earlier chapters, the overriding fact that comes through in the surviving documentation about life at Mount Vernon is that George Washington was by no means an easy man to work for. He was a picky, detail-oriented manager who continually looked over the shoulders of those who served him, could always find a better way to have done a job, and was not above blowing up at a servant, white or black, who did not meet his standards. Balancing these managerial shortcomings was a sense of humor, a thoughtfulness that softened the rough edges of his temper, and the fact that he would listen to, seriously consider, and bother to investigate problems brought to his attention. He could also be counted on to give support and encouragement to those who were trying to overcome personal problems. In all these things he was consistent, exhibiting the same personality traits toward, and expecting the same behavior from, both free men, whether they were of his own social class or not, and slaves alike.

While the daily routine and material well-being of the Mount Vernon slaves were not so different from those of people enslaved on other large Virginia plantations at this period, the identity, character, and personality of their master went a long way toward making their lives both more complicated and better than they might otherwise have been. As was discussed earlier, those people working in the mansion, kitchen, and stables undoubtedly saw their workload increase, especially after the Revolution, as people came from far and wide to see the home of Washington—and perhaps get a glimpse of the man himself. On the other hand, working for Washington could result in extra care and attention. That point becomes clear in the story of Austin's final trip home to Mount Vernon from the executive mansion in Philadelphia. On December 17, 1794, the trusted house servant was given twenty dollars to pay for "his expenses to & from Virginia."[93] Three days later, a letter was sent from Havre de Grace, Maryland, to let the president know that Austin had encountered some type of trouble while trying to cross a river near Harford, had only "with Great Difficulty" been "Dragged out of the water," and was "likely to Lose his Life."[94] A second letter from another correspondent on that same day provided details about the accident:

> This Morning before Sun Rise your Mullatto Man in attempting to cross the Run by this place . . . fell from his Horse & went a small distance down the Stream[.] a Negro Man of Mrs Stiles'[s] who keeps the Public Inn at this place & went with him to see him cross the Run got him out speechless he was taken to Mrs Stiles & a Physician procured immediately but nothing could save his life. [H]e expired about the middle of the day[.] I thought it my duty to inform you by first Post. . . . A Coffin is bespoke & I expect he will be Burried to Morrow.[95]

One might expect that this would be the last reference in the record to Austin, but the fact that he was a member of the president's household meant that many people were anxious to show that he had been well cared for in his final illness. The following day, John Carlile wrote from Harford with some additional details, which he assumed "cannot be uninteresting to an indulgent Master," including the fact that Austin had received "every possible care and attention" from both "Mrs. Stiles and her family" and that he died "about One of the Clock."[96] A letter from the doctor who attended Austin indicated that the cause of death was attributable to either brain damage resulting from the fall from the horse or apoplexy (stroke). Given the fact that there were no external marks on Austin's body to indicate that he had hit his head in the fall, together with "his Age [he would have been about thirty-six] & the conformation of his Body" (presumably he was heavyset), the doctor concluded that the death, which occurred three to five hours after the fall, was probably due to stroke.[97] Among his effects, which were carefully enumerated, were fifteen dollars in bank notes, another two in silver, "1 valice, with Sundries," a mare and colt, a saddle and bridle, his clothing, and five letters, which had been sent on.[98] Very few slaves would have received such attention when they fell ill at an inn.

Of all the descriptions of Washington as a slave owner, only a few are critical of his behavior. For example, Thomas Jefferson—by this time a political enemy—informed a houseguest at Monticello that "George Washington is a hard master, very severe, a hard husband, a hard father, a hard governor. From his childhood he always ruled and ruled severely. He was first brought up to govern slaves, he then governed an army, then a nation. He thinks hard of all, is despotic in every respect, he mistrusts every man, thinks every man a rogue and nothing but severity will do."[99]

Another negative description, written by an Englishman who lived near Mount Vernon, is especially important and perhaps becomes understandable both in the light of Washington's high expectations of himself and those who worked for him, and his interest in scientific farming. When Richard Parkinson remarked that "it was the sense of all his [Washington's] neighbors that he treated [his slaves] with more severity than any other man," neighborhood gossip may well have hinged on Washington's strict management of the estate, which became progressively modern and scientific over the years. By increasing the scope of supervision to closely track the amount of time spent on each type of work, the number of days lost to illness, the amount of corn used by each of his five farms, and other minute observations and calculations, Washington was becoming more like a modern industrialist than a traditional gentleman farmer. In the course of that transformation, in the opinion of neighbors whose own slaves may well have had dealings with those from Mount Vernon and thus knew how they felt about these changes, Washington was also increasing the burden on his slaves. Changes in crops and techniques over the years not only forced the Mount Vernon slaves to learn new ways of doing things but transformed them. In the words of historian Lorena Walsh, "By the close of the 18th century, the men and women who toiled year-round on Mount Vernon's unforgiving soils were far from 'ordinary field hands.' Through a largely undocumented and largely unrecognized high pressure stint of learning by doing, Mount Vernon's enslaved laborers became some of the most skilled mixed-crop farmers, fishermen, and stock breeders in the region."[100]

Not surprisingly, members of the extended Washington family tended to see George Washington as a kind and benevolent slave owner. Stepgrandson George Washington Parke Custis recalled that "as a master of slaves, General Washington was consistent, as in every other relation of his meritorious life." Custis went on to break down some of the elements he considered benevolent—he remembered those enslaved at Mount Vernon as "comfortably lodged, fed, and clothed." While they were "required to do a full and fair share of duty," they were "well cared for in sickness and old age, and kept in strict and proper discipline." According to Custis, "These, we humbly conceive, comprise all the charities of slavery." He closed with the thought that "to his old servants, where long and faithful services rendered them worthy of attachment and esteem, he was most kind."[101] Custis's sister Nelly Custis Lewis remembered her step-grandfather as "a generous & noble master" who was "feared & loved" by those he kept in bondage.[102]

More typical of the descriptions of Washington as a slave owner was an account left by a foreign visitor traveling in America who recorded that Washington dealt with his slaves "far more humanely than do his fellow citizens of Virginia." It was this traveler's opinion that Virginians typically treated their slaves harshly, providing "only bread, water and blows."[103] And yet it was this same visitor who could not bring himself to refer to the slave cabins at Mount Vernon as "houses" because he considered them worse than "the most miserable of the cottages of our peasants."[104] Washington himself once criticized other large plantation owners, "who are not always as kind, and as attentive to their [the slaves'] wants and usage as they ought to be."[105] Toward the end of his life, he looked back on his years as a slave owner, reflecting that

> the unfortunate condition of the persons, whose labour in part I employed, has been the only unavoidable subject of regret. To make the Adults among them as easy & as comfortable in their circumstances as their actual state of ignorance & improvidence would admit; & to lay a foundation to prepare the rising generation for a destiny different from that in which they were born; afforded some satisfaction to my mind, & could not I hoped be displeasing to the justice of the Creator.[106]

Time and again since the end of the Civil War, interviews with former slaves and letters written by them have sometimes expressed the idea that they were better off before they were freed and showed a remarkable attachment to former masters.[107] While Tom and Wagoner Jack, who were sold in the West Indies; Oney Judge and Hercules, who ran away during the presidency; and undoubtedly others who maintained lower profiles probably would have disagreed, at least some of the slaves who labored for George and Martha Washington at Mount Vernon came to feel a similar loyalty to them that lasted beyond the grave. Writing a decade after Washington's slaves were freed, Pennsylvania jurist Richard Peters, who founded the Philadelphia Agricultural Society, wrote that, as a slaveholder, Washington "*would* be obeyed, but his servants were devoted to him; and especially those more immediately about his person. The survivors of them still venerate and adore his memory."[108] As an old man, freed for many years, former Mount Vernon carpenter Sambo Anderson told a white acquaintance that he "was a much happier man when he was a slave than he had ever been since," because he then "had a good kind master to look after all my wants, but now I have no one to care for me." The narrator remarked that he had known quite a few former Washington slaves, and "they all spoke in the highest terms of their master."[109]

These sentiments were more than mere words. On at least one occasion, former Washington slaves came back to the plantation to perform a service for their late master. More than thirty years after Washington's death, a visitor to Mount Vernon noticed a work party, consisting of eleven black men, making some improvements to the ground around Washington's new tomb, which had been constructed a few years before. Intrigued by their "earnest expression of feeling," the visitor struck up a conversation with them. He learned that they were some of the slaves freed by the terms of George Washington's will and had returned to Mount Vernon to undertake this work, volunteering "their services upon this last and melancholy occasion, as the only return in their power to make to the remains of the man who had been more than a father to them." The men planned to "continue their labors as long as any thing should be pointed out for them to do."[110]

Local Celebrity

Like Anderson, another African-born slave came to appreciate what George Washington had done for him—and responded by taking the surname "Washington." About two years before the Revolution, Simon was one of several slaves sent by Washington to work his lands in western Pennsylvania with a partner named Gilbert Simpson. The business relationship between Washington and Simpson was always rocky—Washington received only one of the payments he was supposed to get from Simpson during the entire eight years of the war—and shortly afterward in 1784, Washington decided to settle affairs with Simpson and make new arrangements for his lands.[111] Washington also made a decision about that time concerning the slaves he had sent out to work those western lands. He wrote in October 1785 that he would prefer they be sent back to Mount Vernon, "if the measure can be reconciled to them." He went on to remind them, as an inducement to come back to Virginia, that "Simon's countrymen, & Nancy's relations are all here, & would be glad to see them; I would make a Carpenter of Simon, to work along with his shipmate [S]ambo."[112] This statement is particularly interesting because it indicates that whatever Simon's ethnic origins in Africa, they were shared by a number of people then at Mount Vernon. By this time there were nine slaves on the Pennsylvania property—Washington had originally sent out four—and, as his agent expressed it, "they would not be Prevailed with to come down [to Mount Vernon] from any Argument I could use." This attitude is understandable given the fact that they had had thirteen years in their new home to make new friends and build families on the frontier. As a consequence, these individuals were sold in Pennsylvania. Simon's purchase price was the highest of all, one hundred pounds, paid by Bazil and Thomas Brown.[113]

Simon's new owners, the Browns in western Pennsylvania, at some point sold him to a Colonel Edward Cook. He eventually became free and took the last name Washington, "in honor of his good master," the man who had given him an important choice about how and where he would live the remainder of his life.[114] The fact that he assumed the surname Washington alone would have made Simon stand out from most of the other slaves from Mount Vernon, less than a handful of whom appear to have taken Washington's last name for their own.[115] Simon also took part in a public tribute to George Washington on July 4, 1853, when a large stone, five feet long and eighteen inches in width and depth, was sent from Pennsylvania to Washington, DC, to become part of the Washington monument. On that day, a large procession, including a band, escorted the stone from the quarry to the town of Perryopolis. After being placed on a wagon decorated with flowers and evergreens to which "four fine horses" were harnessed, "an old Negro called 'Funty Munty,' or Simon Washington" was seated on the stone, dressed in "regimentals." A description of the day's events continued, "This old man, with a stone hammer in his hand, occasionally pecked the stone, so that it might truthfully be said not only that the block was taken from land once owned by Gen. Washington, but that it was worked by one of his former slaves. The celebration was attended by nearly three hundred people, and great enthusiasm was manifested on the occasion."[116] Simon was still living the following year when he was said to be 120 years old, undoubtedly an exaggeration that seems to have been rather common in the nineteenth century, a period when white Americans were especially receptive to claims of unbelievable age and connections to famous people by elderly slaves and former slaves.

More work needs to be done on this topic, but it is clear that past ownership by, or association with, George Washington was a claim used by a number of elderly free blacks in the nineteenth century to win attention or as a means of getting better care. For example, an eleven-page pamphlet written about 1900 details the life of Hammet Achmet, who is said to have died at the age of 114 and became something of a local celebrity in Middletown, Connecticut. Achmet claimed to have been "a servant of General Washington" who began "as a little boy, holding the General's horse." When he was slightly older, Achmet waited on the Washingtons' table. The pamphlet claimed that "many long stories he could tell of the fine dinners and grand company in 'Massa Washington's mansion.'" Still later, he served as a drummer boy in the American Revolution. On his cottage door in Middletown, Achmet, then a drum maker, placed the inscription, "Drums, large and small, made and sold by General Washington's waiter." He was granted a pension for his Revolutionary War service and courted by P. T. Barnum to join his traveling show as a curiosity—an "honor" Achmet declined. The author of the booklet opined that "Hammet was undoubtedly a servant of Washington," and went on to give as evidence the fact that he owned a number of Washington relics, including a "waistcoat of flowered silk" worn by George Washington. This special garment was shown to friends "with due reverence" but never worn, "for notwithstanding the added glory it would have given his costume, it was sacred to Washington." There was also a lock of Washington's hair inside a "tiny silver box, shaped like a coffin, [e]nclosed in a wooden case of similar shape." In addition, he owned a "rapier, or small dress sword, gold handled, and engraved with the initials of its former owner." These objects are said to have been buried with Achmet following his death on November 19, 1842. The elderly man was also indulged by the community:

> A favorite custom of his was to walk through the town, and meeting one and another, to tell his dreams. "Massa Hosmer," he would say to the stately Judge, "I dreamed you gave me a shilling." Of course the dream would be realized. Once someone said to him: "Dreams go by contraries Hammet." He quickly replied: "Oh, Massa, I dreamed again you didn't give me any." Meeting a troop of merry boys, Hammet would say: "John, I dreamed you gave me a penny." The boys were kind to him.[117]

A number of details of his later life were recorded in newspapers of the period, including his obituary, which gave his age as "about 90" and stated that he was "brought a slave from Africa; said he had lived as a waiter with Gen Washington, and was continually talking about Massa Washington."[118]

The most notorious case of this type was that of Joice Heth, who was promoting herself in the 1830s as the 161-year-old former nurse of an infant George Washington, before she was taken up by P. T. Barnum for even wider exhibition and then determined to be a fraud.[119] So common was it for elderly African Americans to claim to be former Washington slaves that noted humorist Mark Twain wrote a short story in 1868 poking fun at "George Washington's Negro Body-Servant," who, allegedly based on newspaper articles, died in 1809, 1825, 1840, 1855, 1864, and again in 1868, even though he was also making appearances at patriotic holidays throughout the country.[120]

Sambo Anderson and Simon Washington both came to feel a strong affection for George Washington, born of gratefulness in the first case for having been given the opportunity to end his life as he had begun it, as a free man, and in the second, from having been given the chance to spend the rest of his life in the place that had become his home. For Simon, having been uprooted twice before in his life—once from his family in Africa and secondly from his countrymen at Mount Vernon—it must have been overwhelming to be given a choice about where he would spend the rest of his days. Given the worsening situation for both slaves and free blacks in the early nineteenth century, neither man probably had an easy life after leaving Washington's service. Despite the fact that he was living in a part of the country he had chosen, Simon continued in slavery for many years before he attained freedom. A large part of Anderson's statement that "he was a much happier man when he was a slave than he had ever been since," because he then "had a good kind master to look after all my wants, but now I have no one to care for me," is probably the infirmities of old age talking.[121] Still, both men had become minor celebrities in their hometowns, a fact that relates directly to their connection to George Washington, the same connection that guaranteed Austin better quality care when he fell ill on his way home from Philadelphia. These were not isolated cases. A description by a nineteenth century visitor to Mount Vernon shows this happening, from the perspective of a free white person, even in the case of a slave whose relationship to Washington would have been pretty tenuous: "The Negro, who gave us the history of this plant, was a slave born, I think he said, on the Mount Vernon estate. He had seen Washington once or twice, when quite a boy, and though his remembrance of the great man was very imperfect, to have *seen* Washington, seemed to have ennobled him in his own estimation, as it certainly did in ours."[122]

Centuries of Hurt

In the lives of two of the house servants at Mount Vernon, Austin and Charlotte, it is also possible to see some of the emotional complexity inherent in the institution of slavery, for both master and slave. Both were clearly trusted by the Washingtons, who relied on them for personal service, information, and, perhaps in Austin's case, protection, as he accompanied Martha Washington to and from winter quarters during the Revolution. In turn, Charlotte felt comfortable enough in her relationship with Martha Washington to go to her with a grievance about the farm manager. And yet, as we saw earlier, the Washingtons quite willingly deceived both their slaves and other whites in order to protect their property rights during the presidency. Austin and the other slaves who worked in the executive mansion likely had friends in the black community in Philadelphia and were aware of the Pennsylvania law through which they might gain their freedom. Given Austin's personality, which came across as quiet—the sort of person who would stew and fret inside, without letting on—the incredible stress he must have felt, perhaps caring for the people for whom he worked while also resenting the subterfuge that kept him enslaved, these circumstances might very well be what led to his death by stroke in his mid-thirties. Knowing this aspect of Austin's story also makes it easier to understand the origins of some of the continuing problems among ethnic groups in our country today. George Washington, is after all, almost universally revered for his honesty, yet, as we have seen, he did on occasion lie to his slaves, leading some of their descendants to tell a different narrative about him.

Several years ago, I was contacted by a local woman who is a descendant of a former Augustine Washington slave. When I expressed interest in getting a typescript of a 1980 interview she had done with an older relative, she was hesitant, commenting that we might not like what he had to say. I told her that we were really interested in everything, that we needed to know their story, and that our director, Jim Rees, had always said that if there were negative stories about Washington out there, it was necessary for us to know about them and better that they came from us. She sent a copy of the typescript. In the interview, when the elderly gentleman was asked what kind of men George Washington and his father had been, his response was that the Washingtons "were big liar's, and never keep a promise."[123] This was likely how that family, over multiple generations, experienced members of the Washington family.

A number of times in the last twenty years or so, people have contacted me to investigate family stories that their ancestors had been enslaved by the Washingtons at Mount Vernon. Those times when I have been able to let them know that their ancestors had in fact been here, the news has elicited a variety of responses, ranging from delight at having those stories confirmed to tears upon realizing that those ancestors had "belonged" to another human being and been considered property. In order for the bitterness and distrust among races in this country to heal, all of these stories need to be told, the complexities of the slavery experience—for both master and slave—need to be acknowledged and discussed, so that almost four hundred years of hurt, anger, and denial can stop festering in people's souls and come to an end.

Mount Vernon, as the most visited historic house in America and as the home of one of the greatest—but still not perfect—men who ever lived, is uniquely situated to play an important role in this process. Several international surveys have shown that museums are among the most trusted of learning institutions. According to a 2001 report by the American Association (now Alliance) of Museums, 87 percent of Americans "find museums to be one of the most trustworthy or a trustworthy source of information about a wide range of choices."[124] Three years later, a survey conducted for the National Museum Directors' Conference on the attitudes of British parents noted that 80 percent either "strongly agree" or "tend to agree" that "museums and galleries are among the most important resources for educating our children."[125] Similarly, a Canadian survey found in 2011 that 84 percent of those polled expressed either "very strong" or "somewhat strong" levels of trust in the way museums present historical eras, issues, people, and events.[126] Research into the lives of all the enslaved families and individuals at Mount Vernon will continue in the coming years. Many aspects of slave life that were touched on briefly in previous chapters could be expanded as well, either by the staff at Mount Vernon or by outside researchers.

Several years ago, two of Mount Vernon's first-person interpreters—actors who portray actual people from the eighteenth century—were interviewed for a local newspaper. William Little III and Dhakeria Cunningham were both senior theater arts majors at Howard University and were doing a wonderful job bringing to life Tom Davis, the hunter for Washington's table, and the volatile seamstress Charlotte. On the record, Will commented, "I never was much of a history buff. . . . I tried to stay true to the culture and the historical setting, and show the reality of these enslaved people—my people. It made me realize how strong African American people are. Our history is very rich and shouldn't be forgotten. I have the opportunity to educate people. . . . My job is to tell the story of my people, not sugarcoat it. It has been a life-changing experience." Off the record, he confided to the interviewer that learning what he had about the enslaved residents of Mount Vernon so long ago had made him proud to be African American. An audience member that day, who also agreed to be interviewed, noted in response to Little's and Cunningham's performances, "In some measure, this program will help bring about a kind of healing; an understanding between the races."[127] It is my hope that this book will continue those processes—both developing pride in their heritage by the African American community and healing the wounds of our racially difficult past—for others, regardless of ethnicity, who may never be able to visit Mount Vernon or, having visited, would still like to learn more.

It is a difficult and painful story, but it is also a story of progress and change for the better. In the case of George Washington, he changed into someone who saw that slavery was wrong, that freedom was a right of every human, regardless of race. In thinking about the enslaved families at Mount Vernon, it is impossible not to relate to the words of modern African American writer Audre Lorde, who wrote, "survival is the greatest gift of love. Sometimes, for Black mothers, it is the only gift possible."[128] Those enslaved mothers—and fathers—at Mount Vernon made sure their families survived, to eventually become free.

APPENDIX

Some of the concepts discussed in the text of the book can be easier to understand in the form of a graph or table. This section includes some of that detailed information. In certain cases, a table or tables illuminate the source for figures used in the text itself. In others, they enable the reader to visualize processes such as the growth of the plantation and changes in population makeup over many years. There are also tables that show the origins of names used by enslaved people at Mount Vernon, and try to provide order to an often confusing—and frequently changing—set of individuals in management roles. See the list of abbreviations on page 364 for noted sources.

TABLE 1. George Washington's acquisition of slaves

DATE	NAME, AGE, AND OCCUPATION (IF KNOWN)	SOURCE AND LOCATION (IF KNOWN)	TYPE OF ACQUISITION
1750	Fortune George Long Joe Winna Bellindar Jenny Adam Nat London Milly Frank	Augustine Washington	Bequest
7 August 1752	Unknown number	Colonel Champe	Purchase: £75 Duty: £3.15.0
1754	Peter Jenny Phebe Tom Lucy (child of a slave named Lett) Tom (Jenny's child)	Lawrence Washington	Bequest
31 October 1754	A "Negro Fellow"	John Wake	Purchase: £40.5.0
1755	Two men and one woman	Charles Washington	Rental: £20
9 January 1755	Clio (seamstress)	William Buckner, Caroline County, Virginia	Purchase: £50
9 January 1755	Jack	William Buckner, Caroline County, Virginia	Purchase: £52.5.0
14 February 1755	Kitt (carpenter)	Buckner family, Caroline County, Virginia	Purchase: £39.5.0
25 May 1755	Harry	Mr. Bowee	Purchase: £45
1756	Two men and one woman	Charles Washington	Rental: £20
11 January 1756	Two men and one woman	Mrs. Brooks	Purchase: £86
15 February 1756	James (carpenter)	Mrs. Frances Thornton, Spotsylvania County, Virginia	Rental: £79.3.0
27 November 1756	A "Negro Woman and Child"	"Bought of the Governor"	Purchase: £60

DATE	NAME, AGE, AND OCCUPATION (IF KNOWN)	SOURCE AND LOCATION (IF KNOWN)	TYPE OF ACQUISITION
1757	Two men and one woman	Charles Washington	Rental: £20
7 February 1757	One man (carpenter)	Mary Timson Buckner, Caroline County, Virginia	Purchase: £107.10.0
13 February 1757	Unknown number	"Brookes"	Purchase: £150
30 April 1757	Unknown number	Maryland	Purchase: £79.10.0
1758	One man and one woman	Charles Washington	Rental: £14
6 January 1758	Gregory	Colonel Catesby Cocke	Purchase: £60.9.0
1759	Morrice (29; carpenter) Isaac (28; carpenter) Tom (30; carpenter) Scomberg (42; shirt maker) Breechy (24; waiter) Mulatto Jack (41; waiter) Doll (38; cook) Beck (23; scullion) Jenny (39; washer) Sally (15; lady's maid) Betty (21; seamstress) Austin (child)	Daniel Parke Custis Estate	Marriage
24 April 1759	Will (probably a carpenter)	James Oglesby	Purchase: £50
4 May 1759	Nine slaves	Colonel William Churchill, Middlesex County, Virginia	Purchase: £406
4 May 1759	"A Negro"	Doctor Symmes	Purchase: £60
16 June 1759	Hannah and child	William Cloptan, New Kent County, Virginia	Purchase: £80
1760[?]	Judy and child	Gawin Corbin's estate, Westmoreland County, Virginia	Purchase: £63
5 August 1761	Unknown number	Charles Graham, William Fitzhugh, and Benjamin Fendall, Calvert and Charles Counties, Maryland	Purchase: £259
23 December 1761[1]	Unknown number	Thomson Mason, Fairfax County, Virginia	Purchase: £120.19.0 Tax: £9.12.6

TABLE 1 (*continued*)

DATE	NAME, AGE, AND OCCUPATION (IF KNOWN)	SOURCE AND LOCATION (IF KNOWN)	TYPE OF ACQUISITION
1762	Kate George Maria Kate's first child Kate's second child	Lawrence Washington, via Ann Fairfax Washington Lee	Bequest
22 February 1762	Seven slaves	Lee Massey, King George County, Virginia	Purchase: £300
18 March 1762	Charles	Samuel Washington	Purchase: £30
2 May 1762	Guy (bricklayer)	William Daingerfield	Rental, May 1762–October 1763: £30/year
20 July 1762	Frederick Judy	Fielding Lewis, Fredericksburg, Virginia	Purchase: £115
1763[2]	Harry (£45) Topsom (£43) Nan (£25.5) Toney (£17.5)	Daniel Tebbs's estate	Purchase: £131
23 January 1764	Robin (£65) Charles (£74) Jerry (£65)	Colonel Samuel Buckner's estate	Purchase: £204
23 January 1764	Ben (£72) Lewis (£36.10.0) Sarah (£20)	Francis Stubbs's estate	Purchase: £128.10.0
24 January 1764	Lewis	Sarah Alexander	Purchase: £76
1765	James	Samuel Washington	Rental for one year: £10
11 April 1765	Unnamed man, who would remain until 12 June 1766 (bricklayer)	Mrs. Lettice Corbin, Essex	Rental at the rate of £25/year
1 January 1767	Davy (carpenter)	Lund Washington	Rental at the rate of £18/year (would remain four years)
15 October 1767	Mulatto Will (£61.15) Ditto Frank (£50) Negro boy Adam (£19) Jack (£19)	Mary Smith Ball Lee, Westmoreland County, Virginia	Purchase: £149.15.0

DATE	NAME, AGE, AND OCCUPATION (IF KNOWN)	SOURCE AND LOCATION (IF KNOWN)	TYPE OF ACQUISITION
16 October 1767	Sarah	Henry Self, probably Fairfax County, Virginia	Purchase: £40
11 June 1770	Frank (£31) James (£55)	Thomas Moore's estate sale, West Point	Purchase: £86
November 1770	Twenty-two slaves (sixteen adults, six children [Poll to Janey]) Sam Kitt Cupit Parros Ceasar Moll Bettey Hannah Lucey Moll Dafney Doll Brunswick Jamy Fanney Old Brunswick Alce Poll Billey Suckey Cloe Rachal Janey	Daniel Parke Custis estate	Marriage
16 October 1771	Giles	Lund Washington	Purchase: £76.5.0
4 May 1772	Anthony London Strephon (boy)	Robert Adam & Company	Purchase: £185
15 February 1773	Ned (£72) Murria (a girl) (£49)	Thomas Colvill estate	Purchase: £121.10.0
4 March 1773	Orson	Gilbert Simpson	Purchase: £55
April 1773[3]	James Isaac	Robert Washington (brother of Lund Washington)	Purchase: £180
16 December 1773	Naize (cooper)	Philip Langfit	Rental: £50 for three years

TABLE 1 *(continued)*

DATE	NAME, AGE, AND OCCUPATION (IF KNOWN)	SOURCE AND LOCATION (IF KNOWN)	TYPE OF ACQUISITION
25 December 1773	One man and one woman	Alexander Cleveland	Rental: £18 for one year
1774	Two slaves	Alexander Cleveland	Rental: £14 for one year, as per agreement with Lund Washington
18 February 1775[4]	Thomas (Tom)	John Harper	Purchase: £52.10.0
March 1775 (?)	One male slave	Josias Adams estate, Charles County, Maryland	
21 April 1775	Jack	Robert Adam & Company	Purchase: £60

Sources: *GWP.Col.Series,* vols. 1, 4, 6–10; Ledger A, FWSNL; Ledger B, FWSNL.

1. At least some of these people may have been among those advertised by Thomson Mason (the brother of Washington's neighbor George Mason IV of Gunston Hall) in the *Maryland Gazette,* 24 September 1761, as coming from Gambia on the *Upton,* a ship under the command of Captain Samuel Pemberton. Washington may have purchased them at the fall sale and only got around to paying for them in December, or they may have not sold at the earlier public sale. See "September 24, 1761, Thomson Mason Slave Dealing Advertisement in the Maryland Gazette," *The Enslaved Children of George Mason,* 2017, http://ecgm.omeka.net/items/show/1.

2. According to the editors of the *Papers of George Washington,* in 1763 Washington gave his bond for the total purchase price of four slaves he bought to send to the Dismal Swamp to the executors of Daniel Tebbs's estate, "payable last of June 1764"; he paid the bond on 30 April 1764. See GW, "Cash Accounts," [April 1764], *GWP.Col.Series,* 7:299, 300n17. Other sources list the former owner as Daniel Tibbs. See Ledger A, 173a, 176a.

3. GW made his final payment for these slaves on 25 March 1774. See *GWP.Col.Series,* 9:222, 224n12, 505n7. See also GW, "Account with Robert Washington," April 1773, Ledger B, 86a.

4. GW paid the note, via his cousin LW, on 24 July 1776. See GW, "Promissory Note to John Harper," 18 February 1775, *GWP.Col.Series,* 10:269, 269n1.

TABLE 2. Growth of the Mount Vernon plantation, 1760–1774

YEAR	HIRED OR INDENTURED	WORKING SLAVES OVER AGE SIXTEEN	TOTAL
1760	5	In and around the mansion: 9 Carpenters: 7 Smiths: 2 Fieldworkers: 25	48
1761	6 men	In and around the mansion: 10 (4 men, 6 women) Carpenters: 7 men Smiths: 2 men Fieldworkers: 37 (21 men, 16 women)	62
1762	8 men	In and around the mansion: 10 (3 men, 7 women) Carpenters: 8 men Smiths: 2 men Miller: 1 man Fieldworkers: 41 (25 men, 16 women)	70
1763	9 men	In and around the mansion: 17 (9 men, 8 women) Carpenters: 9 men Tradesmen: 4 men Fieldworkers: 34 (18 men, 16 women)	73[1]
1764	10 men	In and around the mansion: 11 (3 men, 8 women) Tradesmen: 11 men Fieldworkers: 43 (25 men, 18 women)	75[2]
1765	9 men	In and around the mansion: 10 (3 men, 7 women) Tradesmen: 10 men Miller: 1 man Fieldworkers: 47 (26 men, 21 women)	77
1766	7 men	In and around the mansion: 13 (4 men, 9 women) Tradesmen: 9 men Miller: 1 man Fieldworkers: 53 (28 men, 25 women)	83
1767	7 men	In and around the mansion: 15 (6 men, 9 women) Tradesmen: 10 men Miller: 1 man Fieldworkers: 51 (28 men, 23 women)	84
1768	6 men	In and around the mansion: 15 (6 men, 9 women) Tradesmen: 12 Fieldworkers: 55 (30 men, 25 women)	88
1769	7 men	In and around the mansion: 16 (6 men, 10 women) Tradesmen: 12 Fieldworkers: 58 (32 men, 26 women)	93
1770	7 men	In and around the mansion: 15 (5 men, 10 women) Tradesmen: 10 Ferrymen: 2 Fieldworkers: 54 (29 men, 25 women)	88

TABLE 2 (*continued*)

YEAR	HIRED OR INDENTURED	WORKING SLAVES OVER AGE SIXTEEN	TOTAL
1771	6 men	In and around the mansion: 16 (6 men, 10 women) Tradesmen: 8 Ferrymen: 2 Fieldworkers: 69 (37 men, 32 women)	101
1772	6 men	In and around the mansion: 12 (5 men, 7 women) Tradesmen: 7 Fieldworkers: 76 (40 men, 36 women)	101
1773	10 men	In and around the mansion: 14 (5 men, 9 women) Tradesmen: 10 Fieldworkers: 77 (40 men, 37 women)	111
1774	15 men	In and around the mansion: 15 (6 men, 9 women) Tradesmen: 13 Fieldworkers: 91 (49 men, 42 women)	134

Source: GWP.Col.Series, annual Tithables Lists.

1. *GWP.Col.Series,* 7:227–28. This year the slaves at the Mansion House Farm were not divided between domestic workers and fieldworkers, including them all as house servants, hence the jump in the number in this category.

2. *GWP.Col.Series,* 7:313. This year the slaves at the Mansion House Farm were once again divided between domestic workers and fieldworkers.

TABLE 3. Growth of the Mount Vernon plantation, 1786

FARM	ADULT SLAVES (WORKING, DISABLED, RETIRED)	CHILDREN TOO YOUNG TO WORK	TOTAL
Dogue Run	Overseer and wife: 2 Fieldworkers: 18 (9 men; 9 women) Too sick or old to work: 1 man (disabled), 1 woman (elderly)	17 (8 boys, 9 girls)	GW slaves: 21 (12 adults, 9 children) Dower slaves: 18 (10 adults, 8 children) Total: 39
Ferry Farm	Fieldworkers: 15 (5 men, 10 women)	15 (9 boys, 6 girls)	GW slaves: 5 (3 adults, 2 children) Dower slaves: 25 (12 adults, 13 children) Total: 30
Mansion House Farm	In and around the mansion and stable: 26 (12 men, 14 women) Fieldworkers: 10 men Tradesmen: 6 men Mill: 4 men Too sick or old to work: 1 man (elderly)	24 (8 boys, 16 girls)	GW slaves: 31 (26 adults, 5 children) Dower slaves: 38 (19 adults, 19 children) Rented Custis slaves: 2 (adults) Total: 71
Muddy Hole Farm	Overseer: 1 man Fieldworkers: 13 (4 men, 9 women)	11 (5 boys, 6 girls)	GW slaves: 22 (11 adults, 11 children) Dower slaves: 3 (all adults) Total: 25
River Farm	Overseer and wife: 2 Fieldworkers: 27 (10 men, 17 women)	23 (13 boys, 10 girls)	GW slaves: 25 (15 adults, 10 children) Dower slaves: 27 (14 adults, 13 children) Total: 52
Total	127 (65 men, 62 women)	90 (43 boys, 47 girls)	GW slaves: 104 (67 adults, 37 children) Dower slaves: 111 (58 adults, 53 children) Rented Custis slaves: 2 Total: 217

Source: 1786 Slave List.

TABLE 4. Growth of the Mount Vernon plantation, 1799

FARM	ADULT SLAVES (WORKING, DISABLED, RETIRED)	CHILDREN TOO YOUNG TO WORK	TOTAL
Dogue Run Farm	Fieldworkers: 22 (7 men, 15 women) Too sick or old to work: 2 women	21 (10 boys; 11 girls)	GW slaves: 27 (17 adults, 10 children) Dower slaves: 18 (7 adults, 11 children) Total: 45
Mansion House Farm	In and around the mansion and stable: 38 (15 men, 23 women) Tradesmen: 16 men Mill and distillery: 11 men Too sick or old to work: 5 (3 men, 2 women)	28 (11 boys; 17 girls)	GW slaves: 27 (27 adults) Dower slaves: 70 (42 adults, 28 children) Rented slaves: 1 adult[1] Total: 98
Muddy Hole Farm[2]	Fieldworkers: 22 (7 men, 15 women) Too sick or old to work: 1 woman (?)	19 (8 boys; 11 girls)	GW slaves: 36 (18 adults, 18 children) Dower slaves: 5 (4 adults, 1 child) Rented slaves: 1 adult[3] Total: 42
River Farm	Fieldworkers: 36 (15 men, 21 women) Unable to do fieldwork, but cooks: 1 woman Too sick or old to work: 1 woman	19 (11 boys; 8 girls)	GW slaves: 27 (18 adults, 9 children) Dower slaves: 30 (20 adults, 10 children) Total: 57
Union Farm[4]	Fieldworkers: 39 (18 men; 21 women) Too sick or old to work: 3 women	32 (14 boys; 18 girls)	GW slaves: 6 (4 adults, 2 children) Dower slaves: 30 (16 adults, 14 children) Rented slaves: 38 (22 adults; 16 children) Total: 74
Total	197 (92 men; 105 women)	119 (54 boys; 65 girls)	GW slaves: 123 (84 adults, 39 children) Dower slaves: 153 (89 adults, 64 children) Rented slaves: 40 (24 adults, 16 children) Total: 316

Source: 1799 Slave Lists.

1. See GW, "A List of Negroes Hired from Mrs. French," *GWW,* 37:308. The one rented slave was twenty-four-year-old James, who worked at the distillery.

2. Ibid., 37:264–65. On this list, Washington noted that, among the dower slaves, there was one person who "does nothing" and one who was "young." He did not count either of those individuals among the workers. For purposes of the figures here, I inferred that seventy-six-year-old Molly was too old to work and eleven-year-old Mary was young. In the latter case, I included her among the children, since Washington typically did consider young people listed this way as workers, but this was not so with her.

3. See ibid., 37:308. The one rented slave was twenty-nine-year-old Isaac, who was a plowman.

4. Ibid., 37:266–67, 308–9. Note: two of the rented slaves lived on Washington's other farms. Isaac lived at Muddy Hole Farm, while James worked at the distillery. Washington did not include them with the people on those other farms but grouped them with the others rented from Mrs. French.

TABLE 5. Farm managers and overseers at Mount Vernon, 1754–1799

NAME	POSITION AND STATUS	YEARS AND FARM
John Augustine Washington I	Farm manager (family)	1755–58
Humphrey Knight	Farm manager (hired)	1757–58
Lund Washington	Farm manager (hired and family)	1765–85
James Bloxham	Master farmer (hired)	1786–90
George Augustine Washington	Farm manager (family)	1786–93
Robert Lewis	Farm manager (family)	1790–92
Anthony Whiting or Whitting	Farm manager (hired)	1790–93
Howell Lewis	Farm manager (family)	1793–94
William Pearce	Farm manager (hired)	1793–96
James Anderson	Farm manager (hired)	1797–1802
Lawrence Lewis	Assisting with farm management (family)	1797–1802
John Alton	Overseer (hired)	1755–85
William Fairfax	Overseer (hired)	1758 Mansion House Farm
Burgess Mitchell	Overseer (hired)	1762 Mansion House Farm
Thomas Nicholas	Overseer (hired)	1764 Mansion House Farm
Francis Tunley or Turnley	Overseer (hired)	1765–66 Mansion House Farm
John Fairfax	Overseer (hired)	1784–90 Mansion House Farm
James Butler	Overseer (hired)	1792–94 Mansion House Farm
John Allison or Allistone	Overseer (hired)	1794–97 Mansion House Farm
Roger Farrell	Overseer (hired)	1799 Mansion House Farm
John Foster	Overseer (hired)	1759–62 Dogue Run Farm
John Alton	Overseer (hired)	1762 Dogue Run Farm
Nelson Kelly	Overseer (hired)	1762–63 Dogue Run Farm
James Davenport or Devenport	Overseer (hired)	1763–65 Dogue Run Farm

NAME	POSITION AND STATUS	YEARS AND FARM
[Israel] Morris	Overseer (dower slave)	1766–94 Dogue Run Farm
Davy [Gray]	Overseer (dower slave)	1790 Dogue Run Farm
Henry Jones	Overseer (hired)	1792 Dogue Run Farm
Will	Overseer (dower slave)	1792 Dogue Run Farm
Henry McCoy or McKoy	Overseer (hired)	1793–96 Dogue Run Farm
Joseph Cash	Overseer (hired)	1796–98 Dogue Run Farm
Robert Garrett	Overseer (hired)	1798–99 Dogue Run Farm
Richard Stephens or Stevens	Overseer (hired)	1760–? Muddy Hole Farm
Edward Violette/Violet/Violett	Overseer (hired)	1761–62 Muddy Hole Farm
John Alton	Overseer (hired)	1762 Muddy Hole Farm
John Chowning	Overseer (hired)	1762 Muddy Hole Farm
Alexander Cleveland	Overseer (hired)	1765 Muddy Hole Farm
John Alton	Overseer (hired)	1774 Muddy Hole Farm
Davy [Gray]	Overseer (dower slave)	Prior to 1785 Muddy Hole Farm
Will	Overseer (dower slave)	Late 1785 Muddy Hole Farm
Davy [Gray]	Overseer (dower slave)	1792–99 Muddy Hole Farm
Samuel Johnson or Johnston, Jr.	Overseer (hired)	1761–63 River Farm
John Chowning	Overseer (hired)	1764 River Farm
James Cleveland	Overseer (hired)	1765–75 River Farm
Alexander Cleveland	Overseer (hired)	1773–74 River Farm

TABLE 5 (*continued*)

NAME	POSITION AND STATUS	YEARS AND FARM
John Alton	Overseer (hired)	1785 River Farm
Davy [Gray]	Overseer (dower slave)	1785–86 River Farm
Ignatius Dodson	Overseer (hired)	1790–91 River Farm
William Garner	Overseer (hired)	1788–92 River Farm
William Stewart or Stuart	Overseer (hired)	1793–97 River Farm
Moses Dowdell	Overseer (hired)	1798–99 River Farm
Jesse Brummit	Overseer (hired)	1773–74 or 1775 Ferry Farm
Hezekiah Fairfax	Overseer (hired)	1780s Ferry Farm
Hiland or Highland Crow	Overseer (hired)	1790–92 Ferry and French's Farms (later called Union Farm)
Highland Crow	Overseer (hired)	1792–94 Union Farm
John Groves or Grover	Overseer (hired)	1794–95 Union Farm
John Violett or Violet	Overseer (hired)	1796–97 Union Farm
George Rawlins	Overseer (hired)	1798–99 Union Farm
Robert Stephens	Overseer (hired)	1760–61 Williamson's Quarter (later Creek Quarter)
Josias or Josiah Cook	Overseer (hired)	1761–64 Creek Quarter
John Alton	Overseer (hired)	1765–69 Mill Plantation

Sources: Table compiled from references in the published writings of George Washington.

TABLE 6. Age of enslaved first-time mothers at Mount Vernon

NAME (AGE) IN 1799	MARITAL STATUS IN 1799	AGE AT BIRTH OF FIRST CHILD	NUMBER OF CHILDREN IN 1799
Dogue Run Farm			
Peg (30)	Married	24	3
Charity (42)	Married	22	3
Linney (27)	Single	21	2
Grace (35)	Married	25	3
Priscilla (36)	Married	22	6
Sall Twine (38)	Married	27	4
Agnes (25)	Married	23	2
Sarah (20)	Single	18	1
		Average: 22.75	
Muddy Hole Farm			
Darcus (36)	Married	17	4
Peg (34)	Married	14–15	5
Amie (30)	Single	22	2
Letty (19)	Single	17	2
Alce (38)	Married	20	4
Nancy (28)	Married	17	3
Sacky (40)	Single	16	1
Molly (26)	Single	16	2
		Average: 17.44	
River Farm			
Sall (30)	Married	19	5
Rose (28)	Single	22	4
Agnes (36)	Married	19	3
Betty (20)	Married	19	1
Alce (26)	Married	22	2
		Average: 20.2	

TABLE 6 (*continued*)

NAME (AGE) IN 1799	MARITAL STATUS IN 1799	AGE AT BIRTH OF FIRST CHILD	NUMBER OF CHILDREN IN 1799
Union Farm			
Edy (26)	Married	20	2
Fanny (36)	Married	22	2
Jenny (34)	Married	27	3
Rachel (34)	Single	24	5
Milly (22)	Single	21	1
		Average: 22	
		Overall average: 20.54	

Sources: Information on this chart was primarily taken from the 1786 and 1799 Slave Lists from Mount Vernon. Women who were older than forty-five in 1799 were omitted from this sample because information from the 1786 list about teenage children who may have been theirs was not available. Slaves at Union Farm who were rented from Mrs. French were also left out because they were only enumerated on the 1799 list, and without the data from thirteen years before, imperfect though it may be, it was not possible to get anywhere near complete information for these women. The most glaring omission, of course, are individuals at the Mansion House Farm. Unfortunately, on neither the 1786 nor 1799 lists were the ages of adult slaves listed, and many children's were left off the latter one as well. As a result, it was not possible to work out meaningful figures for that farm.

TABLE 7. Age ranges of slaves on the four outlying farms at Mount Vernon, 1799

AGE	NUMBER OF INDIVIDUALS: RIVER FARM	NUMBER OF INDIVIDUALS: DOGUE RUN	NUMBER OF INDIVIDUALS: MUDDY HOLE	NUMBER OF INDIVIDUALS: UNION FARM	TOTAL
90–99	0	0	0	0	0
80–89	1	0	0	0	1
70–79	2	1	1	2	6
60–69	1	2	1	4	8
50–59	8	3	1	4	16
40–49	2	4	1	1	8
30–39	4	4	5	5	18
20–29	8	4	4	12	28
10–19	11	13	11	17	52
1–9	19	14	15	28	76
Unknown	1 "old"	0	2 "old"	1 "old" 2 "in prime"	6
Average age	23.82	21.19	18.74	19.76	20.94
Percent people 60 or over	8.77%	6.67%	9.76%	9.21%	8.68%
Percent people 19 or younger	52.63%	60%	63.41%	59.21%	58.45%
Percent people 9 or younger	33.33%	31.11%	36.59%	36.84%	34.7%

Source: 1799 Slave Lists.

TABLE 8. Births at Mount Vernon, January 1763–December 1774

	MOTHER'S NAME	DATE	MIDWIFE'S NAME	INTERVAL BETWEEN BIRTHS
Dogue Run Farm				
	Sue	July 31, 1767	Susannah Bishop	
	Moll	July 3, 1769	Ann Knowland	
	Hannah	October 1774	Susannah Bishop	
	Jone	October 1774	Susannah Bishop	
Ferry Farm				
	Doll	April 19, 1774	Susannah Bishop	
	Betty	May 2, 1774	Susannah Bishop	
Mansion House Farm				
	Lydia	July 4, 1768	Elizabeth Simpson	
	Phillis	February 27, 1769	Susannah Bishop	
	"House" Sall	June 16, 1772	Susannah Bishop	
	Kitt	June 16, 1772	Susannah Bishop	
	"House" Betty	April 19, 1774	Susannah Bishop	
	"House" Alice	December 21, 1771	Susannah Bishop	
	"House" Alice	December 11, 1774	Susannah Bishop	36 months
Mill Farm				
	Silla	July 23, 1773	Mrs. Parker	
Muddy Hole Farm				
	Kate	July 8, 1767	Susannah Bishop	
	Kate	July 6, 1769	Susannah Bishop	24 months
	Kate	July 7, 1772	Susannah Bishop	36 months
	Kate	October 1774	Susannah Bishop	27 months
River Farm				
	Peg	June 27, 1767	Elizabeth Simpson	
	Judy	July 4, 1768	Elizabeth Simpson	
	Judy	January 3, 1774	Elizabeth Simpson	66 months

	MOTHER'S NAME	DATE	MIDWIFE'S NAME	INTERVAL BETWEEN BIRTHS
Unknown				
	No name given	January 25, 1763	Mrs. Brasenton	
	No name given	January 25, 1763	Mrs. Brasenton	
	No name given	April 11, 1763	Mrs. Brasenton	
	No name given	April 11, 1763	Mrs. Brasenton	
	No name given	April 11, 1763	Mrs. Brasenton	
	No name given	April 11, 1763	Mrs. Brasenton	
	No name given	December 2, 1763	Mrs. Brasenton	
	No name given	December 2, 1763	Mrs. Brasenton	
	Peg	June 4, 1764 (?)	Mrs. Brasenton	
	No name given	June 4, 1764	Mrs. Brasenton	
	Betty (from either Mansion House Farm or Dogue Run Farm)	February 21, 1767	Susannah Bishop	
	Doll (from either River Farm or Mansion House Farm)	June 27, 1767	Elizabeth Simpson	
	Sarah	March 4, 1768	Susannah Bishop	
	Catherine	July 6, 1769	Susannah Bishop	
	Sarah	October 26, 1769	Susannah Bishop	
	Moll	September 4, 1771	Susannah Bishop	
	Betty	October 9, 1771	Susannah Bishop	
	Doll	January 10, 1772	Susannah Bishop	

Source: GWP.Col.Series.

TABLE 9. Births at Mount Vernon, December 1775–May 1779

MOTHER'S NAME	DATE	MIDWIFE'S NAME	INTERVAL BETWEEN BIRTHS
Dogue Run Farm			
Jane	February 20, 1776	Mrs. French's Jane	
Jane	December 2, 1776	Susannah Bishop (money given to her husband, Thomas Bishop)	10 months
Jone	April 16, 1779	Susannah Bishop	
Charity	May 21, 1779	Susannah Bishop	
Ferry Farm			
Betty	April 20, 1776	Susannah Bishop	
Betty	April 18, 1778 (twins)	Susannah Bishop	24 months
Betty	April 16, 1779	Susannah Bishop	12 months
Flora	May 18, 1777	Susannah Bishop (money given to her husband)	
Doll	May 18, 1777	Susannah Bishop (money given to her husband)	
Doll	December 13, 1778	Susannah Bishop	19 months
Mansion House Farm			
Doll	Fall 1775		
Kitty	September 27, 1776	Susannah Bishop	
Kitty	April 18, 1778	Susannah Bishop	19 months
Alice	September 27, 1776	Susannah Bishop	
Alice	April 16, 1779	Susannah Bishop	31 months
Betty	December 2, 1776	Susannah Bishop (money given to her husband)	
Betty	July 10, 1777 (possible miscarriage)	Susannah Bishop	7 months
Betty	July 13, 1778	Susannah Bishop	12 months

	MOTHER'S NAME	DATE	MIDWIFE'S NAME	INTERVAL BETWEEN BIRTHS
	Myrtilla	June 27, 1777	Darcus Parker (money given to her husband)	
	Lame Alice	November 27, 1777	Susannah Bishop	
	Sooky	December 13, 1778	Susannah Bishop	
	Sall	April 16, 1779	Susannah Bishop	
Mill				
	Judah	November 27, 1777 (miscarriage)	Susannah Bishop	
Muddy Hole Farm				
	Kate	May 21, 1779	Darcus Parker	
The Neck (an early name for River Farm)				
	Daphne	April 20, 1776	Susannah Bishop	
	Daphne	July 13, 1778	Susannah Bishop	27 months
	Lydda	April 18, 1778	Susannah Bishop	
	Peg	July 13, 1778	Susannah Bishop	
	Doll	December 13, 1778	Susannah Bishop	
	Suky	December 13, 1778	Susannah Bishop	
	Suky	May 21, 1779 (probable miscarriage)	Susannah Bishop	5 months
Unknown				
	3 women, names not given	December 1775	Susannah Bishop (money given to her husband)	
	Total: 24 (8 gave birth more than once)			Average: 17.27 months (1.4 years)

Source: LW Account Book.

TABLE 10. Births at Mount Vernon, May 1782–August 1787

	MOTHER'S NAME	DATE	MIDWIFE'S NAME	INTERVAL BETWEEN BIRTHS
Dogue Run Farm				
	Susy	May 15, 1782	Susannah Bishop	
	Jane	May 15, 1782	Susannah Bishop	
	Lucy	August 6, 1783	Susannah Bishop	
	Lucy	April 25, 1785	Darcus Parker	20 months
	Charity	November 29, 1783	Darcus Parker	
	Charity	September 28, 1785	Darcus Parker	22 months
	Betty	April 25, 1785	Darcus Parker	
	Sall	April 25, 1785	Darcus Parker	
	Sall	October 28, 1786		18 months
	Peg	April 25, 1785	Darcus Parker	
	Silla	September 28, 1785	Darcus Parker	
Ferry and French's Farms				
	Doll	July 11, 1782	Darcus Parker	
	Doll	April 28, 1783	"Mrs. Frenches Negroe Woman"	9 months
	Doll	December 24, 1784	Susannah Bishop	20 months
	Doll	October 21, 1786		22 months
	Lucy	October 4, 1782	Susannah Bishop	
	Lucy	September 28, 1785	Darcus Parker	35 months
	Betty	August 6, 1783	Susannah Bishop	
	Betty	September 28, 1785	Darcus Parker	25 months
	Fanny	November 6, 1783	Susannah Bishop	
	Tabeen	January 13, 1787		
Mansion House Farm				
	Lame Alice	May 15, 1782	Susannah Bishop	
	Lame Alice	August 6, 1783	Susannah Bishop	15 months
	Sall	July 11, 1782	Darcus Parker	
	Myrtilla	October 4, 1782	Susannah Bishop	
	Myrtilla	November 8, 1784	Susannah Bishop	25 months
	Myrtilla	November 24, 1785	Susannah Bishop	12 months
	Kitty	November 29, 1783	Darcus Parker	
	Alice	April 28, 1784	Susannah Bishop	

	MOTHER'S NAME	DATE	MIDWIFE'S NAME	INTERVAL BETWEEN BIRTHS
Muddy Hole Farm				
	Sarah	August 6, 1783	Susannah Bishop	
	Peg	April 28, 1784	Susannah Bishop	
	Peg	April 29, 1786		24 months
	Amy	September 28, 1785	Darcus Parker	
	Dorchus	September 28, 1785	Susannah Bishop	
The Neck (an early name for River Farm)				
	Leddy or Lydda	October 4, 1782	Susannah Bishop	
	Leddy or Lydda	August 15, 1783	Susannah Bishop	10 months
	Suky	August 6, 1783	Susannah Bishop	
	Doll	1783	Mrs. Williams	
	Doll	December 24, 1784	Susannah Bishop	at least 12 months
	Daphne	November 8, 1784	Susannah Bishop	
River Farm				
	Agnes	July 12, 1784	Susannah Bishop	
	Bath Suzy	week of April 14, 1787		
	Doll	April 28, 1787		
Unknown				
	Dorchus's Charlotte	July 15, 1782	Susannah Bishop	
	Dorchus's Charlotte	May 17, 1785	Susannah Bishop	34 months
	Carolina	November 6, 1783	Susannah Bishop	
	Carolina	March 18, 1785	Susannah Bishop	16 months
	Total: 31 (13 gave birth more than once)			Average: 21.59 months (1.8 years)

Sources: LW Account Book; Weekly Work Reports., FWSNL.

TABLE 11. Births at Mount Vernon, April 1792–August 1798

	MOTHER'S NAME	DATE	INTERVAL BETWEEN BIRTHS
Dogue Run Farm			
	Sall	January 5, 1793	
	Sall	February 8, 1794	13 months
	Charity	February 1793	
	Lynna	February 1793	
	Jinny	August 30, 1794	
	Silla or Sillar	November 8, 1794	
	Silla or Sillar	January 16, 1796	14 months
	Silla or Sillar	July 7, 1798	30 months
	Grace	February 14, 1795	
	Sarah	February 21, 1795	
Mansion House Farm			
	Lucy	April 21, 1798	
	Alice	August 18, 1798	
Muddy Hole Farm			
	Nancy	October 27, 1792	
	Nancy	April 21, 1798	66 months
	Molly	February 1793	
	Darchas	November 8, 1794	
	Peg	January 16, 1796	
River Farm			
	Cornelia	April 7, 1792	
	Cornelia	March 4, 1797	59 months
	Peg	February 14, 1795	
	Sal	July 30, 1796	
	Sal	April 14, 1798	21 months
	Bet	July 30, 1796	
	Agnes	February 18, 1797	

	MOTHER'S NAME	DATE	INTERVAL BETWEEN BIRTHS
Union Farm			
	Grace	August 8, 1793	
	Daphne	May 31, 1794	
	Rose	June 21, 1794	
	Pat	May 30, 1795	
	Pat	March 11, 1797	22 months
	Fanny	April 16, 1796	
	Fanny	March 31, 1798	23 months
	Rachel	April 16, 1796	
	Unknown	April 14, 1798	
	Milley	April 14, 1798	
	Total: 26 (7 gave birth more than once)		Average: 31 months (2.58 years)

Source: Weekly Work Reports, FWSNL. Information about names of midwives is not available for this period.

TABLE 12. Origins of names on Mount Vernon slave lists, 1786 and 1799

Note: Italicization indicates a name of possible African origin

AFRICAN NAMES	NUMBER OF INDIVIDUALS WITH THIS NAME IN 1786	NUMBER OF INDIVIDUALS WITH THIS NAME IN 1799
Juba (Male)	0	1
Sambo (Male)	1	1
Total: 2 (.96%)	Total: 1 (.48%)	2 (.64%)

BIBLICAL NAMES	NUMBER OF INDIVIDUALS WITH THIS NAME IN 1786	NUMBER OF INDIVIDUALS WITH THIS NAME IN 1799
Abram (Male)	0	1
Adam (Male)	2	1
Anna (Female)	1	1
Andrew (Male)	1	0
Ben (Male)	5	5
Charity (Female)	1	2
Cyrus (Male)	1	1
Daniel (Male)	3	4
Davy (Male)	2	4
Elias (Male)	0	1
Elijah (Male)	0	1
Ephraim (Male)	0	1
Esther (Female)	1	1
Eve or Evey (Female)	1	1
Gabriel (Male)	1	1
Gideon (Male)	0	1
Grace (Female)	2	4
Hagar (Female)	0	1
Hannah (Female)	3	6
Isaac (Male)	1	3
Israel (Male)	0	1
Jacob (Male)	1	1
James (Male)	2	4
Jemima (Female)	0	1
Joe (Male)	5	5
John or Johnny (Male)	2	3
Jonathan (Male)	0	1
Jude (Male)	0	1
Lidia or Lydia (Female)	1	2

BIBLICAL NAMES	NUMBER OF INDIVIDUALS WITH THIS NAME IN 1786	NUMBER OF INDIVIDUALS WITH THIS NAME IN 1799
Mary or Maria (Female)	0	2
Matt (Male)	1	0
Mike (Male)	1	1
Moses (Male)	2	3
Nat (Male)	3	3
Nathan (Male)	1	1
Patience (Female)	0	1
Paul (Male)	1	1
Peter (Male)	3	4
Phil (Male)	1	1
Priscilla or Silla (Female)	1	1
Rachel (Female)	1	2
Ruth (Female)	1	1
Sam (Male)	2	2
Sarah (Female)	2	2
Simon (Male)	1	2
Timothy (Male)	1	0
Tom (Male)	3	5
Uriah (Male)	1	1
Virgin (Female)	1	1
Total: 49 (23.44%)	Total: 63 (30%)	Total: 93 (29.62%)

CLASSICAL NAMES	NUMBER OF INDIVIDUALS WITH THIS NAME IN 1786	NUMBER OF INDIVIDUALS WITH THIS NAME IN 1799
Agnes (Female)	1	2
Alce (Female)	0	5
Alexander (Male)	0	1
Augusta (Female)	0	1
Caesar (Male)	1	1
Cloe (Female)	1	1
Cornelia (Female)	1	0
Cupid (Male)	1	0
Daphne (Female)	3	3
Darcus (Female)	1	2
Diana (Female)	0	2
Eneas (Male)	0	1
Flora (Female)	1	1

TABLE 12 (*continued*)

CLASSICAL NAMES	NUMBER OF INDIVIDUALS WITH THIS NAME IN 1786	NUMBER OF INDIVIDUALS WITH THIS NAME IN 1799
Hercules (Male)	1	0
Julia (Female)	0	1
Julius (Male)	0	1
Jupiter (Male)	1	0
Leanthe (Female)	0	1
Lucretia (Female)	1	1
Marcus (Male)	0	1
Paris (Male)	1	0
Phoebe (Female)	1	1
Phoenix (Male)	0	1
Sabine (Female)	0	1
Silvia (Female)	1	1
Total: 25 (11.96%)	Total: 16 (7.62%)	Total: 29 (9.24%)

ENGLISH NAMES	NUMBER OF INDIVIDUALS WITH THIS NAME IN 1786	NUMBER OF INDIVIDUALS WITH THIS NAME IN 1799
Aggy (Female)	1	0
Alice (Female)	4	0
Ambrose (Male)	1	1
Amy or Amie (Female)	1	1
Anderson (Male)	0	1
Anthony (Male)	1	0
Austin (Male)	1	0
Barbara (Female)	0	1
Barbary (Female)	0	1
Bartley (Female)	0	1
Beck (Female)	1	1
Bett or Betty (Female)	5	5
Bill or Billy (Male)	3	2
Bob (Male)	0	1
Burwell (Male)	0	1
Caroline (Female)	1	1
Cecelia (Female)	0	2
Charles (Male)	1	4
Charlotte (Female)	1	1
Christopher (Male)	1	2

ENGLISH NAMES	NUMBER OF INDIVIDUALS WITH THIS NAME IN 1786	NUMBER OF INDIVIDUALS WITH THIS NAME IN 1799
Cynthia (Female)	1	0
Delia (Female)	1	2
Dennis (Male)	0	2
Dick (Male)	1	2
Doll or Dolly (Female)	5	4
Edmund (Male)	1	0
Edy (Female)	1	0
Eliza (Female)	0	1
Elizabeth (Female)	0	1
Elly (Female)	1	0
Emery (Male)	0	1
Fanny (Female)	2	2
Felicia (Female)	0	1
Fendal (Male)	0	1
Frank (Male)	2	2
George (Male)	1	4
Giles (Male)	1	0
Godfrey (Male)	1	1
Gus (Male)	0	1
Guy (Male)	0	1
Hanson (Male)	1	1
Harry (Male)	1	1
Henriette (Female)	0	1
Henry (Male)	0	2
Isbel (Female)	1	1
Jack (Male)	6	5
Jamie (Male)	0	1
Jenny (Female)	4	4
Judy (Female)	3	4
Kate (Female)	3	4
Kitty (Female)	2	1
Laurence or Lawrence (Male)	1	1
Letty (Female)	2	2
Lewis (Male)	0	1
Lilly (Female)	1	0
Lucinda (Female)	0	1
Lucy (Female)	5	8

TABLE 12 (*continued*)

ENGLISH NAMES	NUMBER OF INDIVIDUALS WITH THIS NAME IN 1786	NUMBER OF INDIVIDUALS WITH THIS NAME IN 1799
Martin (Male)	0	1
Matilda or Myrtilla (Female)	1	3
Milly (Female)	2	3
Moll or Molly (Female)	4	5
Morgan (Male)	0	1
Morris (Male)	2	0
Nancy (Female)	2	10
Ned (Male)	3	3
Nelly (Female)	0	1
Oliver (Male)	0	1
Pat or Patty (Female)	1	1
Peg (Female)	3	4
Penny (Female)	1	2
Polly (Female)	0	3
Ralph (Male)	0	1
Randolph (Male)	0	1
Robert (Male)	1	0
Robin (Male)	1	1
Roger (Male)	0	1
Rose (Female)	1	1
Sall or Sally (Female)	4	5
Sandy (Male)	0	1
Simms (Male)	1	1
Sophia (Female)	1	1
Spencer (Male)	0	1
Sue (Female)	1	1
Tomison (Female)	0	1
Townshend (Male)	0	1
Will (Male)	7	3
Wilson (Male)	1	1
Total: 87 (41.63%)	Total: 104 (49.52%)	Total: 149 (47.45%)

NAMES BASED ON OCCUPATIONS	NUMBER OF INDIVIDUALS WITH THIS NAME IN 1786	NUMBER OF INDIVIDUALS WITH THIS NAME IN 1799
Boatswain (Male)	2	1
Forrister or Forrester (Male)	1	1
Gunner (Male)	1	1
Nanny (Female)	1	1
Total: 4 (1.91%)	Total: 5 (2.38%)	Total: 4 (1.27%)

NAMES BASED ON PLACES	NUMBER OF INDIVIDUALS WITH THIS NAME IN 1786	NUMBER OF INDIVIDUALS WITH THIS NAME IN 1799
Bath (Male)	1	0
Bristol (Male)	1	0
Brunswick (Male)	1	0
Delphy (Female)	1	0
Dundee (Male)	0	1
Essex (Male)	1	0
London (Male)	1	1
Richmond (Male)	1	1
Total: 8 (3.83%)	Total: 7 (3.33%)	Total: 4 (1.27%)

NAMES OF UNKNOWN ORIGINS	NUMBER OF INDIVIDUALS WITH THIS NAME IN 1786	NUMBER OF INDIVIDUALS WITH THIS NAME IN 1799
Abbay (Female)[1]	0	1
Alla or Ally (Female)	1	1
Breechy (Male)	1	1
Briney (Male)	0	1
Crager (Male)	1	0
Dolshy (Female)	0	1
Elvey (Female)	0	1
Gutridge (Male)	0	1
Hellam (Male)	0	1
Henky (Male)	0	1
Hukey (Female)	0	1
Isras (Male)	0	1
Lavina (Female)	0	1
Mima	1	1
Mucles (Male)	0	1
Murria (Female)	1	0
Opey or Oney (Female)	1	1
Paschall (Male)	0	1

TABLE 12 (*continued*)

NAMES OF UNKNOWN ORIGINS	NUMBER OF INDIVIDUALS WITH THIS NAME IN 1786	NUMBER OF INDIVIDUALS WITH THIS NAME IN 1799
Rainey (Female)	0	1
Raison (Female)	0	1
Renney (Female)	0	1
Sabra (Female)	1	0
Sackey or Sacky (Female)	1	1
Savary (Female)	0	1
Schomberg (Male)	1	0
Sinah (Female)	1	1
Siss (Female)	0	2
Stately (Male)	0	1
Suck or Suckey (Female)	2	5
Teney (Female)[2]	0	1
Urinah (Female)	0	1
Vina or Viner (Female)	1	1
Winny (Female)	1	0
Total: 33 (15.79%)	Total: 14 (6.67%)	Total: 33 (10.51%)

Sources: 1786 Slave List; 1799 Slave Lists.

1. Holloway, "Africanisms in African American Names in the United States," 85, 87, 88.

2. Possibly a derivation of the name Tinah. See ibid., 88.

NOTES

The roughly thirty years when I was doing research for and writing this book were a time of almost constant change in the status of the surviving papers from George Washington. When I began, the staff at Mount Vernon made regular use of the *Writings of George Washington,* which were published in honor of Washington's two hundredth birthday between the years 1931 and 1944. With the exception of an occasional footnote, these thirty-nine volumes only included Washington's outgoing correspondence. Looking for the incoming mail around a given topic or incident involved going through a variety of media, including microfilms of the Washington Papers at the Library of Congress, and typescripts or photocopies of letters in private collections or at other libraries.

In those early days, we had just given up using the four-volume set of Washington's diaries from the early twentieth century and had started using a brand-new six-volume set, published between 1976 and 1979 by the Washington Papers Editorial Project at the University of Virginia. This project, financially supported by Mount Vernon's governing board since the beginning and still ongoing, is producing the definitive version of Washington's papers, done to the current standards in the field of documentary editing. The project includes both Washington's incoming and outgoing correspondence, as well copious footnotes identifying people, places, and events mentioned in the text. The project plans to complete its work within the next ten years or so.

In the meantime, those papers already published are available in both hardcover versions and online at several websites: Library of Congress (https://www.loc .gov/collections/george-washington-papers/); National Archives (https.founders .archives.gov/about/Washington); and the University of Virginia Press (rotunda .upress.virginia.edu/founders/GEWN.html). Washington's financial papers were only available as typescripts, microfilm, or photostats of the original documents in the early days of this project. Within the last few years, the Washington Papers Project has made them a priority, and they are now also available online at financial .gwpapers.org.

All of this serves as background and an explanation for the variety of sources mentioned in the endnotes for this book. The papers I examined to learn about George Washington and slavery at Mount Vernon were in a wide variety of formats over the years. Sometimes I looked at a given document in several formats at different times. In preparing for publication, I have tried to catch places where I am quoting from differing versions of the same source, and tried to get them from the newest edition, but it was something of a Herculean task—and I wanted to get the book out before I get any older. My apologies to the readers.

Abbreviations

AW	Anthony Whiting
FBW	Fanny Bassett Washington
FWSNL	Fred W. Smith National Library for the Study of George Washington, Mount Vernon, Virginia
GAW	George Augustine Washington
GW	George Washington
GWD	*Diaries of George Washington* (6 vols., 1976–79)
GWP.Col.Series	*Papers of George Washington, Colonial Series*
GWP.Con.Series	*Papers of George Washington, Confederation Series*
GWP.Pres.Series	*Papers of George Washington, Presidential Series*
GWP.Ret.Series	*Paper of George Washington, Retirement Series*
GWP.Rev.Series	*Papers of George Washington, Revolutionary War Series*
GWPC	George Washington Parke Custis
GWW	*Writings of George Washington*
LW	Lund Washington
MVLA	Mount Vernon Ladies' Association
MW	Martha Washington
NCL	Nelly Custis Lewis
OED	*Oxford English Dictionary*
WHAB	"Washington's Household Account Book, 1793–1797"
WP	William Pearce

Preface

1. Innes, "Fulfilling John Smith's Vision," 10.

2. See, for example, Daniel Kovalik, "Our Original Sin," *Pittsburgh Post-Gazette,* 16 March 2012, http://www.post-gazette.com/stories/opinion/perspectives/our-original-sin-401000, or Phil Ebersole, "Slavery Was America's Original Sin," Phil Ebersole's Blog, 5 July 2011, http://philebersole.wordpress.com/2011/07/05/

3. Farrand, *Records of the Federal Convention of 1787,* 2:370.

4. Abraham Lincoln, Second Inaugural Address, 4 March 1865, Lincoln, *Lincoln: Speeches and Writings,* 687.

Introduction

1. GW to WP, 23 November 1794, *GWP.Pres.Series,* 17:203.

2. Griffith, *Rev. Morgan John Rhys,* 99.

3. Lindsay Lowe, "How Many People Visit Graceland Every Year?" *Parade,* 16 August 2014, http://parade.com/327562/linzlowe/how-many-people-visit

-graceland-every-year/; Kathy Turner, "Hearst Castle Visits Rise Along with SLO County's Fortunes," *The Tribune* (San Luis Obispo, CA), 21 January 2015, www.sanluisobispo.com/news/local/community/cambrian/article39509952 .html.

4. Nicholls, "Alexandria and African Americans in the Age of Washington," 2–3; Jim Mackay, "Alexandria Housed over 270 Taverns," *Mount Vernon (Virginia) Gazette,* 14 November 1996.

5. Miller, *Pen Portraits,* 33, 37, 38–39.

6. Ibid., 39–40.

7. Ibid., 17. For the identities of John and Thomas Kirkpatrick and the former's affiliation with George Washington, see *GWP.Col.Series,* 2:108n25; 6:380n14.

8. Rice, *Nature and History,* 158–59. For an unfortunate incident involving Washington's great-grandfather John Washington and local Indians, see ibid., 147–148, and Hoppin, *The Washington Ancestry,* 1:188–94.

9. For an overview of the economic system in Virginia in Washington's lifetime, see Ragsdale, *A Planters' Republic,* especially the first chapter. For the quotation, see ibid., 20.

10. Walsh, *Motives of Honor, Pleasure, and Profit,* 255–56, 463–71, 521, 534–36.

11. GW to Robert Cary & Co., 1[–6] August 1761, *GWP.Col.Series,* 7:61–62. For the order of the liquor case, see ibid., 6:463; 7:27.

12. Ellis, *His Excellency,* 49–50.

13. GW to Robert Cary & Co., 20 September 1765, *GWP.Col.Series,* 7:398–402. See also GW to James Gildart, 20 September 1765, ibid., 7:397.

14. For a good overview of the changes to George Washington's agricultural practices over his lifetime, see Fusonie and Fusonie, *George Washington: Pioneer Farmer.*

15. Ellis, *His Excellency,* 52–53.

16. GW to Arthur Young, 1 November 1787, *GWW,* 29:297.

17. GW to Arthur Young, 4 December 1788, ibid., 30:152.

18. GW to Henry Lee, 16 October 1793, ibid., 33:132–33.

19. Riley, "To Build a Barn," 32–37; Fusonie and Fusonie, *George Washington: Pioneer Farmer,* 19–22.

20. Since about the late 1960s, the standard historical interpretation has been the following: the first Africans to arrive in Virginia in 1619, and for the next few decades, were not slaves and probably had the status of indentured servants. Over the middle decades of the 1600s, however, English settlers faced more work than they could do themselves. As civil war and later improved economic conditions in their home country dried up the supply of immigrant servants willing to work for their passage to America, the colonists tapped into an existing labor pipeline—the slave trade on the African coast. The belief was that the status of these unwilling African immigrants gradually deteriorated as their numbers increased. By the last decades of the seventeenth century, virtually all were enslaved. As mentioned in the body of the text, almost all of these assumptions have been disproven by more recent research. For examples of the earlier interpretation, see Jordan, *White over Black,* 44–98, and Morgan, *American Slavery, American Freedom.*

21. Act 12: "Negro Womens Children to Serve According to the Condition of the Mother," December 1662; act 3: "An Act Declaring That Baptisme of Slaves Doth

Not Exempt Them from Bondage," September 1667; act 1: "An Act about the Casuall Killing of Slaves," October 1669; act 8: "An Act for the Apprehension and Suppression of Runaways, Negroes, and Slaves," September 1672, Virginia, *Statutes at Large,* 2:170, 260, 270, 299.

22. Coombs, "Beyond the 'Origins Debate,'" 258–59, 262, 258 (quotation).

23. Pettigrew, "Transatlantic Politics and the Africanization of Virginia's Labor Force," 280–81.

24. Eltis and Richardson, *Atlas of the Transatlantic Slave Trade,* 200.

25. Sweig, *Slavery in Fairfax County,* 4, 8, 15.

26. Toner, *Wills,* 13–16. Historian John Coombs has compiled a comprehensive database of Virginia slaveholders, which shows that George Washington's great-grandfather John, as well as his grandfather Lawrence and great-uncle John Washington II, all owned slaves. This information was gleaned from Westmoreland County court records and shared with historian Lorena Walsh, who very kindly passed it along to me, via Richard Holway, one of the editors at the University of Virginia Press, 28 July 2010.

27. Warren, "The Childhood of George Washington," 5786–87.

28. Zagarri, *David Humphreys' "Life of General Washington,"* 6.

29. For the slaves inherited by Washington from his father, see Ford, *Wills,* 42, 42n, and *GWP.Col.Series,* 7:173n.

30. For the slaves inherited from Lawrence Washington's estate, see *GWP.Col.Series,* 1:231; 7:172. Lawrence's widow, Ann Fairfax Washington Lee, leased both the land at Mount Vernon and her share of the slaves there to George Washington between 1754 and her death, at which point the land was inherited by him, while the slaves were divided among the five surviving Washington brothers. See ibid., 7:4; 9n60, 172–74. Lawrence's father-in-law, William Fairfax of Belvoir Plantation, had married as his second wife Deborah Clarke, whose brother Gedney Clarke, Sr., was a prominent businessman in Barbados, with a far-flung empire in both North America and the Caribbean. Clarke was involved in legal and illegal aspects of the slave trade in both English and Dutch colonies, an enterprise that drew in William Fairfax. For more on Clarke, see Smith, *Slavery, Family and Gentry Capitalism in the British Atlantic,* 91–138. A business ledger from the Fairfax family, acquired by Mount Vernon in 2013, contains about fifteen pages of an account with Gedney Clarke in the 1740s. It includes numerous transactions involving the sale of slaves from Barbados in Virginia, among whom were two boys and two girls, all unnamed, to George Washington's older half-brother, Lawrence Washington, for the sum of one hundred pounds. Fairfax Family Ledger, 1742–72, bound manuscript, FWSNL. George Washington may also have acquired an additional slave by inheritance in 1762, although the circumstances of that acquisition are unclear. There was some confusion about whether the young man in question, Davy, was part of the estate of Martha Washington's father, who died in 1756, or that of her first husband, who died the following year, and several letters and conversations were necessary to determine whether Davy would come to Mount Vernon, where Mrs. Washington wanted to train him as a gardener. GW to William Dandridge, 20 May 1762, *GWP.Col.Series,* 7:133, 133n1, 134n2.

31. For slaves Washington purchased prior to his marriage (at least one in 1754, at least four in 1755, five in 1756, an unknown number in 1757, and one in 1758), see

Ledger A, October 31, 1754, January 9, February 14, May 25, 1755, November 27, 1756, February 13, April 30, 1757, January 6, 1758, 10a, 11, 18a, 19a, 21a, 31a, 33a, 34a, 37a, bound photostat, FWSNL, and *GWP.Col.Series,* 1:313n4; 2:276; 3:58n7; 4:96–97, 98n2, 108.

32. Walsh, *Motives of Honor, Pleasure, and Profit,* 440–47. Walsh further notes that production fell on the Custis estates following Martha's marriage to George Washington, a fact Walsh attributes to several factors including the "absence of Custis's careful oversight in sorting and packing" the tobacco crop and "high levels of anxiety among the enslaved," who were being separated as the new Mrs. Washington brought slaves to Mount Vernon. Ibid., 448.

33. For all the slaves who were part of the dower share of the Custis estate, and the smaller number who came to Mount Vernon on the Washingtons' marriage (three Custis slaves—Julius, Moll, and Rose—accompanied the new family to Mount Vernon, in order to look after Mrs. Washington's children), see Washington, *"Worthy Partner,"* 105–7, 126. For twenty-two dower slaves (seven men, nine women, and six children) being brought up to Mount Vernon from the Custis plantations in November 1770, see *GWP.Col.Series,* 7:67n5; 8:400–401, 401n2.

34. Gunderson and Gampel, "Married Women's Legal Status in Eighteenth-Century New York and Virginia," 116.

35. For Virginia law concerning the disposition of slaves in intestate estates, see Virginia, *Statutes at Large,* 5:444–46; 12:140, 145–46.

36. For slaves purchased by Washington following his marriage (there were at least fifteen in 1759, an unknown number in 1761, ten in 1762, thirteen in 1764, five in 1767, two in 1770, one in 1771, three in 1772, four in 1773, and two in 1775), see *GWP.Col. Series,* 6:198, 200n15, 313, 314nn3, 4, 321, 321n8; 7:4, 9n67, 62, 66, 106, 109, 110, 299, 300n17, 304–5, 336–37, 469; 8:41, 42n3, 82, 83n2, 347n6, 532n13; 9:35, 36n4, 222, 224n12, 239nn2, 4, 505n7; 10:269, 269n1, 303, 304n3, 319n21. Earlier, less complete accounts of Washington's slave purchases can be found in Mazyck, *George Washington and the Negro,* 5–6n, and Ford, *Washington as an Employer and Importer of Labor,* 8–9.

37. Sweig, "The Importation of African Slaves to the Potomac River," 514–17.

38. See entry for 25 February 1778, LW Account Book, 1772–86, typescript, 67, W-693, FWSNL.

39. See *GWD,* 12 January 1787, 5:93.

40. GW to AW, 3 March 1793, *GWW,* 32:364–65. See also GW to Howell Lewis, 11 August 1793, *GWP.Pres.Series,* 13:422, 423n18.

41. GW to Howell Lewis, 18 August 1793, *GWP.Pres.Series,* 13:487.

42. Morgan and Nicholls, "Slave Flight," 197.

43. For the fact that few of the slaves arriving in the British colonies on the American mainland had been "either born or socialized in the Caribbean," due to a prejudice against them by American slave owners, see Hall, *Slavery and African Ethnicities,* 70. Gregory O'Malley discusses the practice of bringing African slaves to West Indian ports for a very short stay, in order to recuperate from the Middle Passage, before being shipped on to ports in North America for sale. Over seventy thousand newly arrived Africans (about 2.6% of the total arriving in British colonial ports between the mid-seventeenth and early nineteenth centuries) were transshipped from the

West Indies to Britain's North American colonies. See O'Malley, *Final Passages*, 5–7, 35–60.

44. See "Chesapeake: African Coastal Origins of Slaves and Home Ports of Vessels Carrying Them, 1619–1775," in Eltis and Richardson, *Atlas of the Transatlantic Slave Trade*, 212. For an earlier source, see Minchinton et al., *Virginia Slave-Trade Statistics*, 157–89.

45. See Eltis and Richardson, *Atlas of the Transatlantic Slave Trade*, 212. For the identification of the modern countries comprising these areas, see ibid., 302, 304, 306, 307.

46. Hall, *Slavery and African Ethnicities*, 55–79. For a different take on this issue, see Smallwood, *Saltwater Slavery*, 102–5.

47. Hall, *Slavery and African Ethnicities*, 136. For evidence that, in contrast with Virginia, planters in South Carolina cared deeply about the ethnicity of the African slaves being acquired for their rice plantations and developed some decided preferences and prejudices about the traits of various ethnic groups, which are remembered to this day, see Ball, *Slaves in the Family*, 54, 70, 178–80.

48. *Maryland Gazette*, 11, 20 August 1761; the first of these ads can be found in *GWP.Col.Series*, 7:65–66.

49. Old Citizen of Fairfax County, "Mount Vernon Reminiscences," *Alexandria Gazette*, 18 January 1876; W, *Alexandria Gazette*, 25 January 1876, typescripts, FWSNL.

50. For Sambo Anderson, see Old Citizen of Fairfax County, "Mount Vernon Reminiscences," *Alexandria Gazette*, 18 January 1876, and W, *Alexandria Gazette*, 25 January 1876. For "Father Jack" as the "son of a king," see Custis, *Recollections and Private Memoirs*, 456. In this work, Martha Washington's grandson indicates that Jack's contention about his royal background was not unusual. For a period example of Africans from royal, noble, or otherwise prominent families being swept up in the slave trade, see Winter, *The Blind African Slave*, 95, 109, 130–33, 134–36, 137. For the derision shown by some African-born slaves claiming royal blood toward their fellow slaves, see Butler, *Awash in a Sea of Faith*, 157. According to historian Michael Gomez, this emphasis on royal roots in Africa, whether it can be confirmed or not, suggests that these newly enslaved people were affirming "their identity and self-worth in a pernicious environment." "Appealing to Africa" was a form of pride but also served psychologically as a way of resisting "the imposition of class and status as dictated by whites." See Gomez, *Exchanging Our Country Marks*, 239–40. For an example of a former slave claiming African royal status, see the interview with Ann Parker in Hurmence, *My Folks Don't Want Me to Talk about Slavery*, 1, 2.

51. I would like to thank my friend Fante Aw for this information, which she related in a conversation on 12 August 1995. Aw, a native of Mali, was on the staff at American University, where she dealt with international students.

52. Kay and Cary, *Slavery in North Carolina*, 146, 277; Wood, *Black Majority*, 185; Hardesty, *Unfreedom*, 35; Flexner, *I Hear America Talking*, 33; Gomez, *Black Crescent*, 146–47. My colleague Larry Earl, a renowned conveyor of African American history to visitors at museums throughout this country, was so interested in Anderson's story that he went to Nigeria to learn more about his background. In several brief conversations in the summer of 2008 and the fall of 2009, Earl indicated that his

contacts in Nigeria believe Anderson might have been Fula (also known as Fulbe or Fulani), another Islamic ethnic group found throughout West Africa but especially concentrated in Guinea. They were drawn to this conclusion based on the surviving descriptions of Anderson, specifically his tattoos. Earl promises that he will be writing up the results of his research, something to which this author is very much looking forward. For basic information about these ethnic groups, see "Fulani" and "Hausa" in *New Encyclopaedia Britannica,* 5:42, 752. For more on Islam in West Africa, see Walsh, *From Calabar to Carter's Grove,* 60–61, and Johnston, *From Slave Ship to Harvard,* 7–11.

53. Berlin, *Many Thousands Gone,* 112.

54. Elkins, *Slavery,* 92–130, 101, 103 (quotations).

55. Morgan, *Slave Counterpoint,* 18–23.

56. Gomez, *Exchanging Our Country Marks,* 23, 26–27. In contrast to Michael Gomez, Alan Taylor argues that nine out of ten slaves had been born in Virginia by as early as 1765. Taylor, *The Internal Enemy,* 20.

57. For an examination of the kinds of cultural survivals brought to Virginia by enslaved Africans, see Walsh, *From Calabar to Carter's Grove,* 81–108. For the making and use of "head baskets" at Landon Carter's plantation, Sabine Hall, see Carter, *Diary,* 9 August 1758; 15 November 1770; 6 November 1771; 12 December 1774, 1:236, 523; 2:638–39, 895. According to these references by Carter, head baskets were capable of holding two bushels of produce. How common their use might have been in the rest of Virginia is unknown, but the "astonishment" of one of Carter's guests, his own manager from Rippon Hall, at seeing "the wenches merely running . . . for more than a mile" with baskets of corn on their heads suggests that it was not widely practiced.

58. Windley, *Runaway Slave Advertisements,* 34.

59. For the purchase of Billy and Frank Lee from Mary Smith Ball Lee, a childless widow, following the death of her husband, Colonel John Lee, see the entry for 3 May 1768, *GWP.Col.Series,* 8:82, 83n2. For more on Will and Frank's original owners, see "Colonel John Lee," in Lee, *Lee of Virginia,* 285–87.

60. For what happened to the Washington slaves after their emancipation, see Medford, "Beyond Mount Vernon." Readers interested in an excellent study of both slavery and free black labor at Mount Vernon in the nineteenth century should turn to Scott Casper's *Sarah Johnson's Mount Vernon.*

61. *GWP.Rev.Series,* 2:65n; Washington, *"Worthy Partner,"* 464–65.

62. Malone, *Jefferson and His Time,* 397; Harrison, *A Presidential Legacy,* 260.

63. Watson, *Men and Times of the Revolution,* 244.

64. Sargent, Diary, 13 October 1793.

65. John Hancock to John Nicholson, 22 May 1799, *American and Other Autographs and Manuscripts, Property of a Westchester Private Collector and Various Other Owners, Public Auction, Tuesday and Wednesday, February 21 and 22 at 1:45* (New York: Parke-Bernet Galleries, 1961), 100.

66. One of the most poignant details noted by Louis-Philippe concerned the behavior of blacks and whites toward one another, which was typical of Virginia at this period but completely unacceptable to the young Frenchman, who was taken up with ideas of democracy: "Here Negroes are not considered human beings. When

they meet a white man, they greet him from a distance and with a low bow, and they often seem amazed that we [Louis-Philippe and Beaudoin] return their greeting, for no one here does so." Louis-Philippe, *Diary of My Travels,* 32. Hasty reading of the last phrase in Louis-Philippe's description might be taken to mean that white Americans never bowed, perhaps considering it a monarchist custom. Surviving Washington family manuscripts, however, confirm that white Americans did bow to one another and that this custom was a typical social nicety. See Robert Lewis, Diary, July 4–September 1, 1789, typescript, 2 August 1789, H-1199, FWSNL. Given this information, Louis-Philippe was saying that white Americans never returned the bows of slaves.

67. One problem to keep in mind when trying to "reconstruct" families based on 1786 and 1799 slave lists is that, while Washington associated mothers and children in both lists, and linked spouses together in the latter one, it is not possible to say with certainty, given factors such as shorter life expectancies and sexual exploitation, whether a given woman's husband in 1799 was the father of all her children. See George Washington, "A List . . . of All My Negroes," 18 February 1786, *GWD,* 4:277–283 (hereafter 1786 Slave List), and "Negroes Belonging to George Washington in His Own Right and by Marriage," [June 1799], and "A List of Negroes Hired from Mrs. French," [15 July 1799], *GWW,* 37:256–68, 308–9 (hereafter 1799 Slave Lists). For examples from other plantations where enslaved women had children with multiple partners, see Dunn, *A Tale of Two Plantations,* 83–84, 117, 124–25.

68. For this amazing story, see Diouf, *Dreams of Africa in Alabama.*

69. See *GWD,* 26 April 1770, 2:233, 234n, and Cash Accounts, 3 May 1770, *GWP. Col.Series,* 8:329, 329–30n3.

70. Morgan, "Three Planters and Their Slaves," 37–41. For the development of patriarchal society in the ancient Near East and Mediterranean, which was the foundation for the patriarchy of Western Europe and colonial America, see Lerner, *The Creation of Patriarchy.*

71. GW to John Robinson, [20 April 1755], *GWP.Col.Series,* 1:256–57. See also GW to Carter Burwell, [20 April 1755], ibid., 1:252–53, 254n3.

72. GW to Hector Ross, 9 October 1769, ibid., 8:256.

73. GW to James Mercer, 19 July 1773, *GWW,* 3:146–47.

74. GW to David Stuart, 11 December 1787; GW to Edmund Pendleton, 1 March 1788; GW to Charles Lee, 4 April 1788, ibid., 29:335–36, 429, 460–61.

75. Ellis, *His Excellency,* xiv.

76. Wesley Pruden, "Ethnic Cleansing of Dead White Men," *Washington Times,* 18 November 1997.

77. Jessica Chasmar, "U.Va. Professors Ask President to Stop Quoting Thomas Jefferson," *Washington Times,* 14 November 2016.

78. Northup, *12 Years a Slave,* 54–55.

79. Ibid., 106.

80. For a book-length treatment of slavery and involuntary servitude in modern-day Asia, Africa, Europe, South America, and the United States, see Batstone, *Not for Sale.* For a fascinating treatment of the continued exploitation of African Americans (and some whites) as unfree labor for about eighty years following the Civil War, see Blackmon, *Slavery by Another Name.* For United Nations policy and the

continued existence of slavery and the slave trade into the 1950s in the Arabian Peninsula, Southeast Asia, Africa, and South America, see *New Encyclopaedia Britannica,* 27:236. A great deal of information on modern-day slavery throughout the world has appeared in newspapers and on television over the past twenty years. For example, for contemporary slavery or involuntary servitude in South America and Southeast Asia, see "Children for Sale: Dateline Goes Undercover with a Human Rights Group to Expose Sex Trafficking in Cambodia," *NBC News: Dateline,* 9 January 2005, http://www.nbcnews.com/id/4038249/ns/dateline_nbc/t/children-sale/, and David Gagne, "Organized Crime Profits from Modern Slavery in Latin America," *Insight Crime,* 3 June 2016, https://www.insightcrime.org/news/analysis/how-organized-crime-profits-off-modern-slavery-in-latin-america/. For the sale of women in the former Soviet Union, see Genine Babakian, "Ex-Soviets Fall Prey to Sex Trade," *USA Today,* 12 November 1997. For possible slavery in Mauritania, see David Hecht, "Virtual Slavery," *New Republic,* 12 May 1997, 9–10, and Charles Jacobs, Samuel Cotton, and Mohamed Athie, "Master Class," *New Republic,* 16 June 1997. For slavery in the Sudan, see Samuel G. Freedman, "Christians' Indifference Makes Meegan Avery Cringe," *USA Today,* 12 November 1997; William Finnegan, "The Invisible War," *New Yorker,* 25 January 1999, 50–73; and *CBS Evening News,* 1–2 February 1999. For trafficking into the United States, see Amy O'Neill Richard, "International Trafficking in Women to the United States: A Contemporary Manifestation of Slavery and Organized Crime," Center for Intelligence, November 1999, https://www.cia.gov/library/center-for-the-study-of-intelligence/csi-publications/books-and-monographs/trafficking.pdf.

81. Len Cooper, "The Damned: Slavery Did Not End with the Civil War. One Man's Odyssey into a Nation's Secret Shame," *Washington Post,* 16 June 1996; Martha T. Moore and Martin Kasindorf, "Enslavement in America: Terrorized Immigrants Live in Bondage in 'Land of Free,'" *USA Today,* 28 July 1997.

82. Peter Carlson, "The Magazine Reader: Invisible Bondage," *Washington Post,* 26 August 2003.

1. "I Never See That Man Laugh to Show His Teeth"

1. Verme, *Seeing America and Its Great Men,* 66.

2. Maclay, *Diary,* 1 May 1790, 258.

3. Parkinson, *Tour in America,* 2:436.

4. Niemcewicz, *Under Their Vine and Fig Tree,* 87.

5. Hunter, *Quebec to Carolina in 1785–86,* 191–98; Lee, *Experiencing Mount Vernon,* 26–36, 31 (quotation).

6. Jean M. Marengale, transl., *Les carnet de David d'Angers, publies pour la premiere fois avec une introduction par André Bruel* (Paris: Plon, 1958), 133–34.

7. GW to Lieutenant Charles Smith, 24 June 1748, *GWP.Col.Series,* 5:238.

8. For examples of these, see GW, General Orders, 6 January, 3 July 1778, *GWW,* 10:271–72, 12:154, and GW, General Orders, 14 July 1775, 4 July 1777, *GWP.Rev.Series,* 1:114, 10:180.

9. GW, General Orders, 5 July 1777, *GWP.Rev.Series,* 10:194.

10. GW, General Orders, 14 May 1778, *GWW,* 11:387.

11. GW to James McHenry, 29 May 1797, *GWP.Ret.Series,* 1:159–60. For an example of Washington's nephew Bushrod Washington occupied in a similar manner during the years he owned Mount Vernon (1802–29), see excerpt from the *Cyclopedia of Useful Knowledge,* n.d. [probably 1809–36], typescript, Early Descriptions Notebook, FWSNL.

12. John Parke Custis to GW, 12 December 1779, typescript, W-1164/A-196, FWSNL. Writing at a time and place in which the practice of slavery was different from what it had been in eighteenth-century Virginia, a South Carolina planter around 1840 confirmed young Custis's opinion when he noted that it was the master who set the overall tone for life on a plantation. See Breeden, *Advice among Masters,* 31.

13. GW to Brigadier General Alexander McDougall, 25 April 1777, *GWP.Rev.Series,* 9:266.

14. GW to WP, 18 December 1793, *GWP.Pres.Series,* 14:561.

15. GW, Circular to William Stuart, Hiland Crow, and Henry McCoy, 14 July 1793, *GWP.Pres.Series,* 13:225–26.

16. GW to AW, 6 January 1793, *GWW,* 32:293.

17. GW to AW, 2 December 1792, ibid., 32:249.

18. GW to AW, 16 December 1792, ibid., 32:265.

19. GW to WP, 22 December 1793, ibid., 33:196, 207; GW to AW, 4 November 1792, ibid., 32:205; GW to GAW, 17 May 1787, *GWP.Con.Series,* 5:189; GW to AW, 2 December 1792, *GWW,* 32:249–50. For other references to weekly reports, see GW, Circular to William Stuart, Hiland Crow, and Henry McCoy, 14 July 1793, *GWP. Pres.Series,* 13:220, 224.

20. GW to AW, 24 March 1793, *GWW,* 32:402.

21. GW to AW, 2 December 1792, ibid., 32:247.

22. GW to AW, 3 February 1793, *GWP.Pres.Series,* 12:97.

23. GW to AW, 19 May 1793, *GWW,* 32:466.

24. GW to WP, 31 August 1794, ibid., 33:489.

25. GW to Reverend John Witherspoon, 8 March 1785, ibid., 28:99.

26. GW to WP, 23 November 1794, ibid., 34:43.

27. GW to Howell Lewis, 18 August 1793, ibid., 33:52.

28. "A Visit to Mount Vernon," *Parley's Magazine,* October 1838, FWSNL.

29. "Mount Vernon Reminiscences Continued," *Alexandria Gazette,* 22 January 1876, typescript, FWSNL.

30. For more on this transition, especially in the nineteenth century, see Smith, *Mastered by the Clock.*

31. Custis, *Recollections and Private Memoirs,* 427–29.

32. Green, *The Life of Ashbel Green,* 266–67.

33. Sargent, Diary, 13 October 1793; Adams, *Jefferson's Monticello,* 226; Fithian, *Journal and Letters,* 15 December 1773, 31. The use of bells to call people to meals was not limited, however, to plantations in the eighteenth century; among the objects in the kitchen of the Governor's Palace in the town of Williamsburg in 1770 was "1 hand Dinner Bell." See "Kitchen," in "Inventory of the Governor's Palace, Williamsburg, Virginia," 24 October 1770, typescript, FWSNL. Bells were also recommended for use on English farms at this period, first to wake the workers in the morning, then again a bit later when they were expected to be ready with all their equipment for the

day loaded onto wagons or sledges, prepared to set out for the fields. Anyone who was not ready at that point was to be reprimanded and a note of the infraction written in a small book by their supervisor, or "bailey." Eight or nine hours later, the bell rang again to tell the workmen to come home. See [Young], *Rural Oeconomy,* 118–19.

34. GW to George William Fairfax, 17 July 1763, *GWP.Col.Series,* 7:231.

35. Custis, *Recollections and Private Memoirs,* 446.

36. Ibid., 456–57.

37. Wiencek, *An Imperfect God,* 86, 354–55.

38. Winner, *Cheerful and Comfortable Faith,* 112, 213n60. It should be pointed out that Elizabeth Foote Washington was no inexperienced girl at the time of her marriage. Thought to have been about thirty-three years old when she moved to Mount Vernon, she would have had the opportunity to meet and spend time with many slave owners by the time she became a member of the Washington household. "Elizabeth Washington (Foote)," https://www.geni.com/people/Elizabeth-Washington /6000000004047287768, last updated 1 December 2014.

39. For the overall schedule, see Custis, *Recollections and Private Memoirs,* 514, and Berard, "Arlington and Mount Vernon," 162. For sewing, see Berard, "Arlington and Mount Vernon," 162, and Carrington, "A Visit to Mount Vernon," 201. To put Mrs. Washington's activities into context, see Clinton, *Plantation Mistress,* 20.

40. Robert E. Lee to A. Talcott, 10 April 1834, quoted in Nelligan, *Arlington House,* 204.

41. Berard, "Arlington and Mount Vernon," 163–64.

42. MW to FBW, 19 April 1791, Washington, *"Worthy Partner,"* 230.

43. GW to Joseph Whipple, 28 November 1796, *GWW,* 35:298.

44. GW to WP, 12 January 1794, ibid., 33:242.

45. MW to Elizabeth Powel, 1, 20 May 1797; MW to Elizabeth Dandridge Henley, 20 August 1797, Washington, *"Worthy Partner,"* 301, 302, 307.

46. GW to Nathaniel Ingraham, 22 March 1788, *GWP.Con.Series,* 6:170, 171n1.

47. For examples of this, see GW, "Agreement with Edward Violet," [5 August 1762], *GWP.Col.Series,* 7:145; GW to WP, 22 December 1793, *GWW,* 33:201; and GW to James Anderson (of Scotland), 7 April 1797, *GWP.Ret.Series,* 1:79–81. For overseers' wives with similar duties on Burwell family plantations, see Walsh, *From Calabar to Carter's Grove,* 123.

48. GW to WP, 4 December 1796, *GWW,* 35:306.

49. GW to AW, 12 May 1793, ibid., 32:459; MW to FBW, 29 August 1791, 1 July 1792, 4 August 1793, 2 June 1794, Washington, *"Worthy Partner,"* 233, 238–39, 250–51, 267.

50. GW to AW, 23 December 1792, *GWW,* 32:277.

51. "Articles Recd. into the Store," 18 August 1787, Mount Vernon Store Book, 1 January–31 December 1787, typescript, W-676, FWSNL. For similar work done by women on other plantations, see Fox-Genovese, *Within the Plantation Household,* 128, and Clinton, *Plantation Mistress,* 26–28.

52. MW to FBW, 22 April 1792, Washington, *"Worthy Partner,"* 237.

53. MW to FBW, [July 1789], ibid., 217.

54. MW to FBW, 29 August 1791, ibid., 233.

55. MW to FBW, 15 June 1794, ibid., 269.

56. MW to Elizabeth Powel, 20 May 1797, ibid., 302.

57. MW to FBW, 24 May 1795, ibid., 287.

58. GW to Oliver Wolcott, Jr., 1 September [1796], *GWW,* 35:202.

59. GW to Robert Dinwiddie, 29 May 1754, ibid., 1:59–60.

60. MW to FBW, 15 June 1794, Washington, *"Worthy Partner,"* 268. For an earlier mention of her unease at this living situation, see MW to FBW, 13 April 1794, ibid., 264.

61. MW to FBW, 14 July 1794, ibid., 271–72.

62. GW to Bushrod Washington, 15 January 1783, *GWW,* 26:39.

63. Hans-Axel, Comte de Ferson, quoted in Chinard, *George Washington as the French Knew Him,* 62.

64. Abigail Adams to Mary Smith Cranch, 12 July 1789, Adams, *New Letters of Abigail Adams,* 15. For a similar description by Charles Biddle, see Baker, *Washington after the Revolution,* 89.

65. Berard, "Arlington and Mount Vernon," 162.

66. Eisen, *Portraits of Washington,* 3:761.

67. Weld, *Travels through the States of North America,* 1:105–6n. One of Stuart's servants (whether hired or enslaved is unknown) had experienced Washington's temper firsthand. As the story was related by the artist, Washington, always a stickler for punctuality, had arrived at Stuart's rooms at the agreed upon time only to find that the painter was still in bed and the studio not "in order" for the work to begin. He then "flew into a Passion and gave a great Scolding to the Servant, which Stewart overheard as he came up Stairs, but on his entering the Room, he found the General Quite calm as if nothing had happened." Foster, "Caviar along the Potomac," 92–93.

68. Thomas Jefferson to Dr. Walter Jones, 2 January 1814, Bryan, *George Washington in American Literature,* 49. A particularly negative description by Jefferson of Washington as a slave owner can be found in the concluding chapter of this book.

69. Benjamin Rush to John Adams, 4 June 1812; Adams to Rush, 12 June 1812, Kaminski, *The Founders on the Founders,* 518.

70. Jack D. Warren, "George Washington," *Washington Post,* 14 February 1996.

71. Parkinson, *Tour in America,* 2:419–20.

72. Henrietta Liston, quoted in Flexner, *George Washington,* 4:435n.

73. Watson, *Men and Times of the Revolution,* 244.

74. Kolchin, *American Slavery,* 59–61. Paternalism has long been a factor influencing relationships between people in situations where one group has extraordinary control over another. By way of example, for paternalism in the contexts of both Hanoverian Ireland and the feudal estates of tsarist Russia, respectively, see Tillyard, *Aristocrats,* 189, 196–99, 203–4, 313–14, 336–37, 341, and Roosevelt, *Life on the Russian Country Estate,* 158, 173–79.

75. GW to WP, 10 May 1795, *GWW,* 34:193.

76. MW to Mary Stillson Lear, 11 November 1800, Washington, *"Worthy Partner,"* 394. For other uses of the term "family" for slaves, see also MW to FBW, [July 1789], 24 May 1795, ibid., 217, 287.

77. NCL to Elizabeth Bordley Gibson, 29 April 1823, Lewis, *George Washington's Beautiful Nelly,* 134.

78. Custis, *Recollections and Private Memoirs,* 224. Many white historians have had

problems with this story, possibly because of its racist overtones. For instance, one historian at a battlesite from the Revolution said he "wouldn't go near that story," a sentiment with which others agreed. By contrast, in a conversation with military historian Dr. Robert Selig of Hope College on 16 July 1996 about this incident, he indicated that it sounded like something that could well have happened and that he saw no reason to question its authenticity. Still, he is probably the only white historian with whom I have spoken about this who did not have a problem with the story. African Americans with whom I have discussed the tale have no such reservations and believe it probably happened.

79. Anonymous, "The Tomb of Washington," *The Rhetorical Reader,* n.d. [probably 1830s], Early Descriptions Notebook.

80. Nylander, *Our Own Snug Fireside,* 41–43.

81. Gordon-Reed, *Hemingses of Monticello,* 441.

82. Morgan, *Slave Counterpoint,* 282.

83. Abigail Adams to Mary Smith Cranch, 21 December 1800, typescript, PS-605/R-102, FWSNL.

84. Washington, *Rules of Civility,* 34.

85. GW to GWPC, 7 January 1798, *GWP.Ret.Series,* 2:5.

86. GW to GAW, 24 April 1786, *GWP.Con.Series,* 4:28, 29n1.

87. An Old Citizen of Fairfax County, "Mount Vernon Reminiscences," *Alexandria Gazette,* 18 January 1876. This story confirms others about Washington's "correctness." See Parkinson, *Tour in America,* 2:436–40.

88. GW to Elizabeth Washington Lewis, 13 September 1789, *GWP.Pres.Series,* 4:33.

89. Lear, *Letters and Recollections,* 130, 135.

90. Watson, *Men and Times of the Revolution,* 244.

91. Perkins, *Memoir of Thomas Handasyd Perkins,* 199–200.

92. Latrobe, *Virginia Journals,* 1:171.

93. GW to WP, 17 August 1794, *GWW,* 33:469.

94. See 1799 Slave Lists, 37:257. See also GW to Roger West, 19 September 1799, *GWW,* 37:367.

95. *GWD,* 13 April 1760, 1:266; Mazyck, *George Washington and the Negro,* 12–13.

96. GW to AW, 28 April, 26 May 1793, *GWW,* 32:437–38, 474–75.

97. Isaac, *Landon Carter's Uneasy Kingdom,* 187–88.

98. *GWD,* 16 May 1786, 4:330–31.

99. Ibid., 25 July 1786, 5:15–16.

100. Humphreys, "A Poem on the Death of General Washington," Humphreys, *Miscellaneous Works of David Humphreys,* 180, 180n.

101. Flexner, *George Washington,* 4:443. This incident is also described in Hirschfeld, *George Washington and Slavery,* 72, and Wiencek, *An Imperfect God,* 251.

102. Law, "Self-Portrait," 99.

103. Robert Lewis, "A Journey from Fredericksburg—Virginia to New York," 13–20 May 1789, H-1199/b, FWSNL.

104. Watson, *Men and Times of the Revolution,* 244.

105. Ford, *Washington as an Employer and Importer of Labor,* 8–9; GW to Clement Biddle, 28 July 1784, *GWP.Con.Series,* 2:14.

106. Tobias Lear to Clement Biddle, 3 May 1789, quoted in *GWW,* 30:308n.

107. Washington, *Last Will and Testament,* 4. Many years later, Washington's step-grandson, George Washington Parke Custis of Arlington Plantation (now the site of the famous national cemetery), would express a similar affection for his own valet, Philip Lee, who was the son of Mount Vernon butler Frank Lee and his wife, Lucy, the cook: "My old and favorite body servant, Philip Lee . . . is the nephew of Washington's celebrated Revolutionary follower, Will Lee. Philip is a highly intelligent, nay talented man, of gentlemanly manners, and worthy of every confidence and consideration. He will not be my slave much longer—he has been my friend for two-and-thirty years." GWPC to Silas E. Burrows, 17 February 1832, quoted in Nelligan, "'Old Arlington,'" 214.

108. Elizabeth Ambler Carrington, 27 November 1799, Lee, *Experiencing Mount Vernon,* 91.

109. AW to GW, 16 January 1793, *GWP.Pres.Series,* 12:11–12, 14n14. Charlotte's statement about not being whipped for fourteen years indicates that she was last punished in that manner in 1779, under Lund Washington's administration as farm manager during the Revolution.

110. Tobias Lear to William Prescott, 4 March 1788, typescript, PS-636/A-I, FWSNL.

111. GW to AW, 20 January 1793, *GWW,* 32:307.

112. GW to AW, 9 June 1793; GW to Tobias Lear, 21 June 1793; GW to Thomas Jefferson, 30 June 1793, ibid., 32:491, 508, 513.

113. GW to William Tilghman, 21 July 1793, ibid., 33:26.

114. GW to WP, 18 December 1793, ibid., 33:192.

115. GW to Tobias Lear, 25 September 1793, ibid., 33:104–5, 143n.

116. Law, "Self-Portrait," 93–94, 97, 99.

117. GW to WP, 20 April 1794, *GWW,* 33:336–37.

118. GW to Burgess Ball, 27 July 1794, ibid., 33:444.

119. Washington, *Rules of Civility,* 8, 11–12, 42.

120. GW to Edward Pemberton, 20 June 1788, *GWW,* 30:1.

121. Nathanael Greene to GW, 8 August 1783, Kaminski and McCaughan, *Great and Good Man,* 25.

122. Marquis de Lafayette to GW, 17 March 1790, *GWW,* 31:85, 85n.

123. Anne M. Johnson, email communication with author, 19 June 2002.

124. GW to Mary Ball Washington, 15 February 1787, *GWW,* 29:160–61.

125. GW, "Household Expenses, [New York]," 15–22 March 1790, *GWP.Pres.Series,* 5:233.

126. Gordon-Reed, *Hemingses of Monticello,* 171, 178, 179, 180, 181, 209, 236, 237–41, 242, 259, 287, 298, 450, 452, 496, 549.

127. Tobias Lear to GW, 5 April 1791, *GWP.Pres.Series,* 8:67.

128. GW to Tobias Lear, 12 April 1791, ibid., 8:85–86.

129. Ibid.

130. MW to FBW, 19 April 1791, Washington, *"Worthy Partner,"* 230.

131. When Fanny Bassett Washington's first husband, George Augustine Washington, died, he left to her and her heirs those slaves who were inherited from her father's bequest to the young couple. Those individuals were to be divided among Fanny's

heirs when the children either reached their majority or were married, whichever came first. Tobias Lear, as the children's stepfather, would have supervised and been responsible for those slaves until the time came for their dispersal. In his will, George Augustine freed one slave, "my man Charles," leaving him some of George Augustine's clothing (a "Casimire blue coat, my strip'd Great Coat and all my shirts not herein particularly & otherwise disposed of") and an annual payment of ten pounds. See "Copy of the Last Will and Testament of George Augustine Washington," [1795], photocopy, RM-530/MS-4533, FWSNL. George Washington bequeathed Tobias Lear the lifetime use of Walnut Tree Farm, a 360-acre property he was renting to Lear. At Lear's death, the small farm, which was part of a 2,077-acre tract, was to be divided between Fanny's surviving sons with George Augustine Washington. Prussing, *The Estate of George Washington, Deceased,* 59, 62–63, 165–66. At the time of Washington's death, at least three Mount Vernon slaves were married to enslaved people on Lear's rented farm: Grace at the Mansion House Farm was the wife of "Mr Lear's Juba," while twenty-six-year-old Alce (or Alice) and twenty-year-old Betty at River Farm were the wives of "Lears John" and "Lears Reuben," respectively. See 1799 Slave Lists, 37:257, 262.

132. Tobias Lear to William Prescott, 4 March 1788, "A Lear Letter," 23.

133. Tobias Lear to GW, 24 April 1791, *GWP.Pres.Series,* 8:131–32. While this was probably the worst case of duplicity toward a slave or group of slaves, it was not the only such incident to show up in the surviving Washington papers. For another example, see GW to James McHenry, [11 November] 1786; Edward Moyston to GW, 4 April 1787, *GWP.Con.Series,* 4:358–59, 359n1, 5:123.

134. See, for example, Flexner, *George Washington,* 4:112–25; Henriques, *Realistic Visionary,* 158–64; Thompson, *"In the Hands of a Good Providence,"* 84–90; Morgan, "To Get Quit of Negroes"; Pogue, "George Washington and the Politics of Slavery"; and Wiencek, *An Imperfect God.*

2. "A Plant of Rapid Growth"

1. Wiencek, *An Imperfect God,* 178–88. Similarly, two years earlier, Washington, in his role as one of the executors for the estate of Thomas Colvill, paid five shillings for "advertising Sale of Colo. Colvills Negroes." See Ledger A, 242a, 246.

2. The quotation is taken from GW, "To Carter Braxton Esqr. and the Gentn Trustees of Colo. B. Moore," 23 January 1771, *GWP.Col.Series,* 8:430n2; for further information on this transaction, see ibid., 8:427, 429; 9:31, 32n11, 44–45.

3. Nelson, *A Blessed Company,* 221.

4. Genesis 21:10–12. Biblical quotations used here are taken from the King James Version with which Washington and his contemporaries would have been familiar.

5. Genesis 37:27–28, 36; 39:1.

6. See, for example, Deuteronomy 15:15; 16:12; 24:18, 22.

7. Revelation 18:13.

8. For enslavement of war captives, see Deuteronomy 20:10–15. For debt slavery, see 2 Kings 4:1–7.

9. Philemon, verse 16.

10. 1 Timothy 6:1–2.

11. Genesis 1:27.

12. Galatians 3:25, 28.

13. Aesop, *Fables,* 119–20, 147–49, 153–54.

14. George Mason to Colonel George [William] Fairfax and GW, 23 December 1765, *GWP.Col.Series,* 7:424–25n2.

15. Fairfax County Resolves, [18 July 1774], ibid., 10:125, 127n.

16. GW to George William Fairfax, 10[–15] June 1774, ibid., 10:97.

17. GW, General Orders, 27 February 1776, *GWP.Rev.Series,* 3:379.

18. GW, General Orders, 2 July 1776, ibid., 5:180.

19. Samuel Johnson, "Quotes on Slavery," Samuel Johnson Sound Bite Page, http://samueljohnson.com/slavery.html.

20. Cresswell, *Journal,* 13 July 1777, 251–52.

21. GW to James Madison, 2 March 1788, *GWW,* 29:431.

22. GW to LW, 15 August 1778, ibid., 12:327.

23. GW to LW, 24[–26] February 1779, ibid., 14:147–49.

24. GW to John Fowler, 2 February 1788, ibid., 29:398.

25. Berlin, *Many Thousands Gone,* 8, 47.

26. GW, General Orders, 31 October, 12 November 1775, *GWW,* 4:57, 86. See also *GWW,* 4:8n.

27. GW to John Hancock, 31 December 1775, ibid., 4:195.

28. GW to Major General William Heath, 29 June 1780, ibid., 19:93. According to historian Robert A. Selig, the Continental Army exhibited a degree of integration not reached by the American army again for two hundred years until after World War II. See Selig, "The Revolution's Black Soldiers."

29. For Laurens's plan, see Wiencek, *An Imperfect God,* 221–35.

30. GW to Lieutenant Colonel John Laurens, 18 February 1782, *GWW,* 24:4, 88n.

31. Alexander Hamilton, "Attendance at a Meeting of the Society for Promoting the Manumission of Slaves," 4 February 1785; Hamilton, "Memorial to Abolish the Slave Trade," 13 March 1786, Hamilton, *The Papers of Alexander Hamilton,* 597, 654.

32. Marquis de Lafayette to Alexander Hamilton, 13 April 1785, ibid., 604. For correspondence between Washington and Lafayette on the topic of slavery, see Marquis de Lafayette to GW, 5 February 1783; GW to Lafayette, 5 April 1783, *GWW,* 26:300n, 300; and Lafayette to GW, 6 February 1786, *GWP.Con.Series,* 3:121, 544. For a description of Washington and Lafayette discussing the manumission of slaves at Mount Vernon, see William Gordon to GW, 30 August 1784, *GWP.Con.Series,* 2:64.

33. Wheatley, *Poems of Phillis Wheatley,* xi–xv; *GWP.Rev.Series,* 2:243–44n.

34. Phillis Wheatley to GW, [26 October 1775], and enclosure, *GWP.Rev.Series,* 2:242–43.

35. GW to Phillis Wheatley, 28 February 1776, ibid., 3:387. While earlier sources suggested that Wheatley (whose given name is variously given as Phyllis and Phillis) and Washington did meet at Cambridge in March 1776, when she is said to have been given a "very courteous reception," more recent scholarship indicates that Wheatley was in Providence, Rhode Island, at this time and would very likely not have tried to cross British lines to reach Washington's headquarters before the British left Boston on 17 March 1776. According to this source, if Washington and Wheatley were able to meet, it would most likely have been in Providence during the former's stay there

in early April 1776, as he made his way south to New York City. If nothing else, she may have been in the crowds of people greeting him in Providence on that visit. For those earlier sources, see Wheatley, *Poems of Phillis Wheatley,* xv, and *GWP.Rev.Series,* 2:244n. The more recent source is Carretta, *Phillis Wheatley,* 157.

36. See Griffin, *Catalogue of the Washington Collection,* 22, 35, 48, 72, 179, 180, 195. For an analysis of Washington's slavery tracts, see Furstenberg, "Atlantic Slavery, Atlantic Freedom."

37. Coke, *Extracts of the Journals,* 45.

38. James Madison to GW, 11 November 1785, *GWP.Con.Series,* 3:355–56, 357n5.

39. See Thompson, *"In the Hands of a Good Providence,"* 156–57.

40. Robert Pleasants to GW, 11 December 1785, *GWP.Con.Series,* 3:449–51, 451n.

41. Griffith, *Rev. Morgan John Rhys,* 99. Rhys's words associating the Custis slaves with entail indicate that he did not understand that they were held under laws dealing with cases where there was no will (intestate estates), which sought to protect the inheritance of minor children from loss by either their mother, any subsequent husband she might have, or other guardian. Entail involved setting up an estate in such a way as to keep certain properties within one family or line of descendants.

42. GW to Robert Morris, 12 April 1786, *GWP.Con.Series,* 4:16.

43. Tench Tilghman to GW, 25, 31 August 1785; GW to Tilghman, 29 August 1785, *GWP.Con.Series,* 3:205, 214, 208–9. Tilghman was not the only person to see a resemblance between Chinese and Native Americans. In 1818, the Tuscaroras met a Chinese merchant named Punqua Wingchong in New York and were reportedly "so struck with his physiognomy, that they insisted he was one of their people. They made earnest inquiry who he was, and were astonished on being told that he was a Chinese." The *Edinburgh Magazine and Literary Miscellany,* where the story was published, concluded, "Such is the physiognomonical resemblance of these races of Americans and Asiatics." See "The Servant Left Behind," *Boston 1775,* 17 November 2013, http://boston1775blogspot.com/.

44. For examples of the Chinese goods acquired by the Washingtons, see Cadou, *The George Washington Collection,* 44–45, 54–55, 108–9, 110–11, 149, 191, 194, 196–97, 247, 258. Eleven years after his written exchange with Tilghman, Washington was discussing tensions on the border between the United States and the Cherokee nation with his secretary of state, Timothy Pickering, which led him to comment, "But I believe scarcely any thing short of a Chinese wall, or a line of troops, will restrain Land jobbers, and the encroachment of settlers upon the Indian territory." The reference to the "Chinese wall" suggests that by that time, if not earlier, Washington had learned even more about the long and storied history of the Chinese empire. See GW to Timothy Pickering, 1 July 1796, *GWW,* 35:112.

45. Marquis de Lafayette to GW, 10 February [1786]; GW to Thomas Hutchins, 20 August 1786; Hutchins to GW, 8 November 1786; GW to Richard Butler, 27 November 1786; James Madison to GW, 18 March 1787; GW to Madison, 31 March 1787; Butler to GW, 30 November 1787; "Richard Butler's Indian Vocabulary," [ca. 30 November 1787]; "Extract of Letter from Richard Butler," [ca. 30 November 1787], *GWP.Con.Series,* 3:555–56; 4:222, 343–44, 398–400; 5:92, 94n1, 116, 456, 456–58n, 458–60, 461–64.

46. GW to Richard Butler, 10 January 1788, ibid., 6:26–27.

47. GW to Jonathan Edwards, 28 August 1788, ibid., 6:479–80, 480n1.

48. GW to Marquis de Lafayette, 10 January 1788, ibid., 6:29–31. For other correspondence on the subject of Native American languages and origins, see John Ettwein to GW, 28 March 1788; GW to Jonathan Edwards, 28 August 1788, *GWP.Con.Series*, 6:181–82, 479–80.

49. Charles Willson Peale to Robert Patterson, 7 October 1791; Peale, "Account of a Black Man Turned White," 31 October 1791, Peale, *Selected Papers*, 1:619–21; 5:185–86.

50. Many readers may be familiar with vitiligo, a disease from which singer Michael Jackson suffered; there is no cure. For more on this disease, see "Vitiligo: Symptoms and Causes," Mayo Clinic, 8 March 2018, https:www.mayoclinic.org/diseases -conditions/vitiligo/symptoms-causes/syc-203559012.

51. GW to Joseph Reed, 15 February 1780; GW to Reverend William Smith, [15 November 1780]; GW to Dr. Thomas Bond, 28 December 1781; GW to the American Philosophical Society, 13 December 1783; GW to Thomas Jefferson, 31 December 1793, *GWW*, 18:11–12, 11n19, 20:348–49, 348n95, 23:412–13, 27:269–70, 33:221; GW to Timothy Pickering, 6 November 1797, *GWP.Ret.Series*, 1:461, 461n3. See also *GWW*, 35:335n76, for a description of the Washingtons attending a special church service at which Benjamin Rush gave the eulogy for the Philosophical Society's late president David Rittenhouse.

52. Prussing, *The Estate of George Washington, Deceased,* 412.

53. For Peale's portraits of Washington in this period, see Richardson, Hindle, and Miller, *Charles Willson Peale and His World,* 75, 77, 78, 190, 248, 249, 259; for Washington's visits, gifts, and subscriptions to Peale's museum, see ibid., 80, 81, 88, 142, 143, 145, 159.

54. "Virginia, Winchester, July 1. Curious Phenomena," *Independent Gazetteer* (Philadelphia), 13 July 1796.

55. "Extract of a Letter from a Gentleman in Philadelphia, to His Friend in This City, Respecting Henry Moss, Whom We Gave Some Account of in Our Paper of Monday," *Minerva, and Mercantile Evening Advertiser* (New York), 12 October 1796.

56. Melish, *Disowning Slavery,* 140–62; Martin, *White African Body,* 34–43.

57. GW to James McHenry, 30 September 1798, *GWP.Ret.Series*, 3:59.

58. Martin, *White African Body,* 44.

59. GW to James Athill, 4 September 1798, *GWP.Ret.Series*, 2:584.

60. For the early statements, see *GWD*, 23 March, 4 April 1748, 1:13, 18. For examples from the French and Indian War and the Revolution, see GW to Captains William Cocke and John Ashby, 10 October 1755, *GWW*, 1:193–94, 193n; GW to George William Fairfax, 10[–15] June 1774, *GWP.Col.Series*, 10:96, 97; and GW to Major General Robert Howe, 13 January 1778, *GWP.Rev.Series*, 13:221–22.

61. See Thompson, "*In the Hands of a Good Providence,*" 101–2, 157–58, 167–68.

62. GW to Edmund Pendleton, 22 January 1795, *GWW*, 34:99–100.

63. NCL to Elizabeth Bordley Gibson, 1 December 1826, typescript, FWSNL; NCL to Jared Sparks, 26 February 1833, Sparks, *Life of George Washington,* 522.

64. For some of the other reasons for the change in Washington's communion practices, see Thompson, "*In the Hands of a Good Providence,*" 79–84.

65. GW to William Triplett, 25 September 1786, *GWW*, 29:18.

66. Thomas Jefferson, "Notes on a Conversation with Edmund Randolph," [after 1795], Jefferson, *The Papers of Thomas Jefferson,* 28:568.

67. GW to Samuel Langdon, 28 September 1789, *GWP.Pres.Series,* 4:104.

3. "To Remain Constantly with the People"

1. NCL to Elizabeth Bordley Gibson, 29 April 1823, Lewis, *George Washington's Beautiful Nelly,* 133.

2. The primary sources on these individuals are George Washington's papers, diaries, and financial records. Much of this information is gathered in Mary V. Thompson, comp., "A Compendium of Hired and Indentured Laborers at George Washington's Mount Vernon," 16 October 2003–12 January 2016, unpublished manuscript, FWSNL.

3. The Irishmen were Cavan Boa (tailor), Thomas Branagan (joiner), James Butler (overseer), Thomas Mahoney (house carpenter/joiner), Cornelius McDermott Roe (stonemason/bricklayer), Edward McDermott Roe (ditcher), Timothy McDermott Roe (ditcher), Thomas Ryan (shoemaker), Farrell Slattery (millwright), Richard Tharpe (stucco artisan), and Michael Tracy (bricklayer). The English workers were a Mrs. Anderson (nursemaid to Custis children), Matthew Baldridge (joiner), Philip Bates/Bater or Bateman (gardener), Thomas Bishop (a longtime servant in a variety of roles), James Bloxham (master farmer), Eleanor Forbes (housekeeper), Andrew Judge (tailor), John Rawlins (stucco worker), and Thomas Spears (joiner). The German servants were Catherine Ehlers (wife of J. C. Ehlers; supervised spinners), Johann Christian Ehlers (gardener), Dominicus Gubner (blacksmith), Johann Lutz (gardener), Daniel Overdonck (ditcher/mower), Margarett Overdonck (wife of Daniel Overdonck; spinner/washer/milker), John Stedlar (music teacher), and possibly a cooper, whose name was not recorded. The Scots included James Anderson (farm manager), John Anderson (distillery worker), James Donaldson (carpenter supervisor), William Spence (gardener), and William Webster (brickmaker). It should be noted that one of Washington's earliest secretaries, who served on the frontier with him during the French and Indian War, was a Scotsman named John Kirkpatrick. The Frenchmen working at Mount Vernon were Peter Gillig or Gilling (cook), Charles Meunier (steward), and an unnamed plaster worker.

4. Sciagusta, for example, was described by Washington as "a prisoner from the Indians" who came to Mount Vernon "to work with my People" on the millrace on 26 April 1770. He worked at Mount Vernon for a very short time and was paid three shillings on 3 May 1770. See *GWP.Col.Series,* 8:329, 329–30n3.

5. Those whose status was identified as indentured were John Askew (joiner), Matthew Baldridge (joiner), Cavan Boa (tailor), Catherine Boyd ("Servant woman"), Thomas Branagan (joiner), John Broad (joiner), Andrew Judge (tailor), John Knowles (bricklayer/laborer), Rachel Knowles (wife of John Knowles; spinner/house servant), Thomas Mahoney (house carpenter/joiner), an unnamed painter, Anna Overdonck (daughter of Daniel and Margaret), Daniel Overdonck (ditcher), Margaret Overdonck (wife of Daniel Overdonck; spinner/washer/milker), Cornelius McDermott Roe (stonemason/bricklayer), Thomas Ryan (shoemaker), Farrell Slattery (millwright), Michael Tracy (bricklayer), Isaac Webb (bricklayer), William

Webster (brickmaker), Thomas Wight (no trade listed), John Winter (painter), and Henry Young (stonemason). For the immigration figures on indentured servants, see Innes, "Fulfilling John Smith's Vision," 7, 10.

6. The convicts were John Broad (joiner), John Smith (no trade given), William Webster (brickmaker), Thomas Wight (no trade given), John Winter (painter), and Henry Young (stonemason).

7. Ekirch, *Bound for America,* 26–27.

8. Ibid., 173–74.

9. Reverend Jonathan Boucher, "Description of George Washington," from Boucher's *Autobiography,* ca. 1789, quoted in *GWW,* 2:486–87n91.

10. The midwives included Susannah Bishop, a Mrs. Brasenton, a Mrs. Kinney, a Darchus Parker, Elizabeth Simpson, a Mrs. Williams, and two enslaved women belonging to neighbors Thomson Mason and a Mrs. French, respectively.

11. Those women identified as housekeepers were a Mrs. Barnes, Eleanor Forbes, Sarah Harle, Rachel McKeaver or McIver, a Mrs. Skinner, and Mary Wilson. The two males were Richard Burnet Wilson (housekeeper/butler) and Thomas McCarty (housekeeper/steward).

12. GW to William Tilghman, 21 July 1793, *GWW,* 33:25.

13. Ibid., 33:25–26.

14. Mount Vernon Farm Ledger, 1797–98, 14, 18, 20, 26, 42, bound photostats, FWSNL.

15. *GWP.Col.Series,* 7:376, 442, 515, 8:104, 220, 356, 479, 9:54, 238, 10:137; Lund Washington (1767–1853), "Lund Washington's History of His Family," ca. 1849, FWSNL; Bishop Frank M. Bristol, "Copy of Lund Washington's Manuscript," ca. 1900, 12–13, bound photostat, FWSNL.

16. MVLA, *Mount Vernon Commemorative Guidebook 1999,* 28.

17. Throughout this book, I refer to this farm manager as Anthony Whiting, since that is the name by which he is known in John C. Fitzpatrick's *The Writings of George Washington.* The modern edition of *The Papers of George Washington* uses Whitting.

18. Heitman, *Historical Register.*

19. GW to Marquis de Lafayette, 20 October 1782, *GWW,* 25:281.

20. GW to GAW, 14 November 1782, ibid., 25:342, 343. See also GW to Marquis de Lafayette, 15 December 1782, ibid., 25:435.

21. GW to Governor William Greene, 7 June 1783; GW to David Parry, governor of Barbados, 25 April 1784, ibid., 26:478, 478nn21–22; 27:393.

22. *GWD,* 15 October 1785, 4:206.

23. GAW to GW, 26 March 1790, *GWP.Pres.Series,* 5:280. For GW's acquisition of Mrs. French's property, an especially complicated transaction, see *GWD,* 3 February 1785, 9 September, 18, 20, 24 October 1786, 4:84, 84–85n, 5:37, 52, 53–54, 57, 57n; Charles Lee to GW, 13 September 1786, *GWP.Con.Series,* 4:247–48, 249n4; GW to Benjamin Dulany, 15 July 1799, *GWP.Ret.Series,* 4:189, 189–90n1.

24. For General John Cadwalader's death date and the location of his estate, see Wikipedia, s.v. "John Cadwalader (general)."

25. GW to AW, 14 April 1790, *GWP.Pres.Series,* 5:330–31.

26. "Articles of Agreement between George Augustine Washington and Anthony Whiting," 20 May 1790, ibid., 5:332–33n1.

27. GAW to GW, 20 August 1790, ibid., 6:311, 313.

28. GW to Fanny Bassett Washington, 17 March 1793, *GWW,* 32:393–94.

29. Thomas Jefferson to James Madison, 23 June 1793, Jefferson, *The Papers of Thomas Jefferson,* 26:346, 346n.

30. *GWP.Pres.Series,* 12:389n.

31. GW to Charles Carter of Ludlow, 19 May 1792, ibid., 10:397–98. See also Betty Washington Lewis to GW, 19 April 1792, ibid., 292, 292n2; ibid., 15:225n5.

32. GW to William Tilghman, 21 July 1793, ibid., 13:262; GW to James Anderson (farm manager), 18 August 1796, *GWW,* 35:182–83.

33. James Anderson (farm manager) to GW, 11 September 1796, *GWP.Ret.Series,* 1:21–22n.

34. Esther White, Memorandum, 22 July 2002, MVLA, Mount Vernon, VA, based on *GWP.Ret.Series* and Anderson family genealogical notes filed at Mount Vernon.

35. James Anderson (farm manager) to GW, 11 September 1796, *GWP.Ret.Series,* 1:21–22n.

36. WP to GW, 31 August 1794, *GWP.Pres.Series,* 16:621, 622n1.

37. GW to WP, 24 August 1794, *GWW,* 33:473, 473n, 474.

38. GW to WP, 14 December 1794, ibid., 34:58.

39. NCL to Elizabeth Bordley Gibson, 29 April 1823, Lewis, *George Washington's Beautiful Nelly,* 133–34.

40. *GWD,* 19 May 1785, 4:141–42n.

41. Ibid., 2 November 1799, 6:373, 373n.

42. For Alton's experiences with Washington in the army, see GW to John Augustine Washington, 28 June 1755, and GW, "Notes on Journey to Boston," [February 1756], *GWW,* 1:145, 297n, 298, 299. For Alton's early years at Mount Vernon, see GW to Mary Ball Washington, 30 September 1757, and GW to John Alton, [1 April 1759], ibid., 2:137, 318–19.

43. For an overall look at Alton's relationship with Washington, see *GWD,* 21 April, 27 October 1762; 13, 17, 19, 20, 23, 29, 31 August, 7 September, 25 October, 4 December 1785; 12 August, 13 November 1786, 1:296, 296n, 307; 4:182, 183, 184, 185, 187, 188, 190, 212, 244; 5:26, 66. For Alton's final illness and death, see ibid., 23 August, 4 December 1785, 4:185, 244.

44. For payments for Mrs. Alton, see "Dr. . . . John Alton Dcsd. . . . Cr.," LW Account Book, 160. For the bequest, see GW, "Last Will and Testament," [July 1799], *GWW,* 37:287.

45. For Morris's career, see Washington, *"Worthy Partner,"* 61, 105, 126, and *GWD,* 3 January 1760, 1:214, 214–15n.

46. *GWD,* 19 December 1785, 4:252. For Davy Gray's presence at Muddy Hole between 1792 and 1799, see GW to WP, 18 December 1793, *GWW,* 33:192–194; GW to WP, 5 July 1795, *GWP.Pres.Series,* 18:291–92, 292n4; and 1799 Slave Lists.

47. GAW to GW, 26 March 1790, *GWP.Pres.Series,* 5:281.

48. Howell Lewis to GW, 31 July 1793, ibid., 13:313, 314n1.

49. Catherine Hollan to Ellen McCallister, 10 March 1981, photocopy, FWSNL; Norton, "A Penchant for Noble Patronage," February 1962, 12.

50. GW to WP, 22 December 1793, *GWW,* 33:200–201.

51. GW to AW, 23 December 1792, ibid., 32:275.

52. Norton, "A Penchant for Noble Patronage," May 1962, 12.

53. GW to WP, 22 December 1793, *GWW,* 33:200–201.

54. GW to John Christian Ehlers, 23 December 1793, ibid., 33:215.

55. Bushrod Washington to GW, 8 November 1797, *GWP.Ret.Series,* 1:466–67.

56. GW to Robert Brooke, 27 October 1797, ibid., 1:432.

57. GW to Bushrod Washington, 3 November 1797, ibid., 1:455. For the salary Forbes required, see Bushrod Washington to GW, 30 October, 22 November 1797, ibid., 1:422n2, 446, 482.

58. For the problems of getting Forbes to Mount Vernon, see GW to George Lewis, 13 November 1797; GW to Bushrod Washington, 22 November 1797; Burwell Bassett, Jr., to GW, 26 November 1797; Bushrod Washington to GW, 26 November 1797, *GWP.Ret.Series,* 1:470, 482, 486, 487. For the start of Forbes's employment at Mount Vernon, see GW to Bushrod Washington, 18 December 1797, ibid., 1:522, and ibid., 1:84n3. For her use of one of the rooms on the second floor of the kitchen, see MVLA, *Mount Vernon: A Handbook,* 96. For the furnishings of her room, see "Up the Kitchen Stairs," in Prussing, *The Estate of George Washington, Deceased,* appendix 2, 434–35.

59. GW to Bushrod Washington, 18 December 1797, *GWP.Ret.Series,* 1:522.

60. For Forbes's presence in the sickroom, see "Tobias Lear's Narrative Accounts of the Death of George Washington," [15 December 1799], ibid., 4:546, 552.

61. John Riley to the Education Department, "Brickmaking Exhibit, George Washington: Pioneer Farmer," 17 May 1993, memorandum, FWSNL; *GWD,* 7 September 1785, 4:191n; Mesick, Cohen & Waite, "Building Trades," Historic Structures Report, bound notebook, 2–41, FWSNL. According to one source, "The three 'Roe' brothers who worked for Washington were actually part of a family whose surname was spelled 'McDermottroe' or 'McDermott Roe.' That family was almost entirely confined to County Roscommon, Ireland, in the nineteenth century (and probably before), according to Griffith's Valuation of Ireland 1848–1864 and the International Genealogical Index." Nathan Murphy, email communication with author, 11 October 2006.

62. Mesick, Cohen & Waite, "Building Trades," 2–41.

63. Smith, *Colonists in Bondage,* 16–17.

64. GW, "Indenture with John Askew," [1 September 1759], *GWP.Col.Series,* 6:340–41.

65. *GWD,* 31 July 1762, 1:304, 304n; GW, "Agreement with Burgis Mitchell," [1 May 1762], *GWP.Col.Series,* 7:131–32.

66. GW, "Agreement with David Cowan," [11 January 1773], *GWP.Col.Series,* 9:155, 156, 238, 239n1; 10:138n1. For the clothing made by the tailor, see entry for "David Cowan Gardner—Dr.," 29 July 1773, LW Account Book, 14.

67. See entries for 15, 20 May 1773; 12, 25 May, 11 [unknown], 17 September, 3 November 1774, "William Roberts Miller—Dr.," LW Account Book, 17–17a.

68. See entries for 5 June 1775, January, 2 February, April, 1, 22 May 1776, "William Roberts—Dr.," ibid., 44; "William Roberts—Dr . . . Cr.," ibid., 72; "Wm. Roberts—Dr . . . Cr.," ibid., 115.

69. *GWD,* 11 August 1786, 5:25.

70. GW, "Articles of Agreement with Benjamin Buckler," 25 February 1771, Ford,

Washington as an Employer and Importer of Labor, 41–43. For more on Buckler, see *GWP.Col.Series,* 8:438n12; 9:58.

71. *GWD,* 30 July 1768, 2:93.

72. GW, "Articles of Agreement with James Bloxham," [31 May 1786]; James Bloxham to "Mr. Peacey," 23 July 1786, *GWP.Con.Series,* 4:86–87, 4:193–94.

73. GAW to GW, 20 August 1790, *GWP.Pres.Series,* 6:312.

74. WP to GW, 7 January 1796, typescript, FWSNL.

75. *GWD,* 30 July 1768, 2:83.

76. GW, "Articles of Agreement with James Bloxham," [31 May 1786], *GWP.Con.Series,* 4:87. See also *GWD,* 29 May 1786, 4:337.

77. GAW to GW, 20 August 1790, *GWP.Pres.Series,* 6:312.

78. LW to GW, 2 September 1778., *GWP.Rev.Series,* 16:500.

79. *GWD,* 11 August 1786, 5:25, 25n.

80. GW, "Agreement with Edward Violet," [5 August 1762], *GWP.Col.Series,* 7:144, 145.

81. GW, "Articles of Agreement with James Bloxham," [31 May 1786], *GWP.Con.Series,* 4:86–87.

82. GW to WP, 22 December 1793, *GWW,* 33:200–201.

83. GW, "Agreement with Philip Bater," 23 April 1787, ibid., 29:206–7.

84. LW to GW, 30 December 1775, typescript, FWSNL.

85. LW to GW, 31 January 1776, *GWP.Rev.Series,* 3:232–33.

86. LW to GW, 22 February 1776, ibid. 3:355.

87. "Report of the Joiners and Carpenters," Mount Vernon Weekly Report, 20 March 1790, photostat, FWSNL.

88. Harrower, *Journal,* 130–31.

89. GAW to GW, 28 December 1790, *GWP.Pres.Series,* 7:141–42.

90. GW to WP, 19 January 1794, *GWW,* 33:244.

91. GW to WP, 8 June 1794, ibid., 33:399–400.

92. GW, "Agreement with Burgis Mitchell," [1 May 1762], *GWP.Col.Series,* 7:132. For similar stipulations by other plantation owners at this period, see Sobel, *World They Made Together,* 48.

93. GW to Burges Ball, 27 July 1794, *GWW,* 33:444.

94. GW to AW, 2 December 1792, ibid., 32:246.

95. GW, "Circular to William Stuart, Hiland Crow, and Henry McCoy," 14 July 1793, *GWP.Pres.Series,* 13:226.

96. LW to GW, 15 February 1776, *GWP.Col.Series,* 3:317.

97. GW to AW, 19 May 1793; GW to WP, 18 December 1793, 23 November 1794, *GWW,* 32:463; 33:189; 34:43.

98. GW to WP, 18 December 1793, ibid., 33:191.

99. GW to AW, 13 January 1793, ibid., 32:298.

100. Louis-Philippe, *Diary of My Travels,* 32.

101. GW to WP, 10 May 1795, *GWW,* 34:193. Similarly, many years earlier, Washington's uncle Joseph Ball had cautioned, "Let not the overseers abuse my People." Joseph Ball to Joseph Chinn, 18 February 1744, quoted in Morgan, *Slave Counterpoint,* 329.

102. GW to AW, 14 October 1792, *GWW*, 32:184. See also GW to AW, 28 October 1792, ibid., 32:197.

103. For Cupid's illness, see *GWD*, 28, 30, 31 January 1760, 1:230, 230n. For his purchase from a slave ship, the escape attempt, and later information about his life, see *GWP.Col.Series*, 7:66, 67n5, 68n6.

104. "Articles of Agreement with Edward Violett and Benjamin Buckler," 5 August 1762, 25 February 1771, quoted in Ford, *Washington as an Employer and Importer of Labor*, 29, 42.

105. Despite the efforts of Washington and other plantation owners to hire experienced managers and closely regulate their behavior, some of the concerns they expressed may have been based in fact. According to one historian's analysis of the situation, the typical overseer was "poorly educated, poorly motivated, and inadequate" to his job. See Fogel, *Without Consent or Contract*, 170. A nineteenth-century Virginia planter complained that "many overseers are vain, weak tyrants, 'dressed' in a little brief authority," while another in Mississippi cautioned that hiring a good overseer was "one of the most difficult things in the world." Another planter from the Deep South recorded a "phrase common among a certain class of overseers" to the effect that they were "getting their satisfaction out of a negro." He went on to say that it "is this unrelenting, brutalizing, drive, drive, watch and whip that furnishes facts to abolition writers that cannot be disputed, and that are infamous." See Breeden, *Advice among Masters*, 296, 297–98. For a similar problem in feudal Russia, see Roosevelt, *Life on the Russian Country Estate*, 231–33.

106. GW to WP, 7 December 1794, *GWW*, 34:52.

107. GW to WP, 18 December 1793, ibid., 33:193, 194. Other plantation owners also recognized the need for emotional distance. Washington would have agreed wholeheartedly with one Virginia planter who counseled in the 1830s that "Too much familiarity with negroes ought never to be indulged in by the master or overseer, as it causes them to lose the proper respect for them. But kind words may be used whenever they deserve them, without being too familiar with them." See Breeden, *Advice among Masters*, 52–53.

108. GW to WP, 4 May 1794, *GWW*, 33:351.

109. GW to WP, 18 December 1793, ibid., 33:191.

110. GW to WP, 16 November 1794, ibid., 34:25.

111. GW to WP, 2 November 1794, ibid., 34:13.

112. GW to Arthur Young, 12 December 1793, ibid., 33:181.

113. GW to WP, 25 January 1795, ibid., 34:103–4. See also Sobel, *World They Made Together*, 47.

114. GW to WP, 18 December 1793, *GWW*, 33:192–94. A letter written by Washington's longtime secretary Tobias Lear describes the situation in the late 1780s, when supervision of the four outlying farms was entrusted to several enslaved men: "He [Washington] raises no tobacco on his lands here, but is introducing the present mode of Husbandry practi[c]ed in Eng[lan]d. on his farms—The body of Land Cultivated here is abt. 8000 Acres divided into 5 farms—worked by abt. 200 hands—he has no white overseers—an active negro is foreman at each plantation." Tobias Lear to William Prescott, 4 March 1788, "A Lear Letter," 24.

115. GW to Howell Lewis, 11 August 1793, *GWP.Pres.Series*, 13:420, 421, 423n12.

116. Ibid., 13:422.

117. GW to Robert Lewis & Sons, 1 February 1785, *GWP.Con.Series,* 2:317.

118. GW to Nathaniel Ingraham, 22 March 1788, ibid., 6:170, 171n1.

119. For examples of this, see "Agreement with Edward Violet," [5 August 1762], *GWP.Col.Series,* 7:145; GW to WP, 22 December 1793, *GWW,* 33:201; and GW to James Anderson (of Scotland), 7 April 1797, *GWP.Ret.Series,* 1:79–81.

120. Ledger A, 8 December 1765; February 1766, 124a. For the identification of Breechy, see "The Estate of Daniel Parke Custis," [ca. 1759], Washington, *"Worthy Partner,"* 126.

121. LW to GW, 12 March 1783, typescript, FWSNL; *GWD,* 12 August 1786, 5:26, 26n. For more on the Walkers' associations with the Washingtons, see GW to Clement Biddle, 17 August 1785, *GWP.Con.Series,* 3:185, 186n4.

122. See "Paper Money Pd. for the Genrl.," LW Account Book, 108.

123. See "Cash Pd. on Acct. of General Washington," ibid., 121.

124. "George Washington's Last Will and Testament," [9 July 1799], *GWP.Ret.Series,* 4:487, 505–6n26, 506–7n27.

125. William Roberts to GW, 25 November 1784, *GWP.Con.Series,* 2:151–52.

126. William Booker to GW, 6 June 1799, *GWP.Ret.Series,* 4:102.

127. GW to JA, 8 September 1799, ibid., 4:286, 287n2.

128. GW to Howell Lewis, 4 August 1793, *GWW,* 33:41–42n.

129. GW to WP, 21 September 1794, ibid., 33:502.

130. "George Washington's Last Will and Testament," [9 July 1799], *GWP.Ret.Series,* 4:487, 505–6n26. For Washington's continued interest in the family, see GW to WP, 16 November 1794; GW to WP, 30 November 1794, *GWW,* 34:24–25, 48, and "George Washington's Last Will and Testament," [9 July 1799], *GWP.Ret.Series,* 4:487, 505–6n26.

131. Washington, "Lund Washington's History of His Family"; Bristol, "Copy of Lund Washington's Manuscript," 12–14.

132. For Sarah Harle's time at Mount Vernon, see *GWP.Col.Series,* 7:342n1, 430, 430n1, 441, 451, 458, 461, 482, 491, 508, 508n6; 8:91n3. For the treatment by Doctor Thompson and the final payment of Harle's salary, see "Cash . . . Contra," entries for 2, 22 May 1767, Ledger A, 249a.

133. *GWP.Col.Series,* 8:91, 91n3, 112, 121, 127.

134. *GWD,* 17 December 1768, 2:115, 115n; Ledger A, 2 June, 28 April, 27 May 1769, 288a, 290a, 291a.

135. See "Account with Captain George Johnston," 20 May 1767; "Account with Thomas Bishop," Ledger A, 181a, 247a.

4. "So Exact and So Strict"

1. GW to John Fairfax, "A View of the Work at the Several Plantations in the Year 1789," 1 January 1789, *GWW,* 30:175n. For a detailed analysis of the work done by slaves at Mount Vernon in the last years of Washington's life and how it compared to plantations in Jamaica and Barbados, see Roberts, *Slavery and the Enlightenment in the British Atlantic.*

2. "A Visit to Mount Vernon," *Parley's Magazine,* October 1838, typescript, FWSNL.

3. *GWD,* 5 February 1760, 27 June, 10 July 1786, 1:233, 4:353, 5:6; LW to GW, 2 September 1778, typescript, FWSNL.

4. GW to the Overseers at Mount Vernon, 14 July 1793, *GWW,* 33:12.

5. GW to AW, 13 January 1793, ibid., 32:297–98.

6. GW to WP, 18 December 1793, ibid., 33:190–91.

7. Carter, *Diary,* 6 November 1771, 2:639.

8. GW to James McHenry, 29 May 1797, *GWW,* 35:455.

9. GW to James Anderson (farm manager), 11 June 1798, ibid., 36:287. For an example of Washington's nephew and principal heir, Bushrod Washington, engaged in a similar activity, see the description by a visitor to Mount Vernon who found "the benevolent man" "at an early hour" "visiting the cabins of the slaves, inquiring about the sick, and ascertaining personally what were their wants," in *Cyclopedia of Useful Knowledge,* n.d. [probably 1809–36], Early Descriptions Notebook.

10. *GWD,* 5 February 1760, 1:233.

11. The figures for sunrise and sunset at various times of the year are based on information provided by the Astronomical Applications Department at the U.S. Naval Observatory in Washington, DC, as calculated for the year 1779 in Alexandria, Virginia. My very great thanks to historian Lorena Walsh for pointing me toward this helpful resource. "Alexandria, Virginia, Rise and Set for the Sun for 1779, Eastern Standard Time," Sun or Moon Rise/Set Table for One Year, Astronomical Applications Department, U.S. Naval Observatory, http://aa.usno.navy.mil/data/docs/RS_OneYear.php. Using the navy's figures and an online time-card calculator conversant with military time, I worked out the hours for each working day in 1779 and added the totals for each month. By way of comparison, a modern worker scheduled for a 40-hour workweek puts in 2,080 hours per year, which means that the Mount Vernon slaves were working 1,110 hours and 55 minutes more per year (or more than half a year's extra work) than a modern worker. Looking at it slightly differently, the slaves were putting in almost 139 days more than the modern worker. Note: this does not take into account holidays given to either the modern worker or slaves. Sunny Walker, "Time Sheet Calculator," Miracle Salad, http://www.miraclesalad.com/webtools/timesheet.php.

12. Fairbanks and Bates, *American Furniture,* 197.

13. Knock, "New Insights into Slave Life at Woodlawn Plantation," 1, 6. Woodlawn had originally been part of the Mount Vernon estate's Dogue Run Farm. It was given to Washington's step-granddaughter Nelly Custis and her husband, Washington's nephew Lawrence Lewis. See Washington, *Last Will and Testament,* 22–23, 38n40, 39nn41, 42.

14. Kamoie, *Irons in the Fire,* 107.

15. For the slaves at Mount Vernon in 1799, see 1799 Slave Lists.

16. See ibid.

17. *GWD,* 3 May 1762, 1:297, 297–98n. See also "Mr. Willm. Daingerfield . . . Contra," Ledger A, 130a.

18. See "Account with Lund Washington," entry for 1 January 1770, Ledger A, 297a.

19. "Cash Paid on Act. of Colo. Washington by L. Washington," 11 September 1773; "Cash Pd. on Acct. of Genrl. Washington," 22 November 1784, LW Account Book, 47, 140. For another example, see entry for May 1774, "Cash Paid on Act. of Colo. Washington by L. W.," ibid., 48, which shows that "a Negro" was hired from John Taylor for seine hauling.

20. GW to David Stuart, 18, 22 January 1788, *GWW,* 29:387, 390. For Peter's extended presence at Mount Vernon, see 1786 Slave List, 4:279, and 1799 Slave Lists, 37:257, 258, which identify the dower slave Caroline Branham (or Brannum) as Peter's wife and record the names of her children. Peter's surname also appears in the records as Hardman and Harden.

21. William Fitzhugh to GW, 2 November 1785, *GWP.Con.Series,* 3:336, 336n1.

22. "Cash Recd. on Acct. of Genrl Washington," 5 November 1782, LW Account Book, 114.

23. GW to Benjamin Dulany, 15 July 1799, *GWW,* 37:307.

24. Weekly Reports, 18, 25 November, 2 December 1786, 6, 13 January, 10, 17 February 1787, Mount Vernon Weekly Reports of Managers, 18 November 1786–28 April 1787, 1, 2, 3, 8, 16, 19, typescript, FWSNL.

25. See Weekly Reports, 20, 28 January, 4, 11, 18, 25 February, 4, 11, 18, 25 March, 6, 13, 20, 27 May, 3, 10, 24 June, 22, 29 July, 3 September 1797, Mount Vernon Farm Accounts, 7 January–10 September 1797, [13], [18], [21], [27], [33], [38], [44], [48], [55], [59], [96], [101], [107], [114], [119], [124], [135], [151], [155], [174], FWSNL.

26. See Weekly Reports, 29 April, 20 May 1797, Mount Vernon Farm Accounts, [91], [107].

27. See Weekly Reports, 31 March 1787, Mount Vernon Weekly Reports of Managers, 18 November 1786–28 April 1787, 36; Weekly Reports, 7, 14 January, 11 March 1797, Mount Vernon Farm Accounts, [4], [9], [49].

28. See Weekly Reports, 24 February, 31 March 1787, Mount Vernon Weekly Reports of Managers, 18 November 1786–28 April 1787, 22, 37.

29. LW to GW, 31 January, 29 February 1776, *GWP.Rev.Series,* 3:232, 397.

30. See Weekly Reports, 7 January, 4, 11, 18, 25 March 1797, Mount Vernon Farm Accounts, [5], [45], [50], [55], [61].

31. See "Taylors Act 2 Dec.," Mount Vernon Weekly Reports of Managers, 18 November 1786–28 April 1787, 3.

32. Glasse, *The Servants Directory,* 1.

33. Ibid., 2–10.

34. For a description of Martha Washington's bedtime routine during the presidency, see Thane, *Mount Vernon Family,* 74.

35. Glasse, *The Servants Directory,* 11–24.

36. GW to Tobias Lear, 31 August 1794, Lear, *Letters and Recollections,* 79.

37. *GWD,* 18 February 1786, 4:277.

38. Detweiler, *George Washington's Chinaware,* 112, 118.

39. Wansey, *An Excursion to the United States of North America,* 112.

40. Brookes, "A Dinner at Mount Vernon," 76.

41. 1799 Slave Lists, 37:256.

42. Reverend Ashbel Greene, quoted in Custis, *Recollections and Private Memoirs,* 436n.

43. [Trusler], *The Honours of the Table,* 10–15.

44. Louis-Philippe, *Diary of My Travels,* 32–35.

45. Stanton, "'Those Who Labor for My Happiness,'" 152.

46. Niemcewicz, *Under Their Vine and Fig Tree,* 101. For the singling out of mulatto slaves for skilled and indoor jobs, see Roberts, *Slavery and the Enlightenment in the British Atlantic,* 210, 236, 255, 259, 260.

47. *GWD,* 12 January 1760, 1:222, 222n.

48. *Columbian Mirror and Alexandria Gazette,* 12 April 1800; *Philadelphia Gazette and Universal Daily Advertiser,* 16 May 1800.

49. GW to WP, 27 October 1793, 18 May 1794, *GWW,* 33:142, 367.

50. For Austin's earlier work with Frank Lee, see 1786 Slave List. For the fact that Austin was of mixed race, see Herman Stump to GW, 20 December 1794; Thomas Archer to GW, 22 December 1794, microfilm, FWSNL.

51. Chase, "Mrs. [?] Staines," 248.

52. Reverend T. H. Adams, "Washington's Runaway Slave, and How Portsmouth Freed Her," *Portsmouth, New Hampshire, Weekly,* 2 June 1877, reprinted from *Granite Freemason,* May 1845.

53. GW to Joseph Whipple, 28 November 1796, *GWW,* 35:298; GW to Burwell Bassett, 11 August 1799, manuscript, A-301, FWSNL.

54. An example of an older house servant initiating a younger family member in the requirements of a position in the mansion was related by Martha Washington's great-granddaughter Britannia Peter Kennon, as a story told by her father, Thomas Peter (1769–1834), which took place at the home of his father, Robert Peter (1726–1806), who was a contemporary of George and Martha Washington. The elderly slave who waited on the table during meals was "always assisted" by his granddaughter, who was described as "a young girl." One day during dinner, a guest told a "very funny story." While her grandfather "never cracked a smile," the girl laughed out loud. "The old man gave her a look and commenced to edge towards her gradually until she left the room when he followed her out, such a box on the ears as he gave her I shall never forget. No one at the table failed to hear it or to divine its cause." See Armistead Peter, Jr., "Reminiscences of Britannia Peter Kennon (1815–1911)," 53–54, MS14, box 69, folder 24; box 70, folder 1, Tudor Place Archives, Tudor Place Historic House and Gardens, Washington, DC. For another culture in which positions within domestic staffs were passed down in the same serf families for generations, see Roosevelt, *Life on the Russian Country Estate,* 105.

55. "The Estate of Daniel Parke Custis," [ca. 1759], Washington, *"Worthy Partner,"* 126.

56. See 1786 Slave List and 1799 Slave Lists.

57. Nelligan, "'Old Arlington,'" 214.

58. See 1786 Slave List and 1799 Slave Lists. See also Lear, *Letters and Recollections,* 140.

59. GW to GAW, 10 June 1787, *GWW,* 29:233; 1799 Slave Lists.

60. See 1786 Slave List; 1799 Slave Lists; and GW to AW, 28 October 1792, *GWW,* 32:195.

61. For the fact that Sears trained Anderson, see An Old Citizen of Fairfax, "Mount Vernon Reminiscences Continued," *Alexandria Gazette,* 22 January 1876,

and W, *Alexandria Gazette,* 25 January 1876. For Sears's background and work at Mount Vernon, Gunston Hall, Mount Airy, and Pohick, see Dalzell and Dalzell, *George Washington's Mount Vernon,* 103, 104–7, 164–69. For work done by Sears at Pohick Church, see *GWD,* 25 February 1774, 3:235n.

62. Washington, "Articles of Agreement," 20 September 1770, *GWP.Col.Series,* 8:377n3.

63. GW, "Indenture with John Askew," [1 September 1759], ibid., 6:340–41.

64. WP to GW, 16 June 1798, *GWP.Ret.Series,* 2:255n2.

65. GW, "Indenture with Peter Gollatt," [19 March 1770], *GWP.Col.Series,* 8:320.

66. MW to FBW, 2 June 1794, 24 May 1795, Washington, *"Worthy Partner,"* 267, 288; Garrett, *At Home,* 191–93, 206–14; Nylander, *Our Own Snug Fireside,* 103–5, 120–24.

67. For the distilling of rose and mint waters, see MW to FBW, 22 April 1792, Washington, *"Worthy Partner,"* 237, and GW to AW, 12 May 1793, *GWW,* 32:459. For the preservation of gooseberries, cherries, and strawberries, see MW to FBW, 5 June 1791, 24 May 1795, Washington, *"Worthy Partner,"* 231, 288. For the preparation of slave clothing, see GW to AW, 28 April 1793, *GWW,* 32:436, and Weekly Reports, 19, 26 May 1798, Mount Vernon Farm Accounts II, 31 March 1798–7 January 1799, bound photostat, FWSNL.

68. For cleaning, scalding, whitewashing, and the making of "Babe clothes," see MW to FBW, 1 July 1792, 4 August 1793, Washington, *"Worthy Partner,"* 238, 250. For the preparation of slave clothing at this season, see GW to WP, 10 August 1794, *GWW,* 33:467.

69. GW to AW, 28 October, 9 December 1792, *GWW,* 32:198, 256; Nylander, *Our Own Snug Fireside,* 97–98; McMahon, "Laying Foods By," 171–75, 172n.

70. GW to AW, 4 November 1792, *GWW,* 32:205.

71. GW to AW, 4 November 1792, 3 February 1793, ibid., 32:205, 330; MW to FBW, 4 August 1793, Washington, *"Worthy Partner,"* 250; GW to WP, 28 December 1794, 5 November, 4 December 1796, *GWW,* 34:74, 35:263–64, 307.

72. GW to AW, 9 December 1792, 6 January 1793; GW to WP, 28 December 1794, *GWW,* 32:256–57, 295; 34:74.

73. GW to WP, 5 July 1795, ibid., 34:231.

74. GW to AW, 24 February 1793, ibid., 32:357.

75. *GWD,* 4 July 1786, 5:3–4.

76. Weekly Report, 18 March 1797, Mount Vernon Weekly Reports, 10 January 1795–18 March 1797, bound photostat, PS-140, FWSNL; Weekly Report, 31 March, 7 April, 16 June 1798, Mount Vernon Farm Accounts II. In addition to these reports, see also those for 14, 21, 28 April, 5 May 1798, Mount Vernon Farm Accounts II, for evidence that slaves from outlying farms were also being brought to the fishing landing to work during this season.

77. See 1799 Slave Lists.

78. GW, "Articles of Agreement with James Bloxham," [31 May 1786], *GWP.Con.Series,* 4:86–87.

79. "Articles of Agreement between George Augustine Washington and Anthony Whiting," 20 May 1790, *GWP.Pres.Series,* 5:332–33n1.

80. Mount Vernon Weekly Reports, 26 November 1785–30 December 1786,

photostat, PS-134, FWSNL; Carr and Walsh, "Economic Diversification and Labor Organization," 185–88.

81. See *GWD*, 22 April 1785, 4:125.

82. See ibid., 1 March 1788, 5:281.

83. LW to GW, 10 December 1775, *GWP.Rev.Series*, 2:527.

84. See *GWD*, 29 December 1797, 5:236.

85. GW, "Cash . . . Contra," 29 December 1797, Ledger B, bound photostat, 257a, FWSNL.

86. See *GWD*, 9 November 1788, 5:420.

87. GW, General Orders, 13 September 1777, 31 May 1778, *GWW*, 9:213, 11:497; Richard Kidder Meade to Nathanael Greene, 11 November 1778, Greene, *Papers of General Nathanael Greene*, 3:62.

88. LW to GW, 25 January, 29 February 1776, *GWP.Rev.Series*, 3:187–88, 397.

89. See Clark, "A Wartime Incident," 25.

90. 1786 Slave List; 1799 Slave Lists. For an example of elderly slaves on the Custis properties, described as "Old wenches . . . that cant worke out[side]," being considered for positions as spinners, see James Hill to GW, 30 August 1772, *GWP.Col.Series*, 9:86.

91. For information about the 1750 division of slaves, see *GWP.Col.Series*, 7:173n.

92. GW, Tithables Lists, [16 June 1766], [15 June 1767], [20 June 1768], [16 July 1770], [14 June 1771], [10 June 1772], [9 June 1773], [July 1774], ibid., 7:442–43, 515; 8:104, 220, 356, 479; 9:54, 55n, 238; 10:137.

93. AW to GW, 9 January 1793, typescript, PS-10, FWSNL.

94. *GWD*, 22 April 1785, 1 March 1788, 4:125, 125n, 5:281; GW to WP, 18 May 1794, *GWW*, 33:367; 1799 Slave Lists.

95. LW to GW, 25 January 1776, *GWP.Rev.Series*, 3:188.

96. *GWD*, 14 February 1786, 4:275.

97. GW to WP, 5 July 1795, *GWW*, 34:231.

98. James Anderson (farm manager) to GW, 19 June 1798, *GWP.Ret.Series*, 2:347–48.

99. Weekly Report, 11 March 1797, photostat, PS-141, FWSNL.

100. 1799 Slave Lists, 37:308.

101. GW to William Baynham, 30 July 1799, *GWP.Ret.Series*, 4:217, 217n. For Dr. Craik's bill for treating Tom with *Aqua ophthalmic* (an eye lotion) and pulverized ophthalmic, see entries dated 24 April, 8 May 1799, Dr. James Craik, "Receipted Medical Bill," 25 August 1797–14 June 1799, photostat, FWSNL, and Wall, "Dr His Excly Geo. Washington to James Craik," 322, 327.

102. *GWD*, 5, 7 December 1785, 4:244, 245n; George William Fairfax to GW, 23 June 1785, *GWP.Con.Series*, 3:77.

103. *GWD*, 20 February 1799, 6:335.

104. GW to Robert Lewis, 17 August 1799, *GWP.Ret.Series*, 4:257.

105. GW to William Baynham, 30 July 1799, ibid., 4:217.

106. William Baynham to GW, 10 August 1799, ibid., 4:229.

107. William Baynham to GW, 21 August 1799, ibid., 4:263.

108. GW to William Baynham, 27 August 1799, ibid., 4:271.

109. Fithian, *Journal and Letters*, 96, 137. For an example of slaves on another

Virginia plantation of this period having Saturday afternoon free, see Anburey, *Travels through the Interior,* 2:332. In this latter case, the plantation owner did not provide food rations, so the slaves' Saturday afternoons were specifically intended for working in their gardens to provide themselves with food.

110. See Weekly Reports, 24, 31 December 1785, 30 December 1786, Mount Vernon Weekly Reports, 26 November 1785–30 December 1786; Weekly Report, 29 December 1798, Mount Vernon Farm Accounts II; *GWD,* 29 December 1786, 5:85; and GAW to GW, 28 December 1790, *GWP.Pres.Series,* 7:141.

111. *GWD,* 7 April 1760, 1:264; Weekly Report, 14 April 1798, Mount Vernon Farm Accounts II.

112. Weekly Report, 30 May 1795, Mount Vernon Weekly Reports, 10 January 1795–18 March 1797; Weekly Report, 2 June 1798, Mount Vernon Farm Accounts II.

113. Weekly Report, 12 May 1798, Mount Vernon Farm Accounts II. For the president's proclamation, see "Proclamation of Day of Fasting, Humiliation and Prayer (23 March 1798), John Adams," http://millercenter.org/scripps/archive/speeches /detail/3942; Hutson, *Founders on Religion,* 100–101, 100n; McCullough, *John Adams,* 501; and Holmes, *Faiths of the Founding Fathers,* 77.

114. *GWD,* 12 July 1786, 5:6.

115. Weekly Report, 30 July 1796, photostat, FWSNL.

116. "Cash Pd. on Act. of Colo. Washington by L. W.," May 1775, LW Account Book, 49.

117. William Pearce, "Cash . . . Contra," 13 May 1794, Mount Vernon Farm Ledger, January 1794–December 1796, 4; "Fish Account," 12 May 1797, Mount Vernon Farm Ledger, 1797–98, 83. Many thanks to my colleague Bruce Ragsdale for sharing the 1794 reference with me.

118. "Fishery," 15 March 1798, Mount Vernon Farm Ledger, 1797–98, 147; "Mill," 5 March 1798, ibid., 123. For similar examples from the next season, see Mount Vernon Distillery and Fishery Ledger, 1799–1801, March, 28 April 1799, 41, 42, bound photostat, RM-297/PS-2915, FWSNL, as well as an undated entry on page 9 of the same manuscript. This latter reference also indicates that slaves were hired for this fishing season, although it is unclear if this means that people (in this case twelve men for one month, ten men for two weeks, and ten women for two weeks) were brought in from outside or if this was a way of tracking the work of slaves from the Mansion House Farm who were moved to the fishery for a few weeks. Another entry on page 9 records that the overseer from the Mansion House Farm, Moses Dowdal, was in charge of the operation at the fishery that year.

119. Mount Vernon Distillery and Fishery Ledger, 18, 25 December 1799.

120. Weekly Report, 22 October 1787, FWSNL.

121. Gaspar, "Antigua Slaves and Their Struggle to Survive," 133, 134, 137.

122. NCL to Elizabeth Bordley Gibson, 29 April 1823, Lewis, *George Washington's Beautiful Nelly,* 134.

123. Whatman, *Susannah Whatman,* 12, 16, 24.

124. AW to GW, 20 February 1793, *GWP.Pres.Series,* 12:197.

125. Weekly Reports, 15, 22 July 1797, Mount Vernon Farm Accounts, 7 January–10 September 1797, [147], [151], bound photostats, FWSNL.

126. Weekly Reports, 2 December 1786; 20 January, 3, 10, 17, 24 February 1787,

Mount Vernon Weekly Reports of Managers, 18 November 1786–28 April 1787, 2, 9, 13, 15, 16, 18, 21; "Memorandum of Things Delivered to the Different Plantations from the 12th of April, 1786 [to 31 August 1786]," typescript, W-1174, FWSNL.

127. Weekly Report, 23 June 1798, Mount Vernon Farm Accounts II.

128. Weekly Report, 7 April 1792, Mount Vernon Weekly Reports, 8 January 1792–8 November 1794, PS-10, PS-11, PS-136, A-283, PS-140, FWSNL; Weekly Report, 9 June 1798, Mount Vernon Farm Accounts II. For another reference to the illness of Delia's son, see Niemcewicz, *Under Their Vine and Fig Tree,* 100. For another example of a mother getting time off to care for a sick child, see Weekly Report, 5 January 1793, Mount Vernon Weekly Reports, 8 January 1792–8 November 1794.

129. Weekly Reports, 3, 10, 17 March 1787, Mount Vernon Weekly Reports of Managers, 18 November 1786–28 April 1787, 23, 26, 29. For the earlier examples, see *GWD,* 12–15 October 1785, 4:205–6.

130. LW to GW, 2 September 1778, typescript, A-283, FWSNL.

131. Weekly Report, [16] February 1793, Mount Vernon Weekly Reports, 8 January 1792–8 November 1794.

132. *GWD,* 15 February, 25 March 1786, 4:275, 294. For a plan to have slaves at the Custis properties under Washington's supervision keep occupied with spinning when the weather would not permit outside work, see James Hill to GW, 30 August 1772, *GWP.Col.Series,* 9:85.

5. "They Appear to Live Comfortable Together"

1. GW to Daniel Jenifer Adams, 20 July 1772, *GWP.Col.Series,* 9:69–70, 71n2.

2. The tithables lists from 1760–74 can be found in ibid., 6:428; 7:45, 139, 227–28, 313, 376–77, 442–43, 515–16; 8:104, 220–21, 356–57, 479; 9:54–55, 238–39; 10:137.

3. 1786 Slave List. Note that the term "adult" is used here, as well as later in the same paragraph, for anyone who was old enough to work. This included a number of people as young as eleven, as well as those who were no longer working because they were too old or infirm.

4. For the slaves at Mount Vernon in 1799, see 1799 Slave Lists, as well as *GWP.Ret.Series,* 4:527–42. For another historian's view of family life at Mount Vernon, see Stevenson, *Life in Black and White,* 209–12, 329–39.

5. GW to Burwell Bassett, 23 May 1785, *GWW,* 28:152.

6. See 1799 Slave Lists.

7. Kay and Cary, *Slavery in North Carolina,* 165–66, 295–97; Gutman, *Black Family,* 50; Schulz, "Children and Childhood in the Eighteenth Century," 79. Note, however, that the experience of a given individual could differ quite a bit from these average figures, and given the small size of the Mount Vernon sample, can also skew the statistics. The range of ages at which the enslaved women at Mount Vernon gave birth for the first time actually varied between roughly 14.5 and 27 years.

8. Virginia, *Statutes at Large,* 13:182. See also a similar law of October 1748 in ibid., 6:109.

9. GW to Roger West, 19 September 1799, *GWW,* 37:367–68.

10. On some plantations, an enslaved couple would jump over a broom (an early, pre-Christian, Anglo-Saxon cultural artifact) as the ritual signifying their marriage,

while on others a master would read from the Bible, or more rarely, a minister might be called in to officiate. See Stevenson, *Life in Black and White,* 228–29. Historian David Hackett Fischer describes both white and African American couples in Virginia taking part in jumping the broom: "The bride and groom in Virginia were often united in two ceremonies. . . . The first was a Christian ceremony. . . . The other ceremony was an ancient pagan practice in which the bride and groom were made to jump over a broomstick. This ritual had long been observed throughout Britain and much of western Europe, and especially in the kingdoms of Wessex and Mercia. The custom of the broomstick marriage came to be widely practiced by white families throughout the southern colonies in addition to the Christian ceremony. For black slaves, it was the only type of marriage ceremony that was permitted, and rapidly acquired a special meaning in Afro-American culture." See Fischer, *Albion's Seed,* 282. For recollections of former nineteenth-century slaves about jumping the broom as the ceremony used by both poor whites and slaves, see the interview with Willis Cozart in Hurmence, *My Folks Don't Want Me to Talk about Slavery,* 90; interview with James V. Deane and Jenny Procter, Howell, *I Was a Slave,* 1:49–50, 56; and interviews with Hilliard Yellerday, Jephtha Choice, and Allen Sims, Howell, *I Was a Slave,* 4:20, 27, 50. For jumping the broom as a Welsh custom, see Philips, "The African Heritage of White America," 392.

11. For another historian's suggestion that Washington was "perhaps more so" (that is, aware and sympathetic to his slaves' family ties) than most of his peers, see Stevenson, *Life in Black and White,* 210.

12. GW to LW, 24–26 February 1779, *GWW,* 14:148.

13. GW to John Francis Mercer, 24 November 1786, ibid., 29:83.

14. GW to John Fowler, 2 February 1788, ibid., 29:398.

15. GW to David Stuart, 7 February 1796, ibid., 34:452–53; Washington, *Last Will and Testament,* 2.

16. GW to Clement Biddle, 28 July 1784, *GWW,* 27:451.

17. GW to John Lawson, 10 April 1787, ibid., 29:199.

18. GW to David Stuart, 18, 22 January 1788, ibid., 29:387, 390; 1799 Slave Lists. For other examples of masters trying to keep married slaves together and seeking their permission for a physical breakup, see Mullin, *Flight and Rebellion,* 27, 71, 180n109, and Fox-Genovese, *Within the Plantation Household,* 299.

19. For Hannah and Morris's marriage, see *GWD,* 3 January 1760, 1:214–15n.

20. GW to WP, 28 December 1794, *GWW,* 34:74. See also Herman Stump to GW, 20 December 1794; John Carlile to GW, 21 December 1794; Thomas Archer to GW, 22 December 1794, microfilm, FWSNL.

21. LW to GW, 3 December 1775, 17 January 1776, *GWP.Rev.Series,* 2:478; 3:126, 130n1.

22. LW to GW, 18 February, 4 March 1778, *GWP.Rev.Series,* 13:587. 14:60, 61n4.

23. LW to GW, 11 March 1778, ibid., 14:151.

24. GW to LW, 3 April 1779, *GWP.Rev.Series,* 19:735, 736n5. For the rented slaves, see *GWP.Col.Series,* 10:348, 349.

25. Weekly Report, 21 February 1795, Mount Vernon Weekly Reports, 10 January 1795–18 March 1797.

26. GW to WP, 1 March 1795, *GWW,* 34:128; 1799 Slave Lists. For other examples

of a master intervening in a slave marriage, see Mullin, *Flight and Rebellion,* 28, 65, and Fox-Genovese, *Within the Plantation Household,* 299. Although Washington's actions may have been the best way to protect Fanny, whose husband was unlikely to change his behavior without counseling (which had not yet been invented), it is also possible that she was not ready to end the marriage. While perhaps not directly comparable, modern statistics indicate that abused women try to leave their abusive spouses/partners an average of seven times before they are finally able to leave for good. See Domestic Abuse Shelter of the Florida Keys, http://www.domesticabuseshelter.org/InfoDomesticViolence.htm.

27. GW to AW, 3, 24 February 1793, *GWW,* 32:331, 357.

28. For the source of these figures, see 1799 Slave Lists.

29. Gutman, *Black Family,* 87–93, 131.

30. Figures based on 1799 Slave Lists and Sweig, *Slavery in Fairfax County,* 13.

31. See 1799 Slave Lists.

32. Walsh, "A 'Place in Time' Regained," 17, 30n; Samford, *Subfloor Pits,* 40, 177.

33. For the fact that wealthy and powerful men in West Africa could have many wives, see Osifekunde, "The Land and People of Ijebu," 259, 259n3, and Walsh, *From Calabar to Carter's Grove,* 60. For Muslim men being allowed to have as many as four wives, see Shakir, *Holy Qur'an,* 4:3. In earlier papers and talks on family life in the Mount Vernon quarters, I indicated that the family of carpenter Sambo Anderson might have been an example of polygamy. A younger staff member, Molly Kerr, who was heading up Mount Vernon's slavery database project, discovered, however, that George Washington had made a copying mistake in the 1799 Slave Lists. That document very clearly showed that Anderson was married to a thirty-six-year-old woman at River Farm named Agnes, with whom he had three children: Henky (17), Cecelia (14), and Anderson (11). Also living on River Farm at that time were three other children: Ralph (9), Charity (2), and Charles (1), whose mother, Sall, had died not long before. Sambo Anderson was among the slaves freed by the terms of George Washington's will and, as a free man, later made his home on Little Hunting Creek, near Mount Vernon. Unfortunately, Agnes, her children, and Sall's little ones, as dower slaves of Martha Washington, could not be freed and were eventually divided among the latter's four grandchildren. Eleven years later, in the summer of 1810, a local newspaper alerted its subscribers to the escape of a young man named Ralph, then about twenty-one years old, who had run away from his owner, Thomas Peter, the husband of Martha Washington's second granddaughter. Ralph was believed to be heading for the home of his father, "a free negro man named Sambo, living on Judge [Bushrod] Washington's estate, Mount Vernon." For Ralph and the identity of his father, see *Alexandria Gazette,* 12 June 1810. I noted that it was entirely possible that Anderson had two wives, both Agnes and Sall, a fact George Washington might not have recognized because it was outside the scope of his experience and cultural expectations. Besides polygamy, however, I explained that there might have been other explanations for Anderson's family situation. Given the seven-year gap in age between Ralph and his next youngest sibling, a likely possibility is that Sambo and Sall were involved in an extramarital relationship, which resulted in the birth of Ralph. An end to their relationship and Sall's eventual marriage or involvement with another man several years later could well explain the spacing of her younger

children. Another possibility is that Sall and Agnes were related, and that Sambo and Agnes "adopted" Sall's children after her death. Kerr, however, pointed out that the ages of all the children involved (both those attributed to Agnes and those who were recorded as Sall's) matched up with dates in Mount Vernon's childbirth records for times when Agnes was giving birth. Kerr surmised that Sall, who does not otherwise appear in the records, was entered as the mother of the younger children by mistake.

34. See 1786 Slave List and 1799 Slave Lists.

35. Wiggins, "The Play of Slave Children," 182–83.

36. GW to Hector Ross, 9 October 1769, *GWP.Col.Series*, 8:255.

37. GW to AW, 19 May 1793, *GWW*, 32:465.

38. Parkinson, *Tour in America*, 2:448.

39. These figures are derived from the 1799 Slave Lists. The fact that the population was growing rapidly suggests that neither the work done by enslaved women at Mount Vernon nor their diets were having a negative effect on their fertility. For comparisons of fertility among enslaved women in the West Indies with those of their counterparts on a plantation in Virginia, see Dunn, *A Tale of Two Plantations*, 153–55, 159–61.

40. Louis-Philippe, *Diary of My Travels*, 31, 32.

41. Information taken from the 1786 and 1799 Slave Lists.

42. Kiple and King, *Another Dimension to the Black Diaspora*, 99–100; Schulz, "Children and Childhood in the Eighteenth Century," 68–69; Fogel, *Without Consent or Contract*, 142–47.

43. Fogel, *Without Consent or Contract*, 149–51.

44. For early references to the use of midwives on the Custis plantations near Williamsburg, see "General Account of the Estate, 1758–1759," [ca. November 1761]; "John Parke Custis's Estate Account, 1759–1761, [ca. November 1761], *GWP.Col.Series*, 6:266, 272. For early references to a midwife at Mount Vernon, see Ledger A, November 1761; 11 April 1763, 81a, 160a. The former shows Samuel Brasenton being paid £0.11.6 "by laying a Negroe Wench & findg. a bottle of Rum," undoubtedly intended for work done by his wife. The second entry notes that Mrs. Brasenton was paid two pounds that day for "layg. 4 Negroe Women."

45. Weekly Reports, [16] February, 23 March 1793, Mount Vernon Weekly Reports, 8 January 1792–8 November 1794; AW to GW, 27 March 1793, *GWP.Pres.Series*, 12:386, 387n6.

46. See *GWP.Col.Series*, 6:329n4; 7:179, 190, 276, 308, 352n1. See also "Account with Samuel Brasenton," November 1761, August 1763, September 1763, Ledger A, 81a, 158a, and Cash Accounts, 25 January, 11 April 1763, 4 June 1764, Ledger A, 160a 178a.

47. For the reference to the miscarriage, see "Cash Paid on Acct. of General Washington," 27 November 1777, LW Account Book, 66. For the identity of these midwives and examples of payments for their services, see *GWP.Col.Series*, 7:482, 482n2, 515, 515n2, 8:5, 5nn3, 6, 112, 112n2, 70, 70n1, 169, 169n5, 222, 250, 250n6, 521, 527, 557, 557n5, 9:1, 2n4, 53, 58, 228n5, 432, 10:19, 20n11, 39, 168, 168n9, 194, 196n17, and Sandy Newton, "Research Notes on Midwives and Childbirth at Mount Vernon," 31 May 1992, typescript, 2–3, FWSNL. The exact identity and status of two other midwives, Martha Lawrie and Ann Knowland, are not as yet known. See "Account with Lund

Washington," 25 April 1765, Ledger A, 190a; Cash Account, 3 July 1769, *GWP.Col.Series,* 8:221; and Ledger A, 291a.

48. "Cash Paid on Act. of General Washington by L.W.," 20 February 1775; "Cash Pd. on Acct. of General Washington," 28 April 1783, LW Account Book, 51, 121.

49. "Cash Paid," 25 July 1796, Mount Vernon Farm Ledger, January 1794–December 1796, 75.

50. GW to WP, 17 August 1794, *GWW,* 33:469.

51. See Mount Vernon Distillery and Fishery Ledger, 6 February 1799, 35.

52. For the description and prevalence of tongue-tie, which ranges from about 4–10 percent, see Lauren M. Segal et al., "Prevalence, Diagnosis, and Treatment of Ankyloglossia: Methodologic Review," *Canadian Family Physician* 53, no. 8 (June 2007), http://www.ncbi.nlm.nih.gov/pmc/articles/PMC1949218/; Lori Ricke et al., "Newborn Tongue-Tie: Prevalence and Effect on Breast-Feeding," *Journal of the American Board of Family Practice* 18, no. 1 (1 January 2005), http://www.jabfm.org/content/18/1/1.full. For how the condition was treated in the eighteenth century, see Memis, *Midwife's Pocket-Companion,* 121, and [Brown], *Letter to a Lady on the Management of the Infant,* 10.

53. *GWD,* 4 December 1786, 5:75.

54. WP to GW, 31 August 1794, *GWP.Pres.Series,* 16:621, 622n3.

55. Ulrich, *Midwife's Tale,* 170–73.

56. Fogel and Engerman, *Time on the Cross,* 123. To put these figures into perspective, in 1980 the maternal death rate in the United States was one death in ten thousand deliveries. Historians note, however, that most of this phenomenal increase in maternal safety has come about only in the last sixty years, with the advent of prenatal care to identify high-risk cases, blood transfusions to deal with hemorrhaging, and antibiotics to treat infections, for even as late as 1930 about six to seven women died out of every thousand who gave birth. See Leavitt, *Brought to Bed,* 25, 194, 259n43, 268.

57. Rum Account, entries for 13 April, 2, 27 July, 9 September 1787, Mount Vernon Store Book; "Store Account . . . Contra," 27 May 1795, Mount Vernon Farm Ledger, January 1794–December 1796, 32.

58. Although the custom came under increasing fire from medical writers at the end of the eighteenth century who feared it would cause fevers, alcoholic drinks, including rum, were typically given to women recuperating from childbirth, both in England and northern New England, generally in the form of caudle or thick gruel mixed with rum. See Ulrich, *Midwife's Tale,* 190.

59. At the end of Washington's life, the Mount Vernon slaves who were probably mulatto were Frank and Billy Lee, Betty and Tom Davis, Delphy Judge, Christopher Sheels, Marcus, and blacksmith George Young (all at the Mansion House Farm); Forrester Gray (at the mill/distillery complex); Tomison Gray, Sarah, Bartley Clark, and Matilda Clark (at Dogue Run Farm); Lucy (a rented slave at Union Farm); Dennis and Polly (at River Farm); and Alce, Letty, Billy, and Davy Gray (at Muddy Hole Farm). Sources indicating that these individuals were mulatto include family letters and free black registers from the nineteenth century.

60. Morgan and Nicholls, "Slave Flight," 212. Looking at a later period, census data from 1860 indicates that 10 percent of slave children in the United States at that time were mulatto. Fogel, *Without Consent or Contract,* 182. According to one

recent article, based on DNA testing, in the early twenty-first century the average African American has 24 percent European ancestry, while about 4 percent of American whites have at least 1 percent or more of African ancestry. Henry Louis Gates, Jr., "How Many White People Have Hidden Black Ancestry?" *The Root,* 17 March 2014, http://www.theroot.com/articles/history/2014/03/how_many_white_people_have_hidden_black_ancestry/. When considering the issue of sexual exploitation of slaves in North America, it is necessary to say that black men were also sexually abused by both white men and women in the eighteenth and nineteenth centuries. In describing a possible sexual relationship between a white parson and his black manservant in eighteenth-century Jamaica, historian Thomas A. Foster reminds us that it is "worth noting that this act occurred between a slave owner and a close personal servant rather than with a field hand. As such, this type of abuse follows a broader pattern that suggests the closer the proximity to whites, the more likely that sexual abuse was to occur." Foster, "Sexual Abuse of Black Men under American Slavery," 453–54.

61. See 1786 Slave List and 1799 Slave Lists.

62. "Account of Weaving Done by Thomas Davis at Mount Vernon," 1767–71, bound photostat, MF-94, FWSNL.

63. Professor David Coon, Department of History, Washington State University, conversation with author, summer 1982.

64. *GWP.Col.Series,* 8:424, 425n4, 431, 437, 474, 527, 556.

65. For the hire of George Young, see ibid., 9:440–41, 441nn1, 2; 10:137, 137n1.

66. "Complete Inventory, by Counties, of the Estate," n.d., Washington, *"Worthy Partner,"* 61. See also "Schedule A: Assignment of the Widow's Dower," [ca. October 1759], *GWP.Col.Series,* 6:217. Regarding Austin's age, he was not listed, for example, in GW's tithables lists prior to the Revolution, suggesting that he was under the age of sixteen when the last one was done in the summer of 1774, probably two or three months before the birthday that would elevate him to adult status for tax purposes. For the tithables list, see Memorandum, List of Tithables, [ca. July 1774], *GWP.Col.Series,* 10:137. Evidence from other financial papers documents that Austin had started working by 1774. Two months before the tithables list was drawn up, two pairs of shoes were purchased for Billy Lee, George Washington's valet, and for Austin. Seven shillings and six pence were paid for each pair, suggesting not only that the shoes were similar but that the men were engaged in similar work, presumably in the mansion as well. In November of the same year, Austin was described as one of the "Boys" who received their basic clothing issue for the year, comprising a jacket, breeches, two shirts, two pair of stockings, and a pair of shoes. The receipt of two pairs of shoes during the course of the year, together with the fact that the first pair came to Austin in late spring, would also point to a position in or around the mansion. For the shoes purchased for Billy Lee and Austin, see Cash Accounts, [May 1774], *GWP.Col.Series,* 10:40, 41. For the November clothing issue, see "Dr Home House Plantation for Workmens Wages & Exps. Eca.," 2 November 1774, LW Account Book, 7–7a.

67. *GWP.Col.Series,* 9:132, 134n9, 238, 239n1; 10:137. For the work done by Andrew Judge for Washington, see "Andrew Judge . . . Dr. . . . Cr.," LW Account Book, 78; see this same page for a record of work done by Judge between 1776 and 1781.

For other references to Judge, see LW to GW, 15, 22 October 1775, *GWP.Col.Series,* 2:174, 175n23, 219; entries dated 17 January, 27 March 1784, GW Cash Memoranda, September 1783–November 1784, 99, 103 [6], photostat, FWSNL.

68. 1786 Slave List.

69. GW to AW, 17 February 1793, *GWW,* 32:347. For the purchase of "Itch ointment for Daphney's family" to treat the condition, see Ledger B, 2 February 1793, 349a. Tobias Lear initially came to Mount Vernon as tutor to the Custis grandchildren and secretary to George Washington, and later married two of Martha Washington's nieces, Fanny Bassett Washington, then Fanny Henley. Descendants of slaves from Mount Vernon believe that Lear had a mulatto son named George Lear with a slave named Rose at River Farm. See Bernice Johnson Reagon, "Interview of Loretta Carter Hanes," [mid-1985]; Rohulamin Quander, "Second Interview of Loretta Carter Hanes," 14 September 1992, Quander, *Telling Histories,* 2:543–45, 563–64, 566–67.

70. Harrower, *Journal,* 27 December 1775, 130.

71. GW to AW, 14 August 1791, *GWW,* 31:338. See also GW to AW, 9 December 1792, ibid., 32:257.

72. LW to GW, 2 September 1778, *GWP.Rev.Series,* 16:499.

73. GW to WP, 22 December 1793, *GWW,* 33:201.

74. GW to John Christian Ehlers, 23 December 1793, ibid., 33:215.

75. "Contract between GW and Edward Violett," 5 August 1762, quoted in Ford, *Washington as an Employer and Importer of Labor,* 30–31. See also "Agreement with Philip Bater," 23 April 1787, *GWW,* 29:206–7.

76. William North to Ben Walker, 9 March 1784, typescript, FWSNL.

77. Many years after the fact, Charles Biddle, who was prominent in Pennsylvania political circles and a neighbor of the Washingtons in Philadelphia, related an incident when George Washington tried to protect one of the women working in the presidential mansion from sexual abuse, although Biddle did not say whether she was enslaved, indentured, or hired. Biddle, who died in 1821, did not witness the incident himself but quoted "an aged Philadelphia mechanic" who was asked if he remembered Washington. The man replied, "'General Washington! Oh yes, I remember General Washington well; I once see General Washington kick a fellow down stairs.' He proceeded to relate that he and a fellow journeyman were once sent to the President's house to do a job involving painting or glazing. Arriving early, they were admitted by a servant-maid who led the way up the stairs. Whilst ascending the stairs his companion attempted some liberties with the girl, who gave a loud shriek as they reached the second story. Immediately the General sallied forth from the front room, half dressed and half shaved, and demanded the cause of the disturbance. Hearing the girl's story, he rushed at the man in a rage and started him down stairs with a violent kick from behind; at the same time he cried out, 'I will have no woman insulted in my house,' and called for Colonel Lear to put the rascal out the front door." Biddle closed the story with the statement, "The language of the narrator was more graphic, if less decorous, than in the above repetition." Biddle, *Autobiography of Charles Biddle,* 285n.

78. For an example of a rumored relationship between a male slave and a female member of the extended Washington family, see Henriques, "Major Lawrence

Washington versus the Reverend Charles Green," 257. In this case, rumors made their way around Virginia in early 1746 about Ann Fairfax Washington, who was George Washington's sister-in-law, the wife of his older half-brother, Lawrence, the daughter of William Fairfax of Belvoir Plantation, and sister of George Washington's friends George William and Bryan Fairfax. According to the young woman's mother, while gossips told of a black man attempting to seduce Ann, the truth was that a ten-year-old enslaved boy had tried to kiss her when she was eight years old.

79. Wiencek, *An Imperfect God,* 84–85, 284–90, 383n13; Bryan, *Martha Washington,* 24–26, 239–40, 258, 384–85. Mount Vernon has had a similar check from George Washington Parke Custis to William Costin, dated 5 June 1834, in its collection for decades; the check records the transfer of twenty-seven dollars to Costin, drawn on the Bank of the Metropolis. See W-946/b, A-140, FWSNL.

80. Provine, *District of Columbia Free Negro Registers,* 1:52n. William Costin manumitted a number of other enslaved people: Oney Fortune, who was described as "a bright mulatto . . . about thirty-five years old," was freed by him, "in consideration of one dollar," on 13 October 1827. She is very likely the former Mount Vernon dower slave of the same name who in 1799 was the six-year-old daughter of spinner Betty Davis. Similarly, two months later, on 30 December 1827, Costin manumitted "his mulatto woman named Eliza, aged about thirty, and her son, Montgomery, aged about four years," in exchange for a dollar. There appears to be a second reference to this manumission in the records of the District of Columbia: apparently Eliza had died by 25 July 1833, when Costin registered the manumission of a "mulatto boy, Montgomery Parke, the son of Eliza Washington, now deceased but heretofore manumitted by Costin." Montgomery Parke was then said to be eight years old. See ibid., 1:114, 139, 236.

81. 1820 U.S. Federal Census, District of Columbia, Washington, Washington Ward 4, 62–63 [100–101]; 1830 U.S. Federal Census, District of Columbia, Washington, Washington Ward 4, 2[–3].

82. District of Columbia Marriage Records, 1810–53, index, Ancestry.com.

83. Provine, *District of Columbia Free Negro Registers,* 1:52n.

84. For the material from the Costin descendants, see Marcia W. Carter to Christine Meadows, 21 January 1981, Washingtoniana Unowned Files, Curatorial Department, FWSNL, as well as Craig C. Evans, personal communication with author, 16 September 1994.

85. For more on members of the Costin and Holmes families, see Provine, *District of Columbia Free Negro Registers,* 1:51–52, 81–82, 148, 245, 282–83; 2:327–28. Ann Holmes was head of a large household of fifteen free black people in Ward 5 in the District of Columbia on 7 August 1820. Interestingly, the oldest person in the home was a woman between the ages of twenty-six and forty-four. Presumably this was Ann herself and indicates that she was born between 1776 and 1794, knocking holes in the theory that she was the daughter of John Dandridge, who died in 1756. See 1820 U.S. Federal Census, District of Columbia, Washington, Washington Ward 5, 90–91 [128–29].

86. See, for example, Morgan, "To Get Quit of Negroes," 420n26. Peter Henriques and Phil Morgan have both discussed with me their problems with the story of Ann Dandridge.

87. Byrd, *William Byrd's Histories of the Dividing Line,* 113–15. See also Godbeer, *Sexual Revolution in Early America,* 175–76. There were also connections to Native Americans on the other side of Martha Washington's family. Her maternal great-grandfather William Woodward worked as a trader with the Pamunkey Indians and served as an interpreter for them in their dealings with the Virginia governor. See Brady, *Martha Washington,* 15–16.

88. Yagoda, "A Short History of 'Hack.'"

89. Eliza Parke Custis to John Law, 12 October 1808, box Thomas Peter, MSSVII, Papers of John Law, Peter Collection, FWSNL.

90. Eleanor Parke Custis Lewis to William Costin, 12 June 1816, box Thomas Peter, MSSXI, Peter Collection.

91. Lawrence Lewis to William Costin, 6 October 1813, box Thomas Peter, MS-SXI, Peter Collection.

92. Sobel, *World They Made Together,* 150–52; Morgan, "Interracial Sex in the Chesapeake and the British Atlantic World," 52–55; Custis, *Recollections and Private Memoirs,* 20n; Berard, "Arlington and Mount Vernon," 159–60.

93. Calvert, *Mistress of Riversdale,* 378–86; Morgan, "Interracial Sex in the Chesapeake and the British Atlantic World," 64–66.

94. References to GWPC derived from conversations with Christine Meadows, former curator of Mount Vernon, and Agnes Mullins, former curator of Arlington House. See also Dana Priest, "Arlington Bequest a Footnote in Black History," *Washington Post,* 27 February 1990; Liza Mundy, "When Presidents and Slaves Mingled at the White House," *Washington Post,* 15 February 2010; Alexandria Court House Deed Book E (1803), 153, quoted in Anna Lynch to Nancy Hayward, assistant director of education, Mount Vernon, 22 March 1995, FWSNL; Smith, *Black Americana at Mount Vernon,* 52; Rose, *Arlington County Virginia,* 72n; Powell, *History of Old Alexandria,* 243; and Freeman, *R. E. Lee,* 1:392.

95. The statement about Mary Anna Randolph Custis Lee having forty mulatto half-siblings came from "Virginia F. F.'s," *Cleveland Daily Leader,* 26 September 1865. The interview with Maria Syphax was taken from "Lovely Arlington," *Atchison [Kansas] Daily Globe,* 15 September 1888. Many thanks to Hollis Gentry of the Smithsonian's National Museum of African American History and Culture, and Stephen Hammond, a descendant of the Syphax family, for sharing these articles and several others with me.

96. Powell, "Scenes of Childhood," 9. Suggestions that Martha Washington's great-nephew James Dandridge Halyburton fathered a child with one of his slaves came from conversations with Shirlee Taylor Haizlip, a descendant of James Halyburton and one of his slaves, fall 1994 and 5 October 1995; Mary Ann French, "Subtle Shades of the Rainbow: Writer Shirlee Taylor Haizlip on Blacks and the Color Conundrum," *Washington Post,* 7 February 1994; and Haizlip, *The Sweeter the Juice,* 38–50.

97. Information on West Ford can be found in Clark, "Letter of West Ford"; Chase, *Gum Springs,* 9–15; Corbin, "Gum Springs Community"; Gidget Fuentes, "Gum Springs Holding on to Past: Historic Black Community Tries to Replenish Family Roots," *Fairfax Journal* (Springfield, Virginia), 29 November 1991; Sweig, "'Dear Master'"; and Robinson, "Who Was West Ford?" 167, 170–71. For the source of the quotation about Ford as the "venerable Lieutenant," see John A. Washington

III to Jane C. Washington, 28 December 1849, typescript, FWSNL. For examples of West Ford's role at Mount Vernon in the first half of the nineteenth century, see Jane C. Washington to John A. Washington III, January 1838; Jane C. Washington to Rice Levy, 20 February 1839; John A. Washington III to Eleanor Love Selden Washington, 17 April, November 1857, 25 February 1859; Eleanor Love Selden Washington to John A. Washington III, 1857, typescript, FWSNL; "Rambler," 1850, Lee, *Experiencing Mount Vernon,* 184–87; Lossing, *Mount Vernon and Its Associations,* 337–39; and *1876 Visitors' Guide to Mount Vernon,* 30. For the West Ford descendants' take on who his father is thought to be, see Allen, *Tomorrow Came Yesterday,* 68–127; Bryant, *I Cannot Tell a Lie,* 9–57; Saunders-Burton, "A History of Gum Springs, Virginia," 17–39; and Rohulamin Quander, "Bicentennial Celebration of the Freeing of George Washington's Slaves at George Washington's Mount Vernon Estate and Gardens: My Impressions and Recollections," January 2001, photocopy, 6, 6n, FWSNL.

98. GW to "Robin," GW to "John," and GW to "Sally," all [1749–50]; and GW to William Fauntleroy, 20 May 1752, *GWP.Col.Series,* 1:41, 41n1, 42, 43, 49, 50n1.

99. William La Péronie to GW, 5 September 1754, ibid., 1:203, 205n1. Péronie was born in France and had acquired some level of military experience before coming to Virginia about 1750. While serving as an ensign in the Virginia regiment, he was wounded at Fort Necessity; later promoted to adjutant, he was killed at Braddock's defeat. See *GWD,* 11 May 1754, 1:185, 185n39.

100. For Washington's whereabouts at this time, see GW to William Fairfax, 11 August 1754; GW to Robert Dinwiddie, 21 August 1754; and GW, Advertisement, 28 August 1754, *GWP.Col.Series,* 1:183, 192, 196. For another historian's take on Washington's relationship with Nel, see Henriques, *Realistic Visionary,* 74.

101. Fogel and Engerman, *Time on the Cross,* 134.

102. GW to GAW, 25 October 1786, *GWW,* 29:29.

103. For contraceptive options available in England in the eighteenth century, which included breastfeeding infants for eighteen months or longer; abstinence; withdrawal or *coitus interruptus;* nonvaginal sex; and herbs or medicines, which could both prevent or terminate a pregnancy, see Stone, *The Family, Sex and Marriage,* 63–66, 417, 422, 489, 498, 501, 543, 644–45. Condoms were at that time difficult to get in England (to say nothing of the American colonies) and were primarily used to prevent venereal disease, although there is some evidence that both condoms and vaginal sponges were used for contraception. See ibid., 422–23, 536–37, 543, 567, 600–601.

104. "Division of Slaves from Bushfield Plantation," [1787], photocopy, FWSNL.

105. "List of John Auge. Washingtons Negroes 3d March 1783," John Augustine Washington I, Ledger C, typescript, RM-73/MS-2166, FWSNL.

106. Hannah Bushrod Washington, "Last Will and Testament," [April 1801], photocopy and typescript, FWSNL.

107. John Augustine Washington I, "Last Will and Testament," 22 June 1784, manuscript and typescript, RM-502/MS-4086, FWSNL.

108. Additional evidence on wills for the entire period between 3 March 1783 and 19 November 1785 is available for study at FWSNL. George Washington's diaries show that he made no visits to his brother John Augustine's plantation at any time between his return from the Revolution in late December 1783 through his brother's

death in 1787. Unfortunately, while the diaries are complete from 1785 through 1787, if Washington kept a diary for 1784 it either no longer exists or its whereabouts are unknown, except for a journal of a trip to his western lands in the late summer/early fall. It is possible, however, to piece together Washington's whereabouts using information in letters, financial records, and visitor descriptions. Doing that leaves very few times when Washington's location is unknown, though he might have made a trip to Bushfield. There are five instances in 1784 when Washington could possibly have made a trip to his brother's home (this is figuring at least two days to make the ninety-five-mile trip down, one day visiting, and two days to return home) and become involved with Venus there: 5–9 March, 17–24 April, 3–7 June, 12–16 August, and 11–24 October. Correspondence on either side of these periods does not indicate that he was planning to travel away from home. John Augustine's family came to Mount Vernon to visit on several occasions during these years. The times when his wife, Hannah, is known to have come and so might have brought Venus along as a maid (Venus was not her only maid; there were several other women Hannah could have brought with her) were 2 September 1784, 26 November 1784, and 19–23 October 1785. As several people who have looked at the evidence have indicated, while it may have been possible for George Washington to have fathered West Ford, it is not probable.

109. Mount Vernon has encouraged historians from other institutions to examine the evidence, just to be sure we are not looking at it with blinders. Academic historians who have examined this matter include W. B. Allen, Scott E. Casper, Peter R. Henriques, Jean B. Lee, Philip D. Morgan, and Philip J. Schwarz. For their thoughts on this matter, see Allen, *George Washington: America's First Progressive,* 112–16; Casper, *Sarah Johnson's Mount Vernon,* 24–26, 235n37; Henriques, *Realistic Visionary,* 165; Morgan, "To Get Quit of Negroes," 419–420, 420n; Philip Schwarz to Henry Wiencek, 18 October 2002 (my thanks to Phil Schwarz for sharing this); and Nicholas Wade, "Descendants of Slave's Son Contend That His Father Was George Washington," *New York Times,* 7 July 1999. For a very recent discussion of West Ford's paternity and the fact that Peter Henriques also believes John Augustine Washington's third son, William, to be Ford's father, see Fleming, *Intimate Lives of the Founding Fathers,* 68–70, 420–21n16.

110. Weekly Reports, 21 April 1787, Mount Vernon Weekly Reports of Managers, 42.

111. Weekly Reports, [16] February 1793, Mount Vernon Weekly Reports, 8 January 1792–8 November 1794.

112. This time period was determined through an examination of the surviving Weekly Reports from the spring of 1798 in Mount Vernon Farm Accounts I, 16 September 1797–24 March 1798, FWSNL, and Mount Vernon Farm Accounts II. This figure compares fairly well with statistics from one eighteenth-century New England family, where the length of time between giving birth and the resumption of household duties ranged from twenty-one to fifty-one days, with the average being not quite thirty-four days. See Beales, "Nursing and Weaning in an Eighteenth-Century New England Household," 52, 62.

113. James Hill to GW, 30 August 1772, *GWP.Col.Series,* 9:85.

114. Dr. Karin Calvert, associate professor, American Civilization Department,

University of Pennsylvania, talk on the history of childhood, 1600–1830, Mount Vernon, VA, 2 July 1991; Christy Coleman Matthews, director of the Department of African-American Interpretation at Colonial Williamsburg, conversation with author, 22 July 1995; White, "Female Slaves in the Plantation South," 109; Schulz, "Children and Childhood in the Eighteenth Century," 79. For evidence of slave infants being placed on the ground near where their mothers were working, see page 5 of the WPA interview of Sarah Frances Shaw Graves, born 23 March 1850 near Louisville, Kentucky, who recalled that her mother "worked in the field, even when I was a little baby. She would lay me down on a pallet near the fence while she plowed the corn or worked in the field." "Born in Slavery: Slave Narratives from the Federal Writers' Project, 1936–38," Federal Writers' Project: Slave Narrative Project, vol. 10, Missouri, Abbot–Young, image 135, Manuscript Division, Library of Congress, https://www.loc.gov/item/mesn100. For the African practice of carrying infants on their mothers' backs and the argument that it was probably not permitted by American masters, see Walsh, *From Calabar to Carter's Grove*, 99–100. To further muddy the waters about the practice of carrying babies and small children on the backs of their mothers, there is an interesting description by a visitor to Mount Vernon in the fall of 1784 who got lost on his way to the plantation, "but by good luck . . . met a woman with a child on her back," who told him "that she came two or three miles out of her way, because she knew she could have lodgings at the General's, for he gave orders to his servants to entertain all that came; that she had lain there two or three times before, though she lived above two hundred miles distance." See Varlo, *The Floating Ideas of Nature,* 1:90–94. Thanks to Richard L. Flaig for sharing this description with Mount Vernon from his 2014 unpublished work "Sketches of George Washington by Those Who Were in His Presence," copy in FWSNL. The author never mentions the ethnicity of the woman, but the fact that the woman was walking suggests that she was poor.

115. GW to GAW, 2 September 1787, *GWP.Con.Series,* 5:311.

116. GW to WP, 29 November 1795, *GWW,* 34:379.

117. Entry for 6 September 1783, LW Account Book, 125; "Cash . . . Contra," 6 February 1794, Mount Vernon Farm Ledger, January 1794–December 1796, 2; MW to FBW, 4 August 1793, Washington, *"Worthy Partner,"* 250. For the definition of "slazy," see *OED,* s.v. "Sleazy, sleezy," 9:189. For examples of the special care given to new mothers and the material goods used as incentives for women to produce and successfully raise children on other plantations, see Gutman, *Black Family,* 76–77.

118. Katz-Hyman, "In the Middle of This Poverty Some Cups and a Teapot," 88.

119. GW to WP, 29 November 1795, 16–17 March 1794, *GWW,* 34:379, 33:295–96; Gorham, "'The People Shall Be Cloathed,'" 12.

120. Gorham, "'The People Shall Be Cloathed,'" 12.

121. See Gutman, *Black Family,* 194–95; Kay and Cary, *Slavery in North Carolina,* 138–39; and Dunn, *A Tale of Two Plantations,* 112.

122. Kay and Cary, *Slavery in North Carolina,* 139–49, 268–77; Wood, *Black Majority,* 181–86, 181n.

123. Dunn, *A Tale of Two Plantations,* 77.

124. Weekly Report, 8 November 1794, Mount Vernon Weekly Reports, 8 January 1792–8 November 1794; WP to GW, 12 July 1795, *GWP.Pres.Series,* 18:312.

125. See 1786 Slave List.

126. "An Old Man," *Alexandria Gazette,* 26 September 1854; Ellis, *History of Fayette County, Pennsylvania,* 718. In contrast to this case, carpenter Sambo Anderson, who came to America in the same ship as Simon, retained his original name, perhaps because it was close to the English name Sam (another possibility is that Anderson resisted the name change).

127. Custis, *Recollections and Private Memoirs,* 422–23.

128. *Columbian Mirror and Alexandria Gazette,* 12 April 1800; *Philadelphia Gazette and Universal Daily Advertiser,* 16 May 1800.

129. Information taken from the 1786 and 1799 Slave Lists.

130. Kay and Cary, *Slavery in North Carolina,* 163; Gutman, *Black Family,* 186–87. While the slaves studied by Gutman named their children after a number of relatives, he found that they overwhelmingly chose to name children after their fathers, rather than their mothers, probably because of a desire to preserve the connection, when it was more likely that children would be separated from the former than from the latter. Kay and Cary's study of slaves in colonial North Carolina found that they "also tended to name their children after their fathers more frequently than their mothers: 50 to 60 percent as compared with 16 to 20 percent" (163).

131. MW to FBW, 24 May 1795, Washington, *"Worthy Partner,"* 287.

132. See 1799 Slave Lists and *GWP.Ret.Series,* 4:530.

133. "Lot #1 for Mrs. Law's," "List of the Different Drafts of Negros," [1802], Peter Family Collection, FWSNL.

134. *GWD,* 1–6, 8 January 1760, 1:211, 214, 215, 217.

135. MW to Hannah Stockton Boudinot, 15 January 1784, Washington, *"Worthy Partner,"* 193.

136. For references to chicken pox, see Tobias Lear to GW, 12, 19[–20], 23 June 1791, *GWP.Pres.Series,* 8:262, 280–281, 283n10, 297.

137. AW to GW, 22 January 1792, ibid., 9:497.

138. Weekly Report, 18 February 1797, Mount Vernon Weekly Reports, 10 January 1795–18 March 1797. For another, possibly fatal case of intestinal parasites in an enslaved child, see LW to GW, 22 April 1778, *GWP.Rev.Series,* 14:589, 590n10.

139. GW to WP, 31 August, 14 September 1794, *GWW,* 33:490, 499–500. For young Boatswain's approximate birthdate of 1780, see 1786 Slave List.

140. Weekly Report, 8 November 1794, Mount Vernon Weekly Reports, 8 January 1792–8 November 1794.

141. Weekly Report, 9 June 1798, Mount Vernon Farm Accounts II.

142. *GWD,* 24 May 1785; 29 December 1787, 4:145; 5:236.

143. Dr. James Craik to GW, receipted bill, 25 August 1797–22 January 1799, 1, photostat, H-1197, FWSNL.

144. Sweig, *"Registrations of Free Negroes,"* 14, 11, 10.

145. Ulrich, *Midwife's Tale,* 243–48.

146. Weekly Reports, 14, 21 February, 30 May, 5, 12, 19 December 1795, Mount Vernon Weekly Reports, 10 January 1795–18 March 1797.

147. Stanton, "'Those Who Labor for My Happiness,'" 156; Ulrich, *Midwife's Tale,* 243. For examples of other children from a variety of cultures being looked after by siblings, see Mergen, *Play and Playthings,* 39; Schulz, "Children and Childhood in the Eighteenth Century," 79; Smith, "Autonomy and Affection," 55; Wiggins, "The

Play of Slave Children," 175, 187; and Strickland and Ambrose, "The Baby Boom, Prosperity, and the Changing Worlds of Children," 549. As a personal example, my mother, the sixth of fourteen children in her family, was about six years old when she took over the day-to-day supervision of an infant brother, who was the ninth child, on a tenant farm in Arkansas in the 1930s.

148. GW to WP, 27 October, 22 December 1793, *GWW*, 33:142–43, 201. See also GAW to GW, 14 December 1790, *GWP.Pres.Series*, 7:80–81; Wiggins, "The Play of Slave Children," 178–79, 180, 182; Mergen, *Play and Playthings*, 43, 51–52. For evidence that Washington found the presence of small, noisy children of all races "disagreable," see GW to LW, 20 November 1785, *GWW*, 28:318, and AW to GW, 16 January 1793, *GWP.Pres.Series*, 12:8.

149. Interviews conducted in the 1930s with former slaves who grew up throughout the South in the mid-nineteenth century indicate that at least 10 percent of their former masters made similar efforts to control where and when the children played. See Mergen, *Play and Playthings*, 41.

150. GW to WP, 6 October 1793, *GWW*, 33:111; WP to GW, 19 October 1793, *GWP.Pres.Series*, 14:235.

151. Parkinson, *Tour in America*, 2:435–36. Historian Mechal Sobel has found that these attitudes were not unusual in the eighteenth century and discusses some of the values white children were learning from their enslaved caretakers, as well as from their young black playmates, in *World They Made Together*, 64–67, 135–39.

152. *GWD*, 5 July 1786, 5:4.

153. Agnes Lee, *Growing up in the 1850s*, 23 March 1856, 80.

154. GW to the Overseers at Mount Vernon, 14 July 1793, *GWW*, 33:11.

155. GW to WP, 27 October 1793, ibid., 33:142–43. See also, GW to AW, 25 November 1792; GW to James Anderson (farm manager), 1 November 1798, ibid., 32:240; 37:2.

156. GAW to GW, 20 August 1790, *GWP.Pres.Series*, 6:312. For evidence that these chores were fairly typical for slave children in the American South, see Wiggins, "The Play of Slave Children," 175.

157. 1799 Slave Lists; *GWD*, 15 July 1785, 5:8–10; Weekly Reports, 24 February, 3, 10, 17, 24, 31 March, 7, 14, 21 April 1787, Mount Vernon Weekly Reports of Managers, 18 November 1786–28 April 1787, 21, 23, 24, 26, 28, 29, 31, 32, 34, 35, 38, 39, 40, 42. The fact that enslaved children at Mount Vernon started work at the ages of eleven to fourteen should not be seen as anything unusual for the period. Depending on their sex, slave children at Monticello began working at the age of ten in either the nailery or as spinners and spent the next six years at those positions, until they were able to start fieldwork or entered a trade. See Stanton, "'Those Who Labor for My Happiness,'" 150, 156. Interviews with freed slaves from throughout the South recorded in the 1930s suggest that a similar pattern was followed on other plantations. See Wiggins, "The Play of Slave Children," 175. Nor was it only children in the South who began working at an early age. Young girls, both black and white, in eighteenth-century New England were typically hired out by their parents to live and labor in the homes of other families when they were about eleven or twelve years old. See Nylander, *Our Own Snug Fireside*, 48.

6. "A Mean Pallet"

1. Morse, *American Geography,* 381. Morse was not the only visitor to be struck by the village-like appearance of Mount Vernon. Robert Hunter, Jr., wrote in 1785: "It's astonishing what a number of small houses the General has upon his estate for his different workmen and Negroes to live in. He has everything within himself—carpenters, bricklayers, brewers, blacksmiths, bakers, etc., etc.—and even has a well-assorted store for the use of his family and servants." Robert Hunter, Jr., 1785, Lee, *Experiencing Mount Vernon,* 33–34.

2. GW to Arthur Young, 12 December 1793; 1799 Slave Lists.

3. Wells, "Eighteenth-Century Landscape of Virginia's Northern Neck," 4219, 4239–4240.

4. Pogue, "Archaeology of Plantation Life," 75, 79. For the possibility that the House for Families might have been built by George William Fairfax's carpenters about the time that Washington began renting Mount Vernon from his sister-in-law in late 1754, see "Account with George Fairfax," Ledger A, 1a.

5. GW, "Memorandum of Carpentry Work to Be Done," [June 1791], *GWW,* 31:308.

6. LW to GW, 12 November 1775, *GWP.Rev.Series,* 2:356.

7. GAW to GW, 8 April 1792, *GWP.Pres.Series,* 10:233.

8. "The West Quarter," 24; Pogue, "Archaeology of Plantation Life," 79. With two people in each bunk, the new quarters could house pretty much every enslaved person on the Mansion House Farm, but we also know that people were living in other types of quarters on this farm, so there was very likely no need to double up.

9. "Greenhouse-Quarters Reconstruction," 34–40.

10. Morgan, *Slave Counterpoint,* 104–6, 144.

11. Burnaby, *Travels through the Middle Settlements in North America,* 142n.

12. Louis-Philippe, *Diary of My Travels,* 2–3, 35–36.

13. See the work listed for the mansion house and the joiners and carpenters, 7 April 1792, and for the joiners and carpenters, 14 April 1792, Mount Vernon Weekly Reports, 8 January 1792–8 November 1794.

14. Wall, "Housing and Family Life of the Mount Vernon Negro," 5–8, 33.

15. Morse, "Special Report on the Quarters," 3–4.

16. GW to WP, 27 October 1793, *GWW,* 33:142–43.

17. Wall, "Housing and Family Life of the Mount Vernon Negro," 19; Morse, "Special Report on the Quarters," 8; WP to GW, 13 November 1796, typescript, PS-10, FWSNL; GW to WP, 20 November 1796, *GWW,* 35:286.

18. Weld, *Travels through the States of North America,* 1:92.

19. Brookes, "A Dinner at Mount Vernon," 77.

20. Brissot de Warville, *On America,* 1:429.

21. For the daubing, see GW to WP, 7 September, 2 November 1794, *GWW,* 33:495, 34:15.

22. GW to AW, 14 August 1791, *GWP.Pres.Series,* 8:426.

23. Humphrey Knight to GW, 2 September 1758, *GWP.Col.Series,* 5:448.

24. For the practicality of this type of chimney in the event of a fire, see Kelso, "Mulberry Row," 32. For the children injured in the chimney collapse, see GW to

WP, 4 January 1795, *GWW,* 34:78. For the quarter and slaves struck by lightning, see *GWD,* 18 May 1760, 1:281.

25. LW to GW, 8 February 1776, *GWP.Rev.Series,* 3:271; GW to WP, 22 December 1793, *GWW,* 33:196. Although the dimensions of the double cabins at Mount Vernon are unknown, they might have been similar in size to those on a plantation in Virginia's Northern Neck, where similar quarters measured 30 feet by 16 feet, giving those on each side 480 square feet of living space (240 each on the main floor and the loft). See Wells, "Eighteenth-Century Landscape of Virginia's Northern Neck," 4238.

26. LW to GW, 31 January 1776, *GWP.Rev.Series,* 3:232.

27. GW to Arthur Young, 12 December 1793, *GWW,* 33:178; Sobel, *World They Made Together,* 113.

28. Wells, "Eighteenth-Century Landscape of Virginia's Northern Neck," 4237.

29. Kelso, "Mulberry Row," 31, 32; Sobel, *World They Made Together,* 103–4, 112.

30. Nylander, *Our Own Snug Fireside,* 6–7.

31. Schulz, "Children and Childhood in the Eighteenth Century," 79–80.

32. Anburey, *Travels through the Interior,* 2:322–23. For other examples of such quarters, see Vlach, *Back of the Big House,* 155–60.

33. LW to GW, 24 November 1775, *GWP.Rev.Series,* 2:423.

34. GW, "Memorandum of Carpentry Work to Be Done," [June 1791], *GWW,* 31:307.

35. Louis-Philippe, *Diary of My Travels,* 32; Niemcewicz, *Under Their Vine and Fig Tree,* 100.

36. AW to GW, 16 January 1793, *GWP.Pres.Series,* 12:8.

37. Niemcewicz, *Under Their Vine and Fig Tree,* 100. The cabin and its accompanying garden belonged to the family of Delia, one of the fieldworkers at Union Farm who was rented by Washington from a neighbor, Mrs. French. The fact that this was Union Farm—and Delia's cabin—was discovered in 1992. Earlier in the account of his activities on this day (4 June), Niemcewicz mentioned visiting Washington's mill and distillery, which were situated on the creek separating Dogue Run Farm and Union Farm. The cabin, therefore, was most likely on one of those two farms. Later, Niemcewicz mentioned the presence in the cabin of a fifteen-year-old boy who was very ill, suffering from convulsions, and that the doctor had been sent to treat him. Interestingly, a weekly report survives for the period of 2–9 June 1798. During that week, Delia was off for all six workdays in order to care for her son Daniel, who was sick. The 1799 Slave Lists show a reference to Delia, age thirty-five, who worked as a spinner, had no husband, and was the mother of at least six children, the oldest of whom was sixteen-year-old Daniel. The previous year, when Niemcewicz had been to Mount Vernon and seen a very ill fifteen-year-old boy in the quarter, Daniel had been fifteen years old and very sick. It followed from these facts that Niemcewicz had visited and described the quarter at Union Farm and, more specifically, Delia's cabin.

38. Vail, "Two Early Visitors to Mount Vernon," 355, 361–62.

39. LW to GW, 10 December 1775, *GWP.Rev.Series,* 2:527.

40. GW to James Anderson (farm manager), 11 June 1798, *GWW,* 36:287.

41. GW, General Orders, 14, 27 May 1778, *GWW,* 11:387, 463. The author's mother lived in a log cabin as a child and remembered that the chinking between the logs was

regularly removed during the summer as a means of increasing ventilation, so that practice, at least, was still being done in the American South in the 1930s.

42. NCL to Frances Parke Lewis Butler, 8 April 1832, quoted in Knock, "New Insights into Slave Life at Woodlawn Plantation," 6.

43. Martin, *Buying into the World of Goods,* 175, 177–78, 179–81, 180 (quotation); the spiritual traits of mirrors are discussed at 188–90, 238n45.

44. Pogue, "Archaeology of Plantation Life," 76–78; Pogue and White, "Summary Report on the 'House for Families' Slave Quarter Site," 19.

45. MVLA, "Archaeological Artifact Catalogue, House for Families, 1984–1985," photostat, FWSNL; Pogue and White, "Summary Report on the 'House for Families' Slave Quarter Site," 13–36.

46. GW to WP, 28 December 1794, *GWW,* 34:74; John Carlile to GW, 21 December 1794, *GWP.Pres.Series,* 17:297.

47. GW to GAW, 2 September 1787, *GWP.Con.Series,* 5:311; GW to WP, 29 November 1795, *GWW,* 34:379. See also Gorham, "'The People Shall Be Cloathed,'" 4–5.

48. GW to Tobias Lear, 7 October 1791, *GWW,* 31:383–84, 385. For other, but by no means all, examples of correspondence concerning blankets, see GW to Clement Biddle, 15 May, 11 June, 2 October 1783, 30 June 1784, 18 May, 30 July 1786; GW to Daniel Parker, 18 June 1783, ibid., 26:435, 436; 27:6, 175–76, 428, 21; 28:430, 492.

49. GW to GAW, 2 September 1787, ibid., 29:268–69.

50. See "Account of Blankets Received . . . Contra . . . Delivered," Mount Vernon Farm Ledger, January 1794–December 1796, 51.

51. Entry for 14 August 1784, LW Account Book, 137.

52. GW, General Orders, 1 September 1782, *GWW,* 25:101–2. For the use of similar beds at a Virginia tavern in 1785, described by the user as "a straw paliasse with blankets and no sheets," see Hadfield, *Englishman in America,* 4.

53. GW, "River Farm: Crops for, and Operations Thereon, for the Year 1800," *GWW,* 37:468.

54. GW to "Richard," [1749–50], ibid., 1:17.

55. GW to John Augustine Washington, 14 June 1755, ibid., 1:140.

56. See Ledger B, 8 May 1772, 5a.

57. GW to LW, 10[–17] December 1776, *GWP.Rev.Series,* 7:290.

58. See LW Account Book, 1–7a, and Gorham, "'The People Shall Be Cloathed,'" 2–4. With the exception of the people working in the mansion and on the carriage, the slaves probably wore the single pair of shoes received each year only in cooler weather and on Sundays and special occasions. This does not seem to have been unusual for even upper-class white Americans at this period. For an example of a well-educated white American at this period, the eminent botanist William Bartram, hoeing his garden while barefooted, see Cutler and Cutler, *Life Journals and Correspondence of Rev. Manasseh Cutler,* 1:272–73. Devereux Jarratt, an eighteenth-century Anglican minister who was the son of a carpenter in New Kent County, Virginia, recalled that in his family, "our raiment was altogether my mother's manufacture, except our hats and *shoes,* the *latter* of which we never put on, but in the winter season." Jarratt, *Life of the Reverend Devereux Jarratt,* 14. For an example of one of

Thomas Jefferson's teenaged grandsons coming into the drawing room at Monticello barefoot, see Augustus John Foster, "1807: The Visit of a British Diplomat," in Peterson, *Visitors to Monticello,* 39. For a comment about enslaved women driving plows while barefoot, see the interview with Henry James Trentham in Hurmence, *My Folks Don't Want Me to Talk about Slavery,* 7. As a child, my mother grew up on a tenant farm in Arkansas during the Great Depression and was seven years old before she received her first pair of shoes. She noted that, prior to getting shoes, she and her siblings had developed such thick calluses on their feet that they could break glass with them without getting cut. Something similar was probably true for the feet of the fieldworkers and children at Mount Vernon.

59. David Humphreys to Thomas Jefferson, 29 November 1788, Jefferson, *The Papers of Thomas Jefferson,* 14:303.

60. GW, Enclosure, Invoice to Robert Cary & Co., 20 September 1759, *GWP.Col.Series,* 6:353, 355n; GW to Clement Biddle, 4 April 1788, *GWP.Con.Series,* 6:197; Queen, *Textiles for Colonial Clothing,* 28, 30, 35.

61. Baumgarten, *What Clothes Reveal,* 133–34; Morgan, "Interracial Sex in the Chesapeake and the British Atlantic World," 63.

62. Verme, *Seeing America and Its Great Men,* 47. A few months later, this same man referred to the "nakedness" of the slaves on the West Indian island of Antigua; see ibid., 64.

63. GW to Philip Marsteller, 15 December 1786, *GWP.Con.Series,* 4:454, 455n2.

64. See "Union Farm," June 1794; "Dogue Run Farm," June 1794; "Muddy Hole Farm," 6 May, 3 July 1794; "River Farm," June 1794, Mount Vernon Farm Ledger, January 1794–December 1796, 40–43.

65. WP to GW, 22 February 1795, *GWP.Pres.Series,* 17:559, 560n2.

66. James Anderson (farm manager) to GW, 23 June 1799, *GWP.Ret.Series,* 4:147, 148. The figures for clothing are taken from an interesting letter in which Anderson outlined a plan for reducing the number of slaves needed on the outlying farms and sending the surplus workers to settle on Washington's western lands.

67. See LW Account Book, 1–7a, and Gorham, "'The People Shall Be Cloathed,'" 2–4.

68. Baumgarten, *What Clothes Reveal,* 128–32; Gorham, "'The People Shall Be Cloathed,'" 10.

69. GW to Richard Washington, 6 December 1755, Enclosure, Invoice, [6 December 1755], *GWP.Col.Series,* 2:208, 209. For other references to the purchase of the Washington livery, see GW to Robert Cary & Co., 20 September 1759; GW to Charles Lawrence, 10 August 1764; GW to Clement Biddle, 8, 17 January, 10 March, 7 May, 30 June 1784, 3, 24 March 1788, 30 March 1789, 9 March 1797; GW to John Gill, 26 November 1799, *GWW,* 2:332, 420, 27:296, 304, 304n, 356, 398, 428, 29:434, 446, 30:254, 37:443, 576; Invoice from Robert Cary & Co., 13 February 1765, *GWP.Col.Series,* 7:353, 355; Biddle to GW, 16 March 1788, *GWP.Con.Series,* 6:156; "Household Expenses, [Philadelphia]," 15–22 March 1790, *GWP.Pres.Series,* 5:233. See also the entry dated 8 July 1790, Decatur, *Private Affairs,* 138; and entries regarding William Hunter and William Hartshorn, "Cash Pd. on Acct. of Genrl. Washington," November 1782, LW Account Book, 114.

70. For a published version of this portrait, which is in the collection of the Smithsonian Institution's National Gallery of Art, see Miles, *George and Martha Washington,* 48.

71. GW, "Invoice of Sundry's to Be Shipd by Robert Cary Esq. & Co.," 12 October 1761; GW to Charles Lawrence, 20 June 1768, *GWW,* 2:370, 493. For another reference to the Custis livery, see "Invoice of Goods Shipped on Board the Unity . . . on the Proper Acct. & Risque of Master John Custis but Consignd to Geo: Washington," 10 April 1762, Washington Invoices and Letters, 1755–66, bound photostat, FWSNL.

72. "[Account with] Andrew Judge," 1776, LW Account Book, 78.

73. Ibid., 57, 78, 79, 106, 116. For the definition of a surtout, see *OED,* 10:248. A "fustian" coat was generally made of a linen-cotton blend, although by the end of the eighteenth century might be made completely from cotton. See Queen, *Textiles for Colonial Clothing,* 35.

74. See entries for 7 July, 4 November 1789, 18 August 1790, Decatur, *Private Affairs,* 39, 41, 77, 147, 151; and WHAB, 6 June, 30 November 1793, 21 April, 31 May, 21 June, 8 September, 6 December 1794, 29:402; 30:50, 176, 182, 185, 318, 328. When another enslaved house servant, Marcus, ran away in early April 1800, the advertisement noted that when he left, he was wearing a coat and jacket of dark mixture (black and white) and black breeches. It went on to say, however, that Marcus had "various suits," and people might see him in either a black suit or one of very light "drab," a woolen fabric. For Marcus's clothing, see *Federal Gazette and Baltimore Daily Advertiser,* 30 April 1800; for the definition of "drab," see Queen, *Textiles for Colonial Clothing,* 12.

75. GW, Enclosure, Invoices to Robert Cary & Co., 15 November 1762; Invoice from Robert Cary & Co., 13 April 1763, *GWP.Col.Series,* 7:167, 168n10, 196.

76. See entries for 23 June, 10 July, 8 August, 4 November 1789; 18 August 1790; 15 January, 1, 4 June 1791; 23 May, 14 June, 12, 15 December 1792, Decatur, *Private Affairs,* 32, 41, 48, 77, 147, 188, 239, 260, 272, 314, 318. For the definition and uses of "Lawn," see Queen, *Textiles for Colonial Clothing,* 25. For the definition of "habbits," many thanks to my colleague, Samantha Dorsey, and her self-styled "Clothing Mafia," conversation with author, 12 January 2010.

77. See WHAB, 13 April, 15 May, 16 July, 4, 6 September, 21, 26 December 1793; 22 April, 2 May, 13 June, 29 July, 23 August, 24 December 1794; 12 [or 13] January, 27 March, 20 May, 14, 15 July, 9 December 1795; 30 January, 10 May, 11 June, 22 November 1796; 4 March 1797, 29:392, 398; 30:32, 45, 53, 54, 176, 178, 184, 312, 316, 330, 461, 471, 477; 31:59, 60, 70, 78, 182, 189, 327, 344. For the definition and uses of "Checks," see Queen, *Textiles for Colonial Clothing,* 26.

78. Hannah Bushrod Washington, "Last Will and Testament," n.d. [proved 26 April 1801], typescript, FWSNL.

79. See Store Account, 4 November 1785, Mount Vernon Farm Ledger, January 1794–December 1796, 85. For the definition of "calico," see Queen, *Textiles for Colonial Clothing,* 31.

80. See Store Account, 11 May 1796, Mount Vernon Farm Ledger, January 1794–December 1796, 87.

81. See Mount Vernon Distillery and Fishery Ledger, 1 March 1799, 36.

82. See ibid., 29 January 1800, 47.

83. Louis-Philippe, *Diary of My Travels*, 32.

84. See Brookes, "A Dinner at Mount Vernon," 76.

85. Heath and Bennett, "'The Little Spots Allow'd Them,'" 39–44, 39, 43 (quotations).

86. Niemcewicz, *Under Their Vine and Fig Tree*, 100–101.

87. Atkins, "Mount Vernon: Identified Taxa." The cat remains might also relate to African spiritual practices, as explained in the next chapter.

88. GW to AW, 16 December 1792, *GWW*, 32:264.

89. Anburey, *Travels through the Interior*, 2:452–53.

90. Latrobe, *Latrobe's View of America*, 270–72.

91. Savitt, *Medicine and Slavery*, 50; MW to FBW, 9 March 1794, Washington, *"Worthy Partner,"* 261.

92. *GWD*, 1, 3, 4, 8, 19 January, 7 February, 26 April, 5 May 1760, 1:211, 214, 215, 217, 226, 235, 273, 276.

93. Ibid., 7, 8 May 1760, 1:276–77. The nurse hired to look after the sick slaves appears to have been Mary Thomas. See "Cash . . . Contra," 1761, Ledger A, 143a.

94. For the hospital for sick slaves, see LW to GW, 23 December 1775, *GWP.Rev.Series*, 2:594–95.

95. For the story of Washington's actions in regard to the threat of smallpox early in the Revolution, see Thompson, "'More to Dread,'" and Fenn, *Pox Americana*.

96. For the Washington quotations about inoculation, see GW to John Augustine Washington, 1 June 1777, *GWW*, 8:157–58.

97. Jean-Pierre Brissot-Warville, "General Observations on Maryland and Virginia," quoted in Chinard, *George Washington as the French Knew Him*, 87.

98. James Anderson (farm manager) to GW, 22 May 1798, *GWP.Ret.Series*, 2:291–92.

99. GAW to GW, 16 July 1790, *GWP.Pres.Series*, 6:92.

100. Savitt, *Medicine and Slavery*, 71–73. For references to fleas infesting the cabins of white settlers on the frontier, see Ulrich, *Midwife's Tale*, 188.

101. See, for example, WP to GW, 31 August 1794, *GWP.Pres.Series*, 16:621.

102. GW to WP, 14 September 1794, *GWW*, 33:499.

103. Savitt, *Medicine and Slavery*, 61, 63.

104. GW to WP, 31 August, 14 September 1794, *GWW*, 33:489, 499. Jesuit's or Peruvian bark was the powdered bark of the cinchona tree, from which quinine is extracted.

105. Savitt, *Medicine and Slavery*, 64–66, 89–90.

106. LW to GW, 22 April 1778, *GWP.Rev.Series*, 14:589, 590n10; Lewis, *Nelly Custis Lewis's Housekeeping Book*, 107; Hess, *Martha Washington's Booke of Cookery*, 125, 383, 426. For the death of another child, also attributed to worms, see Weekly Report, 18 February 1797, Mount Vernon Weekly Reports, 10 January 1795–18 March 1797.

107. Ulrich, *Midwife's Tale*, 246–47. In the antebellum South, not realizing that malnutrition was the actual cause of the deaths, some 1,709 deaths were attributed to worms in 1849–50. Of this number, 77 percent of the sufferers were black, and 96 percent of the total were children, nine years of age or younger. See Kiple and King, *Another Dimension to the Black Diaspora*, 113–15.

108. MW to FBW, 5 June 1791; 15 June 1794, Washington, *"Worthy Partner,"* 232, 268.

109. GW to WP, 27 October 1793, *GWW,* 33:142–43.

110. GAW to GW, 8[–9] April 1792, *GWP.Pres.Series,* 10:233.

111. GW to Howell Lewis, 3 November 1793, *GWW,* 33:144.

112. For references to slave children and the chore of drawing water, see GW to AW, 25 November 1792; GW to James Anderson (farm manager), 1 November 1798, ibid., 32:240; 37:2. For the gathering of wood, see Weekly Report, [16] February 1793, Thom Collection.

113. GW, "Memorandum of Carpentry Work to Be Done," [June 1791], *GWW,* 31:307.

114. GW to WP, 29 May 1796, ibid., 35:72.

115. MVLA, "Archaeological Artifact Catalogue, House for Families"; Pogue and White, "Summary Report on the 'House for Families' Slave Quarter Site," 19, 20.

116. Vlach, *Back of the Big House,* 21.

117. Ibid., 230–36.

7. "And Procure for Themselves a Few Amenities"

1. AW to GW, 22 January 1792, *GWP.Pres.Series,* 9:498–99.

2. White and White, "Slave Hair and African American Culture in the Eighteenth and Nineteenth Centuries," 46, 47, 69–73. In addition to complex hair styles, African and African American culture has long placed an emphasis on headcoverings as well. See Paul Richard, "On Top of the World: Museum of African Art's 'Crowning Achievements,'" and Robin D. Givhan, "Hat Tricks: Headgear Speaks Volumes," both *Washington Post,* 12 May 1996.

3. *Columbian Mirror and Alexandria Gazette,* 12 April 1800.

4. GW to WP, 1 May 1796, *GWW,* 35:34.

5. See entry dated 9 June 1797, GW Cash Memoranda, September 1794–December 1799, 32, A-55, FWSNL.

6. Mullin, *Flight and Rebellion,* 76, 80–81, 93–94, 111, 114, 121, 130, 190n68; Sobel, *World They Made Together,* 184–85; Kolchin, *American Slavery,* 141–42; Nicholls, "Alexandria and African Americans in the Age of Washington," 18. For estimates on the percentage of slaves who were literate in the eighteenth century, see Fogel, *Without Consent or Contract,* 156–57. Laws prohibiting the teaching of reading and writing to slaves were passed in Virginia in the nineteenth century but were largely ignored. See Kolchin, *American Slavery,* 129, and Loth, *Virginia Landmarks of Black History,* 41. For a discussion of education among slaves, see Genovese, *Roll, Jordan, Roll,* 561–66, and Cornelius, *When I Can Read My Title Clear.*

7. GW to James Anderson (farm manager), 5 September 1796, photocopy, A-283, FWSNL. Thank you to David Hoth at the Papers of George Washington project for bringing this quotation to my attention.

8. Weekly Reports, 11, 25 February 1786, Mount Vernon Weekly Reports, 26 November 1785–30 December 1786.

9. "Account with Davie Gray," 12 January 1801, Letterbook, 1800–1829, Peter Family Collection, box 4, F.

10. GW to Roger West, 19 September 1799, *GWW,* 37:367–68.

11. GW to WP, 21 February 1796, ibid., 34:476.

12. Morgan and Nicholls, "Slave Flight," 204.

13. Chase, "Mrs. [?] Staines," 249; Adams, "Washington's Runaway Slave." From this statement, it would appear that training in the rudiments of reading and writing were not provided by the Washingtons as a routine part of slave life at Mount Vernon, as they would be in the next century at Thomas Jefferson's Monticello and at Martha Washington's grandson's home, Arlington. See Stanton, "'Those Who Labor for My Happiness,'" 167; Lee, *Growing up in the 1850s,* 9; Coulling, *Lee Girls,* 38; and Nelligan, "'Old Arlington,'" 153.

14. See Ledger B, 25 December 1773, 98a.

15. See entries dated 18 May, 29 September, 5 October, 13, 20 November 1784, GW Cash Memoranda, September 1783–November 1784, 113, 129, 131. For similar payments to slaves from before the Revolution, see Ledger B, 4, 9, 17 September; 21 October; 16 November 1772, 60a, 61a.

16. Niemcewicz, *Under Their Vine and Fig Tree,* 99.

17. Paston-Williams, *Art of Dining,* 108, 221–22. See also Gordon-Reed, *Hemingses of Monticello,* 209–10.

18. See the editors' translation of Philipe de Létombe to Thomas Jefferson, 26 March 1801, Jefferson, *The Papers of Thomas Jefferson,* 33:450. According to this letter, the man hired by Jefferson, Honoré Julien, had worked for the Washingtons in Philadelphia during the last four months of the presidency, when Hercules was at Mount Vernon.

19. Custis, *Recollections and Private Memoirs,* 423.

20. "Flour Accompt . . . Contra," "Cash," 14, 15, 22 December 1798, Mount Vernon Farm Ledger, 1797–98, 168, 191.

21. Charles MacIver to GW, 17 June 1786, *GWP.Con.Series,* 4:113–15, 115n3. This incident gives evidence of the secondhand market, which was utilized by lower-class whites and slaves alike. Reverend Devereux Jarratt, a contemporary of the Washingtons, recalled that as a young man of nineteen, around 1752, he set off for Albemarle County, Virginia, to start a school. So concerned was he with appearances that he made use of this market in used goods to acquire a wig, "which, perhaps, being cast off by the master, had become the property of his slave, and from the slave it was conveyed to me." Jarratt, *Life of Devereux Jarratt,* 26.

22. Christy Coleman Matthews, Department of African-American Interpretation, Colonial Williamsburg, conversation with author, mid-1990s.

23. For Sukey Washington, the daughter of Robert Washington of Westmoreland County, Virginia, in the eighteenth century, see Wayland, *Washingtons and Their Homes,* 342. For the fact that Susannah Bishop, the wife of Washington's longtime white servant Thomas Bishop, was also known as "Suekey," see *GWP.Col.Series,* 10:19, 20n11.

24. Flexner, *I Hear America Talking,* 33; Holloway, "Africanisms in African American Names in the United States," 100. See also "Bambara" and "Wolof" in *New Encyclopaedia Britannica,* 1:852–53; 12:731.

25. Niemcewicz, *Under Their Vine and Fig Tree,* 100.

26. District of Columbia Land Records, 26 November 1805, Liber O, no. 14, p. 18.

Historian Lorena Walsh notes that the furnishings in Nancy's home suggest that she supported herself by washing clothing and other textiles for residents of the District of Columbia. Lorena Walsh to Richard Holway, email communication, 28 July 2010, in author's possession.

27. *Alexandria Gazette,* 27 October 1798.

28. GW, "Cash Accounts," 20 May 1768, *GWP.Col.Series,* 8:83; "Cash Pd. on Acct. of General Washington," 18 August 1783; "Cash Pd. on Acct. of Genrl. Washington," 22 April 1785, LW Account Book, 125, 149.

29. Charles MacIver to GW, 17 June 1786, *GWP.Con.Series,* 4:113.

30. Niemcewicz, *Under Their Vine and Fig Tree,* 101.

31. See Ledger B, 13 September 1792, 344a.

32. Custis, *Recollections and Private Memoirs,* 456–57; An Old Citizen of Fairfax County, "Mount Vernon Reminiscences," *Alexandria Gazette,* 18 January 1876.

33. Miller, *Pen Portraits,* 281–82; Powell, *History of Old Alexandria,* 58–59.

34. *Columbian Mirror and Alexandria Gazette,* 12 June 1798; Virginia, *Statutes at Large,* 12:183. For an example of a pass from a later owner of Mount Vernon, John Augustine Washington II, allowing one of his slaves to sell things from the Mount Vernon greenhouse, see *Alexandria Gazette,* 11 August 1831.

35. Ledger B, 11 September 1790, 320a. Washington's fondness for nuts also encouraged enslaved people to sell them to him, as when Harry sold nuts to Washington at least twice in 1765. See "Account with Joseph Devenport," Ledger A, 210a.

36. Isaac, *Landon Carter's Uneasy Kingdom,* 199.

37. Virginia, *Statutes at Large,* 12:182. An interesting entry in a financial ledger notes that Isaac, Mount Vernon's head carpenter, was paid four dollars in 1799 "for one Gun, by the Generals Order, & for his [Behest?]." It is unclear from this reference if Isaac was being given the money to purchase a gun or if he was being rewarded for turning in a firearm confiscated from a poacher. See undated entry in the account with Mansion House Farm overseer Moses Dowdal in Mount Vernon Distillery and Fishery Ledger, 2.

38. Entry for 19 January 1787, Mount Vernon Store Book.

39. Ledger B, 3 October 1792, 346a.

40. Custis, *Recollections and Private Memoirs,* 457–58.

41. Provine, *Alexandria County, Virginia, Free Negro Registers,* 105, 209; M. to Mr. Snowden, "Communicated," *Alexandria Gazette,* 16 November 1835; "Mount Vernon Reminiscences," *Alexandria Gazette,* 18, 22, 25 January 1876.

42. *Alexandria Gazette,* 10 August 1786; GW to Archibald Johnston, 30 October 1787, *GWW,* 29:295–96.

43. Joseph Lewis, Jr., to GW, 12 November 1787, *GWP.Con.Series,* 5:431–32.

44. Bennion, *Antique Dental Instruments,* 82; Weinberger, *Introduction to the History of Dentistry,* 1:357, 366; Woodforde, *The Strange Story of False Teeth,* 28, 61–63, 83. For a fine overview of Washington's dentures as an artifact, their role in the early history of the United States, and issues relating to the purchase of teeth from the poor, including slaves, see Van Horn, "George Washington's Dentures."

45. Woodforde, *The Strange Story of False Teeth,* 81–83.

46. Forbes, *Paul Revere and the World He Lived In,* 127; *GWD,* 15 September 1785, 4:193–94n; *GWP.Con.Series,* 3:337–38n; Weinberger, *Introduction to the History of*

Dentistry, 1:355, 366. The information on Le Moyer's string of failed transplants in Philadelphia is taken from Woodforde, *The Strange Story of False Teeth,* 84–85.

47. "Cash Pd. on Acct. of Genrl. Washington," May 1784, LW Account Book, 134.

48. *GWD,* 15, 19, 25, 26 September 1785, 15, 17, 23, 28 June, 1 July, 14, 22, 26 December 1786, 5, 9 February 1787, 20 November 1788, 4:193, 193–94n, 195, 198, 348, 349, 352, 354, 5:1, 78, 83, 84, 101, 103, 426; *GWP.Con.Series,* 1:63–64, 64n, 64n2, 148–49, 149n3, 149n4, 2:38–39.

49. GW to Richard Varick, 22 February 1784, *GWW,* 27:342–43; Woodforde, *The Strange Story of False Teeth,* 83–84.

50. GW to WP, 16, 30 November 1794, *GWW,* 34:24–25, 48.

51. GW to AW, 18 November 1792, ibid., 32:232. For the fact that bells and "buck[le]s for sheep bells" were purchased for the Mount Vernon sheep, see Ledger B, 8, 15 December 1792, 348a. For other references to slaves using dogs for hunting and efforts to control the same, see Carter, *Diary,* March 1752, February 1764, 1:72–73, 75, 77, 86, 87, 89, 254, 258, 261; Custis, *Recollections and Private Memoirs,* 66; Virginia, *Statutes at Large,* 6:295–296; and Parkinson, *Tour in America,* 2:446. For further information on slaves and dogs, see Campbell, "'My Constant Companion.'"

52. GW to AW, 16 December 1792, *GWW,* 32:264. For an example of Washington ordering his soldiers' dogs hanged during the French and Indian War, after they had become "a great Neausance in Camp," see Orderly Book, [24 November 1758], *GWP.Col.Series,* 6:156.

53. Boorer, *World of Dogs,* 61.

54. Hay, "Poaching and the Game Laws on Cannock Chase," 193, 194, 196, 215, 238; McEwan, *Thomas Jefferson,* 128; Zanne McDonald, Research Department, Thomas Jefferson Memorial Foundation, Monticello, Virginia, conversation with author, 5 October 1993. For additional examples of George Washington and other members of the Custis, Lewis, and Washington families prohibiting hunting on their estates, see *Alexandria Gazette,* 10 August 1786; 28 October 1800; 30 July, 3 November 1801; 3 December 1802; 16 September 1805; 14 September 1822; 20 November 1827; 23 July 1829; 1 September 1832.

55. Bilali, "Salih Bilali's Recollections of Massina," 150; Osifekunde, "The Land and People of Ijebu," 252.

56. GW to WP, 9 February 1794, *GWW,* 33:267. For the importance of these hours to the slave children, see Wiggins, "The Play of Slave Children," 182–83.

57. GW to WP, 18 May 1794, *GWW,* 33:369; GW to James Anderson (farm manager), 20 February 1797, Thom Collection. For similar complaints by Washington's contemporaries Thomas Jefferson and John Tayloe II about their slaves, see Stanton, *Slavery at Monticello,* 39, and Kamoie, *Irons in the Fire,* 45.

58. See 1786 Slave List. In much the same way, former slaves raised on nineteenth-century plantations recalled traveling away from their home farms in order to enlarge their circle of playmates. See Wiggins, "The Play of Slave Children," 175–76.

59. Pogue and White, "Summary Report on the 'House for Families' Slave Quarter Site," 24–27. It is unfortunate that there is so little physical or documentary evidence for music by slaves at Mount Vernon during Washington's lifetime, something that is not true for Monticello or for the Tayloes' plantations; for music on those estates, see Stanton, *Slavery at Monticello,* 39–40, and Kamoie, *Irons in the Fire,* 45.

Washington's hire of a slave named Charles to play for an election ball in Alexandria may suggest that he either did not feel any of the slaves at Mount Vernon had the talent to entertain at such a venue or that he did not like the types of music they played. See *GWD*, 4 December 1771, 3:74, 74n. Although it was not published until 1805, Richard Parkinson's description of American slaves was based on his experiences as Washington's neighbor in the late eighteenth century. In speaking of Washington as a slave owner, this reference might be to slaves in general or specifically to those at Mount Vernon: "They are so lazy by nature, that they would do little or nothing, but take pleasure in fine weather, cook victuals, and play on music and dance all winter, if they had no master." Parkinson, *Tour in America*, 2:419. There are some wonderful descriptions of slaves and music at Mount Vernon and its surrounding area in the nineteenth century. A visitor in 1844 recorded, "Just before arriving at the Mount Vernon plantation, the tympanum of our ears was aroused by the loud singing of some twenty slaves, who were chopping by the wayside. These poor fellows became silent as we approached, and taking off their apologies for hats, bowed to us as reverentially, as though we had been the autocrat of Russia." See "Visit to Mount Vernon from the *Woonsocket Patriot*," *Herald*, November 1844, Early Descriptions Notebook. In the late 1840s, a later Washington at Mount Vernon would write of Christmas as practiced at the plantation at that period: "The real frolic however was out of doors, the negroes dressed in their 'Sunday Best' with a horn, a fiddle & a tambourine, passed around the yard, & house to the Portico to give us a serenade, when with such singing, fiddling, music dancing, jumping & scraping, as I have not seen for many a day, they performed a variety of quadrilles and intricate manouvres to our great amusement and their own infinite satisfaction." See John Augustine Washington III to Jane Charlotte Blackburn Washington, 28 December 1849, typescript, RM-732/4926, FWSNL. The granddaughters of Caroline Branham, a maid at Mount Vernon, were described many years later as having sung "the old plantation songs," as well as the popular ballad of Kitty Wells, in the 1850s, when they acted as the nursemaids for a family in Alexandria. See Powell, "Scenes of Childhood," 3. For the nineteenth-century song "Kitty Wells," written by Thomas Sloan, Jr., see "America Singing: Nineteenth-Century Song Sheets," Rare Book and Special Collections Division, Library of Congress, https://www.loc.gov/resource/amss.as107320/?st=text/.

60. Pogue and White, "Summary Report on the 'House for Families' Slave Quarter Site," 24–27. For pipes found in other slave dwellings, see Heath, *Hidden Lives*, 56–58, and Howard, "Slavery in Our Midst," 26. For use of pipes and tobacco by both sexes in Africa, see Walsh, *From Calabar to Carter's Grove*, 60, 61–63.

61. Custis, *Recollections and Private Memoirs*, 456.

62. See Stanton, "'Those Who Labor for My Happiness,'" 166–67, for a discussion of music among the slaves at Monticello and a similar example of slaves telling stories to Thomas Jefferson's daughter Martha. For an example of a young girl who grew up near Philadelphia in the eighteenth century and remembered hearing African songs from an elderly slave who had been born there, see Saltar, "Fanny Saltar's Reminiscences of Colonial Days in Philadelphia," 189. For general information on storytelling on nineteenth-century plantations, see Wiggins, "The Play of Slave Children," 182.

63. Powell, "Scenes of Childhood," 3.

64. Levine, *Black Culture and Black Consciousness,* 81–83, 103, 106–20; Bickley, "Joel Chandler Harris"; Werner, "Brer Rabbit in Africa."

65. Pogue and White, "Summary Report on the 'House for Families' Slave Quarter Site," 33. For marbles found at other slave sites, see Heath, *Hidden Lives,* 55, and Howard, "Slavery in Our Midst," 26.

66. Mergen, "Top-Time's Gone, Kite-Time's Come"; Mergen, *Play and Playthings,* 8, 11, 41, 42, 45; Wiggins, "The Play of Slave Children," 180.

67. LW to GW, 2 September 1778, *GWP.Rev.Series,* 16:497–98, 501n4. By way of contrast, for a description of upper-class white urbanites going swimming at this period, see entry for 12 August 1789, Robert Lewis, Diary, 4 July–1 September 1789, typescript, H-1199/D, FWSNL.

68. Niemcewicz, *Under Their Vine and Fig Tree,* 101.

69. Carson, *Colonial Virginians at Play,* 44; Mohr, *Games Treasury,* 310–11; Opie, *Children's Games,* 7, 9–10, 143–46; Mergen, *Play and Playthings,* 8, 74.

70. See entry dated 26 October 1784, GW Cash Memoranda, September 1783–November 1784, 129; *GWD,* 9 October, 11–12 October 1786, 5:49, 50; Charles MacIver to GW, 17 June 1786, *GWP.Con.Series,* 4:113.

71. Decatur, *Private Affairs,* 233; WHAB, 1 April, 24 June, 13 July 1793, 29:391, 405; 30:32.

72. Custis, *Recollections and Private Memoirs,* 501–2; Lossing, *Mary and Martha,* 103; Lossing, *Mount Vernon and Its Associations,* 50–51.

73. Lee, *Growing up in the 1850s,* 80–81.

74. Lear, *Letters and Recollections,* 138–41. Another family story passed down by slaves and former slaves to much later generations of Washington descendants dealt with the funeral of Martha Washington's son, John Parke Custis, who died at the home of his uncle Burwell Bassett in early November 1781. "Uncle Jimmy," who lived to be 103 years old, described Custis being brought from Yorktown to Eltham and how, when the young man died, "dey wrapped his body in flags—dey took him [a]way to bury him." Uncle Jimmy went along with the funeral party, although he did not specify his own role in this occasion. See MVLA, *Minutes of the Council,* 1931, 82–83.

75. Chase, "Mrs. [?] Staines," 249.

76. Elizabeth Bordley, n.d. [1790–97], quoted in Thane, *Mount Vernon Family,* 74.

77. Kolchin, *American Slavery,* 54, 55; Nelligan, "'Old Arlington,'" 118. See also Berard, "Arlington and Mount Vernon," 161, and Lossing, "Mount Vernon as It Is," 445.

78. Kay and Cary, *Slavery in North Carolina,* 195.

79. Tate, *Negro in Eighteenth-Century Williamsburg,* 119–29. For more on the writing off of African-born slaves as candidates for conversion, see Butler, *Awash in a Sea of Faith,* 133. For owner fears about conversion changing about 1740, see Walsh, *From Calabar to Carter's Grove,* 152–53.

80. Walsh, *Motives of Honor, Pleasure, and Profit,* 445.

81. Elizabeth Foote Washington, Journal, typescript, 6–7, FWSNL.

82. Charles Green, "Fairfax County List of Titheables for 1749," photostat, FWSNL. For an example of a different situation in another Virginia parish, St. Mary's in Caroline County, in which the only "infidels" were "negroes" and "particular

means" for converting them were "discouraged," see Mays, *Edmund Pendleton,* 1:18. By 1765, the situation in St. Mary's had changed with the coming of a new rector, Jonathan Boucher, who would later take over the education of George Washington's stepson. Boucher recorded that on 24 November 1765, he baptized 115 "negro adults" at his church. Several months later, on 31 March 1766, which was the Easter Monday holiday, he baptized another 313 and "lectured extempore to upwards of one thousand." He noted that he had "under my care many negroes as well-informed, as orderly and even as regularly pious, as country people usually are, even in England." He set up a school to teach reading to the slaves on Sunday afternoons and eventually had twenty to thirty who could "use their prayer-books, and make the responses" during the services. By the time he left the congregation there were thirteen slaves who had qualified to take communion. See Boucher, *Reminiscences of an American Loyalist,* 57–59.

83. Register of Bruton Parish Church, Williamsburg, Virginia, transcribed in Linda H. Rowe, historian at the Colonial Williamsburg Foundation, to Susan Fincke, 29 May 1997, Education Department, Mount Vernon, VA. For a description of Washington's nephew Lawrence Lewis kneeling at the communion rail beside one of his slaves "after the white members had communed" at the Episcopal Church in Berryville, Virginia, sometime prior to his death in 1839, see Meade, *Old Churches, Ministers, and Families,* 2:231–32. Bishop Meade surmised, without providing evidence, that Lewis felt "no doubt that one God made them and one Saviour redeemed them."

84. Louis-Philippe, *Diary of My Travels,* 32. See Stanton, "'Those Who Labor for My Happiness,'" 168, for a discussion of the religious life of the slaves at Monticello, and Walsh, *From Calabar to Carter's Grove,* 151–59, for religion on Burwell family plantations. For material on religion among African American slaves in general, see Kolchin, *American Slavery,* 55–57; Morgan, "Slave Life in Piedmont Virginia," 472–79; and Sobel, *World They Made Together,* 187–98. Church membership figures for African Americans in 1790 are from Tate, *Negro in Eighteenth-Century Williamsburg,* 157.

85. Elizabeth Foote Washington, Journal, 28–29.

86. For Alexandria and the abolition society, see Schwarz, "George Washington and the Developing Law of Slavery in Virginia"; Nicholls, "Alexandria and African Americans in the Age of Washington," 17–19, 24–25; and Fasy, "After Prayer and Praise," 27.

87. Fasy, "After Prayer and Praise," 125; Lynch, *Compendium of Early African Americans,* 83, 84. For continued ties to the Baptist church in Alexandria, see the story of Charles Syphax, who was enslaved at both Mount Vernon and Arlington, and was a member later in the nineteenth century, in Preston, "William Syphax," 448–49.

88. Agnes Mullins, curator at Arlington House; Anna Lynch, historical researcher with the Alexandria Department of Archaeology; and Wilson Gaines, historian for First Baptist Church of Alexandria, conversations with author, 1992. For the location of the Back Lick Baptist Church and additional information on the early Baptist church in Alexandria, see Wallace, *I Once Was Young,* 7–24.

89. For other enslaved ministers in Virginia at this period, see Morgan, "Slave Life in Piedmont Virginia," 479.

90. For the runaway advertisement, see *GWP.Ret.Series,* 2:615n1, and Morgan and Nicholls, "Slave Flight," 204.

91. For this tradition, see "The Syphax Family," Arlington House, National Park Service, http://www.nps.gov/archive/arho/tour/history/syphax.html; Preston, "William Syphax," 448–49.

92. In earlier papers on this subject, I also identified Will, an older man who belonged to the estate of Martha Washington's first husband and lived at Muddy Hole Farm, as a minister to the enslaved community. The basis for this assessment was George Washington's 1799 Slave List, which shows several almost illegible letters after Will's name. In the Fitzpatrick edition of Washington's writings, those initials were interpreted as "Mintr." See *GWW,* 37:264. It has been suggested by at least one other historian that those letters indicated Will's role as a "minister." See Wall, "Housing and Family Life of the Mount Vernon Negro," 25–26. The more recent version of the slave list, published by the University Press of Virginia, interprets the letters after Will's name as "Mink." See *GWP.Ret.Series,* 4:532. Many thanks to my colleague Phil Morgan for pointing out both my error and the fact that "Mink Will" also showed up in other places in Washington's writings.

93. Stanton, "'Those Who Labor for My Happiness,'" 168; Walsh, *From Calabar to Carter's Grove,* 154; Bill Broadway, "Digging up Some Divining Inspiration," *Washington Post,* 16 August 1997; Linda Wheeler, "Common Objects Are an Uncommon Find: Extensive Collection of African American Hoodoo Artifacts Uncovered in Annapolis," *Washington Post,* 16 February 2000; Butler, *Awash in a Sea of Faith,* 157; Kay and Cary, *Slavery in North Carolina,* 178–79; Gomez, "Muslims in Early America"; Kolchin, *American Slavery,* 54–55; Samford, *Subfloor Pits,* 155–56, 172. See also Leone and Fry, "Conjuring in the Big House Kitchen," for an excellent example of using the strengths of both archaeology and folklore to fill in the gaps of those disciplines, in order to get a better picture of African conjuring traditions in British North America.

94. Butler, *Awash in a Sea of Faith,* 159.

95. For examples of Muslim slaves and/or their descendants continuing to practice certain ceremonies or rituals from Africa, as well as mixing elements of Christianity, Islam, and/or traditional African religions at the same time, see Curtis, *Muslims in America,* 17–21.

96. Samford, *Subfloor Pits,* 151. Of these elements, both the belief in a creator God who rules the universe and the understanding of intermediaries acting between humans and God would mesh well with traditional Christian teachings about the nature of God and the role of saints.

97. Ibid., 129–37, 139–41, 147–48, 154–72.

98. Martin, *Buying into the World of Goods,* 238n45.

99. Pogue and White, "Summary Report on the 'House for Families' Slave Quarter Site," 44–46; Howell, *I Was a Slave,* 1:41; Bowen, "Faunal Remains from the House for Families Cellar," 28; Atkins, "Archaeological Perspective on the African-American Slave Diet," 84–85; Leone and Fry, "Conjuring in the Big House Kitchen," 395. It is impossible to say at this point exactly what the meaning of the baculum and owl talons might have been. Electronic correspondence with a voodoo practitioner

in Haiti indicates that there, at least, owls are thought to embody malevolent spirits, so cutting off the talons of an owl might have been a symbolic means of taking evil power away from someone or something. The practitioner suggested that the raccoon baculum might be a power object as well, and that these two objects might reflect beliefs learned or adapted from Native Americans. Mambo Racine, Jacmel, Haiti, email correspondence, 2 October 2000.

100. Haworth, *George Washington: Country Gentleman,* 213. For descriptions by former slaves about the practice of conjuring in nineteenth-century Virginia, see Perdue, Barden, and Phillips, *Weevils in the Wheat,* 221–22, 244, 246, 263, 267–68, 278, 310–11, 324. Some of these beliefs have continued down to the present day in the local African American community; for an example of a modern murder case in which the alleged perpetrator killed his sister because he thought she had put a spell, or "done roots," on him, see Neely Tucker and Petula Dvorak, "NE Shooting Linked to 'Curse,' Prosecutors Say," *Washington Post,* 29 July 2000.

101. See I. A. Ibrahim, "What Are the Five Pillars of Islam?" A Brief Illustrated Guide to Understanding Islam, 1996–2002, http://www.islam-guide.com/ch3–16 .htm. Historians of the slave trade have provided varying estimates for the percentage of Muslims among the African-born slaves imported to the Americas, generally ranging from 10 to 20 percent. See Curtis, *Encyclopedia of Muslim-American History,* 1:20, and Kelley, *Voyage of the Slave Ship Hare,* 2, 218n2.

102. Actually, in several places, the Koran allows Muslims to eat pork and other forbidden foods, if it is necessary for survival. According to Surah 2:173, "He [Allah] has only forbidden you what dies of itself, and blood, and flesh of swine, and that over which any other (name) than (that of) Allah has been invoked; but whoever is driven to necessity, not desiring, nor exceeding the limit, no sin shall be upon him; surely Allah is Forgiving, Merciful." Again, in Surah 5:3, "Forbidden to you is that which dies of itself, and blood, and flesh of swine, and that on which any other name than that of Allah has been invoked, and the strangled (animal) and that beaten to death, and that killed by a fall and that killed by being smitten with the horn, and that which wild beasts have eaten, except what you slaughter, and what is sacrificed on stones set up (for idols) and that you divide by the arrows; that is a transgression. This day have those who disbelieve despaired of your religion, so fear them not, and fear Me. This day have I perfected for you your religion and completed My favor on you and chosen for you Islam as a religion; but whoever is compelled by hunger, not inclining willfully to sin, then surely Allah is Forgiving, Merciful." For these and other similar examples, see Shakir, *Holy Qur'an,* 16, 65–66, 88, 91, 177.

103. GW, "Memorandum: List of Titheables," [ca. July 1774], *GWP.Col.Series,* 10:137, 138n2.

104. "Fatimah," in *New Encyclopaedia Britannica,* 4:697.

105. 1799 Slave Lists, 37:256–68; Washington, *Last Will and Testament,* 2–4, 31n; Provine, *Alexandria County, Virginia, Free Negro Registers,* 10. The connection between the names Nila and Naailah, and the Arabic meaning of the name as well, were brought to the author's attention in a conversation with Nila Chowdry of the Pakistani Embassy in Washington, DC, and confirmed through the reference desk in the library at the Islamic Center in Washington, DC, 14 August 1995. For an example of the use of another Muslim name, Ozman, at Mount Vernon in the

nineteenth century, see Bushrod Washington, Slave List, 24 July 1815, Mount Vernon Farm Book, John A. Washington III, 1842, bound manuscript, FWSNL. For more information about the practice of Islam in the New World in the early nineteenth century, see Abu Bakr Al-Siddiq, "Abu Bakr Al-Siddiq of Timbuktu," 163–66; Curtis, *Muslims in America,* 6–22; and Johnston, *From Slave Ship to Harvard,* which tells the story of Yarrow Mamout, an enslaved man from the Fulani people of Senegambia who was brought to America in the early 1750s, practiced Islam throughout his life in Maryland and the District of Columbia, wrote in Arabic, and became a prominent figure in eighteenth-century Georgetown. Certain details of Mamout's life—his connection to the Fulani and the fact that he arrived in the 1750s—are similar to those in the story of Mount Vernon carpenter Sambo Anderson.

106. For the Washingtons' support of the religious practices of their hired and indentured servants, see Thompson, *"In the Hands of a Good Providence,"* 137.

107. For archaeological evidence of the mixing of Christian and African elements in the belief system of slaves at a plantation in Maryland, see John Noble Wilford, "Ezekiel Wheel Ties African Spiritual Traditions to Christianity," *New York Times,* 7 November 2016.

108. GW to the General Committee of the United Baptist Churches in Virginia, May 1789, *GWW,* 30:321.

109. "Genealogy: Harrison of James River," 277–78.

110. Sherman, "An Old Virginia Landmark."

111. Interview with Silas Jackson, Howell, *I Was A Slave,* 1:42.

112. Hurmence, *My Folks Don't Want Me to Talk about Slavery,* 8.

113. Howell, *I Was A Slave,* 1:50, 58. For another plantation where no funeral services were held for slaves, see interview with Adeline Marshall, ibid, 1:52.

114. For references to another burial ground on former Mount Vernon property, see "Firm Seeks to Empty Old Cemetery," *Washington Post,* 8 August 1967, and "Virginia: In the Circuit Court of Fairfax County, United States Plywood Corporation . . . vs. Any and All Persons Having an Interest in Any Body or Bodies Buried in an Old Cemetery, Graveyard or Burial Ground," *Fairfax Herald,* 11 August 1967. This property would become the neighborhood known as Wessynton. Many thanks to colleagues Joe Downer, Molly Kerr, and Esther White from Mount Vernon's Historic Preservation and Archaeology Departments and Maddy McCoy from Fairfax County for sharing these articles with me.

115. Caroline Moore, 30 April 1833, Lee, *Experiencing Mount Vernon,* 139.

116. "The Tomb of Washington," 162.

117. "Visit to Mount Vernon," *Cincinnati Enquirer,* 1846, Early Descriptions Notebook.

118. Documentation for the number of anomalies discovered through remote sensing comes from Downer, "Hallowed Ground, Sacred Place," 64–66, and Dennis J. Pogue, director of restoration at Mount Vernon, conversation with author, 7 February 1995.

119. For the possible meaning behind the siting of the graves, see MVLA, "The Slave Memorial at Mount Vernon," 1.

120. "Archaeologists Survey the Slave Cemetery: Beginning with a Blessing," *George Washington's Mount Vernon: Yesterday, Today, Tomorrow,* Fall 2014, 1–2. As of

the closing of the dig for the 2017 season, seventy graves had been located in the slave burial ground. Luke Pecoraro, director of archaeology, Mount Vernon, conversation with author, 29 September 2017.

121. Talk given by Jessie MacLeod and Jason Boroughs, "Updates from the Field: Lives Bound Together and the Slave Cemetery," Mount Vernon Historic Preservation and Collections Department and FWSNL, 1 November 2016.

122. For similar examples of coffins being made for slaves on the Carter and Burwell family plantations, see Carter, *Diary,* 27 July 1774, 2:841; Isaac, *Landon Carter's Uneasy Kingdom,* 190; and Walsh, *From Calabar to Carter's Grove,* 105–6. For descriptions of coffins made by "slave men on the plantation" for fellow slaves in the nineteenth century, see interview with Henry James Trentham in Hurmence, *My Folks Don't Want Me to Talk about Slavery,* 8.

123. Weekly Report, 30 August 1794, Mount Vernon Weekly Reports, 8 January 1792–8 November 1794; Carpenter's Work Report, 30 August 1794, photostat, PS-140, FWSNL; "Store Accompt . . . Contra," 11 May 1795, Mount Vernon Farm Ledger, January1794–December 1796, 32; Weekly Report, 7 April 1798, Mount Vernon Farm Ledger II, 31 March 1798–7 January 1799, 8, bound photostat, FWSNL. For other examples of coffins being made for slaves, see Weekly Report, 4 March 1797, Mount Vernon Weekly Reports, 10 January 1795–18 March 1797, and Weekly Reports, 27 May, 3 June, 22 July 1797, Mount Vernon Farm Accounts, [114], [119], [151].

124. Rum Account, 9 September 1787, Mount Vernon Store Book; Leni Ashmore Sorenson, consultant on African American history and graduate student at the College of William and Mary, conversation with author, 4 November 1994. Further evidence for some type of ceremony to mark the end of a life comes from a weekly work report showing that in the week ending 18 February 1797, Davy, an enslaved carpenter, missed one day of work because he was "Burying his Child," whose coffin was made by two of his colleagues, Nase and Joe, in the carpenter's shop. See Weekly Report, 18 February 1797, photostat, PS-141, FWSNL.

8. "Better . . . Fed Than Negroes Generally Are"

1. GW to Arthur Young, 18[–21] June 1792, *GWW,* 32:65.

2. GW to WP, 22 December 1793, ibid., 33:202.

3. GW, "Estimate of the Cost of Mrs. French's Land and Negroes on Dogue Creek, Compared with the Produce by Which It Will Be Seen What the Tenant Is to Expect," [ca. 1790], ibid., 31:186–87.

4. Niemcewicz, *Under Their Vine and Fig Tree,* 101.

5. For the size of eighteenth-century herring, see Leach, "George Washington: Waterman-Fisherman," 14.

6. U. S. Bureau of the Census, *Historical Statistics of the United States,* 755, 774.

7. Kiple and King, *Another Dimension to the Black Diaspora,* 88. There is considerable discrepancy in the figures given by various historians about the calories provided by such a diet. Todd L. Savitt, in *Medicine and Slavery,* demonstrates that such rations, which work out to about one quart of cornmeal and a half-pound of pork per day, could not sustain an adult for long. According to him, these rations would

provide 2,348 calories, or 352 less than the 2,700 calories required by a moderately active man. There would not be nearly enough calories for an adult, male or female, doing hard physical labor or to meet the caloric needs of pregnant or nursing women. Pork and cornmeal would provide more than enough protein, phosphorus, thiamine, and niacin, but a person eating such a limited diet would face significant shortages in calcium, iron, vitamin A, riboflavin, and vitamin C, which might predispose them to disease. See Savitt, *Medicine and Slavery,* 91–92. Federal government figures, however, indicate that these same rations would provide between 4,187 and 5,287 calories per day. See U. S. Bureau of the Census, *Historical Statistics of the United States,* 774. Still other studies have looked at a wider range of foods known to have been eaten by nineteenth-century slaves, consisting of the basic ration plus other kinds of meat (beef and mutton), dairy products, legumes, and other grains besides corn, and suggest that the average slave consumed about 4,200 calories per day. However, problems in the preparation and storage of corn and pork, due to the technology of the period, would have reduced the amount of thiamine available, while other nutritional shortages in the diet would have prevented the body from properly utilizing niacin. All agree that an individual eating such a limited diet might well come to suffer from beriberi, pellagra, tetany, rickets, or kwashiorkor, which are characterized by such symptoms as sore muscles, feet, and legs; night blindness; abdominal swelling; bowed legs; skin problems; and convulsions. While nineteenth-century slaves complained of all these symptoms, they may or may not have been caused by these particular diseases, because the same symptoms are rather vague and could be the result of other problems as well. See Fogel and Engerman, *Time on the Cross,* 109–15; Fogel, *Without Consent or Contract,* 132–38; and Savitt, *Medicine and Slavery,* 86–87, 86–87n.

8. Savitt, *Medicine and Slavery,* 91–92. Because of their darker skin, Africans and African Americans also faced deficiencies in vitamin D, resulting from changes in the angle and strength of sunlight caused by the difference in latitude between Africa and North America. The colder climate also necessitated wearing clothing over most of the skin for months each year, preventing the absorption of sunlight. This shortage would have had a negative impact on a number of things, including immune status and the ability to absorb calcium, which were less likely to be a problem for white southerners. See Kiple and King, *Another Dimension to the Black Diaspora,* 91–93.

9. This is discussed further in the next chapter. Historian Lorena Walsh reminded me that days a given slave was off from work because of illness should not be viewed as a "straightforward category, since they could be exaggerated by slaves feigning illness as a form of resistance, or understated because overseers forced sick slaves to work or slaves who were ailing but able to go to work preferred to do so rather than to undergo heroic European medical treatments." Lorena Walsh to Richard Holway, email communication, 28 July 2010, in author's possession.

10. Sargent, Diary, 13 October 1793.

11. GW to Arthur Young, 18[–21] June 1792, *GWW,* 32:65.

12. Fithian, *Journal and Letters,* 38.

13. Kelso, "Mulberry Row," 32.

14. Anburey, *Travels through the Interior,* 2:331–32.

15. GAW to GW, 7 December 1790, *GWP.Pres.Series,* 7:42. Unfortunately,

the corn produced for human consumption in the American South tended to be white corn, which contains no vitamin A. See Kiple and King, *Another Dimension to the Black Diaspora,* 89.

16. GW to WP, 21 December 1794, *GWW,* 34:63. I have occasionally been asked if slaves ever ate fresh corn, in addition to cornmeal. The answer is probably yes, but I do not have documentation for it at this point. Slaves may well have grown this crop in their gardens. Corn on the cob was certainly eaten by people in the eighteenth century, as recorded by a foreign traveler in New England who was served this novel dish one night for supper, noting that it was typically "either boiled in water or roasted over a grate and seasoned with fresh butter, salt, and pepper—a hearty beggar's meal." See Verme, *Seeing America and Its Great Men,* 21. Butter, salt, and pepper would only have been available to slaves at Mount Vernon if they purchased or traded for those items, but they may still have enjoyed corn cooked in this manner.

17. GW to Alexander Spotswood, 13 February 1788, *GWW,* 29:416.

18. Latrobe, *Virginia Journals,* 1:170. Richard Parkinson, a British immigrant who settled near Mount Vernon, commented on the popularity of cornmeal and cornbread among all Americans, not just the enslaved, noting that "General Washington had so habituated himself to eating the Indian corn bread, that I know of some instances of tavern-keepers having to send several miles for it, for his breakfast." Quoted in *GWD,* 1:xxxi.

19. *GWD,* 13 September 1786, 5:39.

20. GW to GAW, 26 August 1787, *GWW,* 29:265–66. For an example of George Washington's nephew Bushrod Washington feeding potatoes to his slaves about thirty years later when the cornmeal allowance ran short, see Mount Vernon Farm Book, John A. Washington III, 24, 25, 41–43.

21. LW to GW, 12 March 1783, typescript, FWSNL.

22. Weekly Report, 21 July 1798, Mount Vernon Farm Accounts II.

23. "Flour Accompt," October 1797–October 1798, Mount Vernon Farm Ledger, 1797–98, 168.

24. "Flour Account," 1797, ibid., 82.

25. GW to Howell Lewis, 18 August 1793, *GWW,* 33:54.

26. GW to Howell Lewis, 25 August 1793, ibid., 33:64.

27. GW to WP, 21 December 1794, ibid., 34:63.

28. George Grieve, eighteenth-century translator of Chastellux, quoted in the latter's *Travels in North America,* 2:597.

29. GW to WP, 23 March 1794, *GWW,* 33:303.

30. Paston-Williams, *Art of Dining,* 25–26, 211.

31. Niemcewicz, *Under Their Vine and Fig Tree,* 103, 106.

32. MVLA, "Archaeological Artifact Catalogue, House for Families"; Atkins, "Mount Vernon: Identified Taxa," 1.

33. LW to GW, 8 February 1776, *GWP.Rev.Series,* 3:271.

34. LW to GW, 1 April 1778, ibid., 14:382.

35. GW to WP, 20 April 1794, *GWW,* 33:337. For more on the practice of issuing food at Mount Vernon, at one point on a daily basis, see LW to GW, 17 January 1776, *GWP.Rev.Series,* 3:129.

36. Moore, "'Established and Well Cultivated,'" 73–74; Hume, *Food,* 14–15;

Mullin, *Flight and Rebellion*, 50. For nineteenth-century slaves receiving extra meat, fish, vegetables, molasses, milk, and buttermilk to supplement their rations, see Postell, *Health of Slaves on Southern Plantations*, 34–35, and Savitt, *Medicine and Slavery*, 91–96. For a good picture of the opinions and concerns of antebellum slave owners regarding the diet of their slaves, see Breeden, *Advice among Masters*, 89–113.

37. LW to GW, 2 September 1778, *GWP.Rev.Series*, 16:501.

38. "Mudyhole Farm," Mount Vernon Farm Ledger, 1797–98, 6.

39. GW to WP, 22 December 1793, *GWW*, 33:202. For the use of offal by free white people at this period see Glasse, *"First Catch Your Hare,"* 187, and Hume, *Food*, 14–16. For evidence that the particular cuts, in this case haslets, given to the slaves would not necessarily be considered too lowly by poorer white Americans at this period, see Ulrich, *Midwife's Tale*, 275, 337.

40. LW to GW, 17 January 1776, *GWP.Rev.Series*, 3:129.

41. GW to WP, 16 November 1794, *GWW*, 34:26.

42. Weekly Report, 4 December 1790, Mount Vernon Weekly Reports, 19 April 1789–17 September 1791, PS-11, FWSNL; Weekly Report, 5 December 1795, Mount Vernon Weekly Reports, 10 January 1795–18 March 1797; "Mudyhole Farm," Mount Vernon Farm Ledger, 1797–98, 6.

43. Weekly Report, 8 July 1786, Mount Vernon Weekly Reports, 26 November 1785–30 December 1786. For examples of beef and pork being sent during the harvest at River Farm in 1797, see "River Farm," 14 February 1798, Mount Vernon Farm Ledger, 1797–98, 111.

44. Weekly Reports, 30 June, 7 July 1798, Mount Vernon Farm Accounts II, 51, 54; "Mudyhole Farm," "Union Farm," June 1798, Mount Vernon Farm Ledger, 1797–98, 113, 115. For evidence that many planters believed that fresh meat was harmful to slaves, see Kiple and King, *Another Dimension to the Black Diaspora*, 82.

45. Weekly Report, 19 May 1798, Mount Vernon Farm Accounts II, 33.

46. Weekly Report, 23 December 1786, Mount Vernon Weekly Reports, 26 November 1785–30 December 1786.

47. "Pork," Mount Vernon Farm Ledger, 1797–98, 196.

48. See GW to Arthur Young, 18[–21] June 1792, *GWW*, 32:65.

49. "Agreement between GW and Edward Violett," 5 August 1762, *GWP.Col.Series*, 7:144.

50. Moore, "'Established and Well Cultivated,'" 77; Kiple and King, *Another Dimension to the Black Diaspora*, 83.

51. WP to GW, 11 November 1794, *GWP.Pres.Series*, 17:159.

52. Savitt, *Medicine and Slavery*, 45–46; Kiple and King, *Another Dimension to the Black Diaspora*, 11, 83–85.

53. Moore, "'Established and Well Cultivated,'" 77.

54. Bowen, "Faunal Remains from the House for Families Cellar," 9, 39–41; Pogue, "Slave Lifeways at Mount Vernon," 118–19, 132. Information about the consumption of fish bones in late nineteenth- and early twentieth-century Virginia was gleaned in conversations with Viola Prince of Alexandria, Virginia, and one of her tenants, Forrest Dishman, between 1980 and 1984, and a conversation with John Payne, curatorial steward at Mount Vernon, 15 December 1995.

55. Atkins, "Mount Vernon: Identified Taxa"; Pogue, "Archaeology of Plantation

Life," 76. For more information about hunting, see Joseph Lewis, Jr., to GW, 12 November 1787, *GWP.Con.Series,* 5:431–32; Custis, *Recollections and Private Memoirs,* 457–58; and "Mount Vernon Reminiscences," *Alexandria Gazette,* 18, 22, 25 January 1876. These small mammals were not just eaten by slaves at this period. A European visitor during the Revolution recorded his experience hunting flying squirrels on an estate in the middle colonies and later eating them served in "a fricassee." He described the flavor as "good, but not like that of a fowl, as the local people say." Verme, *Seeing America and Its Great Men,* 30–31. In other words, it did not taste like chicken.

56. Moore, "'Established and Well Cultivated,'" 74–75, 78. In considering the foods slaves acquired for themselves, it is necessary to remember that, depending on a given family's situation and their priorities, the members of that household may not have eaten those things themselves. See Shick, "An Analysis of Archaeobotanical Evidence," 65–66. Several times in the course of conversations with the late Gladys Quander Tancil, a longtime Mount Vernon employee and descendant of George Washington slaves, she related to me that in the early twentieth century, her family in Fairfax County, Virginia, always raised chickens, but that they almost never ate eggs because those had to be saved for customers. Personal communication with author, 1990s.

57. Niemcewicz, *Under Their Vine and Fig Tree,* 100–101.

58. GW to AW, 4 November 1792, *GWW,* 32:203.

59. *Columbian Mirror and Alexandria Gazette,* 12 June 1798; Nicholls, "Recreating a White Urban Virginia," 30. An Italian visitor to Antigua in 1784 recorded similar markets at which "every Sunday the Negroes bring to the market what garden produce they do not consume. Like our peasants they are permitted to keep on their place chickens, pigs, sheep, etc." Verme, *Seeing America and Its Great Men,* 64.

60. Gaspar, "Antigua Slaves and Their Struggle to Survive," 132, 135; Pulsipher, "Galways Plantation, Montserrat," 152, 156. One visitor reported that slaves on eighteenth-century Antigua received "a fixed ration of corn, salt fish, and a kind of potato called *yames,*" as well as "a piece of land which, with good cultivation, can supplement the lean diet provided by the master." Verme, *Seeing America and Its Great Men,* 64.

61. Fithian, *Journal and Letters,* 96.

62. MVLA, "Archaeological Artifact Catalogue, House for Families"; Shick, "An Analysis of Archaeobotanical Evidence," 49–62; Esther White to Christine Messing, Nancy Hayward, Steven Bashore, Ken Johnston, Eleanor Breen, and Mary V. Thompson, 17 April 2007, FWSNL.

63. See Ledger B, 29 September 1791; 3 October 1792, 333a, 346a.

64. Ibid., 23 July, 13 September 1792, 342a, 344a.

65. Ledger A, January 1758, xxii.

66. "Cash Pd. on Act. of Colo. Washington by L. W.," July 1775, LW Account Book, 49; Ledger B, 2 August, 15 September 1792, 342a, 344a.

67. See Ledger B, 7, 27 September 1788; 19 July 1789; 28 March 1791, 270a, 275a, 306a, 325a.

68. Carter, *Diary,* 20 April 1777, 2:1095–96.

69. Randolph, Monticello Household Accounts.

70. "Flour Accompt," October 1797–October 1798, Mount Vernon Farm Ledger, 1797–98, 168.

71. "Cash," entries for 14, 15, 22 December 1798, ibid., 191.

72. GW to Arthur Young, 18[–21] June 1792, *GWW*, 32:65.

73. Rum Account, "Weekly Allowances Deld. out of the Store," Mount Vernon Store Book.

74. "Cash Pd. on Acct. of Genrl. Washington," 9 June 1783, LW Account Book, 122.

75. Rum Account, entries for 4, 6, 7, 9 January 1787, Mount Vernon Store Book.

76. Rum Account, entry for 13 February 1787, ibid.

77. Rum Account, entry for 16 February 1787, ibid.

78. Rum Account, entries for 8 April, 7 May 1787, ibid.

79. Rum Account, entry for 20 March 1787, ibid.

80. Rum Account, entries for 3, 7 April 1787, ibid.

81. Rum Account, entries for 18, 26, 31 May, 23 June, 11 July, 5 August, 18 September 1787, ibid.; Ledger B, 12 June 1789, 305a. For one gallon of whiskey given to slaves at Christmas, see "Account with Christopher Hardwick, Contra," 1762, Ledger A, 91a.

82. Rum Account, entry for 18 January 1787, Mount Vernon Store Book.

83. Rum Account, entry for 9 September 1787, ibid.

84. GW to Major General William Heath, 8 June 1781, *GWW*, 22:182.

85. GW to President Meshech Weare, 5 August 1781, ibid., 22:467.

86. GW to Robert Morris, 27 September 1781, ibid., 23:144–45. See also GW to Robert Morris, 27 October 1781, 4 September 1782, ibid., 23:279; 25:124.

87. "Cash," entry for 9 October 1798, Mount Vernon Farm Ledger, 1797–98, 188.

88. Wargee, "African Travels of Wargee," 182; "To Make Small Beer," *GWP.Col.Series*, 4:405n13; "Agreement between GW and James Bloxham," 31 May 1786, *GWW*, 28:446.

89. Randolph, Monticello Household Accounts; Nicholls, "Recreating a White Urban Virginia," 30.

90. LW to GW, 4 March 1778, *GWP.Rev.Series*, 14:60.

91. For the fact that persimmon remains were so common, see Shick, "An Analysis of Archaeobotanical Evidence," 56, and Esther White to Christine Messing et al., 17 April 2007, FWSNL. For references to slaves and persimmon beer, as well as to recipes for making this beverage, see Edmonston, *"Journal of a Secesh Lady,"* 22; Hill, *Mrs. Hill's New Cookbook*, 342; Page and Wigginton, *Foxfire Book of Appalachian Cookery*, 55; and Perdue, *Pigsfoot Jelly and Persimmon Beer*, 33–34. For a discussion of making and using persimmon beer in Virginia, and specifically at Montpelier, the home of James and Dolley Madison, see Campo, "Wine Not?" 5. According to African American foodways specialist Michael Twitty, persimmons the slaves found growing in America would have reminded them of the fruit of the ebony or jack-alberry tree in West and Central Africa, known as the *alom* to the Wolof and *kuku* to the Fula peoples, who are known to have used it as a medicine, dried fruit, ingredient in bread, and source for making beer. See Twitty, *Fighting Old Nep*, 19, and Melissa D. Corbin, "Persimmon Beer," Edible Communities, 15 February 2016, www.ediblecommunities.com/recipes/persimmon-beer.

92. GW to AW, 3 February 1793, *GWW,* 32:331.

93. Custis, *Recollections and Private Memoirs,* 157n.

94. Gaspar, "Antigua Slaves and Their Struggle to Survive," 133; Mullin, *Flight and Rebellion,* 60–61.

95. Carter, *Diary,* 26 April 1770, 1:396.

96. GW to WP, 23 November 1794, *GWW,* 34:42.

97. LW to GW, 19 February 1776, *GWP.Rev.Series,* 3:396.

98. GW to AW, 9 December 1792, *GWW,* 32:257; WP to GW, 11 November 1794, *GWP.Pres.Series,* 17:160.

99. Niemcewicz, *Under Their Vine and Fig Tree,* 97.

100. WP to GW, 31 May 1795, *GWP.Pres.Series,* 18:187.

101. GW to WP, 7 June 1795, *GWW,* 34:212.

102. James Anderson (farm manager) to GW, 19 June 1798, *GWP.Ret.Series,* 2:347.

103. Carter, *Diary,* 31 July 1771, 2:602.

104. Blassingame, *Slave Community,* 172, 179; Moore, "'Established and Well Cultivated,'" 74; Savitt, *Medicine and Slavery,* 97–98; Stampp, *Peculiar Institution,* 286–87.

105. Breeden, *Advice among Masters,* 89–90, 99; Savitt, *Medicine and Slavery,* 95–96; Stampp, *Peculiar Institution,* 287–88.

106. *GWD,* 15 July 1769, 2:172.

107. "Fishery," 15 March 1798, Mount Vernon Farm Ledger, 1797–98, 147.

108. 1799 Slave Lists.

109. Weekly Reports, 5, 12, 19 December 1795, Mount Vernon Weekly Reports, 10 January 1795–18 March 1797.

110. *GWD,* 11 August 1786, 5:25.

111. GAW to GW, 20 August 1790, *GWP.Pres.Series,* 6:312.

112. Bowen, "Faunal Remains from the House for Families Cellar," 44, 51, 55; MVLA, "Archaeological Artifact Catalogue, House for Families"; Pogue, "Archaeology of Plantation Life," 76, 78–79; Moore, "'Established and Well Cultivated,'" 76, 78–79. For a good description of the transfer of West African cooking methods to the Americas, see Yentsch, *Chesapeake Family and Their Slaves,* 196–215.

113. Hafner, *Taste of Africa,* 16, 20, 28, 38, 47. For examples of similar dishes, which came to the New World from Africa, see ibid., 118, 132.

114. Tillery, *African-American Heritage Cookbook,* 93; Mariani, *Dictionary of American Food and Drink,* 77; Hafner, *Taste of Africa,* 34. The starch used in the African version of these "meatballs" was rice.

115. Anburey, *Travels through the Interior,* 2:335.

116. Oliver, "Using Barm to Make Bread," 4.

117. NCL to Elizabeth Bordley Gibson, 7 January 1821, typescript, FWSNL.

118. Hafner, *Taste of Africa,* 24–25, 120, 121.

119. *GWD,* 5 February 1760; 27 June 1786, 1:232–33; 4:353.

120. Pulsipher, "Galways Plantation, Montserrat," 152, 156, 157.

121. LW to GW, 2 September 1778, *GWP.Rev.Series,* 16:497–98. While this incident was treated as an unfortunate accident, it may be that Jack committed suicide. Studies of suicide among slaves in North American have shown that this was a route taken by newly enslaved people who hoped to return in spiritual form to Africa, and

by more acculturated slaves as the ultimate means of resisting a master or the institution of slavery, or of dealing with the despondency brought on by continual mistreatment or separation from loved ones. See Snyder, "Suicide, Slavery, and Memory in North America."

122. Anburey, *Travels through the Interior,* 2:331–33.

123. Carney and Rosomoff, *In the Shadow of Slavery,* 55–57.

124. Samford, *Subfloor Pits,* 127.

125. Moore, "'Established and Well Cultivated,'" 75–78.

126. Bilali, "Salih Bilali's Recollections of Massina," 150; Osifekunde, "The Land and People of Ijebu," 252, 266; Wargee, "African Travels of Wargee," 182; Crowther, "Narrative of Samuel Ajayi Crowther," 303–4. See also Hall, "Savoring Africa in the New World," 169. For the fact that, much like corn, pineapples and sweet potatoes were also brought to Africa by the Portuguese and quickly became agricultural staples, see Smallwood, *Saltwater Slavery,* 13–14.

127. Equiano, "The Early Travels of Olaudah Equiano," 73–74; Bilali, "Salih Bilali's Recollections of Massina," 150; Osifekunde, "The Land and People of Ijebu," 251–53; Wargee, "African Travels of Wargee," 182–83.

128. Moore, "'Established and Well Cultivated,'" 78.

129. Brookes, "A Dinner at Mount Vernon," 75–76.

130. Lucy Flucker Knox to General Henry Knox, 29 September, 23 October 1781, Knox and Knox, *Revolutionary War Lives and Letters,* 157, 161; General Henry Knox to Clement Biddle, 11 November 1781, RM-481/PS-3908, FWSNL. For the ages of the Knox children at this time, see Knox and Knox, *Revolutionary War Lives and Letters,* 143, 145, 175n42.

131. Custis, *Recollections and Private Memoirs,* 451–52.

132. Carney and Rosomoff, *In the Shadow of Slavery,* 183–85.

133. For examples of these chicken recipes, see "To Make a Frykecy" and "To Make a Frykacy of Chikin Lamb Ueale or Rabbits," in Hess, *Martha Washington's Booke of Cookery,* 40–45, and "Chickens *Chiringrate*," in Glasse, *"First Catch Your Hare,"* 39.

134. Randolph, *The Virginia House-Wife,* 253.

135. Carter, *Diary,* 29 July 1766, 1:323.

136. Carney and Rosomoff, *In the Shadow of Slavery,* 177, 178.

137. Gaspar, "Antigua Slaves and Their Struggle to Survive," 133.

138. GW to AW, 28 April 1793, *GWW,* 32:437–38.

139. GW to AW, 26 May 1793, ibid., 32:474–75.

140. GW to WP, 22 December 1793, ibid., 33:201.

141. GW to James Germain, 1 June 1794, ibid., 33:391.

9. "An Idle Set of Rascals"

1. GW to AW, 23 December 1792, *GWW,* 32:277.

2. GW to AW, 19 May 1793, ibid., 32:463. For an example of another case of demotion, in this case a coachman who was set to ditching on the Custis properties managed by Washington, see James Hill to GW, 11 May 1773, *GWP.Col.Series,* 9:232. For a fellow plantation owner's demotion of an enslaved gardener to fieldwork at Sabine Hall, see Isaac, *Landon Carter's Uneasy Kingdom,* 202–3.

3. GW, Cash Accounts, 13 June 1766; GW to Joseph Thompson, 2 July 1766; GW, Cash Accounts, 3 March 1767, *GWP.Col.Series*, 7:441, 442n4, 453–54, 491, 492n1.

4. James Hill to GW, 5 February, 11 May 1773, ibid., 9:172–73, 173n8, 232. For the identification of Hill, see ibid., 8:574n, 574–75n1. A partial set of iron shackles has been found at the former sites of the Mount Vernon carpenter's shop and a barn or storehouse, in a context suggesting a date of the late eighteenth or early nineteenth century. They are currently being studied to determine a more exact date. They do provide evidence that shackles were used at Mount Vernon during the years the estate was owned by George and/or Bushrod Washington.

5. Louis-Philippe, *Diary of My Travels*, 31–32.

6. Humphrey Knight to GW, 2 September 1758, *GWP.Col.Series*, 5:447.

7. AW to GW, 16 January 1793, *GWP.Pres.Series*, 12:11–12; GW to AW, 20 January 1793, *GWW*, 32:307.

8. GW to AW, 24 February, 3 March 1793, *GWW*, 32:358, 366. While Matilda's son Ben is the most likely perpetrator of the assault on Sambo Anderson, primarily because he was continually getting into trouble at this time, another possibility is that the culprit was Ben the miller. For evidence that the word "correction" was a typical contemporary term for physical punishment, see Virginia, *Statutes at Large*, 6:111; 12:681.

9. GW to WP, 14 November 1796, *GWW*, 35:279. In this case, seven dollars had been stolen from the saddle bags of a hired white servant, James Wilkes; the stolen money was found by farm manager William Pearce. See WHAB, 2 December 1796, 31:328. For another example of a "correction" being made "by way of example," see GW to WP, 30 March 1794, *GWW*, 33:309. See also Stanton, "'Those Who Labor for My Happiness,'" 159, for information on whipping as a punishment at Monticello.

10. GW, General Orders, 13 March, 9, 19 April 1783, *GWW*, 26:220–21, 310–11, 339.

11. Fogel and Engerman, *Time on the Cross*, 146.

12. Ibid.

13. Mays, *Edmund Pendleton*, 1:20.

14. GW, General Orders, 3 January 1780, 30 September, 23 November 1782, 9, 28 January, 8 February, 9 April 1783, *GWW*, 17:345, 25:220, 368–69, 26:24, 73, 110, 310–11; Lewis and Clark, *Journals*, 27, 27n.

15. Virginia, *Statutes at Large*, 6:111. Those not allowed to testify included people convicted of perjury in the past, blacks, mulattoes, and Indians, unless, in the case of the last three groups, they were giving evidence against one of the same. See ibid., 9:411; 12:748.

16. Peterson, *Visitors to Monticello*, 30.

17. Tobias Lear to William Prescott, 4 March 1788, "A Lear Letter," 24. Similarly, Lear wrote to his future brother-in-law George Long, "The negroes are not treated as blacks in general are in this Country, they are clothed and fed as well as any laboring people whatever and they are not subject to the lash of a domineering Overseer—*but still they are slaves.*" See Decatur, *Private Affairs*, 315.

18. GAW to GW, 7 December 1790, *GWP.Pres.Series*, 7:41.

19. Fogel and Engerman, *Time on the Cross*, 146.

20. GAW to GW, 26 March 1790, *GWP.Pres.Series*, 5:280.

21. GW to WP, 30 March 1794, *GWW*, 33:309. Interestingly, seven months earlier,

Washington had acknowledged to Crow that "your Crop was the most productive of any I had made last year." Perhaps Crow's crop turned out so well because he was especially harsh in driving and punishing the slaves under his supervision. GW to Hiland Crow, 4 August 1793, *GWP.Pres.Series,* 13:336. For the identification of Abram, see 1799 Slave Lists and *GWP.Ret.Series,* 4:540.

22. GW to Colonel Burgess Ball, 27 July 1794, *GWW,* 33:444.

23. John Gadsby Chapman, "Notes from a Meeting with Lawrence Lewis," June 1833, 1–2, McGuigan Collection, Harpswell, Maine. Much gratitude to John F. McGuigan, Jr., for sharing this material with Mount Vernon.

24. John Gadsby Chapman, "Wash[ingto]n Sketches, Forwarded to Mr. Paulding under Date 14 November 1833," 3, McGuigan Collection.

25. Ibid., 3–4.

26. Foster, "Caviar along the Potomac," 92.

27. The Franklin/Washington cane is now at the Smithsonian. "George Washington's Last Will and Testament," [9 July 1799], *GWP.Ret.Series,* 4:486, 502–3n17. It could be argued, however, that the widespread publication of George Washington's will in the early nineteenth century made the gift of the cane more well-known than it would otherwise have been; see the next chapter for a description of the publication of the will.

28. A second example of Washington's temper flaring up with a slave was given in a nineteenth-century biography, in association with stories about his interest in the proper care of his horses, but lacks credibility due to the attribution to tradition rather than a more specific source: "It is traditionally said that he once, with a good deal of unction, tried the stirrup-leather on the shoulders of a groom who had left a favorite horse uncared for, after Washington had ridden him pretty hard on the preceding evening. The servant thought he would be up so early that his master would never find out the omission; but Washington was too prompt for him, and while Cupid, or perhaps Apollo, was dreaming of last night's frolic, the sound of the stable-bell just at dawn announced that the unhappy steed had mutely told his own story. The result would certainly have afforded amusement to a bystander, especially as the President had doubtless lost some of the strength of arm which distinguished him in early times when he flogged the poacher, or when he shook the two fighting soldiers at Cambridge." See Kirkland, *Memoirs of Washington,* 447–48.

29. Ann Chinn, compiler, Family History, conversation with author, 21 March 2006.

30. Virginia, *Statutes at Large,* act 22, March 1642/43; act 11, March 1655/56; act 16, March 1657/58, 1:254–55, 401, 440.

31. Henry Knox to GW, 15 September 1792, *GWP.Pres.Series,* 11:115.

32. Henry Knox to GW, 17 August 1792; GW to Knox, 26 August 1792, ibid., 11:41, 41n2.

33. Anthony Wayne to Henry Knox, 7 September 1792; Knox to Wayne, 14 September 1792, ibid., 11:11n1, 117–18n2.

34. *GWD,* 1 November 1765, 1:343; invoice from Robert Cary & Co., 20 December 1765, *GWP.Col.Series,* 7:419. For the identity of the Neck Plantation, see *GWP.Pres.Series,* 6:314–15n6.

35. *GWD*, 3 April, 22 December 1772, 3:99n, 149n. See also Thomas Newton, Jr., to GW, 11 January 1773, *GWP.Col.Series*, 9:156n1.

36. William Ramsay, Robert Adam, and Carlyle & Dalton to GW and John West, 16 May 1774, *GWP.Col.Series*, 10:63n4. For GW's purchase of "Sundry Branding Irons" from Philadelphia, see Cash Accounts, [January 1772], *GWP.Col.Series*, 9:1, 1n1.

37. GW to LW, 11 June 1783, *GWW*, 27:2–3.

38. Trenton Cole Jones, email communication with author, 9 October 2015.

39. Marion Dobbins, Mount Vernon, conversation with author, 18 December 2015.

40. Jessie MacLeod, Mount Vernon, conversation with author, October 2015. It might be instructive at this point to look at another memory from the Revolutionary War that descended in several families whose ancestors were formerly enslaved at Monticello. In June 1781, a party of British dragoons under the command of Colonel Banastre Tarleton arrived at Monticello with the intent of capturing Thomas Jefferson, who was then serving as governor of Virginia. According to the story, by the time of their arrival, Jefferson had escaped on horseback with the assistance of the slaves, who had reshod the horse putting the shoes on backward so that, in the words of one, when the British "thought Jefferson was coming, he was going in the opposite direction." Research into this oft-repeated tale showed a number of problems with the story. For example, the two men variously described as the blacksmith in the story were only one and eleven years old, respectively, at the time of the British raid. A particularly significant issue was that it is impossible to shoe a horse backward. According to Monticello historian Lucia Stanton, "In the Revolutionary stories, the substitution of recognizable family members for forgotten protagonists and the embellishment with mythical elements like the reversed horseshoes reinforced their central messages. Every step of the way, Jefferson was supported by his slaves.... Their skills and resourcefulness were essential to the safety of someone who was not just a plantation owner in Albemarle County but one of the most important men in Virginia." See Stanton, "Those Who Labor for My Happiness," 100–101.

41. GW to Captain Josiah Thompson, 2 July 1766, *GWP.Col.Series*, 7:453–54. For more on this incident, see Ledger A, 245a.

42. Morgan and Nicholls, "Slave Flight," 199. According to these historians, Sam proved just as problematic for his next owner and was sold at least twice more.

43. Joseph Valentine to GW, 24 August 1771, *GWP.Col.Series*, 8:520, 520–21n1.

44. GW to AW, 3 March 1793, *GWW*, 32:366.

45. Ledger B, 3 December 1791, 336a; Haworth, *George Washington: Country Gentleman*, 204; Mazyck, *George Washington and the Negro*, 122.

46. GW to Brigadier General Anthony Wayne, 27 November 1779, *GWW*, 17:198–99. For other examples of Washington using leniency to shape behavior in the army, see GW to Brigadier General William Woodford, 13 January 1780; GW, General Orders, 4 February 1780; GW to Colonel Lewis Nicola, 5 February 1780; GW, General Orders, 24 February 1780; GW, General Orders, 3 August 1781, ibid, 17:388, 485, 491–92; 18:48; 22:455–56.

47. Peterson, *Visitors to Monticello*, 28. See also Fogel, *Without Consent or Contract*, 189, 191–92.

48. GW to AW, 5 May 1793, *GWW*, 32:442–43.

49. GW to AW, 3 March 1793, ibid., 32:366.

50. GW to AW, 19 May 1793, ibid., 32:463.

51. GW to WP, 22 December 1793, 15 March, 13 December 1795, 1 May 1796, ibid., 33:199, 34:145, 393–94, 35:34; Lear, *Letters and Recollections,* 131.

52. GW to WP, 29 November 1795, *GWW,* 34:379.

53. GW to AW, 11 November 1792, ibid., 32:215–16.

54. "Cash . . . Contra," 4 April 1795; "Cash Paid," [December 1796], Mount Vernon Farm Ledger, January 1794–December 1796, 55, 114.

55. Entries dated 19 January 1798, 16 February 1799, GW Cash Memoranda, September 1794–December 1799, 13, 43.

56. "Cash . . . Contra," 25 October 1799, Mount Vernon Distillery and Fishery Ledger, 41.

57. Olwell, "'Reckoning of Accounts,'" 41. See also Fogel and Engerman, *Time on the Cross,* 148–51.

58. GW to WP, 11 January 1795, *GWW,* 34:85.

59. Davis, "At the Heart of Slavery," 51; Wallach, *Desert Queen,* 345.

60. GW to AW, 27 January 1793, *GWW,* 32:319.

61. GW to WP, 12 January 1794, ibid., 33:242.

62. GW to WP, 18 May 1794, ibid., 33:369.

63. GW to WP, 27 July 1794, ibid., 33:447.

64. GW to WP, 8 March 1795, ibid., 34:135.

65. GW to WP, 20 March 1796, ibid., 34:502–3.

66. LW to GW, 2 September 1778, *GWP.Rev.Series,* 16:498, 501–2n6.

67. For the story of John Broad's injury and death, see LW to GW, 30 December 1775, and LW to GW, 31 January, 22 February 1776, *GWP.Rev.Series,* 3:232–33, 355.

68. "Schedule B: General Account of the Estate," [ca. October 1759], *GWP.Col.Series,* 6:252.

69. "General Account of the Estate, 1758–1759," [ca. November 1761], ibid., 6:266.

70. "Cash Accounts," [October 1759]; "Cash Accounts," [November 1763], [December 1763], [August 1766], ibid., 6:365; 7:268, 276, 458. See also Ledger A, 13 November, 8 December 1763; 1 August 1766, 171a, 172a, 234a.

71. For Doctor Laurie, see "Cash Accounts," [March 1760], *GWP.Col.Series,* 6:390, 390n4. For the "Negro Doctr," see Ledger B, 23 December 1773, 98a.

72. GW to James Anderson (farm manager), 20 February 1797, typescript, FWSNL.

73. GW to WP, 22 March 1795, *GWW,* 34:153–54.

74. GW, "General Instructions for the Colonels and Commanding Officers of Regiments in the Continental Service," [ca. 1777], ibid., 10:241.

75. Mary V. Thompson, "Statistics on Slave Illness," 1992, FWSNL.

76. Lee, "Laboring Hands and the Transformation of Mount Vernon Plantation," 15.

77. *Mount Vernon Employee Handbook* (MVLA, April 1987), 18; Robin Woodward, National Guard Bureau, conversation with author, 27 November 1995.

78. Fogel and Engerman, *Time on the Cross,* 126.

79. LW to GW, 7 March 1776, *GWP.Rev.Series,* 3:431.

80. GW to AW, 4 November 1792, *GWW,* 32:204–5.

81. GW to AW, 24 February 1793, ibid., 32:357. For other complaints about laziness, see GW to WP, 12 January 1794, ibid., 33:242.

82. Tobias Lear to Charles Vancouver, 5 November 1791, *GWP.Pres.Series,* 9:144n2.

83. GW to Governor Henry Lee, 16 October 1793, *GWW,* 33:132.

84. GW to AW, 23 December 1792, ibid., 32:277.

85. GW to WP, 22 February 1795, *GWP.Pres.Series,* 17:557. This same letter was published earlier in *GWW,* 33:275, with the erroneous date of 22 February 1794. See also GW to Howell Lewis, 18, 25 August 1793; GW to WP, 18 December 1793, 3 August 1794, 15 February 1795, *GWW,* 33:52–53, 64, 194, 454–55; 34:117.

86. GW to AW, 3 March 1793, *GWW,* 32:365. For another example of Washington's thoughts on the use of his carpenters for this project, see GW to AW, 6 January 1793, ibid., 32:293. For examples of sloppy work by other slaves, see GW to AW, 28 April 1793, ibid., 32:435.

87. James Hill to GW, 30 August 1772, *GWP.Col.Series,* 9:85.

88. GW to WP, 13 July 1794, *GWW,* 33:428.

89. GW to AW, 30 December 1792, ibid., 32:279–80.

90. Howell Lewis to GW, 6 August 1793, *GWP.Pres.Series,* 13:369.

91. GW to WP, 6 October 1793, *GWW,* 33:111–12.

92. GW to AW, 14 October 1792, ibid., 32:184–85; GW to James Anderson (farm manager), 22 January 1797, typescript, FWSNL. See also numerous entries in the Mount Vernon Store Book; GW to AW, 19 May, 2 June 1793, *GWW,* 32:462–63; and James Anderson (farm manager) to GW, 19 June 1798, *GWP.Ret.Series,* 2:346.

93. GW to James Anderson (farm manager), 21 December 1797, *GWP.Ret.Series,* 1:526.

94. AW to GW, 16 January 1793, *GWP.Pres.Series,* 12:11–12, 14n14.

95. GW to WP, 20 April 1794, *GWW,* 33:336–37.

96. See, for example, the entry dated 6 April 1799 in one of Washington's financial ledgers, which shows that on that day the hired gardener William Spence was given two dollars to "buy a pair of Garden Shears." Under the entry is a note which says that the money was returned because there were "no shears to be had." GW Cash Memoranda, September 1794–December 1799, 46.

97. GW to AW, 3 February 1793, *GWW,* 32:330.

98. GW to AW, 17 February 1793, ibid., 32:348. For an example of Washington's suspicions that raw wool was being pilfered, see GW to AW, 2 June 1793, ibid., 32:482–83.

99. For the theft of rum, see LW to GW, 29 February 1776, *GWP.Rev.Series,* 3:396. For the loss of wine, see GW to WP, 23 November 1794, *GWW,* 34:42. For the stealing of apples, see *GWD,* 10 September 1785, 4:192. For other fruits, see Niemcewicz, *Under Their Vine and Fig Tree,* 97. For the loss of milk and butter, see GW to AW, 9 December 1792, *GWW,* 32:257. For potatoes having been "made way with," see WP to GW, 11 November 1794, *GWP.Pres.Series,* 17:160. For the theft of corn, see GW to AW, 21 April 1793, *GWW,* 32:424. For the theft of meat, see WP to GW, 31 May 1795, *GWP.Pres.Series,* 18:187, 188n3. For Washington's concern about the construction delays at Dogue Run, see GW to AW, 24 February, 21 April 1793, *GWW,* 32:357, 426.

100. For thefts from the greenhouse and corn lofts, see GW to AW, 21 April 1793,

GWW, 32:424. For the theft from the smokehouse, see WP to GW, 31 May 1795, *GWP.Pres.Series*, 18:187, 188n3

101. GW to AW, 21 April 1793, *GWW*, 32:424–25, 426. See also Howell Lewis to GW, 6 August 1793, *GWP.Pres.Series*, 13:369–70, and GW to WP, 26 January 1794, *GWW*, 33:254.

102. For the locks in the mansion, see the account with Philip Wanton in Mount Vernon Distillery and Fishery Ledger, 9. For the lock on the stable loft, see "Cash . . . Contra," 6 February 1794, Mount Vernon Farm Ledger, January 1794–December 1796, 2. For locks on the corn houses, see "Agreement with Edward Violet," [5 August 1762], *GWP.Col.Series*, 7:144; GW to AW, 9 December 1792, *GWW*, 32:257; and Mount Vernon Distillery and Fishery Ledger, 2 March 1799, 36. For "that trusty old negro Jack," see GW to WP, 25 October 1795, *GWW*, 34:343.

103. GW to WP, 4 December 1796, *GWW*, 35:306.

104. GW to WP, 11 January 1795, ibid., 34:84.

105. For similar concerns at Landon Carter's Sabine Hall, see Isaac, *Landon Carter's Uneasy Kingdom*, 203.

106. GW to James Anderson (farm manager), 1 November 1798, *GWW*, 37:2–3.

107. Howell Lewis to GW, 6 August 1793; GW to Lewis, 18 August 1793, *GWW*, 33:50–51.

108. GW to AW, 19 May 1793, ibid., 32:463.

109. GW to WP, 1 June 1794, ibid., 33:394–95. See also letters of 8 June, 16, 30 November 1794, ibid., 33:398–400; 34:24, 48. For a detailed treatment of theft by slaves, including collusion with free blacks and working-class whites, see Schwarz, *Twice Condemned*, 118–32.

110. *Columbian Mirror and Alexandria Gazette*, 12 June 1798. For an example of a pass from a later Washington, John Augustine Washington II, allowing one of his slaves to sell plants from the Mount Vernon greenhouse, see *Alexandria Gazette*, 11 August 1831.

111. Parkinson, *Tour in America*, 2:432–33.

112. J. T. Trowbridge, "A Visit to Mount Vernon," *Our Young Folks*, February 1866, 88. See also Fox-Genovese, *Within the Plantation Household*, 96, 315, and Schwarz, *Twice Condemned*, 118–20, 214, 214n.

113. See *GWD*, 8 March 1787, 5:115.

114. GW to AW, 16 December 1792, *GWW*, 32:263.

115. GW to AW, 9 December 1792, ibid., 32:258.

116. Peale, *Selected Papers*, 696. See also *Commercial Advertiser* (New York), 11 May 1804, and Bushrod Washington to Judge Richard Peters, 21 May 1804, microfilm, FWSNL. Especially interesting is Dolley Payne Madison to Anna Cutts, [May–June] 1804, Madison, *Selected Letters of Dolley Payne Madison*, 58, relating that five fires had been set at Mount Vernon.

117. GAW to GW, 7 December 1790, *GWP.Pres.Series*, 7:41.

118. Chambers, *Murder at Montpelier*, 7–10, 8 (quotation).

119. Joseph Valentine to GW, 29 July, 6 August 1764, *GWP.Col.Series*, 7:318, 320.

120. James Bloxham to William Peacy, 23 July 1786, typescript, FWSNL.

121. Washington, "Lund Washington's History of His Family"; Bristol, "Copy of Lund Washington's Manuscript," 12–13.

122. *Pennsylvania Gazette,* 31 December 1767, quoted in *GWP.Col.Series,* 8:215n4.

123. Schwarz, *Twice Condemned,* 100; Custis, *Recollections and Private Memoirs,* 157–58. For an example of poisoning at Mount Vernon during Bushrod Washington's tenure as proprietor of the estate, when a female slave tried to poison a farm manager, see *Alexandria Gazette,* 11 October 1821, and Casper, *Sarah Johnson's Mount Vernon,* 18–24.

124. Anburey, *Travels through the Interior,* 2:435–36. See also Fox-Genovese, *Within the Plantation Household,* 306–7, 315–16, and Schwarz, *Twice Condemned,* 92–113. For poisoning in African tradition, see Schwarz, *Twice Condemned,* 97–98, 103–4. For another example of poisoning where the perpetrator and victims were both enslaved, see *Alexandria Gazette,* 14 August 1833.

125. Morgan and Nicholls, "Slave Flight," 197, 203–4, 206, 208–13. For the barriers to female slaves escaping, see Gordon-Reed, *Hemingses of Monticello,* 412–13.

126. GW, Advertisement for Runaway Slaves, *Maryland Gazette,* 20 August 1761, reprinted in *GWP.Col.Series,* 7:65–66. For the fact that all four men were returned to Mount Vernon, see the excellent footnotes on pages 67 and 68 of the same source.

127. LW to GW, 22 August 1767, ibid., 8:19.

128. Weekly Report, 22 December 1798, Mount Vernon Farm Accounts II; 1799 Slave Lists.

129. GW to WP, 25 January 1795, *GWW,* 34:104.

130. Landon Carter to GW, 9 May 1776, *GWP.Rev.Series,* 4:236–37, 240–41n5.

131. James Hill to GW, 5 February 1773, *GWP.Col.Series,* 9:172–73, 173n8. For the identification of Hill, see ibid., 8:574n.

132. *GWD,* 18 April 1760, 1:269; "Cash," 18 April 1760, Ledger A, 89a.

133. Joseph Valentine to GW, [4] October 1771, *GWP.Col.Series,* 8:529. White people were also typically paid for capturing runaway slaves, as in the case of the Washingtons' pastor, Reverend Charles Green, who was paid two pounds "for taking up one of my Runaway Negroes" in March 1761. See Ledger A, 118a. Eleven years later, Leonard Milsford was given one pound on 23 July 1772 for "taking up a Runaway Negro belonging to Mr. Custis's Estate." See Ledger B, 23 July 1772, 55a.

134. LW to GW, 3 December 1775, *GWP.Rev.Series,* 2:479–80.

135. Berlin, *Many Thousands Gone,* 231–32, 230.

136. For the escapes and the immediate reaction of Landon Carter to them, see Isaac, *Landon Carter's Uneasy Kingdom,* 3–15. The remainder of the book deals with the backstory of life at Sabine Hall and then carries the story forward to the end of Carter's life.

137. George Grieve, notes on conversation with LW, Chastellux, *Travels in North America,* 2:597n24.

138. Ibid., 2:597.

139. Rice, editorial note, ibid., 2:597n24.

140. LW, "List of Runaways," April 1781, *GWW,* 22:14n. For another published version of this list, which differs a bit from that in *GWW,* see Clark, "A Wartime Incident," 25. According to historian Fritz Hirschfeld, John C. Fitzpatrick, the editor of *GWW,* was mistaken when he identified the commander of the *Savage* as Richard Graves, a prominent British naval officer, rather than his brother, Captain Thomas Graves. See Hirschfeld, *George Washington and Slavery,* 23n8.

141. Marquis de Lafayette to GW, 23 April 1781, Lafayette, *Lafayette in the Age of the American Revolution,* 60–61.

142. GW to LW, 30 April 1781, *GWW,* 22:14.

143. See ibid., 22:14n, and Clark, "A Wartime Incident," 25. These two published sources conflict in regard to whether all the men were captured in Philadelphia and the women were picked up after Yorktown, or if only Tom was found in Philadelphia. Examination of the original manuscript, which is in the Mount Vernon collections, suggests that all of the returned slaves were taken up after the siege at Yorktown, but that Tom is the only one who got as far as Philadelphia. Many thanks to Michele Lee, former special collections librarian and my delightful colleague, for helping to work out that conundrum. A second, as yet unsolved problem concerns the identities of three Mount Vernon slaves who appear in the British records at the end of the Revolution, when they were transported to Nova Scotia: Henry Washington, forty-three years old, who is said to have escaped in 1776; Daniel Payne, age twenty-two; and Deborah Squash, twenty years old, who ran away in 1779. The given names of these people match three of those from Lund's 1781 list. Are they the same people? Was Lund providing a comprehensive list of everyone who left in the war or just those who escaped in 1781? These questions still await answers. For the work of other historians on the Mount Vernon slaves who escaped during the war, see Pybus, *Epic Journeys,* 218; Schama, *Rough Crossings,* 16–17, 81, 232, 281, 381, 383; and Whitehead, *Black Loyalists,* 74, 139–40, 149.

144. Taylor, *The Internal Enemy,* 28.

145. GW to Roger West, 19 September 1799, *GWP.Ret.Series,* 4:310–11.

146. For Sheels's presence in Philadelphia, see GW to Tobias Lear, 12 April 1791, *GWP.Pres.Series,* 8:85–86.

147. *GWD,* 14 October 1797, 6:262, 263n; entry dated 18 October 1797, GW Cash Memoranda Book, 1 September 1797–3 December 1799, photostat, FWSNL; GW to Reverend William Stoy, 14 October 1797; Mattias Slough to GW, 20 October 1797; George Washington Motier Lafayette and Felix Frestel to GW, 21 October 1797; GW to Lafayette, 5 December 1797, *GWP.Ret.Series,* 1:404, 404–5n2, 414–16, 417–418, 506, 506n2. See also Stoy to GW, 28 February 1798; GW to Stoy, 17 March 1798, *GWP.Ret.Series,* 2:111–12, 145–46.

148. Lear, *Letters and Recollections,* 135, 136.

149. Custis, *Recollections and Private Memoirs,* 422–23.

150. Entry for 9 September 1787, Mount Vernon Store Book.

151. GW to Tobias Lear, 22 November 1790, *GWP.Pres.Series,* 6:682.

152. Tobias Lear to GW, 5 June 1791, ibid., 8:232.

153. GW to WP, 14 November 1796, *GWW,* 35:279.

154. See Weekly Reports, 7, 14, 20, 28 January, 11, 25 February 1797, Mount Vernon Farm Accounts, [4], [9], [14], [19], [28], [39], and Weekly Reports, 18 February 1797, Mount Vernon Weekly Reports, 10 January 1795–18 March 1797. My thanks to Philadelphia journalist Craig Laban for pointing me toward these references during a phone call on 10 November 2009. Until this time, the standard interpretation was that Hercules left from Philadelphia, despite Washington's very clear statement in a letter to Frederick Kitt, written from Mount Vernon on 10 January 1798, that "we have never heard of Hercules our Cook since he left this [place]; but little doubt

remains in my mind of his having gone to Philadelphia." See Decatur, *Private Affairs*, 296–97; Hirschfeld, *George Washington and Slavery*, 70; and Lawler, "The President's House Revisited," 394. Washington's quotation can be found in *GWW*, 37:578.

155. GW to Tobias Lear, 10 March 1797; GW to Frederick Kitt, 10 January 1798, *GWP.Ret.Series*, 1:27; 2:16.

156. Louis-Philippe, *Diary of My Travels*, 32.

157. MW to Elizabeth Dandridge Henley, 20 August 1797, Washington, *"Worthy Partner,"* 307.

158. GW to George Lewis, 13 November 1797, *GWP.Ret.Series*, 1:469.

159. For the letter noting that Hercules was in Philadelphia, see Frederick Kitt to GW, 15 January 1798, ibid., 2:16. For Washington's instructions about Hercules, see GW to Kitt, 10, 29 January 1798, ibid., 2:25, 60.

160. MW to Colonel Richard Varick, 15 December 1801, Washington, *"Worthy Partner,"* 398.

161. Several years ago, Mount Vernon learned that there is a portrait of a black man in the collection of the Museo Thyssen-Bornemisza in Madrid, Spain, which is attributed to Gilbert Stuart and entitled *Supuestor retrato del cocinero de George Washington* (Supposed Portrait of the Cook of George Washington). There has been considerable speculation about the possibility that the portrait is a depiction of Hercules.

162. GW to Oliver Wolcott, Jr., 1 September [1796], *GWW*, 35:201–2. Although many historians now refer to Martha Washington's maid as "Ona," because that is how she identified herself, throughout this book I have chosen to call her "Oney," the name by which she was known—and appears in the records—from Mount Vernon.

163. Frederick Kitt, "Advertisement," 23 May, *Pennsylvania Gazette and Universal Daily Advertiser* (Philadelphia), 24 May 1796. The information about the exact date and time of the escape is taken from Frederick Kitt, "Ten Dollars Reward," 24 May, *Claypoole's American Daily Advertiser* (Philadelphia), 24, 25 May 1796. My colleague Coxey Toogood, the historian for Independence National Historical Park in Philadelphia, deserves thanks (and a lovely bouquet) for transcribing and sharing these articles with Mount Vernon, as does historian Peter Hinks from the American History Workshop, who found them the old-fashioned way—by slogging through the microfilm. For examples of the fact that Judge had many clothes, see references in Decatur, *Private Affairs*, 32, 48, 314.

164. Adams, *Diary and Autobiography*, 17 July 1796, 3:229, 229n1; GW to Bartholomew Dandridge, 5 June 1796; GW to Oliver Wolcott, Jr., 1 August 1796; GW to James McHenry, 1 August 1796, *GWW*, 35:78, 159, 162.

165. Thomas Lee, Jr., to GW, 28 June 1796, typescript, FWSNL. I would like to thank Coxey Toogood at Independence Hall for her great kindness in sharing this source with us.

166. GW to Oliver Wolcott, Jr., 1 September 1796, *GWW*, 35:201–2. The three young women were close in age: in the summer of 1796, Oney Judge was about twenty-two, Elizabeth Langdon was almost nineteen, and Nelly Custis was seventeen. For an example of another of Custis's Philadelphia friends spending an evening in the company of Martha Washington, Custis, and a maid who was probably Judge, see Elizabeth Bordley Gibson, quoted in Thane, *Mount Vernon Family*, 74.

167. GW to Joseph Whipple, 28 November 1796, *GWW,* 35:297. According to Coxey Toogood, communication with author, 23 September 2009, in *Claypoole's American Daily Advertiser* (Philadelphia), 25 May 1796, there is a reference to a Frenchman named William Boussaret, who worked in a tobacco shop in Philadelphia, running away about this same period. This might be the basis for Washington's idea that Judge had run off with a Frenchman.

168. Joseph Whipple to Oliver Wolcott, 4 October 1796, quoted in "Ona Maria Judge," Weeks Public Library, Greenland, New Hampshire, http://www.weekslibrary .org/ona_maria_judge.htm.

169. GW to Joseph Whipple, 28 November 1796, *GWW,* 35:297.

170. GW to Burwell Bassett, 11 August 1799, *GWP.Ret.Series,* 4:237.

171. Chase, "Mrs. [?] Staines," 249; Adams, "Washington's Runaway Slave." These interviews are also available at http://www.ushistory.org/presidentshouse/slaves /oneyinterview.php. Oney Judge and John Staines were married on 8 January 1797 and had their first child either later that same year or in 1798. See "Ona Maria Judge," Weeks Public Library, Greenland, New Hampshire.

172. Virginia, *Statutes at Large,* 12:145.

173. Even more importantly, according to historians Philip D. Morgan and Michael L. Nicholls, "Oney Judge is the only eighteenth-century Virginia runaway slave who has left her own account of her actions." See Morgan and Nicolls, "Slave Flight," 202.

174. Dunbar, *Never Caught,* 107–8, 113.

175. Chase, "Mrs. [?] Staines," 249–50.

176. Adams, "Washington's Runaway Slave." An excerpt from the latter interview can be found at "Ona Maria Judge," Weeks Public Library, Greenland, New Hampshire.

177. For Austin's death, see Unknown to "Mr. Dandridge," 20 December 1794; Herman Stump to GW, 20 December 1794; John Carlile to GW, 21 December 1794; Thomas Archer to GW, 22 December 1794; "Barney" to Unknown, 22 December 1794; Elizabeth Stiles to Unknown, 22 December 1794, Library of Congress Microfilm Collection, FWSNL; and GW to WP, 28 December 1794, *GWW,* 34:74, 74n. For Betty's death, see GW to WP, 1 February 1795, *GWW,* 34:109.

178. Chase, "Mrs. [?] Staines," 250.

179. Adams, "Washington's Runaway Slave." For the fact that promises or gifts of particular female domestic slaves were often made to young brides at this period, and examples of such transactions from the Jefferson family, see Gordon-Reed, *Hemingses of Monticello,* 422–24.

180. Adams, "Washington's Runaway Slave."

181. Oney Judge Staines's death date is found in the *Pennsylvania Freeman,* 11 May 1848; my thanks to Coxey Toogood for the reference. The most complete treatments of Judge's life to date are Evelyn Gerson's, "A Thirst for Complete Freedom," a master's thesis done for Harvard University in 2000, and Erica Armstrong Dunbar's 2017 work *Never Caught.* Two versions of her story have also been told for younger readers: first, for "young adults," by Ann Rinaldi in *Taking Liberty,* and second, for children, by Emily Arnold McCully in *The Escape of Oney Judge.*

182. GW to Arthur Young, 18[–21] June 1792, *GWW,* 32:66.

Conclusion

1. Richard Allen, "Eulogy of George Washington," 29 December 1799, "The President's House in Philadelphia," http://www.ushistory.org/presidentshouse/history/alleneulogy.htm.

2. Washington, *Last Will and Testament*, 1, 27.

3. Ibid., 2–4. For Virginia laws dealing with the estate issues and manumission requirements faced by the Washingtons, see Virginia, *Statutes at Large*, 5:445, 446, 464; 11:39–40; 12:145, 146, 150. Washington biographer James Thomas Flexner stated in his 1970s work that Washington actually had emancipated a handful of slaves several years earlier, at the end of his presidency: "Washington, as he prepared to return home from the Presidency, saw in the same Pennsylvania law an opportunity secretly to free some of his slaves. By the simple expedient of leaving the blacks behind, he could manumit them so inconspicuously that the southern government opposition to the government need never find out." Flexner noted that "Washington, indeed, covered his tracks so well that his act remained hidden from history until this writer chanced upon it when making a routine check of a seemingly trivial correspondence." The letter in question was between Washington and a Philadelphia tailor, James McAlpin, and dates to the summer after the former's retirement from the presidency. Washington thanked the tailor for information he provided about someone named John Klein (or Cline), "but [I] shall give myself no further concern about him, for it was always my intention to have given him his freedom (as I did the other servants under similar circumstances) when I retired from public life, had he remained with me." See Flexner, *George Washington*, 4:432. For a more recent mention of this manumission, see Henriques, *Realistic Visionary*, 160. For the original correspondence, see James McAlpin to GW, 15 May 1797; GW to McAlpin, 3 July 1797, *GWP.Ret.Series*, 1:140, 230. Klein was a German immigrant indentured to Washington on 22 August 1794 for a period of three years (so his time would have been up in August 1797). In his letter to McAlpin, Washington was simply saying that he let several indentured servants out of their contracts a little early, because he had no need for them at Mount Vernon. For the hire of John Klein, see WHAB, 22 August 1794, 30:316.

4. "Legacies of Washington," *Massachusetts Mercury* (Boston), 17 January 1800.

5. "From a Late London Paper. General Washington," *Providence [Rhode Island] Gazette*, 28 June 1800.

6. GW to Marquis de Lafayette, 10 May 1786, *GWP.Con.Series*, 4:43–44.

7. GW to Robert Morris, 12 April 1786, ibid., 4:16. Interestingly, Washington's step-granddaughter Nelly Custis seems to have taken to heart his ideas about the benefits of gradual abolition, although she also supported colonization and showed considerably more racial disdain than her grandfather. Writing to a friend in 1832, she complained about those who "decry anything to advance colonization, & the *real* interests of those *dark* torments of our lives." She went on to say that "to do good, we must proceed *cautiously,* & *noiselessly.* Emancipation *must* be *gradual*—& all this uproar creates discontent, & induces insurrection & murder." See NCL to Eleanor Bordley Gibson, 19 March 1832, Lewis, *George Washington's Beautiful Nelly*, 199. Much of the difference in the attitudes of Washington and his step-granddaughter may be attributable to three incidents: the Haitian slave revolt of the early 1790s;

Gabriel's Rebellion in Richmond, Virginia, in 1800; and Nat Turner's rebellion in Virginia in 1831, all of which tended to harden white opinions about African Americans and led to more restrictive laws in the antebellum South than had existed in the eighteenth century.

8. GW to John Francis Mercer, 9 September 1786, *GWP.Con.Series,* 4:243. Following his change of heart about slavery, Washington would even refuse to accept slaves in whom he had a legal right. In 1793, in trying to rectify a mistake in settling the estate of his younger brother Samuel's last wife (Samuel outlived four, leaving his fifth wife a widow), which might have brought him several slaves, George Washington learned that one of the people to whom he was definitely entitled was a teenager, who asked that she be sold in the area where she was living, "as she poor Slave wishes to remain among her connections." The executor noted, "I mention this at her request as she begged her master might be told how desireous she was of staying with her relations she is the Daughter of an old favourite Ser[van]t . . . if it is yr will that I should turn her into cash it shall be done for the most that can be got." In response, Washington suggested that the executor pay "me one hundd. pounds which I shall give to my Niece for her immediate support, and I will quit claim to *all* the Negro's which belonged to Mrs Saml Washington, & will releas[e] them accordingly." Francis Willis, Jr., to GW, 4 August 1793; GW to Willis, 25 October 1793, *GWP.Pres.Series,* 13:347, 14:288.

9. GW to Lawrence Lewis, 4 August 1797, *GWP.Ret.Series,* 1:288.

10. GW, July 1798, quoted by British actor John Bernard in his book *Retrospections of America,* 88, 90–91.

11. Walsh, *Motives of Honor, Pleasure, and Profit,* 447, 447n64.

12. GW to Continental Congress Camp Committee, 29 January 1778, *GWP.Rev.Series,* 13:377.

13. GW to John Banister, 21 April 1778, *GWP.Rev.Series,* 14:574.

14. Washington's Farewell Address, 1796, Avalon Project, http://avalon.law.yale .edu/18th_century/washing.asp.

15. Kolchin, *American Slavery,* 76–79; Robinson, *Slavery in the Structure of American Politics,* 23–24, 29–30, 35, 55n. The situation in New England was not straightforward. Vermont abolished slavery for adults in 1777, however, the failure of the legislature to get rid of loopholes that allowed children to be enslaved or to ensure any means of enforcing emancipation, meant that slavery continued to be a fact of life in that state until at least 1806, when the legislature passed the Prevention of Kidnapping Act, prohibiting the kidnapping and sale of black people out of the state, at the risk of severe punishment. See Whitfield, *Problem of Slavery in Early Vermont,* 57, 74–75, 119–20. Rhode Island and Connecticut would not abolish slavery until 1843 and 1848, respectively. The fact that slavery was officially ended in Massachusetts by judicial ruling in 1783, rather than by action of the legislature, is perhaps why the practice continued there, off the record, well into the 1820s. According to historian Joanne Melish, the fact that white New Englanders had lived with slavery for almost 150 years meant that they had a very difficult time accepting "freeborn people of color" as anything but a perpetual underclass and simply could not see them as potential citizens: "What the gradual abolition statutes offered was a framework within which whites could enjoy abolition and slavery at the same time—just

as they had always enjoyed personhood and property together in their slaves." See Melish, *Disowning Slavery*, 76–79. See also Francie Latour, "New England's Hidden History: More Than We Like to Think, the North Was Built on Slavery," *Boston Globe*, 26 September 2010.

16. Virginia, *Statutes at Large*, 6:112; 11:39–40.

17. For Pleasants, see *GWP.Con.Series*, 3:451n; Finkelman, "Thomas Jefferson and Antislavery," 217; and Finkelman, "Jefferson and Slavery," 186–88. In terms of all the slaves in Virginia, free blacks made up 1 percent of that population in 1782 and 7 percent by 1800. Taylor, *The Internal Enemy*, 37.

18. GW to LW, 11 June 1783, *GWW*, 27:2–3. The fact that Washington began to require weekly reports from his farm managers after the Revolution is, I believe, a direct result of his shock at the condition of his farms on his return from the war and his consequent lack of trust in anyone else to stay on top of the situation at Mount Vernon but himself.

19. GW to Pierre Charles L'Enfant, 1 January 1787, ibid., 29:137.

20. GW to Mary Ball Washington, 15 February 1787, ibid., 29:158–59.

21. GW to LW, 7 May 1787, ibid., 29:212

22. GW to Matthew Carey, 29 October 1787, ibid., 29:294.

23. GW to David Stuart, 11 December 1787, ibid., 29:335.

24. GW to Sir Edward Newenham, 2 March 1789, ibid., 30:217.

25. GW to Richard Conway, 4 March 1789, ibid., 30:220–21, 220n64.

26. GW to Richard Conway, 6 March 1789, ibid., 30:223.

27. "An Act to Authorize the Manumission of Slaves," May 1782, Virginia, *Statutes at Large*, 11:39–40. The paperwork would have cost roughly £31 for the manumission of just Washington's slaves or £69 for all, including the dower slaves. In modern currency, this works out to between $2,450 and $5,020 for the former and $5,450 and $11,200 for the latter. The figures are derived from the Measuring Worth website, https://www.measuringworth.com/.

28. Marquis de Lafayette to GW, 5 February 1783, *GWW*, 26:300n.

29. GW to Marquis de Lafayette, 5 April 1783, ibid., 26:300.

30. William Gordon to GW, 30 August 1784, *GWP.Con.Series*, 2:64.

31. Marquis de Lafayette to GW, 6 February 1786, ibid., 3:121, 544. Lafayette initially purchased two plantations, Saint-Régis and La Belle Gabrielle, and forty-eight slaves. With Lafayette's involvement in efforts at governmental reform in France, much of the long-distance supervision of the program was carried out by his wife, Adrienne, who sought to prepare the enslaved workers for freedom through the teaching of religion and morality. When those first purchases proved unsuitable, the Lafayettes bought another plantation called L'Adrienne, worked by twenty-one slaves, who produced cocoa and coffee and were forbidden to be flogged. By 1787, a plantation manager brought changes to La Belle Gabrielle, one of the first two Lafayette estates on Cayenne, where cloves and cinnamon were grown, and the enslaved population had grown to sixty-five. Slaves at La Belle Gabrielle were given wages as well as an education, punishments were the same as those given to a white person for a similar offense, and sales of slaves were not permitted. See Maurois, *Adrienne*, 145–46.

32. GW to Marquis de Lafayette, 10 May 1786, *GWP.Con.Series*, 4:43.

33. GW to Arthur Young, 12 December 1793; GW to Tobias Lear, 11 September 1797; GW to Richard Parkinson, 28 November 1797, *GWW,* 33:174–83; 36:31, 80. See also Advertisement, 1 February 1796; "Terms on Which the Farms at Mount Vernon May Be Obtained," 1 February 1796; GW to William Strickland, to Sir John Sinclair, and to the Earl of Buchan, all 20 February 1796, ibid., 34:433–38, 441–47, 467–68, 469–70, 471–72.

34. GW to Tobias Lear, 6 May 1794, *GWP.Pres.Series,* 16:25–26, 28n13.

35. Wiencek, *An Imperfect God,* 335–43.

36. GW to William Pearce, 27 January, 7 February 1796, *GWW* 34:427, 448.

37. GW to David Stuart, 7 February 1796, typescript, FWSNL.

38. Wiencek, *An Imperfect God,* 340–41.

39. Pogue, *Founding Spirits,* 106–9, 261n96.

40. Niemcewicz, *Under Their Vine and Fig Tree,* 99–100.

41. James Welch to GW, ca. 24, 29 November 1797; GW to James Keith, 12 December 1797; GW, "Schedule of Property," 9 July 1799, *GWP.Ret.Series,* 1:490, 483, 483n1, 490–91n1, 512–14, 514nn1, 2; 4:514–15, 523n10.

42. GW to Robert Lewis, 18 August 1799, *GWW,* 37:338–39.

43. GW to Robert Lewis, 7 December 1799, ibid., 37:453.

44. Madison, *Notes of Debates,* 295.

45. Ibid., 502–3.

46. Ibid., 504.

47. Ibid., 505.

48. Ibid., 504–6.

49. Ibid., 506–8, 522, 530–32, 621.

50. For earlier treatments of Washington's views on slavery, see Mazyck, *George Washington and the Negro;* Ellis, *His Excellency,* 160–69, 255–65; Flexner, "Washington and Slavery"; Flexner, "George Washington and Slavery," in *George Washington,* 4:112–25; and Twohig, "'That Species of Property.'"

51. Dr. David Stuart to GW, 25 February 1796, *GWP.Pres.Series,* 19:496.

52. Ibid.

53. Ibid., 19:497.

54. Ibid., 19:497–98. Interestingly, two years later, in a conversation with Polish guest Julian Ursyn Niemcewicz, Stuart sounded much more pessimistic—and racist—than in the letter to Washington. Niemcewicz described the encounter: "He told me: no one knows better than the Virginians the cruelty, inconvenience and the little advantage of having Blacks. Their support costs a great deal; their work is worth little if they are not whipped; the *Surveyor* [overseer] costs a great deal and steals into the bargain. We would all agree to free these people; but how to do it with such a great number? They have tried to rent them a piece of land; except for a small number they want neither to work nor to pay their rent. Moreover this unfortunate black color has made such a sharp distinction between the two races. It will always make them a separate caste, which in spite of all the enlightenment of philosophy, will always be regarded as an inferior class which will never mix in the society of Whites. All these difficulties will increase from day to day, for the Blacks multiply. Only a great increase of the population of Whites, a great emigration from Europe, could render this less apparent." Niemcewicz, *Under Their Vine and Fig Tree,* 104.

55. For the primary breakdown of the enslaved population at Mount Vernon into rented, Washington-owned, and dower slaves, see 1799 Slave Lists. In addition, as discussed elsewhere in this work, the Washingtons rented Peter Hardiman and Moll from Martha Washington's former daughter-in-law and her new husband, Dr. David Stuart, while Martha would, following George's death, acquire a male slave called Elish.

56. For Virginia law concerning the disposition of slaves in intestate estates and other estate issues concerning slavery faced by the Washingtons, see Virginia, *Statutes at Large,* 5:445, 446, 464; 11:39–40; 12:145–46, 150.

57. Washington, *Last Will and Testament,* 2. Many years later, Washington's step-grandson George Washington Parke Custis, a supporter of the American Colonization Society, would make provisions in his own will to free the 196 slaves he owned at the time of his death, within five years of that 1857 event. See Sara B. Bearss, "Custis, George Washington Parke," in *Dictionary of Virginia Biography,* 3:631, 633. For earlier manumissions by Custis, see Provine, *Alexandria County, Virginia, Free Negro Registers,* 32, 43, 218–19, 233. For manumissions by Thomas Law, the husband of Custis's older sister Eliza prior to their divorce, see Provine, *District of Columbia Free Negro Registers,* 1:52n.

58. *Federal Gazette and Baltimore Daily Advertiser,* 30 April 1800.

59. MW to Burwell Bassett, 22 December 1777, Washington, *"Worthy Partner,"* 175.

60. MW to Bartholomew Dandridge, 2 November 1778, ibid., 180.

61. Abigail Adams to Mary Smith Cranch, 21 December 1800, typescript, PS-605/R-102, FWSNL.

62. Bushrod Washington to unknown, 27 December 1799, Washington, *"Worthy Partner,"* 329.

63. Custis, *Recollections and Private Memoirs,* 157–58.

64. Binney, *Bushrod Washington,* 25–26. For evidence that arson continued to be a problem for several years, see Dolley Payne Madison to Anna Cutts, [May–June] 1804, Madison, *Selected Letters of Dolley Payne Madison,* 58, in which she says that "Mount Vernon has been sett on fire five different times & tis suspected some malicious persons are determined to reduce it to ashes—Oh the wickedness of Men & women. I'm affraid to accept their invitations."

65. Registrations nos. 52, 53, Provine, *Alexandria County, Virginia, Free Negro Registers,* 10.

66. "A List of Negroes Belonging to Mrs. Washington," 5 March 1801, Peter Family Collection, Thomas Peter Papers, box 1, folder 32.

67. The other possible woman who was "Old Judy" would have been fifty-two years old in 1801 and was described in an earlier list as "blind." She had been living earlier at Dogue Run Farm, while her husband, Gabriel, a George Washington slave who was twenty years younger than herself, lived at Muddy Hole Farm. Information about the slaves at Mount Vernon after the emancipation comes from 1799 Slave Lists, 37:256–67, and "A List of Negroes Belonging to Mrs. Washington."

68. "Mrs. Washington's Account with Dr. Hamilton," 6 December 1801–6 September 1802; "The Estate of Mrs. Washington of Mt Vernon To Peter Hawk," 14 August 1802, Letterbook, 1800–1829, Peter Family Collection, box 4, F.

69. "Account with Davie Gray," 12 January 1801, ibid.

70. Peter Family Collection, Thomas Peter Papers, box 1, folder 36.

71. Washington, *Last Will and Testament,* 2–4, 12–13. The figures given here are based on slave lists compiled by Washington in the summer before his death, which would not necessarily be accurate at the time of the manumission of the slaves and the division two years later of the Custis dower slaves. This is because there were undoubtedly a few births and perhaps a few deaths (and at least one escape—that of Marcus) in the intervening eighteen months and three years, respectively, between the time the lists were drawn up and the occurrence of the later events. The value of George Washington's slaves at Mount Vernon was about £4,640 or $19,163.20 in 1799 (based on an exchange rate of $4.13 to £1 sterling), as well as the sale prices of slaves inherited by Martha Washington's second granddaughter from the estate of her late father, John Parke Custis, upon her marriage to Thomas Peter in the mid-1790s. Thomas Peter, Day Book, 1796, MS2, Papers of Thomas and Martha Parke Custis Peter, box 1, folder 18, Tudor Place Archives. From those sales figures, each of the slaves was assigned an approximate worth based on the following criteria: older men (over forty, no skills)—£45; older men (over forty, with skills)—£50; younger men (under forty)—£75; older women (over forty)—£40; younger women (under forty)—£50; nonworking children (over the age of two)—£25; toddlers and babies (two years old and under)—£5; invalids and those too old to work—£0. The value of those slaves in 2015 dollars was $361,000. See Measuring Worth website.

72. Washington, *Last Will and Testament,* 2. The value of the dower slaves in 1799 was approximately £6,055 or $25,007.15 (based on values of slaves inherited by Martha Washington's second granddaughter from the estate of her late father upon her marriage to Thomas Peter in the mid-1790s). To put this figure into perspective, George Washington's salary as president of the United States was $25,000 per year, and in 1805, Bushrod Washington insured the mansion and primary outbuildings at Mount Vernon for $33,920. See Bushrod Washington, "Insurance Policy on Mount Vernon," 5 June 1805; "Insurance on Barn," 6 June 1805; "Insurance Declaration," 6 June 1805, photostat, FWSNL. The value of the dower slaves in 2015 dollars was approximately $471,000. Taking the two sets of figures together, the combined value of the Washington and dower slaves in 1799 was £10,695 or $44,170.35, which is equivalent to $832,000 in 2015 dollars. To further put this into perspective, Washington estimated the value of his lands, livestock, bank and company stocks (everything but the slaves, furnishings, house, outbuildings, and lands at Mount Vernon) at $530,000 in 1799, which would be equivalent to $9.98 million in 2015. Adding up the appraised value of the contents of Mount Vernon ($27,158.34), the omissions noted at the end ($668), the cash on hand ($254.70), stocks and other securities ($29,212), and Washington's appraisal of his lands elsewhere ($546,428.04), and adding in the combined value of the Washington and dower slaves ($44,170.35), while leaving out redundancies (livestock and securities), yields a total figure of $590,598.39, which is equivalent to $11.1 million in 2015 dollars. The combined value of the Washington (3.24%) and dower slaves (4.2%), therefore, made up about 7.5 percent of Washington's overall wealth, *not* counting the value of the land and structures at Mount Vernon estate. For Washington's estimation of his net worth—minus the Mount Vernon property— see Washington, *Last Will and Testament,* 50. For the appraised value of the contents

of Mount Vernon and the schedule of property, see Prussing, *The Estate of George Washington, Deceased,* 72, 73, 447. As mentioned earlier, slaves made up 33 percent of the financial assets (not including land) of Martha Washington's first husband, Daniel Parke Custis; on large Virginia estates on the eve of the American Revolution, the figure was closer to 75 percent. See Walsh, *Motives of Honor, Pleasure, and Profit,* 447, 447n64. Determining the equivalent percentage for Washington based on the inventoried contents of Mount Vernon plus the value of cash, shares in stocks and bonds, and slaves, which came to $101,463.39 (not including any of the land or buildings at Mount Vernon or elsewhere), the slaves ($44,170.35) made up 43.53 percent of his financial wealth.

73. For Washington's attempts to return Mrs. French's slaves to the family prior to his death (as shown earlier, they were a financial liability), see GW to Benjamin Dulany, 15 July, [12 September] 1799, *GWP.Ret.Series,* 4:189, 189n1, 190nn2–3, 295–96, 296n2.

74. MW, "The Will of Martha Washington," Washington, *Last Will and Testament,* 62; Prussing, *The Estate of George Washington, Deceased,* 392. In recent years, Martha Washington has come under criticism for not being as forward thinking on the issue of slavery as her second husband. My own take on this matter is that from the time she became a widow for the first time in 1757, an event that left the twenty-six-year-old woman with two small children who were relying on her, she would have seen it as one of her primary responsibilities to ensure that the third of the estate in which she had a life interest was not squandered but held together for the benefit of those heirs, who were first her children and then, after their deaths, her four grandchildren. Having grown up in a Virginia Anglican home in the 1730s and 1740s, she would have been trained that doing one's duty to one's family and community was a religious obligation. See Thompson, *"In the Hands of a Good Providence,"* 15.

75. Many of the questions we would like to know about what happened to the former Mount Vernon slaves between the deaths of George and Martha Washington and the Civil War cannot be answered at this time. Official lists that might have enumerated the individuals freed by Martha Washington on 1 January 1801 or itemized the dower slaves going to each grandchild, which should have been recorded in local court records, are missing, rather ironically because the Fairfax County Courthouse was ransacked by Union soldiers during the Civil War. For the damage to the papers at the courthouse, and the fact that Martha Washington's will was almost destroyed by the soldiers, who were burning papers in order to kindle fires, see James E. Hoofnagle, "Introduction," in Washington, *Last Will and Testament,* ii–iii, and Prussing, *The Estate of George Washington, Deceased,* 393–400.

76. "List of the Different Drafts of Negros," [1802], Letterbook, 1800–1829, Peter Family Collection, box 4, F. Granddaughter Eliza's husband, Thomas Law, a wealthy and well-connected Englishman, had signaled even before their marriage that the couple's relationship in regard to property would be different. Eliza's stepfather told George Washington in a letter written about a month before the wedding that he expected to be able to rent Eliza's share of her late father's slaves "allways . . . for very little: As I am told, Mr Law say's she may do as she pleases with her fortune." Dr. David Stuart to GW, 25 February 1796, typescript, FWSNL.

77. William Short to Thomas Jefferson, 18 September 1800, Jefferson, *The Papers of Thomas Jefferson*, 32:155.

78. Binney, *Bushrod Washington*, 26.

79. Edward George Washington Butler to Charles Gayarré, 16 July 1853, photostat, FWSNL. My thanks to David D. Plater of Thibodaux, Louisiana, for providing the copy in a letter to the author, 2 October 2014. For more on the life and career of Edward G. W. Butler, see Plater, *The Butlers of Iberville Parish*.

80. Custis, *Recollections and Private Memoirs*, 158.

81. Edward George Washington Butler to Charles Gayarré, 16 July 1853, FWSNL.

82. Bristol, "Copy of Lund Washington's Manuscript," 14–15.

83. Those legal barriers included an 1806 Virginia law requiring newly freed slaves to leave the state within one year and a series of increasingly restrictive laws that prevented slaves from learning to read and write. For example, see Stanton, *"Those Who Labor for My Happiness,"* 6, 164, 197, 219, 221, 224, 225, 226–27, 231, 333n160.

84. Ibid., 223.

85. Hellman and McCoy, "Soil Tilled by Free Men," 48, 49.

86. Paula Elsey, "Another Day on Harley Road," *South County Chronicle* (Fairfax County, VA), 1 November 2004, 1, 5.

87. Shawn Costley, descendant of former Mount Vernon slaves Davy and Edy Jones, conversation with the author, 30 September 1994; Medford, "Beyond Mount Vernon," 150.

88. For the obituaries of Frank Lee and "Samuel" Anderson, see *Alexandria Gazette,* 30 July 1821; 22 February 1845.

89. "Samuel Anderson," Friends of Freedmen's Cemetery, http://www .freedmenscemetery.org/resources/families/documents/anderson.shtml.

90. An Old Citizen of Fairfax, "Mount Vernon Reminiscences Continued," *Alexandria Gazette,* 22 January 1876.

91. See "Registration No. 6 . . . William Anderson, 7 May 1842"; "Registration No. 9 . . . Eliza Anderson, 23 May 1842"; "Registration No. 448 . . . Eliza Anderson, 6 August 1847," Provine, *Alexandria County, Virginia, Free Negro Registers,* 105, 209.

92. For a fuller treatment of the freed families from Mount Vernon and their lives after they were manumitted, see Medford, "Beyond Mount Vernon."

93. WHAB, 30:329.

94. John Holland Barney to Bartholomew Dandridge, Jr., 20 December 1794, *GWP.Pres.Series,* 17:294.

95. Herman Stump to GW, 20 December 1794, ibid., 17:294–95.

96. John Carlile to GW, 21 December 1794, ibid., 17:296–97.

97. Thomas Archer to GW, 22 December 1794, ibid., 17:303; Elizabeth Stiles to GW, 22 December 1794, ibid., 17:294n.

98. John Carlile to GW, 21 December 1794, ibid., 17:297.

99. Brookes, "A Dinner at Mount Vernon," 82.

100. Parkinson, *Tour in America,* 2:420; Walsh, "Slavery and Agriculture at Mount Vernon," 47–50, 70–73, 49–50 (quotation). For a discussion of the change to "industrial farming" in the New World and elsewhere, see Fogel, *Without Consent or Contract,* 25–29.

101. Custis, *Recollections and Private Memoirs,* 157.

102. NCL to Elizabeth Bordley Gibson, 29 April 1823, Lewis, *George Washington's Beautiful Nelly,* 134.

103. Niemcewicz, *Under Their Vine and Fig Tree,* 101. An Englishman, writing about twenty years before Niemcewicz about the Eastern Shore of Maryland, described similar treatment of slaves: "Many agreeable Plantations, many of them bearing the Appearance of our better kind of Farms in England, are interspersed every where; though the Country is not cleared one tenth Part, except near the Shore. Scarce a white person was to be seen; but negroes appeared in great abundance. These live in Huts or Hovels near the Houses of their Owners, and are treated as a better kind of Cattle, being bought or sold, according to Fancy or Interest, having no Property not even in their Wives or Children. Such is the Practice or Sentiment of Americans, while they are bawling about the Rights of *human Nature,* and oppose the freest Govt. and most liberal System of Polity known upon the Face of the Earth!" Serle, *American Journal,* 249.

104. Louis-Philippe, *Diary of My Travels,* 32; Niemcewicz, *Under Their Vine and Fig Tree,* 100.

105. GW to Arthur Young, 18–21 June 1792, *GWW,* 32:65.

106. Comment by GW, recorded by David Humphreys in the latter's biography of Washington, now in the Rosenbach Library in Philadelphia, quoted in Wall, "Housing and Family Life of the Mount Vernon Negro," prefatory note, and in Zagarri, *David Humphreys' "Life of General Washington,"* 78.

107. For examples of these kinds of statements, see interviews with Simuel Riddick, Josephine Smith, Mary Anderson, Sarah Debro, Patsy Mitchner, and Parker Pool in Hurmence, *My Folks Don't Want Me to Talk about Slavery,* 31, 32, 49–50, 59–60, 78–80, 87. One thing to keep in mind when reading these opinions is that, for the most part, the people doing the interviews were white and the work was undertaken during a highly racist period in American history, characterized by Jim Crow laws, lynchings, and the incarceration of many black men for minor infractions of the law, which left them vulnerable to virtual reenslavement on southern farms and industries. The realities of the period may well have led those being interviewed to edit what they were saying on the record, for fear of some sort of retribution. For more on the larger culture's interactions with African Americans in these years and on former slaves telling interviewers what they wanted to hear, see Douglas A. Blackmon's *Slavery by Another Name,* and Halee Robinson's "Black Women's Voices and the Archives," Black Perspectives, 15 November 2017, http://www.aaihs.org/black-womens-voices-and-the-archive/.

108. Peters, "Fac-Simile of General Washington's Hand Writing," viii. Many thanks to historian Bruce Ragsdale, a colleague since our days in a graduate seminar on colonial America four decades ago, for sharing Peters's character sketch with Mount Vernon.

109. "Mount Vernon Reminiscences Continued," *Alexandria Gazette,* 22 January 1876.

110. M., "[Communicated]," *Alexandria Gazette,* 16 November 1835. Sambo Anderson would remain a well-known figure in Alexandria for another decade. He died

on 20 February 1845, an event that was noted in the local newspaper, the *Alexandria Gazette,* on 22 February 1845.

111. For the slaves sent out with Simpson in 1773 and Washington's partnership with him, see "Cash Accounts," [May 1772]; Gilbert Simpson to GW, 5 October 1772, GW to Simpson, 23 February 1773; Simpson to GW, [?] July, 1 October 1773, *GWP.Col.Series,* 9:35, 36n4, 113–14, 114–15n, 185, 186nn1, 2, 291, 342, 342–43n2.

112. GW to Thomas Freeman, 16 October 1785, *GWP.Con.Series,* 3:309. See also the same letter in *GWW,* 28:294, in which Sambo Anderson's name is given correctly. For the importance of the shipmate relationship, see Kelley, *Voyage of the Slave Ship Hare,* 112–13.

113. Thomas Freeman to GW, 18 December 1786, *GWP.Con.Series,* 4:463, 464n1.

114. "An Old Man," *Alexandria Gazette,* 26 September 1854.

115. Another former Mount Vernon slave who took Washington's last name was Henry Washington. He was probably the "Harry" who left the estate on the British ship *Savage* during the Revolution, although that story disagrees with details provided by him to the British at the end of the war. However he left Mount Vernon, he eventually made his way to Sierra Leone, where he took part in a revolt against the Sierra Leone Company in 1800. For Henry Washington's life, see Frey, *Water from the Rock,* 198, and Clark, "A Wartime Incident," 25. For more on his life, with a different description of when he left Mount Vernon, see Pybus, *Epic Journeys,* 218; Schama, *Rough Crossings,* 16–17, 81, 232, 281, 381, 383; and Whitehead, *Black Loyalists,* 74, 139–140, 149. The only other Mount Vernon slave believed to have used Washington's last name was a woman originally known as Mary Simpson. She is said to have been born at Mount Vernon and to have lived there until George Washington's death, after which she made her way to New York City where she ran "a small cake store." She later was well known in New York for her annual celebration of Washington's birthday and "became known as Mary Washington." The phrasing suggests that the surname was bestowed on her, rather than one she chose for herself. The only known slave named Mary who was at Mount Vernon in 1799 was an eleven-year-old girl at Muddy Hole Farm who was a dower slave and would not have been freed upon Washington's death. For Mary Simpson/Washington, see *Alexandria Phoenix Gazette,* 4 March 1826, and Moscow, *Book of New York Firsts,* 85. Recent email conversations with independent researcher Brad Hillis reveal that Simpson was actually Mary's married name and that Thompson was her original surname. Hillis has located her will, dated 22 December 1832, which was probated on 6 April 1836 and left part of her estate to her cousins William Costen of Washington, DC, and Peggy Holmes. Brad Hillis, email correspondence, 15 July 2015. Clearly the references to William Costen and another cousin named Holmes have opened up a new area for additional research.

116. Ellis, *History of Fayette County, Pennsylvania,* 718. I would like to thank Art Louderback of the Library and Archives Division of the Historical Society of Western Pennsylvania for providing Mount Vernon with this source.

117. Stedman, *Hammet Achmet.*

118. "Died," *Boston Courier,* 5 December 1842, as illustrated in Mary Harrell-Sesniak, "Hammet Achmet: Washington's Waiter and Revolutionary War Patriot,"

18 February 2014, http://blog.genealogybank.com/hammet-achmet-washingtons-slave-revolutionary-war-patriot.html. For a similar case, this time involving Richard Stanhope in Ohio, see the letter from T. S. McFarland, from Urbana, Ohio, dated 14 March 1859, as published in the *Columbian Register,* 9 April 1859, and Medford, "Beyond Mount Vernon," 152–53.

119. For a wonderful study of Barnum and the Joice Heth case, see Reiss, *The Showman and the Slave.*

120. Mark Twain, "General Washington's Negro Body-Servant: A Biographical Sketch," *The Galaxy* (New York), February 1868, http://www.twainquotes.com/Galaxy/186802.html. For a fuller treatment of Twain's story and the phenomenon of George Washington's many faithful body servants, see Muller, *Mark Twain in Washington, D.C.,* 121–35.

121. An Old Citizen of Fairfax, "Mount Vernon Reminiscences Continued," *Alexandria Gazette,* 22 January 1876.

122. Ann S. Stephens, "A Ride to Mount Vernon," *Ladies Companion,* [April?] 1841, 4, FWSNL.

123. H. Pernell Taylor, interview with Madeleine Lindsey Green, 30 September 1980, typescript, FWSNL. I would very much like to thank Green for sharing this interview with Mount Vernon.

124. Nina Simon, "Trust Me, Know Me, Love Me: Trust in the Participatory Age," Museum 2.0, 28 March 2008, http://museumtwo.blogspot.com/2008/03/trust-me-know-me-love-me-trust-in.html.

125. "Attitudes of Parents towards Museums: Omnibus Survey," National Museum Directors' Council, February 2004, http://www.nationalmuseums.org.uk/media/documents/publications/parents.

126. Randy Boswell, "Museums Trusted as Source for History," *Edmonton Journal,* 27 December 2011.

127. Ruth Baja Williams, "Interpreting Slave Life at Mount Vernon," *South County Chronicle* (Fairfax County, Virginia), February 2008; Ruth Williams, conversation with author, 2009.

128. Lorde, *Sister Outsider,* 150.

BIBLIOGRAPHY

Abu Bakr Al-Siddiq. "Abu Bakr Al-Siddiq of Timbuktu." In *Africa Remembered: Narratives by West Africans from the Era of the Slave Trade,* edited by Philip D. Curtin, 152–69. Madison: University of Wisconsin Press, 1967.

Adams, Abigail. *New Letters of Abigail Adams, 1788–1801.* Edited by Stewart Mitchell. Boston: Houghton Mifflin, 1947.

Adams, John. *Diary and Autobiography of John Adams.* Edited by L. H. Butterfield. 4 vols. Cambridge, MA: Belknap Press of Harvard University Press, 1961.

Adams, William Howard. *Jefferson's Monticello.* New York: Abbeville Press, 1983.

Aesop. *Aesop's Fables, with His Life, Morals, and Remarks, Fitted for the Meanest Capacities.* 11th edition. Glasgow: John McCallum, 1751.

Allen, Janet S. *Tomorrow Came Yesterday: The Story of George Washington, a Slave Named Venus and a Negro Son Named West Ford.* New York: Vantage Press, 2012.

Allen, W. B. *George Washington: America's First Progressive.* New York: Peter Lang, 2008.

Anburey, Thomas. *Travels through the Interior Parts of America; in a Series of Letters.* 2 vols. London: William Lane, 1789.

Atkins, Stephen C. "An Archaeological Perspective on the African-American Slave Diet at Mount Vernon's House for Families." M.A. thesis, College of William and Mary, 1994.

———. "A Closer Look: Reconstructing Slave Diet from the House for Families Cellar." Unpublished paper prepared for the College of William and Mary and the Mount Vernon Ladies' Association, 1990.

———. "Mount Vernon: Identified Taxa." Unpublished paper prepared for the Mount Vernon Ladies' Association, 1993.

Baker, William Spohn. *Washington after the Revolution, 1784–1799.* Philadelphia: J. B. Lippincott, 1898.

Ball, Edward. *Slaves in the Family.* New York: Farrar, Straus and Giroux, 1998.

Bates, Elizabeth Bidwell, and Jonathan L. Fairbanks. *American Furniture: 1620 to the Present.* New York: Richard Marek, 1981.

Batstone, David. *Not for Sale: The Return of the Global Slave Trade—and How We Can Fight It.* New York: Harper San Francisco, 2007.

Baumgarten, Linda. *What Clothes Reveal: The Language of Clothing in Colonial and Federal America.* Williamsburg, VA: Colonial Williamsburg Foundation and Yale University Press, 2002.

Beales, Ross W., Jr. "Nursing and Weaning in an Eighteenth-Century New England Household." In *Families and Children: The Dublin Seminar for New England Folklife: Annual Proceedings, June 29 and 30, 1985,* edited by Peter Benes and Jane Montague Benes, 48–63. Boston: Boston University, 1987.

Bennion, Elisabeth. *Antique Dental Instruments.* New York: Sotheby's, 1986.

Berard, Augusta Blanche. "Arlington and Mount Vernon 1856 as Described in a Letter of Augusta Blanche Berard." Edited by Clayton Torrence. *Virginia Magazine of History and Biography* 57, no. 2 (April 1949): 140–75.

Berlin, Ira. *Many Thousands Gone: The First Two Centuries of Slavery in North America.* Cambridge, MA: Belknap Press of Harvard University Press, 1998.

Bernard, John. *Retrospections of America, 1797–1811.* New York: Harper and Brothers, 1887.

Bickley, R. Bruce. "Joel Chandler Harris (1845–1908)." New Georgia Encyclopedia. https://www.georgiaencyclopedia.org.

Biddle, Charles. *Autobiography of Charles Biddle, Vice-President of the Supreme Executive Council of Pennsylvania, 1745–1821.* Philadelphia: E. Claxton, 1883.

Bilali, Salih. "Salih Bilali's Recollections of Massina." In *Africa Remembered: Narratives by West Africans from the Era of the Slave Trade,* edited by Philip D. Curtin, 147–51. Madison: University of Wisconsin Press, 1967.

Binney, Horace. *Bushrod Washington.* Philadelphia: C. Sherman and Son, 1858.

Blackmon, Douglas A. *Slavery by Another Name: The Re-Enslavement of Black Americans from the Civil War to World War II.* New York: Doubleday, 2008.

Blassingame, John W. *The Slave Community: Plantation Life in the Antebellum South.* New York: Oxford University Press, 1979.

Boorer, Wendy. *The World of Dogs.* London: Hamlyn, 1969.

Boucher, Jonathan. *Reminiscences of an American Loyalist, 1738–1789: Being the Autobiography of The Revd. Jonathan Boucher, Rector of Annapolis in Maryland and Afterwards Vicar of Epsom, Surrey, England.* Boston: Houghton Mifflin, 1925.

Bowen, Joanne. "Faunal Remains from the House for Families Cellar." Unpublished report prepared for the Mount Vernon Ladies' Association, 3 November 1993.

Brady, Patricia. *Martha Washington: An American Life.* New York: Viking, 2005.

Breeden, James O., ed. *Advice among Masters: The Ideal in Slave Management in the Old South.* Westport, CT: Greenwood Press, 1980.

Brissot de Warville, Jacques Pierre. *On America: New Travels in the United States of America Performed in 1788.* 2 vols. London: J. S. Jordan, 1792. facsimile edition, New York: Augustus M. Kelley, 1970.

Brookes, Joshua. "A Dinner at Mount Vernon: From the Unpublished Journal of Joshua Brookes (1773–1859)." Edited by R. W. G. Vail. *New-York Historical Society Quarterly* 31, no. 2 (April 1947): 72–85.

[Brown, Sarah]. *A Letter to a Lady on the Management of the Infant.* London: Baker and Galabin, 1779.

Bryan, Helen. *Martha Washington: First Lady of Liberty.* New York: Wiley, 2002.

Bryan, William Alfred. *George Washington in American Literature, 1775–1865.* New York: Columbia University Press, 1952.

Bryant, Linda Allen. *I Cannot Tell a Lie: The True Story of George Washington's African-American Descendants.* Lincoln, NE: Writer's Showcase, 2001.

Burnaby, Andrew. *Travels through the Middle Settlements in North America in the Years 1759 and 1760, with Observations upon the State of the Colonies.* 1798. Reprint edition, New York: Augustus M. Kelley, 1970.

Butler, Jon. *Awash in a Sea of Faith: Christianizing the American People.* Cambridge, MA: Harvard University Press, 1990.

Byrd, William Byrd, II. *William Byrd's Histories of the Dividing Line Betwixt Virginia and North Carolina.* Edited by William K. Boyd. Gloucester, MA: Peter Smith, 1984.

Cadou, Carol Borchert. *The George Washington Collection: Fine and Decorative Arts at Mount Vernon.* Manchester, NY: Mount Vernon Ladies' Association and Hudson Hills Press, 2006.

Calvert, Rosalie Stier. *Mistress of Riversdale: The Plantation Letters of Rosalie Stier Calvert, 1795–1821.* Edited and translated by Margaret Law Callcott. Baltimore: Johns Hopkins University Press, 1991.

Campbell, Edward D. C., Jr., and Kym S. Rice, eds. *Before Freedom Came: African-American Life in the Antebellum South.* Richmond: Museum of the Confederacy and University Press of Virginia, 1991.

Campbell, John. "'My Constant Companion': Slaves and Their Dogs in the Antebellum South." In *Working toward Freedom: Slave Society and Domestic Economy in the American South,* edited by Larry E. Hudson, Jr., 53–76. Rochester, NY: University of Rochester Press, 1994.

Campo, Ally. "Wine Not? Investigating Alcohol Consumption within Montpelier's Enslaved Community." *The Scoop: A Newsletter of the Friends of Fairfax County Archaeology and Cultural Resources* (May 2016): 2–7.

Carney, Judith A., and Richard Nicholas Rosomoff. *In the Shadow of Slavery: Africa's Botanical Legacy in the Atlantic World.* Berkeley: University of California Press, 2009.

Carr, Lois Green, and Lorena S. Walsh. "Economic Diversification and Labor Organization in the Chesapeake, 1650–1820." In *Work and Labor in Early America,* edited by Stephen Innes, 144–88. Chapel Hill: University of North Carolina Press, 1988.

Carretta, Vincent. *Phillis Wheatley: Biography of a Genius in Bondage.* Athens: University of Georgia Press, 2014.

Carrington, Eliza Ambler Brent, "A Visit to Mount Vernon—A Letter of Mrs. Edward Carrington to Her Sister, Mrs. George Fisher." *William and Mary College Quarterly Historical Magazine,* 2nd ser., 18, no. 2 (April 1938): 198–202.

Carson, Jane. *Colonial Virginians at Play.* Williamsburg, VA: Colonial Williamsburg Foundation, 1989.

Carter, Landon. *The Diary of Colonel Landon Carter of Sabine Hall, 1752–1778.* Edited by Jack P. Greene. 2 vols. Charlottesville: University Press of Virginia, 1965.

Casper, Scott E. *Sarah Johnson's Mount Vernon: The Forgotten History of an American Shrine.* New York: Hill and Wang, 2008.

Chambers, Douglas B. *Murder at Montpelier: Igbo Africans in Virginia.* Jackson: University Press of Mississippi, 2005.

Chase, Benjamin. "Mrs. [?] Staines." In *Slave Testimony: Two Centuries of Letters,*

Speeches, Interviews, and Autobiographies, edited by John W. Blassingame, 248–50. Baton Rouge: Louisiana State University Press, 1977.

Chase, John Terry. *Gum Springs: The Triumph of a Black Community.* Fairfax, VA: Fairfax County Board of Supervisors, 1990.

Chastellux, François Jean, Marquis de. *Travels in North America in the Years 1780, 1781 and 1782.* Translated by Howard C. Rice, Jr. 2 vols. Chapel Hill: University of North Carolina Press 1963.

Chinard, Gilbert, ed. and trans. *George Washington as the French Knew Him: A Collection of Texts.* Princeton, NJ: Princeton University Press, 1940. Reprint edition, New York: Greenwood Press, 1969.

Clark, Ellen McCallister. "A Letter of West Ford." In *Annual Report, 1985,* 34–35. Mount Vernon, VA: Mount Vernon Ladies' Association, 1986.

———. "Two Unpublished Letters." In *Annual Report, 1986,* 29–36. Mount Vernon, VA: Mount Vernon Ladies' Association, 1987.

———. "A Wartime Incident." In *Annual Report, 1986,* 23–25. Mount Vernon, VA: Mount Vernon Ladies' Association, 1987.

Clinton, Catherine. *The Plantation Mistress: Woman's World in the Old South.* New York: Pantheon, 1982.

Coke, Thomas. *Extracts of the Journals of the Rev. Dr. Coke's Five Visits to America.* London: G. Paramore, 1793.

Coombs, John C. "Beyond the 'Origins Debate': Rethinking the Rise of Virginia Slavery." In *Early Modern Virginia: Reconsidering the Old Dominion,* edited by Douglas Bradburn and John C. Coombs, 239–78. Charlottesville: University of Virginia Press, 2011.

Corbin, David A. "The Gum Springs Community." *Fairfax Chronicles* 4, no. 2 (Spring 1980): 1–2, 5.

Cornelius, Janet Duitsman. *When I Can Read My Title Clear: Literacy, Slavery, and Religion in the Antebellum South.* Columbia: University of South Carolina Press, 1991.

Coulling, Mary P. *The Lee Girls.* Winston-Salem, NC: John F. Blair, 1987.

Cresswell, Nicholas. *The Journal of Nicholas Cresswell, 1774–1777.* New York: Lincoln McVeagh/The Dial Press, 1924.

Crowther, Samuel Ajayi. "The Narrative of Samuel Ajayi Crowther." In *Africa Remembered: Narratives by West Africans from the Era of the Slave Trade,* edited by Philip D. Curtin, 298–316. Madison: University of Wisconsin Press, 1967.

Curtis, Edward E., IV, ed. *Encyclopedia of Muslim-American History.* 2 vols. New York: Facts on File, 2010.

———. *Muslims in America: A Short History.* New York: Oxford University Press, 2009.

Custis, George Washington Parke. *Recollections and Private Memoirs of Washington, by His Adopted Son, George Washington Parke Custis, with a Memoir of the Author, by His Daughter; and Illustrative and Explanatory Notes, by Benson J. Lossing.* 1860. Reprint edition, Bridgewater, VA: American Foundation, 1999.

Cutler, William Parker, and Julia Perkins Cutler. *Life Journals and Correspondence of Rev. Manasseh Cutler, LL.D. by His Grandchildren.* 2 vols. Cincinnati, OH: Robert Clarke, 1888.

Dalzell, Robert F., Jr., and Lee Baldwin Dalzell. *George Washington's Mount Vernon: At Home in Revolutionary America.* New York: Oxford University Press, 1998.

D'Avezac-Macaya, Marie Armand Pascal. "The Land and People of Ijebu." In *Africa Remembered: Narratives by West Africans from the Era of the Slave Trade,* edited by Philip D. Curtin, 223–88. Madison: University of Wisconsin Press, 1967.

Davis, David Brion. "At the Heart of Slavery." *New York Review of Books,* 17 October 1996, 51–54.

Dawes, Frank. *Not in Front of the Servants: A True Portrait of English Upstairs/ Downstairs Life.* New York: Taplinger, 1973.

Decatur, Stephen, Jr. *Private Affairs of General Washington: From the Records and Accounts of Tobias Lear, Esquire, His Secretary.* Boston: Houghton Mifflin, 1933.

Detweiler, Susan Gray. *George Washington's Chinaware.* New York: Harry N. Abrams, 1982.

Dictionary of Virginia Biography. 3 vols. Richmond: Library of Virginia, 1998–2006.

Diouf, Sylviane A. *Dreams of Africa in Alabama: The Slave Ship Clotilda and the Story of the Last Africans Brought to America.* New York: Oxford University Press, 2007.

———. *Servants of Allah: African Muslims Enslaved in the Americas.* New York: New York University Press, 1998.

Downer, Joseph A. "Hallowed Ground, Sacred Place: The Slave Cemetery at George Washington's Mount Vernon and the Cultural Landscapes of the Enslaved." M.A. thesis, George Washington University, 2015.

Duke, Lynne. "This Harrowed Ground." *Washington Post Magazine,* 28 August 1994, 8–13, 20–25.

Dunbar, Erica Armstrong. *Never Caught: The Washingtons' Relentless Pursuit of Their Runaway Slave, Ona Judge.* New York: 37 Ink/Atria Books, 2017.

Dunn, Richard S. *A Tale of Two Plantations: Slave Life and Labor in Jamaica and Virginia.* Cambridge, MA: Harvard University Press, 2014.

Edmonston, Catherine Ann Devereux. *"Journal of a Secesh Lady": The Diary of Catherine Ann Devereux Edmonston, 1860–1866.* Edited by Beth G. Crabtree and James W. Patton. Raleigh, NC: Division of Archives and History, Department of Cultural Resources, 1979.

1876 Visitors' Guide to Mount Vernon. Washington, DC: E. B. Johnston, 1876.

Eisen, Gustavus A. *Portraits of Washington.* 3 vols. New York: Robert Hamilton and Associates, 1932.

Ekirch, A. Roger. *Bound for America: The Transportation of British Convicts to the Colonies, 1718–1775.* Oxford: Clarendon Press, 1987.

Elkins, Stanley M. *Slavery: A Problem in American Institutional and Intellectual Life.* 3rd edition. Chicago: University of Chicago Press, 1976.

Ellis, Franklin, ed. *History of Fayette County, Pennsylvania, with Biographical Sketches of Many of Its Pioneers and Prominent Men.* Philadelphia: L. H. Everts, 1882.

Ellis, Joseph J. *His Excellency: George Washington.* New York: Knopf, 2004.

Eltis, David, and David Richardson. *Atlas of the Transatlantic Slave Trade.* New Haven, CT: Yale University Press, 2010.

Equiano, Olaudah. "The Early Travels of Olaudah Equiano." In *Africa Remembered:*

Narratives by West Africans from the Era of the Slave Trade, edited by Philip D. Curtin, 69–98. Madison: University of Wisconsin Press, 1967.

Farrand, Max, ed. *The Records of the Federal Convention of 1787.* 4 vols. Revised edition. New Haven, CT: Yale University Press, 1966.

Fasy, Jennifer Jacquelyn Ione. "After Prayer and Praise: The Record Book of the Alexandria Baptist Church, 1803–1816." M.A. thesis, Utah State University, 1992.

Fenn, Elizabeth. *Pox Americana: The Great Smallpox Epidemic of 1775–82.* New York: Hill and Wang, 2001.

Finkelman, Paul. "Jefferson and Slavery: "Treason against the Hopes of the World." In *Jeffersonian Legacies,* edited by Peter S. Onuf, 181–221. Charlottesville: University Press of Virginia, 1993.

———. "Thomas Jefferson and Antislavery: The Myth Goes On." *Virginia Magazine of History and Biography* 102, no. 2 (April 1994): 193–228.

Fischer, David Hackett. *Albion's Seed: Four British Folkways in America.* New York: Oxford University Press, 1989.

Fithian, Philip Vickers. *Journal and Letters of Philip Vickers Fithian, 1773–1774: A Plantation Tutor of the Old Dominion.* Edited by Hunter Dickinson Farish. Williamsburg, VA: Colonial Williamsburg, 1957.

Fleming, Thomas. *The Intimate Lives of the Founding Fathers.* New York: Smithsonian, 2009.

Flexner, James Thomas. *George Washington.* 4 vols. Boston: Little, Brown, 1965–72.

———. "Washington and Slavery." *Constitution* 3 (Spring–Summer 1991): 5–10.

Flexner, Stuart Berg. *I Hear America Talking: An Illustrated History of American Words and Phrases.* New York: Touchstone, 1979.

Fogel, Robert William. *Without Consent or Contract: The Rise and Fall of American Slavery.* New York: Norton, 1989.

Fogel, Robert William, and Stanley L. Engerman. *Time on the Cross: The Economics of American Negro Slavery.* New York: Norton, 1989.

Forbes, Esther. *Paul Revere and the World He Lived In.* Boston: Houghton Mifflin, 1942.

Ford, Worthington C. *Washington as an Employer and Importer of Labor.* Brooklyn: Privately printed, 1889.

———, ed. *Wills of George Washington and His Immediate Ancestors.* Brooklyn, NY: Historical Printing Club, 1891.

Foster, Augustus John. "Caviar along the Potomac: Sir Augustus John Foster's 'Notes on the United States,' 1804–1812." Edited by Margaret Bailey Tinkcom. *William and Mary Quarterly,* 3rd ser., 8, no. 1 (January 1951): 68–107.

Foster, Thomas A. "The Sexual Abuse of Black Men under American Slavery." *Journal of the History of Sexuality* 20, no. 3 (2011): 445–64.

Fowble, E. McSherry. *Two Centuries of Prints in America, 1680–1880: A Selective Catalogue of the Winterthur Museum Collection.* Charlottesville: University Press of Virginia, 1987.

Fox-Genovese, Elizabeth. *Within the Plantation Household: Black and White Women of the Old South.* Chapel Hill: University of North Carolina Press, 1988.

Freeman, Douglas Southall. *George Washington: A Biography.* 6 vols. New York: Charles Scribner's Sons, 1948–54.

———. *R. E. Lee: A Biography.* 4 vols. New York: Charles Scribner's Sons, 1934–35.

Frey, Sylvia R. *Water from the Rock: Black Resistance in a Revolutionary Age.* Princeton, NJ: Princeton University Press, 1991.

Furstenberg, François. "Atlantic Slavery, Atlantic Freedom: George Washington, Slavery, and Transatlantic Abolitionist Networks." *William and Mary Quarterly,* 3rd ser., 68, no. 2 (April 2011): 247–86.

Fusonie, Alan, and Donna Jean Fusonie. *George Washington: Pioneer Farmer.* Mount Vernon, VA: Mount Vernon Ladies' Association, 1998.

Garrett, Elisabeth Donaghy. *At Home: The American Family, 1750–1870.* New York: Harry N. Abrams, 1989.

Gaspar, David Barry. "Antigua Slaves and Their Struggle to Survive." In *Seeds of Change: A Quincentennial Commemoration,* edited by Herman J. Viola and Carolyn Margolis, 130–37. Washington, DC: Smithsonian Institution Press, 1991.

Gaynor, Joanne Bowen. "Preliminary Notes on the House for Families Faunal Assemblage." Unpublished paper in the collections of the Mount Vernon Ladies' Association, 15 October 1989.

"Genealogy: Harrison of James River." *Virginia Magazine of History and Biography* 36 (July 1928): 271–82.

Genovese, Eugene D. *Roll, Jordan, Roll: The World the Slaves Made.* New York: Vintage Books, 1974.

Gerson, Evelyn B. "A Thirst for Complete Freedom: Why Fugitive Slave Ona Judge Staines Never Returned to Her Master, President George Washington." M.A. thesis, Harvard University, June 2000.

Girouard, Mark. *Life in the English Country House: A Social and Architectural History.* New Haven, CT: Yale University Press, 1978.

Glasse, Hannah. *"First Catch Your Hare...": The Art of Cookery Made Plain and Easy.* Facsimile edition. Totnes, Devon, UK: Prospect Books, 1995.

———. *The Servants Directory, Improved; or, House-Keepers Companion.* 4th edition. Dublin: J. Potts, 1762.

Godbeer, Richard. *Sexual Revolution in Early America.* Baltimore: Johns Hopkins University Press, 2002.

Gomez, Michael A. *Black Crescent: The Experience and Legacy of African Muslims in the Americas.* New York: Cambridge University Press, 2005.

———. *Exchanging Our Country Marks: The Transformation of African Identities in the Colonial and Antebellum South.* Chapel Hill: University of North Carolina Press, 1998.

———. "Muslims in Early America." *Journal of Southern History* 60, no. 4 (November 1994): 671–710.

Gordon-Reed, Annette. *The Hemingses of Monticello: An American Family.* New York: Norton, 2008.

———. *Thomas Jefferson and Sally Hemings: An American Controversy.* Charlottesville: University Press of Virginia, 1997.

Gorham, Anne Huber. "'The People Shall Be Cloathed': Slave Clothing at Mount Vernon." Unpublished report prepared for the Mount Vernon Ladies' Association, 1993.

Green, Ashbel. *The Life of Ashbel Green, V.D.M.* Edited by Joseph H. Jones. New York: Robert Carter and Brothers, 1849.

Greene, Nathanael. *The Papers of General Nathanael Greene.* Edited by Richard K. Showman and Dennis M. Conrad. 9 vols. Chapel Hill: University of North Carolina Press, 1976–97.

"Greenhouse-Quarters Reconstruction." In *Annual Report 1951,* 34–40. Mount Vernon, VA: Mount Vernon Ladies' Association, 1952.

Griffin, Appleton P. C. *A Catalogue of the Washington Collection in the Boston Athenæum . . . in Four Parts . . . with an Appendix . . . by William Coolidge Lane.* Cambridge, MA: Boston Athenæum, 1897.

Griffith, John T. *Rev. Morgan John Rhys: The Welsh Baptist Hero of Civil and Religious Liberty of the 18th Century.* Lansford, PA: Leader Job Print, 1899.

Gundersen, Joan R., and Gwen Victor Gampel. "Married Women's Legal Status in Eighteenth-Century New York and Virginia." *William and Mary Quarterly,* 3rd ser., 39, no. 1 (January 1982): 114–34.

Gutman, Herbert G. *The Black Family in Slavery and Freedom, 1750–1925.* New York: Vintage Books, 1977.

Hadfield, Joseph. *An Englishman in America, 1785, Being the Diary of Joseph Hadfield.* Edited by Douglas S. Robertson. Toronto: Hunter-Rose, 1933.

Hafner, Dorinda. *A Taste of Africa.* Berkeley, CA: Ten Speed Press, 1993.

Haizlip, Shirlee Taylor. *The Sweeter the Juice: A Family Memoir in Black and White.* New York: Touchstone, 1994.

Hall, Gwendolyn Midlo. *Slavery and African Ethnicities in the Americas: Restoring the Links.* Chapel Hill: University of North Carolina Press, 2005.

Hall, Robert L. "Savoring Africa in the New World." In *Seeds of Change: A Quincentennial Commemoration,* edited by Herman J. Viola and Carolyn Margolis, 160–69. Washington, DC: Smithsonian Institution Press, 1991.

Hamilton, Alexander. *The Papers of Alexander Hamilton.* Edited by Harold C. Syrett and Jacob E. Cooke. Vol. 3. New York: Columbia University Press, 1962.

Handler, Jerome S., and Robert Corruccini. "Weaning among West Indian Slaves: Historical and Bioanthropological Evidence from Barbados." *William and Mary Quarterly,* 3rd ser., 43, no. 1 (January 1986): 111–17.

Harbin, Billy J. "Letters from John Parke Custis to George and Martha Washington, 1778–1781." *William and Mary Quarterly,* 3rd ser., 43, no. 2 (April 1986): 267–93.

Hardesty, Jared Ross. *Unfreedom: Slavery and Dependence in Eighteenth-Century Boston.* New York: New York University Press, 2016.

Harrison, Lee-Langston. *A Presidential Legacy: The Monroe Collection at the James Monroe Museum and Memorial Library.* Fredericksburg, VA: James Monroe Museum, 1997.

Harrower, John. *The Journal of John Harrower: An Indentured Servant in the Colony of Virginia, 1773–1776.* Edited by Edward Miles Riley. Williamsburg, VA: Colonial Williamsburg, 1963.

Haworth, Paul Leland. *George Washington: Country Gentleman.* Indianapolis: Bobbs-Merrill, 1925.

Hay, Douglas. "Poaching and the Game Laws on Cannock Chase." In *Albion's Fatal*

Tree: Crime and Society in Eighteenth-Century England, by E. P. Thompson et al., 189–253. New York: Pantheon Books, 1975.

Heath, Barbara J. *Hidden Lives: The Archaeology of Slave Life at Thomas Jefferson's Poplar Forest.* Charlottesville: University Press of Virginia, 1999.

Heath, Barbara J., and Amber Bennett. "'The Little Spots Allow'd Them': The Archaeological Study of African-American Yards." *Historical Archaeology* 34, no. 2 (2000): 38–55.

Heitman, Francis B. *Historical Register of Officers of the Continental Army during the War of the Revolution, April, 1775, to December, 1783.* Washington, DC: Rare Book Shop, 1914.

Hellman, Susan, and Maddy McCoy. "Soil Tilled by Free Men: The Formation of a Free Black Community in Fairfax County, Virginia." *Virginia Magazine of History and Biography* 125, no. 1 (January 2017): 38–67.

Henisch, Bridget Ann. *Cakes and Characters: An English Christmas Tradition.* London: Prospect Books, 1984.

Henriques, Peter R. "Major Lawrence Washington versus the Reverend Charles Green: A Case Study of the Squire and the Parson." *Virginia Magazine of History and Biography* 100, no. 2 (April 1992): 233–64.

———. *Realistic Visionary: A Portrait of George Washington.* Charlottesville: University of Virginia Press, 2006.

Hess, Karen, ed. *Martha Washington's Booke of Cookery.* New York: Columbia University Press, 1981.

Hill, Mrs. A. P. *Mrs. Hill's New Cookbook: A Practical System for Private Families, in Town and Country. With Directions for Carving and Arranging the Table for Dinners, Parties, etc., Together with Many Medical and Miscellaneous Receipts Extremely Useful in Families.* New York: Carleton, 1872.

Hirschfeld, Fritz. *George Washington and Slavery: A Documentary Portrayal.* Columbia: University of Missouri Press, 1997.

Holloway, Joseph E. "Africanisms in African American Names in the United States." In *Africanisms in American Culture,* edited by Joseph E. Holloway, 82–110. Bloomington: Indiana University Press, 2005.

Holmes, David L. *The Faiths of the Founding Fathers.* Oxford: Oxford University Press, 2006.

Hoppin, Charles Arthur. *The Washington Ancestry and Records of the McClain, Johnson, and Forty Other Colonial American Families.* 3 vols. Greenfield, OH: Privately printed, 1932.

Howard, Hugh. "Slavery in Our Midst: The Remains of a New England Plantation Reveal a Side of Colonial Life the History Books Forget to Mention." *Tufts Magazine,* Summer 2010, 22–27.

Howell, Donna Wyant, comp. *I Was a Slave: Books 1–6.* Washington, DC: American Legacy Books, 1995–2004.

Hume, Audrey Noel. *Food: Colonial Williamsburg Archaeological Series no. 9.* Williamsburg, VA: Colonial Williamsburg Foundation, 1978.

Humphreys, David. *The Miscellaneous Works of David Humphreys.* New York: T. and J. Swords, 1804.

Hunter, Robert, Jr. *Quebec to Carolina in 1785–86, Being the Travel Observations of*

Robert Hunter, Jr., a Young Merchant of London. Edited by Louis B. Wright and Marion Tinling. San Marino, CA: Huntington Library, 1943.

Hurmence, Belinda, ed. *My Folks Don't Want Me to Talk about Slavery: Twenty-One Oral Histories of Former North Carolina Slaves.* Winston-Salem, NC: John F. Blair, 1984.

Hutson, James H., ed. *The Founders on Religion: A Book of Quotations.* Princeton, NJ: Princeton University Press, 2005.

Innes, Stephen. "Fulfilling John Smith's Vision: Work and Labor in Early America." In *Work and Labor in Early America,* edited by Stephen Innes, 3–47. Chapel Hill: University of North Carolina Press, 1988.

Isaac, Rhys. *Landon Carter's Uneasy Kingdom: Revolution and Rebellion on a Virginia Plantation.* Oxford: Oxford University Press, 2004.

Jarratt, Devereux. *The Life of the Reverend Devereux Jarratt: Rector of Bath Parish, Dinwiddie County, Virginia.* Baltimore: Warner and Hanna, 1806.

Jefferson, Thomas. *The Papers of Thomas Jefferson.* Edited by Julian P. Boyd et al. Vol. 14. Princeton, NJ: Princeton University Press, 1958.

———. *The Papers of Thomas Jefferson.* Edited by John Catanzariti et al. Vol. 26. Princeton, NJ: Princeton University Press, 1995.

———. *The Papers of Thomas Jefferson.* Edited by John Catanzariti et al. Vol. 28. Princeton, NJ: Princeton University Press, 2000.

———. *The Papers of Thomas Jefferson.* Edited by Barbara B. Oberg et al. Vol. 32. Princeton, NJ: Princeton University Press, 2005.

———. *The Papers of Thomas Jefferson.* Edited by Barbara B. Oberg et al. Vol. 33. Princeton, NJ: Princeton University Press, 2006.

Johnston, James H. *From Slave Ship to Harvard: Yarrow Mamout and the History of an African American Family.* New York: Fordham University Press, 2012.

Jordan, Winthrop D. *White over Black: American Attitudes toward the Negro, 1550–1812.* Chapel Hill: University of North Carolina Press, 1968.

Kaminski, John P., ed. *The Founders on the Founders: Word Portraits from the American Revolution.* Charlottesville: University of Virginia Press, 2008.

Kaminski, John P., and Jill Adair McCaughan, eds. *A Great and Good Man: George Washington in the Eyes of His Contemporaries.* Madison, WI: Madison House, 1989.

Kamoie, Laura Croghan. *Irons in the Fire: The Business History of the Tayloe Family and Virginia's Gentry, 1700–1860.* Charlottesville: University of Virginia Press, 2007.

Katz-Hyman, Martha B. "'In the Middle of This Poverty Some Cups and a Teapot': The Material Culture of Slavery in Eighteenth-Century Virginia and the Furnishing of Slave Quarters at Colonial Williamsburg." Unpublished report prepared for the Colonial Williamsburg Foundation, January 1993.

Kay, Marvin L. Michael, and Lorin Lee Cary. *Slavery in North Carolina, 1748–1775.* Chapel Hill: University of North Carolina Press, 1995.

Kelley, Sean M. *The Voyage of the Slave Ship Hare: A Journey into Captivity from Sierra Leone to South Carolina.* Chapel Hill: University of North Carolina Press, 2016.

Kelso, William M. "Mulberry Row: Slave Life at Thomas Jefferson's Monticello." *Archaeology* 39 (September–October 1986): 28–35.

Kiple, Kenneth F., and Virginia Himmelsteib King. *Another Dimension to the Black Diaspora: Diet, Disease, and Racism.* New York: Cambridge University Press, 1981.

Kirkland, Mrs. C. M. *Memoirs of Washington.* New York: D. Appleton, 1870.

Klein, Herbert S., and Stanley L. Engerman. "Fertility Differentials between Slaves in the United States and the British West Indies: A Note on Lactation Practices." *William and Mary Quarterly,* 3rd ser., 35, no. 2 (April 1978): 357–74.

Knock, Patricia Ilura. "New Insights into Slave Life at Woodlawn Plantation." *Fairfax Chronicles* 16 (1994): 1, 6–7.

Knox, Henry, and Lucy Knox. *The Revolutionary War Lives and Letters of Lucy and Henry Knox.* Edited by Phillip Hamilton. Baltimore: Johns Hopkins University Press, 2017.

Kolchin, Peter. *American Slavery, 1619–1877.* New York: Hill and Wang, 1993.

Lafayette, Marquis de. *Lafayette in the Age of the American Revolution: Selected Letters and Papers, 1776–1790.* Edited by Stanley J. Idzerda et al. Vol. 4. Ithaca, NY: Cornell University Press, 1981.

Lamire, Elise. *Black Walden: Slavery and Its Aftermath in Concord, Massachusetts.* Philadelphia: University of Pennsylvania Press, 2008.

Latrobe, Benjamin Henry. *Latrobe's View of America, 1795–1820: Selections from the Watercolors and Sketches.* Edited by Edward C. Carter II, John C. Van Horne, and Charles E. Brownell. New Haven, CT: Yale University Press, 1985.

———. *The Virginia Journals of Benjamin Henry Latrobe, 1795–1798.* Edited by Edward C. Carter II. 2 vols. New Haven, CT: Yale University Press, 1977.

Law, Eliza Parke Custis. "Self-Portrait: Eliza Custis, 1808." Edited by William D. Hoyt, Jr. *Virginia Magazine of History and Biography* 53, no. 2 (April 1945): 89–100.

Lawler, Edward, Jr. "The President's House Revisited." *Pennsylvania Magazine of History and Biography* 129 (2005): 371–410.

Leach, Donald B. "George Washington: Waterman-Fisherman, 1760–1799." *Yearbook of the Historical Society of Fairfax County* 28 (2001–2): 1–28.

Lear, Tobias. *Letters and Recollections of George Washington.* New York: Doubleday, Page, 1906.

"A Lear Letter." In *Annual Report 1958,* 19–24. Mount Vernon, VA: Mount Vernon Ladies' Association, 1959.

Leavitt, Judith Walzer. *Brought to Bed: Childbearing in America, 1750–1950.* New York: Oxford University Press, 1986.

Lee, Agnes. *Growing up in the 1850s: The Journal of Agnes Lee.* Edited by Mary Custis Lee deButts. Chapel Hill: University of North Carolina Press, 1984.

Lee, Edmund Jennings, ed. *Lee of Virginia, 1642–1892: Biographical and Genealogical Sketches of the Descendants of Colonel Richard Lee.* 1895. Reprint edition, Baltimore: Genealogical Publishing, 1983.

Lee, Jean B., ed. *Experiencing Mount Vernon: Eyewitness Accounts, 1784–1865.* Charlottesville: University of Virginia Press, 2006.

———. "Laboring Hands and the Transformation of Mount Vernon Plantation, 1783–1799." Paper presented at "Re-Creating the World of the Virginia Plantation, 1750–1820," conference, Charlottesville, Virginia, 31 May 1990.

Leone, Mark P., and Gladys-Marie Fry. "Conjuring in the Big House Kitchen: An Interpretation of African-American Belief Systems Based on the Uses of Archaeology and Folklore Sources." *Journal of American Folklore* 112, no. 445 (Summer 1999): 372–403.

Lerner, Gerda. *The Creation of Patriarchy*. New York: Oxford University Press, 1986.

Levine, Lawrence W. *Black Culture and Black Consciousness: Afro-American Folk Thought from Slavery to Freedom*. Oxford: Oxford University Press, 1977.

Lewis, Eleanor Parke Custis. *George Washington's Beautiful Nelly: The Letters of Eleanor Parke Custis Lewis to Elizabeth Bordley Gibson, 1794–1851*. Edited by Patricia Brady. Columbia: University of South Carolina Press, 1991.

———. *Nelly Custis Lewis's Housekeeping Book*. Edited by Patricia Brady Schmit. New Orleans: Historic New Orleans Collection, 1982.

Lewis, Jan Ellen, and Peter S. Onuf, eds. *Sally Hemings and Thomas Jefferson: History, Memory, and Civic Culture*. Charlottesville: University Press of Virginia, 1999.

Lewis, Meriwether, and William Clark. *The Journals of Lewis and Clark*. Edited by John Bakeless. New York: Penguin Books, 1964.

Lincoln, Abraham. *Abraham Lincoln: Speeches and Writings, 1859–1865*. Edited by Don E. Fehrenbacker. New York: Library of America, 1989.

Lorde, Audre. *Sister Outsider: Essays and Speeches*. Berkeley, CA: Crossing Press, 1984.

Lossing, Benson J. *Hours with the Living Men and Women of the Revolution: A Pilgrimage*. New York: Funk and Wagnalls, 1889.

———. *Mary and Martha: The Mother and the Wife of George Washington*. New York: Harper and Brothers, 1886.

———. *Mount Vernon and Its Associations, Historical, Biographical, and Pictorial*. New York: W. A. Townsend, 1859.

———. "Mount Vernon as It Is." *Harper's New Monthly Magazine*, March 1859, 433–51.

Loth, Calder, ed. *Virginia Landmarks of Black History: Sites on the Virginia Landmarks Register and the National Register of Historic Places*. Charlottesville: University Press of Virginia, 1995.

Louis-Philippe, King of France. *Diary of My Travels in America*. Translated by Stephen Becker. New York: Delacorte Press, 1977.

Lynch, Anna, comp. *A Compendium of Early African Americans in Alexandria, Virginia*. Alexandria, VA: Alexandria Archaeology, Office of Historic Alexandria, City of Alexandria, 1993.

Maclay, William. *The Diary of William Maclay and Other Notes on Senate Debates*. Edited by Kenneth R. Bowling and Helen E. Veit. Baltimore: Johns Hopkins University Press, 1988.

Macomber, Walter M. "The Rebuilding of the Greenhouse-Quarters." In *Annual Report 1952*, 18–26. Mount Vernon, VA: Mount Vernon Ladies' Association, 1953.

Madison, Dolley Payne. *The Selected Letters of Dolley Payne Madison*. Edited by David B. Mattern and Holly C. Shulman. Charlottesville: University of Virginia Press, 2003.

Madison, James. *Notes of Debates in the Federal Convention of 1787 Reported by James Madison*. New York: Norton, 1987.

Malone, Dumas. *Jefferson and His Time,* vol. 1, *Jefferson the Virginian.* Boston: Little, Brown, 1948.

Mariani, John. *The Dictionary of American Food and Drink.* New York: Hearst Books, 1994.

Martin, Ann Smart. *Buying into the World of Goods: Early Consumers in Backcountry Virginia.* Baltimore: Johns Hopkins University Press, 2008.

Martin, Charles D. *The White African Body: A Cultural and Literary Exploration.* New Brunswick, NJ: Rutgers University Press, 2002.

Maurois, André. *Adrienne: The Life of the Marquise de La Fayette.* Translated by Gerard Hopkins. London: Jonathan Cape, 1961.

Mays, David John. *Edmund Pendleton, 1721–1803: A Biography.* 2 vols. Richmond: Virginia State Library, 1984.

Mazyck, Walter H. *George Washington and the Negro.* Washington, DC: Associated, 1932.

McCullough, David. *John Adams.* New York: Simon and Schuster, 2001.

McCully, Emily Arnold. *The Escape of Oney Judge: Martha Washington's Slave Finds Freedom.* New York: Farrar Straus Giroux, 2007.

McEwan, Barbara. *Thomas Jefferson: Farmer.* Jefferson, NC: McFarland, 1991.

McMahon, Sarah F. "Laying Foods By: Gender, Dietary Decisions, and the Technology of Food Preservation in New England Households, 1750–1850." In *Early American Technology: Making and Doing Things from the Colonial Era to 1850,* edited by Judith A. McGaw, 164–96. Chapel Hill: University of North Carolina Press, 1994.

Meade, Bishop [William]. *Old Churches, Ministers, and Families of Virginia.* 2 vols. Philadelphia: J. B. Lippincott, 1857.

Medford, Edna Greene. "Beyond Mount Vernon: George Washington's Emancipated Laborers and Their Descendants." In *Slavery at the Home of George Washington,* edited by Philip J. Schwartz, 136–57. Mount Vernon, VA: Mount Vernon Ladies' Association, 2001.

Melish, Joanne Pope. *Disowning Slavery: Gradual Emancipation and "Race" in New England, 1780–1860.* Ithaca, NY: Cornell University Press, 1998.

Memis, John. *The Midwife's Pocket-Companion; or, A Practical Treatise of Midwifery.* Aberdeen, Scotland: John Memis, 1786.

"Memoirs of a Monticello Slave as Dictated to Charles Campbell by Isaac." In *Jefferson at Monticello,* edited by James A. Bear, Jr., 3–24. Charlottesville: University Press of Virginia, 1967.

Mergen, Bernard. *Play and Playthings: A Reference Guide.* Westport, CT: Greenwood Press, 1982.

———. "Top-Time's Gone, Kite-Time's Come, and April Fool's Day Will Soon Be Here: Making Time for Play in the Early Republic." Paper presented at "Pleasant Diversions: Americans at Leisure, 1750–1875," seminar, George Mason University, 19 March 1993.

Miles, Ellen G. *George and Martha Washington: Portraits from the Presidential Years.* Washington, DC: Smithsonian Institution, 1999.

Miller, T. Michael, ed. *Pen Portraits of Alexandria, Virginia, 1739–1900.* Bowie, MD: Heritage Books, 1987.

Minchinton, Walter, Celia King, and Peter Waite, eds. *Virginia Slave-Trade Statistics, 1698–1775.* Richmond: Virginia State Library, 1984.

Mohr, Merilyn Simonds. *The Games Treasury.* Shelburne, VT: Chapters, 1993.

Moore, Stacy Gibbons. "'Established and Well Cultivated': Afro-American Foodways in Early Virginia." *Virginia Cavalcade,* Autumn 1989, 70–83.

Morgan, Edmund S. *American Slavery, American Freedom: The Ordeal of Colonial Virginia.* New York: Norton, 1975.

———. *The Puritan Family: Religion and Domestic Relations in Seventeenth-Century New England.* New York: Harper and Row, 1966.

Morgan, Philip D. "Interracial Sex in the Chesapeake and the British Atlantic World, c. 1700–1820." In *Sally Hemings and Thomas Jefferson: History, Memory, and Civic Culture,* edited by Jan Ellen Lewis and Peter S. Onuf, 52–84. Charlottesville: University Press of Virginia, 1999.

———. *Slave Counterpoint: Black Culture in the Eighteenth-Century Chesapeake and Lowcountry.* Chapel Hill: University of North Carolina Press, 1998.

———. "Slave Life in Piedmont Virginia, 1720–1800." In *Colonial Chesapeake Society,* edited by Lois Green Carr, Philip D. Morgan, and Jean B. Russo, 433–85. Chapel Hill: University of North Carolina Press, 1988.

———. "Three Planters and Their Slaves: Perspectives on Slavery in Virginia, South Carolina, and Jamaica, 1750–1790." In *Race and Family in the Colonial South,* edited by Winthrop D. Jordan and Sheila L. Skemp, 37–79. Jackson: University Press of Mississippi, 1987.

———. "'To Get Quit of Negroes': George Washington and Slavery." *Journal of American Studies* 39 (2005): 403–29.

Morgan, Philip D., and Michael L. Nicholls. "Slave Flight: Mount Vernon, Virginia, and the Wider Atlantic World." In *George Washington's South,* edited by Tamara Harvey and Greg O'Brien, 197–222. Gainesville: University Press of Florida, 2004.

Morse, Frank E. "Special Report on the Quarters for the Regent and the Vice-Regent for Illinois." Unpublished paper prepared for the Mount Vernon Ladies' Association, n.d. (ca. 1954–62).

Morse, Jedidiah. *The American Geography; or, A View of the Present Situation of the United States of America.* London: John Stockdale, 1792.

Moscow, Henry. *The Book of New York Firsts: Unusual, Arcane, and Fascinating Facts in the Life of New York City.* Syracuse, NY: Syracuse University Press, 1995.

Mount Vernon Ladies' Association. *Minutes of the Council, 1931.* Mount Vernon, VA: Mount Vernon Ladies' Association, 1932.

———. *Mount Vernon: A Handbook.* Mount Vernon, VA: Mount Vernon Ladies' Association, 1985.

———. *Mount Vernon Commemorative Guidebook 1999: George Washington Bicentennial Edition.* Mount Vernon, VA: Mount Vernon Ladies' Association, 1998.

———. "The Slave Memorial at Mount Vernon." Brochure from the 11th anniversary of the Slave Memorial. Mount Vernon, VA: Mount Vernon Ladies' Association of the Union, 1994.

Muller, John. *Mark Twain in Washington, D.C.: The Adventures of a Capital Correspondent.* Charleston: History Press, 2013.

Mullin, Gerald W. *Flight and Rebellion: Slave Resistance in Eighteenth-Century Virginia*. London: Oxford University Press, 1972.

Nelligan, Murray H. *Arlington House: The Story of the Robert E. Lee Memorial*. Burke, VA: Chatelaine Press, 2001.

———. "'Old Arlington': The Story of the Lee Mansion National Memorial." Unpublished report prepared for the U.S. Department of the Interior, National Park Service, Washington, DC, 1953.

Nelson, John K. *A Blessed Company: Parishes, Parsons, and Parishioners in Anglican Virginia, 1690–1776*. Chapel Hill: University of North Carolina Press, 2001.

The New Encyclopaedia Britannica. 15th edition. Chicago: Encyclopaedia Britannica, 1986.

Nicholls, Michael L. "Alexandria and African Americans in the Age of Washington." Unpublished paper prepared for the Mount Vernon Ladies' Association, December 1995.

———. "Recreating a White Urban Virginia." In *Lois Green Carr: The Chesapeake and Beyond—A Celebration*, 27–36. Crownsville: Maryland Historical and Cultural Publications, 1992.

Niemcewicz, Julian Ursyn. *Under Their Vine and Fig Tree: Travels through America in 1797–1799, 1805*. Edited and translated by Metchie J. E. Budka. Elizabeth, NJ: Grassman, 1965.

Northup, Solomon. *12 Years a Slave: Narrative of Solomon Northup, a Citizen of New-York*. Vancouver: Engage Books, 2013.

Norton, Elizabeth Rosemary. "A Penchant for Noble Patronage." *National Society—Daughters of American Colonists*, February 1962, 6–7, 9, 12; May 1962, 12–14; August 1962, 9–10; November 1962, 10–12.

Nylander, Jane C. *Our Own Snug Fireside: Images of the New England Home, 1760–1860*. New York: Knopf, 1993.

Oliver, Sandra. "Using Barm to Make Bread." *Food History News*, Summer 1993, 3–4.

Olwell, Robert. "'A Reckoning of Accounts': Patriarchy, Market Relations, and Control on Henry Laurens's Lowcountry Plantations, 1762–1785." In *Working toward Freedom: Slave Society and Domestic Economy in the American South*, edited by Larry E. Hudson, Jr., 33–52. Rochester, NY: University of Rochester Press, 1995.

O'Malley, Gregory E. *Final Passages: The Intercolonial Slave Trade of British America, 1619–1807*. Chapel Hill: University of North Carolina Press, 2014.

Opie, Frederick Douglass. *Hog and Hominy: Soul Food from Africa to America*. New York: Columbia University Press, 2008.

Opie, Iona, and Peter Opie. *Children's Games in Street and Playground*. London: Oxford University Press, 1969.

Osifekunde, "The Land and People of Ijebu." In *Africa Remembered: Narratives by West Africans from the Era of the Slave Trade*, edited by Philip D. Curtin, 223–88. Madison: University of Wisconsin Press, 1957.

O'Toole, Marjory Gomez. *If Jane Should Want to Be Sold: Stories of Enslavement, Indenture and Freedom in Little Compton, Rhode Island*. Little Compton, RI: Little Compton Historical Society, 2016.

Oxford English Dictionary. Edited by James A. H. Murray, Henry Bradley, W. A. Craigie, and C. T. Onions. 13 vols. Oxford, UK: Clarendon Press, 1933.

Page, Linda Garland, and Eliot Wigginton, eds. *The Foxfire Book of Appalachian Cookery*. Chapel Hill: University of North Carolina Press, 1992.

Parkinson, Richard. *A Tour in America, in 1798, 1799, and 1800. Exhibiting Sketches of Society and Manners, and a Particular Account of the American System of Agriculture, with Its Recent Improvements.* 2 vols. London: J. Harding and J. Murray, 1805.

Paston-Williams, Sara. *The Art of Dining: A History of Cooking and Eating.* London: National Trust, 1993.

Peale, Charles Willson. *The Selected Papers of Charles Willson Peale and His Family.* 5 vols. Edited by Lillian B. Miller et al. New Haven, CT: Yale University Press, 1983.

Perdue, Charles L., Jr., ed. *Pigsfoot Jelly and Persimmon Beer: Foodways from the Virginia Writers' Project.* Santa Fe: Ancient City Press, 1992.

Perdue, Charles L., Jr., Thomas E. Barden, and Robert K. Phillips, eds. *Weevils in the Wheat: Interviews with Virginia Ex-Slaves.* Charlottesville: University Press of Virginia, 1992.

Perkins, Thomas Handasyd. *Memoir of Thomas Handasyd Perkins; Containing Extracts from His Diaries and Letters. With an Appendix.* Edited by Thomas G. Cary. Boston: Little, Brown, 1856.

Peters, Richard. "Fac-Simile of General Washington's Hand Writing; and Sketches of His Private Character." In *Memoirs of the Philadelphia Society for Promoting Agriculture,* 2:i–ix. Philadelphia: Johnson and Warner, 1811.

Peterson, Merrill D., ed. *Visitors to Monticello.* Charlottesville: University Press of Virginia, 1989.

Pettigrew, William A. "Transatlantic Politics and the Africanization of Virginia's Labor Force, 1688–1712." In *Early Modern Virginia: Reconsidering the Old Dominion,* edited by Douglas Bradburn and John C. Coombs, 279–99. Charlottesville: University of Virginia Press, 2011.

Philips, John Edward. "The African Heritage of White America." In *Africanisms in American Culture,* edited by Joseph E. Holloway, 372–96. Bloomington: Indiana University Press, 2005.

Plater, David D. *The Butlers of Iberville Parish, Louisiana: Dunboyne Plantation in the 1800s.* Baton Rouge: Louisiana State University Press, 2015.

Pogue, Dennis J. "The Archaeology of Plantation Life: Another Perspective on George Washington's Mount Vernon." *Virginia Cavalcade,* Autumn 1991, 74–83.

———. *Founding Spirits: George Washington and the Beginnings of the American Whiskey Industry.* Buena Vista, VA: Harbour Books, 2011.

———. "George Washington: His Troubles with Slavery." *American History,* February 2004, http://www.historynet.com/george-washington-his-troubles-with-slavery.htm/print/.

———. "George Washington and the Politics of Slavery." *Historic Alexandria Quarterly,* Spring–Summer 2003, 1–10.

———. "Slave Lifeways at Mount Vernon." In *Annual Report 1989,* 35–40. Mount Vernon, VA: Mount Vernon Ladies' Association, 1990.

———. "Slave Lifeways at Mount Vernon: An Archaeological Perspective." In *Slavery at the Home of George Washington,* edited by Philip J. Schwarz, 110–35. Mount Vernon, VA: Mount Vernon Ladies' Association, 2001.

Pogue, Dennis J., and Esther C. White. "Summary Report on the 'House for Families' Slave Quarter Site (44 Fx 762/40–47), Mount Vernon Plantation, Mount Vernon, Virginia." Unpublished report prepared for the Mount Vernon Ladies' Association, December 1991.

Pool, Daniel. *What Jane Austen Ate and Charles Dickens Knew: From Fox Hunting to Whist—the Facts of Daily Life in 19th-Century England.* New York: Simon and Schuster, 1993.

Postell, William Dosite. *The Health of Slaves on Southern Plantations.* Baton Rouge: Louisiana State University Press, 1951.

Powell, Mary G. *The History of Old Alexandria, Virginia from July 13, 1749 to May 24, 1861.* Richmond, VA: William Byrd Press, 1928.

———. "Scenes of Childhood." *The Fireside Sentinel: The Alexandria Library, Lloyd House Newsletter,* January 1990, 1–12.

Preston, E. Delorus, Jr. "William Syphax, A Pioneer in Negro Education in the District of Columbia." *Journal of Negro History* 20, no. 4 (October 1935): 448–76.

Provine, Dorothy, comp. and ed. *Alexandria, County, Virginia, Free Negro Registers, 1797–1861.* Bowie, MD: Heritage Books, 1990.

———, comp. and ed. *District of Columbia Free Negro Registers, 1821–1861.* 2 vols. Bowie, MD: Heritage Books, 1996.

Prussing, Eugene E. *The Estate of George Washington, Deceased.* Boston: Little, Brown, 1927.

Pulsipher, Lydia M. "Galways Plantation, Montserrat." In *Seeds of Change: A Quincentennial Commemoration,* edited by Herman J. Viola and Carolyn Margolis, 138–59. Washington, DC: Smithsonian Institution Press, 1991.

Pybus, Cassandra. *Epic Journeys of Freedom: Runaway Slaves of the American Revolution and Their Global Quest for Liberty.* Boston: Beacon Press, 2006.

Quander, Rohulamin, ed. *Telling Histories: A Collection of Transcribed Interviews of Quander Family Members.* 2 vols. Washington, DC: Quander Historical Society, 1998.

Queen, Sally A. *Textiles for Colonial Clothing: A Workbook of Swatches and Information.* Arlington, VA: Sally Queen and Associates, 2000.

Ragsdale, Bruce A. *A Planters' Republic: The Search for Economic Independence in Revolutionary Virginia.* Madison, WI: Madison House, 1996.

Randolph, Anne Cary. Monticello Household Accounts, early 19th century. Thomas Jefferson Papers. Library of Congress, Washington, DC.

Randolph, Mary. *The Virginia House-Wife.* Edited by Karen Hess. Facsimile edition. Columbia: University of South Carolina Press, 1991.

Rediker, Marcus. *The Slave Ship: A Human History.* New York: Viking, 2007.

Reiss, Benjamin. *The Showman and the Slave: Race, Death, and Memory in Barnum's America.* Cambridge, MA: Harvard University Press, 2001.

Rice, James D. *Nature and History in the Potomac Country: From Hunter-Gatherers to the Age of Jefferson.* Baltimore: Johns Hopkins University Press, 2009.

Richardson, Edgar P., Brooke Hindle, and Lillian B. Miller. *Charles Willson Peale and His World.* New York: Harry N. Abrams, 1983.

Riley, John P. "To Build a Barn." In *Annual Report 1992,* 32–37. Mount Vernon, VA: Mount Vernon Ladies' Association, 1993.

Rinaldi, Ann. *Taking Liberty: The Story of Oney Judge, George Washington's Runaway Slave*. New York: Simon and Schuster, 2002.

Roberts, Justin. *Slavery and the Enlightenment in the British Atlantic, 1750–1807*. Cambridge: Cambridge University Press, 2013.

———. "Sunup to Sundown: Plantation Management Strategies and Slave Work Routines in Barbados, Jamaica and Virginia, 1776–1810." Ph.D. diss., Johns Hopkins University, 2008.

Robinson, Donald L. *Slavery in the Structure of American Politics, 1765–1820*. New York: Harcourt Brace Jovanovich, 1971.

Robinson, Henry S. "Who Was West Ford?" *Journal of Negro History* 66, no. 2 (Summer 1981): 167–74.

Roosevelt, Priscilla. *Life on the Russian Country Estate: A Social and Cultural History*. New Haven, CT: Yale University Press, 1995.

Rose, C. B., Jr. *Arlington County Virginia: A History*. Baltimore: Arlington Historical Society, 1976.

Rutman, Darrett B., Charles Wetherell, and Anita H. Rutman. "Rhythms of Life: Black and White Seasonality in the Early Chesapeake." *Journal of Interdisciplinary History* 11, no. 1 (Summer 1980): 29–53.

Saltar, Fanny. "Fanny Saltar's Reminiscences of Colonial Days in Philadelphia." *Pennsylvania Magazine of History and Biography* 40, no. 2 (1916): 187–98.

Samford, Patricia M. *Subfloor Pits and the Archaeology of Slavery in Colonial Virginia*. Tuscaloosa: University of Alabama Press, 2007.

Sargent, Winthrop. Diary. Ohio Historical Society, Ohio State Museum, Columbus. Transcript at Mount Vernon Ladies' Association, Mount Vernon, VA.

Saunders-Burton, Judith. "A History of Gum Springs, Virginia: A Report of a Case Study of Leadership in a Black Enclave." Ph.D., George Peabody College for Teachers of Vanderbilt University, 1986.

Savitt, Todd L. *Medicine and Slavery: The Diseases and Health Care of Blacks in Antebellum Virginia*. Urbana: University of Illinois Press, 1978.

Schama, Simon. *Rough Crossings: Britain, the Slaves and the American Revolution*. London: BBC Books, 2005.

Schulz, Constance B. "Children and Childhood in the Eighteenth Century." In *American Childhood: A Research Guide and Historical Handbook*, edited by Joseph M. Hawes and N. Ray Hiner, 57–109. Westport, CT: Greenwood Press, 1985.

Schwarz, Philip J. "George Washington and the Developing Law of Slavery in Virginia." Unpublished paper prepared for the Mount Vernon Ladies' Association, October 1995.

———, ed. *Slavery at the Home of George Washington*. Mount Vernon, VA: Mount Vernon Ladies' Association, 2001.

———. *Twice Condemned: Slaves and the Criminal Laws of Virginia, 1705–1865*. Baton Rouge: Louisiana State University Press, 1988.

"A Scot Recently Come Over." March 1823. Early Descriptions Notebook, Mount Vernon Ladies' Association, Mount Vernon, VA.

Selig, Robert A. "The Revolution's Black Soldiers: They Fought for Both Sides in Their Quest for Freedom." *Colonial Williamsburg*, Summer 1997, 15–22.

Serle, Ambrose. *The American Journal of Ambrose Serle, Secretary to Lord Howe.* Edited by Edward H. Tatum. San Marino, CA: Huntington Library, 1940.

Shakir, M. H., transl. *Holy Qur'an.* Elmhurst, NY: Tahrike Tarsile Qur'an, 1986.

Sherman, Caroline Baldwin. "An Old Virginia Landmark." *William and Mary College Quarterly Historical Magazine,* 2nd ser., 7 (April 1927): 90–91.

Shick, Laura A. "An Analysis of Archaeobotanical Evidence from the House for Families Slave Quarter, Mount Vernon Plantation, Virginia." M.A. thesis, American University, 2004.

Smallwood, Stephanie E. *Saltwater Slavery: A Middle Passage from Africa to American Diaspora.* Cambridge, MA: Harvard University Press, 2007.

Smith, Abbot Emerson. *Colonists in Bondage: White Servitude and Convict Labor in America, 1607–1776.* Chapel Hill: University of North Carolina Press, 1947.

Smith, Daniel Blake. "Autonomy and Affection: Parents and Children in Eighteenth-Century Chesapeake Families." In *Growing up in America: Children in Historical Perspective,* edited by N. Ray Hiner and Joseph M. Hawes, 46–58. Urbana: University of Illinois Press, 1985.

Smith, Gloria L. *Black Americana at Mount Vernon: Genealogy Techniques for Slave Group Research.* Tucson, AZ: G. L. Smith, 1984.

Smith, Mark M. *Mastered by the Clock: Time, Slavery, and Freedom in the American South.* Chapel Hill: University of North Carolina Press, 1997.

Smith, S. D. *Slavery, Family and Gentry Capitalism in the British Atlantic: The World of the Lascelles, 1648–1834.* New York: Cambridge University Press, 2006.

Snyder, Terri L. "Suicide, Slavery, and Memory in North America." *Journal of American History* 97, no. 1 (June 2010): 39–62.

Sobel, Mechal. *The World They Made Together: Black and White Values in Eighteenth-Century Virginia.* Princeton, NJ: Princeton University Press, 1987.

Sparks, Jared. *The Life of George Washington.* Boston: Ferdinand Andrews, 1839.

Stampp, Kenneth M. *The Peculiar Institution: Slavery in the Ante-Bellum South.* New York: Vintage Books, 1956.

Stanton, Lucia. *Free Some Day: The African-American Families of Monticello.* Charlottesville, VA: Thomas Jefferson Foundation, 2000.

———. *Slavery at Monticello.* Charlottesville, VA: Thomas Jefferson Memorial Foundation, 1996.

———. "'Those Who Labor for My Happiness': Thomas Jefferson and His Slaves." In *Jeffersonian Legacies,* edited by Peter S. Onuf, 147–80. Charlottesville: University Press of Virginia, 1993.

———. *"Those Who Labor for My Happiness": Slavery at Thomas Jefferson's Monticello.* Charlottesville: University of Virginia Press, 2012.

Stedman, Emile T. *Hammet Achmet: A Servant of George Washington.* Middletown, CT: E. T. Stedman, 1900.

Stevenson, Brenda E. *Life in Black and White: Family and Community in the Slave South.* New York: Oxford University Press, 1996.

Stone, Lawrence. *The Family, Sex and Marriage in England, 1500–1800.* New York: Harper and Row, 1977.

Strickland, Charles E., and Andrew M. Ambrose. "The Baby Boom, Prosperity, and the Changing Worlds of Children, 1945–1963." In *American Childhood:*

A Research Guide and Historical Handbook, edited by Joseph M. Hawes and N. Ray Hiner, 533–85. Westport, CT: Greenwood Press, 1985.

Svalesen, Leif. *The Slave Ship Fredensborg.* Translated by Pat Shaw and Selena Winsnes. Bloomington: Indiana University Press, 2000.

Sweig, Donald M. "'Dear Master': A Unique Letter from West Ford Discovered." *Fairfax Chronicles,* May–July 1986, 1–3, 5.

———. "The Importation of African Slaves to the Potomac River, 1732–1772." *William and Mary Quarterly,* 3rd ser., 42, no. 4 (October 1985), 507–24.

———, ed. *"Registrations of Free Negroes Commencing September Court 1822, Book No. 2" and "Register of Free Blacks 1835 Book 3."* Fairfax: History Section, Office of Comprehensive Planning, Fairfax County, Virginia, 1977.

———. *Slavery in Fairfax County, Virginia, 1750–1860.* Fairfax County, VA: History and Archaeology Section, Office of Comprehensive Planning, 1983.

Tate, Thad W. *The Negro in Eighteenth-Century Williamsburg.* Williamsburg, VA: Colonial Williamsburg Foundation, 1965.

Taylor, Alan. *The Internal Enemy: Slavery and War in Virginia, 1772–1832.* New York: Norton, 2013.

Taylor, Elizabeth Dowling. "The Plantation Community Tour." Unpublished paper prepared for Monticello, February 1993, revised March 1994.

Thane, Elswyth. *Mount Vernon Family.* New York: Crowell-Collier Press, 1968.

Thompson, Mary V. *"In the Hands of a Good Providence": Religion in the Life of George Washington.* Charlottesville: University of Virginia Press, 2008.

———. "'More to Dread . . . than from the Sword of the Enemy': Smallpox, the Unseen Killer." In *Annual Report 2000,* 22–27. Mount Vernon, VA: Mount Vernon Ladies' Association, 2001.

———. "'They Appear to Live Comfortable Together': Private Lives of the Mount Vernon Slaves." In *Slavery at the Home of George Washington,* edited by Philip J. Schwartz, 78–109. Mount Vernon, VA: Mount Vernon Ladies' Association, 2001.

Tillery, Carolyn Quick. *The African-American Heritage Cookbook.* Secaucus, NJ: Carol, 1996.

Tillyard, Stella. *Aristocrats: Caroline, Emily, Louisa, and Sarah Lennox, 1740–1832.* New York, NY: Farrar, Straus and Giroux, 2000.

"The Tomb of Washington." In Ebenezer Porter, *The Rhetorical Reader; Consisting of Instructions for Regulating the Voice, with a Rhetorical Notation, Illustrating Inflection, Emphasis, and Modulation; and a Course of Rhetorical Exercises, Designed for the Use of Academies and High-Schools,* 159–62. Andover, MA: Gould and Newman, 1838.

Toner, Joseph M., ed. *Wills of the American Ancestors of General George Washington in the Line of the Original Owner and the Inheritors of Mount Vernon: From Original Documents and Probate Records.* Boston: New-England Historic Genealogical Society, 1891.

[Trusler, John]. *The Honours of the Table; or, Rules for Behaviour during Meals.* London: Literary Press, 1788.

Twitty, Michael. *Fighting Old Nep: The Foodways of Enslaved Afro-Marylanders, 1634–1864.* N.p.: Michael Twitty, 2008.

Twohig, Dorothy. "'That Species of Property': Washington's Role in the Controversy over Slavery." In *George Washington Reconsidered,* edited by Don Higginbotham, 114–38. Charlottesville: University Press of Virginia, 2001.

Ulrich, Laurel Thatcher. *A Midwife's Tale: The Life of Martha Ballard Based on Her Diary, 1785–1812.* New York: Knopf, 1992.

U.S. Bureau of the Census. *Historical Statistics of the United States, Colonial Times to 1957.* Washington, DC: U.S. Government Printing Office, 1960.

Vail, R. W. G. "Two Early Visitors to Mount Vernon." *New-York Historical Society Quarterly* 42, no. 4 (October 1958): 349–65.

Van Horn, Jennifer. "George Washington's Dentures: Disability, Deception, and the Republican Body." *Early American Studies* 14, no. 1 (Winter 2016): 2–47.

Varlo, Charles. *The Floating Ideas of Nature, Suited to the Philosopher, Farmer, and Mechanic.* 2 vols. London: Charles Varlo, 1796.

Verme, Francesco dal. *Seeing America and Its Great Men: The Journal and Letters of Count Francesco dal Verme, 1783–1784.* Translated and edited by Elizabeth Cometti. Charlottesville: University Press of Virginia, 1969.

Virginia. *The Statutes at Large: Being a Collection of All the Laws of Virginia, from the First Session of the Legislature, in the Year 1619.* 13 vols. Edited by William Waller Hening. Richmond, VA: Samuel Pleasants, Jr., 1809–23.

"Visit to Mount Vernon." *Western Literary Messenger: A Family Magazine of Literature, Science, Art, Morality, and General Intelligence* 5 (1845–46): 200–201.

Vlach, John Michael. "Afro-American Domestic Artifacts in Eighteenth-Century Virginia." In *By the Work of Their Hands: Studies in Afro-American Folklife,* 53–71. Charlottesville: University Press of Virginia, 1991.

———. *Back of the Big House: The Architecture of Plantation Slavery.* Chapel Hill: University of North Carolina Press, 1993.

Wall, Charles C. "'Dr His Excly Geo. Washington to James Craik': Notes on a Medical Bill." *Virginia Magazine of History and Biography* 55, no. 4 (October 1947): 318–28.

———. "Housing and Family Life of the Mount Vernon Negro." Unpublished paper prepared for the Mount Vernon Ladies' Association, May 1962.

Wallace, Alton S. *I Once Was Young: History of Alfred Street Baptist Church, 1803–2003.* Littleton, MA: Tapestry Press, 2003.

Wallach, Janet. *Desert Queen: The Extraordinary Life of Gertrude Bell: Adventurer, Adviser to Kings, Ally of Lawrence of Arabia.* New York: Doubleday, 1996.

Walsh, Lorena S. *From Calabar to Carter's Grove: The History of a Virginia Slave Community.* Charlottesville: University Press of Virginia, 1997.

———. *Motives of Honor, Pleasure, and Profit: Plantation Management in the Colonial Chesapeake, 1607–1763.* Chapel Hill: University of North Carolina Press, 2010.

———. "A 'Place in Time' Regained: A Fuller History of Colonial Chesapeake Slavery through Group Biography." In *Working toward Freedom: Slave Society and Domestic Economy in the American South,* edited by Larry E. Hudson, Jr., 1–32. Rochester, NY: University of Rochester Press, 1994.

———. "Slavery and Agriculture at Mount Vernon." In *Slavery at the Home of George Washington,* edited by Philip J. Schwarz, 46–77. Mount Vernon, VA: Mount Vernon Ladies' Association, 2001.

Wansey, Henry. *An Excursion to the United States of North America, in the Summer of 1794*. Salisbury, England: J. Easton, 1798.

Wargee. "The African Travels of Wargee." In *Africa Remembered: Narratives by West Africans from the Era of the Slave Trade,* edited by Philip D. Curtin, 175–89. Madison: University of Wisconsin Press, 1967.

Warren, Jack D., Jr. "The Childhood of George Washington." *Northern Neck of Virginia Historical Magazine* 49, no. 1 (December 1999): 5785–5809.

Washington, George. *The Diaries of George Washington*. Edited by Donald Jackson and Dorothy Twohig. 6 vols. Charlottesville: University Press of Virginia, 1976–79.

———. *The Diaries of George Washington, 1748–1799*. Edited by John C. Fitzpatrick. 4 vols. Boston: Houghton Mifflin, 1925.

———. *The Last Will and Testament of George Washington and Schedule of His Property to Which Is Appended the Last Will and Testament of Martha Washington*. 4th edition. Edited by John C. Fitzpatrick. Mount Vernon, VA: Mount Vernon Ladies' Association, 1972.

———. Papers. Microfilm series 1–8. Library of Congress, Washington, DC.

———. *The Papers of George Washington, Colonial Series*. Edited by W. W. Abbot and Dorothy Twohig. 10 vols. Charlottesville: University Press of Virginia, 1983–95.

———. *The Papers of George Washington, Confederation Series*. Edited by W. W. Abbot and Dorothy Twohig. 6 vols. Charlottesville: University Press of Virginia, 1992–97.

———. *The Papers of George Washington, Presidential Series*. Edited by W. W. Abbot, Dorothy Twohig, and Philander D. Chase. 19 vols. to date. Charlottesville: University Press of Virginia, 1987–.

———. *The Papers of George Washington, Retirement Series*. Edited by W. W. Abbot and Dorothy Twohig. 4 vols. Charlottesville: University Press of Virginia, 1998–99.

———. *The Papers of George Washington, Revolutionary War Series*. Edited by W. W. Abbot, Dorothy Twohig, Philander D. Chase, and Theodore J. Crackel. 26 vols. to date. Charlottesville: University Press of Virginia, 1985–.

———. *Rules of Civility and Decent Behaviour in Company and Conversation*. Annotated by Ann M. Rauscher. Mount Vernon, VA: Mount Vernon Ladies' Association, 1989.

———. *The Writings of George Washington: From the Original Manuscript Sources, 1745–1799*. Edited by John C. Fitzpatrick. 39 vols. Washington, DC: U.S. Government Printing Office, 1931–44.

Washington, George, and James E. Hoofnagle. *The Last Will and Testament of General George Washington*. Fairfax County, VA: Clerk of the Circuit Court, 1980.

Washington, Martha. *"Worthy Partner": The Papers of Martha Washington*. Compiled by Joseph E. Fields, with an introduction by Ellen McCallister Clark. Westport, CT: Greenwood Press, 1994.

"Washington's Household Account Book, 1793-1797." *Pennsylvania Magazine of History and Biography* 29, no. 4 (1905): 385–406; 30, nos. 1–4 (1906): 30–56, 159–86, 309–31, 459–78; 31, nos. 1–3 (1907), 53–82, 176–94, 320–50.

Watson, Elkanah. *Men and Times of the Revolution; or, Memoirs of Elkanah Watson,*

Including Journals of Travels in Europe and America, from 1777 to 1842, with His Correspondence with Public Men and Reminiscences and Incidents of the Revolution. Edited by Winslow C. Watson. New York: Dana and Company, 1856.

Wayland, John W. *The Washingtons and Their Homes.* Berryville: Virginia Book Company, 1944.

Weinberger, Bernhard Wolf. *An Introduction to the History of Dentistry.* 2 vols. St. Louis: C. V. Mosby, 1948.

Weld, Isaac, Jr. *Travels through the States of North America, and the Provinces of Upper and Lower Canada, during the Years 1795, 1796, and 1797.* 2 vols. London: John Stockdale, 1799.

Wells, Camille. "The Eighteenth-Century Landscape of Virginia's Northern Neck." *Northern Neck of Virginia Historical Magazine* 37, no. 1 (December 1987): 4217–55.

Werner, Alice. "Brer Rabbit in Africa." In *Myths and Legends of the Bantu.* London: George G. Harrap, 1933.

"The West Quarter." In *Annual Report 1962,* 22–25. Mount Vernon, VA: Mount Vernon Ladies' Association, 1963.

Whatman, Susanna. *Susanna Whatman: Her Housekeeping Book.* Cambridge: Cambridge University Press, 1952.

Wheatley, Phillis. *The Poems of Phillis Wheatley.* Edited by Julian D. Mason, Jr. Chapel Hill: University of North Carolina Press, 1966.

White, Deborah Gray. *Ar'n't I a Woman? Female Slaves in the Plantation South.* New York: Norton, 1985.

———. "Female Slaves in the Plantation South." In *Before Freedom Came: African-American Life in the Antebellum South,* edited by Edward D. C. Campbell, Jr., and Kym S. Rice, 100–121. Richmond: Museum of the Confederacy and University Press of Virginia, 1991.

White, Shane, and Graham White. "Slave Hair and African American Culture in the Eighteenth and Nineteenth Centuries." *Journal of Southern History* 61, no. 1 (February 1995): 45–76.

Whitehead, Ruth Holmes. *Black Loyalists: Southern Settlers of Nova Scotia's First Free Black Communities.* Nimbus, CA: Nimbus, 2013.

Whitfield, Harvey Amani. *The Problem of Slavery in Early Vermont, 1777–1810: Essay and Primary Sources.* Barre: Vermont Historical Society, 2014.

Wiencek, Henry. *An Imperfect God: George Washington, His Slaves, and the Creation of America.* New York: Farrar, Straus and Giroux, 2003.

Wiggins, David K. "The Play of Slave Children in the Plantation Communities of the Old South, 1820–60." In *Growing up in America: Children in Historical Perspective,* edited by N. Ray Hiner and Joseph M. Hawes, 173–90. Urbana: University of Illinois Press, 1985.

Windley, Lathan A., comp. *Runaway Slave Advertisements: A Documentary History from the 1730s to 1790.* Vol. 1. Westport, CT: Greenwood Press, 1983.

Winner, Lauren F. *A Cheerful and Comfortable Faith: Anglican Religious Practice in the Elite Households of Eighteenth-Century Virginia.* New Haven, CT: Yale University Press, 2010.

Winter, Kari J., ed. *The Blind African Slave; or, Memoirs of Boyrereau Brinch, Nicknamed Jeffrey Brace.* Madison: University of Wisconsin Press, 2004.

Wood, Peter, H. *Black Majority: Negroes in Colonial South Carolina from 1670 through the Stono Rebellion.* New York: Norton, 1974.

Woodforde, John. *The Strange Story of False Teeth.* London: Routledge and Kegan Paul, 1968.

Yagoda, Ben. "A Short History of 'Hack.'" *New Yorker,* 6 March 2014, https://www.newyorker.com/tech/elements/a-short-history-of-hack.

Yentsch, Anne Elizabeth. *A Chesapeake Family and Their Slaves: A Study in Historical Archaeology.* Cambridge: Cambridge University Press, 1994.

[Young, Arthur]. *Rural Oeconomy; or, Essays on the Practical Parts of Husbandry.* Dublin: J. Exshaw, 1770.

Zagarri, Rosemarie, ed. *David Humphreys' "Life of General Washington," with George Washington's "Remarks."* Athens: University of Georgia Press, 1991.

INDEX

Note: Page numbers in italics refer to illustrations, and a "t" following a page number designates a table. GW and MW refer to George Washington and Martha Washington.

[Smith], Dolshy (dower slave; Mansion House Farm), 119, 309

Smith, Josephine, 450n107

Snowden, Mr., 144–45

Sobel, Mechal, 407n151

socializing, 132–33, 140–41, 182, 209, 286, 287

Sophia (GW slave; Dogue Run Farm), 276

South, the, 39, 182, 188–89, 203, 212, 228, 235, 244, 289, 305–6, 395n10

South Carolina, 57, 66, 129, 153–54, 211, 306–7, 368n47, 372n12

Southern cuisine, African influence on, 243–44, 245–46

Southern Tour, 36, 59–60

Spain, 193, 440n161

Spence, William (hired Scottish gardener), 436n96

spinners, 110, 114, 115, 116, 117, 120, 139, 157, 167, 249, 267, 392n90

spiritual objects, 212–13

Spotswood, Alexander, 193

Squash, Deborah (runaway slave from Mount Vernon), 439n143

Staines, Eliza, 288

Staines, John, 288

Staines, Oney Judge (dower slave; Mansion House Farm), 40, 42, 58, 110, 113, 139, 143, 181, 191, 192, 204, 206–7, 285–90, 322, 440n166, 441n171, 441n173

Stanhope, Richard, 452n118

Stanton, Lucia Cinder, 317, 434n40

Stephen (enslaved cooper; runaway), 279–80

Steuben, General Friedrich Wilhelm von, 142

stewards, 40, 42, 115, 245, 284, 285, 286

Stiles, Mrs., 320

Stockholm Syndrome, 17

stolen goods, 200

Stoy, Doctor William, 282

Stuart, Doctor David, 196, 197, 204, 251, 288, 304, 307–9, 445n54, 446n55, 448n76

Stuart, Eleanor Calvert Custis, 41, 56, 76, 108

Stuart, Gilbert (artist), 43–44, 374n67, 440n161

Stuart or Stewart, William (hired overseer), 80, 94–95, 99, 160

Stuart family, 41

Suck (Bushfield slave), 181

suicide, 430–31n121

"Suke," 195

Sukey (enslaved girl; mill, 1774), 179

Sukey (enslaved seamstress at Woodlawn), 172

Sullivan, Teresa, 26

"Sunday Best," 418n59

Sunday markets, 124, 197, 230–31, 271, 428n59

Supuestor retrato del cocinero de George Washington (portrait attributed to Gilbert Stuart), 440n161

surveying, 196

swamps, 83, 91, 126, 240

swearing, 44

Sweig, Donald M., 14

Syphax, Charles (Custis family slave), 211, 420n87

Syphax, Maria (Custis family slave; Arlington), 146

tailors, 67, 90, 139, 177, 233, 381n3, 442n3

talons, owl, 212–13

Tancil, Gladys Quander, 428n56

Tar Baby, 203

Tarleton, Colonel Banastre, 434n40

Tarquin (racehorse), 108

Tartars (Tarters; Mongols), 71

taverns, 2, 58, 72, 94–95, 148, 175, 410n52, 426n18

taxes, 14, 76, 68–69, 89, 90, 299, 305, 307

Tayloe, John (II), 107, 417n57

Taylor, Alan, 281

Taylor, H. Pernell, 452n123

Taylor, John, 389n19

teeth and tooth transplants, 16, 199–200, 312

tenants, 298–99, 302, 303, 304–5

Texas, 211, 216

textiles, 4, 41, 88, 110, 146, 151–52, 153, 172, 173, 175–77, 207, 211, 243, 260, 269–70, 410n52, 412n74; tasks and equipment for production and maintenance, 4, 39, 40, 41–42, 55, 89, 101, 107, 110, 115, 116, 120, 151, 160, 172–73, 178–79, 190, 267, 394n132. *See also* clothing and accessories; fabrics; rags

theft, 40, 55–56, 94–96, 159, 175, 190, 195, 197, 200, 201, 234, 235–37, 239, 244, 245, 249–50, 259–60, 269–72, 284, 290–91, 316, 436nn98–99, 436–37n100

weavers, 120, 139, 280

weekly reports, 19–20, 33–34, 41, 55, 78, 94, 101, 109, 124, 132, 151, 157, 191–92, 222, 225, 262, 264, 284, 444n18

Welch, James, 304

Weld, Isaac (visitor), 167

well and pump, 187

Wells, Camille, 162

Wessex, Kingdom of, 395n10

West, Roger, 119, 129, 282

West Africa, 16, 182, 212, 219, 228, 229, 234, 239, 242, 243, 244, 396n33, 429n91

West Indies, 15, 46, 81, 127, 136, 178, 229, 231, 235, 240, 248, 258–59, 275, 302, 322, 367n43, 387n1, 397n39, 399n60. *See also* Antigua

Westmoreland County, VA, 79, 146–47, 415n23

Wheatley, John, 67

Wheatley, Mary, 67

Wheatley, Phillis/Phyllis (enslaved poet), 67–68, 378–79n35

Wheatley, Susanna, 67

White, Esther, 423n114

White House (official home of American presidents after 1800), 59, 194

"white Negroes," 74

Whiting (Whitting), Anthony (hired English overseer), 20, 34–35, 55–56, 81–83, 117, 134, 156–57, 170, 190, 201, 248, 249, 266, 269, 382n17

Wiencek, Henry, 38, 142, 143, 304

wildlife, 2, 52, 87, 119, 198–99, 212–13, 214, 229, 232, 236, 309–10, 318–19, 421–22n99, 428n55

Wilkes, James (hired white servant), 249–50, 284, 432n9

Will (dower slave; overseer), 86, 132, 192, 233, 234

Will (dower slave; Mansion House Farm), 312

Will/"Mink Will" (dower slave; Muddy Hole Farm), 421n92

Will (slave rented from Mrs. French; Union Farm), 260–61, 276–77

Williamsburg, VA, 16, 114, 148, 208–9, 248, 257, 258, 277, 372n33

wills, 11, 102, 181, 252, 254–55, 274, 285, 288, 294–95, 298, 307, 309, 310, 313, 315–16, 318, 323, 377n131, 433n27, 443n8, 451n115

Wilson (dower slave; Mansion House Farm), 114, 206

Wilson, James, 307

Wilson, Mary (hired housekeeper), 103–4

Wingchong, Punqua (Chinese merchant), 379n43

Winna or Winny (GW slave; house servant and spinner), 120

Winner, Lauren F., 38

wives of hired and indentured workers, 40, 55, 79, 80, 87, 92–93, 94–95, 101, 137, 270

Wolof (people and language), 195, 429n91

Woodlawn (plantation), 107, 145, 172, 313, 316, 388n13

Woodward, William (maternal great-grandfather of MW), 402n87

workday, 90, 91, 105–7, 240, 241, 264, 265

working boys and girls, 160

work reports. *See* weekly reports

Works Progress Administration (WPA) interviews, 216, 450n107

workweek, 122–23, 124, 223, 231, 388n11, 392–93n109

World War II, 31, 378n28

writing, 34, 191, 192

yards, 182–83, 282

York River, 12–13

Yoruba (people), 228

Young, Arthur (English agronomist), 8, 98–99

Young, George (hired white clerk), 139

Young, George (mixed-race GW slave; Mansion House Farm), 139, 221, 232, 398n59